D1432706

Edging the Boundaries of Children's Literature

Carol J. Winters
Grand Valley State University

Gary D. Schmidt
Calvin College

Allyn and Bacon

Boston • *London* • *Toronto* • *Sydney* • *Tokyo* • *Singapore*

Vice President: *Paul A. Smith*
Senior Editor: *Aurora Martinez Ramos*
Editorial Assistant: *Beth Slater*
Executive Marketing Manager: *Lisa Kimball*
Editorial Production Service: *Chestnut Hill Enterprises, Inc.*
Manufacturing Buyer: *Julie McNeill*
Cover Administrator: *Kristina Mose-Libon*

Copyright © 2001 by Allyn & Bacon
A Pearson Education Company
160 Gould Street
Needham Heights, MA 02494

Internet: www.ablongman.com

Between the time Website information is gathered and published, some sites may have closed. Also, the transcription of URLs can result in typographical errors. The publisher would appreciate notification where these occur so that they may be corrected in subsequent editions.

Library of Congress Cataloging-in-Publication Data

Winters, Carol.
    Edging the boundaries of children's literature / Carol Winters and Gary Schmidt.
       p. cm.
    Includes bibliographical references and index.
    ISBN 0-205-28775-1 (pbk.)
      1. Children's literature—History and criticism.   I. Schmidt, Gary D.   II. Title.

PN1009.A1 W56 2001
809'.89282—dc21   00-052566

Poetry credits are found on page 392, which should be considered an extension of the copyright page.

Printed in the United States of America

10 9 8 7 6 5 4 3 2 1   05 04 03 02 01

"To my dear and loving husband"

CW

For Clara E. Hutchins, with love from her nephew

GS

Contents

Preface

In writing a textbook with the word *boundaries* in its title, we run the risk of seeming to write a book about limits. In fact, on one level, this is a book about limits. It examines the genres of children's literature, focusing on the nature of those genres and arriving at some type of definition. And as soon as one defines, one limits. A given genre might include some works, for example, but it may not include others. Definition is limitation.

But we do not see the boundaries as limitations; certainly writers of children's literature do not see them in this way. Boundaries of genres are conventional agreements about the workings of a genre. Writers use those agreements to order and structure their work. A writer working in historical fiction, for example, will use the boundaries of the genre to decide whether he or she will include the Roman Empire's defeat of the Huns. A writer of realism will not allow a main character to metamorphose into a crow.

But sometimes writers will push at these boundaries. A writer in biography may decide to invent dialogue: Has she left the genre of biography and entered historical fiction? A writer in fantasy might have his character meet a historical figure: Has he left fantasy for historical fiction? A writer in nonfiction might use fictional characters to introduce the elements of physics: Has she left the genre of nonfiction? In short, writers work within boundaries, using those boundaries to think about and order material in their writings. At the same time, they may stretch and push at those boundaries to create certain kinds of effects in their work.

Genres suggest probabilities. They reduce random events. They lead to certain lines of narrative progression. The reader comes to a genre with certain expectations, expectations that the writer may follow or, perhaps, play with, subvert, thwart, change, or fulfill. Any of those choices necessitates, however, primary agreement about the nature of the genre.

In this textbook, a book designed for those coming into the field of children's literature, those already advanced in the field, and those interested in the issues of writing and bringing books and children together, we first look at each of the major genres of children's literature, establishing the definitions of those genres and the boundaries that those definitions engender, particularly as they relate to the field of children's literature. We then turn to the principal issues in each of those genres, issues often established by the generic expectations of both writer and reader. In each of these sections we examine the ways those issues work within the field of children's literature.

We conclude each chapter with the examination of several major writers in children's literature who have worked within the genre at hand. Our interest here lies in how those writers and illustrators have handled the issues previously discussed, and how they have used the boundaries of the genre in their own work to create works of beauty and meaning.

This is a textbook and not a reference work, so we have been purposefully selective rather than inclusive in our choice of books and authors. To choose only a handful of writers in each genre is, on the one hand, frustrating; on the other, it allows us to explore them more fully than if we had allowed that number to grow. In exploring the ways that they have handled these generic issues, we believe that we are also exploring the ways that readers may handle those issues. Further, it is our belief that anyone who brings children and books together will face the kinds of issues we describe here—issues of aesthetics, of identification, of meaning and significance, of propriety, of censorship, of literary quality, of the nature of reading and age appropriateness. This text provides one discussion of how some of the great writers have faced the boundaries of their genres.

When one writes a book, one gathers a host of obligations. Among the many that we both owe are our debts to Mary Feenstra and Ginny Klingenburg of the Department of English at Grand Valley State University; Sherry Levy of the Department of English at Calvin College; Laurel Balkema, Children's Librarian at Grand Valley State University; and Conrad Bult, Reference Librarian at Calvin College. Our thanks also to Charlotte F. Otten of the Department of English of Calvin College for her encouragement and her cheerful willingness to discuss any and all matters in the field. In addition, we thank the following reviewers whose insightful comments were most helpful: Joanne E. Bernstein, Brooklyn College; Dr. Kelly Foth, University of Dubuque; Karen Pinter, Sauk Valley Community College; and Sam Sebesta, University of Washington.

To our children and spouses go all praise and thanks for the ways, small and large, in which they have kept the candles burning by the window while we have been writing and writing and writing.

1

The Boundaries of Children's Literature

In the spring of 1997, the children's book author and illustrator David Small wrote a review for the *Hungry Mind Review* of a new and somewhat unusual picture book for children by Audrey and Don Wood: *Bright and Early Thursday Evening* (1996). The book, with its paradoxical cover illustration of a rooster looking at the egg he has just laid, is a constellation of "whimsical paradoxes and playful contradictions," Small writes, in which a young woman wakes up and dresses for her own funeral. There she meets joyful guests who weep, billionaires who are poor, a naked potato wearing gabardine pants, and an alligator dancing on a stage. She falls in love with the potato and eats him. The potato is rescued from her innards and they marry, and soon there is a bald and hairy baby. The conclusion— "Although I'm a liar my story is true"—brings the reader back to the beginning and the opening of the dream. It is a strange and unsettling book, with its mixture of funeral and marriage motifs, with computer-generated illustrations that create disturbing images that hint at violence and sexuality, without any kind of stable center, any element of narrative coherence.

Small's appraisal is a biting one:

> Figure it yourself: Don Wood gives the protagonist the face of a pretty, older teen-ager and the body of a twelve-year-old girl. She is first seen with her legs spread wide. In a series of provocative poses, she works her way into a skintight outfit, applies makeup, and is then pursued through Hell by legions of phallic symbols. A terrifying crocodile and some skeletons are also there, lending an aura of threat and death to the proceedings. The old man whom she eventually weds doubles as a potato with a huge false nose strapped to its waist, and the baby that results from their union is shown in monstrous close-up, its face revoltingly smeared with cake frosting…. All of this tumult is offered up in high camp style with characters who act like terrible clowns. They bug their eyes and purse their lips. They bend over and look at you through their legs. This sweaty posturing is meant to mug its way into your heart; in fact, it is simply obnoxious.

> No need to flip back through the pages of this magazine; yes, you *are* in the children's section, though the question of this book's appropriateness for children seems not to have entered the minds of its creators. (30)

The interpretation that Small gives to the book is clearly a sexual one, and one justified particularly by the illustrations. The review continues on to call for some sort of accountability to readers, and to reject the use of glitzy illustrations to cover the inadequacy of a text. Readers, he concludes, should "recognize a hustle when they see one."

Who are these readers that Small is calling up? The innocent child some authors construct or the real child who comes with a less than perfect background? The Victorian writers of children's literature had a dual audience in mind: idealized, innocent children and the nostalgic adults who wanted to reexperience their childhood through the reading, buying, and giving of books to children. Is this dual audience the same today? And what is true about the nature of children's literature that allows it to appeal to such a dual audience?

Small is not merely interpreting in this review; he is asking a basic question: Does children's literature have boundaries? Are there some works that are clearly in the arena, and some that are left outside—that must be left outside if the ones inside are to be recognizable as children's literature? Put another way, Small is suggesting that certain kinds of presentations of certain kinds of materials exclude a work from the arena of children's literature.

The question here is one of definition. How does one define a book as a children's book? What are the criteria for deciding that this one is a children's book and that one is not? How do these criteria help to decide these categories, and how do they help a reader to appreciate a children's book as a children's book?

Blurred Boundaries

At first the boundaries of children's literature do not seem to be difficult to describe. Certainly it is the case that there are books for children and there are books for adults. There are elements that readers can readily recognize that distinguish the two. Or, at least, it seems intuitively that there should be. But as soon as those elements begin to be enumerated, the distinctions begin to blur. *Bright and Early Thursday Evening* is a picture book. It uses quick and paradoxical turns of phrase: "To expand my tale I'll summarize," "That stranger was my best friend." It employs fantasy, both in text and illustration, to suggest the exotic turns of experience a dream might take. None of these elements is unique to an adult book; in fact, all of these seem as though they might, instead, be qualities of a children's book.

The paradox here is that the qualifying *children's* in "children's literature" seems to work from the assumption that this literature has certain boundaries. It is children's literature as distinct from adult literature. It seems as though it must be a subset of "literature" that could be described and, in being described, bound.

But *children's literature* turns out to be the most slippery of terms. It is not a term that limits by period or date, such as seventeenth-century literature or medieval literature. It is not a term that limits by authorship, as women's literature. It is not a term that bounds by culture or ethnicity, as Russian literature or Inuit literature. In fact, it is a remarkably unusual term in that it does not define at all in terms of the creators of the literature.

Instead, it is a term that defines by audience. This is literature written for children. But even that apparently simple formula is problematic. It suggests that there is a single, understood way of defining *children.* In fact, it suggests that children are a homogenous audience that may be defined and characterized, though this is clearly not the case. Even if we were to define *childhood,* as society has tried to do, by limiting it according to age—say, twelve or thirteen—there is still the recognition that literature that appeals to an audience of five year olds will probably not appeal to an audience of twelve year olds. Defining by audience does not bring with it a uniform audience; it brings with it a group of readers at many developmental stages, some of whom will be reading what are clearly regarded as "adult" books long before they leave the age of childhood.

Historical perspective yields little in resolving the issue of how to understand the audience for what are purportedly children's books. The earliest children's books, other than primers, didactic Sunday School tracts and educational texts, were, in fact, works that had not been written for a child audience. John Bunyan's *Pilgrim's Progress,* Jonathan Swift's *Gulliver's Travels,* and Daniel Defoe's *Robinson Crusoe*—all are works adopted by a child audience. Each of these works claimed child readers because of its strong narrative line, its engaging protagonist, its fabulous elements, its high drama. This does not mean that children were engaged, however, by some of these books' heavy didacticism, long moralizations, or cutting satire. Despite these elements, the books came to be read by children.

If we are to take *children's literature* to be a term that describes books that find a child audience, then we must classify *Pilgrim's Progress, Gulliver's Travels,* and *Robinson Crusoe* as works of children's literature. But most readers will sense that something is not quite right here. Today, each of these books has been revised and adapted to make them more accessible to a contemporary child audience. Were these works of children's literature when they were first written? Certainly their authors would not have seen them in such a manner. Nor would their early reviewers and readers. These were adult works, written for and to an adult audience.

The shift in audience works in the other direction as well, as children's books become popular for an adult audience. J. K. Rowling's Harry Potter series is, on the surface, a series of fantasies for a child audience in which the young Harry Potter attends Hogwarts, a school for witches, and there meets close friends and establishes a true family for the first time. Yet the books have achieved enormous popularity, both in North America and across the Atlantic, and have reached into the best-seller lists of major newspapers, prompting the question of whether a children's book belongs on such a list. The argument by those who would assert that they do not is an argument of definition—a children's book does not belong on a best-seller list of adult books. But if adults are reading the books—if, in fact, the adult audience has claimed Harry Potter as its own—then in what sense is a Harry Potter book *not* an adult book? The question of audience muddles the definition considerably.

So, if children as audience are at the center of the definition of this genre, how are we to understand the meaning of the qualifier?

Exclusive and Inclusive Boundaries

If we do understand the term *children's literature* to be focused on a description of audience, the corollary question is whether that term is meant to be exclusive or inclusive. If it is exclusive, then the term suggests that this is literature that is meant only for the child, not for the adult. Children's literature in this sense is completely other, a set of works completely separate from those works judged to be adult literature. In this model, a reader is involved with children's books for a time, then matures and leaves them behind forever. Certainly, it does seem that there are many books marketed for children that do fall into such a category; they are the books one buys at the supermarket checkout lane, the spin-off books marketed after a hit film or television series, the instantly manufactured biographies of a teen star of some sort.

But writers of children's literature have argued vigorously against such an understanding of children's literature. The Victorian fantasist George MacDonald set the pace when he asserted that, "I write not for the child, but for the childlike." C. S. Lewis, the author of the *Narnia Chronicles,* argued eloquently that "where the children's story is simply the right form for what the author has to say, then of course readers who want to hear that will read the story or reread it at any age.... I am almost inclined to set it up as a canon that a children's story which is enjoyed only by children is a bad children's story. The good ones last. A waltz which you can like only when you are waltzing is a bad waltz." In this sense, children's literature is not only for children, but about childhood—a subject worthy of any reader, any writer.

An inclusive definition begins not with the word *children's,* but with the word *literature.* Children's literature is, first of all, literature. It shares all the aesthetic and structural and ethical principles that govern any work worthy of the title *literature.* It must pass all the aesthetic criteria that mark any book that wishes to be considered literature rather than the stuff of supermarket aisles.

Still, *children's* qualifies the term *literature.* This body of literature, this subset, is work that can be enjoyed by any reader, but it can also be enjoyed by child readers. Charles Dickens's *Bleak House* or Samuel Beckett's *Waiting for Godot* may speak powerfully to adult readers and viewers; they are unlikely to speak at all to a child audience. On the other hand, E. B. White's *Charlotte's Web,* Kenneth Grahame's *The Wind in the Willows,* J. R. R. Tolkien's *The Hobbit,* Maurice Sendak's *Where the Wild Things Are,* Katherine Paterson's *Bridge to Terabithia,* Patricia MacLachlan's *Sarah, Plain and Tall*—all of these works of children's literature speak to the adult reader as well. Their boundaries of readership are inclusive, not at all exclusive.

This does not mean that a child reader and an adult reader might be able to articulate the same meanings after reading a work of children's literature. The best works of children's literature, like Walt Whitman, contain multitudes. It may be that child readers and adult readers will take away complementary meanings or even distinctly different meanings. Maurice Sendak's *Where the Wild Things Are* (1963) may be read by a child as an adventure story. Max, sent off to bed because he is naughty, finds his room mysteriously changed into a forest and, finally, "the world all around." He gets into a boat and comes to the land of the monstrous Wild Things, whom he tames through his magic. Finally he wants to return home, and leaves the land of the Wild Things to come back to his own room.

An adult reader may find the same sense of adventure, but go beyond as well. For the adult reader, this may be the story of a young boy who is bored because his parents are absent; thus, he makes "mischief of one kind and another." When his mother responds in anger, so, too, does he. But, while his mother is an adult, he is a child and cannot deal with the enormously conflicting emotions that are in him: He is angry at the person he loves most in the world, a conflict that adults can assimilate but that may be difficult for a child. So Max enters into fantasy to find a situation he can control in the midst of emotions he cannot: the land of the Wild Things. Once the emotions are played out and resolved, he can return to his own room, out of the fantasy, to find that his mother has gone through a similar ordeal. She has left supper on the table, "and it was still hot."

The point here is that both readings are absolutely legitimate. The adult should be able to enjoy the book as an adventure story even as she enjoys the book on a deeper psychological level. But the child, though he may sense the deeper story, may simply enjoy the book as Max's adventure, and that is a sufficient reading. The day will come when that reading becomes more complex, but, for now, the book can be enjoyed and understood on that level.

Libby Hathorn's *Way Home* (1994) also supports this kind of multiple reading—indeed, it calls for it. This is a picture book with less resolution than *Where the Wild Things Are*. In it, the young boy Shane finds a cat and brings it home, carrying it from all dangers until he reaches his place of relative security. The landscape is urban; the dangers inherent to that landscape are very real, very threatening. And young Shane's final place of security is, in the end, only a makeshift shack at the end of an alley; he lives by himself. The conclusion is, therefore, poignant; he now has company, but the only company he has is a cat.

The adult reader will recognize particularly Gregory Rogers's visual clues about the nature of Shane's relationships. The pictures on the walls of the alley in which Shane finds the cat suggest the spiritual desolation of this urban landscape: One image is the face of one of the damned in Michaelangelo's "Last Judgment"; the other is of the hand of God reaching for the lifeless hand of Adam, taken from the Sistine Chapel. However, a tear has made their connection impossible. At the end of the book the same image appears, only this time the tear is covered over by a picture of a cat, suggesting a repairing of relationships. On the other wall of Shane's shack is a picture of a house that Shane has pinned up, clearly something for which he longs. These elements, which a child reader might not recognize, add to the depth of the aloneness—both of the cat and of Shane himself. But the child reader does not need to understand all of these images to comprehend and enjoy the work.

Children's literature, then, is, first, literature. As children's literature, it is available to all readers, to both adults and children.

The Child Audience as a Defining Boundary

Yet, even if children's literature is indeed for all ages, there are still some distinctions that establish its boundaries as a subset within literature. While children's literature shares the qualities of all literature, it must also have its unique identifying qualities.

It is at this crux that so many difficulties in definition arise. The question here revolves around the constitution of the subset. If there are certain books that are distinctly children's literature with identifiable qualities, one is first faced with the difficulty of deciding which books constitute the subset from which those identifiable qualities will be derived. Here there is a plurality of voices. P. L. Travers and Maurice Sendak would suggest that children's literature is literature about children, or perhaps about childhood. Others might argue that children's literature is that body of literature that children read and enjoy, both now and in a given period of time. Others suggest that children's literature is that literature that educators and parents have judged to be written for children. Some authors might agree with Lewis that children's literature is a form within which the writer works. Other authors might disagree, suggesting that children's literature is a literature purposefully aimed at a child readership. Working from the perspective of marketing, others argue that children's literature is that set of works that are distinctly marketed for a child audience.

There is a single common denominator to all of these approaches: the child as audience.

Is children's literature for the child? Yes.
Is children's literature about the child? Yes.
Is children's literature directed by the author to the child? Yes.

The commonality in children's literature is a concern on the part of author and illustrator to deal with the experience of the child in a way that the child can access, understand, and enjoy. Emily Brontë's *Wuthering Heights* and Charlotte Brontë's *Jane Eyre* may in many ways be about childhood, among other things, but neither is written with a child audience in view. More than one reader has had the experience of having a book "ruined" by a too early reading.

For a book to be a work of children's literature, there needs to be some sense that the work is, in fact, being read by a child audience. This does not mean that the work is to be dumbed down, or the vocabulary necessarily controlled, or the ending sweetened, or even certain topics avoided. It does mean that the writer and illustrator must recognize the nature of the audience. It would be odd, for example, to include an explicit sexual scene in a novel for the very young child. Aside from the ethical questions, which are legion, there is the fact that the young child will simply have no experience by which to understand and enjoy such a scene, aside, perhaps, for some half-understood titillation. Such a mature scene would be inappropriate for the audience, at least on one level, because it is completely outside the experience of the audience.

It is this very sensitivity to the experience of the child that marks the best in children's literature. In Robert McCloskey's *Blueberries for Sal* (1948), this sensitivity is quite subtle. When Sal loses her mother on Blueberry Hill while gathering fruit for the next winter, Little Bear simultaneously wanders away from his mother. Little Bear will eventually find Little Sal's mother, and Little Sal find Little Bear's. When Little Bear's mother turns to see Sal, McCloskey writes that "she took one good look and backed away. (She was old enough to be shy of people, even a very small person like Little Sal.) Then she turned around and walked off very fast to hunt for Little Bear." (42) McCloskey, understanding his audience, has no desire to frighten; Little Bear's mother is not going to gobble up Little Sal. So he has the mother back quickly away to search for her own child.

The accompanying illustration shows the same kind of sensitivity to audience. Little Sal stands beside Little Bear's mother, showing her the pail with three blueberries she has just picked; Little Bear's mother stares at her in astonishment. When McCloskey first drew the illustration, he had Little Sal and Little Bear's mother quite close together, but, at the suggestion of his editor May Massee, he moved them farther apart, recognizing that, for a little child, even an inquisitive and fearless little child like Sal, the mere proximity to something so large would be terribly daunting. Moving them apart responded to this difficulty.

In such a case, McCloskey has responded to his perceptions—as well as his editor's—of the nature of his child audience. He is true to the experience of childhood, and aware of how his child readers will respond.

The Experience of Childhood
as a Defining Boundary

Both McCloskey and Sendak recognize that they are writing for a child audience, but they also recognize that they are writing about childhood. They are writing about an experience that a child can understand and enjoy, using a child's perceptions about the world that lies so closely around, though those perceptions are mediated by an adult artist.

Here, historical perspective is helpful. Up until the latter decades of the nineteenth century, children's literature—if children's literature could be said to exist at all—did not work towards such perceptions. Children's literature was in fact *prescriptive* in its approach. Adults prescribed through education, so that children's books taught the current acceptable morals and values of society, indoctrinating children into a particular set of social beliefs. This meant that children's literature sought to define the manner in which a child's experience should be conducted and understood, as in this passage from *First Lessons on the Great Principles of Religion* (1833). Here, Susan, who has a sickly mother (of course), decides that she will deceive.

> Now Susan, like other naughty children, did not like school much, and she used often to wish she could be walking about the streets instead of sitting there all day. One day she determined to take a walk, instead of going to school. When she set out she saw that her mother was watching her from the window, so she went along the road, and turned round the corner that led to the school-house, so as to make her mother think that she was going there. Was not that lying? Susan took a long walk, and came home about the time when the scholars came back from school. Her mother thought she had been at school, and her teacher thought she must be sick, or something had happened to keep her away. So, you see, she deceived them both. (35–36)

The strong narrator carries the stern, judgmental voice of the adult who uses the story for a didactic purpose: One should not become a liar. (It is little wonder that poor Susan comes to a bad end.) This is literature suggesting what a child's experience should be, and showing the dangers of what will happen should it not be so.

Later in the century, illustrators like Kate Greenaway and, especially, Randolph Caldecott moved from this prescriptive form of literature to a much more *descriptive form;* they described the child's experience, rather than suggesting what form that experience should take. Caldecott's series of picture books created a completely new approach to children's literature. Here were drawings that showed a child's perspective that undercut the seriousness and pretensions of the adult world. William Goldsmith's comic "Elegy on the Death of a Mad Dog," for example, takes on a wickedly funny perspective as Caldecott arranges it in his *Picture Book No. 1* (1879); Caldecott laughs at the stuffy pretensions of the man, the arrogant self-righteousness of the fellow who makes show of his piety. Once the dog turns against the man, the illustrations depict riotous and ridiculous flights by the adult world that clambers over walls, up trees, around corners; one woman hides behind an umbrella. After the bite, Caldecott focuses on the gossip about the event, the assertion by many that the man would die, and the lack of real concern by anyone over the possible death. The conclusion—in which the dog dies of the bite—underscores Caldecott's subversive interpretation. It would be hard to exaggerate the huge character of the change that Caldecott represented. From his time on, though the didactic vision would continue, children's literature would focus on the child's experience, the child's vision of the world, describing what that world is like to and for a child.

Such a change made possible books like *The Snowy Day* (1962) and *Louie* (1975) by Ezra Jack Keats. In these works, Keats explores the inner life of the child. In *The Snowy Day,* he uses collage to create the sensations felt by Peter when he goes out into a snowfall in an urban landscape. The piles are huge, piling up well over his head, and the fields of snow are vast, as they would be to a very young child. The snowballs of the big boys are similarly huge, as are the hills Peter

Randolph Caldecott's illustration for William Goldsmith's "An Elegy on the Death of a Mad Dog" (1879); later published in *R. Caldecott's Picture Book No. 1* (London: Frederick Warne, n.d.).

slides down. Keats is not interested in representing the snow exactly as it might be; instead, he represents it as the child Peter perceives it.

In *Louie*, Keats shows the interior life of a very shy boy, a boy with no father and no friends; he has, however, a rich interior life that is filled with an imagination that takes him far from his dark and bare room. Here Keats uses dark, somber colors and varying perspective to show Louie's inner world. In one image, Louie walks home alone, bowed over, while a wall filled with torn and dirtied advertisements looms over him. Here, too, Keats is describing the experience of childhood, not prescribing the nature of that experience.

In this sense, children's literature is literature with a child as audience, and with a focus on the experience and world of the child reader. In fact, such a focus is necessary for the child reader to understand the work.

Distinguishing Qualities of the Literature as Boundaries

Thus, though children's literature is literature, it is literature that a child reader must be able to access, understand, and enjoy. It is literature that responds to a specific audience and to which a specific audience responds. This kind of mutual responsiveness necessitates certain distinctive characteristics. None of these distinctions is marked by totality; there are exceptions to all. Yet there are a number of qualities that are accurate generalizations about a work of children's literature.

- Children's literature is generally shorter than adult literature. This is, of course, true of picture books, which generally extend to about thirty-two pages. But it is also true for the novels, which are generally below two hundred pages.
- Children's literature often has a strong dependence on the visual elements of the book. Again, this is true, of course, in the picture books that depend on the illustrations to convey much of the narrative. But it is also true of those novels that employ illustrations to establish character, setting, perspective.
- The language and sentence structure of a work of children's literature generally recognize the needs of its audience. This does not mean that the vocabulary must necessarily be limited, or the sentence structures all simple. It does mean that the author recognizes that diction is crucial in reaching this audience, and that sentence structures that become so convoluted as to lose a young reader will not be effective in this context.
- The plot of a work of children's literature is usually active rather than passive. While protagonists certainly are seen thinking, much more time is spent on doing.
- The narrative perspective of a work in children's literature is often either that of a strong, omniscient voice or that of a child. In either case the narrator is usually to be trusted. An untrustworthy narrator is generally not part of the field, though some certainly occur.
- The protagonists of a work in children's literature are most often children themselves. This is not always the case, but it often is, even when the principal characters are animals. Here the focus of children's literature on the world and experience of the child comes into play.
- The conclusions of works of children's literature are often strongly resolved, or point toward strong resolution. Generally the plot narratives and character developments are rounded off, completed, and not left ambiguous or unresolved. Most often it is the child character who actively solves the plot complication, or who at least changes in some significant way to suggest the resolution.
- Though all narrative structures of children's literature are generally available to the writer of children's literature, this is generally not the arena for the use of the more complex structures. Elements such as stream-of-consciousness narrative, metafictive discourse, simultaneous narrative plotlines, flashback—in short, those elements difficult for a young reader to follow—are usually not part of children's literature.
- Children's literature is generally tightly controlled in terms of the multiplicity of its perspectives. Usually there is only a single narrative perspective in the work; if there are more, they are of a limited number and clearly distinguished.

- Children's literature is generally clear in depicting distinct moral worlds. Though there are moral ambiguities, it is generally quite clear who is on what side of the fence when that fence represents an ethical dimension. There is an assumption of a moral and ethical world where choices are made that respond to moral and ethical questions.
- The tone of a work of children's literature is generally optimistic. This does not mean that the work must conclude with a "happily ever after" ending, but it is the case that most works of children's literature do not end with bleak despair, but with a sense that at least the right direction, if not total happiness, has been achieved. However, as with all of these generalizations, there are significant exceptions, and certainly a number of children's books end with a resolution that leaves the reader with ambiguity.

A work like Robert McCloskey's *Blueberries for Sal* (1948) demonstrates a number of these qualities. Though the narrator is third-person omniscient, the perspective of the book is consistently that of Little Sal or Little Bear, the two child protagonists of the story, though one is in fact a bear cub. The story is set in the world of a child, focusing on a child's experience: the adult gathering many berries, but the impossibility of picking enough berries without eating them to fill even the bottom of the child's pail. Bored, the child wanders.

The structure of the plot places two identical stories side by side; their parallelism makes their connections easy to follow. That same parallelism establishes a tight perspective; even though the perspective switches back and forth from Little Sal to Little Bear, the similarities in their stories seem to minimize the shift in perspective. The conclusion is well resolved: Little Bear and his mother go off to sleep for the winter with full bellies, while Little Sal and her mother return to their kitchen to can the berries for next winter. The parallel structure is maintained even here, as the book concludes on the optimistic note of plenitude and security for the child.

Rachel Isadora paints a less secure world in her *At the Crossroads* (1991), but still keeps her work well within the boundaries of children's literature. Set in one of the villages of corrugated metal in South Africa, it is the story of a group of children who are waiting for their fathers to come home from the mines; they have not been home for ten months. The children play at center stage here, and the perspective is universally theirs. The first-person narrative perspective emphasizes this child-centeredness: "We eat quickly and leave for school. On the way we meet our friends. 'Our fathers are coming home!' we shout."

The simplicity of the story is complemented by the simplicity of the sentence structures. The very structure of the story itself is quite simple, as the children leave school to wait at the crossroads for their fathers. While they wait, they play on makeshift instruments, which are not at all makeshift to them. It is only in the illustrations, not in the voice of the narrator, that the reader sees that the guitar is a can with metal wire, and the drum a plastic canister. The children wait all through the night until dawn, when their fathers finally do come. The resolution is a joyous one, as they take up their instruments and lead their fathers home. Though there is the clear sense that their fathers will leave again for another ten months, there is also the intense joy and optimism of the reunion of the family that concludes this work.

This is not to say, however, that all works of children's literature must demonstrate all the above-mentioned qualities; there will be many exceptions. Wanda Gág's *Millions of Cats* (1928), for example, contains "a very old man and a very old woman" as its protagonists; there is no child in sight, although there is a young cat whom they choose to keep. The narrative perspective of William Mayne's novel *Drift* (1985) is radically altered as the story of a young boy's abduction by two Native American women is told first from his perspective, then from that of a young girl who follows him. Bijou Le Tord uses difficult diction in lines such as "to live harmoniously" in her *The Deep Blue Sea* (1990), a creation story for the very young child, and Jonathan London will include foreign terms such as *Shoukran* and *kesrah* in his picture book, *Ali: Child of the Desert* (1997). Katherine Paterson uses an unreliable narrator in her *Jacob Have I Loved* (1980), so that the reader must sort through the terrible jealousy that clouds Louise's description of her life with her sister Caroline to understand that Louise is filled with hatred. Lois Lowry, in *The Giver* (1993), uses an ambiguous ending, so that the reader must decide if Jonas and the baby Gabriel have indeed escaped to freedom, or if the novel concludes with their death. And the conclusion of David Wisniewski's *Golem* (1996) is haunting: The giant that has saved the Jewish community from the barbarism of its persecutors has himself been destroyed by those he has saved, and there is the terrible sense that he may have to be resurrected again—and used—when there is "the desperate need for justice"; that is, the Golem's purposes have not been fulfilled forever.

All of these exceptions—and the many, many others not mentioned—suggest that children's literature is not easily definable, not easily pinned down. It is a vast and wide-ranging arena where there is experimentation, where there are boundaries that are pushed, where there are works firmly in the center and works swirling around the edges. But all are marked, in the end, by a concern for the child reader as audience.

One Thematic Center of Children's Literature: The Boundary Marked by Home

Children's literature is marked by a number of thematic centers that commonly focus on the experience of the child; often this is a boundary marked by the need for belongingness. Here, thematic centers such as school, friendship, a relationship with an animal, and, quite often, home, show common concerns that bring works of children's literature together. Though these themes will be understood differently by different readers, the emphasis on home stands as one of the dominant centers.

In Robert McCloskey's *Make Way for Ducklings* (1941), Father and Mother Mallard search the streets of Boston for a safe place to bring their children up. They settle at first in the Public Gardens, but soon find that the bicycles are too busy for them. They fly over the State House, past Louisburg Square, and finally to an island in the Charles River, where they settle and have eight ducklings. Mr. Mallard flies back up the river while Mrs. Mallard trains the children, and they agree to meet in the Public Gardens. When the ducklings are ready, Mrs. Mallard brings them safely through the traffic of Boston, aided by Michael the policeman. Together they arrive at the Public Gardens, and "there was Mr. Mallard waiting for them, just as he had promised." *Make Way for Ducklings* is about a search for home. Home here is a place of security, where there is plenty to eat, a place to sleep safely at night, the pleasure of the family, and, most importantly, a sense that here, at the very least here, promises will be kept.

In *Time of Wonder* (1957), a later picture book, McCloskey again uses an island to suggest home, only this time the island is his own, and the characters are he and his wife, and their two daughters. McCloskey takes the reader through a summer on the island, showing his daughters on the beach and in the water, depicting the delights of the Maine shore. But, at the center of the story is a storm, and McCloskey spends a great deal of the story preparing for it. The parents gather in the boats and check the house. During the height of the storm, they are singing and battening down, using cloths to keep out the driving salt air. When McCloskey pictures the scene outside, he shows a wild, chaotic rain that covers the island and seems to splinter the air, but in the center is a yellow light, standing firm. It is the light of their house. Home is a place of absolute, unquestioned security.

Home may not always be a place of absolute, unquestioned security; in *Way Home* and *At the Crossroads*, for example, home is quite threatened. But the large emphasis in children's literature is towards the establishment or the finding or the securing of home. Generally the plotlines of a work of children's literature center around this thematic center: Home. One of the distinguishing marks of adolescent or young adult literature is the shifting of that thematic center: Adolescent literature is often about the protagonist's movement away from home and towards the establishment of the individual self. But in children's literature, the movement is much more strongly back to the security and presence of home.

A number of works in children's literature deal with this thematic center very explicitly. Eve Bunting's *Fly Away Home* (1991) tells the story of a father and son forced to live secretly in an airport; as the father tries to find work and a place to live, they also must try to live without attracting attention. When the boy sees people greeting passengers to take them home, he is frustrated: "Sometimes I get mad, and I want to turn at them and push them and shout, 'Why do *you* have homes when we don't? What makes *you* so special?'" (30) The work concludes with the young boy seeing a trapped bird escape from the airport, and he hopes that they too will eventually find a home.

In Beverly and David Fiday's *Time to Go* (1990), the story is of the loss of home: "The acres of my family's farm stretch endlessly before me. We've been here for as far back as anyone can remember. But today all that will change. Today we

Illustration by Ronald Himler for Eve Bunting's *Fly Away Home.*
Copyright © 1991. Reprinted by permission of Clarion Books.

are leaving. Papa says it's time to go." The book juxtaposes brightly colored images from the boy's memory of the good, fertile times on the farm, with brown, blander pictures of the empty and poor acres and buildings. The still tractor is set against the tractor plowing the field, with the boy and his father on top. The straight rows of the garden are set against the wreck of the scare-crow and the marauding crows that eat at the plants. One day, the boy re-solves, he will return, but it is not clear if the concluding illustration is set in the future, where an older boy looks over fertile fields, or if that image too comes from his imagination.

In Judith Hendershot's quiet pic-ture book, *In Coal Country* (1987), a young girl recounts the life of her family in a small, coal-mining town in Ohio. The reader may come to the book with some preconceptions of the life of a coal miner, but here the story is told from the point of view of the young girl, where all the world around her is extraordinary. Life is hard: Papa works very long hours in the mine and the air is so acrid that it peels paint off the houses. Mixed with that is the beauty established in a home: "The houses were huddled in a hollow between two softly rising hills. In the spring the hills were covered with lady's-slippers and yellow and white violets. Mama always had a jar of spring flowers on the kitchen table. Weeping willow trees lined the banks of the creek that flowed behind Company Row." This mixing of the beautiful with the difficult dominates the book; everyone works hard, but there is the joy of a created home where the children have the whole wide world to play and where, back home, they find security and love.

In each of these stories, the search for a secure and loving home dominates. Such a search is at the center of children's literature. Often, however, that ques-tion is addressed more obliquely, in an infinite variety of ways.

Sometimes the emphasis is on the search for a home. In Robert San Souci's *Nicholas Pipe* (1997), San Souci recasts a twelfth-century folktale about a merman who loves a woman whose father has him caged and taken away; far from the sea, he dies on the road. In San Souci's version, however, the story is slanted to emphasize the mutual searching for a home, so that in the end he is rescued and brought back to the water. He and his wife-to-be resolve to marry, realizing that, though they are creatures of land or sea, their children will be at home in both; they will create a home, then, in an impossible situation. In Keizaburo Tejima's *Fox's Dream* (1985), a lonely fox wanders through the landscape of Hokkaido, his loneliness emphasized by the images he constructs in the ice of his childhood with his mother and other cubs. By the end of the book, however, he has found a vixen, and the suddenly bright colors suggest the creation of a new home.

In Sarah Stewart's *The Gardener* (1997), Lydia Grace Finch must leave her home during the Depression and live with Uncle Jim in the city. Lydia sets out to make Uncle Jim's bakery a home, and she does this through her own instinctual goodness and through her love of flowers and color, which she spreads everywhere. Her goal is to make Uncle Jim smile, and, though he never does, he finds another way to show the enormity of his love for Lydia, who succeeds in establishing home. In Allen Say's *Grandfather's Journey* (1993), Say depicts the story of his own family's search for a home. Coming from Japan, he travels all over the United States, but eventually is drawn back to his home. Say himself repeats the cycle, but in reverse. "The funny thing is," he concludes, "the moment I am in one country, I am homesick for the other." (31) Say here respects his child readers' ability to understand and accept the complex, the ambiguous, and the contradictory emotions that mark us all, children and adults.

Other works approach this theme by dealing with the needs of home. Sherry Garland's *My Father's Boat* (1998) deals with the passing on of traditions, as Garland recounts a day in the life of a Vietnamese shrimp fisherman who teaches his son about fishing even as he was taught by his father. The poignancy of this story comes from the sense of separation, for the young narrator's grandfather remains in Vietnam, but the boy and his father now live in the United States. But "the heart does not count the years" of separation, and home is still preserved in memory. Leo Lionni's *Frederick* (1967) suggests the mutuality of life at home. Certainly the grains and foods that the other mice gather are necessary for a secure home in this book, but just as necessary is the poetry and imagery collected by Frederick. Patricia Polacco's *Just Plain Fancy* (1990) similarly suggests the mutuality of family needs, as a peacock is integrated into the farmlife of a young Amish girl with the acknowledgement that "this be God's handiwork": he is fancy because God made him that way, even if he is in a community that celebrates the plain.

In each of these books, home is at the center of the concern, whether that home is established and well secured, or whether that home is being defined, or whether that home is being threatened. Home is one powerful center of children's literature, one organizing—though not exclusive—boundary. It is itself part of the larger thematic concern for belonging that marks so very much children's literature.

Pushing the Boundaries: Books on the Edge of Children's Literature

Because of the difficulties in strictly defining the boundaries of children's literature, those boundaries remain somewhat amorphous. Clearly, *Make Way for Ducklings* is inside the circle; clearly, *Bleak House* is outside the circle. But many works are not so easily placed. If *Bleak House* is outside, is Dickens's *A Christmas Carol*?

And what to do with those classic works that have come into the field, works like *Robinson Crusoe* and *Pilgrim's Progress*? Are they children's literature only when adapted, as in Selina Hastings' *The Canterbury Tales* (1988), James Riordan's *Gulliver's Travels* (1992), or Geraldine McCaughrean's *Moby Dick* (1996)?

Here, a work like Maurice Sendak's *Dear Mili* (1988) illustrates the difficulty. This story, collected by Wilhelm Grimm, seems like it must be a work of children's literature; it is, after all, a folktale and illustrated as a picture book. But the story itself presents real difficulties and reminds the adult reader that folktales were never originally meant for a child audience. When a young girl is sent from home because of a war, she escapes into the woods for three days and is comforted by a guardian angel and St. Joseph. In Sendak's vivid illustrations, the woods are terribly threatening, almost overwhelming. When the girl returns home, she finds that each day has been a decade, and she falls into her ancient mother's arms. That night, they lie down and die together.

The hard ending makes this text difficult to be understood as a work of children's literature. Sendak's vivid illustrations complement this difficulty. In one illustration set in the woods, refugees clamber over a bridge, their faces haunted and discolored. Behind them looms the shape of a concentration camp; none of this is part of the text, but certainly part of its tenor. Yet, if children's literature is about the experience of the child, it certainly may be about the experience of loss, of grief, and hope quashed. These too, regrettably, are part of the child's experience. In this sense *Dear Mili,* despite its very unhappy ending, does fit into the arena of children's literature.

One way in which children's literature has traditionally been bounded has been through subject matter. There have simply been certain experiences that children's literature did not explore, or at least did not explore without euphemism and indirection. This extended also to illustration, which abjured problematic visuals. Nudity, excessive violence, sometimes even the dirty griminess of life were all avoided. In later years, those boundaries have come down, and books like Charles Mikolaycak's *Orpheus* (1992), with quite explicit nudity and gruesome violence, have been published and marketed as children's literature. Even the standard of children's literature as being about the experience of childhood, or at least working within the experience or perspective of the child, has been breached. Tom Feelings's brilliant *The Middle Passage* (1995), for example, is a vivid and powerful visual depiction of the horrors of the slave trade, using illustrations that are both realistic and allegorical. But the horror of the pictures—the branding, the sexual assault, the whipping, the murders, the drowning, the sharks eating slaves thrown overboard—surely these are not the stuff of children's literature.

To be children's literature, a work must speak to and about the experience of the child. Though boundaries in terms of subject matter are open, that principle is still unchanged. It may be that a book will deal with harsh realities, but to be a work of children's literature, the book must somehow deal with those realities in a way that the child reader can understand from within his or her experience.

A recent illustrated edition of Martin Luther King, Jr.'s *I Have a Dream* (1997) suggests the possibility of using material that is, on the one hand, adult, but presenting it in a manner that a child can understand and appreciate. Though the child reader may not fully understand the context of the speech, the message of tolerance, brotherhood, and community that it espouses is captured in the fifteen illustrations of the book. The speech is broken down into small segments, and each is illustrated with a picture that often focuses on the child: the African American drummer in the Civil War, the young family standing together while every valley is exalted, the two young children of different races dancing close together, the table of brotherhood where folks of all races gather around, the "unspeakable horror" when two young children stand below the baton of a policeman. In each case there is the perspective of the child to mediate the meaning of the text.

I Have a Dream does what all works of children's literature must do: It works from the experience and the perspective of the child. It is not cast at the adult looking over the child's shoulder, but engages the child reader. This is why neither *Orpheus* nor *The Middle Passage* is a successful children's book. Neither engages the child in a way that allows the child to understand the experience of the book.

Children's literature must speak about the child reader and about that reader's world in a way that the reader can comprehend. It must use all the aesthetic principles that any literature uses to provide a full and meaningful experience, one worthy of the name of literature—and, in that sense, it must speak to all audiences. And it must create the kind of experience that delights, that engages. In the end, it must be a literature that a child enjoys.

Thinking and Writing about and from within Children's Literature

Thinking and Writing about Children's Literature

1. Choose one of the following books and argue whether or not it is a work of children's literature:

    Nancy Willard, *Pish, Posh, Said Hieronymus Bosch* (1991). Illustrated by Leo and Diane Dillon.

    Paul Goble, *Love Flute* (1992).

    Robert Frost, *Birches* (1988). Illustrated by Ed Young.

    Ed Young, *Voices of the Heart* (1997).

    Jim McGugan. *Josepha, A Prairie Boy's Story* (1994). Illustrated by Murray Kimber.

    Geraldine McCaughrean. *El Cid* (1988). Illustrated by Victor Ambrus.

2. Browse through a local children's library until you find a book that you remember from your own childhood reading. Choose a book here that has particularly powerful associations for you. After reading it over, reflect in an informal essay about whether the book is still meaningful for you. Are your responses to it mere emotion and sentimentality—nostalgia for the past—or is the book still able to convey a strong reading experience?

3. Can a child's story be openly didactic and still be an enjoyable reading experience? Choose a contemporary book that you feel to be heavily didactic and examine whether or not it works as a successful children's book.

4. Choose one of the following novels to read: Cynthia Voigt's *Building Blocks* (1984), Christopher Paul Curtis's *The Watsons Go to Birmingham—1963* (1995), Beverly Cleary's *Dear Mr. Henshaw* (1983), Phyllis Reynolds Naylor's *Shiloh* (1991), or Lois Lowry's *Gathering Blue* (2000). All of these novels put children in problematic situations, often situations centered in the adult world. In a book review for one of these, show how the author is able to provide the child reader with a way of entering into the significance of these problems, while still maintaining the perspective of the child.

Thinking and Writing from within Children's Literature _____

1. Think about a hot, hot day in the city. Write a story about a very young child, say five or six, who spends the day trying to get cool. Keep in mind the perspective of the child.

2. Choose a monument that celebrates an event in North American history. Probably this will reflect an event that requires an adult understanding to grasp its full import, but tell a story of a young child's trip to the monument with parents, grandparents, or, perhaps, schoolmates. How will you go about making that monument meaningful to a young audience?

3. Retell an experience from your own childhood that centers on a specific holiday. Holiday stories can be very clichéd, so you will have to avoid the expected. Tell the story as a child's story, avoiding the adult narrator looking back on childhood but still speaking to an adult audience.

4. Retell a story that involves injustice for a child audience. The injustice may be on a national scale, or it may be on a very private scale. Think about how you will make the child respond to that injustice. How will he or she deal with a potentially new and unsettling view of the nature of the world?

Selected Bibliographies

Works Cited _____

Bunting, Eve. *Fly Away Home.* New York: Clarion, 1991. Illustrated by Ronald Himler.

Caldecott, Randolph. *Randolph Caldecott's Picture Book No. 1.* London: Frederick Warne, n.d.

Cleary, Beverly. *Dear Mr. Henshaw.* New York: William Morrow, 1983.

Curtis, Christopher Paul. *The Watsons Go to Birmingham—1963.* New York: Delacorte, 1995.

Feelings, Tom. *The Middle Passage.* New York: Dial, 1995.

Fiday, Beverly and David. *Time to Go.* New York: Harcourt, Brace, 1990. Illustrated by Thomas Allen.

First Lessons on the Great Principles of Religion. Philadelphia: American Sunday-School Union, 1833.

Frost, Robert. *Birches.* New York: Henry Holt, 1988. Illustrated by Ed Young.

Gág, Wanda. *Millions of Cats.* New York: Coward-McCann, 1928.

Garland, Sherry. *My Father's Boat.* New York: Scholastic, 1998. Illustrated by Ted Rand.

Goble, Paul. *Love Flute.* New York: Bradbury, 1992.

Grimm, Wilhelm. *Dear Mili.* New York: Farrar, Straus, 1988. Illustrated by Maurice Sendak.

Hastings, Selina. *The Canterbury Tales.* New York: Henry Holt, 1988. Illustrated by Reg Cartwright.

Hathorn, Libby. *Way Home.* New York: Crown, 1994. Illustrated by Gregory Rogers.

Hendershot, Judith. *In Coal Country.* New York: Alfred Knopf, 1987. Illustrated by Thomas Allen.

Isadora, Rachel. *At the Crossroads.* New York: William Morrow, 1991.

Keats, Ezra Jack. *Louie.* New York: William Morrow, 1975.

———. *The Snowy Day.* New York: Viking, 1962.

King, Jr., Martin Luther. *I Have a Dream.* New York: Scholastic, 1997.

Le Tord, Bijou. *The Deep Blue Sea.* New York: Orchard, 1990.

Lionni, Leo. *Frederick.* New York: Pantheon, 1967.

London, Jonathan. *Ali: Child of the Desert.* New York: Lothrop, Lee and Shepherd, 1997. Illustrated by Ted Lewin.

Lowry, Lois. *Gathering Blue.* Boston: Houghton Mifflin, 2000.

———. *The Giver.* Boston: Houghton Mifflin, 1993.

Mayne, William. *Drift.* New York: Doubleday, 1985.

McCaughrean, Geraldine. *El Cid.* Oxford: Oxford University Press, 1988. Illustrated by Victor G. Ambrus.

———. *Moby Dick.* Oxford: Oxford University Press, 1996. Illustrated by Victor G. Ambrus.

McCloskey, Robert. *Blueberries for Sal.* New York: Viking, 1948.

———. *Make Way for Ducklings.* New York: Viking, 1941.

———. *Time of Wonder.* New York: Viking, 1957.

McGugan, Jim. *Josepha, a Prairie Boy's Story.* San Francisco: Chronicle, 1994. Illustrated by Murray Kimber.

Mikolaycak, Charles. *Orpheus.* New York: Harcourt, Brace, 1992.

Naylor, Phyllis Reynolds. *Shiloh.* New York: Doubleday, 1991.

Paterson, Katherine. *Jacob Have I Loved.* New York: Crowell, 1980.

Polacco, Patricia. *Just Plain Fancy.* New York: Bantam, 1990.

Riordan, James. *Gulliver's Travels.* Oxford: Oxford University Press, 1992. Illustrated by Victor G. Ambrus.

Rowling, J. K. *Harry Potter and the Sorcerer's Stone.* New York: Scholastic, 1997.

San Souci, Robert D. *Nicholas Pipe.* New York: Dial, 1997. Illustrated by David Shannon.

Say, Allen. *Grandfather's Journey.* Boston: Houghton Mifflin, 1993.

Sendak, Maurice. *Where the Wild Things Are.* New York: Harper and Row, 1963.

Stewart, Sarah. *The Gardener.* New York: Farrar, Straus, 1997. Illustrated by David Small.

Tejima, Keizaburo. *Fox's Dream.* New York: Philomel, 1985.

Voigt, Cynthia. *Building Blocks.* New York: Random House, 1984.

Willard, Nancy. *Pish, Posh, Said Hieronymous Bosch.* New York: Harcourt, Brace, 1991. Illustrated by Leo and Diane Dillon.

Wisniewski, David. *Golem.* New York: Clarion, 1996.

Wood, Audrey. *Bright and Early Thursday Evening.* New York: Harcourt, Brace, 1996. Illustrated by Don Wood.

Young, Ed. *Voices of the Heart.* New York: Scholastic, 1997.

Works on the Definition of Children's Literature

Barron, Pamela Petrick and Jennifer Q. Burley, eds. *Jump over the Moon.* New York: Holt, 1984.

Binghan, Jane and Gayce Scholt. *Fifteen Centuries of Children's Literature.* Westport, CT: Greenwood, 1980.

Collinson, Roger. "The Children's Author and His Reader." *Children's Literature in Education* 10 (1973): 37–49.

Eakin, Mary K. *Good Books for Children.* Chicago: Chicago University Press, 1966.

Gooderham, David. "Still Catching Them Young? The Moral Dimension in Young Children's Books." *Children's Literature in Education* 24 (1993): 155–172.

Hughes, Felicity. "Children's Literature: Theory and Practice." *ELH: English Literary History* 45 (1978): 542–561.

Hunt, Peter. *Children's Literature: The Development of Criticism.* New York: Routledge, 1990.

Knoepflmacher, U. C. and Mitzi Myers. "'Cross-Writing' and the Reconceptualizing of Children's Literary Studies." *Children's Literature* 25 (1997): vii–xvii.

Lesnik-Oberstein, Karin. *Children's Literature: Criticism and the Fictional Child.* Oxford: Clarendon, 1994.

Lewis, C. S. "On Three Ways of Writing for Children." In Sheila Egoff, ed., *Only Connect: Readings on Children's Literature."* New York: Oxford University Press, 1969: 207–220.

Lundin, Anne H. and Carol W. Cubberley. *Teaching Children's Literature.* Jefferson, NC: McFarland, 1995.

May, Jill. *Children's Literature and Critical Theory.* New York: Oxford, 1995.

McDowell, Myles. "Fiction for Children and Adults: Some Essential Differences." *Children's Literature in Education* 10 (1973): 50–63.

Meek, Margaret. "What Counts as Evidence in Theories of Children's Literature?" *Theory into Practice* 21 (Autumn 1982): 284–292.

Mills, Claudia. "The Ethics of the Author/Audience Relationship in Children's Fiction." *Children's Literature Association Quarterly* 22 (Winter, 1997–1998): 181–187.

Nodelman, Perry."Pleasure and Genre: Speculations on the Characteristics of Children's Fiction." *Children's Literature* 28 (2000): 1–14.

———. *The Pleasures of Children's Literature.* White Plains, NY: Longman, 1996.

Rose, Jacqueline. *The Case of Peter Pan, or The Impossibility of Children's Fiction.* Philadelphia: University of Pennsylvania Press, 1984.

Small, David. "Virtual Involvement." *Hungry Mind Review* 41 (Spring, 1997): 30.

Steig, Michael. *Stories of Reading.* Baltimore: Johns Hopkins University Press, 1989.

Stephens, John. *Language and Ideology in Children's Literature.* New York: Longmans, 1992.

2

Picture Books and the Narrative Role of Illustration

John Schoenherr's curiously named *Rebel* (1995) opens with an illustration that recalls Robert McCloskey's *Make Way for Ducklings* (1941): Two geese fly over a landscape looking for a safe place to raise their young. The text of both books seems similar as well. Both tell of the adult birds' concern for their young; they train them to keep close, they care for their needs, and they protect them well. "The world is cold, but the nest is warm. They huddle close under their mother," writes Schoenherr. "They nibble tender blades of grass and juicy shoots of weeds. As close as peas they stay together, never going far." It seems that this is a world as secure as that of the Mallard family.

As the title hints, there is something quite different here. The rebel gosling's story, told only in the illustrations, is a story of near abandonment. While the new goslings "huddle close under their mother," the illustration shows that the rebel has wandered to the other side of the island, where it stares at a young fawn; the father goose is racing across the island to bring it back. Though the goslings are all "as close as peas," in one scene the father goose rushes to protect the wandering rebel from a marauding hawk. Though the parents keep the goslings close to them and protect them through the night, the illustrations show that the rebel, in fact, wanders off the island and is pursued by two raccoons until he finds a place to hide beneath a log. When he returns, his family has all left: "They'll go together to a brooding ground, where all the families gather." The illustration shows the returned rebel alone against an empty landscape; the diction carries tremendous irony: *together, all, families, gather*. These are words that suggest union. But the rebel is entirely alone.

The next spread, however, presents restoration. As the rebel stands up high on his legs, he sees his family returning from the distance. The final illustration shows him standing still apart from his other siblings, but now under the very watchful care of his father. They will soon "all fly south together," the final line for the first time indicating a togetherness that is mirrored in the illustration.

Boundaries and Definitions

The Illustration as Narrative

Rebel suggests much about the role of illustration in a picture book. If the reader were to follow only the text of the book, then much of the full story would be lost. The title would seem irrelevant, and the story of the dangers that one gosling undergoes would be completely missing. The full meaning of the story can only be perceived through a union of text and illustration in which both the text and the illustration work together to produce the narrative.

A picture book, then, is a work in which the illustrations and the written text combine to form a single work of art. It is in the combination of text and illustration that meaning occurs. One without the other is impossible—or at least severely limits the experience of the reader and probably prohibits full understanding of the book's meaning.

Thus, the illustrations in a picture book are not merely decorative, nor do they merely function as literal representations of the text. Instead, the illustrations of a picture book extend the textual narrative and carry much of the narrative meaning itself. Reading a picture book, therefore, demands much more than simply reading the text. The reader must link the reading of the text with the reading of the pictures so that the two forms of reading combine to create a single experience.

Thus, a text that asserts the secure world of the geese comes across with one kind of reading. But, as the illustrations of *Rebel* are read, they convey a very different kind of story. They faithfully depict the landscape of the text, but they also are the exclusive carriers of the story of the rebellious gosling. Together these two readings yield a story of danger and protection, of loneliness and togetherness, of losing a family and regaining it. The full meaning comes only with the combination of these readings.

Michael Foreman's *Seal Surfer* (1996) suggests this same quality in the picture book. It is the story of Ben who has "carefully climbed down" to a rocky beach, where he finds what seems to be a a wounded seal; in fact, it is a seal about to give birth, and Ben and his grandfather bring it fish. Through the spring they watch the seal family, and the next summer, when Ben is learning to surf, he establishes a closeness with the seal, who, in fact, saves him when his board flips and his head strikes a rock. But life is hard for the seal, and Ben worries as she must endure the terrible winter storms. The next summer, when the seal returns with her own pup, Ben realizes that "he would ride the waves with the seals that summer and every summer."

The story could have been simply the clichéd tale of a boy and his pet, and it would have lacked power. But the illustrations add another side to the tale. This time the illustrations do not contradict the text, as in *Rebel,* but instead present a wholly different interpretive slant. Ben is handicapped, unable to walk—a fact not represented at all in the text, and represented in the pictures through the presence of his crutches and, once, his wheelchair. Nevertheless, he can climb down to the rocks and swim strongly; the final illustration shows him with his grandchildren, still with his crutches. The merger of the two "readings" suggests the parallel worlds of Ben and the pup, who must endure real hardships but who, together, forge a good and happy life for themselves. This larger and more poignant meaning is lost without the dual reading.

Some picture books will go so far as to convey not just some, but all of their narrative information through illustration. Peter Spier's *Rain* (1982) and *Christmas* (1983) all work with virtually no text to focus on the experiences of a single family. In *Rain,* for example, the children play with umbrellas while in their slickers, walk through puddles, dump wheelbarrows filled with water, shake water from a pine branch, watch rabbits staying dry in their pen. Spier is not so much telling a story as he is recreating the experience of a child on a rainy day. He needs no text to do this.

In *Tuesday* (1991), *Free Fall* (1988), and *Sector 7* (1999) by David Wiesner, the illustrations also carry all of the narrative. In *Tuesday,* Wiesner depicts an evening when frogs can fly on lily pads; they invade a town, scaring the birds, startling a man up for a late snack, tearing down laundry left up overnight, and watching television with a woman who has fallen asleep. At dawn the lily pads fall from the sky and the frogs make their way back to the pond. In *Free Fall,* Wiesner recreates the weird logic of the dream, as each of his illustrations merges to establish a seamless pattern that a young boy moves through, carrying images as though in a wake behind him. His quilt becomes a landscape of square fields that becomes a chessboard, whose rooks become a castle, whose towers become a forest, whose trunks become the pages of huge books that open into stone columns that become classical arches, that become rock formations in a canyon, that become a cityscape. The power of the book lies in the continuing metamorphoses of the visual elements. In *Sector 7,* Wiesner tells the tale of an artistic boy who, while atop the Empire State Building, is befriended by a small cloud who takes him to the floating contraption that defines how clouds shall be shaped. The artist in the boy expands as he draws exotic aquatic shapes for the clouds to assume, delighting the clouds, frustrating those who would confine them to already established shapes, and amazing those who witness the new cloud formations. A work that subtly speaks to the necessity of artistic freedom and development, *Sector 7* tells its tale solely through illustration.

There is, then, something of a continuum in illustration. On the one end, there are those illustrated books whose illustrations convey only the literal meaning of the text; there is nothing, or very little in them that suggests anything but what is already in the text. On the other end, there are those illustrated books in which the illustrations alone convey the narrative of the book, where there is no text at all other than visual text. And, perhaps, standing outside that continuum are those books whose illustrations subvert the meaning of their texts, so that the reader comes on a completely different story in the visual narrative of the book.

The Experience of Reading the Picture Book

Reading the picture book demands reading both text and illustration. But Arnold Lobel (1977) argues that there is yet another dimension to the reading of a picture book.

> A picture book is an audiovisual thing. It's both, and in a good picture book you shouldn't know where the words stop and the pictures begin. Certainly a child doesn't, particularly a small child who's being read to. He looks at a picture and hears the words from the parent's mouth, or somebody reading, and I don't think he dissociates the two. It comes from him as we'd watch a movie. We see an image and we hear a voice. It's one thing. And that makes it a whole different cup of tea.

Lobel is arguing here for a unity of sensory experience. There is the reading of the picture. There is the oral quality of the reading of the text. And for older children there is the visual reading of the text. All of these combine to form a single reading experience, while books for older readers might only work as a singular sensory experience.

This means that, for the child reader, there is a constant evaluation and re-evaluation of what the pictures are doing along with the text. Do they simply support the textual and oral readings, replicating exactly the settings, characters, and action of the plot? Are they adding to those textual elements, contributing new information on such things as plot action, characterization, and the meaning of the setting? Are they, as in *Rebel*, working against the textual reading? As these questions are asked—and of course they are asked quite unself-consciously—the reader is able to merge the sensory experiences of the reading.

In Jim Aylesworth's *Country Crossing* (1991), the author attempts to give the reader the experience of standing at a railroad crossing while a train thunders past. Ted Rand sets the illustrations in the dark of the night, the only light coming from a large yellow moon reflected in the puddles by the tracks, and the two yellow headlights of the old Model T. The horizontal formatting of the book encourages the sense of long roads and lengthy tracks, and the text encourages the auditory senses of the experience.

> *Soon, a train whistle rose in the distant night.*
> Whooawoo
> Whooawoooooo
> *And as the old car waited, a strong yellow light*
> *began to poke its way through the trees,*
> *and the roar of an engine began*
> *to rumble out of the darkness.*
> Chooachoo choo choo choo
> Chooachoo choo choo choo
> Chooachoo choo choo choo

Aylesworth has captured the sounds of the train here, and in doing so has tried to replicate the experience for the reader. Rand complements this by carefully manipulating shape and perspective: When the engine finally bursts on them, it is huge and dominating, taking over an entire spread. And if that were not large

Pointers for Teachers: Interactive Connections

- At several points during the reading of a picture book, ask the child listener, "What has happened just before this picture? What is going to happen right after it? What is happening outside the picture's frame? What is happening inside the picture in places that we cannot see, such as behind a building or tree? What would you hear if you were in the picture? What would you smell, or feel?"
- Stop at individual illustrations and ask why the illustrator chose to do it this way and not another way. Where does the illustrator seem to be standing, and why has he or she chosen that spot? What is the illustrator adding to the story with this picture?
- After the reading of the book, engage in a discussion using the following critical thinking skills:

  Observing: "What colors does the illustrator use? Why do you think these particular colors were chosen? What kind and shapes of objects appear? Why?"

  Comparing: "Does any character change from the beginning to the end of the story? How and why?"

  Classifying: "How many large objects appear? Small objects? Does the classification contribute to the story's meaning? How?"

  Hypothesizing: "Why do you think the illustrator made the main character look like this? Why is the landscape made to look the way it does?"

  Organizing: "How does the author arrange the time sequence of the story?"

  Summarizing: "What would you say are the important events of the story? What do you think the larger point of the story might be?"

- Show the book again, and ask the children to look closely at the illustrations to find something they had not noticed before. Why do they think they had not seen this the first time around? Do they think that the illustrator wanted them to see it the first time around? What does it add to the story?

enough, the next spread is taken over by the racing wheels of the train alone, clattering past the gate at the crossroads. And, once the train is past and silence descends, Rand shows the long and empty expanse of tracks; the text supports the quietness of the night.

> *The night became as peaceful as before.*
> *The moonlight sparkled in the puddles*
> *on the narrow road and gleamed*
> *like silver on the rails.*
> *Crickets sang in the weeds.*
> Chirp Chirp Chirp Chirrp

Here the auditory experience—whether the book is read aloud or read silently—must be united with the visual experience for the reader to experience the crossing of the train as the author and illustrator hope to portray it.

It is generally the case that the illustrations of a picture book will be narrative in quality rather than static. Instead of still lifes or landscapes, the illustrations will carry the action of the story in some manner. This means that the illustrations will often be filled with action. That action might be frenetic or quite quiet, but still it is action that the child reader can interpret—intriguing detail, elements that suggest interior thought and motivation, and details suggesting character relationships and plot directions. These are the elements that contribute to the narrative quality of the illustrations. The issue here is to learn to read these elements in such a way that they contribute to the overall meaning of the book.

The Literalism of the Child Reader

One large overriding principle in the reading of illustration is that children are rather stern literalists. If Mr. and Mrs. Mallard in *Make Way for Ducklings* are said to have eight ducklings, then the child reader will expect there to be eight ducklings. If one is missing—as one is in one illustration—then it needs to be clear why that duckling is not there. (In this case, the tire of a parked car hides the second duckling in line.) This means that, in general, despite works like *Rebel*, picture books for the child reader usually work quite hard at synchonizing text with illustration; the picture must have some clear relationship to the textual reading on any given spread. If Mr. and Mrs. Mallard are said to be flying over the State House, then McCloskey needs to have them flying over the State House in that spread, and not in a later spread.

It is this literalism with which Chris Van Allsburg will often play in his fantasy picture books. Here the literal reading of the story seems insufficient, or the literal reading does not seem to match with the illustration, and it is in that tension that Van Allsburg produces his meaning. In *The Sweetest Fig* (1993), for example, Van Allsburg tells the story of a dentist who acquires a fig that will fulfill his dreams. Greedy and eager, Bibot the dentist practices the control of his dreams, all the while being cruel to his small dog, Marcel. When Marcel instead eats the fig, Bibot is heartbroken and goes to bed vowing to take vengeance on the dog the next day. But, in the final illustration, Bibot is reaching under the bed and he seems to be smiling. The text, however, undercuts that apparent literal meaning: "A hand reached down and grabbed him. Bibot tried to yell, but all he could do was bark." It is left to the reader to perceive that this discordance suggests that Marcel, having eaten the fig, has dreamed that he transposed places with the dentist.

Most picture books do not call for that kind of a sophisticated reading, however; most clearly synchonize the action of the text with the action of the illustration. Gerald McDermott, in his speech (1975) accepting the Caldecott Award for his picture book *Arrow to the Sun* (1974), argues that learning to "read" illustrations, learning to develop the aesthetic consciousness, is one of the crucial things that picture books can teach the young reader; it is a kind of reading, he suggests, often neglected.

> Imagination. Image-ination. The ability to call up spontaneously the visual forms of our inner life. Children seem to possess the open eye, a direct access to 'the unpolluted rivers of perception and imagination.' But early in childhood, swiftly,

almost inexorably, our natural perceptual responses, instead of being cultivated, are eradicated.... As Herbert Read has described it,

> "Somewhere in the process of upbringing, in the environment we have made for ourselves, there exists a corroding influence [that]...prevents the development of aesthetic consciousness...."

> A picture book of artistic integrity will often be the only place where a child can expand his imagination and direct his gaze toward beauty. In this medium, it is possible to create a dynamic relationship between the visual and the verbal. The techniques of storytelling and the compelling serial imagery together convey the force of exciting ideas. In form and content, the picture book can become an essential element in the child's evolving aesthetic consciousness, and the artist creating a picture book has an opportunity—and a special responsibility—to nurture the development of his young audience's visual perception.

This plea by McDermott is a call for the development of the aesthetic consciousness. There is a kind of urgency to the plea, a sense that for many children the picture book will be the one moment—both in time and place—where he or she may learn about the principles of art and beauty. This urgency, McDermott claims, points to a particular responsibility on the part of the picture book artist, a responsibility that other artists may not share to the same degree.

Reading the Narrative Illustration

Robert Lawson's Caldecott-winning *They Were Strong and Good* (1940) is a series of vignettes that focus on his family tree. Each spread combines a short text suggesting some element of an ancestor's life with a full-page illustration that captures that element in the particular setting of the ancestor's story. The illustrations are particularly telling, in that they often capture much of a character's personality that is not conveyed by the rather spare text.

Pointers for Teachers: Hands-On Possibilities

- Choose a picture book that includes a handmade object in a significant role, such as Valerie Flourey's *The Patchwork Quilt* (1985), or Donald Hall's *Ox-Cart Man* (1979). Make that object in class and display it.
- Give children one photocopied page from a picture book that you have read to them. Talk about the texture of the illustrations, and ask why the illustrator made that particular choice for the texture. Have the students then draw a full-page illustration for a family story that they would be willing to share with the group, and ask them to add texture to the illustration by using materials that are provided. When the illustrations are finished, have the children share their stories and their pictures, and talk for a moment about the reasons for choosing the textures that they did.
- Record each child reading his or her favorite book. After the class listens to the tapes, ask them how the auditory element has contributed to the story's meaning.

In one illustration of his father, Lawson draws a random landscape. Confederate troops retreat across it, their lines ragtag, their rifles and bayonets held at many different angles. The wagon that draws the single cannon up to position is about to lose one of its wheels and the bombs are bursting ever nearer. Abandoned rifles and packs lie about on the ground, and it is clear that the Confederates have had a hard time of it. Even the flag is simply flying from a makeshift branch, and the uniform of the boy that holds it is ragged and tattered; the ends of his pants come up past his shins.

In the midst of this random world, Lawson's father—only a boy here—stands rigidly straight, directly in the center of the illustration. The strongly vertical line of his thin body complements the vertical line of the flagpole and is reflected in the distance by the strong verticality of a stand of trees that has endured the bombing. This striking use of line suggests much about the boy's character: He does not care that his side might be losing; he will perform his duty, and he will perform it proudly and heroically, never bending. It is a picture whose lines suggest pride and optimism, even in desperate circumstances.

Two pages later, the boy returns home, wounded. Again Lawson puts him in the center of the illustration, but now he is much smaller, perhaps only a third the size of the earlier illustration. The strong verticality is gone; one shoulder is hunched and the flagpole is now halved to a walking cane. The road on which he walks is drawn in one-point perspective, but it seems to lead nowhere. There is nothing in front but blankness; on either side lies the ruin of war, with buildings devastated by the fighting. A thick and heavy sky broods above him. Here is an illustration that suggests a world of sorrow and heaviness, where the optimism and energy and pride of the earlier illustration has not led to the preservation of a way of life, but only to destruction.

In each of these illustrations, the reader needs to "read" the narrative that is suggested in the pictures. This demands the development of what Gerald McDermott calls the aesthetic consciousness. It means that the reader must ask certain kinds of questions of the illustrations to determine what meaning they are conveying and how they are conveying it. The answers to these questions point the way towards the fusion of text and illustration that creates meaning.

Pointers for Teachers: Evaluating Picture Books

- How do the illustrations convey the narrative?
- How does the text convey the narrative? How does the book create a union of text and illustration?
- How do the illustrations develop a child's aesthetic consciousness?
- How does the artist use shape, perspective, line, texture, movement and direction, color, the medium, and the form to convey narrative meaning?

How does the artist arrange the elements of each spread? In drawing his illustrations of his father, Robert Lawson could have changed a great many elements. In the first illustration, he could have placed the boy far off on a distant hill. In the forefront he might have placed the ragged Confederate army, with the cannon leaning crazily to the side. The principal effect of this would have been to emphasize the difficulties of the army; the boy would have stood apart as a single exception, but would not at all have been the focus of the illustration.

Similarly, Lawson might have changed the elements in the second illustration. He might have created greater perspective by using a bird's eye point of view to emphasize the bleakness of the ruined landscape. Or he might have focused strongly on one of the ruined houses, perhaps showing the boy trudging past through the empty frame of a window. In making these choices, Lawson would have emphasized the ways in which the Civil War had ruined the once peaceful and prosperous southern world.

In making the choices he did, Lawson emphasized instead the character of the boy—and that was his principal intent. As the artist arranges elements on a single page or across a spread, he or she is making choices about how to draw the reader's eye, about how to emphasize certain kinds of information, about negotiating space with the text, about conveying the narrative and its meaning.

Perhaps the illustrator wants to convey a sense of motion across a page. In doing this, she might place certain elements at the top left, and then slant other elements to the bottom right, suggesting a sense of downward motion. Perhaps the artist wishes to indicate something about propotions and size relationships. In doing this, she might place certain elements on the same plane, perhaps next to each other, or behind each other. Perhaps the artist wishes to establish contrast. In this case, she might set elements on either side of an illustration so that the eye suggests a kind of opposition. Perhaps the artist wishes to create a sense of distance. In this case, the artist might foreground some element of which we see only a small part, then use perspective to distance other elements. The artist does not work randomly; in making these decisions, the illustrator is making decisions about how to convey narrative information.

In Patricia Polacco's *Pink and Say* (1994), Polacco wants to focus on relationships between Pink, Say, and Moe Moe Bay. Set during the Civil War, it is the story of how Pink, from a Negro Regiment, finds and saves the wounded Say and brings him back to own mother, Moe Moe Bay. There, Say finds healing, but when Moe Moe Bay is killed by outriders, he returns to the war, only to be captured with Pink and sent to Andersonville, where Pink is executed. In each of her spreads, Polacco emphasizes the nature of their relationships by placing the characters in close proximity to each other; they are almost always touching, and almost always foregrounded. When they are finally driven apart at Andersonville, Polacco focuses on their hands, clasped on one side of the spread; on the other side are strong arms pulling Say away. The final effect is a cumulative one: For the first time in the book, Pink and Say are not together. Much of the poignancy of this loss is conveyed simply through Polacco's arrangement of elements on the page.

In each decision, the illustrator is weighing advantages and disadvantages, making choices in the layout of a spread that will affect emphasis and meaning. All such choices reflect the illustrator's understanding and interpretation of the text.

How does the illustrator convey narrative information through shape?   In Lynd Ward's *The Biggest Bear* (1952), a young boy finds a small bear cub while out hunting. Delighted, he brings the cub back home and resolves to keep him as a pet. Through each succeeding illustration, the bear cub grows larger and larger as he begins to roam through the valley. But, then, Ward presents a series of illustrations that do not show the cub; instead they show the wreckage he causes in smokehouses and cornfields. When the bear cub is finally shown again, he is fully grown, huge and dominating, taking up the entire page as he drinks maple syrup by the gallon. Ward uses surprise to show the reader that the bear is now clearly too large for a pet.

This surprise comes about because of Ward's handling of shape. Had he shown the bear from a distant perspective, the meaning would have been lost; the bear needs to appear huge to the reader to make the narrative point. Here is the artist controlling shape in order to create and convey some kind of meaning.

In his illustrations for Hildegarde Swift's *The Little Red Lighthouse and the Great Gray Bridge* (1942)—the title itself suggests an interest in shape—Lynd Ward was particularly adept at using shape to illustrate the story. In the beginning of the tale, the red lighthouse has for many years controlled the traffic on the river; in the scenes picturing this control, he is large and dominant. But when the huge gray bridge is built, Ward makes the bridge enormous in comparison to the now diminutive lighthouse. It arches over it in long spreads, and the lighthouse that once controlled the river is now tiny. When a dense fogs rolls in—something that Ward personifies and makes larger than either the lighthouse or the bridge—the bridge calls out to the lighthouse to guard the river, and so the lighthouse's role is renewed. Ward emphasizes this renewal by showing the lighthouse large again and by manipulating the perspective so that the size distinction between the two is not so great anymore.

In handling shape, the illustrator is once again working with the arrangement of elements on the page. But here, in addition, the illustrator is using the size and shape of elements to draw attention to them, or to diminish them, or to suggest relationships. In creating a large, dominating shape, the illustrator is suggesting something of the role of that element in the plot narrative. But in addition to size, the illustrator may make other decisions about shape. Through the manipulation of line, she may make the shape of an element distinct and sharp, or blurred and amorphous. The shape may be simple and easy to discern, or the shape may be complex and difficult to perceive. The shape may dominate a page, or it may be pushed back to a less central place. In making any of these decisions, the illustrator is once again making decisions about the layout of a page and the best means of conveying narrative information.

How does the illustrator use point of view to convey narrative information?   In making decisions about the arrangement of elements on a page and about shape, the artist is often making decisions as well about point of view, the perspective that the viewer is granted. That point of view suggests to the reader certain meanings, certain understandings, certain possibilities of narrative. And, like an author's use of point of view, the illustrator's use both creates certain meanings and sets boundaries around the creation of those meanings.

Sometimes the point of view will be that of the child, looking upward to something or someone larger and more powerful. Generally, a point of view that makes the reader look up puts the reader in a more vulnerable position, as a child might be looking up to a powerful adult. In the image of the witch in Chris Van Allsburg's *The Widow's Broom* (1992), for example, the reader looks up towards the witch's face and is immediately put in the position of being the smaller, vulnerable character. In his *The Polar Express* (1985), however, Van Allsburg reverses this posture, placing the reader above the flying Santa Claus while looking down on the gathered elves; here the reader is in a dominant position, high above everything. In making such decisions, the illustrator is conscious of creating certain meanings. In the first, the witch becomes powerful and threatening; in the second, the reader is encouraged to participate in Santa's perspective. In either case the illustrator has consciously used point of view to achieve certain effects.

In Robert Lawson's illustration of the young boy walking home through the ruined southern countryside, for example, the point of view seems omniscient. The reader is behind the young boy, seeing him as one element in the midst of a larger set of elements. This creates a certain kind of meaning: The reader sees him as part of and reacting to the terrible ravages of war. The point of view also limits, however. We do not see the point of view of the young boy, for example, and so are left to surmise what his feelings might be. Is he feeling devastated by the loss of the Confederates? Is he frustrated by the way that his wound prevents him from hurrying home? Is he so filled with thoughts of home that he does not even see the ruin around him? None of these questions is answered. Instead, the point of view that Lawson gives the reader suggests only one set of meanings. The perspective bounds the meaning.

Point of view can at times suggest the presence of the reader. In *Make Way for Ducklings,* for example, McCloskey draws the first gathering of the eight ducklings after their hatching. Two of the ducklings look right out at the reader, and they hide behind their mother's leg or a clump of grasses. In his *One Morning in Maine* (1952), McCloskey draws his daughter Sal looking out at the reader again; here she is distraught because she has lost her tooth. More recently, David Shannon's *A Bad Case of Stripes* (1998), a tale about conformity and individuality, includes several pictures of Camilla Cream looking out at the reader, as if to involve the reader in her plight: She keeps changing color and form depending on the expectations of others. The last image of the book is of Camilla eating lima beans—a sign of her individuality—and looking at the reader to suggest the pleasure of having gained new insights into herself.

Stripes also suggests another use of point of view: the expansion of the illustrated space. In one of the opening illustrations, Camilla holds a dress in front of her and looks out of the page. Though Shannon is illustrating a closet, suddenly that space has expanded as the reader recognizes that the character is looking into a mirror. Later, "an old woman who was just as plump and sweet as a strawberry" comes to bring lima beans to Camilla, and the first illustration of her shows her looking again directly out of the page; she is, in fact, speaking to Camilla's parents, who the reader imagines in the expanded space of the illustration. Shannon's use of point of view has created larger dimensions than even a page can hold, and involved the reader in the space of the characters.

In making choices about point of view, the illustrator is making choices about the set of eyes through which the reader will look. When the characters seem to be looking directly out at the reader, the reader is pulled into the world of the illustration, perhaps even made to take on the point of view of one of the characters. When the point of view is further back, perhaps omniscient, the reader is encouraged to read the illustration a step removed from the action.

How does the illustrator use line to create narrative meaning?   The line that the illustrator chooses both bounds and creates shape. It is the way that the illustrator gives form to blank space. And here, once again, the artist chooses certain kinds of lines for certain kinds of forms, certain kinds of effects, even certain kinds of meanings.

The illustrator chooses a form of line because it gives advantages. Peter Spier, for example, uses a very thin line, perhaps one of the thinnest in all of children's literature. The advantage to him is that it allows him to create an astonishing number of details within watercolored backgrounds. Any single illustration in his *Rain* or *Christmas* is marked by what seems an infinitude of tiny details, and the delight of the illustrations comes, at least partially, through the discovery of those details. Strikingly different, Keizaburo Tejima's illustrations are woodcuts that use bold, very distinct and obvious lines. This means that, in books like *The Bears' Autumn* (1986), *Owl Lake* (1987) and *Woodpecker Forest* (1984), the illustrations do not show the plenitude of detail that marks a Spier illustration, but they do show a drama and startling boldness that draws the eye to the dominant figure and to the landscape. This is particularly true of those light lines that distinguish figures against a night sky.

Both Tejima and Spier use distinct lines, in the sense that they are easily perceived. But another option is to use lines that are blurred, not distinct at all. In *Time of Wonder* (1957), for example, Robert McCloskey blurs overlapping layers of watercolors to create a sense of depth in the ocean water around a Maine island; had he used distinct lines to show this, the water would have seemed stilted and unreal. Chris Van Allsburg uses blurred lines in his *Polar Express* to suggest the dreamlike state of the narrator as he boards the train for the North Pole. Here, distinct lines would have destroyed the ambiguity and scarcely real nature of the story, which allows a reader to interpret it as a dream or not. A blurred line suggests a kind of uncertainty, whether that uncertainty might be about the nature of reality, or whether it might simply be an inability to distinguish where one thing starts and another leaves off.

The illustrator can use line to suggest emotional states. Harsh diagonals may suggest a kind of frenzy, where soft, blurred lines might suggest an easy, pacific state of mind. Bold, sharp lines may suggest action, where loose lines may instead suggest rest or ease. Thin lines may suggest movement; thick lines may suggest permanence or solidity. In any case, the illustrator chooses the line to convey the state appropriate to the illustration.

In general, lines that are at right angles to a side of the page—lines that are strongly horizontal or vertical—work to orient the reader. The effect is similar to that of a straight horizon. Lines that angle off in unexpected ways or that thwart the desire for a horizon tend to disorient. The first suggests stability and centeredness; the second suggests a lack of stability or a kind of uncertainty of place. Here again, the illustrator makes choices according to his or her sense of the desired effect.

How does the illustrator use texture to generate narrative meaning?   Perhaps no question depends more on artistic techniques than the question of texture. Texture is generated by the illustrator consciously choosing a certain kind of application that will yield a certain kind of effect. This effect may be generated, as with McCloskey's illustrations in *Time of Wonder*, by a series of overlapping watercolors. But the choices in application are infinite. Perhaps the paint will be brushed on thickly to create texture, or perhaps it will be layered. The paint may be applied with brushes, with sponges, with a knife, with fingers; it may simply be dripped or splashed onto the page. The paint may be merged with other materials to yield surprising forms and combinations. But the illustrator does not experiment with such techniques for mere pleasure, though there is pleasure in the experimentation. Instead, the illustrator tries to find a texture for the illustration that is appropriate to the matter, mood, and tones of the illustration. Thus, texture in an illustration creates a tactile sense that is appropriate to the textual narrative.

Dennis Nolan's *The Castle Builder* (1987) is a story about a young boy who builds a sand castle on a beach and imaginatively enters into it, encountering dragons, Vikings, and destructive waves from which he must eventually save himself by leaving behind his imaginative play. Because the action takes place entirely on the beach and in a sand castle, Nolan decided to draw each illustration with a crow quill pen, using only black dots. The closer these came, the darker the space. The result is a seemingly sandy texture, as if the illustrations are printed on sandpaper—appropriate to the beach setting.

For Judith Hendershot's *In Coal Country* (1987), illustrator Thomas Allen wanted to create the texture of the coarse penny paper that a child might have used before the middle of the century. His pictures thus reflect a kind of coarse graininess so that dots seem to pop through the lines, which become indistinct and blurred. Because the story is told from the point of view of a child narrator, the illustrations reflect the way that a child might illustrate the scene, so the texture is particularly appropriate.

Paul Morin similarly allows the material of his art to show through and influence the picture itself. In works like *The Orphan Boy* (1990), Morin uses thick, thick paint to give a sense of texture to the clothing and the landscape; at times he will affix objects to the painting, such as grass. In manipulating his texture, Morin creates effects that complement the text. When he wants to show a land lush with water and growth, he uses thick greens to give a strong texture to the landscape; when he wants to show the drought that has infected the land, he will instead hold back on the paint and allow the canvas to show through, suggesting the sparsity of the land. In all of these cases the artist has used texture to suggest a tactile sense that is appropriate to the narrative.

As with line, the illustrator can use texture to create certain emotional states in the reader. A smooth texture is created by minimizing changes in color and dimension and the fine dots that make up an illustration. The eye sees such an illustration as smooth, perhaps even soft. This is the kind of texture that marks the landscapes of Kate Kiesler's *Twilight Comes Twice* (1997), in which the illustrator shows the light of dawn and dusk, emphasizing the way elements merge into one another. Conversely, the artist may highlight contrasts, using many lines and many distinctions in color—slight and subtle, or harsh and bold—to suggest a much rougher texture. This is the technique Ted Lewin uses in *Cowboy Country* (1993), where at times he will blur watercolors into one another, but more often show the distinct texture of the landscape through highlighting contrasts in color. The result is a world that is not at all soft, but detailed and rough. Each choice of texture is appropriate to the narrative text.

How does the illustrator use a sense of movement and direction to create narrative meaning? Any picture book illustrator who wants to create movement is faced with the limitations of two-dimensional, static space. Given such limitations, the artist needs to find ways of generating a sense of movement, a sense of direction that the reader can perceive. Lacking this, the illustrations of a picture book may seem stilted and posed, a grouping of set scenes rather than an enlivened illustration of figures and elements that are in motion.

Direction is suggested by the arrangement of shapes on a page. Shapes and elements that are arranged or organized horizontally and vertically have the most stable presentation; shapes and elements arranged diagonally are less stable and will often suggest a kind of movement, due to the directional flow of the eye. Curves and diagonals both work to create a sense that the illustration is dynamic rather than static. This is not to suggest that motion is inherently better than stasis in an illustration, but to show that the illustrator makes certain kinds of choices in her composition to create the effect of motion and direction.

In Byrd Baylor's *Desert Voices* (1981), for example, illustrator Peter Parnall wants to create a sense of direction and movement to suggest the rapid running of a jackrabbit. To do this, he creates diagonal lines across a two-page spread. He draws the landscape as fading from the upper left to the lower right, strongly downhill. The angles of the rocks all contribute to that directional flow, as do the angled leaves of the sharp plants. The rabbit is shaped in such a way that he, too, suggests the downward diagonal, with ears back and front legs extended downward. Then Parnall colors in only those spaces of the sky that will contribute to this downward motion. Together the whole is directional and strongly suggestive of motion, precisely the point of the poem it illustrates.

Direction and a sense of motion are complementary, but not necessarily paired; a sense of direction can be established without a sense of motion being established. In Robert Lawson's illustration of his father holding the flag, the sense of direction is strongly vertical, suggested by the body of the boy as well as his flagpole. But the scene is principally static, which is important for its meaning. The boy is meant to seem very, very still. Had Lawson angled the boy forward and mirrored that angle by setting the flagpole at a diagonal, he would have created a sense of motion: The boy would seem to be moving right off the page. But then this would have created a very different kind of meaning in the illustration than Lawson had intended.

An illustrator who seeks to add a sense of motion to the illustrations has decided to use certain techniques to avoid a series of set scenes; instead, she wants to create a work full of action and vigor. For a text that requires such a tone, the illustrator must be careful to suggest both direction and motion. In his *Owl Lake*, Keizaburo Tejima wishes to show the downward motion of the owl as it catches salmon. To do this, he creates a series of three panels across a single spread, each panel angled at the bottom to stress a downward motion. The downward flight of the owl is accentuated by the angles of his wings. The eye follows the owl down and down until it extends its claws directly over the fish.

Similarly Dennis Nolan, in order to show Icarus's fall from the sky in Jane Yolen's *Wings* (1991), shows the boy plummeting on the left side of a spread, a triangle of individual feathers floating free above him; the triangle points directly downward. In addition, the arrangement of the gods in the clouds moves from the upper right to the lower left, again suggesting a fall. Not all motion is associated with diagonals, however. In Toshi Yoshida's *The Young Lions* (1989), the sense of direction is strongly horizontal. Yoshida wishes to show the difficulties of the hunt, even for a lion, and to do this he suggests intense speed by using long spreads in which he blurs the animals—antelope, cheetah, gnu—in order to show that they are moving so quickly that they cannot be easily perceived. To this he adds thin, coarse parallel horizontal lines that cross the entire spread. He has created in this way a sense of the speed and motion of the animals on the African plains.

Not all artists choose this sense of motion. Barry Moser, for example, consistently presents series of portraits; his focus is not on action as much as it is on character. Barbara Cooney employs a folk art style with characters and settings that seem almost posed; their flatness and lack of motion come out of the folk art style. Tomie DePaola uses the techniques of the theater in books like *Fin M'Coul* (1981) and *The Clown of God* (1978), in which the characters seem to pose on a stage.

But, even in these apparently still illustrations, there is a sense of direction. The eye generally flows first along a vertical line, and the illustrator will take advantage of this to suggest something of the nature of the shapes that are arranged. In Barbara Cooney's first illustration of the protagonist's house in *Miss Rumphius* (1982), for example, the scene may be quite still, but the strong angles of the house and the spit of land jutting above the sea still give an organizational sense of direction to the illustration. The artist, always aware of how his or her elements work together, uses this organizational sense to create meaning in the illustration.

How does the illustrator use color in the illustration to create narrative meaning? When one asks a question about the use of color, one is really asking several questions. Certainly one is asking first what colors are used. Even when the color seems as though it must be predetermined—say, the color of grass, or a fire engine, or the sky—there are still many hues that the artist can choose that fit into the realism of the color scheme if realism is what the artist wishes to achieve. One need only see an Eric Carle illustration of a leaf to see the many greens that the artist uses in the composition of a single element.

But there may be reasons other than realism that lead an artist to choose certain colors. He or she might want to choose the warm hues—red, orange, yellow. Or the artist might choose cooler hues—blue and its associated colors. The artist may choose a color because he or she wants it to be dominant thematically in the book. Choices may be made so that colors clash, so that colors complement, so that colors tell something of a landscape or character. In any case, the first inquiry into color is simple identification; then comes the investigation as to the reasons for those choices.

In asking about color, one is also asking about value, or the intensity of light and darkness in a given color. Value is often manipulated to create effects of light and darkness in an illustration; a work set principally in darkness will have a low value, for example. The effect is created by placing objects of higher value directly beside an object of lower value. The object with higher value will seem to be more lit. Value is, therefore, in some sense relative. But value may be used for more than light. It can create and suggest shape and the boundaries of space. It can also be used to suggest movement, as the eye travels from a lower value to a higher value. It is one more set of choices the illustrator uses to create effects.

One other question one is asking when speaking of color is about saturation, which, simply defined, is the amount of gray in the color. The more gray in a color, the less saturated it is, until there is an absence of color and the image is in black and white. The purer a color is, the more saturated it is. A less saturated image might be used to create a colorless night scene, or a scene in a gray fog. It is often used as well to suggest the past, as though the image had been reproduced in the sepia tones of the nineteenth century. The effect of unsaturation is often one of stillness, of quietness. Bold bright colors, however—those that are saturated—are arresting to the eye and anything but still and quiet. They draw the eye to themselves and call for attention. They highlight, emphasize, and take command of the visual reading.

In asking these three large questions of color, value, and saturation, one begins to get to the reasons for the choices that illustrators have made. Are the colors bold (saturated) or quite subtle (unsaturated)? Do they clash and shock, or are they peaceful and quiet complements? Do they establish form and shape? Do they draw the eye to certain elements? Do they complement and seem appropriate to the text of the story and its tones? And, most importantly, do they add to the meaning of the text?

For Eve Bunting's *Night of the Gargoyles* (1994), illustrator David Wiesner chose to use very unsaturated colors, drawing the entire book in shades of gray. The text follows the mischievous adventures of a group of stone gargoyles who come alive during the night. Wiesner chose the unsaturated colors to emphasize not only the nighttime setting of the work, but to match the stone character of the gargoyles. As they wrestle and tumble through the air, falling into fountains and washing off the mess of the pigeons, Wiesner consistently keeps them stone gray, suggesting their entrapment in the world of night.

Illustrators use color frequently to highlight meaning. David Diaz's illustrations for Eve Bunting's *December* (1997) show a frequent use of a rose-red color, particularly after an angel unbeknownst comes into the small shelter of the narrator and his mother, wearing a rose. The color quickly comes to suggest charity and hospitality. In *Fair!* (1997), Ted Lewin manipulates the values of his colors to highlight the color and light and panorama of the bright fair, particularly as it is set against the night sky. And in *Heckedy Peg* (1987), illustrator Don Wood juxtaposes scenes dominated by cool—perhaps even cold colors—with scenes where warm colors dominate to create distance between the witch and the rescuing mother. In each of these works the illustrator has made a set of very specific choices in order to further the meaning of the narrative.

In some works the color will itself carry the meaning of the book by suggesting tone, or perhaps emphasis, or perhaps thematic connections. In such a case the illustrator is expecting the reader to react to colors in very specific ways so that the narrative meaning can, in fact, be extended. In Keizaburo Tejima's *Fox's Dream* (1987) for example, Tejima tells the story of a lonely fox who wanders into a section of the forest that he has never seen before. Though the opening spreads had been dominated by blues and even some warm yellows, the new section of the woods is pictured in highly unsaturated colors, and this increases as the fox moves further into the woods. As he looks up into the ice-laden trees, he seems to see an image of his mother with her three young cubs, and the colors switch dramatically: they become highly saturated and very, very warm as the fox remembers his childhood.

But when that memory is over, Tejima returns to the unsaturated colors; the next spread is almost completely gray; the fox is alone and there is nothing warm in the world around him. These colors continue for two spreads, until suddenly the fox spies a vixen in the distance. Again Tejima dramatically switches colors, changing again to highly saturated colors—yellows and light purples. In the final spread, Tejima has lightened the values of the colors, so that the world seems bright with promise. The changes in the fox's perceptions, as well as the bright hopefulness of the book's ending, are shown, not necessarily in the spare, unemotional text, but instead in the manipulation and choice of color.

In all of these decisions, the illustrator is conscious that choices have consequences, and that those consequences affect the ways in which a text is read. That
means that the illustrator needs to choose in such a way that everything in the
visual illustration contributes precisely in the way it is supposed to contribute to
the meaning of the picture. This allows the reader to "read" the illustration and
the text and to arrive at the single experience for which both author and illustrator strive.

Pointers for Teachers: Writing Possibilities

- Working in pairs, have students choose a favorite picture book illustrator and read a
  number of his or her works. Then have the students address questions that examine
  the aesthetic elements of picture books.

  Line: What kinds of lines has the illustrator chosen? Dark, light, heavy, thin, jagged,
  straight, curved? What relationship does this choice have to the story's meaning? In
  what directions do the lines move? Vertically, horizontally, at right angles, diagonally,
  jaggedly, curved? When you remember that vertical lines suggest something standing
  still, that horizontal lines suggest a placed environment, that things joined at right
  angles suggest something man-made, that diagonal lines suggest a loss of balance and
  uncontrolled motion, that jagged lines suggest destruction and curved lines suggest
  fluid motion, what comments can you make about the illustrator's attempt to convey
  the story through the illustration?

  Color: If red, yellow, and orange suggest warmth and heat, how does that choice fit
  with the story's meaning? Comment on the use of color to define a mood, create
  character, establish a setting, and underscore a theme.

  Shape: If irregular and organic shapes are natural, and regular, angular shapes man-
  made, how does the artist use shape to create meaning in the story? Geometric
  shapes often convey complexity, stability, assertion, and even severity. Is there evidence of this in the picture book? Regular shapes often suggest calm tranquillity;
  asymmetrical shapes may suggest dynamism. Is there evidence for this in the book?

  Texture: How is the texture introduced, and how does it contribute to the meaning?

  Design: How does the illustrator show readers the most important figures? Size, contrasting colors, centrality, strong line, repetition? How formal is the design? Is the
  text placed opposite the illustration? (This is the most formal composition.) Is the text
  placed above or below the illustration? Are the boundaries and text regular or varied?
  What relationship does this have to the story's meaning?

  Media: What media style has the artist chosen for the story, and how appropriate is
  this choice, given the text?

  Artistic Style: What artistic style has the author chosen, and why? Is the art representational (trying to capture real life), impressionistic (using the art form to suggest), or
  perhaps expressionistic (in which mood is crucial), or abstract? How does this choice
  flow from and contribute to the meaning of the story?

Illustrators of Picture Books

The illustrator of children's literature has available to him or to her all artistic media, from pen and ink to computer animation. Though the illustrator is more confined than the artist painting a picture, because the illustrator must, in some measure, illustrate a text or narrative, still the range of media options for illustration is as open, as free, as unlimited as it might be for any artist. But the illustrator needs to choose a medium appropriate to the textual material to be illustrated.

It may be that the illustrator will choose the conventional medium of paints. But even here, choices need to be made. The artist may choose oil paints, or she may choose acrylics, whose colors can be more brilliant than oils. Each of these paints provides a solid covering of the page, though they may be thinned. Watercolors are much more transparent and are used in layers, one layer set on another over white paper. This allows the paper to show through the transparent layers and creates impressions of depth. Watercolors may also be opaque, in which case they are called *gouache* or *tempera*. Some artists using colored illustrations turn instead to colored pencil, crayon, or pastels, which are colored chalk, to create a more grainy texture.

The illustrator may also choose to approach the illustration in a black-and-white portrayal. Here the artist may choose the simplest medium of all: pencil. For more precise lines, the artist may choose pen and ink, a medium sometimes used in conjunction with watercolors to outline the shapes more definitively. The artist might also use woodcuts, in which the artist uses prints made from engraved wood or linoleum, a technique that creates thicker lines and bolder shapes. In scratchboard, the artist has scratched away the black surface treatment of a white board to create the illustrations, which often have a distinct sense of movement.

Some artists choose to avoid media such as paints and chalks and, instead, turn to a medium that allows them to explore the relationships of shapes: collage. Here the illustrator brings together what might once have been disparate shapes and uses them to suggest new shapes, new relationships, and even new meanings as they work in combination with each other. The result is a work that needs to be photographed before it may be reproduced. A not very dissimilar technique is the use of cut paper, in which the artist makes intricate cuttings that suggest landscapes, characters, and other visual elements. As with collage, the result is a three-dimensional art form.

In making any of these choices, the artist is also free to mix the media, so that several different forms might be used at once. Pen and ink might be used to complement watercolors. Watercolors might be used to color in the white space of woodcuts or scratchboard. Collage might be combined with acrylics and pastels, the first providing background, the second establishing action and character. In mixing media, the artist is able to take advantage of the strengths of each.

The choice of art form depends on the artist's competencies and interests, and, most especially, on the narrative itself. A text that calls for a very realistic portrayal of its subject may not be at all suitable for collage. A text that is dreamlike might benefit from the blurring possibilities in watercolors. A text that stresses the fine details of a story or setting might call for pen and ink rather than pastels. A text in which landscape is critical in the carrying forward of the story might call for watercolors rather than woodcuts. All of these choices affect the reader's perception of meaning.

Maurice Sendak (b. 1928)

Though Maurice Sendak drew illustrations for books edited by the famed Ursula Nordstrom beginning in the mid-1950s, he came into his own with the publication of *Where the Wild Things Are* in 1963; it quickly became one of the most well-known and universally recognized books in North American children's literature. He continued to draw through the next decades, achieving tremendous heights for his line drawings for books by Randall Jarrell and Isaac Bashevis Singer especially, but achieved prominence most especially for the two books that followed in the *Wild Things* trilogy: *In the Night Kitchen* (1970) and *Outside Over There* (1981).

The three books of the trilogy are moving, poignant explorations of the deep and powerful emotions of childhood. In *Where the Wild Things Are,* Sendak explores the ways in which a child will deal with emotions that are new, unfamiliar, and strong. When Max is angry at his mother—he is making mischief of one kind or another because no one pays attention to him—his mother responds with equal anger and sends him to bed. Confronted with the terrible oddity of being angry at the one he loves best in the world, Max deals with his frustration by entering into a world of fantasy, where he can be king of all wild things. Achieving that mastery, he commands at will and is finally the center of attention. But, after a time, those emotions having played out, he wants to come back home. Once there he finds his supper waiting for him, still hot.

Sendak manipulates the size of the illustrations themselves in the book, so that they grow bigger and bigger as Max's fantasy begins to take control; eventually the illustrations are so large that they squeeze the text off the page and expand to the borders of the two-page spread. Conversely, they quickly shrink in size as Max's emotions play out. Within the illustrations, Sendak similarly controls shape, so that the Wild Things are huge in proportion to Max, yet he is still able to control them—the child controlling the larger adult world around him. Throughout, the mixture of watercolor and detailed pen and ink cross-hatching allowed Sendak to achieve the effect of a dream while maintaining a sense of intricate detail.

For *In the Night Kitchen,* Sendak turned to his own childhood for inspiration, finding it in the cartoons of Walt Disney and the comedies of Laurel and Hardy. In this tale, Mickey—the name is, obviously, from Disney—climbs out of bed at night because he is eager to hear what is going on down in the kitchen while he is supposed to be asleep. The dream reflects the desire of all children to pierce the veil that separates them from the adult world. In the kitchen, Mickey finds three bakers working on a wonder cake, and, when they falter for need of milk, Mickey becomes the hero by securing it for them. Then, satisfied with his role, he yawns and climbs back into bed, having made discoveries, he believes, about what goes on while he is asleep.

Sendak wanted to suggest the dreamlike nature of this experience, as well as the sensuality of it. To this end, he wanted to capture the energetic movement of a comic book from his childhood. Thus, he focused in this book on creating a sense of direction and motion. Mickey moves up and down, across the page in several different directions. His movement is so energetic that he seems to be always breaking out of the boxes in which he is pictured. When he creates a plane from bread dough, he flies at a diagonal across the spreads until he reaches the top of what turns out to be a giant milk bottle. Here Sendak plays up the sense of shape to give a sense of the enormity of the size, and even Mickey seems a bit daunted by it. Nevertheless, he is always in control, and the rounded forms, soft textures, and muted colors all create a sense of security and ease.

Sendak's very painterly *Outside Over There* is not a book that creates a sense of ease. The text of the book is very sparse, less than 350 words. The story tells of Ida, whose Papa is away at sea. Here again Sendak will explore the powerful emotions of childhood. Because her mother is distraught with the father's leaving, Ida is left with the baby, a task that seems to her unfair. When goblins come and steal the baby, they are, in fact, only doing what she wishes. But, when she realizes the baby is gone, she resolves to find him again. Thus she, like Max, enters into fantasy to resolve what seems unresolveable. In the end she discovers him and brings him home, resolution having been achieved, and she leaves the brother to play happily by the dog while the mother clasps her tightly. Ida still has the task of taking care of the child, but at least there is affirmation by her parents.

The paintings here are lush, with none of the posed forms and unrealities of *Where the Wild Things Are,* none of the bright Disney-esque colorations of *In the Night Kitchen.* There is something deadly serious about this book, and the lush landscapes and starker realities complement that meaning. Sendak manipulates value here, so that, as Ida moves deeper and deeper into her fantasy, the values become lower and lower until it is clearly night; once having found the child, the values change, and Ida stoops over him with hands that seem to be inspired by Michelangelo's hands of God reaching to Adam on the Sistine Chapel ceiling.

Since the publication of *Outside Over There,* Sendak has continued to explore the passions of childhood in books like *Dear Mili* (1988), a Grimm folktale, and *We Are All in the Dumps with Jack and Guy* (1993). These are disturbing books; some have argued that they are not children's books at all. In *Jack and Guy,* for example, two children at first show no compassion to a young boy, but then are moved to rescue him when he is attacked. They bring the young boy home with them, bruised and beaten, but home is only a cardboard shack, and all their good impulses seem ultimately unable to rescue them from this devastating poverty. In each of his works, Sendak suggests the power and passion of childhood emotions. For almost forty years he has found many different ways of depicting that power in a manner that speaks to both the child and adult reader.

Leo Lionni (1910–1999)

Since the 1950s, Leo Lionni has been known as a writer and illustrator whose fable-like tales are marked by gentleness, quietness, and affirmation. They are stories such as those of *Frederick* (1967), in which a mouse shows that, though he is not helpful in gathering supplies for the cold winter along with the other mice, still, he gathers something else. When the winter storms come and they huddle together, Frederick brings color and warmth through his poetry—the thing he has gathered all summer. In *Swimmy* (1968), a small, isolated fish teaches a large school to swim "close together, each in his own place," and thus survive through cooperation. In *Tillie and the Wall* (1989), the young mouse Tillie teaches the other mice not to be afraid of barriers, as she burrows under the wall to find another colony of mice waiting for her.

Lionni's books all work in this affirming manner. They are each a celebration of human potentiality and grace, and suggest moral meanings without heavy didacticism. Lionni's illustrations are known for their playfulness and simplicity, as well as their effective use of collage, which he creates with soft shapes made from torn paper. The backgrounds are white pages, contributing to the simplicity as well as the brightness of the illustrations. The characters are animals: fish, frogs, and—most often—mice, and they are usually shown on a small scale and rather brightly. At times his work is very bright indeed, as in *Matthew's Dream* (1991), in which Matthew visits a museum and later has a colorful dream that he then replicates in his own art. Sometimes the unsaturated colors can be subdued and somber, as in *Frederick,* in which Lionni is trying to capture the essence of a gray, colorless world. In *It's Mine* (1986), Lionni uses both saturations for a story that begins with selfishness and bitterness and ends with community and joy.

Though Lionni uses a number of art forms—in *Swimmy,* for example, he puts on his watercolors with stamps and sponges to depict the undersea world—Lionni is best known for his work with collage. Sometimes he will use patterned paper, something he uses to brilliant effect in *Alexander and the Wind-Up Mouse* (1969), in which he depicts china cups, bottles, wallpaper, toys, blankets, and boots. Here, as Ezra Jack Keats will do, he allows the reader to determine and define the shapes that the patterns are suggesting. In books like *Frederick,* Lionni creates the collage with paper that he has first painted, then ripped or cut. This allows him to experiment playfully with the relationships between shapes. In *Tillie and the Wall* he uses cut paper that he has painted to depict the changing hues of the landscape, their values contrasting sharply with the glossy black spread that illustrates Tillie's journey underground.

Colorful, bright, and simple, Lionni's illustrations are recognizable for their continuity. Though his mice will sometimes be brown, sometimes gray, he depicts them consistently, so that any one mouse book will recall the others. The effect here is one of pleasurable sameness, as though the reader returns to an old friend.

Ezra Jack Keats (1916–1983)

In the 1960s, Ezra Jack Keats broke new ground by choosing to write about and illustrate the urban experiences of young minority children. Like Maurice Sendak, Keats grouped his books together; but, unlike Sendak, Keats grouped by character, rather than meaning and concerns. His Peter books explore the world of a young boy who is fascinated by the small things around him. Energetic, sensitive, exploring, eager, he travels happily through a landscape renewed by snow in *The Snowy Day* (1962), plays with Willie his dachshund and learns, surprisingly, how to whistle in *Whistle for Willie* (1964), struggles with the arrival of a new sibling in *Peter's Chair* (1967), and grows in sensitivity toward girls in *A Letter to Amy* (1968). In each of these stories Peter is surrounded by strong and loving parents who understand his concerns. The stories are dominated by hopefulness and the joy of growth.

In his *Louie* books, Keats works with a very different kind of boy. In *Louie* (1975), the protagonist rarely speaks and is very, very alone. When he goes to a neighborhood puppet show, he is entranced by the spectacle and calls out to the puppets; the other children are astonished to hear his voice. When he returns home, he walks, hunched over, past looming billboards and to a lonely apartment, where he sits in an empty, dark room. But his mind is filled with bright, colorful images, and they enter his dreams. At the end of the book, he finds that the children have given him a puppet, which is colored bright green and is set off against the darkness of the wall behind it. A dramatic sense of movement shows Louie racing towards it happily.

Unlike Sendak, Keats suggests that, though there is real pain and passion in childhood, what dominates is joy and hope and, if not security, a sense that there are at least loving parents who stand behind the child. Keats will not minimize emotions such as loneliness, but he suggests that they are not the last word in a child's experience. His is a world somewhat harsher than Robert McCloskey's, but much gentler than that of Maurice Sendak.

Keats works with gouache and collage, though in fact he will happily mix his mediums. In *The Snowy Day*, for example, he uses stamps and paint to create the effect of snowflakes. In *Whistle for Willie* he uses paper that he has fashioned by mixing oil paints and water, then floating the sheet of paper on top to absorb the swirling paint. This allows him to juxtapose certain colors to suggest moods and emotions. Dark gray swirling patterns suggest loneliness, for example.

But Keats is perhaps best known for his use of collage, which is common in almost all of the books. At times he will use patterned paper, and other times he will use real images that he has clipped from a magazine—a building, a boy, a Tiffany lamp—and incorporate them into a landscape or setting. At other times he will tear paper and use it to indicate something such as a battered billboard. In this use of collage Keats allows the reader to create meaning through the new relationships he establishes between his patterns, so that brown textured paper turns out to be a fence, and other patterned paper turns out to be curtains, but only in the eye of the reader.

Vera B. Williams (b. 1927)

In books like *A Chair for My Mother* (1982), *Something Special for Me* (1983), *Cherries and Cherry Pits* (1986), and *More, More, More* (1990), Vera B. Williams tells stories about simple, unadorned, but deeply felt pleasures that a child experiences within the confines of a strong family. Frequently using strong, confident, bold, and imaginative female characters, Williams creates plots that focus on characters rather than intense plots, that show those characters warmly and joyfully interacting with others as well as their environment, and that suggest the real and very deep beauty and joy that lies within those things that are close around us, as in the ending of *A Chair for My Mother:* "Mama sits down and watches the news on TV when she comes home from her job. After supper, I sit with her and she can reach right up and turn out the light if I fall asleep in her lap." The accompanying illustration pictures the two close together, the mother reaching for the pull string; there seems nothing else around them, as if they are in the strong center of their world, together.

The leap, of course, is to find a way to visually represent what is an abstract notion: recognizing joy and beauty in the simple and close at hand. Williams chooses to make the visual connection through the use of bold, bright colors and large shapes that dramatically catch the eye of the reader. When the narrator comes to meet her friend Bidemmi in the opening to *Cherries and Cherry Pits,* half of the page is the bright textured green of Bidemmi's door, the other half her face. The illustrations for *More, More, More* focus on the intense and joyful relationships between a father and Little Guy, a grandmother and Little Pumpkin, and a mother and her Little Bird. Each pictures the two characters with almost nothing else around them, so that the focus on the relationship is intense and centered.

To achieve her texture and intensity, Williams uses several different techniques. The playfulness and exuberance of *More, More, More* is enhanced with bright gouache paintings; the imagined stories of *Cherries and Cherry Pits* that are drawn by Bidemmi are done in magic marker, Bidemmi's medium; the postcards of *Stringbean's Trip to the Shining Sea* (1988) are done with watercolors, magic markers, and colored pencils. In each case, Williams chooses a medium to heighten the effects that she is after in a given text, and to connect the style of her drawings to her characters.

The pictures themselves, which suggest a child's perspective, are drawn with the textures, simple shapes, and bold colors that a child might use, even in the borders, which Williams carefully crafts to mirror and reflect the action of the illustration. In *A Chair for My Mother,* for example, the border will sometimes show the pattern of the chair, or, after the fire that destroys their apartment, a line of burned and wilted flowers to suggest their devastation and disappointment. At times, Williams's shapes are more complicated, as in *Stringbean's Trip to the Shining Sea,* in which Williams illustrates a series of black-and-white photographs and postcards that Stringbean sends home to his family as he travels west from Kansas with his brother Fred. Though the postcards are much more detailed than her other illustrations, the use of bold colors and simplified shapes, as well as the focus on people rather than things or plot moments, connects these illustrations to Williams's other work.

Eric Carle (b. 1929)

Whereas Leo Lionni's illustrations are soft and gentle, subdued, and somewhat unsaturated, Eric Carle's illustrations are bold and saturated, bursting with hues that startle by their conjunctions and vividness. Whereas Ezra Jack Keats's illustrations ask readers to interpret the meaning of shapes and to give form in the imagination, Eric Carle uses his shapes dramatically to create very distinct forms. And, while all three of these illustrators use collage, Carle's are distinguished by their strong hues and fantastic suggestions, as well as by a distinctly individualized desire to experiment with the boundaries of a book's nature.

Like Lionni, Carle frequently turns to the world of animals to tell tales that have a fable-like tenor to them, as well as a pleasing narrative simplicity. Carle's *Do You Want to Be My Friend?* (1971) is an almost wordless picture book of a mouse who searches for a friend, finally finding one in another mouse. Together they outwit the snake searching for them. Similarly, *The Very Quiet Cricket* (1990) tells the story of a cricket searching for a way to make a sound; he is finally able to once he meets another cricket. *The Very Lonely Firefly* (1995) depicts the nighttime journey of a firefly who is finally able to find other fireflies with which to shine his light. In all of these books there is a sense of community, of pleasure in being together, that is reminiscent of a Leo Lionni book.

More than any other illustrator, however, Carle depends on the reader's senses, often the tactile sense. In *The Very Busy Spider* (1984), Carle depicts the growing web of the spider by raising its lines off the page so that a reader can follow its growth by touch. In *The Very Hungry Caterpillar* (1969), Carle cuts holes in several of the pages so that the reader can follow the voracious eating of the young caterpillar. *The Very Lonely Firefly* boasts a final spread that shows a grouping of fireflies that acutally lights up randomly, and *The Very Quiet Cricket* ends with a spread that is accompanied by a recorded chirping sound, the sound the cricket has finally found. This extension of the boundaries of the book shows a kind of inventiveness and playfulness on the part of Carle, a playfulness also reflected in books like *Papa, Please Get the Moon for Me* (1986), a book whose spreads open wide to the left, wide to the right, up and down, and finally to an expansive fullness that more than quadruples the size of the page.

Carle is most conscious of his choice of dramatic colors, which are often highlighted by placing them, like Lionni, against a white background. In *The Very Lonely Firefly* he juxtaposes warm red, yellows, and oranges against the cool blue and green background of the night to suggest their contrast. In *Animals, Animals* (1989) he painted paper in vivid acrylics, meshing together many shades of brown. He then cut these out to form the shapes of the animals he wished to depict, using the various shades of the meshed paint to create the texture he wanted. In his counting book *1, 2, 3 to the Zoo* (1968), he used this same technique in combination with crayon to create effects such as the lion's mane, the alligators' ridges, and the monkeys' expressions. In his *A House for a Hermit Crab* (1987), he combined collage with intricately cut paper, crayon, and a watercolor wash that he allowed to spread in order to create the texture of the hermit crab's shell. Like Ezra Jack Keats, Eric Carle mixes media to create his effects.

Carle's collage is easily recognizable. Unlike the torn and soft edges of Lionni, Carle's are cleanly cut and placed in combination, a series of saturated hues that strike the eye both in themselves and in their values. The bold colors, however, are placed in conjunction with gentle texts that most frequently tell of a search, usually a search for something with which a child reader can readily empathize: companionship, growth, love, a home.

Ted Lewin (b. 1935)

Though *precision* and *watercolor* are not terms that are generally linked, this union is precisely what marks the work of illustrator Ted Lewin. His illustrations boast an astonishing array of colors, and he achieves his textures through the multiple layering of the paint and through a willingness to allow the paint to spread in surprising patterns. But, in addition, his illustrations are marked by precise and intricate detail, so that facial expressions, the sides of buildings, the banister of a stairway, the reedwork on a basket are all closely rendered.

Such a union allows Lewin to create unusually textured watercolor paintings, so that the sea, for example, may be many distinct shades of blue, or a hillside and its rocks may seem to be made of a thousand different hues. Instead of creating large spaces of color that gradually blur into each other, Lewin is adept at breaking those large spaces down into small units and varying the hues and values significantly, thereby creating patterns within those large spaces. The result is an illustration with a complex color patterning.

In Ann Herbert Scott's *Cowboy Country* (1993), for example, Lewin wants to show the intricate contrasts in the texture of the landscape of the U.S. West. Every landscape thus becomes a patterning of hues, so that there hardly seems to be a single brushstroke uncomplicated by another brushstroke, or a single sweep of green uncomplicated by a slightly different hue or value. In *Ali, Child of the Desert* (1997), Lewin restrains this technique, for he wants to show the broad and unchanging expanse of sand, the world in which Ali lives. Here he does use large expanses of the same hue, particularly in the depictions of a sandstorm that changes everything to the same color. The intricate variety of watercolor comes instead in the depiction of the animals, who are complicated by many hues.

Lewin is particularly sensitive to the use of color to support the meaning of a text. In *Peppe the Lamplighter* (1993), Lewin uses color thematically to tell the tale of an Italian American family that has recently immigrated. When Peppe, still a young boy, is forced to find work, he becomes a lamplighter, a job that shames his father. Though Peppe values his work, he faces the daily scorn of his father, until one night his sister is lost and the father recognizes the importance of what Peppe does. The overriding metaphor here is that of light, and so Lewin paints most of the illustrations in the darkness of night, or in the darkness of a small, overcrowded apartment. In each of the illustrations, Lewin places a strong light source that remains the source of all hope, all illumination, as it were. The notion of light as hope begins to dominate and finally culminates in the last spread in which Peppe is lighting a lamp that "is a small flame of promise for tomorrow."

In each of these books, Lewin maintains his interest in creating many different hues and values to give texture to the large illustration. Blank walls, shades, wood floors, polished bars—all carry with them a spectrum of shades and hues. And all are marked by the precise detail that characterizes Lewin's work.

Allen Say (b. 1939)

Whereas illustrators like Eric Carle use bold, bright colors, and illustrators like Ted Lewin create scenes filled with varying and contrasting hues and values, Allen Say is more to be noted as an illustrator whose watercolors are subdued, even, at times, quite unsaturated. His illustrations are marked by large sections of single textured color, particularly in the backgrounds. His scenes often have the look of being posed, where the child protagonist is caught in the middle of contemplation. This lends a quiet, meditative quality to his work.

Illustration by Allen Say for his *Emma's Rug.* Copyright © 1996. Reprinted by permission of Houghton Mifflin Company.

Emma's Rug (1996), for example, is the story of a young girl who finds artistic inspiration in the pictures that she sees in the textures of her rug. She becomes well known for her exceptional talent. When her mother washes the rug, however, she is in despair and throws away her paints; she believes she will no longer see the images that so enthralled her. Then, on a bare wall, she sees a bird just flying away, then looks out and sees all the images that had been in the rug, but are now in the world about her. She begins to draw again.

For his illustrations, Say focuses on quiet, still moments in Emma's life: watching the rug, drawing in the kitchen, standing by her blue ribbon. Emma herself is quiet and reserved, and the unsaturated hues suggest this quality in her personality. When Emma hears of her rug being washed, she is shown in an agony of anger, her hands drawn up; behind her is a brown-gray background with nothing else in it. When she sees the bird that marks her new artistic awareness, the background is similarly blank, but filled in now with the flying crane. It is as if the uncluttered backgrounds are meant to suggest the empty canvas.

In *Grandfather's Journey* (1993), the illustrations depicting Say's grandfather's journey from Japan to the United States and back to Japan also have the posed quality of those in *Emma's Rug,* but here that quality comes from the fact that these illustrations are meant to depict photographs. Characters pose in stilted positions, seemingly aware of the presence of the camera. Again, Say uses many tones of a single hue to create the illustration; sometimes these are the sepia tones of early photography, but at other times they are the greens of a pond, or the golden yellow of fertile fields. The sense of action and movement is missing here; all the characters are caught in time.

In *A River Dream* (1988) and *The Lost Lake* (1989), Say uses much higher values than in his later work. Both books have the quality of a dream: In *A River Dream,* a young boy imagines, during a fever, that he is out on a river with his uncle, who teaches him the value of reverence for life. In *The Lost Lake,* a boy and his father come to a closer relationship as they search for a lake that is unspoiled and find it unexpectedly one morning. Both books are marked by cool blues and greens, and the warmer colors are used to suggest sudden warmth: a sunrise, for example, or the flash of a rainbow trout, or the first sight of a lost lake. The colors point to the startled wonder of the characters, a wonder in which readers can participate as well.

Say's work shows that effective illustration does not have to be chock-full to the gun'ls with detail, nor does it have to be dominated by bright and bold color, nor does it depend on dramatic action. Say shows that quite the opposite is possible, that illustration of subdued hues and quiet tones may also capture the meaning and impact of the text. In *The Lost Lake,* father and son wake up to a vision of a lake that they had not expected. The direction of the illustration is all directed downward to them, as cool blues give way to warm yellows. Father and son are small against the huge landscape, and the lake, by contrast, is majestic. Though the text indicates their mutual wonder—"Dad didn't say a word the whole time. But then, I didn't have anything to say either" (30)—it is the illustration that captures the distinc-

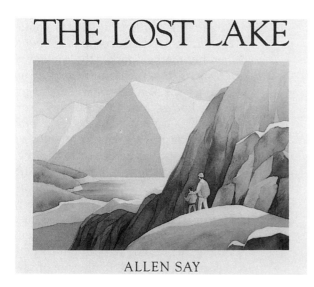

Illustration by Allen Say for his *The Lost Lake.* Copyright © 1989. Reprinted by permission of Houghton Mifflin Company.

tion between the small and the great. The subdued, quiet illustration carries the meaning.

Patricia Polacco (b. 1944)

In Patricia Polacco's *Just Plain Fancy* (1990), two young Amish girls find an egg by the side of the road; when it hatches, it is a peacock, and they are stunned to find that it is so fancy that they name it Fancy. When it gets older and begins to show its feathers, they are sure that it cannot be allowed to remain in the Amish community because it is not plain. They hide it for a time until it escapes and displays during a barn raising; though the girls fear it will be sent away, old Martha reassures them. "This be one of God's most beautiful creations. He is fancy, child, and that's the way of it."

The illustration depicting the girls' first discovery of Fancy's tail feathers is indicative of Polacco's techniques. The directional movement is from the upper right to the lower left, a line suggested by the angle of the sunlight in the barn, the line from Naomi's eyes to the chickens' eye to the peacock, the line designated by the hem of Naomi's dress, and even the line given by the angle of the barn seen outside the open door. Much of the left-hand page is white, a typical background for Polacco, but here, especially, meaningful because it is so plain. The tail is itself hidden off the page, left to the reader to imagine.

But beyond this sense of direction, the illustration suggests much about Polacco's creation of meaning. The children are caught in midaction, as they express their concern, their horror. Much of the emotion of the scene is given through facial expression, to which Polacco pays special attention; here the eyebrows are raised, the eyes big, the mouth circled in an O. Not dissimilar expressions are given to the chickens, who are also struck by Fancy's display. The plain browns and grays—the subdued colors in general—all connect to the thematic contrast of the story, plainness versus fanciness, though Polacco calls this contrast into question at times with her display of quilts. When Fancy is finally shown displaying, the vibrant greens, blues, and purples are iridescent, strongly distinguished from the earlier illustrations, especially those many spreads dominated

From *Just Plain Fancy* by Patricia Polacco. Copyright © 1990. Used by permission of Bantam Books, a division of Random House, Inc.

by white backgrounds. But, put together, as in the final illustration showing the white and black-clad Naomi sitting with Fancy, the centrality of the thematic meaning comes clear: Both of these ways—plain and fancy—are part of God's world.

All of these techniques can be found in Polacco's work, some of the most easily recognizable work done in children's literature. Her stories are moving, passionate, simple stories of families that are created, homes that are made, insights gathered and shared. *The Bee Tree* (1993) tells of a raucous, delightful romp through the countryside to follow a bee to its hive; its honey becomes a metaphor for the sweetness of books. *Mrs. Katz and Tush* (1992) is a tale of loneliness overcome, as Mrs. Katz is visited by Larnel, who brings her a cat. The closeness that develops between the two spans generations and races, as they become part of each others' families. *Chicken Sunday* (1992) similarly shows a multiracial, multigenerational bond, as the young Patricia, Stewart, and Winston come to love Eula Mae Walker and, later on, Mr. Kodinski, who shares with them his Ukrainian heritage. The tattooed number on his forearm—never mentioned in the text—suggests another heritage he has survived but chooses not to share with the children.

One of Polacco's more potent artistic elements is the care she takes with the placement of elements on a page. Often this placement indicates relationships between characters. In *Mrs. Katz and Tush*, the opening spread shows Larnel's mother and Mrs. Katz side by side on a couch, holding each other; Larnel sits on another chair, somewhat uneasy and embarassed. But later illustrations that show their growing relationship put him closer and closer, until, at the end, he has taken his mother's place and now holds Mrs. Katz, who in fact holds his child. In *Just Plain Fancy*, Polacco shows the relative ages of Naomi and Ruth by setting them back to back; Ruth plays with a snowman, but Naomi feeds the chickens, one playing while the other works, indicating their ages. In *Chicken Sunday* Polacco suggests the closeness of the three children by always placing them close together physically; when loving adults come into their world, they, too, are added in the close proximity. In these ways, Polacco uses her arrangement of elements to complement the meaning of her stories.

In all of these works, Polacco uses a mixed-media approach. Allowing her large white spaces to define areas, she uses pencil to define shapes, and watercolor and crayon to give color and texture. At times she will turn to collage, adding in actual photographs of family members to connect the story to real history, as in *Pink and Say* (1994). Her values are carefully chosen. The darker, subdued values and tones of *Pink and Say* suggest the darker quality of that story; the much higher values of *Chicken Sunday* reflect the riotous joy and happiness of that book. In *The Keeping Quilt* (1988), Polacco uses only pencil and no color except that of the quilt itself, which shows brightly against the browns of the pencilled sketches. But in each of these books the intense attention to the facial expression, mostly created through pencil, conveys much of the powerful emotion of Polacco's work.

Thinking and Writing about and from within Children's Literature

Thinking and Writing about Children's Literature _____

1. When Robert McCloskey first began to illustrate *Make Way for Ducklings,* he wanted to illustrate it in color. His editor suggested otherwise. Was she right? What advantages does he gain with the use of sepia tones throughout?

2. Examine Chris Van Allsburg's *The Widow's Broom.* How do his choices about color, the placement of elements on a page, texture, and sense of direction contribute to the meaning of this book?

Thinking and Writing from within Children's Literature _____

1. In a brief paragraph, explain how you would organize the elements of a spread that is meant to illustrate the following situations:
   a. While standing at the North Pole, a character sees the first moments of the flight of Santa's sleigh.
   b. On the plains of Africa, the sun heats the land.
   c. On a farm during winter, a father and young daughter head out to the forest during the night.
   d. A young boy looks up at a huge mansion.

   Later, compare your ideas to the handling of the subject in Chris Van Allsburg's *The Polar Express,* Toshi Yoshida's *Rhinoceros Mother,* Jane Yolen and John Schoenherr's *Owl Moon,* and Chris Van Allsburg's *The Garden of Abdul Gasazi.*

2. Think about a color scheme that might be appropriate for each of the following situations, explaining, in each case, why such a color scheme would be appropriate.
   a. A story set on an ocean liner
   b. A story about a lonely child
   c. A story about a child moving to a new school
   d. A story set during a snowstorm
   e. A fantasy story set in the darkness of a cave

Selected Bibliographies

Works Cited _____

Aylesworth, Jim. *Country Crossing.* New York: Atheneum, 1991. Illustrated by Ted Rand.

Baylor, Byrd. *Desert Voices.* New York: Charles Scribners, 1981. Illustrated by Peter Parnall.

Bunting, Eve. *Night of the Gargoyles.* New York: Clarion, 1994. Illustrated by David Wiesner.

———. *December.* New York: Harcourt, Brace, 1997. Illustrated by David Diaz.

Cooney, Barbara. *Miss Rumphius.* New York: Viking, 1982.

dePaola, Tomie. *The Clown of God.* New York: Harcourt, Brace, 1978.

———. *Fin M'Coul: The Giant of Knockmany Hill.* New York: Holiday House, 1981.

Fletcher, Ralph. *Twilight Comes Twice.* New York: Clarion, 1997. Illustrated by Kate Kiesler.

Flournoy, Valerie. *The Patchwork Quilt.* New York: E. P. Dutton, 1985.

Foreman, Michael. *Seal Surfer.* New York: Harcourt, Brace, 1996.

Hall, Donald. *The Ox-Cart Man.* New York: Viking Press, 1979.

Hendershot, Judith. *In Coal Country.* New York: Knopf, 1987. Illustrated by Thomas Allen.

King, Dr. Martin Luther, Jr. *I Have a Dream.* New York: Scholastic Press, 1997.

Lawson, Robert. *They Were Strong and Good.* New York: Viking, 1940.

Lewin, Ted. *Fair!* New York: Lothrop, Lee and Shepard, 1997.

McCloskey, Robert. *Make Way for Ducklings.* New York: Viking, 1941.

———. *One Morning in Maine.* New York: Viking, 1952.

———. *Time of Wonder.* New York: Viking, 1957.

McDermott, Gerald. *Arrow to the Sun.* New York: Viking, 1974.

Mollel, Tolowa M. *The Orphan Boy.* New York: Clarion, 1990. Illustrated by Paul Morin.

Nolan, Dennis. *The Castle Builder.* New York: Macmillan, 1987.

Polacco, Patricia. *Pink and Say.* New York: Philomel, 1994.

Schoenherr, John. *Rebel.* New York: Philomel, 1995.

Scott, Ann Herbert. *Cowboy Country.* New York: Clarion, 1993. Illustrated by Ted Lewin.

Shannon, David. *A Bad Case of Stripes.* New York: Scholastic, 1998.

Spier, Peter. *Christmas.* New York: Doubleday, 1983.

———. *Noah's Ark.* New York: Doubleday, 1977.

———. *Rain.* New York: Doubleday, 1982.

Swift, Hildegarde. *The Little Red Lighthouse and the Great Gray Bridge.* New York: Harcourt, Brace, 1942. Illustrations by Lynd Ward.

Tejima, Keizaburo. *The Bears' Autumn.* LaJolla, CA: Green Tiger, 1986.

———. *Fox's Dream.* New York: Philomel, 1987.

———. *Owl Lake.* New York: Philomel, 1987.

———. *Woodpecker Forest.* New York: Philomel, 1984.

Van Allsburg. *The Garden of Abdul Gasazi.* Boston: Houghton Mifflin, 1979.

———. *The Polar Express.* Boston: Houghton Mifflin, 1985.

———. *The Sweetest Fig.* Boston: Houghton Mifflin, 1993.

———. *The Widow's Broom.* Boston: Houghton Mifflin, 1992.

Ward, Lynd. *The Biggest Bear.* Boston: Houghton Mifflin, 1952.

Wiesner, David. *Free Fall.* New York: Lothrop, Lee, and Shepard, 1988.

———. *Sector 7.* New York: Clarion, 1999.

———. *Tuesday.* New York: Clarion, 1991.

Wood, Audrey. *Heckedy Peg.* New York: Harcourt, Brace, 1987. Illustrated by Don Wood.

Yolen, Jane. *Owl Moon.* NY: Philomel, 1987. Illustrated by John Schoenherr.

———. *Wings.* New York: Harcourt, Brace, 1991. Illustrated by Dennis Nolan.

Yoshida, Toshi. *Rhinoceros Mother.* NY: Philomel Books, 1991.

———. *The Young Lions.* New York: Philomel, 1989.

Works by Selected Illustrators

Maurice Sendak

Grimm, Wilhelm. *Dear Mili.* New York: Farrar, Straus, 1988. Illustrated by Maurice Sendak.

In the Night Kitchen. New York: Harper and Row, 1970.

Outside over There. New York: Harper and Row, 1981.

We Are All in the Dumps with Jack and Guy. New York: HarperCollins, 1993.

Where the Wild Things Are. New York: Harper and Row, 1963.

Leo Lionni

Alexander and the Wind-Up Mouse. New York: Pantheon, 1969.

Frederick. New York: Pantheon, 1967.

It's Mine. New York: Knopf, 1986.

Matthew's Dream. New York: Knopf, 1991.

Swimmy. New York: Pantheon, 1968.

Tillie and the Wall. New York: Knopf, 1989.

Ezra Jack Keats

A Letter to Amy. New York: Harper and Row, 1968.

Louie. New York: Morrow, 1975.

Louie's Search. New York: Four Winds, 1980.

Peter's Chair. New York: HarperCollins, 1967.

The Snowy Day. New York: Viking, 1962.

The Trip. New York: Morrow, 1978.

Whistle for Willie. New York: Viking, 1964.

Vera Williams

A Chair for My Mother. New York: Greenwillow, 1982.

Cherries and Cherry Pits. New York: Greenwillow, 1986.

More, More, More. New York: Greenwillow, 1990.

Something Special for Me. New York: Greenwillow, 1983.

Stringbean's Trip to the Shining Sea. New York: Greenwillow, 1988.

Eric Carle

1, 2, 3 to the Zoo. New York: Philomel, 1968.

Animals, Animals. New York: Philomel, 1989.

Do You Want to Be My Friend? New York: Thomas Crowell, 1971.

Dragons, Dragons. New York: Philomel, 1991.

A House for a Hermit Crab. Saxonville, MA: Picture Book Studio, 1987.

Papa, Please Get the Moon for Me. Saxonville, MA: Picture Book Studio, 1986.

The Very Busy Spider. New York: Philomel, 1984.

The Very Hungry Caterpillar. Cleveland: Collins World, 1969.

The Very Lonely Firefly. New York: Philomel, 1995.

The Very Quiet Cricket. New York: Philomel, 1990.

Ted Lewin

Bartone, Elisa. *Peppe the Lamplighter.* New York: Lothrop, Lee and Shepard, 1993. Illustrated by Ted Lewin.

Fair! New York: Lothrop, Lee and Shepard, 1997.

London, Jonathan. *Ali, Child of the Desert.* New York: Lothrop, Lee and Shepard, 1997. Illustrated by Ted Lewin.

Oberman, Sheldon. *The Always Prayer Shawl.* Honesdale, PA: Boyds Mill, 1994. Illustrated by Ted Lewin.

Scott, Ann Herbert. *Cowboy Country.* New York: Clarion, 1993. Illustrated by Ted Lewin.

Weller, Frances Ward. *I Wonder If I'll See a Whale.* New York: Philomel, 1991. Illustrated by Ted Lewin.

Yolen, Jane. *Bird Watch.* New York: Philomel, 1990. Illustrated by Ted Lewin.

Allen Say

Emma's Rug. Boston: Houghton Mifflin, 1996.

Grandfather's Journey. Boston: Houghton Mifflin, 1993.

The Lost Lake. Boston: Houghton Mifflin, 1989.

A River Dream. Boston: Houghton Mifflin, 1988.

Snyder, Diane. *The Boy of the Three-Year Nap.* Boston: Houghton Mifflin, 1988. Illustrated by Allen Say.

Stranger in the Mirror. Boston: Houghton Mifflin, 1995.

Patricia Polacco

The Bee Tree. New York: Philomel, 1993.

Chicken Sunday. New York: Philomel, 1992.

Just Plain Fancy. New York: Bantam, 1990.

The Keeping Quilt. New York: Simon and Schuster, 1988.

Mrs. Katz and Tush. New York: Bantam, 1992.

Pink and Say. New York: Philomel, 1994.

Works on the Narrative Art of the Picture Book

Alderson, Brian. *Sing a Song of Sixpence: The English Picture Book Tradition and Randolph Caldecott.* Cambridge: Cambridge University Press, 1986.

Bader, Barbara. *American Picturebooks: From Noah's Ark to the Beast Within.* New York: Macmillan, 1976.

Cahn, Annabelle Simon. "Leo Lionni, Illustrator and Philosopher." *Children's Literature* 2 (1973): 123–129.

Carle, Eric. *The Art of Eric Carle.* New York: Philomel, 1996.

Cech, John. *Angels and Wild Things: The Archetypal Poetics of Maurice Sendak.* University Park: Pennsylvania State University Press, 1995.

———. "Remembering Caldecott: *The Three Jovial Huntsmen* and the Art of the Picture Book." *Lion and the Unicorn* 7/8 (1983–1984): 110–119.

Cleaver, Elizabeth. "Idea to Image: The Journey of a Picture Book." *Lion and the Unicorn* 7/8 (1983–1984): 156–170.

Cooney, Barbara. "Narrating Chaucer, Grimm, New England, and Cooney." In Charlotte F. Otten and Gary D. Schmidt, eds., *The Voice of the Narrator in Children's Literature* (Westport, CT: Greenwood Press, 1989): 25–31.

Cummings, Pat, ed. *Talking with Artists.* New York: Macmillan, 1991.

Goldstone, B. P. "Visual Interpretation of Children's Books." *The Reading Teacher* 42 (1989): 592–595.

Hannah, Kathleen. "'Acknowledgement for What I Do, to Fortify Me to Go Ahead': Family, Ezra Jack Keats, and Peter." *Children's Literature Association Quarterly* 22 (Winter, 1997–1998): 196–203.

Hubbard, R. *Authors of Pictures, Draughtsmen of Words.* Portsmouth, NH: Heinemann, 1989.

Keifer, Barbara. *The Potential of Picturebooks.* Englewood Cliffs, NJ: Merrill, 1995.

Lacy, L. E. *Art and Design in Children's Books: An Analysis of Caldecott Award Winning Illustrations.* Chicago: American Library Association, 1986.

Landes, S. "Picture Books as Literature." *Children's Literature Association Quarterly* 10 (1985): 51–54.

Lanes, Selma. *The Art of Maurice Sendak.* New York: Abrams, 1980.

Lobel, Arnold. "An Interview with Arnold Lobel." By Roni Natov and Geraldine DeLuca. *Lion and the Unicorn* 1 (1977): 72–96.

McDermott, Gerald. "Caldecott Award Acceptance." *Horn Book* 51 (August, 1975): 349–354.

Moebius, W. "Introduction to Picturebook Codes." *Word and Image* 2 (1986): 141–152.

Nodelman, Perry. *Words about Pictures: The Narrative Art of Children's Books.* Athens, GA: The University of Georgia Press, 1988.

Pope, Martin and Lillie. "Ezra Jack Keats: A Childhood Revisited." *New Advocate* 3 (1990): 13–23.

Roxburgh, Stephen. "A Picture Equals How Many Words?: Narrative Theory and Picture Books for Children." *Lion and the Unicorn* 7/8 (1983–1984): 20–33.

Schmidt, Gary. "The Elemental Art of Keizaburo Tejima." *Lion and the Unicorn* 14 (1990): 77–91.

———. *Robert McCloskey.* Boston: Twayne, 1990.

Shaddock, Jennifer. "*Where the Wild Things Are:* Sendak's Journey into the Heart of Darkness." *Children's Literature Association Quarterly* 22 (Winter, 1997–1998): 155–159.

Spitz, Ellen Handler. *Inside Picture Books.* New Haven, CT: Yale University Press, 1999.

Stanton, Joseph. "The Dreaming Picture Books of Chris Van Allsburg." *Children's Literature* 24 (1996): 161–179.

———. "Maurice Sendak's Urban Landscapes." *Children's Literature* 28 (2000): 132–146.

Steig, Michael. "Reading *Outside over There.*" *Children's Literature* 13 (1985): 139–153.

3

Alphabet and Counting Books: Teaching More Than Letters and Numbers

Alphabet and counting books are among the first genres that children experience. And, as one of the first genres, they are often regarded as books whose primary purpose is to teach. For that reason, writers often keep the colors bright, the objects clear and familiar, the text uncluttered. After all, teaching tools ought to be bright and easy if they are going to instruct young children in letters and numbers.

But one of the large questions of this genre is that of purpose. Are alphabet and counting books designed primarily to teach? Certainly they do this, particularly if they are read in conjunction with an adult reader. But the number of books that require sophisticated reading skills in this genre suggest that these books do something else as well. They instruct in design, incorporating organized material as diverse as zoo animals and airplanes. They instruct in establishing correspondence between a thing and its symbolic representation. They instruct in sound. Through the use of language and numerical systems, they instruct in a culture's art and life. They instruct the reader in the unlimited possibilities of words and visual choices. And they delight in their ingenuity. Above all, they delight.

Boundaries and Definitions

The nature of an alphabet book or a counting book is suggested by its name. Each is what might be termed a concept book, a book that uses text and illustration to establish connections between a symbol—"B" or "4"—and an object or number of objects. Generally the books are aimed at a juvenile audience, with the result that these correspondences are made easily discernible, both in terms of the idea of the correspondence (A is for Apple, B is for Barn) and in terms of the visual correspondences (A is placed next to the Apple, B is placed beside the barn).

One of the traditional boundaries of alphabet and counting books is their reliance on recognizable objects from a child's world: B is for Ball, C is for Crayon. The advantage here is that the child reader is able to identify correspondences between the symbol, the sound, and the object because all of the elements on the page are a part of his or her own direct experience. This means that the illustrator of such a book, to take advantage of this direct experience, uses as many visual elements as possible to enable the child reader to identify these correspondences. The letters will be large, the objects familiar and bright. Those objects will be central in the space of the page so that the reader can easily pick out the pertinent element. White space highlights the important object and avoids distraction. In short, the illustrator in this genre, perhaps more than in any other, must be intimately concerned *in a pedagogical sense* with balance, emphasis, and form, as well as the selection and the arrangement of subject matter.

Tana Hoban's *Let's Count* (1999)—the title itself suggesting an invitation—uses vigorously-colored photographs to highlight the items that the child reader is to count. Five, for example, uses five crushed soda cans to illustrate the number, the image surrounded by a blue background that also holds a large yellow 5, the word written in uppercase letters, and five white dots in a vertical line. The images are sharp and arresting, easily counted, while the number is represented as a digit, as a word, and as a series of dots. Carol Saul's *Barn Cat* (1998), illustrated by Mary Azarian's tinted woodcuts, is for a slightly more sophisticated audience, one that can place a series of items to count within the context of a narrative. Here, the barn cat is searching for something, passing by one grasshopper, two crickets, three monarch butterflies, and so on. The narrator begins each spread by asking the barn cat what she is looking for, each time suggesting something that sees the cat and flies, whirrs, and bounds away. Finally, the cat finds what she is looking for: the narrator herself, a young girl with a bowl of milk.

But must a writer rely solely on readily recognizable objects? Can the writer push back the boundary and move into arenas previously unknown to a child? In other words, is it possible for alphabet and counting books to do more, to function as narratives or as cultural histories, or as information books?

Insofar as they move in these kinds of directions, such books move beyond traditional boundaries. Instead of focusing on one-to-one correspondences, they add larger concerns to their texts. For example, in *Grandmother's Alphabet* (1996) Eve Shaw is interested in commenting on women's roles. She begins, "Grandma is an Artist, she paints with colors bright. Grandma can be...an actress, an author, or an architect...and so can I." Readers are taken through an alphabet of grandmothers who can do anything and who also look like anyone. They are young and old, slender and round, white and people of color. They cannot only paint, but also be doctors and lawyers as well as teachers and nurses. Current questions of diversity and female roles are packaged into an alphabet format as the author goes beyond the role of simply teaching the alphabet and moves into the area of influencing readers' views.

In Virginia A. Stroud's *The Path of the Quiet Elk: A Native American Alphabet* (1996), a wise, older man instructs a young boy in the ways of his Native American people, walking with him in nature and pointing out their people's interpretation of the world around them. Stroud uses a narrative to introduce the customs of the Native Americans and to incorporate important philosophical elements: "remember our interconnectedness with everything." The alphabetical arrangement demonstrates that philosophy through depicting the older man's relationship to the environment. Here, too, the writer has moved well beyond traditional boundaries.

This movement beyond the boundaries of alphabet and counting books functioning solely as ways to teach a juvenile audience suggests that those books may be much more complicated in terms of purpose than they might at first appear. In fact, no alphabet or counting book is successful if its entire purpose is simply didactic. It must imaginatively engage the child reader, so that delight will precede—and sometimes even supersede—learning.

The decisions about the boundaries of an alphabet or counting book are influenced by the writer's idea of presentation, which, in turn, suggests what should be included, what excluded. If the work is using a narrative approach, each letter or number must contribute to the development of the story. If the work is interested in presenting information about a subject, then each letter should engage readers and excite their interest in the subject. What is important here is that inclusion is not random but logical and even imperative, given the presentation choices of the writer.

The Stable Elements of an Alphabet and Counting Book

This is a genre dominated by flexibility. While the alphabet and number systems are grounds for organization, the content is open to an almost limitless number of subjects and arrangements. Yet, at the same time, there are certain elements of the alphabet and counting books that are stable.

Pointers for Teachers: Evaluating ABC and Counting Books

Narrative
- How is the text presented for its audience? Clear and uncluttered for the young? Playful for the young and older? Mysterious and perhaps even challenging for the older? Interactive for all ages?
- Is the text a fresh presentation of well-known material? How so?
- What thematic elements hold the separate spreads of the book together?

Illustrations
- How do the text and illustrations work together to create an imaginative world for the reader?
- How does the artist arrange the illustrations to accommodate the level of complexity to the level of the audience?

There is, foremost, the objective of clarity. All books within this genre need to present the numbers and the letters clearly, so that they are well attached to the concept or element that they represent. The more concrete and physical the connection, the easier it is for the child to comprehend.

The correspondence between element and letter or number may come about because the illustration uses an object that is well known to the child. But it may also come about through other means. The book may work thematically, for example, as in Anita Lobel's *Alison's Zinnia* (1990), in which Lobel uses the names of young girls, the names of flowers, and an appropriate verb to bring the reader through the alphabet.

> Alison acquired an Amaryllis for Beryl.
> Beryl bought a Begonia for Crystal.
> Crystal cut a Chrysanthemum for Dawn.
> Dawn dug a Daffodil for Emily.

Each of these lines is on a single page, each illustrated by a large picture of the appropriate flower and a smaller one of the child performing the action. Jerry Pallotta's and Fred Stillwell's *The Airplane Alphabet Book* (1997) similarly uses the names of airplane models to take the child reader through the alphabet, linking a type of plane to its appropriate letter. In a thematic book the elements being connected to numbers and letters may be exotic, but the theme contributes to a kind of predictability that allows for easy correspondence.

Clarity is also achieved when the letters or numbers are large and prominent, easy to pick out from the welter of the page. The connecting elements, too, need to be easy to discern, even when they are part of a larger background. Alphabet books for older readers, in fact, play with this kind of discernment. Stephen T. Johnson's *Alphabet City* (1995) places the objects in large drawings of urban scenes; set in order as they are, it is not difficult for the child reader to find the letters. Lucy Micklethwait's *I Spy: An Alphabet in Art* (1992) is more difficult, in that the child reader has to be able to discover objects in a work of art that connect to the letter.

Works like those of Johnson and Micklethwait suggest that, while there are certain stable elements in an alphabet book, there is also a range of flexibility, a context within which the artist may roam freely and imaginatively.

The Flexible Elements in an Alphabet and Counting Book

Despite the stable elements of the alphabet and counting book, there is indeed enormous flexibility. The range of approaches to the handling of what seem simple elements suggests something of the range of the human imagination, and is shown most fully by a sampling of those books.

Eve Merriam's *Where Is Everybody?* (1989) uses personified animals, alliteration, and rhyme to illustrate the alphabet. Readers meet the "giraffe...in the garage" and the "Hippopotamus...in the hardware." Mnemonic devices such as rhyming alliteration and sentence pattern repetition both teach and entice through repeated sounds. She also puts unusual animals in unusual places, so that she taps the mind's ability to instantly see and remember the animals that are out of place: a giraffe stooping to get out of the garage, a hippo squeezing his way into narrow store aisles.

In *Chica Chica Boom Boom* (1989) Bill Martin, Jr. and John Archambault use bright colors and bold shapes to tell a story of the alphabet letters—lowercase in the illustrations and uppercase in the text—who crowd up a coconut tree and then find themselves summarily dumped on the ground when the tree cannot hold their weight. The text's strongly rhythmic lines have the same kind of energy as the letters cavorting up the tree, as the artists use the letters both as sounds and as characters.

Lois Ehlert's *Fish Eyes: A Book You Can Count On* (1990) uses bright primary colors and cutout fish to plunge the child into a tropical world of multicolored and multishaped fish swimming. As promised in the title, the fish eyes stand out most of all and are used to count the number of fish that correspond to the number in the upper left-hand corner of the page.

The flexibility of the alphabet and counting book allows for a kind of endless inventiveness on the part of both authors and illustrators. The incongruity of two ordinary things juxtaposed, such as a handle adorning a hat, forms the basis of Beau Gardner's *Have You Ever Seen...? An ABC Book* (1986). This incongruity also enhances Robert Tallon's *ABC in English and Spanish* (1970). For A, the word *airplane* is written in both English and Spanish, but the picture shows an open-topped airplane jammed with a World War I-style pilot, a white bird wearing a beanie and glasses and holding an umbrella, an alligator, a woman traveler clutching her suitcase outside the airplane, a flower that towers over everyone, and a man wearing a hat. Added to this is an array of birds flying in the air and a chain that keeps the capital letter A close behind the airplane. The master at devising startling combinations is Dr. Seuss. In his *Dr. Seuss's ABC* (1963), readers can see a policeman standing in a pail of water, an antelope painting his pajamas pink, and Peter Pepper, who looks half human, half animal.

Kate Duke's *The Guinea Pig ABC* (1983) uses adjectives to illustrate her alphabet. Thus, the guinea pig mother pounding on a drum to wake up her sleeping child illustrates "A Awake," while the bouncing guinea pig on a pogo stick introduces "B Bouncy." *Pigs from A to Z* (1986) by Arthur Geisert relies on grammatical construction to organize an alphabet. For G, the pigs are working feverishly to move lumber from one side of a gorge to the other. When readers see "G is for getting the lumber over the gorge," the gerund phrase and noun interpret the effort involved in the movement. Sandra Boynton, in *A Is for Angry* (1983) uses a similar technique. When readers see a cartoon turkey tangled in telephone cords and wrapped around the letter T and then read "T is for Tangled," they connect the sound and letter with the meaning of the adjective, rather than the traditional noun, though even here the animal does fulfill traditional expectations.

In Suse MacDonald's *Alphabatics* (1986) readers see the alphabet itself transformed from abstract representation to the representation of an object. She uses bold, primary colors in her printed letters, but, as they move from abstract representation to more organic shapes, they lose that brilliance. McDonald finally places the new shapes into a more concrete picture. Thus, M is presented in clear type at the beginning of the sequence. It is then transformed to a curving two-mounded shape, finally taking its place on a man's face as a mustache. Readers then follow the movement from restraint to freedom as the circle is closed back to hardedged print, as the word *mustache* is boldly spelled out.

This flexibility, this endless inventiveness, encourages the child's imagination and contributes, more than anything else, to the delight so essential in this genre, particularly if the book is to instruct as well.

The Alphabet Book's Appeal to the Imagination

Alphabet and counting books must create a relationship with the child reader so that the reader is actively involved in the fusion of symbol and object. The presentation of the progression of letters and numbers is a base for a flexible and highly varied structure, but the book must deliberately appeal to the imagination. Such books often appeal by merging the predictable and the unpredictable in such a way that the child feels grounded in a comfortable area while exploring the terrain beyond that area.

Alphabet and counting books do have as one of their constraints a particular structure. In order for a book to be an alphabet book, it must organize its information around the twenty-six letters of the alphabet presented in order from A to Z. Similarly, a counting book moves from one, or sometimes zero, to a considered numerical terminus. With some alphabet or counting books this constraint is hardly an issue. A book such as Gerald Hausman's *Turtle Island ABC* (1994) is concerned with telling the Native American stories of "The Things the Old Turtle carries on her back," and the order of those things is not particularly important; it hardly matters in terms of the presentation of information whether or not "Hummingbird" comes before "Wolf," except in terms of fulfilling the constraints of the genre.

But, in other works, this order is indeed crucial. In *Anno's Counting Book* (1975), Mitsumasa Anno depicts the passage of the months and the growth of a small town as he moves from zero to twelve. In the New England village that grows up, a building is constructed for each new number added to the text. The flight of imagination for children is to internalize the fact that the addition of an entire building only adds one counter. In order to reinforce this, Anno draws counting blocks on the left side of the page and the graphic number on the right side of the page to introduce the concept of only one count added, no matter how large that one thing is. This is complicated by the addition of other elements besides the houses: hardwood trees that grow to twelve in number, evergreen trees, flowers, children, adults, trucks, all needing to be differentiated and counted separately to make sense of the narrative. The expectation of the reader is that the book will proceed along familiar routes; this, after all, seems to be part of the role of the book as a teaching tool. But Anno is willing to complicate those expectations. And, in complicating them, he insures that children who come back to the book will review his illustrations, finding new connections—perhaps each time.

Maurice Sendak's *One Was Johnny* (1962) uses the expected order of one to ten and back again, but the elements of the text are hardly expected. Johnny is a young boy sitting quietly in his room reading a book; he is smiling and happy to be by himself. But, as the story develops, all kinds of animals and people come crowding in on Johnny's solitude, insisting that they be counted. In order to preserve his sanity, Johnny begins to count backward, so the "robber who left looking pale" is followed by all the other intruders until once again Johnny is in the same pleasurable solitude in which he began.

But if expectations and predictability are a large part of the alphabet and the counting book, Judith Viorst's *The Alphabet from Z to A (with much confusion on the way)* (1994) suggests an author's willingness to subvert those expectations, and to intrigue the child reader through that very subversion. Her text turns the alphabet around and begins with the letter Z. Not only does she change the order, but she also uses finely drawn, even confusing illustrations that puzzle more than clarify. Further, she shows that the sounds don't always match what tradition says, nor do the animals necessarily stand for the letter under consideration. It is the sound the owl makes—"who"—that stands for W, but that leads Viorst to speculate that the owl also makes the sound of "Hoot," suggesting a sound relationship between the two but not a letter relationship.

Richard Wilbur and David Diaz's *The Disappearing Alphabet* (1998) is built around the premise that changes in language affect changes in our perception of reality. Wilbur playfully moves through the alphabet to give instances of such changes.

> *It would be bitter, if there were no L,*
> *To bid the LEMON or the LOON farewell,*
> *And if the LLAMA, with its two-L name,*
> *Should leave us, it would be a* double *shame;*
> *But certainly it would be* triply *sad*
> *If LOLLIPOPS no longer could be had.*

Here is a sophisticated alphabet book, asking the child reader to connect the letter, the word, and the reality that the word represents, and not only to connect those elements, but also to play with them. Diaz's illustrations, colorful and strongly lined, capture the playfulness of the text, both combining to present a rather sophisticated notion about language and perception.

Thus, the interaction between the adult or older child reading the alphabet book to the child is of immeasurable importance. In this genre, as in no other, do the readers talk out loud and think about the meaning they are making with the print symbols: the lines, shapes, points, thickness or thinness of the letters are all parts of the discussions between the knowledgeable reader and the inexperienced one. To automatically consign such sophisticated alphabets as Viorst's or Wilbur's to only adult understanding is to not take into account the flexibility and imagination of the child.

Pointers for Teachers

The following Pointers are based on Izhar Cohen's *ABC Discovery!* (1998).

Interactive Possibilities
- Hold the book up quite closely to the children so that they can see and reach a two-page spread. Ask the children to read the words and then point to the objects in the illustrations.
- Ask children to point to and name any objects they see. Sound out the beginning letters of their words to see if any match the letter that Cohen is using to organize the page.
- Cut open an apple, and have students name each part to see what beginning sounds they might match. Give each child a taste of the apple as you put words on the board and ask where those beginning sounds might appear in the alphabet.

Hands-on Possibility
- Ask students to choose an object from one spread of *ABC Discovery!* and reproduce it in papier mâché.
- As students listen to different styles of music, have them write upper- and lowercase letters. Make available a variety of writing tools, including pencils, ink, broad-tipped colored markers, crayons, paints. At the end of the session, have students explain to a buddy or the class why they chose those particular tools and shapes for their letters. Display all the drawings around the room.

Issues in the Genre of Alphabet and Counting Books

In a genre concerned with creativity and inventively teaching skills, it might seem that there would be few issues raised. After all, the primary reason for the existence of these books would seem to be a simple, instructive one. But, in fact, the teaching function of these books is precisely the area in which issues come to play, for as these books teach skills, they also teach much more.

What is the intended audience of these books?

The first and easy answer to this question is that alphabet and counting books are for young children just learning their letters and numbers. In that case, the letters and numbers are to be distinct and readable, with any accompanying pictures clear and unambiguous. However, all alphabet books are not just for a young audience. They can be used with older children, sometimes even adults as a method of organizing information in a familiar format. Marie Heinst's *My First Number Book* (1992), for example, uses brightly colored objects and then asks the readers to read, match, sort, and tell which objects are the same and different, later asking readers to put the objects in the proper order. In such books, young readers must not only identify, but also think about and articulate meaning.

Here, in sophisticated and pleasurable ways, the artist has used the alphabet or the number system as a structuring device; much of the delight comes in the apparently simple organization of what might be complicated and certainly unexpected matter. *The Butterfly Alphabet* (1999) by Kjell B. Sandved is another good example of such sophistication. Using close-up photography of different species' butterfly wings, Sandved finds letters in the wings' configurations. The colors are bright, their combinations startling, and the readers' growing realization that such geometry can be found with a microscope makes for an unusual and pleasing alphabet. Another unusual alphabet is David Pelletier's *The Graphic Alphabet* (1996), which uses a graphic artist's tool to make an alphabet. Thus, A crumbles on the page, B bounces across the pages, and the W consists of a black field with two white v's at the top that resemble vampire's teeth. There is an interactivity between reader and text that will be too sophisticated for a very young audience.

Other alphabet and counting books call for similar sophisticated interactivity between reader and text and illustration. Chris Van Allsburg's *The Z Was Zapped* (1987) presents the alphabet as a play in twenty-six acts. For the young child, Van Allsburg gives the familiar alphabet; for the more sophisticated child, he constructs a rich context around each letter both visually and textually. For "A was in an avalanche," the A is being pelted with rocks. But the illustration appears while the accompanying text is kept hidden, so readers must make their own texts. What the older reader brings is the imagination able to make a play out of a picture.

CHRIS VAN ALLSBURG

Another such opportunity comes in Marty Neumeier and Byron Glaser's black-and-white *An Action Alphabet* (1984). On the right-hand side of the page, the authors present the letter in both upper- and lowercase, followed by a colon and the name of an action. On the left page is an abstracted representation of that action. For example, the letter F is shown falling from a crosshatched grid. It takes close inspection of that grid to see how the F broke away and fell. For the young child, the F occurs four times; older children not only see the letters, but also experience the action and interconnectedness between the letters and their abstraction.

Mitsumasa Anno's *Anno's Alphabet* (1975) calls for a different kind of interactivity; he wants readers to enter imaginatively into the techniques he might have used to create his wood designs. His letters are made completely out of wood, and, in order to set the context for them, he first shows the tree, the ax, and the piece of wood in a vise that make the letters possible. Twisting the wood shows its grain and movement as it is bent into letters. But, beyond this, Anno asks the reader to peer at his illustrations to find other appropriate words. Thus, the borders surrounding each letter are also part of the natural world, made up, in the instance of the B, of a bean vine, but they hide other objects such as a bell, a bird, and a button.

Alphabet and counting books, then, certainly seem like they must appeal to a young, relatively unsophisticated audience in terms of its reading abilities. But they do not end there. They also work in very complex ways to appeal to those readers who have already mastered the system of the alphabet, and much of their pleasure comes from the reader's ability to flex this mastery in new, complex, and sometimes surprising ways.

How do alphabet books combine the roles of delighting and instructing?

Certainly alphabet and counting books are designed to entertain the child and teach the alphabet at the same time. In fact, it might be argued that such a combination is imperative if the book is to succeed. But the artist needs to find a way to combine these two elements, to allow each to play its appropriate role, to establish the appropriate scale and emphasis of each role. That combination and balance will often be determined by the nature of the perceived audience.

Alphabet and counting books for the very young child are frequently balanced so that they attract visually, but maintain the primary purpose of instruction. Celestino Piatti's *Animal ABC* (1966), for example, uses a bold, primitive style of painting to engage the child's imagination. The Ural owl looks as if he may be posing for flight right at the reader, and Piatti adds to the drama by drawing the owl in the shape of the letter U. The rhyming text helps with naming the letters: "The Ural Owl / His hoots advise, / It is wise to those / In night's disguise." Anita Lobel's *On Market Street* (1981) also uses rhyme and illustration to both entertain and teach. A young girl visits the farmer's market where the apple seller, intriguingly, not only looks like a giant letter A but also is made up of a variety of apples. An older woman is made of books, while the clock lady's arms are jointed with grandfather clock weights and her body is filled with clocks. The narrator happily discovers all sorts of just such interesting "people" on Market Street, just as the child reader connects the letters with objects.

Gail Kredenser's and Stanley Mack's *1 One Dancing Drum* (1971) entertains and teaches through a combination of pen-and-ink drawings that show numbers three ways: the numeral itself, the word, and a cartoon drawing of the appropriate number of figures. For the number one, an enthusiastic bass drummer marches his way onto the page and toward a gazebo. Next come two "tinkling triangles" played by two band members. The band members gather until finally they take over the gazebo and every available space on the page.

In all of these cases the artist has found a means to balance instruction and pleasure.

As one of the earliest genres associated with child readers, how were alphabet and counting books first used?

The tension of purpose has long been an issue with alphabet and counting books. If they are, on the one hand, books to delight, then their insistence on instruction seems extraneous. If they are, on the other hand, books to teach the concept of the number or the letter, then their dual nature in terms of their ability to delight seems more useful. But early texts of this genre were designed to instruct in more than letters and concepts; they were introductions to a culture, introductions that were sometimes disturbingly prescriptive.

In the late seventeenth century, the *New England Primer* used religious subject matter to teach the alphabet so that children could learn to read and internalize the Bible. Thus, the *Primer* begins, "In Adam's Fall, We sinned all," and moves to such advice as "Heaven to find, The Bible to mind." No child could miss the fact either in word or illustration that reading was a serious business whose end result was to learn the ways of God and apply those ways to the devout life.

But, by the nineteenth century, delight had established itself; contexts were not always heavy-handed and were couched in more humorous terms. Walter Crane used humor in his *An Alphabet of Old Friends and The Absurd ABC*, originally published in the 1870s.

> *A*   *A carrion crow sat on an oak,*
> *Watching a tailor shape his cloak.*
> *"Wife, bring me my old bent bow,*
> *That I may shoot yon carrion crow."*
> *And shot his own sow quite through the heart,*
> *"Wife, wife, bring brandy in a spoon,*
> *For our old sow is in a swoon."*

The illustrations that accompany this demonstrate Crane's sense of what children of the day liked best: bright colors, bold shapes, objects presented in profile, and a definite theme. Children, he believed, have a view of the world that centers on society's expectations, but they branch off in delightful ways, hence the integrated world of romance and reality in his alphabet books.

Crane was virtually unchallenged until Kate Greenaway's *A Apple Pie* (1886) was published. Greenaway's preference for pastel colors and realistic actions mark her as a clear departure from Crane. However, her portrayal of humor and fun keeps her firmly in Crane's tradition of alphabet writing. Young children dressed in clothing of the day play decorous games and do work appropriate to the period. Children play "Ring around the Rosy" circling a huge apple pie for A, two girls stand with hoops and sticks in their hands while watching a boy eat the pie for B. The depiction of the period as a time of grace and elegance promoted a child's learning the alphabet, but it also promoted imitation of the manners of the day, as well as a certain romantic vision of childhood as a time of miniature adulthood.

But alphabet and counting books did not always present grace and elegance; these genres could also promote and inculcate views about the "other" in a society. Not only is the actual number of African Americans small in nineteenth-century alphabets, but their representation is consistently stereotypical. For instance, in *Little Pets Picture Alphabet* " (from the 1860s) 'N' was a NEGRO chasing a coon"; the picture of a comical, very black person with heavy features doing something silly is portrayed in an exaggerated fashion. Again, "Alice's Alphabet" from *Babyland* (1884) depicts a little white mistress receiving her newspaper from a

> *Nimble Negro Named Ned*
> *who is never tired or sleepy 'tis said,*
> *But is smiling and bright*
> *With a bow most polite*
> *He brings up the news*
> *Every morning and night (46).*

The front view picture of Ned shows a deferential African American touching his cap to the world at large and the little miss in particular.

The quintessential alphabet from the late 1800s that shows disdain for African Americans was Edward Kemble's *A Coon Alphabet* (1898). Kemble was a self-taught illustrator whose popularity led him to illustrate the first edition of *Huckleberry Finn* (1884). In his alphabet, every letter portrays stereotypical elements.

> *A is of Amos*
> *What rides an ole mule*
> *So he can be early*
> *Each mornin ter school.*

Amos is seated on the back of a mule and is depicted with exaggerated features as he self-importantly goes to school. The mother watching her son is shown in an elongated headrag and standing in a bent-over position. The second scene shows Amos surprised as the mule bucks him off and in through the door of the "gramer schole." The mule, whose head is closest to the reader, smiles at his trick on Amos. Each letter has its own set of stereotypes, but the overall effect is the nineteenth-century impression that African Americans are childlike, foolish, lazy, watermelon eaters who smile at their own sad lives while wishing they were white.

The question of how women are historically treated in alphabets is more complicated. Women are generally seen in very traditional roles. Thus in "Alice's Alphabet" from *Babyland* (1884), it is not surprising to see an image of a little girl raking the field while watching the baby, a girl at school learning her letters, a girl looking on while the boy skates and falls on the ice, or a mother comforting her small child. The images of men, on the other hand, are active ones—farming (without watching children), playing ball, calling the time out to the town, guarding the queen, and running. The only image of an active woman is a shrew, "Xantippe, who scolds by the hour." This stereotyping of women is hardly limited to the nineteenth century; in *The Sounds the Letters Make* (1940), Lucille Schoolfield and Josephine Timblake show girls as teachers, mothers, cooks, and actresses, while boys are explorers and fishermen.

In all these works, the illustrators are doing more than teaching letters and numbers; they are using cultural assumptions to depict their world. The appropriateness of these cultural assumptions is at question here, and when those assumptions stereotype and suggest bias, the assumptions should be challenged.

How do alphabet and counting books convey information about a culture?

The most popular form of information conveyed through alphabet and counting books is cultural. Many of these books depict worlds that are a part of the North American experience, but that may not be very familiar to many readers. Luci Tapahonso and Eleanor Schick's *Navajo ABC: An Indian Alphabet Book* (1995), for example, gives readers the essentials of the Navajo culture. Drawn in the pastels of the Southwest, representations like "C Cradle board" allow readers to observe not only a baby prepared for carrying, but also the way in which a baby is held on the cradle board. Indeed the entire attitude of the culture is expressed in such representation. James Rice's *Cowboy Alphabet* (1990) informs readers about the life of a cowboy. With pen-and-ink drawings, some of which are in color, Rice re-creates the Old West. The text for the letter B says, "B is for barbed wire that's crippled up many a good horse and few head of spirited stock." The illustration shows a cowboy on his horse surrounded by cattle being stopped by barbed wire and further circled in by other objects beginning with B, such as a bronco and a bog. At the same time, the text captures the diction and the idiom of the culture. Similarly, Chris Demarest's *The Cowboy ABC* (1999) tries to evoke the world of the U.S. cowboy, though it uses rhyming couplets and the thematic motif of a cattle drive to organize its material. Combining the text with bold and dramatic illustrations, Demarest portrays a way of life in a wide landscape. The union of text and illustration, in effect, conjures up an entire world and pleasingly organizes what might be disparate material.

A number of alphabet and counting books suggest a culture through their illustration style and medium. Kathleen Thorne-Thomsen and Paul Rocheleau's *A Shaker's Dozen* (1999) focuses on the art of the Shakers. Each photographic illustration suggests a number—"One Shaker house / Entered through two Shaker doors / Guarded by three Shaker doves...." Each of the three photographs depicts the proper number of items, and includes below it, in rather small print, a short

A SHAKER'S DOZEN
- COUNTING BOOK -

by Kathleen Thorne-Thomsen and Paul Rocheleau

Illustration for *A Shaker's Dozen* by Kathleen Thorne-Thomsen and Paul Rocheleau copyright © 1999. Published by Chronicle Books, San Francisco. Used with permission.

statement about the significance of the item. For the two Shaker doors, Thorne-Thomsen notes that "Shaker houses had two doors. The men, or brothers, entered through one, and the women, or sisters, entered through the other." The culture of Vermont is captured in Mary Azarian's *A Farmer's Alphabet* (1981), in which Azarian uses the wood block technique to make her imprints. Ann Whitford Paul's *Eight Hand Round: A Patchwork Alphabet* (1991) uses a U.S. patchwork quilting motif to capture a time when every scrap of clothing was reused many times, until it ultimately ended up in beautifully designed quilts. And, to capture the rugged world of the northwoods of Minnesota, Betsy Bowen uses bold woodcuts in her *Gathering: A Northwoods Counting Book* (1999) to depict the annual rhythm of preparing for the frozen winter. For Jewish Americans, Malka Drucker's *A Jewish Holiday ABC* (1992) uses bright, celebratory illustrations as the alphabet organizes the succession of Jewish holidays. In such works as these, the culture essentially functions as the theme of the work, so that the alphabet or number system provides the structure for organizing the theme's matter.

Of course, not all alphabet and counting books that depict a culture are set in North America. Arthur and Adrienne Yorinks's *The Alphabet Atlas* (1999) assigns a country to each letter of the alphabet. The text is simply a short, intriguing statement about the country—"Luxembourg has many castles, so many, in fact, that it is sometimes called the 'land of haunted castles'"—while the illustrations, works of textile art, depict the country's culture both in its very materials. Margot Musgrove's *From Ashanti to Zulu* (1976), with illustrations by Leo and Diane Dillon, is the only alphabet book to win a Caldecott Award, and it, too, conveys cultural information. Each letter of the alphabet represents an African tribe, and the illustrators have been careful to recreate accurate pictures of these peoples. They present the clothing, body type, housing, and environment of each tribe in order to give readers a visual sense of the tribe. Each text begins with a capital letter that is also the first letter of a tribe's name, and a repeated frame ties all the portraits together. In "A/Ashanti" the illustration shows in its background the weavers who make material for the people. In the middle ground readers see a woman wearing the material called "Gold Dust" and another woman probably wearing "When the Queen comes to Africa." In the foreground is a rooster whose stylized representation demonstrates the natural inspiration for the weavers. Part of the aesthetic success is that the Dillons give life to the timelessness of Africa and its appeal to readers.

In *Moja Means One* (1971), a counting book, and *Jambo Means Hello* (1974), an alphabet book, Muriel and Tom Feelings again depict African culture. In the first, numbers correspond with geographical sites in Africa: for the number one, the Feelings picture Mount Kilimanjaro, and, at the number 10, the illustration presents an old man telling stories of the village's children around a campfire. In the second work, the letter J stands for the African word *jambo,* which is the beginning of a "long courteous greeting." The illustrations by Tom Feelings amplify the text by showing body language, facial expressions, and the surrounding landscape. In all the pictures, the simple act of counting or reciting the alphabet has grown to include an entire culture, one that relies on the storyteller to pass its traditions down to the next generation.

Alphabet and counting books can, thus, reinforce learning about the child's own culture when they deal with the world close to home. However, they can also expand a child's cultural horizons when they depict communities far afield from a typical North American experience.

In what ways might alphabet and counting books examine the nature of language itself?

In the 1960s, new interpretations of the alphabet itself came into play as the nature of language, as well as the ownership of language's governance, was questioned. In children's literature, this was manifested in a willingness to manipulate playfully the perceived boundaries of the alphabet.

George R. Bodmer, in "The Post-Modern Alphabet: Extending the Limits of the Contemporary Alphabet Book, from Seuss to Gorey," argues that two of Dr. Seuss's books, *The Cat in the Hat Comes Back* (1958) and *On beyond Zebra* (1955) present such a challenge. In *The Cat in the Hat* (1957), children read with delight about the outrageous actions of the cat who came into the children's lives and turned them upside down. In the sequel, *The Cat Comes Back,* readers meet the alphabet in the service of the Cat: letters jump out from underneath his hat, ready to help get rid of the pink cat stain that threatens to get the children in trouble. Cats ABCDE and F hurry to the work at hand. G through Y spread the cat stain through the yard, and finally Z comes along with spot remover. While the traditional A–Z order has not been tampered with, aligning the letters with the unpredictable cats puts them squarely on the side of disorder. Having those letters work hard *with* the cat and against the establishment makes them part of the anarchy.

In *On Beyond Zebra* (1955), Seuss invents an entirely new set of letters that allows the narrator to use freely his or her imagination. The not so subtle message—to throw off the bonds of conformity—comes through the characterization of Conrad Cornelius O'Donald O'Dell's encounter with the narrator. Dr. Seuss created Conrad as a nerdy little teacher's pet, who, with hair carefully parted down the middle and wearing a preppy sweater and pants, writes a traditional alphabet on the blackboard. Eager to show how much he knows, he brags to the narrator standing by the blackboard. The narrator, with a spiked haircut and scruffy clothes, is unimpressed, declaring that he will not stop with Z, but go right on to "Yuzz."

The imaginative letters tumble one after the other with the narrator as a confident guide and Conrad as an open-mouthed onlooker, mirroring the role of the reader. Conrad must have enjoyed his foray into the narrator's imagination because, when he gets home, he draws a most intricate, imaginary letter of his own on the blackboard. The narrator stands off to the side, gesturing as if to say, "I present my first convert," and Dr. Seuss makes that same gesture to the readers by asking them what they think Conrad's new letter will stand for.

Graeme Base, in *Animalia* (1987), exploits the culture's tendency for fragmentation and ambivalence. He too uses the traditional form of A to Z, but consistently empties it of meaning. A is "An Armored Armadillo/Avoiding an Angry Alligator." While older children will probably know both animals, they would not know that the two would never be found together in the same location. On close examination of the crowded picture—with an angel standing behind the letter A, an ambulance, anchovies, another alphabet book, an ant, an ace, an anaconda, an abacus, even aliens hatching from an egg, Noah's ark, a Roman aqueduct, allegro time in music, an algebra equation, and an accordion—the many layers of civilization that he has fragmented come into view. What is the organizing principle? All begin with A, of course; but all are equally unimportant when stripped of their meaningful context.

Alphabet and counting books have provided a medium for instruction in language and number systems, but they have also provided a medium for cultural awareness. They have passed on rudimentary knowledge, and have passed on visions of life. They have been simplified to instruct and complicated to delight. They have given a context in which the pleasures of teaching and delighting may be intermingled, where the artist, facing the challenge of a limited set of numbers or letters, may develop an entirely new way of using old material so that what is familiar may still startle. They have provided, in sum, a vehicle for the imagination of the artist.

Thinking and Writing about and within the Genre of the Alphabet and Counting Book

Thinking and Writing about the Genre of the Alphabet and Counting Book _____

1. Choose alphabet and counting books that you think have been written for different audiences, ranging from the very young to adult. Think about subject matter, complexity of presentation, and illustration to establish your divisions. Then present your findings to the class along with a rationale for your choices.

2. Look for alphabet and counting books that have the same subject matter. How do the presentations of the information differ? How are they the same? What

purpose do you think each of the authors had for writing his or her book? Which books do you prefer for use with young children? Why? With older children? Why? Then, take the book you like the best, read it to a child of the appropriate age and report back to the class about the success of that reading. Why do you think the reading went the way it did? You might want to begin here with Jo Bannatyne-Cugnet's *A Prairie Alphabet* (1993) and George Shannon's *Tomorrow's Alphabet* (1996).

3. Trace the representation of women, men, and children in alphabet and counting books through three time periods: the 1940s, the 1960s, and current books. What do you notice about who the main characters are, what kind of things they are doing in the story, what kind of language they use, what others say about them? You might want to begin with books like *Alison's Zinnia* (1990) by Anita Lobel, Eve Shaw's *Grandmother's Alphabet* (1996), and Leland Jacobs's *Alphabet of Girls* (1969).

4. Trace the current representation of minorities in alphabet and counting books found at a local bookstore. How are minorities presented? What kinds of jobs are they doing? How do they dress? Where do they live? What kind of language do they use? How many different minorities are represented? Are the stories about minorities in modern times, or are they confined to stories of the past? What difference does it make? You might want to begin with Ashley Bryan's *ABC of African American Poetry* (1997).

Thinking and Writing from within the Genre of the Alphabet and Counting Book

1. An editor has set you the task of coming up with a theme that will help to structure an alphabet book. Make a dummy for the book, complete with sketchy illustrations, that uses that theme.

2. Make a dummy for a counting book that uses a setting as its organizing factor: a beach, a mountain, a rain forest, the plains, the tundra. Or, you may be more specific and use an individual city or town. After finishing the dummy, write a letter to your editor that explains some of your choices.

3. Taking on the role of editor, read Laura Rankin's *The Hand Made Alphabet* (1991), a work that reproduces the hand formation for each letter. The marketing department in your publishing house wonders whether the book will have a limited audience. You are to respond in a memo to their concerns.

Selected Bibliographies

Works Cited

Anno, Mitsumasa. *Anno's Alphabet.* New York: Thomas Crowell, 1975.

———. *Anno's Counting Book.* New York: Thomas Crowell, 1975.

Azarian, Mary. *A Farmer's Alphabet.* Boston: David R. Godine, 1981.

Baldwin, Ruth M. *100 Nineteenth-Century Rhyming Alphabets.* Carbondale: Southern Illinois University Press, 1972.

Bannatyne-Cugnet, Jo. *A Prairie Alphabet.* Plattsburgh, NY: Tundra Books, 1993.

Base, Graeme. *Animalia.* New York: Harry N. Abrams, 1997.

Bowen, Betsy. *Gathering: A Northwoods Counting Book.* Boston: Houghton Mifflin, 1999.

Boynton, Sandra. *A Is for Angry.* New York: Workman, 1983.

Bryan, Ashley. *ABC of African American Poetry.* New York: Athenaeum, 1997.

Cohen, Izhar. *ABC Discovery!* New York: Dial, 1998.

Crane, Walter. *An Alphabet of Old Friends and the Absurd ABC.* New York: Metropolitan Museum of Art, 1981.

Demarest, Chris. *The Cowboy ABC.* New York: DK Publishing, 1999.

Drucker, Malka. *A Jewish Holiday ABC.* New York: Harcourt, Brace, 1992. Illustrated by Rita Pocock.

Duke, Kate. *The Guinea Pig ABC.* New York: E. P. Dutton, 1983.

Ehlert, Lois. *Fish Eyes: A Book You Can Count On.* San Diego: Harcourt Brace, Jovanovich, 1990.

Ernest, Edward. *The Kate Greenaway Treasury.* Cleveland: World, 1967.

Feelings, Muriel. *Moja Means One.* New York: Dial, 1971. Illustrated by Tom Feelings.

———. *Jambo Means Hello.* New York: Dial, 1974. Illustrated by Tom Feelings.

Ford, Paul, ed. *The New England Primer.* New York: Columbia, 1962.

Gardner, Beau. *Have You Ever Seen…? An ABC Book.* New York: Dodd, Mead, 1986.

Geisert, Arthur. *Pigs from A to Z.* Boston: Houghton Mifflin, 1986.

Greenaway, Kate. *A Apple Pie.* London: Frederick Warne, 1886.

Hausman, Gerald. *Turtle Island ABC.* New York: Harpercollins, 1994. Illustrated by Cara and Barry Moser.

Heinst, Marie. *My First Number Book.* New York: DK Publishing, 1992.

Hoban, Tana. *Let's Count.* New York: Greenwillow, 1999.

Jacobs, Leland. *Alphabet of Girls.* New York: Holt, Rinehart, and Winston, 1969.

Johnson, Stephen T. *Alphabet City.* New York: Viking, 1995.

Jonas, Ann. *Aardvarks, Disembark!* New York: Greenwillow, 1990.

Kemble, Edward. *A Coon Alphabet.* New York: R. H. Russell, 1898.

Kitchen, Burt. *Animal Alphabet.* New York: Dial, 1984.

Kredenser, Gail and Stanley Mack. *1 One Dancing Drum.* New York: S. G. Phillips, 1971.

Lobel, Anita. *Alison's Zinnia.* New York: Greenwillow, 1990.

———. *On Market Street.* New York: Greenwillow, 1981.

MacCarthy, Patricia. *Ocean Parade/A Counting Book.* New York: Dial, 1990.

Mac Donald, Suse. *Alphabatics.* New York: Bradbury, 1986.

Martin, Bill, Jr. and John Archambault. *Chicka Chicka Boom Boom.* New York: Simon and Schuster, 1989. Illustrated by Lois Ehlert.

Merriam, Eve. *Where Is Everybody?* New York: Simon & Schuster, 1989. Illustrated by Diane deGroat.

Micklethwaite, Lucy. *I Spy: An Alphabet in Art.* New York: Greenwillow, 1992.

Moore, Yuetle. *A Prairie Alphabet.* Montreal: Tundra, 1992. Illustrated by Jo Bannatyne-Cugnet.

Musgrove, Margot. *From Ashanti to Zulu.* New York: Dial, 1976. Illustrated by Leo and Diane Dillon.

Neumeier, Marty and Byron Glaser. *An Action Alphabet.* New York: Greenwillow, 1984.

Pallotta, Jerry and Fred Stillwell. *The Airplane Alphabet Book.* Watertown, MA: Charlesbridge, 1997.

Paul, Ann Whitford. *Eight Hand Round: A Patchwork Alphabet.* New York: HarperCollins, 1991.

Pelletier, David. *The Graphic Alphabet.* New York: Orchard, 1996.

Piatti, Celestino. *Celestino Piatti's Animal ABC.* Trans. Jon Reid. New York: Athenaeum, 1966.

Rankin, Laura. *The Hand Made Alphabet.* New York: Dial, 1991.

Rice, James. *A Cowboy Alphabet.* Dallas, TX: Pelican Publishing, 1990.

Rubin, Cynthia Elyce. *ABC Americana from the National Gallery of Art.* San Diego: Gulliver, 1989.

Sandved, Kjell. *The Butterfly Alphabet.* New York: Scholastic, 1999.

Saul, Carol P. *Barn Cat.* Boston: Little, Brown, 1998. Illustrated by Mary Azarian.

Schoolfield, Lucille D. and Josephine B. Timberlake. *The Sounds the Letters Make.* Boston: Little, Brown, 1940. Illustrated by Catherine Wheeler.

Sendak, Maurice. *Alligators All Around.* New York: Harper & Row. 1962.

———. *One Was Johnny.* New York: Harper & Row, 1962.

Seuss, Dr. [Theodor S. Geisel]. *The Cat in the Hat.* New York: Random House, 1957.

———. *The Cat in the Hat Comes Back.* New York: Random House, 1958.

———. *Dr. Seuss's ABC.* New York: Random House, 1963.

———. *On beyond Zebra.* New York: Random House, 1955.

Shannon, George. *Tomorrow's Alphabet.* New York: Greenwillow Books, 1996. Illustrated by Donald Crews.

Shaw, Eve. *Grandmother's Alphabet.* Duluth, MN: Pfeifer-Hamilton, 1996.

Steig, Jeanne and William Steig. *Alpha, Beta, Chowder.* New York: HarperCollins, 1992.

Stroud, Virginia. *The Path of the Quiet Elk: A Native American Alphabet.* New York: Dial, 1996.

Tallon, Robert. *ABC in English and Spanish.* New York: Lion Press, 1970.

Tapahonso, Luci and Eleanor Schick. *Navaho ABC: An Indian Alphabet Book.* New York: Macmillan, 1995.

Thorne-Thomsen, Kathleen and Paul Rocheleau. *A Shaker's Dozen.* San Francisco: Chronicle, 1999.

Van Allsburg, Chris. *The Z Was Zapped: A Play in Twenty-Six Acts.* Boston: Houghton Mifflin, 1987.

Viorst, Judith. *The Alphabet from Z to A (with much confusion on the way).* New York: Atheneum, 1994. Illustrated by Richard Hull.

Wilbur, Richard. *The Disappearing Alphabet.* New York: Harcourt, Brace, 1998. Illustrated by David Diaz.

Yorinks, Arthur and Adrienne Yorinks. *The Alphabet Atlas.* Alexandria, VA: Winslow, 1999.

Works on Alphabet and Counting Books in Children's Literature

Baldwin, Ruth M. *100 Nineteenth-Century Rhyming Alphabets.* Carbondale: Southern Illinois University Press, 1972.

Bodmer, George R. "The Post-Modern Alphabet: Extending the Limits of the Contemporary Alphabet Book, from Seuss to Gorey." *Children's Literature Association Quarterly* 14 (1989): 115–117.

Coffman, Gerry A. and Judy Jackson Spohn. "From A to Z: Using Alphabet Books as an Instructional Tool with Older Readers." *Reading Horizons* 37 (1996): 3–15.

Fielding, Linda and Cathy Roller. "Making Difficult Books Accessible and Easy Books Acceptable." *The Reading Teacher* 45 (May, 1992): 678–685.

Holt, Elvin. "A Coon Alphabet and the Comic Mask of Racial Prejudice." *Studies in American Humor* 5 (1991): 307–318.

McGee, Lea M. and Donald J. Richgels. "'K is Kristen's': Learning the Alphabet from a Child's Perspective." *The Reading Teacher* 43 (December, 1989): 216–225.

Smolkin, Laura B. and David B. Yader, Jr. "O is for Mouse: First Encounters with the Alphabet." *Language Arts* 69 (1992): 432–440.

Taylor, Mary-Agnes. "Notes from a Dark Side of the Nursery: Negative Images in Alphabet Books." Sylvia Patterson-Iskander, ed., *The Image of the Child: Proceedings of the 1991 International Conference of the Children's Literature Association.* Hattiesburg, MS: Children's Literature Association, 1991: 32–35.

Vidor, Constance. "Alphabet Books in Upper Grades." *School Library Media Activities Monthly* 1 (1994): 32–37.

4

The Delight and Wisdom of Children's Poetry

The leader of a poetry workshop for children, eager to teach the nature of poetry, asks each of the students to pretend that he or she is a flower. Now, the leader asks, "Quickly write down what you are seeing, feeling, smelling, tasting, hearing." Once the students have all jotted down a list, the leader randomly asks students to read one element from their list. The leader writes these down in a column on the board.

> *I smell the damp ground.*
> *Bees buzz softly around me.*
> *The petals see the blue sky.*
> *I see the wind blowing the other flowers around me.*
> *My leaves are bright green.*

The leader turns to the class. Here, he declares, is poetry!

Down the hall, a teacher wants to introduce fourth-grade students to the delights of poetry, but she decides to do it quite differently. On the board she writes the final two lines from Wallace Stevens's "The Emperor of Ice-Cream," then turns to the class and asks what this means. The students sit stunned, then they begin to guess, focusing on the image of ice cream. With each guess, the teacher shakes her head. After twenty minutes of such guessing, she begins to ask questions. What rules over ice cream? What conditions must exist? Cold, calls one student. She nods, then encourages them to go on guessing. At the end of the period, she announces that cold is a metaphor for death, and that Stevens's poem is focusing on the inevitability of the reality of death. The students groan and pack their books.

Both the workshop leader and the classroom teacher have it wrong, and both approaches suggest something about why it is that so many students so quickly abandon any attempt to find delight in poetry. The workshop leader sends the message that poetry is easy and simple, almost mindless in its construction.

Come up with a series of images, avoid justifying the right-hand margin, and there it is. But poetry is highly controlled langauge, a text that makes uses of poetic techniques to express its meaning both through form and diction. It is not a series of random images randomly displayed, an easy and simple thing to construct, but the effect of concentrated meaning.

The classroom teacher errs on the other side of the spectrum. She uses a poem never meant for children, with a meaning difficult for children to perceive; giving only two cryptic lines from the poem does not make it easier. Though the poem is powerful for an adult reader who can read the poet's use of poetic technique, particularly metaphor, the poem would be opaque to most young children. The result is that the teacher sends the message that poetry is a code, and children do not have the key. The teacher does, and the children may guess at it. But, in the end, it is unlikely that the child will come up with the right answer. And what child would want to go through the agony of deciphering meaning on his or her own? In this sense, poetry becomes a distant, foreign thing that may not be worth the conquering—may not even be conquerable.

Boundaries and Definitions

The opening stanza to X. J. Kennedy's humorous "The Whales Off Wales" suggests something of the nature of poetry for children.

> *With walloping tails, the whales off Wales*
> *Whack waves to wicked whitecaps.*
> *And while they snore on their watery floor,*
> *They wear wet woolen nightcaps.*

The imagery of the poem is vivid, both in terms of the realistic image of the waves and the whales' tails, and the nonsense image of wet woolen nightcaps. The iambic rhythm—which Kennedy varies to avoid a sing-songy effect—the heavy use of alliteration, the pleasurable use of the homonym, all contribute to a concise and striking whole that pleases the ear and the eye.

Children's poetry, like children's literature, is not poetry simplified. It is that poetry that is accessible to a child audience, that speaks to a child audience, and that is able to convey meaningfully the experiences and perceptions of the child. Again, like children's literature, children's poetry is inclusive; it can be enjoyed by adults and children. And, finally, children's poetry is poetry. It is not the easy jingle, the silly rhyme, the poem disencumbered of poetic technique. Instead, it uses all the poetic techniques available to poetry written for an older audience.

In X. J. Kennedy's poem, the poet uses these techniques to summon up certain images, one quite humorous, and to suggest certain sounds: the use of the alliterative "w" connects to the whacking of a broad tail on water. The meaning of the poem is accessible—even if a child has never seen a whale, or whitecaps, for that matter—because the imagery is vivid and uncomplicated, particularly in terms of its diction. This accessibility is created by Kennedy's careful use of poetic techniques, so that the techniques never complicate meaning beyond what a child might be able to decipher.

Certainly this seems obvious, on the one hand. There are poets who write specifically for a child audience, who have in mind the creation of aesthetically pleasing and effective poems that a child will comprehend. Minfong Ho's *Hush!* (1996), for example, is a repetitive poem about a mother in Thailand urging all the animals to be quiet as baby is asleep. But the illustrations show what the mother does not perceive at all: Baby is not asleep, but has snuck from the hammock and is wandering about the house. That illustration contributes to the accessibility of the poem's meaning, but Ho's short lines and easy diction also contribute. In addition, the poem, though set in another culture, clearly is part of any young child's experience—the difficulty of falling asleep when a parent expects the child to nap.

At times, writers of literature for older readers will work at children's literature, and here they will adapt their styles and techniques for a younger audience. John Updike's "August," for example, evokes summer images that any child will recognize: "The sprinkler twirls. / The summer wanes. / The pavement wears / Popsicle stains." Again, the lines are short, the images vivid. The metaphor of the pavement is uncomplicated and evokes a simple and recognizable picture. Here is the poet understanding the needs of the audience and gearing everything in his piece—both language and technique—to the needs and abilities of that audience.

In another sense, however, and perhaps in a more difficult sense, it is impossible to erect an impermeable boundary at the edge of children's poetry. If children's poetry is that poetry that is accessible to the audience, then the boundary will be very flexible and even porous. Though much of the poetry of Robert Frost, for example, is clearly adult poetry, outside of the child's understanding, much of it is accessible, at least in a literal sense. It may be the case that a poem is not understandable in all of its meanings to the child reader, but this does not necessaily mean that the poem should not be a part of the child's literary experience.

In Frost's "Stopping by Woods on a Snowy Evening," the speaker halts his horse to watch the snow fall in the woods. He cannot stop for long, however, because he has commitments and distance in front of him. A child might read that poem and enjoy it as a simple image of a rider stopping by the woods after a busy day to enjoy the sight of the snow. The teacher who shakes a head and asserts that the poem is really about the commitments of our lives, about the discrepancy between pleasure and duty, or between play and work, or between business and art, or even about death, may be right on one level. But the teacher would be in error to say that the child reader was wrong. It is, indeed, about a man who stops in the woods to enjoy the snow.

When children have adopted the work of poets writing for the adult world, they have generally adopted the literal meanings of the poems and ignored deeper meanings. And, for their age, this is absolutely appropriate. It is not the case that they will want to remain at the level of literal interpreters; the time will come when their literary skills will enable them to enjoy other pleasures in poetry. But, for the child, a literal reading of an adult poem is appropriate.

The boundaries of children's poetry, then, are loose. While there are certainly those poems specifically written for the child audience, there are also poems that have been brought into the arena. The commonality here is that all of these poems are able to be enjoyed and understood, at least on the literal level, by a child audience.

The First Organized Language

In many ways, poetry is the first patterned language that a child encounters. Early on, many children hear lullabies, which are, of course, poems set to music. In many cases such lullabies are a multisensory experience, as a parent holds a child and rocks back and forth, or stands and sways to the rhythm of the lullaby. In this way, physical rhythm is added to the oral/aural event, so that several senses are working together at once to reinforce the notion of rhythm. Daily routine songs, the chants that accompany swings, the nonsense songs, and the lyrics that young children learn to sing—all of these represent early encounters with poetry.

As children begin to acquire language themselves, they move to the oral culture of game lore, counting rhymes, chants, tongue twisters, riddles, and songs. Once again it is the rhythm of poetry, as well as its intricacies of sound, that bring delight for the reader or speaker or listener. These are the songs that pattern the rhythm of a swing, the songs that order the steps of a hike, the songs that follow the rhythm of the bus ride. There is poetry in the song that teaches the alphabet, or the song that identifies which months have only thirty days. All of these establish an enormous fund of poetry that children encounter and memorize, and that they remember for many years afterward.

The difficulty for many readers comes as children move from the oral and aural culture to the written culture. Here ballads, narrative poems, humorous lyrics may delight and, as Robert Frost asserts, establish a process that begins in delight and ends in wisdom. But when poems become coded language that must be painstakingly deciphered, they can become too obscure and distance many young readers.

The Mother Goose Poems

Some of the poems encountered in that aural and oral culture are the Mother Goose poems, first collected in the seventeenth century and later used as a kind of umbrella term for short, often nonsense lyrics with a heavy dependence on rhythm. These are poems that are delightful in their sound, more than their meaning, in that the reading or telling of them often involves this strong rhythmic quality. Some of the poems, such as "Pat-a-Cake" and "Ring around the Rosie," may actually involve physical manifestations of that rhythm, so that once again rhythm is created by both sound and movement. The poems, in fact, encourage participation. This rhythmic quality is so strong that even adults who have not thought of the poems in years can identify the poems simply by their rhythm, such as a poem like "Hickory Dickory Dock."

The poems also delight the tongue in their use of clever combinations of sounds. "Hicketty Piggity, my black hen, / She lays eggs for gentlemen." The sounds of the two opening words, with their repetition and hard consonants, are pleasurable even in their pronunciation. This delight also comes from the rhymes of the poems, as in the tale of little Polly Flinders who sat among the cinders, or of Mary who is quite contrary, or of the contrasting towns of Wibbleton and Wobbleton. In each of these works the sound, in addition to making the poem easy to memorize, delights.

But the poems are not only delightful in their rhythm and sound; as Frost suggests, they move to wisdom. The Mother Goose poems may suggest something of the child's inner life, evoking a kind of quiet introspection.

Star light, star bright,
First star I see tonight.
I wish I may, I wish I might
Have the wish I wish tonight.

The repeating rhyme, the repetition of internal sounds, the four references to the quiet word *wish*—all of these point to the child's inner vision, as the speaker experiences a sense of something behind himself or herself. The same is true of "Twinkle, twinkle, little star. / How I wonder what you are." The quiet, inward eye expresses something about the Not Me, and in this sense probes deeply into the wonder of a child. The poems, then, seem at first glance to be one-dimensional, even superficial, but in reality they hold within them a deep wisdom, a deep intuition about the nature of our lives.

These poems are tiny stories, all created in the context of just a few short lines, but not all of the stories are pleasant ones. There is, for example, the story of Old Mother Hubbard, who goes to the cupboard and finds it empty—a story of real starvation and perhaps hopelessness. There is the whipping associated with the old lady who lived in a shoe, or little Polly Flinders, who was whipped for sitting in the cinders. There is the difficulty of old age in the crooked man who walked a crooked mile. There is the curious relationship of Peter and his wife, whom he put into a pumpkin shell, though this is perhaps balanced by the tale of Jack Sprat, who could eat no fat, and his wife, who could eat no lean. Even the tale of Jack and Jill contains the painful episode of Jack falling down and breaking his crown and Jill tumbling after.

Many of the poems do come out of dire circumstances and carry the emotion of those circumstances with them: "Ring Around a Rosie" is, in fact, an incarnation of the medieval dance of death, in which we all turn to ashes and all fall down. But no child needs to know the historical background of the poems to get a sense of their distress. These are poems that are not sentimental and sweet; instead, they frequently take a hard look at the dreadful circumstances of life and paint them unalloyed, as suggested by Maurice Sendak's recent rendition of *We Are All in the*

Dumps with Jack and Guy (1993), which places the lyric in a shantytown of homeless children.

But, in the end, the Mother Goose poems do not lead to melancholy; the delight of their construction overwhelms any possibility of that. They are poems that speak to the imagination.

> *Hey, diddle diddle!*
> *The cat and the fiddle,*
> *The cow jumped over the moon.*
> *The little dog laughed*
> *To see such sport,*
> *And the dish ran away with the spoon.*

The sounds of the opening two lines, though the second lines seems to carry little meaning, bring the child into a world of nonsense, but it is a world filled with astonishing bright images, images that an illustrator such as Tomie dePaola can capture in his *Tomie dePaola's Mother Goose* (1985). In the illustration for this rhyme, the cow jumps within a bright blue background, as the laughing dog looks above. The cat plays blithely in one corner, while in the other the dish and the spoon are dashing away. The whole is marked by the same kind of delight in nonsense that marks the poem itself.

In the end, the Mother Goose poems, in their many editions, suggest the validity of Frost's observations: Poetry does indeed begin in delight. That delight comes not only from meaning, however, but from the very things that make poetry what it is: highly patterned language. The rhythm, the sound, the imagery, the diction, these are the poetic elements that bring delight to the reader.

A Process That Begins with Delight

In suggesting that poetry is a process that begins with delight, Frost was arguing that poetry must first entice the reader through sheer enjoyment. For the child to enter into the world of the poem, he or she must first enjoy the poem. And, as with all poetry written for adults, poetry written for children crafts its delights in many ways.

In terms of content, children's poetry is often marked by experiential humor. The comedy will often arise out of situations that the child reader can recognize, but that have been set on their heads and made ridiculous. In Alfred Noyes's "Daddy Fell into the Pond," for example, the sky is gray and dismal until the normal course of events is disrupted when Daddy falls into the water. Authority is thus subverted. In Theodore Roethke's "The Ceiling," the narrator wonders what might happen if the ceiling decided to walk outside. And in Jack Prelutsky's "The New Kid on the Block," the speaker expresses his fear of the brawny, mean-spirited, muscular new kid, revealing only in the last line that "I don't care for her at all." In these situations the humor is generated by the unexpected, by the common situation reversed, by the clever overturning of predictability.

Poems can also be humorous in depicting the reality of a child's experience, though here the difficulty is to show the humor in that experience without being condescending. John Ciardi's "Some Cook!" describes Johnny's culinary efforts, for example, by listing ingredients such as pepper, mustard, garlic fried in olive oil; when he "brought the custard to a boil, / [He] ate it up and burned his tongue— / You shouldn't cook when you're too young." Similarly, Marchette Chute's "Going to Bed" evokes a common experience for the child: there is so very much to do before the lights go out: "I have to bounce upon my bed / To see if it will sink, / And then when I am covered up / I find I need a drink." In these poems the humor is generated as the poet displays the realities of a child's life and suggests the inherent humor in the situations.

But humor is only one way in which poetry delights, one of a myriad ways. Poems may tell stories, may evoke images, may evoke memory, may suggest new understandings. Poetry may startle, may help the reader see things from a completely new perspective, may suggest the splendid nature of something that seems ordinary. Poetry, by its very nature, heightens the subject and makes the reader more aware. In this sense delight is involved with nothing less than the reader's growth.

Poetry delights through its uses of poetic techniques, not just in its content. Laura Richards's "Eletelephony" works not so much because of its content—which is nonetheless humorous: an elephant trying to use the telephone—but because of the clever interpolations of sound. "Once there was an elephant, / Who tried to use the telephant." John Updike's "January" creates its meaning and imagery through metaphor: "The sun a spark / Hung thin between / The dark and dark." Galway Kinnell's "Crying" strikes with its personification, as he encourages the reader to weep fully, then laugh just as fully once the crying is done: "'Ha ha!' sing back, 'Happiness / was hiding in the last tear! / I wept it! Ha ha!'" All of these are examples of children's poets working at the use of poetic devices and elements to bring delight to a poem.

Charlotte F. Otten's *January Rides the Wind* (1997), a collection of poems about each month, is particularly notable for its use of poetic devices to delight the reader. The poet often combines vivid images that suggest the nature of the months—and here the task is to avoid the expected images and to startle—through personifications so that they seem alive, active, intimate. The poems are short, and the illustrations by Todd L. W. Doney complement their meaning and capture the essence of the month as the poet has illuminated it. Otten creates images notable for their ambiguity and fertility, and also works to suggest striking new ways of seeing the familiar through unexpected diction and metaphor. In "March," the month is personified and the expected images made startlingly new through unexpected twists.

> *March eats the winter;*
> *icicles drip from its mouth*
> *to fall on secret gardens.*
> *Crocuses wake,*
> *stain the melting snow with gold.*

March ends winter by eating it, and the focus remains on the mouth for the second line, which gives back winter's icicles as water that brings out the flowers of March. The gardens are secret, perhaps because they are in the woods (as the illustration suggests) or perhaps because they have been so long hidden under the snows of winter. In either case they wake the crocuses, and, just as John Updike uses *stain* to suggest the coloring of melted popsicles on a sidewalk, here Otten uses it to show the spreading color against the snow. In both cases the reader must struggle with the connotations of the word, which are generally negative, to see that here the image is meant to be one of striking and even un-expected beauty.

Perhaps more than any other genre, poetry can use the patterns of its language to draw the reader into the very sounds of the text. The reader becomes an active oral and aural participant by playing with those sounds, thus participating with the poet to create the experience of the poem. In John Ciardi's "Summer Song," for example, the poet depends on the reader's use of sound to complete the poem:

> By the way the children shout
> Guess what happened? School is....!

The poem invites participation; the reader must guess the final word, using the rhythm of the poem to recognize that each word is only a single syllable, and the content and the rhyme scheme of the poem to figure out which word is appropriate. Ciardi's poem calls for a kind of participation in the creation of the text that would be unusual in a poem written for an adult audience.

Poetry delights in its words and in its sounds. It delights in its humor and in its striking imagery. It delights in its wordplay and in its unexpectedly fertile and evocative meanings. In such things there is no distinction between poetry written for the child and that written for the adult.

A Process That Ends in Wisdom

If the first half of Frost's equation is to work, then the second half must also be true: Poetry is a process that ends in wisdom. At first blush this is a daunting thought. A poem that is going to lead to wisdom would seem to be didactic, but this is not at all what Frost is suggesting. The wisdom of a poem may be quite simple and easy, and it may (sometimes simultaneously) be quite profound. When a child wonders what a star might be, the reader sees a poem that speaks to the very nature of a child who is beginning to understand that the world is more than the self, and that that outside world might in fact have elements in it very much worthy of wonder. When a child reads of a man stopping by woods on a snowy evening, the reader comes to see that there are some things in this busy world that are worth stopping to see, and that it may be the quiet things that are most worthy of our stopping. These are poems that lead to wisdom.

When a poem can move a child, call up emotion, lead to new understandings, help a child reader see something or someone from an entirely new perspective,

Pointers for Teachers

Interactive Possibilities
- Use a communal reading of poetry at different times during the school day, having the students read in pairs, boys and girls, one half of the class followed by the other.
- Ask students to identify words that rhyme after they have listened to a poem or after they have read a poem.
- Ask students to identify the rhythm of the poem by tapping it out on their desks with a pencil, slapping it out on their knees, clapping it out with their hands, or swaying their bodies.

Writing Possibilities
- Bring in an illustration of a common experience from childhood: singing, swimming, eating ice cream. Have the students write in their journal about the humor they already see in the picture, then have them write about the experience as if something odd suddenly happened. Suppose, for example, that the rocky road ice cream really did become a rocky road.
- After reading a poem in class, have the students paraphrase it. Talk about what is lost in such a paraphrasing.

Hands-On Possibility
- Have students choose a favorite poem from Eve Merriam, Myra Cohn Livingston, Joyce Carol Thomas, Shel Silverstein, Jack Prelutsky, Nikki Grimes, or Walter Dean Myers. Ask them to practice reading the poem aloud for a younger audience, or develop an oral interpretation of the poem that includes visuals. Finally, tape or film the production and send it to a younger class.

---

catch a child in striking ways, suggest new ways of looking at the world and at the self, then the poem has led toward wisdom. When Carl Sandburg writes "Buffalo Dusk," for example, he allows the child reader to experience the sense of loss.

> Those who saw the buffaloes by thousands and how they
>   pawed the prairie sod into dust with their great hoofs,
>   their great heads down pawing on in a great pageant
>   of dusk,
> Those who saw the buffaloes are gone.
> And the buffaloes are gone.

The sense of loss comes through the mournful repetition of what is now gone, something suggested as well through the title. Between that repetition comes the great rush of words that strain at the boundaries of the lines, a rush that ends not with the expected repeated *dust*, but with *dusk* to show the ending of the great herds. It is a poem that speaks to the horror of loss, of the sadness of our not being able to see the great herds, of change, of endings.

But the kind of wisdom suggested by the child poet may be much simpler, much more commonplace. Douglas Florian's "The Egret," from his collection *On the Wing* (1996), shows the child reader a striking image, suggesting something of how one might view the commonplace through eyes that work metaphorically: "On morning tide / An egret sat / And gave the beach / A feathered hat." The simplicity of the short lyric comes not only from the number of lines, but from the shortness of those lines; each line has a singular event, a singular meaning: a morning tide, an egret, a beach. In the final line these three combine to create the metaphor, which is notable as the only nonliteral image of the poem. The wisdom of the poem is gained by its pointing out a way of seeing.

Tone and repetition, image, narrative—children's poems use many techniques to move toward wisdom, just as any adult poem. The issues for the children's poet, however, are how to move toward that wisdom and what kind of wisdom is appropriate. The first is suggested by Frost's delight. The poem must be accessible in terms of its literal meaning, and it must draw the child reader in through any number of techniques that create a pleasurable reading experience. But the second issue is more difficult.

As with any genre in children's literature, the work must be accessible not only in terms of its literal meaning, but in terms of its experience. Shakespeare's sonnets would be inappropriate for a young child not chiefly because of the difficulty in language—a good reader, even a young reader, may be able to perceive the literal meaning of some of the sonnets—but because of the distance of the experience. Shakespeare's love for the young man and his urging of him to marry and procreate, or his love for the dark woman and his overturning of conventional expressions of love, are all very far from the experience of the child, and, though the sonnets are unquestionably some of the best poetry in the language, they are not the best poetry for an audience of child readers.

The wisdom that a child's poem leads to may be profound and grand, mighty and spectacular, but it must always be within the child's experience so that the child reader can make sense of its meaning and its import.

David McCord's "Books Fall Open" praises books that allow a reader to fall in and find places and voices never heard before. But he does not just want to talk about the absorption of reading, but of what reading does: "True books will venture, / dare you out, / whisper secrets, / maybe shout." McCord's lines will be recognized in terms of their meaning by any reading child; a book that is true will shout out to those in need, those who hanker for a book to read.

Phyllis McGinley's "Troilet against Sisters" evokes a narrator who complains about the busy-ness of sisters, who are always locked away, posing at the mirror, flying down the stairs to answer the telephone. What is unsaid, but what is quite clear, is that the sisters are not paying attention to the speaker, who sees their lives only from the outside, never from within; the speaker's world has no connection to that of the older sister, though he or she longs for such a connection. The powerful poignancy of the closing lines—which are also the opening lines—is recognizable to any sibling who is closed off from another's world: "Sisters are always drying their hair, / Locked into rooms, alone."

Pointers for Teachers: Evaluating Works of Children's Poetry

- How do the poems in this collection begin in delight? What sounds, images, language, and poetic techniques does the author use to bring pleasure to the reader?
- How do the poems in the collection end in wisdom? What literal meaning is there for the child to understand? Do the poems allow child readers to move beyond themselves? What new understandings, perspectives of world and self, unique visions does the poem bring to the reader?
- How does the poem convey its meaning? What language, rhythm, experience, and imagery does it bring that will create meaning for the child?
- How is the collection organized? By theme? By subject? By technique? By poet?
- How do the illustrations and layout of the collection contribute to the meanings of the poems?

Frank Dempster Sherman's "Blossoms," collected by Donald Hall (1985) tells of the blossoms that hang on a tree like tufts of forgotten snow. But, when the speaker looks out again, they seem like butterflies in the breeze as the rain comes and they flutter away. "With butterflies 'tis etiquette / To keep their wings from getting wet. /" So, when they knew the storm was near, / They thought it best to disappear." The experience of watching blossoms pass and fall in a rainstorm is one that a child will recognize, but the extended metaphor of the poem creates a new way of seeing those blossoms by evoking butterflies, yet another living thing that quickly comes and quickly goes. Behind the metaphor is the sense of the inevitability of passing time, and even, perhaps, of the appropriateness of that inevitability.

Each of these last three poems moves towards wisdom by enabling the reader to imaginatively enter the world of the poem—and its meaning—because the experience is a familiar one. The child reader recognizes the image, or the feeling, or the emotion, or the experience itself. But, in the poem, those are heightened and clarified, so that the reader comes to understand and perceive them to a greater extent. Here, perhaps, is the beginning of some kind of wisdom for the child reader.

Issues in Poetry for Children

The issues that hover at the boundaries of children's literature are principally about form rather than matter, in sharp contrast to many of the other genres. Though children's poetry deals with the broad range of issues and experiences with which other genres in children's literature deal, often the difficulties in poetry, particularly as expressed by young readers, center around questions of understanding.

What, in the end, divides children's poetry from poetry written for adults?

Though the boundaries between these two audiences are not sharp, some general characteristics do divide the two. Certainly the one element that must come into play is accessibility. For the poem to delight, it must be accessible. This means that the poet for the child audience must consider questions not only of diction and matter, but most particularly of how the matter is conveyed. If the poetic devices overwhelm and obscure, the obscurity that might be pleasing to the adult might only frustrate the child and hide meaning. If the organized language of the poem is such that the literal meaning itself is opaque to the child, then, there, too, the poem is no longer reaching its audience. Gerard Manley Hopkins might have written some of the most splendid poems in the language, but to give "The Windhover" to a young child is to misread the audience.

For the poem to work as children's poetry, the organization of the language, the poetic devices used, the elements of matter affected by the organization and the devices all must fuse into a whole that the child can be delighted by and that the child can understand. When A. A. Milne writes in his "Solitude" that he has a place alone where there is no one else, "Where no one says anything—so / There is no one but me," he has evoked in simple diction, yet carefully organized language, the pleasurable solitude a child might feel. When Jack Prelutsky writes in his "The Ghoul" of the monster that waits beside the classroom to eat children up, every single part of them a treat, he touches on the delightful vicarious and yet safe terror that children—and adults—enjoy, for once the ghoul has finished with his latest meal, "he hurries to another school /and waits…perhaps for you." Again the language is highly organized, highly patterned, and quite accessible.

As with all of children's literature, the question in children's poetry is one of audience. Poets who write for a child audience seek to organize their language in appropriate ways, while at the same time using that organization in a sophisticated, highly aesthetic manner. Again, this is not poetry simplified, but poetry distinctly crafted to reach its audience.

What are the benefits of an anthology of poetry versus a picture book edition of a single poem?

In days when the realities of book purchasing weigh heavily on either the parent or the teacher or the librarian, certain severe choices must be made. The librarian who purchases Susan Jeffers's illustrated editions of *Stopping by Woods on a Snowy Evening* (1978) or *Hiawatha* (1983) must recognize that, though he or she has purchased a splendidly illustrated version of a poem, it is still only a single poem. Had he or she purchased Beatrice Schenk de Regniers's *Sing a Song of Popcorn* (1988), the library would have had a splendid collection of many poems.

Given the realities of library budgets, the call here seems easy to make. One would choose the collection that brings the most texts to the eyes of readers. An anthology is a more useful resource for the adult bringing books and children together. It allows for more flexibility and more exposure to various poets and poetic forms. It simply seems to provide more for the child reader.

But, in fact, the choice between an anthology of poems and an edition of a single poem is not a choice simply between many poems and one poem. Both kinds of editions work to provide delight, but they do it in very different ways. The illustrated edition of a single poem delights through the fullness of its illustration. Often a single line or a single stanza might bear an entire spread, so that the meaning of the poem is highly developed through the pictorial narrative. Here the delight comes through the fulsomeness of the illustration.

Susan Jeffers's *Stopping by Woods on a Snowy Evening* uses principally black-and-white illustrations to capture the essence of the poem. Jeffers creates a version of the poem in which the traveller is not troubled by such things as duty or, perhaps, even death, but is on an errand—he is bringing feed to the animals of the forest. The illustrations convey a tone of bright happiness, actually, that is, perhaps, not in keeping with the tone of the poem. Nevertheless, the fact that the poem is the only one that appears in the book enables Jeffers to create this new narrative and to use large spreads with rather little text.

Ted Rand's *Paul Revere's Ride* (1990) sets out to endow a single poem with powerful, dramatic illustrations that capture not only the action of the ride but also the eighteenth-century settings. The lantern, the heights of Boston, the *Somerset*, the uniforms of the British soldiers, even the windows on the Old North Church are accurately rendered, and the fully illustrated edition allows Rand to divide the text in such a way that the child reader feels the strength of the narrative impelling the next page turn.

The anthology, however, delights in a very different manner: through allowing the reader to browse, ramble, search through many poems, in many diverse styles, with many diverse forms, with many diverse meanings. The delight is similar to that of a walk in the woods, where the delight in the whole is composed of a delight in the parts. This is very different from the kind of delight a single illustrated edition yields; it is the delight of a sojourner.

X. J. Kennedy and Dorothy Kennedy's *Knock at a Star* (1982) is subtitled "A Child's Introduction to Poetry," and, in this sense, it strives to bring together poems that illustrate the meanings and the workings of poetry. It is divided into sections that ask questions: What do poems do? What is inside a poem that allows it to do what it does? What are the special forms that create meanings? In deemphasizing the technical vocabulary of poetry and in providing a plethora of examples from both adult poetry and children's poetry, the collection delights with its texts and teaches with its organization.

Nancy Larrick's *Piping Down the Valleys Wild* (1968) collects thematically, though the thematic boundaries are loose. The collection is wide-ranging and focuses on lyrical poems that express sharply some moment of a child's experience, both humorous and serious. It combines children's poets like Karla Kuskin and Eve Merriam with generally perceived adult poets such as Robert Frost, John Ciardi, and Gwendolyn Brooks. Beatrice Schenk de Regniers's *Sing a Song of Pop-*

corn and Jack Prelutsky's *The Random House Book of Poetry for Children* (1983) are more humorous romps through poetry, though they, too, collect poignant poems to express the large dimension of a child's experience. *Sing a Song of Popcorn* is illustrated by nine Caldecott artists, each of whom works on a single grouping of poems organized thematically. The child, then, browses through sections connected by illustration, as well as by content. Prelutsky's *Random House Book of Poetry for Children* is illustrated by Arnold Lobel; its almost six hundred poems are organized thematically as well, with half a dozen or more poems for each spread. The format makes this a busier book than *Sing a Song of Popcorn,* but, like that anthology, this one delights with its plethora of choice.

In the sense that an anthology collects many poems from many writers, it is distinct from a collection of poems by a single poet, a collection such as Judith Viorst's *If I Were in Charge of the World* (1981), Jack Prelutsky's *The New Kid on the Block* (1984), Karla Kuskin's *Dogs and Dragons, Trees and Dreams* (1980), or Shel Silverstein's *A Light in the Attic* (1981). A collection of poems by a single author has its own pleasures, its own delights, in that it too allows the reader to browse, but here the browsing is more focused, more limited. The reader is always working within the vision of a single poet, and, though that vision may be expansive, as is Kuskin's for example, still the reader remains in that single vision.

The choice between an edition of a single poem and the anthology or collection, then, is not so much the choice of one poem over many as it is the choice of one kind of delight over another.

What role does oral presentation play in the reading of poetry?

In the nineteenth and early twentieth centuries, New England towns would hold communal recitals that were not musical, at least in the sense of instrumental music. Instead, they were recitations in which children and adults in the town gave oral voice to the written word. The recitals may have been famous speeches, well-known prose passages from novels, and poems, particularly ballads with strong narrative lines. In giving such readings, the performers gave voice to a silent written text, and, in giving voice, they interpreted and enlivened. Though oral reading is significant for all genres in children's literature, there is no genre—perhaps with the exception of the picture book—that calls for the necessity of oral reading as strongly as children's poetry.

What is especially meaningful in the oral reading is the union of the poetic elements and the narrative, or textual content, of the poem. The listener perceives the significance of the structure of the poem in terms of its meaning, so that rhythm and narrative flow become a single event. This is particularly evident in a ballad, which works with a strong rhyme scheme and a strong sense of rhythm.

Most important of all is the performance quality of the oral reading. If one element of poetry is delight, as Frost writes, then the oral reader—or performer—of poetry for children is able to use a dramatic presentation to generate that delight, and then to send the child reader from the oral performance to the text of the poem, loving it more. No one who has listened to an oral performance of a rollicking narrative like "Casey at the Bat" reads the text without hearing that oral voice once again; no one who hears a performance of "Barbara Allen" forgets the loneliness and longing that are only partially compensated for at the final twining of the red rose and the briar.

In this sense, child readers can come to understand that texts have voices, that reading is not necessarily a speedy activity, that words have muscle and timber and tone, and that those qualities play out in the meaning of the text itself.

Writers of Children's Poetry

Eve Merriam (1916–1992)

In thinking about her own poetry, Eve Merriam believed that the most important element of her work was sound. "The first, and perhaps main strand, is my delight in word play, in the mellifluous and ridiculous aspects of language, in oddities and quirks. I am happy when I am clowning around with language, brandishing slapstick nonsense, falling down over polysyllables, balancing on the thin wire of riddles. I like horseshoe curves and unexpected turns" (1989). In fact, much of the delight that children may take from Merriam's poetry is the delight that her play with sound generates.

The title of her collection, *There Is No Rhyme for Silver* (1964), suggests just this interest, and it is carried throughout the collection. In "Toaster Time" she uses sound to replicate an experience: "Tick tick tick tick tick tick tick / Toast up a sandwich quick quick quick." The delight here comes not only from the repeating sound, but from the use of that same sound in unusual ways. In *Chortles* (1989), which Merriam subtitles "Wordplay Poems," she uses this same kind of repetition of sound: "There's a flicker of a snicker / before Joe tells a joke, / there's a twitter of a titter, / a smiley wily poke." The sound does not only have to come from language as it is commonly understood. In "Cacophony" Merriam recreates the sounds of a garbage truck, beginning with real words, then quickly merging into fabulous language: "Mash, smash, / grink, chong, / goopidy guck, / grabbid slee." This technique is especially apparent in *Bam Bam Bam* (1995), a single poem set in a picture book format. Here Merriam captures the sounds of a building being demolished to make way for a new highrise.

This interest in sound is mirrored by Merriam's interest in the construction of poetry itself, and many of her poems reflect that metapoetic interest. "There Is No Rhyme for Silver," for example, suggests the poet's manipulation of language to make it follow the poem's structure.

> *There is no rhyme for silver,*
> *but if you climb a hill ver-*
> *-y very slowly*
> *you can almost make it go…See?*

There is a sense of invitation here; the poet invites the reader into the world of poetry rather than suggesting that poetry is something that has erected stern barriers around itself. "A rhyme is a jump rope— / Let's begin. / Take a turn and / Jump right in." In thinking about the origins of a poem, Merriam again allows the reader to participate. Merriam's greatest contribution to children's poetry is her sense that a poem's construction depends on the poet's use of elements of sound. And what is particularly important in her poetry is her firm belief that children can apprehend the poet's use of such an element to create meaning.

Myra Cohn Livingston (1926–1996)

If the strength of Eve Merriam's poetry lies in her use of sound, the strength of Myra Cohn Livingston's work lies in her use of vibrant and absorbing imagery.

Illustration by Leonard Everett Fisher for Margaret Cohn Livingston's *Earth Songs*. Copyright © 1986. Published by Holiday House, New York. Used with permission.

Though she, like Merriam, will play with the structure of her poetry, in fact, the dramatic emphasis in her work is on the image itself, so that her poems are in many ways sensory experiences. In work from her collection *4-Way Stop and Other Poems* (1976), the moon peeks out of the sky, "parting thin white cloud curtains." The bees "work in their orange / and black striped sweaters." Power lines are strung from "thin robots, / Spun of wire lace," and October is "the hair of a golden girl / Tangled in leaves, with a wisp of curl." Throughout her work Livingston strings together such strong images, drawn from what she calls "metaphoric observation." For a child reader of Livingston's poetry, the world is charged with potential images, and images that can be cast in dramatically vivid metaphor.

This is particularly true in the four collections celebrating the natural world, books that she created with illustrator Leonard Everett Fisher. In *Earth Songs* (1986), Livingston wrote a dramatic monologue in which the earth speaks of its many features; the effect is the suggestion of the planet's sheer physical size. She writes of the mountains like waves of the waters that splash against the shore and of the evergreens that lean against slopes. In *Sea Songs* (1986) Livingston used a disordered, unrhymed stanza to suggest the unpredictable movement of the sea, but once again she depended on vivid imagery to create her effects: "Heaving ships, plunged into black waters, / Vomit saltspray back to hissing seas, / Sailing over, up and ever on." The apparent randomness of the stanza suggests the randomness of the stormy ocean, but the strongest element here is the image of the persistent ship amidst the hissing seas.

Sky Songs (1984) reverses the monologue of *Earth Songs* and, instead, has the poet speak to the sky. Again, however, the poetry is highly sensory. In "Snow," the poet compares a sheet of snow to a blanket of air. In "Sunset," the sky will don evening dress. And in "Smog," the poet complains about the pollution that cankerous pollutants. In *Space Songs* (1988), Livingston abandoned the dramatic monologue and, instead, turned to the lyrical voice, though still the strength of her poetry is its imagery. In the opening poem "Otherwhere," the moon is a night watchman, stars pinwheel the sky, and comets tumble. Here, too, is the result of metaphoric observation.

The titles of these books with Fisher suggest something of Livingston's interest in thematic organization, and, in fact, she crafted a number of books in which all of her poems centered around a single idea, such as her *Birthday Poems* (1989). She also edited a large number of poetry collections along thematic lines, such as *Dog Poems* (1990), *Halloween Poems* (1989), and the intriguing *Call Down the Moon* (1995), a collection of poems that speak about music, another of Livingston's loves. Of these collections, one of the strongest is her *There Was a Place and Other Poems* (1988), a collection of her own poems about a broken family, all from the point of view of the young child whose parent has died, or who has abandoned or been barred from the family. The poignant voices of the poems are striking, as Livingston explores the crushing sadness of such a break on a child.

Livingston's lyrical poetry is marked by imagery, certainly, but it is also marked by a sensitivity to the interests of a child, both in the outer and the inner life.

Joyce Carol Thomas (b. 1938)

The poet Joyce Carol Thomas writes of the experience of home, of family, of moments of togetherness, of parents. Her poetry is the poetry that celebrates the small, apparently insignificant moments of life by recognizing that there are no insignificant moments when a child and parent are together. Instead, there are moments of forging relationships, of establishing contact, and, most particularly in Thomas's poetry, of loving and enjoying the delights of family life, as a child enjoys the ingredients of gingerbread: molasses, milk, butter, flour, ginger, eggs, vanilla, and nutmeg.

In her *Gingerbread Days* (1995), a book of poems celebrating the months, Thomas focuses on the details of each month with a strong sense of a child's idea of proportions. May, for example, is the imagining of "recess for months / And playmates for lunch." In December the child narrator celebrates his father, a brick-layer, who "smells like houses." Though the book, on one level, seems a celebration of the months, in fact the months are the way in which Thomas structures and organizes the celebration of the family.

In *Brown Honey in Broomwheat Tea* (1993), Thomas focuses on the inner life of the young girl in a series of lyrical poems. These lyrics deal again with the close family unit: "My mother says I am / Brown honey in broomwheat tea / My father calls me the sweetwater / of his days." The first-person narrator suggests the interior examination of the speaker, and it is not an untroubled examination. While she celebrates the family's closeness and security, she is aware of the pressures of her culture: "There are those who / Have brewed a / Bitter potion for / Children kissed by the sun." Yet, there is an interior strength here, supported, as in the stories of Mildred Taylor, by the family, that allows the child to affirm her own interior strength and desire.

As the title of that poem suggests, the poems of *Brown Honey in Broomwheat Tea* are marked by vivid and striking metaphor; those in *Gingerbread Days* are less so, focusing as they do on the simple moments of life. In these poems Thomas notes "the pottery of my skin," and that "I am hewn from the solid ledge of rock." Sometimes the metaphor and tone suggest a biblical psalm: "Oh hide me in the crevice of a rock." The gentle voice, the appealing tone, the diction, and metaphor all work towards this connection.

In *I Have Heard of a Land* (1998), Thomas uses a series of lyrics—all of which begin with the book's title—to tell the story of an African American woman pioneer who staked out her own land in Oklahoma. It is a story based on her own family's experience, and, like the narrator of *Brown Honey in Broomwheat Tea,* the narrator here is strong and sure, knowing what she wants, willing to work hard—and beyond hard—to fulfill the dream. Though the lyrics do not themselves convey an explicit narrative, they do use striking images to suggest the staking of the land and its settling, a plot line emphasized in Floyd Cooper's illustrations. Having claimed the land, the pioneers dig and shelter and, during the long winter, hope for spring's songbirds. When spring does come, neighbors emerge to sing and worship together, build their houses, and "finish the porch /where they sit and tell stories," leaving that night so that the woman can saw "the planks for the steps / by herself." In the end, the pioneer becomes a metaphor herself for possibilities and imagination.

The simplicity of diction, the lyrical and easy rhythm, the focus on the small and common moments of life—all of these characterize Joyce Carol Thomas's poetry. The delight of her work comes through that simplicity and focus, but those very same elements carry with them the wisdom of her poetry as well.

Shel Silverstein (b. 1932)

The world to which Silverstein invites his readers is a world of the humorous and the unexpected, a world filled with twists that take normal experience and subvert it. Three collections contain most of his work: *Where the Sidewalk Ends* (1974), *A Light in the Attic* (1981), and *Falling Up* (1996). In each, the poems smack of the raucous, of the slapstick, of riotous fun.

Like Jack Prelutsky, Silverstein encourages the reader to see the everyday as extraordinary, and it is this shift of perspective that leads to the comedy of his poems. In *Falling Up* there is the birthday party for the dragon who blows his cake's candles on, and there is the Queen who, on hearing her magic mirror insisting that Snow White is the fairest, threatens to let it smash to the ground. The mirror decides to change the answer. In *A Light in the Attic* there is the troublesome traffic signal that turns unusual colors, and the Upside-Down Man who is the reflection of the speaker, though the speaker wonders if he is the Upside-Down Man and the reflection of his reflection. In *Where the Sidewalk Ends* there is Captain Hook who must be careful with an itchy nose, the hippopotamus sandwich that is too big to bite into, and the Christmas Tree that nobody loves because it is March the twenty-fifth. In each of these poems Silverstein has dramatically shifted the reader's perspective.

Silverstein's poems are, unlike those of Merriam and Livingston, quite heavily narrative in scope; each tells a small vignette. At the same time there is a strong union of the narrative and the illustration that he has drawn; frequently the two function like text and illustration in a picture book, so that the effect of the whole depends on reading the two. In "Something Missing" from *A Light in the Attic,* the speaker remembers putting on socks and shoes and tie and coat, but feels like something still is missing. The illustration shows it to be his pants. In "Snake Problem," the illustration of the snake spells out the snake's love but it is not clear from the illustration if this is affection or desire for a meal. In "Invisible Boy" Silverstein has left an empty rectangle and uses it to introduce the boy who cannot be seen. And in "Safe?" the title takes on two meanings as a child looks to the right and left and concludes that it is safe to cross the street, never realizing, as does the reader from the illustration, that a safe is plummeting down.

But perhaps most striking about the poems is the way in which they involve the reader, at times directly addressing the reader. Silverstein's is a strongly oral voice, with a strong narrator speaking to the child as though present. In "The Deadly Eye," the speaker warns against watching the eye, and then concludes with an address that involves the reader:

> *It's a good thing you* didn't…
> *You* did?…
> Good-bye.

Similarly Peggy Ann McKay, after listing a series of terrible illnesses that plague her in "Sick," discovers that it is Saturday: "You say today is…Saturday? / G'bye, I'm going out to play!" The effect of this technique is to have the reader become part of the poem, creating a sense in which the reader is actually speaking to the speaker of the poem.

Silverstein's world is not a gentle one—characters may get eaten by boa constrictors, be accosted by elephants, sprout arms and heads where they should not sprout, or turn into a television set. But the hilarity of these poems speaks directly to moments that a child would recognize, moments of conflict with the adult world, moments of imaginative exaggeration, moments of intense emotion and frustration, moments of exhilaration.

Jack Prelutsky (b. 1940)

The work of Jack Prelutsky, like that of Joyce Carol Thomas, touches on some of the simple, apparently small moments of a child's life. But Prelutsky's approach to these moments is entirely different. His is the world of comic poetry, and there is hardly a single lyric that does not smack of the pen of the humorist who perceives comedy in even the mundane moments of life. Prelutsky's rhymes are apparent; his sense of rhythm is strong and determinative for the poem. But what is distinctive about his work is the funny turn, the unexpected laugh, the clever wit that turns the moment on its head.

Prelutsky generates much of his humor by taking an everyday situation, person, or even character trait and exaggerating it so that it seems ludicrous. In *The New Kid on the Block* (1984), Prelutsky writes of Clara Cleech, a lousy juggler because she juggles only one thing at a time. There is Euphonica Jarre, whose bizarre voice will shatter windowpanes and spoil batter. Granny Grizer who "would charge you for a snowflake," and Dainty Dottie Dee is so immaculate that she "launders every lightbulb." In *Something BIG Has Been Here* (1990), there is the hapless mother and her meatloaf: "She whacked it with a hammer, / and she smacked it with a brick, / but she couldn't faze that meat loaf, / it remained without a nick."

Mixed in with poems of exaggeration are the poems of monsters, which delight Prelutsky. Each of his books boasts a constellation of monstrous forms that, though they seem predatory, also seem rather harmless because of the diction. *Something BIG Has Been Here* boasts the Wooly Wurbbe and the Addle-pated Paddlepuss; *The New Kid on the Block,* in turn, has the exploding Bloders, the Flotz that gobbles dots, the Gloppy Gloppers, and the Yubbazubbies. The very names that he has chosen suggest his delight in sound, as well as his delight in the imaginative creation of fabulous creatures, as in Fretenetica Fluntz, Miss Misinformation, and Quentin Quimble Quamble Quayle of *A Pizza the Size of the Sun* (1996).

Some of Prelutsky's poems are much more contemplative, though still they retain their strong rhythm and humor. In "Life's Not Been the Same in My Family," an older sibling laments the coming of the new baby, and there is the poignant sense of parental loss. In "We Moved about a Week Ago," a young boy remembers the friends who dumped him in the dirt, who wrestled, who bopped him in the nose, who shaved his teddy bear, who sat on him. But despite all this, the poem concludes with his hope for the same kind of friends in his new neighborhood. In *My Parents Think I'm Sleeping* (1985), Prelutsky explores this contemplative side more fully in writing a series of poems that develop the feelings of a young child at night: "What happens to the colors / when night replaces day? What turns the wrens to ravens, / the trees to shades of gray?"

In *Ride a Purple Pelican* (1986) and *Beneath a Blue Umbrella* (1990), Prelutsky plays with the strong rhythms and nonsense language of the Mother Goose poems, creating his own lyrics that recall the tones and diction and even the action of the earlier poetry. There is the same strong presence of dreamlike logic, the strong sense of rhythm, the quick and easy depiction of a vivid and delightful scene. In *Beneath a Blue Umbrella,* Prelutsky writes of a character who seems directly out of Mother Goose: "Nicholas Narrow, tall and thin, / slumbered in a garden. / A sparrow landed on his chin / and chirped, "I beg your pardon!" Here is the scene quickly depicted, filled with a fabulous character doing something seemingly ordinary, yet slightly inappropriate or odd. But, in addition, Prelutsky is able to capture some of the elements of fancy that mark the Mother Goose poems: "A monkey strummed a blue guitar, / a donkey caught a falling star."

Prelutsky also captures the repetitions and consonant sounds of Mother Goose: In *Ride a Purple Pelican* Prelutsky writes, "Rumpitty Tumpitty Rumpitty Tum, / Buntington Bunny is beating the drum." A later poem again turns to the repetition of sound: "Hinnikin Minnikin, / Minnie and Moe." The pleasure of these sounds is the same as that sound in a Mother Goose poem that depends heavily on consonantal repetition.

If the poetry of Joyce Carol Thomas is contemplative and quiet, the poetry of Jack Prelutsky is a romp, a carnival, and loud baseball game, a whoop and a holler. He and Thomas together suggest the kind of range that poets for children can reach to delight their audience.

Nikki Grimes (b. 1950)

In works like *It's Raining Laughter* (1997) and *From a Child's Heart* (1993), Nikki Grimes has used her verse to depict the joyousness of a child's life, focusing especially on the African American child. Mixing blank with rhymed verse, Grimes creates an exuberance both in her diction and, particularly, in her varied lines, which always seem about to break out of order for the sheer pleasure of it all. Like Joyce Carol Thomas, Grimes explores the small moments of a child's life. But where Thomas's verse is quiet and thoughtful, Grimes is boisterous, a poetic romp through a moment of childhood.

Her greatest strength is her ability to recreate the feelings of childhood. In *It's Raining Laughter,* she depicts a child as "a goofy giffler, / a sadness chase, / a good-mood maker." There are interior moments, as when a young girl reads a book, but more often there are children like the boy in "Running," who knows that "All I have to do / is take a deep breath / and go." This is a world of pleasure and happiness, where the child "laughed for no good reason, / needing none."

Throughout the book, the child is affirmed in a world that is safe and secure because of friends and because of family. It may be that taunts come, but there is the parent to secure the world afterwards, a father to say that eyeglasses are "only / picture frames" or a friend to remind the speaker that, after a fight, their anger will be "forgotten as we squinted / at the sun."

Most of Grimes's poems are written from a first-person point of view, as in *From a Child's Heart.* These poems are mostly meditations addressed to God. They are funny, poignant, vivacious, energetic; always they speak directly to the experience of the child. In "One More Year," the speaker prays that her grandmother might live for another year. In "Daddy's Hat," the boy enjoys playing with his father's hard hat, but prays that his father will need to take it to work again. In "Number One," the child hopes that she will be chosen to dance, not because she is the only one in the class with her color of skin, but because she is good. And, in "From a Child's Heart," the child prays for a longer summer, or at least the sense that the days are lasting forever. These are poems that come out of a child's world, that work from within a child's perspective.

If the child's experience organizes *It's Raining Laughter* and *From a Child's Heart*, Grimes instead uses a narrative line to bring together the poems of *Meet Danitra Brown* (1994) and *Come Sunday* (1996). The success in each of these books lies not just in the poems themselves, but in the accumulating images and meanings that come together to form a whole. *Come Sunday* is a series of poems, all told from the perspective of a young girl, that explores the experience of going to Paradise Baptist Church. Here, blue-haired ladies pinch her cheeks and wear "satin ribbons, black as jet, / broad silk bands, and lacy net." Wearing white gloves, she is entranced to see the ushers "high-stepping down the center aisle, / their backs all straight and proud." There is a sense of joy and pleasure in the service, in the Sunday School class, in the church dinner, so that, in the end, she leaves with the sound of the organ following her home.

In *Meet Danitra Brown*, Grimes organizes a series of poems told again by a young girl, but this time about her friend Danitra, who is kind, sensible, exuberant, witty, quick, and going to win the Nobel Prize for her writing. She always wears purple because "she might just be a princess," and together the girls sing and dance and grow quiet together and affirm each other. When the narrator is teased for the dark color of her skin, Danitra tells her "Next time, honey, you just say, / The blacker the berry, the sweeter the juice." She is "the greatest, most splendiferous girl in town," the narrator affirms, and this is suggested by all the poems that celebrate her splendid nature—and friendship.

Grimes's poems work to celebrate, in fact. They celebrate the joy of childhood, the sheer energy and exuberance of being young and the world lying just in front as far as can possibly be seen.

Walter Dean Myers (b. 1937)

As with all genres of children's literature, audience is a large consideration for children's poetry. Walter Dean Myers, known also as a novelist, has recently issued several volumes of poetry that push the boundaries of children's poetry. In *Brown Angels* (1993) and *Glorious Angels* (1995), Myers creates nothing short of a "celebration" of the world of childhood. Illustrating the books profusely with early photographs, Myers creates lyrics that call for the reader to love and cherish and bring joy to the lives of children. The illustrations—moving and funny and startling at times—all contribute to this sense of the innocence and joys and pleasures of the child's world.

The language that Myers uses is both hortatory and celebratory, at times echoing the structures of the Psalms: "Let us parade them to / tambourine and tabla / Sprinkling hallelujahs in their paths." *Glorious Angels* uses photographs from around the world, and Myers divides the book into a song from the Mother, from the Father, and from the Village. But the voice in each section is similar in tone and purpose: "Let us celebrate the children / And bring them peace." The voice is filled with passion and purpose for the cause of childhood.

In *Brown Angels* Myers uses only early photographs of African American families, and his preface suggests much about his purposes: "Seeing their faces scrubbed and beaming, seeing them dressed in their Sunday best for a traveling photographer, told me what our grandparents and great-grandparents thought of their children. These pictures speak to me of hardworking people—of tenant farmers, porters, and teachers of the 'colored' schools—who celebrated the lives of their babies as have all the people before them and since." In these poems the narrative voice—whether the voice is first-person or third—is strong in its identity and in its sense of affirmation of the child, and again there is often a Biblical echo: "For I am dark and precious / And have such gifts to give / Sweet joy, sweet love." Here truly is the celebratory voice, but it is also a celebration with a point: Myers has something to say about the African American experience, as well as about the experience of childhood.

In his long poem *Harlem* (1997), Myers wants to evoke an impression about the city. He deals with it in the abstract—"Harlem was a promise / Of a better life, of a place where a man didn't / Have to know his place"—but also very much in specific, concrete detail to show the harmonies and discordancies of Harlem: "Cracked reed / soprano sax laughter." The poem is dominated by strong metaphor, so that eventually Harlem itself becomes a metaphor for the African American experience; it is "A journey on the A train / That started on the banks of the Niger / And has not ended."

All the poems are strikingly original, passionate in their narrative voice. But all of them also push the boundaries of children's literature in terms of the audience addressed. *Harlem* includes many references—both to the physical city and to the famous people of its history—that would be opaque for many young children. And the poems of *Glorious Angels* and *Brown Angels* seem to be addressed more to the world of the adult than to the child. They are more about children than for children. And yet, at the same time, these poems are about childhood, and evoke that world with great joy and specificity. In this sense they are within the larger arena.

Thinking and Writing about and from within the Genre of Children's Poetry

Thinking and Writing about the Genre of Children's Poetry _____

1. Read a ballad such as "Barbara Allen," or a classic Victorian poem such as "The Charge of the Light Brigade" or "Gunga Dinn." Is it fair to consider such poems to be within the boundaries of children's literature? If not, why? If so, what is it in them that brings them within the boundaries? How does a contemporary child overcome the cultural distinctions that they present to a modern reader?

2. Choose a poem by the Canadian poet Dennis Lee. Analyze the way in which he generates his humor. Is it similar to the humor of a Shel Silverstein or a Jack Prelutsky, or does Lee do something quite different?

3. Read David Small's *George Washington's Cows* (1994), focusing especially on the complex stanza form. In a short critical essay, analyze the ways in which the structure of this stanza form affects the reading and the humor of the poetry.

Thinking and Writing from within the Genre of Children's Poetry

1. Keep a journal in which you try out Myra Cohn Livingston's technique of metaphoric observation (1989). Which of the observations that you gather and cast in metaphor would be appropriate to a child reader? Would any not be appropriate?

2. As the editor of a small collection of poems to be published for children, choose a dozen poems by either Robert Frost, Alfred Tennyson, John Greenleaf Whittier, or Robert Burns. After deciding on the titles, write the introduction to the volume that explains your editorial choices. Your audience here is the child reader of the collection.

3. Choose a simple, ordinary experience and exaggerate it to the point that it becomes humorous. Cast this revised experience in the form of a two-stanza poem, your audience being the child reader.

Selected Bibliographies

Works Cited

Brooks, Gwendolyn. *Bronzeville Boys and Girls.* New York: HarperCollins Publishers, 1994.

Ciardi, John. *The Man who Sang the Sillies.* Philadelphia, PA: Lippincott, 1961.

Chute, Marchette. *Rhymes About the Country.* New York: MacMillan, 1949.

dePaola, Tomie. *Tomie dePaola's Mother Goose.* New York: Putnam, 1985.

de Regniers, Beatrice Schenk, ed. *Sing a Song of Popcorn.* New York: Scholastic, 1988. Illustrated by Marcia Brown, Leo and Diane Dillon, Richard Egielski, Trina Schart Hyman, Arnold Lobel, Maurice Sendak, Marc Simont, and Margot Zemach.

Florian, Douglas. *On the Wing.* New York: Harcourt, Brace, 1996.

Frost, Robert. *The Poetry of Robert Frost.* New York: Holt, Rinehart and Winston, 1969.

———. *Stopping by the Woods on a Snowy Evening.* New York: Dutton, 1978. Illustrated by Susan Jeffers.

Hall, Donald. *The Oxford Book of Children's Verse in America.* New York: Oxford, 1985.

Ho, Minfong. *Hush! A Thai Lullaby.* New York: Orchard Books, 1999. Illustrated by Holly Meade.

Kennedy, X. J. *One Winter Night in August and Other Nonsense Jingles.* New York: Atheneum, 1975.

Kennedy, X. J. and Dorothy, eds. *Knock at a Star.* Boston: Little, Brown, 1982. Illustrated by Karen Ann Weinhaus.

Kinnell, Galway. *Mortal Acts, Mortal Words: The Past.* Boston: Houghton Mifflin Co., 1993.

Kuskin, Karla. *Dogs and Dragons, Trees and Dreams.* New York: Harper, 1980.

Larrick, Nancy. *Piping Down the Valleys Wild.* New York: Dell, 1968. Illustrated by Ellen Raskin.

Longfellow, Henry Wadsworth. *Hiawatha.* New York: Dial, 1983. Illustrated by Susan Jeffers.

———. *Paul Revere's Ride.* New York: Penguin, 1990. Illustrated by Ted Rand.

McCord, David. *One at a Time.* Boston: Little Brown, 1996.

McGinley, Phyllis. *Times Three.* New York: Viking Penguin, 1959.

Milne, A. A. *Now We Are Six.* New York: E.P. Dutton & Co, 1927.

Noyes, Alfren. *Daddy Fell into the Pond and Other Poems.* New York: Sheed and Ward, 1952.

Otten, Charlotte F. *January Rides the Wind.* New York: Lothrop, Lee and Shepard, 1997. Illustrated by Todd L. W. Doney.

Prelutsky, Jack. *The New Kid on the Block.* New York: Greenwillow Books, 1984.

Prelutsky, Jack, ed. *The Random House Book of Poetry for Children.* New York: Random House, 1983. Illustrated by Arnold Lobel.

Richards, Laura. *Tirra Lirra.* Boston, MA: Little Brown, 1935.

Roethke, Theodore. *The Collected Poems of Theodore Roethke.* Garden City, NY: Doubleday, 1966.

Sandburg, Carl. *Smoke and Steel.* New York: Harcourt, Brace, Jovanovich, 1920.

Sendak, Maurice. *We Are All in the Dumps with Jack and Guy.* New York: HarperCollins, 1993.

Small, David. *George Washington's Cows.* New York: Farrar Straus Giroux, 1994.

Stevens, Wallace. *The Collected Poems of Wallace Stevens.* New York: Alfred A. Knopf, 1993.

Updike, John. *A Child's Calendar.* New York: Alfred A. Knopf, 1965.

Viorst, Judith. *If I Were in Charge of the World and other Worries: Poems for Children and Their Parents.* New York: Atheneum, 1981. Illustrated by Lynne Cherry.

Works by Children's Poets

Eve Merriam

Bam Bam Bam. New York: Henry Holt, 1995. Illustrated by Dan Yaccarino.

Blackberry Ink. New York: William Morrow, 1985. Illustrated by Hans Wilhelm.

Chortles. New York: William Morrow, 1989. Illustrated by Sheila Hamanaka.

Fresh Paint. New York: Macmillan, 1986.

Jamboree Rhymes for All Times. New York: Dell, 1984.

Rainbow Writing. New York: Macmillan, 1976.

A Sky Full of Poems. New York: Dell, 1986.

There Is No Rhyme for Silver. New York: Atheneum, 1964. Illustrated by Joseph Schindelman.

Myra Cohn Livingston

Birthday Poems. New York: Holiday House, 1989. Illustrated by Margot Tomes.

Call Down the Moon. [Editor] New York: Margaret McElderry, 1995.

Celebrations. New York: Holiday House, 1985. Illustrated by Leonard Everett Fisher.

Dog Poems. [Editor] New York: Holiday House, 1990. Illustrated by Leslie Morrill.

Earth Songs. New York: Holiday House, 1986. Illustrated by Leonard Everett Fisher.

4-Way Stop and Other Poems. New York: Atheneum, 1976. Illustrated by James J. Spanfeller.

Halloween Poems. [Editor] New York: Holiday House, 1989. Illustrated by Stephen Gammell.

O Sliver of Liver. New York: Atheneum, 1979.

Sea Songs. New York: Holiday House, 1986. Illustrated by Leonard Everett Fisher.

Sky Songs. New York: Holiday House, 1984. Illustrated by Leonard Everett Fisher.

Space Songs. New York: Holiday House, 1988. Illustrated by Leonard Everett Fisher.

There Was a Place and Other Poems. New York: Margaret McElderry, 1988.

Whispers and Other Poems. New York: Harcourt, Brace, 1958.

Joyce Carol Thomas

Brown Honey in Broomwheat Tea. New York: HarperCollins, 1993. Illustrated by Floyd Cooper.

Gingerbread Days. New York: HarperCollins, 1995. Illustrated by Floyd Cooper.

I Have Heard of a Land. New York: HarperCollins, 1998. Illustrated by Floyd Cooper.

Shel Silverstein

Falling Up. New York: HarperCollins, 1996.

A Light in the Attic. New York: HarperCollins, 1981.

Where the Sidewalk Ends. New York: Harper and Row, 1974.

Jack Prelutsky

Beneath a Blue Umbrella. New York: Greenwillow, 1990. Illustrated by Garth Williams.

My Parents Think I'm Sleeping. New York: Greenwillow, 1985. Illustrated by Yossi Abolafia.

The New Kid on the Block. New York: Greenwillow, 1984. Illustrated by James Stevenson.

Nightmares. New York: Greenwillow, 1976.

A Pizza the Size of the Sun. New York: Greenwillow, 1996. Illustrated by James Stevenson.

Ride a Purple Pelican. New York: Greenwillow, 1986. Illustrated by Garth Williams.

Something BIG Has Been Here. New York: Greenwillow, 1990. Illustrated by James Stevenson.

Tyrannosaurus Was a Beast. New York: Greenwillow, 1988. Illustrated by Arnold Lobel.

Nikki Grimes

Come Sunday. Grand Rapids: Eerdmans, 1996. Illustrated by Michael Bryant.

From a Child's Heart. East Orange, NJ: Just Us, 1993. Illustrated by Brenda Joysmith.

It's Raining Laughter. New York: Dial, 1997. Photographs by Myles Pinkney.

Meet Danitra Brown. New York: William Morrow, 1994. Illustrated by Floyd Cooper.

Walter Dean Myers

Brown Angels. New York: HarperCollins, 1993.

Glorious Angels. New York: HarperCollins, 1995.

Harlem. New York: Scholastic, 1997. Illustrated by Christopher Meyers.

Works About the Genre of Children's Poetry

Bremser, Martha. "The Voice of Solitude: The Children's Verse of Walter de la Mare." *Children's Literature* 21 (1993): 66–91.

Butler, Francelia. "'Over the Garden Wall / I Let the Baby Fall': The Poetry of Rope Skipping." *Children's Literature* 3 (1974): 186–195.

Clark, Leonard. "Poetry and Children." *Children's Literature in Education* 9 (Autumn, 1978): 127–135.

Cox, Susan Taylor. "A Word or Two with Eve Merriam: Talking about Poetry." *New Advocate* 2 (1989): 139–149.

Flynn, Richard. "Can Children's Poetry Matter?" *Lion and the Unicorn* 17 (June, 1993): 37-44.

Harmon, William. "Lear, Limericks, and Some Other Verse Forms." *Children's Literature* 10 (1982): 70–76.

Kennedy, X. J. "Disorder and Security in Nonsense Verse for Children." *Lion and the Unicorn* 13 (December, 1989): 28–33.

Livingston, Myra Cohn. "Some Thoughts on Voice in Poetry." In Charlotte F. Otten and Gary D. Schmidt, eds., *The Voice of the Narrator in Children's Literature* (New York: Greenwood, 1989): 215–227.

Lynn, Joanne L. "Runes to Ward Off Sorrow: Rhetoric of the English Nursery Rhyme." *Children's Literature in Education* 16 (Spring, 1985): 3–14.

Merriam, Eve. "Out Loud: Centering the Narrator in Sound. In Charlotte F. Otten and Gary D. Schmidt, eds., *The Voice of the Narrator in Children's Literature* (New York: Greenwood, 1989): 230–235.

Obbink, Laura Apol. "The Primacy of Poetry: Oral Culture and the Young Child." *New Advocate* 3 (1990): 227–234.

Opie, Iona and Peter. *Oxford Dictionary of Nursery Rhymes.* London: Oxford University Press, 1952.

Snipes, Wilson Currin. "Five Ways and One of Looking at Mother Goose." *Children's Literature* 2 (1973): 98–104.

Ten Harmsel, Henrietta. "Annie M. G. Schmidt: Dutch Children's Poet." *Children's Literature* 11 (1983): 135–144.

Vardell, Sylvia. "An Interview with Jack Prelutsky." *New Advocate* 4 (1991): 101–111.

5

The Oral Voices of Folklore

In Doreen Rappaport's *The Journey of Meng* (1991), Meng's husband Wan is taken by the emperor's soldiers to work far to the north on the Great Wall of China. She waits for a year, hearing no word while preparing warm clothing for him against the cold, but no one is willing to take the clothing north. When her husband comes to her in a dream, Meng resolves to venture north herself, even though she has never traveled outside her own village. After weeks of her terrible, lonely journey she is magically able to fly to the wall, but she is too late: Her husband has died and been buried within the wall.

Enraged by the hard-heartedness of the emperor, Meng waits at the wall by the edge of the sea, and, in response, lightning splits the wall and reveals Wan's bones. But now it is the emperor who is enraged, and Meng is dragged before him to account for the ruined wall. On seeing her, he instantly desires her and threatens to behead her if she will not yield to him. But Meng is not cowed and slyly promises to yield if the emperor will give Wan a state funeral at the end of seven weeks of mourning. The emperor agrees, but, after the funeral, Meng turns and leaps into the sea, escaping him. The emperor commands that the body be retrieved, cut into pieces, and her bones ground to dust. When that dust is returned to the sea, it becomes thousands and thousands of silvery fish.

The Journey of Meng is illustrative of the ways in which folktales push at the boundaries of children's literature. Certainly there is much here that is consonant with children's literature: the loyal relationship, the difficult journey successfully completed, magical assistance, the clever tricking of the wicked. But there is also much here that seems discordant, not because it speaks of unpleasant events, but because of the manner in which those unpleasant events are handled. The meaningless death of Wan, the violent suicide, the repulsive retribution against a dead body, the lack of any telling justice—these seem to point toward a world unusual to the arena of children's literature. *The Journey of Meng* might not be, in fact, a work of children's literature; perhaps folklore is not necessarily within the boundaries of children's literature only by virtue of its being folklore.

In *Sam and the Tigers* (1996), Julius Lester retells the story of Little Black Sambo, a story that seems to most contemporary readers to have all the elements of a folktale. This is subtitled as a new retelling, however, and in it Lester transforms the racist elements of the early tale so that Sam becomes a smart, wily trickster, a fully rounded character. In the retelling, Sam goes off to school with his fine suit of clothes, but he is accosted by a series of tigers who threaten to eat him up. "I don't like that idea," he says, and instead trades off piece after piece of his fine suit until there are five tigers each wearing a piece of his clothing.

Each of the tigers now assumes that he is the best dressed, and, when they begin to argue, they shed the clothes—Sam picks them up—and then chase each other until they turn into a pile of golden butter. That night, Sam gathers his friends for a pancake supper to enjoy the butter he has gathered; he wears all his fine clothes.

Lester's afterward says much about the story. Here is a tale that has been viewed as racist and stereotyped for over half a century, and yet it is a story that has at its center an African American hero who outsmarts his antagonists. In his retelling, Lester employs his southern storyteller's voice as he reconceptualizes the story and heightens the playfulness and wit of Sam, as well as his heroic stature, thus eliminating the stereotyped elements. But, even in crafting such a reconceptualization, there is the tacit understanding that this is a story that has, in some of its elements, offended. In this sense, the telling or retelling of a story becomes, on some level, a moral act.

Both retellings raise questions. Are tales of violence and vengeance appropriate for a child audience? Is a story that lacks final justice too difficult for a child to accept? Can retellers from one ethnicity retell the tales of another culture? If the retelling of a tale is a moral act, is it the case that some stories may be inappropriate to tell for some tellers, for some audiences? In what sense does the telling itself become a moral event?

But before such questions can be answered, others of definition must be asked. Little Black Sambo has entered into the cultural consciousness of the West and seems to be a folktale; its multiple retellings suggest continual recasting and new influences. But, in fact, the story was written at the very end of the nineteenth century by Helen Bannerman, who was living in India. Despite the presence of many folklore elements—the trickster hero, the talking beast, the magical transformation, attendant justice—this story is not by strict definition a folktale; it is not a story that originated within a community of people. The question then becomes, when does a story become a folktale?

Boundaries and Definitions

A folktale is a narrative story that literally comes out of the folk; it is a tale with oral origins in a distinct culture, handed down year after year, generation after generation, refined and revised, always changing with the teller, always changing with the audience, always shifting in its detail, usually constant in its basic narrative form and plot situations, often constant in its basic meanings. The genre includes the comic tales told on the front porch and around the campfire, and the serious tales of community origins and meanings. It includes the tales of heroes and tricksters. It includes tales that attach to the past even as they speak about the present. They are stories that have entered the consciousness of a culture and that speak to its members both in an individual sense and a communal sense.

The story of Hansel and Gretel, for example, is one of the best-known folktales in the West; it is a tale of astonishing evil and grace. Though variants will change certain details, the principal narrative outlines are constant. Finding the larder nearly empty, Hansel and Gretel's wicked stepmother convinces their father that he must take the children into the woods and leave them there to die. On the first night, Hansel cleverly leaves white stones along the forest path to guide them home; on the second, he leaves bread crumbs, only to find that they have been eaten by the birds.

In despair, the children wander until they come to a candied house. But when they begin to nibble, they are caught by the wicked witch who lives there. Hansel is caged and Gretel made to work while the witch fattens her brother so she might eat him. Though the children are able to trick the witch for a time by hiding her glasses, the day comes when the witch resolves to eat Hansel. She has Gretel prepare the oven, then commands her to climb in to see to it. When Gretel feigns ignorance, the witch climbs in as an example and Gretel slams the door shut. Then the children flee, taking with them the witch's jewels and wealth. They arrive home to find that their stepmother has died, and the three live together happily ever after.

The narrative of the story is powerfully symmetrical: From a house empty of food, the children move to a house made of food. From a stepmother filled with murderous purpose, they move to a heightened version of a murderous woman. From Hansel's cleverness, which fails, they move to Gretel's cleverness, which succeeds. But the power of the story lies also in its larger meanings. The children are faced with the most dire of evils: Their parents have not only ignored their responsibility, but have, in fact, turned to become their murderers. The witch is only an incarnation of what they have done. The children are unprotected and can respond only with their native cleverness. It turns out that this is enough.

But what is most remarkable is not the success of their cleverness, but the story's conclusion. They return—in some versions they are guided by a bird—to their father, who has just a short time ago left them to die. And they do the most unexpected thing in the whole story: They forgive him. They forgive his blundering and his weakness and his evil, and they reestablish right relationships.

Here is a story strong in its narrative structuring, but stronger still in the potency of its meanings. It may be that this is a story that has specific historical roots: dark European woods, fear of witches, the exigencies of the poor, starvation. But in its portrayal of proper and improper relations between parents and children, it continues to speak powerfully and universally, even outside its own culture.

The fertility of folktales in terms of their meanings, whether they are investigated structurally or through Freudian eyes, attests to the way that artfully simple plot constructions carry deep meaning. That a folktale can support several complex readings suggests that the folktale can speak across cultures and generations.

The Oral Nature of the Folktale

One measure of authenticity of a folktale is its oral origin; this is an origin that allows for immediate and ever-changing adaptations to an audience. In fact, it is a tradition that depends heavily on the immediate audience; it is the connection between audience and teller that provides the impetus for variance in the storytelling.

As a folktale moves into the print medium, however, that immediacy, that high sense of the very present audience, is lost. Recognizing this inevitability, the reteller of a folktale may simply allow the oral quality to disappear and replace it with a more literary aesthetic. In Mercer Mayer's *The Sleeping Beauty* (1984) for example, Mayer chooses a formal literary style to distance her story from the present.

> Somewhere in time, in a faraway land, there lived a great king in a large castle with many courtiers and servants. Nevertheless, the king was lonely. One day he came upon a stable girl who tended the royal horses. So deeply impressed was he by her gentleness, sincerity, and beauty that he fell in love with her and asked her to become his queen.

The oral voice here is silent; the story has become formalized. The pace of the text, the structural repetition, the inverted and passive phrasing, the punctuated pauses—all are qualities that Mayer has chosen to create a very formal presentation of the story.

Other retellers, however, resist this inevitability and instead hope to incorporate the oral voice of the folktale into their retellings. In attempting this, the reteller must bridge the restrictions of the medium and use diction and structures to recreate the oral voice. In his *John Henry* (1994), Julius Lester speaks directly to the reader, addressing the reader and incorporating the informal diction of the oral teller.

> You have probably never heard of John Henry. Or maybe you heard about him but don't know the ins and outs of his comings and goings. Well, that's why I'm going to tell you about him. When John Henry was born, birds came from everywhere to see him. The bears and panthers and moose and deer and rabbits and squirrels and even a unicorn came out of the woods to see him. And instead of the sun tending to his business and going to bed, it was peeping out from behind the moon's skirts trying to get a glimpse of the new baby.

The tone here is very different from that of Mayer's *Sleeping Beauty*. The opening is conversational and directed. The use of conjunctions to open the sentences strongly suggests the stance of the oral storyteller.

In *The People Could Fly* (1985), Virginia Hamilton uses constructions to create a vivid sense of the African voice, as in this selection from the title story in which flying is used as a metaphor for the escape to freedom.

> There was a great out-cryin. The bent backs straightened up. Old and young who were called slaves and could fly joined hands. Say like they would ring-sing. But they didn't shuffle in a circle. They didn't sing. They rose on the air. They flew in a flock that was black against the heavenly blue. Black crows or black shadows. It didn't matter, they went so high. Way above the plantation, way over the slavery land. Say they flew away to *Free-dom.* (171)

The use of dialectal expression, sentence fragments, formulaic openings—all of these contribute to the rhythmic sound of the passage. And it is this rhythm that mimics the oral voice of the storyteller.

But then a complication arises. If an authentic folktale arises only out of an oral culture, then that oral beginning necessarily limits the boundaries of folklore. A tale that arises from the imagination of a distinct individual would be disqualified as a folktale, because it is not out of the folk, not out of the oral culture. Thus, a book like Michael Patrick Hearn's *The Porcelain Cat* (1987) uses the stock characters and repetitive structures of folktales to tell the story of an apprentice gathering the recipe for bringing a china cat to life and so sails close to the shore of folklore, but, though using folkloric elements, it is not a story that itself has oral origins.

If this criterion of orality is used to authenticate a folktale, and used rigorously, then it disqualifies even a tale such as "Beauty and the Beast," which has mid-eighteenth-century French sources as a tale written to entertain the court. There is no evidence for a distinctive oral origin for the tale. And this definition must also leave out much of North American folklore in the tall tale tradition, a tradition that Richard Dorson calls "fakelore" in his *American Folklore* (1959). If it is the case, for example, that the character of Paul Bunyan was, indeed, created as a lumber company advertising image, then this would seem to exclude such tales from folklore.

And there is also the question of Hans Christian Andersen's stories. By strict definition they are the works of an individual writer; they use folklore elements, but they have no oral origin. And perhaps even the tales collected by Jacob and Wilhelm Grimm in the first half of the nineteenth century are suspect. Because the brothers did not replicate the tales exactly as they heard them, but added literary elements and motifs to the oral tales, it might be argued that they have falsified the original stories and that what they eventually produced is no longer folklore.

On the other hand, even as oral tales were retold over and over and eventually split into many variants, so also has "Beauty and the Beast." North American tall tales and the fairy stories of Andersen and the Grimm brothers have also been told and told and told again. They, too, have developed into many variants. Tales of Paul Bunyan appear in Maine, Minnesota, and upper Michigan, each claiming to be the site of his birth. Tales of the real life John Chapman have been developed and exaggerated for over a century. And the story of "Beauty and the Beast," which has itself seen many variants, seems now to be part of the cultural consciousness of the West. At what point may it be said that these stories, too, now have been shaped by multiple retellings and that they, too, now in some measure come out of the folk?

The Cultural Qualities of the Folktale

In James Berry's *Spiderman Anancy* (1989), Anancy is a creature who is half-man, half-spider. He is the clever trickster, the rogue, the charmer. In the story "Anancy and the Making of the Bro Title," Berry uses language to capture the essence and voice of the character.

> At the time, nobody is called Bro.
> Anancy gets everybody to spread news that something special is ready to happen. It's ready to happen because everybody is ready for it. Come to the meeting in the village square. The big new happening will be revealed.
> Anancy is pleased-pleased. A big crowd surrounds him in the early night. Anancy feels good and ready to make a sweetmouth speech.
> "Friends," he starts, "you know and I know, everybody is a good-good person. But every person uses only a little goodness and a little bigness." (11)

The reader knows something about the sweetmouthed Anancy by the end of this opening—his clever flattering, his desire to be the center of attention. But Berry has also announced something about the culture through his diction. There is the use of the present tense, the repetition of words, the use of dialectal terms: "pleased-pleased," "good-good," "sweetmouth." Berry is suggesting here that the stories of Anancy are tied strongly to the culture.

Pointers for Teachers

Interactive Possibilities
- To demonstrate how stories change as they pass from one person to another, whisper a simple three-sentence tale to a child. Ask the child to whisper the same story to the next, and on to the next, until the story has made its way on through the room. Have the final student relate the story to the rest of the class, and discuss the differences and why they might have arisen.
- After reading a folktale, discuss the story's meaning in terms of what the characters needed, desired, hoped for, recognized. What did they accept and reject, given their limitations? What kind of good existed in the world, and what kind of evil? What kind of community developed? What kind of individuality developed?
- Choose a meaningful line or paragraph from a story you have just read and have the students recite it communally.
- Choose a student to represent each character in a story you will be reading. When the action turns to that character, have the student act out the narrative as you read, or directly after you read.

Folktales take their origins from specific cultures. This cultural origin affects everything about the tale: plot situations, characters, settings, language, motivations, and assumptions. More largely the cultural origin will impact the meanings of the stories and how those meanings are carried out. It will affect the way the world is viewed, how the communal life is viewed, how the individual life is viewed. In fact, everything about the story's presentation will be affected by that story's cultural origin.

It is for this reason that folktales cannot be dissociated from their cultural connections. Though a basic story, perhaps even universal in its appeal, might be teased out, the way in which that story is presented and the ways in which it creates its meanings are part of a cultural heritage.

In *The Feather Merchants* (1993), Steve Sanfield, like James Berry, uses his language to suggest cultural connections. Here, Rabbi Faivel of Chelm wonders why the government does not simply mint as many coins as it likes, rather than taxing the poor. Rassi Fishel responds that it is just like God and the angels.

> "God and the angels? What are you talking about, Reb Fishel?"
> "You know, Reb Faivel, that every time a human being does a good deed he creates an angel. Now, God could create all the angels he wants, but he doesn't do so. Why doesn't he? I'll tell you why. He would rather have your angel than his own. It's the same with taxes. Of course the government could produce as many zlotys as it likes, but it would much rather have yours." (75)

The idiomatic nature of the language—"Do you know why? I'll tell you why"— the use of the familiar Reb, the easy connection between matters spiritual and earthly, all point to the Jewish culture out of which the story arises.

But the connections are deeper. Beneath the humor of the exchange there is the pain of a persecuted people who sense the general malice of the government towards the other, particularly when the other is weaker. The response to this is not despair, but a kind of noble endurance and a recognition that the government is no closer to them than God himself. This deep underlying sense is what gives the story power. Put that same story in the mouth of the corporate executives walking down Wall Street, and the entire meaning and power of the story is lost.

Retellers of folktales to a new audience—perhaps a child in North America— are faced with the challenge of finding ways to retain the cultural connections of the story. How to convey these connections to an audience unfamiliar with the language, assumptions, beliefs, communal rituals and practices, and idiosyncracies of the original culture? "One cannot possibly write the stories of a culture," writes Paul Goble, the author of Southwestern Native American folktales, "without this kind of deep understanding. I was once with the Zunis at the invitation of the schools; they wanted me to write stories of their mythology. But how can I? I know almost nothing about them, and would make major and minor mistakes all the time."

In contemporary North America, children's literature is the largest popular venue for the retelling of folktales. This has implications for writers like Paul Goble, who want to connect the story to its parent culture, who want to avoid the major and minor mistakes of a reteller who is not a part of that parent culture, and who want to speak to a child audience. The writer and illustrator need to find some way of establishing those connections, avoiding the cold and distant tone of a narrator that sees the parent culture as very other. In other words, the reteller and illustrator want to find ways not only to put themselves in the context of an artist working out of the original culture, but also to put the audience of the book, whether individual or communal, in the position of an audience from that culture.

Authors and illustrators have taken this task on in a number of ways. For the writer, certainly, one way to establish this connection is through the language. Here again the suggestion of oral origins is important. The writer can establish the connection to a culture by re-creating its oral voice, using its diction and idioms, using conventional structures and rhythms, establishing ways for the voice of that culture to speak.

Writers can also use details of setting and character to establish the cultural connection. Here, Laurence Yep establishes the setting for the Mongolian folktale, *The Khan's Daughter* (1997).

> Domed tents spread all the way to the horizon like so many buttons sewn onto a giant sheet of brown felt. From their tops rose smoke like threads of cotton waving in the wind. And with the horses were tethered haughty camels and oxen and even big, hairy yaks. Everywhere soldiers and citizens hurried to get ready, for the Khan's great enemy was preparing to invade.
> Möngke tried not to stare, but he had never seen so many people in his life.

The accompanying illustration depicts the flying banners of the camp, as well as the barrel-chested Mongolian soldiers who are preparing wagons against the invasion. The elaborate costumes, the tents, the countryside, the mythological demons, the nature of the tests to which Möngke is put, even the instrument he plays, all speak to the culture.

The role of the illustrator in establishing the cultural connections is crucial; the illustrator must make a fundamental decision about how to establish those connections. In *The Journey of Meng*, Yang Ming-Li represents the action through illustrations that are more realistic than representational. Here, the illustrations depict settings, characters, and events much as any observer from any culture might see them, given the perspectives of the story. But in *The Khan's Daughter*, Jean and Mou-Sien Tseng do something somewhat different, though a number of the illustrations work as realistic depictions. Here Jean and Mou-Sien Tseng have not just accurately captured the details of the Mongolian landscape, architecture, and dress, but have, at times, rendered the illustrations in a style appropriate to the culture's art forms. In other words, the illustrators represent the perspectives of an artist from within the culture. This is evident in the stylized depictions of the capturing of wild horses, in the flattened dimensions of the first meeting between Möngke and the Khan, and, most especially, in the vividly colored demons that Möngke must face.

In making this decision, the illustrator argues that the cultural context of the story is conveyed not only through the oral voice, and not only through plot situations and textual detail, but through the illustrations as well. In this sense the illustrations depict not only the cultural setting, but how that cultural setting might be viewed by someone from within the culture.

Other illustrators make this decision even more radically by choosing to depict the entire work in the artistic style of the originating culture. In Katherine Paterson's *The Tale of the Mandarin Ducks* (1990), Leo and Diane Dillon use a distinctive Japanese style, *ukiyo-e,* noted for its flat perspectives, flat characters, and distinctively postured forms. Each illustration depicts the story of Shozo and how his kindness leads him first to disgrace, then to love. In Sumiko Yagawa's *The Crane Wife* (1981), Suekichi Akaba illustrates the familiar story of the man who is kind to a crane and then rewarded by her love, a love destroyed when he becomes too curious. The subtle, deft illustrations use the strong, yet thin lines, the blurred and mysterious background, the formal posturing, and the isolating setting of Japanese art as well, so that the reader enjoys the story from the perspective of a Japanese audience.

In his *Rapunzel* (1997), Paul Zelinsky decided to use the art of the Italian Renaissance to illustrate his story. He used the artistic techniques of the period to capture that art form: the lush colors, the posed forms, the intricate background designs, the dramatic architecture, the vivid reflected light, the use of mirrors and distorted reflections, the significant use of interiors, the stylized exteriors. In using these forms, Zelinsky placed his audience in the cultural world of the story, allowing his audience to see the story as an early listener might have seen it.

The Folktale and Its Variants

In Ed Young's *Lon Po Po* (1989), Sheng, Tao, and Paotze are left alone when their mother goes to visit Po Po, their grandmother. While she is gone, a wolf comes and convinces them that he is their Po Po. Only when she sees the wolf's bushy

Pointers for Teachers

Writing Possibilities
- Rewrite a tale in the language of today, changing the setting and diction to a contemporary one.
- Have students write a simulated folktale by following the motifs suggested here:

  One of the family members is absent from home because of a misfortune

  An interdiction is addressed to the hero

  The villain attempts to deceive the hero

  The villain, falling to the hero's deception, unwittingly helps the hero

  The villain is defeated

  The initial misfortune is overturned

tail and hairy face does Sheng realize they must escape; she cleverly convinces the wolf that they will pick ginkgo nuts for him. Safely up the tree, the children let down a basket to bring the wolf up into the branches. But when he is close, they drop the basket and so kill the wolf, which allows them to return safely home.

In *Sootface* (1994), an Ojibwa story retold by Robert San Souci, two sisters who are lazy and bad-tempered force their other sister to do all the work, and soon she is seared by the fire and covered with ashes. She is laughed at and mocked by the villagers. One day the Invisible Warrior, a great and mighty hunter, sends his sister to Sootface's village to find a wife for him; only the most kind and honest woman, however, will be able to see him. Sootface, who has no fine clothes, drapes herself with birchbark. She is, indeed, able to see the Invisible Warrior, and, when the Warrior's sister dresses and bathes Sootface, she is renamed Dawn-Light.

Both of these stories are familiar. *Lon Po Po* is a Red Riding Hood story, in which the young child—here three children—is threatened by a wolf who affects a disguise. Where the Western tale often ends with disaster and then salvation for Red Riding Hood, this Chinese variant instead emphasizes the cleverness of the children who are able to outwit and kill the wolf. *Sootface* is a Cinderella story in which the younger, despised, apparently ugly sister is, in fact, both gentle and beautiful. Though mocked for a time, eventually her goodness of heart becomes apparent as she wins the heart of the prince—here, the Invisible Warrior. As with all Cinderella stories, this is a tale in which true value is at first hidden, then finally revealed in all its graciousness.

Such tales are variants because of their roots in the oral tradition. Folktales, as they spread, took on new details, new characters, new plot situations. As storytellers added or deleted elements, the stories changed. As the stories moved from one group to another, from one culture to another, the storytellers changed them to adapt them to that group's, that culture's needs. In so doing, the characters, the settings, may have changed, but the essential plotlines remained quite similar. When we read, then, the story of Rhodopis in Shirley Climo's *The Egyptian Cinderella* (1989), we might not recognize the name, but, when a falcon steals her slipper and delivers it to Pharaoh, who in turn begins to search all over Egypt for its tiny-footed owner, the motif is strikingly familiar.

The result is that, though many folktales are no longer dispersed and experienced primarily as oral stories, neither has the print medium frozen them in the sense of having preserved only a single version. The publication of many variants allows contemporary readers to encounter something of the oral experience, to see how the story fares with different tellers, different cultures.

The presence of variants means that authors have yet another choice to make in the retelling of folktales. They could follow what is sometimes called the "traditional" or "classic" story, which is that version most generally known in a culture. Margot Zemach's *The Three Little Pigs* (1988), for example, is faithful to the traditional story, including not only the episodes of the three houses, but also including the three attempts to trick the third little pig out of this house. It also includes the more gruesome—though "traditional"—elements of the story. Here, the first two little pigs do, in fact, get eaten up, and the third little pig boils the wolf and "had wolf soup for supper. Yumm-yum!" The accompanying illustration shows the wolf's tail protruding from the steaming pot.

But the reteller might also decide to tell one of the lesser known variants. When William Hooks came to the tale, he decided to retell an Appalachian version, a version in which there is no wolf at all: *The Three Little Pigs and the Fox* (1989). Tales such as this, Hooks writes in his preface, changed as they were told in the mountains, so that they emerged no longer from a faraway place, but from the hollows of Appalachia. "Every storyteller is unique, adding local color and regional language to capture and enchant an audience. This rendition of *The Three Little Pigs* is based on several oral versions I have heard over the years in the Great Smoky Mountains."

So far, all this is legitimate. Here is a storyteller who is retelling, not the "traditional" tale, but another one that sprang out of it as it encountered yet another oral tradition. The opening of the story reflects that tradition:

> The story happened a long time ago, way back when the animals could still talk around these parts. Back then they could say a whole lot more than *baa-baa, moo-moo, oink-oink,* and stuff like that. They could talk just like human folks.
> Back then there was this humongous mama pig. She built herself a house out of rocks in a pretty green holler over Black Mountain way. As soon as she'd finished, she moved into her fine rock house with her three piglets.

It is the diction that suggests the oral genesis of this story: "way back," "these parts," "humongous," "pretty green holler," "over Black Mountain way." This is the stuff of folklore.

But then there comes a difficulty. "In keeping with one of the truest roles of the storyteller," Hooks writes, "I have added a few flourishes of my own." Hooks is right here; each oral storyteller adds flourishes to the telling. In adding flourishes to the oral versions he heard in the Appalachians, he has simply continued that tradition on into print. But if a folktale is a story with an oral history, it might be argued that Hooks has stepped beyond the boundaries of the genre. Those details—which are uninvolved in the text—have no historical precedent in the "traditional" version, in published variants, or in other oral traditions. Yet, the story is clearly the familiar one.

This problem becomes clearer as the retellings press the boundaries of the genre and its oral tradition even further by adding more original, complex "flourishes." In Jon Scieszka's *The True Story of the Three Little Pigs* (1989), the story is told from the point of view of the wolf, who insists that "Nobody knows the real story, because nobody has ever heard *my* side of the story." He was actually only looking to borrow a cup of sugar, he claims, and it was his terrible cold that led him to sneeze and thus blow down the houses. Afterwards, "it seemed like a shame to leave a perfectly good ham dinner lying there in the straw. So I ate it up. Think of it as a big cheeseburger just lying there." Incapacitated by his sneezing, he is eventually jailed by the pig police and "they jazzed up the story with all of that 'Huff and

Pointers for Teachers

Hands-On Possibilities
- Have the students draw one scene from a folktale that has just been read in class, but have them put it into a different setting. Afterwards, discuss their choices.
- Have the students research a culture's art forms, looking for recurring patterns of shapes, objects, color, and style. Then, match those findings to a folktale from that culture, having students find as many similarities as possible.

---

puff and blow your house down.'" In Eugene Trivizas's *The Three Little Wolves and the Big Bad Pig (1993)*, the outlines of the story are the same, but the position of the characters has changed markedly. Now there are innocent wolves whose brick, concrete, and, finally, metal houses are destroyed by a malicious bully of a pig. In the end, the wolves build a house of flowers, and, when the pig smelled them, "his heart grew tender, and he realized how horrible he had been. Right then he decided to become a good pig. He started to sing and dance the tarantella."

Here the retellers are not retelling a variant; in fact, they are not retelling at all. Instead, they are using elements of the traditional tale in new and innovative ways. The story becomes most meaningful only when the reader is familiar with the traditional story; much of the pleasure in the reading comes from seeing the ways in which the reworking has been accomplished. However, these are not, strictly speaking, folktales, as they have no oral origins; they are not variants that emerge out of a culture but, instead, out of an individual imagination.

Folktales as Vehicles for Meaning in Children's Literature

It may be true, as Bruno Bettelheim argues (1975), that the Jack stories represent the maturing of the adolescent. Jack, climbing up the phallic beanstalk, confronts and defeats the older male figure and secures for himself the central place as mature provider for the household. But it might be argued that now, as folklore has entered into the arena of children's literature, those meanings are extraneous. Though the stories were originally told for an adult audience in many cultures, their new child audience has pushed such deep meanings even deeper.

Yet, the fact that the stories are still repeated, that they are so very familiar, that they appear in variant forms in cultures around the world, suggests that they do continue to convey meanings that are central to our experience as human beings, whether we are children or adults. The stories speak to us of human needs and desires, of our hopes for glory, of our recognition and rejection of limitations, of a world of benevolent and malevolent forces, of our need for community and our need for individual growth. They speak of our terrible longings and our joyous achievements. They focus on what is most significant to us as human beings.

Pointers for Teachers: Evaluating Books of Folktales

- How does the reteller handle issues of violence, vengeance, or other harsh subject matter in a manner appropriate to a child reader?
- What multiple levels of meaning exist in the tale? Can a child reader perceive these? Is it important that that reader be able to perceive all of these?
- How successful is the reteller in maintaining the oral quality of the tales?
- Where do you see evidence of the parent culture in the retelling? in the plot, characters, dress, setting, language, character motivation, assumptions about the ways in which the world works?
- How do the book's illustrations present the parent culture? Where can you see use of a culture's artistic individuality?

Issues in the Retelling of Folktales

Two wives walk through their shtetl. They have spent all day working in their houses, their farmyards, their kitchens, cleaning and cooking and doing chores while their husbands sit and study Torah. Now they are coming back from the sweat bath, and they look up and see the lights on in their husbands' studies.

The first clicks her tongue in scorn, then looks ahead, lifts her skirts, and sits in a bank of snow.

"Why do such a thing!" cries the second.

The first stands and lowers her skirts. "I should bring a warm ass to him?" she says.

This Jewish folktale, with its startling ending, establishes some of the difficulties inherent in retelling folktales for a child audience. Here is a story about adults, with tensions set in the adult world, and with a thinly veiled sexuality. Though this is folklore, is it the stuff of children's literature?

How does the adult character of folktales affect the retelling of those stories for a child audience?

The story of the two wives in the shtetl is a story that may not be within the bounds of children's literature at all. The conflict between the wives and the husbands is an adult conflict, and the tensions involved are not necessarily the stuff of children's stories. The ending, an ending that is bawdy and smacks of the wife's sexual revenge on her husband, is also far from the child's experience.

Because so much of folklore was aimed at a primarily adult audience, the tales are filled with material that may be applicable to an adult world, but not to a child's world. The tales may be filled with violence, sexuality, obscenity, a bawdiness that would not be appropriate to the audience that generally reads picture books. When Steve Sanfield came to write his *The Adventures of High John the Conqueror* (1989), for example, he eliminated the exaggerated, hyperbolic accounts of

High John's amazing sexual prowess, because he felt that such stories were not appropriate to his audience.

Stephen Kellogg faced much the same difficulty when he came to write his tall tales.

> Some of the material simply is not appropriate for a picture book audience. I haven't included some of the off-color stories about John Chapman (Johnny Appleseed), for example. I eliminated Pecos Bill's racism and alcoholism. I'm working on Mike Fink right now, and considering the audience, I'll have to tone down his obsession with violence without diminishing the impact of his vitality and energy-something that is very difficult to do. I don't want to take away from Mike Fink his ragged, rough-and-ready character, but much of his violence is not appropriate for a picture book audience (1992).

If Kellogg had been writing an academic text on the North American tall tale, a text meant to record the stories in their earliest forms, such a revisionist process would have been problematic. But Kellogg is about something very different; he is doing what every storyteller must do: adapt the story to the immediate audience. Again and again Kellogg returns to issues of audience, and, as a storyteller, he has made decisions about that child audience that impact his tales: Protagonists should not be bawdy, alcoholic, or violent.

At issue here is whether or not such decisions violate the integrity of the tales. On the one hand, it does seem to be the case that the optimum way of presenting these cultural stories would be to present them as authentically as possible. To do this, one should find resources that are close to the authentic origins of the stories in order to get a sense of how the original audience might have heard them. On the other hand, all retellers change and adapt the stories to their immediate needs. Even such early sources are themselves adaptations and revisions. Just as a farmhouse is adapted and refashioned to meet the needs of its current occupants, so a story is always being refashioned to speak to its contemporary audience.

In this conflict between preservation and adaptation, writers of children's tales have generally, though not always, leaned toward the side of adaptation. The overwhelming weight that tips the scales here is Kellogg's: The writer needs to consider the audience, though, as C. S. Lewis warned in his famous essay, "On Three Ways of Writing for Children" (1952), most of us do not find "that violence and bloodshed, in a story, produce any haunting dread in the minds of children.

> As far as that goes, I side impenitently with the human race against the modern reformer. Let there be wicked kings and beheadings, battles and dungeons, and let villains be soundly killed at the end of the book. Nothing will persuade me that this causes an ordinary child any kind or degree of fear beyond what he wants, and needs, to feel. For, of course, he wants to be a little frightened."

But the answer to Lewis is that there are substantive and qualitative differences between a knight beheading a terrible dragon, and an ending in which pretty, loving Snow White, having found her true love, traps her stepmother and places her into red hot iron shoes, forcing her to dance until she falls down dead.

(Paul Heins included this ending in his *Snow White* [1974], but the illustrator, Trina Schart Hyman, chose not to illustrate the scene.) A dragon is palpably fantastic, but the torturous death of a stepmother is much closer to realism.

The choices of various retellers reflect this debate. Wanda Gág, in her *Tales from Grimm* (1936), decided that her stories would be more gentle than the originals. In her account of "The Fisherman and His Wife," the bitterness and acrimony and shrewish quality of the wife are softened substantially. In "Hansel and Gretel," the wicked stepmother does not die; instead, she packs up her belongings in a large handkerchief and runs away. In the "Frog Prince," the princess is repelled by the frog, but never commits the kind of violence against him that marks other tellings. Here, Gág has chosen to avoid unpleasantness in retellings for children and to include a strong, reassuring narrator who speaks directly to the reader in a secure voice. When the witch dies in "Hansel and Gretel," the narrator notes, "That was the end of her, and who cares?" (20). At the end of "The Frog Price," she concludes conventionally: "It is not hard to guess, I'm sure, that when they were grown up they were married and lived happily ever after" (188).

Conversely, David Wisnewski's *Golem* (1996) confronts issues that may seem beyond the boundaries of children's literature. In the story, Rabbi Loew creates a giant man of clay who is able to fight back and destroy those who would kill the Jewish community in Prague. The picture book, with disturbing and violent images, poses difficult questions: the uses of force and violence, the dangers of meddling with the supernatural, the vitality of life, the ethics of using another. These are difficult issues, and, when the book concludes with the Rabbi's destruction of the clay giant, they are not resolved.

One of the most difficult tasks for the reteller of folktales for children, then, is to recast the story, considering the audience, without losing the vitality and depth of the story. Insofar as they are adapted to a child audience, folktales may begin to move away from earliest versions. But, at the same time, it is the storyteller's task to adapt and change, as well as to preserve. The balance between these two impulses will often lie directly on the boundary of children's literature.

Who may retell a folktale?

Though one of the shortest questions and one that seems innocuous, the issue of who may retell a folktale is one of the thorniest issues in this field. Must a reteller come from within a culture? If not, does the reteller face insurmountable difficulties? A reteller from outside the originating culture must recognize that he or she might not understand the story as the culture does. Emphasis, character development, significance of setting—all of these elements might be quite different to a writer coming from the outside. Add to these the questions of idiomatic language and the capturing of an authentic oral voice, and the difficulties compound.

But beyond the difficulties of the actual writing is another issue. Does a writer have the right to tell a story from another culture, one not his or her own? Are a culture's stories akin to its artifacts, in the sense that they belong to the parent culture? If so, would retelling these by an outsider be what amounts to cultural theft? And, if the answer to this last question is yes, all the issues of the actual writing are moot.

Certainly there are some writers who would argue that cultural theft is an accurate term. Writers of African American folktales get them right, such critics would argue, precisely because they have heard all their lives the sounds and rhythms of the language that give life to the tales. But, beyond this, such writers come out of the traditional culture; they understand the larger meanings, and sense in their own selves the import of the stories because they emerge out of the consciousness of their own culture. An outsider telling the tales, no matter how well versed in the culture, can never participate in that consciousness. Nor, such critics would argue, should they. Beyond getting the details right, there is the issue of ownership. To such critics, telling stories from outside the writer's culture is, in fact, exactly analogous to appropriating relics and antiquities. The life of one people might be the curios of another.

If this argument was accepted in its most extreme manifestation, it would mean that no writer could legitimately retell the stories of any culture but his or her own. It would mean accepting as axiomatic the belief that no one from another culture could understand the tales of another. And it would mean accepting the belief that no child can learn or grow from the folktale of another culture, because its meanings and subtleties would be forever opaque. Folktales, in this sense, transmit cultural, not human, meanings.

Some writers would soften such a position. Though it might be better for the tales to come out of a writer who comes from within the culture simply because that writer will get the words and language correct, it is not the case that cultures are isolates in which stories carry no meaning beyond the boundaries of the cultural circle. Folktales instead speak to that which is human in all of us, meaning that all listeners and readers can enjoy the stories, at least on some level.

Here the question becomes sharpened. If the tales are only meaningful to the parent culture, then perhaps they cannot be meaningfully retold outside that culture. But if the stories speak to that which is human in all of us, then they are accessible to all of us. We may not all of us come from a northern European or Native American background, but when we read the story of "Hansel and Gretel" or the Native American tale of "The Lost Children," we recognize the pain of childhood loss and abandonment, even if the stories are from outside our cultures.

Given this common humanity, other writers would argue, it is not legitimate to argue that the tales should be told only by someone from within the culture. Because the stories speak to all of us, they should be told by a broader spectrum of writers than that represented by a single culture. At the same time, given that the stories do emerge from a peculiar culture, the reteller is responsible for learning as much as possible about that culture so that he or she will get the details of the story, its assumptions, and its language right.

Steve Sanfield, for example, has written *A Natural Man: The True Story of John Henry* (1986) and *The Adventures of High John the Conqueror,* but the Jewish story-teller has also written tales of Chelm in *The Feather Merchants.* In spanning these cultures, Sanfield argues that the stories speak directly to our common humanity:

"We now share many of these tales and characters, either consciously or unconsciously.... They help us to see beyond ourselves, to speak freely, and ultimately to understand each other." Still, he suggests, the artist is responsible to the parent culture. "Part of the artist's job is to take the unique and make it universal so that we can break down the barriers that seem to separate us, barriers of race, color, language, class, and religion, showing our children and ourselves that we're all in this together. It seems to me that, at the very, very least, this breaking down of barriers must be done in such a way that it honors the tales and the people who originally told them." For Sanfield, the meaning of the tales and their ability to break down barriers legitimizes their retelling; the stance suggests that cultural barriers do not have to be impermeable at all.

In *The Hunterman and the Crocodile* (1997), Baba Wagué Diakité tells a West African story. A crocodile family, caught in the sun during the journey to Mecca, convinces a hunterman to carry them to the water. But, once there, they trap him and prepare to eat him. None of the other animals will help him, because man has universally abused them. But the rabbit tricks the crocodiles by asking them to show him how the hunterman carried all the crocodiles; once captured, the hunterman brings them to his village to eat. But, on the way, he hears that his wife is ill and must have crocodile tears to help. When these are given, the hunterman, in gratitude, returns the crocodiles to the water. "Donso never forgot the lessons he learned from the cow, the horse, the chicken, the mango tree, and the rabbit. From that time forward he has reminded people of the importance of living in harmony with nature and the necessity of placing Man among—not above—living things."

The tale is African, and the illustrations are African designs on hand-painted tiles. But the brisk narrative, the trickery, and the lesson of humanity's place in the world is one to which all children, African or not, can respond. Elements such as these—elemental justice, the need for love, the need for security, the need to be the hero—these are elements that all readers recognize.

How do folktales pass on cultural wisdom?

Certainly one large element of the folktale is delight; the tales survive because they entertain us, move us, show us our foibles and our glories. But the tales also survive because they communicate to us the wisdom of our cultures. They are tales that speak to us about the nature of our world and about our place in that world. They tell us about ourselves and our communities, and show us images—often very stark and explicit images—of the good and the evil. They warn and encourage us by showing and suggesting that our lives are more than the merely physical.

Again and again folklore suggests the presence of a world beyond the senses that is intimately concerned with human life. It suggests that there really are malignant forces in the universe. There are witches and trolls, hobgoblins and demons who are out to trick and damn. And, though these are externalized versions of evil, the folktale suggests that their evil lies within us: the stepmother who will murder her children in the forest, the sisters who scorn and humiliate a younger sibling, the brothers who leave their youngest brother nothing but a cat. The folktales do not quail at all at showing the dark side of human experience. Neither do they quail at showing the light side of life. There is often the wise old woman who warns us—"Do not touch the magic pasta pot!" "Do not take that path!" "Do not choose that casket!" If there is malevolence in the world, there is also benevolence. There is the fairy who will get a young girl to the ball, the clever young girl who will help the beloved through the labyrinth, the mighty swings of hammers that will help a crew escape a cave-in.

In the Chinese folktale retold by Robert San Souci in *The Enchanted Tapestry* (1990) and Marilee Heyer in *The Weaving of a Dream* (1986), an older woman has three sons; two are lazy, while one cuts wood for the family and the mother weaves beautiful tapestries that they sell. But one tapestry she works on for over a year, weaving her own blood and tears into it, and, when it is finished, the youngest, hardworking brother sees, in its fields and gardens and house, his mother's ideal. When his older brothers insist that it be sold, the youngest refuses, until suddenly it is whisked away by the east wind. One by one the brothers go to find it while the mother, stricken by the loss of her dream, lies dying. The two older brothers succumb to temptations and do not proceed in the ardors of the quest. The youngest braves all the difficulties and, finally, finds the tapestry in the hands of the beautiful and elegant Queen of the Fairies, who returns it to him. Home, he spreads it out before his all but dead mother, and, even as she revives, the tapestry continues to expand and expand until the ideal has in fact become reality, and the Queen herself steps out from the house to marry the youngest son. The two older sons, who return to find this fine new house, are whisked away by the wind.

This story of a quest and its fulfillment is delightful merely in the suspense of its narrative plot. But it also tells about the values of its culture, values of hard work, of honoring the parent, of rewards for virtue and faithfulness. There is also a sense here of the potential for evil that lies within all, as well as the sense of beneficent external forces that recognize that potentiality and honor the overcoming of it.

In this way, folktales carry in their plotlines the accumulated wisdom of a culture. That wisdom may speak to large issues of how we live our lives. It may speak to communal justice, or potential warnings: "Stay on the path on your way to Grandmother's house." But it is crucial to recall that such wisdom is not mere didacticism. The stories tell us much about what kind of beings we humans are.

What does the presence of so many repeating patterns and motifs in folktales suggest about their nature?

The easy answer to the question of cause in variation among folktales goes back to their oral nature. These are stories that are told and retold and retold, with the result that, though basic plot structures will remain consistent, the details surrounding those structures will change as one teller stresses one element, while a different teller stresses another. In *A Ring of Tricksters* (1997), for example, Virginia

Hamilton retells African stories that migrated to North America during slavery times, and then migrated back to Africa with freed and escaped slaves. The result is a collection of stories that retain basic African trickster structures, but have been influenced in their details by their sojourns in the southern United States and in the Caribbean West Indies.

Perhaps, however, there are different, deeper causes for the similarities in so many folktales. Perhaps the similarities come out of mythic patterns deeply embedded in human culture. Perhaps the similarities come out of archetypes that lie in the human consciousness. The sense here is that there are certain ways of using and creating stories that express the human experience. That is, stories necessarily fall into certain structures simply because they are told by human beings.

In 1958, Vladimir Propp argued in his *Morphology of the Folktale* that folktales could be examined profitably through their structures; he suggested an examination of the architectural aspects of literature, proposing thirty-one "functions" that are arranged, selected, and finally adapted by a folktale teller. The small details may vary, but the order and presence of a group of the functions would not. So a folktale might proceed as follows:

> Function 1: One of the family members absents himself or herself from home.
>
> Function 2: An interdiction is addressed to the hero.
>
> Function 6: The villain attempts to deceive the victim.
>
> Function 8: The villain causes harm to one of the family.
>
> Function 18: The villain is defeated.
>
> Function 19: The initial misfortune is liquidated.

These functions may suggest the plot of Red Riding Hood, but in broad outlines they may suggest the plot structures of works as complex as *The Iliad*. Propp's structural argument suggests yet another cause for multiple variants of a single tale. He referred to this as a typology of narrative structures.

In children's literature, variants have come about most especially because of the retellers' concern for audience. If there are certain problematic details, then those might be easily left out of a child's version of the story. Many versions of such tales for children work deliberately to tone down or delete such elements, with the result that such elements become institutional as variants. Thus, in most retellings of the Red Riding Hood story, as in Mireille Levert's *Little Red Riding Hood* (1995), the protagonist ends up victorious and the violent and sexual elements are downplayed. This is even true in Ed Young's *Lon Po Po* (1989), a Chinese variant of the Red Riding Hood story in which three children outwit the wolf posing as their grandmother. In Patricia McKissack's *Flossie and the Fox* (1986), Flossie, the Red Riding Hood character, must successfully travel the road to the McCutchin Place with a basket of eggs coveted by the fox. When the fox appears, Flossie is able to outwit him long enough to get to the farm with the eggs intact; there, the fox is chased off by the hounds. In this variant, the young protagonist is much more able, much more adept at dealing with her situation. She defeats the fox by her own wit.

But some versions do adhere to the more disturbing original ending, in which Red Riding Hood is not saved. Christopher Coady ends his *Red Riding Hood* (1991) with the words "gobbled up," and the illustration depicts an empty bed and cloak, both heavily stained with blood. Beni Montresor ends his *Little Red Riding Hood* (1991) with a violent eating scene, followed by three spreads of a pacific Red Riding Hood floating cruciform in the womblike belly of the wolf. Here are two versions that have refused the variant of the typical child's version.

This wide range of variation is especially evident in Cinderella stories, which change small but significant elements. What, for example, happens to the father? How many balls are there that Cinderella attends? How violently do the sisters try to pass the test of the shoe? What happens to the stepsisters? All of these questions are answered in various ways.

But the greatest variances occur when the story is placed in varying cultures. Susan Jeffers's *Cinderella* (1985)—the version of Charles Perrauld—places the story in its traditional Western European context. But in tales like Shirley Climo's *The Egyptian Cinderella* (1989) and *The Irish Cinderlad* (1996), the stories change dramatically. In *The Egyptian Cinderella,* the story focuses almost wholly on the search for the young girl who will fit into the red slipper dropped into Pharaoh's lap by a falcon. In *The Irish Cinderlad,* the search is for a boy who has left behind enormous footprints after performing deeds of bravery. In Rafe Martin's *The Rough-Face Girl* (1992) and Robert D. San Souci's *Sootface* (1994), the story is set in a Native American context in which the protagonist is able to prove herself by being able to see the Invisible Warrior. In Alan Schroeder's *Smokey Mountain Rose* (1997) and Joanne Compton's *Ashpet* (1994), the story is set in Appalachia and the prince is transformed into a "real rich feller" or the doctor's son.

Variants suggest the enormous power and fecundity of the folktale. They show the effects of storytelling, or consideration of place and audience. They, in their very existence, suggest much about the human propensity to story.

Retellers and Illustrators of Folktales

Retellers of folktales for a child audience must begin with the recognition that they are telling and illustrating the stories for a new audience. It is an audience separated from the original both in terms of age and culture. The decisions that each reteller makes are determined by his or her vision of folklore, the perceived meaning and significance of the tale, and the author's perception of the intended audience. The plurality of visions leads to an extraordinary variety in terms of the retellings, as writers decide whether to write from within or without the culture, whether to include all or only selected elements of the tales, and whether to emphasize the common humanity of the story or its cultural uniqueness.

Steven Kellogg (b. 1941)

Steven Kellogg is one of North America's most prolific picture book authors and illustrators, and his exuberant style is easily recognizable. His illustrations burst with the energy of movement, light, clashing and complementary colors, and a thousand details, details so intriguing that, at times, he seems to have many foci.

Kellogg uses this exuberance to expand traditional stories; he does not necessarily feel bound to present the oldest, most established version of a tale, or to preserve original oral elements. Instead, he vigorously and freely adapts stories to create something both old and new. In his *The Three Little Pigs* (1997), for example, Kellogg tells the very familiar story, but even the cover suggests that there will be enormous differences: The three pigs are dressed in baker's outfits and hold an enormous waffle in their hooves. Only the bare outlines of the story are recognizable.

But there is something else striking about his version of *The Three Little Pigs:* the lack of consequential violence. "Often during the course of the story," Kellogg writes in the book's note, "many of the principal characters are devoured, but I decided that there would be no fatalities in my retelling. I opted to go lightly on the wolf as the story concludes." In fact, the final illustration of the wolf puts him on a beach waving a shirt that announces, "Thugs Need Hugs Too." The sense of "opting"—of making choices—suggests how Kellogg sees himself as a reteller. He is not preserving an original version, but participating in the tradition as an active storyteller. "This is a part of the fun of these tales: each person who tells the story brings something unique to it, so that it becomes renewed. And if certain aspects of a given interpretation are banal, those parts will wither, they will not have enough vitality to be accepted. So I see myself as continuing—though in print—a long tradition of oral retellings" (1992).

Kellogg is best known in folklore as a reteller of North American folktales with such books as *Paul Bunyan* (1984), *Johnny Appleseed* (1988), *Pecos Bill* (1986), *Mike Fink* (1992), and *Sally Ann Thunder Ann Whirlwind Crockett* (1995). In these books Kellogg has stayed closer to original versions than in his *Three Little Pigs*. But he has also chosen to play down the violence of the stories, recognizing that the audience is the child reader. Instead, he plays up the exaggerated qualities of the story, maintaining an even tone in the narrative voice while showing the most extraordinary events in the visuals. "Bill's plans were interrupted when he was ambushed by a giant rattlesnake," Kellogg writes in *Pecos Bill*, but it is left to the illustration to show the huge scale of the rattlesnake, which curls around a mountain, hiding the monster that will attack Bill once the snake has taken his opportunity. The drama and movement of the episode are all conveyed visually.

The difficulty Kellogg found with the tall tale lay with the structuring of a picture book. Most of the tall tales are very episodic, with many disparate elements that divide the narrative episodes. But a picture book requires more of a continuous narrative thread. Each of the books found a different center, often involving movement. *Paul Bunyan* centered on lumbering and followed the character from roots in Maine, down to the Southwest, and finally north to Alaska. With *Pecos Bill* and *Mike Fink,* Kellogg focused on a single extraordinary characteristic—ranching and wrestling, respectively—and placed those characters in distinctive regions, Texas and the Mississippi Valley. In *Johnny Appleseed* Kellogg used the westward movement of the pioneers, but also played with the balance between the historical adventures of Johnny Chapman and the more mythical adventures of Johnny Appleseed. These structure what might otherwise be quite disparate.

Rarely has text been so appropriate to illustrator; the utter exuberance and hyperbole of the stories is matched by the energy and high drama and action of the illustrations. Whether it be an explosion on a riverboat, a contest of cutting trees, the whirlwind of a stallion, or Sally Ann's battle with alligators, the illustrations are filled with movement, so that the stories are tall not only in their telling, but in their visuals. In this way Kellogg is not replicating older versions, but using his new version of the tales' large meanings to inspire the art. "When I think of the American tall tale," he writes, "I think of exaggeration, humor, color, movement, action, vitality, and high-spiritedness" (1992); these are precisely the qualities he tries to capture in his work.

Paul O. Zelinsky (b. 1953)

Like Stephen Kellogg, Paul Zelinsky fills his illustrations with very precise and specific detail. But his detailing is of a very different order. Where Kellogg's work is marked by bright, exaggerated action and humor, Zelinsky's illustrations recall the art of the Renaissance and portraiture of the seventeenth-century masters. Where Kellogg's illustrations are filled with almost kinetic movement, Zelinsky's suggest the caught moment in which time is arrested. The bright deft lines and watercolors of Kellogg here give way to the more somber oils, giving the folktales of Zelinsky a much more serious quality.

Zelinsky's *Rapunzel* (1997) is typical of the technique. He decided to allow the illustrations to tell much of the story, so the text itself is spare and concise. The two most dramatic and moving episodes of the story—the taking of the child Rapunzel from her parents, and the reunion of the bereft Rapunzel and her children with the blinded Prince, a moment of loss and a moment of recovery—are both told solely through evocative illustrations in which characters move through backgrounds that one might find in the forms of a Renaissance painting. In fact, the oil paintings are based directly on the Renaissance tradition—particularly the work of Raphael—and the portraits of Rembrandt; the student of art—though not the child reader—will find direct echoes of the work of both these artists. Zelinsky captures the period and culture of the tale through exquisite detail, all rendered through using the artistic techniques of the Renaissance. What the Dillons do for *The Tale of the Mandarin Ducks,* Zelinsky does for *Rapunzel.*

Both *Hansel and Gretel* (1984), whose text was written by Rika Lasser, and *Rumpelstiltskin* (1986) show these same qualities. The oil paintings are marked by enormous precision of detail, shown with great clarity. Zelinsky also borrows the medieval technique of simultaneous action, so that one illustration can show the nurse of *Rumpelstiltskin* in several different places searching for the little man, or

Rapunzel can be shown simultaneously being cursed and, far away, lamenting her wretched state.

But Zelinsky's greatest strength is his ability to balance a dual emphasis. On the one hand, the eye is drawn to the backgrounds, something he establishes in the frontispieces. Often this background is strange and threatening, as in the looming woods of *Hansel and Gretel* or the parched deserts of *Rapunzel.* On the other hand, Zelinsky also turns the eye dramatically to character. Here he is especially powerful with the wicked or unnatural characters, often the most intriguing characters of the stories. The bent and turbaned witch of *Hansel and Gretel,* the pop-eyed and spindly figure of Rumpelstiltskin, and the huge and angry figure of Rapunzel's witch all take center stage. (In one brilliant overturning of these two foci, Zelinsky pictures the vanquished Rumpelstiltskin on a completely blank page.)

Though the illustrations dominate in telling the narrative, Zelinsky is much more willing to probe the subtleties and depths of the folktales than Kellogg, and this probing is more often disturbing than humorous. In *Hansel and Gretel,* the witch is a real alternate mother, providing everything that the childrens' stepmother (who is never called their mother, but their father's wife) does not provide. Still, at the end, both mothers offer death, and both times the father is impotent, yet forgiven by the children. In *Rumpelstiltskin* Zelinsky probes the allure of an innocent girl by the male world, a world she is able to defeat with the help of another woman. Only at the end does the Prince come in, but he has been no help at all in deciphering Rumpelstiltskin's riddle. While the Queen holds her child lovingly and tightly, the Prince is left apart. In *Rapunzel,* the unnatural results of an unnatural love are explored, results that are overcome only with a maturer, natural love.

In each case, Zelinsky allows full play to the more mature—and more difficult—themes of these stories, which all end happily, but which hold out the real possibility of disaster at several levels. Zelinsky's illustrations capture the culture of the story both in terms of its setting and the techniques of the depiction. But those illustrations also depict the human dilemmas posed by the stories, dilemmas that cut across all cultural boundaries, and may, in the subject matter, press at the boundaries of children's literature.

Ed Young (b. 1931)

In stark contrast to the precise detailing of Stephen Kellogg and Paul Zelinsky, Ed Young's artwork is loose, often indistinct and abstract, and, at times, suggestive of two completely different images. His cover illustration for *Night Visitors* (1995), for example, may be an ant or it may be the face of a fierce warrior, an anomaly that is united in the book. The opening image of the wolf in *Lon Po Po* (1989) may be the wolf or it may be the crouching grandmother. The hillside of the first illustration may be a gently rolling yard or it may be the enlarged head of the wolf himself. Instead of precision, there is ambiguity, a quality that is appropriate to the folktales themselves.

Born in Tientsin, China, Young draws on his Chinese past as he illustrates. In works like *The Emperor and the Kite* (1967), he used oriental cut paper techniques. In *Lon Po Po* and *Night Visitors,* he turned to pastels to create his images. In each case the illustrations are marked by bold, large shapes and wide backgrounds that loom hugely against the individual; often his characters seem actually to merge into the darker backgrounds. In *Cat and Rat* (1995), the twelve animals of the Chinese zodiac seem to struggle to pull themselves away from the darkly colored backgrounds, and their frenzied, disturbed motions fill the page with uneasy energy.

The ambiguity and indistinctness of the illustration complement similar qualities in the folktales. In *Lon Po Po,* for example, three children are visited by a wolf disguised as their grandmother, and the children's inability to clearly perceive the difference is suggested by the indistinct illustrations of the wolf, which are dark and overhead and huge—altogether threatening. In *Night Visitors,* Young moves into a dreamlike world where Ho Kuan, the good son who believes in the importance of even the smallest creature, sees ants as warriors, and warriors as ants. In *The Turkey Girl* (1996), a Zuni Cinderella story, the stones of a Zuni temple suggest the forms of the turkeys that have transformed the life of the young Matsaki. For Young, establishing parallels and repeating patterns is the task of his illustrations.

But if there is ambiguity in the illustrations, there is none in the strong morality of the stories. *Night Visitors* is a story about respect, as Ho Kuan comes to understand the importance of respect "for all forms of life, no matter how small"; it is not by accident that the book is dedicated to St. Francis. *The Turkey Girl* warns against the betrayal of the natural world, while *White Wave* (1979), a tale by Diane Wolkstein that Young illustrates with the repeating loopy pattern of the snail shell, focuses on the meaning and significance of commitments. Each of the books is marked by a real concern for how it is that lives are to be lived; they carry a wisdom from their cultural roots.

Though Young's personal background is quite varied—his descent is English, Chinese, and Wyandotle Indian—most of his work is in Chinese folklore. Of these works, *Lon Po Po* is his most accomplished, garnering him the Caldecott Medal. The illustrations always reach over entire spreads, but Young often divides them up to form panels that are sometimes continuous, sometimes discontinuous. By placing these panels in conjunction, Young presents startling contrasts, such as the three worried faces of the young children placed directly beside a panel dominated by the wolf's huge snout and teeth, or the spreads depicting the children pulling the wolf up the nut tree and his cascading fall as they release him. Here, as in many folktales, evil is defeated by goodness and innocence armed with wit and cleverness.

Julius Lester (1939) and Jerry Pinkney (1939)

One of the more successful collaborations in contemporary retellings of folktales is that of the illustrator Jerry Pinkney and the writer Julius Lester. Together, particularly in their *Brer Rabbit* volumes, the two have recast African American folktales, adapting them to a new, more contemporary audience, most especially through the use of language.

In early books, *To Be a Slave* (1968), *Long Journey Home: Stories from Black History* (1988), and *The Knee-High Man and Other Tales* (1985), Lester had shown his fascination with the African American experience, particularly as told through the stories of that tradition. In *To Be a Slave* Lester had gathered together first-person accounts of slavery days, the whole becoming a powerful and moving work that tore at the reader's sense of justice. But it was *The Knee-High Man* that really pointed the way to Lester's more recent work; there he showed how folk stories could express the powerful emotions of the tradition. And here, instead of the rage and horror of *To Be a Slave,* Lester used humor and wit to express the nature of a culture that had to define itself even while it was being enslaved.

In his *John Henry* (1994), Lester retells the familiar story of the man who defeated a steam drill. But it is not just this story that he focuses on; he instead wants to show a man of gigantic stature and of noble heart. He is a man who, armed with strength and good nature, is cloaked with a rainbow around his shoulders. When he hammers, he sings, and all of his actions are witnessed by the sun and the moon, who are eager to see what he is up to. Lester's language is filled with metaphor: a voice "like bat wings on tombstones," a boulder "hard as anger," a rainbow shining "like hope that never dies," a man not bigger "than a wish that wasn't going to come true."

In the end, John Henry dies, but Lester wants to suggest the larger implications of the story: "Dying ain't important. Everybody does that. What matters is how well you do your living." This larger than life message also impacts Jerry Pinkney's watercolors. The illustrations are always large and full, sometimes spanning an entire spread, more often spanning three-quarters of it. John is pictured as large, but not a giant; Pinkney does not want to put him outside human experience, because the story is about human experience. And, usually, he carries the rainbow on his shoulders to suggest the interest the natural world takes in this prodigy.

Though the story is an old one, Lester does not hesitate to add details that are strikingly new, though Pinkney chooses not to duplicate this technique in his illustrations. When John Henry is very young, he "helped his papa rebuild the porch he had busted through, and added a wing onto the house with an indoor swimming pool and one of them jacutzis." The detail is striking when placed in a tale that seems to be so old. Lester uses the same technique in the Brer Rabbit stories he tells, mentioning sneakers and pink halter tops. The inclusion of such contemporary details suggests something of Lester's view of the folktale and its retelling.

When Julius Lester turned to his retelling of the Brer Rabbit stories, he was faced with the difficulty that all retellers of these tales encounter: the character of Uncle Remus himself, a slave. Instead of simply trying to redo Joel Chandler Harris's Uncle Remus, Lester decided that he would focus on the stories themselves and create a narrator, not through the development of a new Uncle Remus, but through the creation of a distinctive voice.

> [T]he personality of my storyteller would be communicated entirely through voice, through his asides, imagery, and allusions. Perhaps because I had grown up during

the Golden Age of Radio, perhaps because I had had a live radio show for eight years, I know the power of the voice and all that can be conveyed through the sound of it. However, I was not aware that anyone had attempted to put on paper the atmosphere created by the unseen human voice, to recreate the sound and feeling of what it was like to sit on the porch late at night and hear voices coming from the darkness as the old people told tales. This is how the slaves had told and heard the tales, and this is how I had heard the tales as a child (1988).

The voice, he decided, would be Southern and rural; it would speak in the vernacular, though not so strongly as to cause misunderstanding. It would be colorful and run-on, somewhat endearing. It would have rhythm and pacing built into its structure. And it would be contemporary.

The last is one of the richest decisions that Lester made. He would not be recreating stories told as they had been told during slavery times, but would, instead, recreate them as contemporary tales, in the manner that he had heard them. Thus, in *The Adventures of Brer Rabbit* (1987), the first of four volumes in *The Tales of Uncle Remus,* Lester pictures this version of the primping Brer Wolf's daughter:

> Brer Wolf's daughter, who had always thought Brer Rabbit kind of cute, put on her mascara and eyeliner and whatever else it is that the women put on their face. She squeezed herself into a pair of jeans four sizes too small. Have mercy! And she put on a pink halter top! When Brer Rabbit saw her, he thought he'd died and gone to heaven. (125)

The voice, as Lester maintains, is the element that holds together the teller and the reader or listener. There is a strong sense of the speaker's presence throughout all of the stories in each of the volumes, to the point that the teller will at times step out from the book to address the reader. At the end of the final story in volume four, for example, we hear that "Simon and Susanna went their way and from what I heard, they lived happily ever after." Then the teller concludes with a personal address: "And I hope you do too" (156).

Jerry Pinkney illustrates all the volumes by alternating colorful watercolors with black-and-white line drawings. As with *John Henry,* Pinkney resists the contemporary and places the images in contexts that would not have been unfamiliar to a nineteenth-century reader. What he uses to strike the eye instead is a union of animal and human lives. The animals all sport rural southern dress, even the grasshoppers. But they also interact with humans, each of whom wears very similar dress, as though there is nothing at all remarkable about such an exchange. At the same time, there is a comic awkwardness about dressed animals: the yellow scarf on the blacksnake, the clumsy trousers of the bear, the pointed shoes of the bullfrog, the problems of the fox's tail and his britches—all in *Further Adventures of Brer Rabbit, His Friends, Enemies, and Others* (1988). They are at home, yet not at home in these duds.

In the introduction to the final volume, Lester suggests the importance of retellings, even when the retellings cross cultural boundaries. "Do not our souls hunger for genuine experiences of others? Are not our spirits revived through contact with others whose spirits touch our spirits in a way that makes us feel better for having sat with them a while? Is not the essence of our lives the desire to live in relationships that will return to us an image of ourselves that we can love?" (xii). The storyteller, Lester suggests, unites "us to the mysteries that will always be, and at the same time animate[s] us with laughter and love."

Paul Morin (1959)

Paul Morin comes to the retellings of folktales as an illustrator. His desire is to involve vividly the culture out of which the story comes. But, instead of doing this through a flat medium, he uses heavily contoured painting, heavily textured canvas, and photographed objects to gain a sense of the nature of culture, particularly as it relates to the story at hand. His technique is the technique of assemblage.

In Tololwa Mollel's *The Orphan Boy* (1990), an old and lonely man is suddenly visited by a young boy who comes to do all of his work and to make him prosperous. But, when the old man's curiosity overcomes the trust that had built up between them, the boy vanishes, leaving the old man lonelier than ever. The story is played out on the African landscape, under the looming presence of the stars; the boy is actually the planet Venus come to earth. To capture the essence of the land and sky, Morin uses luminous blues to evoke the night sky, where shadows balance with the bright light of the stars. The land, however, is heavily textured, with a three-dimensional effect. This accentuates the terribly parched nature of the ground, which is dry as dust, both in look and in feel. Everywhere the grain of the canvas shows through, giving the viewer a powerful tactile sense of this world.

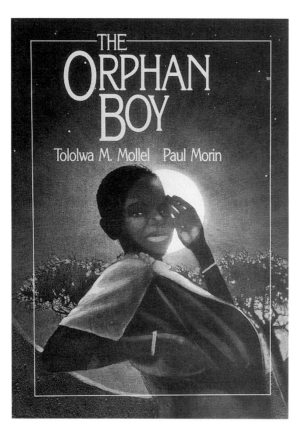

Illustration by Paul Morin for Tololwa M. Mollel's *The Orphan Boy*. Copyright © 1990. Reprinted by permission of Clarion Books.

For Julie Lawson's *The Dragon's Pearl* (1993), Morin adorned the cover with elements appropriate to the story: canvas, long reedy plants, red cloth, twine, bamboo, and a textured image of a Chinese dragon. The overleaf continues these motifs, but adds a gold Chinese coin and a large pearl. In the story, gentle Xiao Sheng cares for his mother during the drought, but, when he finds a magic pearl that makes everything fertile—even gold coins reproduce themselves—they became wealthy, though still generous. When two men come to steal the pearl, Xiao Sheng swallows it and himself becomes a dragon, later using his abilities to bring rain to the land. The people are blessed, though mother and son are forever separated.

Once again the landscape is crucial, and Morin uses his texture to accentuate the forms of the land and the quality of the light that shines down on it. The grass itself is raised and yields shadows. But it is the recurring sight of real elements that contributes to how we see Xiao Sheng's pattern of life: the rough canvas, the simple fishhook, the single gold coin, and the pearl, large and glowing. It sits so oddly against the rugged canvas, as it should, given the role it plays in the tale. Here the artist has expanded the traditional depictions of events through the creation of a strong tactile sense that strikes the eye and projects the meaning of the tale.

Virginia Hamilton (b. 1936)

The prolific author Virginia Hamilton has worked in many genres, but most recently she has turned her hand to folklore, particularly the folklore that emerged out of the African American experience of slavery. In these retellings, Hamilton tries to recapture the oral voice of the tales by creating narrators who seem to speak out of the period. But, in addition to these eloquent voices, Hamilton herself comments on the stories, suggesting that these are tales that depict the dignity and mobility of a voice that was enslaved. In depicting this, Hamilton depicts the innate dignity of all humanity. "These tales were created out of sorrow," she writes in *The People Could Fly.* "But the hearts and minds of the black people who formed them, expanded them, and passed them on to us were full of love and hope. We must look on the tales as a celebration of the human spirit" (xii).

In *The People Could Fly* (1985), Hamilton retells tales that had been told during slavery times. To suggest the oral quality of the stories, she uses a mild dialect, having adapted the language to the ear of a contemporary audience. The tales themselves, such as "Doc Rabbit, Bruh Fox, and Tar Baby," suggest their migratory nature; many were African tales retold in and adapted to the American landscape. They are also stories that elevate the defenseless to the role of the trickster, again echoing the slave experience. This trickster may sometimes take the form of a rabbit as protagonist, sometimes the form of the slave trickster High John. Each of the stories—particularly those moving stories of slaves seeking freedom—speaks to the painful historical context out of which they come, and express poignantly the condition of slavery.

In the companion volume *Many Thousand Gone* (1993), Hamilton shifts her genre slightly and her language changes accordingly. Here she tells nonfictive accounts from the early days of slavery, and the language is much more formal, though Hamilton still crafts the individual accounts in storylike structures. Beginning with the earliest days of slavery in the United States, she recounts the inception and growth of the practice, focusing also on the abolition movement and on slave revolts. The tales themselves are often not the more famous tales, though the book does include stories of Harriet Tubman, Sojourner Truth, and Frederick Douglas. But the most poignant stories are those like that of Wisdom, a slave who escaped to the Union army camp. When his owner came to reclaim his "property," Wisdom was handed over. No one knows what became of him. The historical quality of the collection is framed by an opening illustration by Leo and Diane Dillon of an open stone cage by the sea; a slave ship sails away. At the close, an open slave cabin door looks on a road on which a family travels away to freedom.

Hamilton combined these genres in *Her Stories* (1995), a collection of tales of African American women. It is an eclectic collection, with trickster tales, vampire stories, tales of legendary women, and true accounts of women who endured the degradations of slavery. The stories are told in multiple voices; the stories of women who endured slavery are, in fact, told in their own voices. But, once again, Hamilton works to create an authentic oral voice:

> Black folks tell about Annie Christmas, and so do white folks. Every kind of folk claim her as their own, and there are good reasons why. But let *me* tell you. Who am I? I am the kind of grandmaw man that lives to spin a good yarn. (84)

In creating such vivid voices, Hamilton is trying to recreate her own experience as a child listening to the stories told by her female relations.

In *When Birds Could Talk and Bats Could Sing* (1996) and *A Ring of Tricksters* (1997), Hamilton has collaborated with illustrator Barry Moser to retell African tales and their North American variants. In the first volume, Hamilton retells tales first collected by Martha Young on the plantation of her father. Young had recorded them in heavy African American dialect, but Hamilton recasts them once again in "an easy-to-read colloquial speech" (64). Like the stories of *The People Could Fly,* these stories come out of slavery times and reflect the migration of the stories to a North American context. But, unlike the earlier tales, those stories are more fablelike, ending with a moral of sorts: "It never does a body a bit of good to be hoity-toity. For pride has a way of taking a fall every time. So, children be extra careful you don't trip over yourselves!"(45).

A Ring of Tricksters takes its name from that storytelling ring that spans an ocean. These are all stories with African roots. They came to North America with slaves and then returned as variants to Africa with escaped and freed slaves. The basic patterns of each of these trickster tales is African, and again they reflect the slave/master relationships. "All of these new tales," Hamilton writes, "kept the pattern of the African trickster tales in which a resourceful animal hero having human traits used deceit and sly trickery, and often magic, to get what he needed from bigger and stronger animals" (10).

All of these books are marked by the strongly oral quality of Hamilton's voice. They recreate the early experiences of listening to the tales. In doing so, they recreate the experience of the slave and the extraordinary gift of the human spirit that allowed someone enslaved as property to still be a storyteller.

Thinking and Writing about and from within Folktales

Thinking and Writing about the Genre of Folklore

1. The public school system in your town has decided to ban works like *Snow White* and *Little Red Riding Hood* because of the excessive violence and sublimated sexuality of the stories. The argument for this position is based on questions of audience: Young children, the school board argues, cannot deal with the harshness of the first, nor the presence of the second. Write the editorial for your local paper in which you respond to the school board.

2. A private religious school in your town has questioned whether it should ban Native American folktales because they come out of what some claim to be a pagan religious culture. The initiative for this has come from a small group of parents. You have been asked to lead the meeting that all parents of the school will attend to discuss the issue. Write your opening statement.

3. Examine folktales as they were retold in the *My Bookhouse* set of anthologies from the 1920s. Then write an informal essay about the assumptions made about folktales and "other" cultures that are suggested by the ways in which those tales are handled.

4. May folktales be retold by a writer from outside the tale's culture? Explain your position in a letter to an editor who likes the story you have written, but who wonders about the propriety of your having written it because you are not from the appropriate culture. Are the editor's concerns legitimate? What is the ethical question at stake here?

Thinking and Writing from within the Genre of Folklore

1. You have been asked by a publisher of school textbooks to organize a trio of anthologies of folktales, the first for the very young grades, the second for the middle grades, and the third for an adolescent audience. Write the introduction to this set of anthologies that expresses the principles that you have established for deciding which folktales shall fit into each volume. Illustrate your principles by naming at least one folktale for inclusion and show why it is appropriate to the volume you have chosen, but not, perhaps, to the others.

2. Choose an anthology of folktales from a culture with which you are not familiar. Having read through a number of the tales, choose one to retell for a picture book format. Write the retelling, and include a short Author's Note explaining how you recast the story and how you went about the requisite research about the culture.

3. In *The True Story of the Three Little Pigs,* Jon Scieszka retells a familiar story by slanting it. He allows one of the characters to tell the tale. To do this, he created a character who was unsympathetic to the traditional version of the story and allowed that character to recast the tale in very different ways. Retell one of the following well-known tales from the point of view of one of the more unsympathetic characters.

    The King retells the story of Rumplestiltskin.

    One of the stepsisters retells the story of Cinderella.

    The stepmother retells the story of Hansel and Gretel.

    The wolf retells the story of St. Francis and the Wolf.

Selected Bibliographies

Works Cited

Berry, James. *Spiderman Anancy.* New York: Henry Holt, 1989.

Climo, Shirley. *The Egyptian Cinderella.* New York: HarperCollins, 1989. Illustrated by Ruth Heller.

———. *The Irish Cinderlad.* New York: Harper-Collins, 1996. Illustrated by Loretta Krupinski.

Coady, Christopher. *Red Riding Hood.* New York: Dutton, 1991.

Compton, Joanne. *Ashpet.* New York: Holiday House, 1994. Illustrated by Kenn Compton.

Diakité, Baba Wagué. *The Hunterman and the Crocodile.* New York: Scholastic, 1997.

Gág, Wanda. *Tales from Grimm.* New York: Coward-McCann, 1936.

Hearn, Michael Patrick. *The Porcelain Cat.* Boston: Little, Brown, 1987. Illustrated by Leo and Diane Dillon.

Heins, Paul. *Snow White.* Boston: Little, Brown, 1974. Illustrated by Trina Schart Hyman.

Heyer, Marilee. *The Weaving of a Dream.* New York: Viking, 1986.

Hooks, William H. *The Three Little Pigs and the Fox.* New York: Macmillan, 1989. Illustrated by S. D. Schindler.

Lester, Julius. *John Henry.* New York: Dial, 1994. Illustrated by Jerry Pinkney.

———. *Sam and the Tigers.* New York: Dial, 1996. Illustrated by Jerry Pinkney.

Levert, Mireille. *Little Red Riding Hood.* Toronto: Groundwood, 1995.

Louie, Ai-Ling. *Yeh-Shen: A Cinderella Story from China.* New York: Putnam and Grosset, 1982. Illustrated by Ed Young.

Martin, Rafe. *The Rough-Face Girl.* New York: G. P. Putnam, 1992. Illustrated by David Shannon.

Mayer, Mercer. *The Sleeping Beauty.* New York: Macmillan, 1984.

McKissack, Patricia. *Flossie and the Fox.* New York: Dial, 1986. Illustrated by Rachel Isadora.

Miller, Olive Beaupré. *My Bookhouse.* Chicago: Bookhouse for Children, 1920.

Montressor, Beni. *Little Red Riding Hood.* New York: Doubleday, 1991.

Paterson, Katherine. *The Tale of the Mandarin Ducks.* New York: Dutton, 1990. Illustrated by Leo and Diane Dillon.

Perrault, Charles. *Cinderella.* Amy Ehrhich, re-teller. New York: Dial, 1985. Illustrated by Susan Jeffers.

Rappaport, Doreen. *The Journey of Meng.* New York: Dial, 1991. Illustrated by Yang Ming-Yi.

Sanfield, Steve. *The Adventures of High John the Conqueror.* New York: Orchard, 1989. Illustrated by John Ward.

———. *The Feather Merchants.* New York: Beech Tree, 1993.

———. *A Natural Man: The True Story of John Henry.* Boston: David Godine, 1986.

San Souci, Robert. *The Enchanted Tapestry.* New York: Dial, 1990. Illustrated by Lászlo Gál.

———. *Nicholas Pipe.* New York: Dial, 1997. Illustrated by David Shannon.

———. *The Red Heels.* New York: Dial, 1996. Illustrated by Gary Kelley.

———. *Sootface: An Ojibwa Cinderella Story.* New York: Doubleday, 1994. Illustrated by Daniel San Souci.

Schroeder, Alan. *Smokey Mountain Rose: An Appalachian Cinderella.* New York: Dial, 1997. Illustrated by Brad Sneed.

Scieszka, Jon. *The True Story of the Three Little Pigs.* New York: Viking, 1989. Illustrated by Lane Smith.

Trivizas, Eugene. *The Three Little Wolves and the Big Bad Pig.* New York: Margaret K. McElderry, 1993. Illustrated by Helen Oxenbury.

Wisniewski, David. *Golem.* New York: Clarion, 1996.

Yagawa, Sumiko. *The Crane Wife.* New York: William Morrow, 1981. Illustrated by Suekichi Akaba. Translated by Katherine Paterson.

Yep, Lawrence. *The Khan's Daughter.* New York: Scholastic, 1997. Illustrated by Jean and Mou-Sien Tseng.

Young, Ed. *Lon Po Po.* New York: Philomel, 1989.

Zelinsky, Paul O. *Rapunzel.* New York: Dutton, 1997.

Zemach, Margot. *The Three Little Pigs.* New York: Farrar, Straus and Giroux, 1988.

Works of Selected Retellers

Steven Kellogg
Johnny Appleseed. New York: William Morrow, 1988.
Mike Fink. New York: William Morrow, 1992.
Paul Bunyan. New York: William Morrow, 1984.
Pecos Bill. New York: William Morrow, 1986.
Sally Ann Thunder Ann Whirlwind Crockett. New York: William Morrow, 1995.
The Three Little Pigs. New York: William Morrow, 1997.

Paul O. Zelinsky
Hansel and Gretel. New York: Dodd, Mead, 1984. Text by Rika Lesser.
Rapunzel. New York: Dutton, 1997.
Rumplestiltskin. New York: Dutton, 1986.

Ed Young
Cat and Rat: The Legend of the Chinese Zodiac. New York: Henry Holt, 1995.
The Emperor and the Kite. Cleveland: World, 1967. Text by Jane Yolen.
Lon Po Po. New York: Philomel, 1989.
Night Visitors. New York: Philomel, 1995.
The Turkey Girl. Boston: Little, Brown, 1996. Text by Penny Pollock.
White Wave. New York: Harcourt Brace, 1979. Text by Diane Wolkstein.

Julius Lester and Jerry Pinkney
John Henry. New York: Dial, 1994. Illustrated by Jerry Pinkney.
The Knee-High Man and Other Tales. New York: Viking, 1985.
Long Journey Home: Stories from Black History. New York: Scholastic, 1988.

The Tales of Uncle Remus:
    The Adventures of Brer Rabbit. New York: Dial, 1987. Illustrated by Jerry Pinkney.
    Further Adventures of Brer Rabbit, His Friends, Enemies, and Others. New York: Dial, 1988. Illustrated by Jerry Pinkney.
    Misadventures of Brer Rabbit, Brer Fox, Brer Wolf, the Doodang, and Other Creatures. New York: Dial, 1990. Illustrated by Jerry Pinkney.
    The Last Tales of Uncle Remus. New York: Dial, 1994. Illustrated by Jerry Pinkney.
To Be a Slave. New York: Dial, 1968.

Paul Morin
The Dragon's Pearl. New York: Clarion, 1993. Text by Julie Lawson.
The Orphan Boy. New York: Clarion, 1990. Text by Tololwa M. Mollel.

Virginia Hamilton
Her Stories: African American Folktales, Fairy Tales, and True Tales. New York: Scholastic, 1995. Illustrated by Leo and Diane Dillon.
Many Thousand Gone: African Americans from Slavery to Freedom. New York: Knopf, 1993. Illustrated by Leo and Diane Dillon.
The People Could Fly: American Black Folktales. New York: Knopf, 1985. Illustrated by Leo and Diane Dillon.
A Ring of Tricksters: Animal Tales from America, the West Indies, and Africa. New York: Scholastic, 1997. Illustrated by Barry Moser.
When Birds Could Talk and Bats Could Sing. New York: Scholastic, 1996. Illustrated by Barry Moser.

Works on the Retelling of Folktales in Children's Literature

Apseloff, Marilyn Fain. "The Big, Bad Wolf: New Approaches to an Old Folk Tale." *Children's Literature Association Quarterly* 15 (Fall, 1990): 135–137.

Barchers, Suzanne. "Beyond Disney: Reading and Writing Traditional and Alternative Fairy Tales." *Lion and the Unicorn* 12 (1988): 135–150.

Bettelheim, Bruno. *The Uses of Enchantment.* New York: Random House, 1975.

Bottigheimer, Ruth, ed. *Fairy Tales and Society: Illusion, Allusion, and Paradigm.* Philadelphia: University of Pennsylvania Press, 1986.

Dorson, Richard. *American Folklore.* Chicago: University of Chicago Press, 1959.

Dundes, Alan, ed. *Cinderella: A Casebook*. Madison, WI: University of Wisconsin Press, 1988.

———. *Little Red Riding Hood: A Casebook*. Madison, WI: University of Wisconsin Press, 1989.

Goble, Paul. "On Beaded Dresses and the Blazing Sun." In Gary D. Schmidt and Donald R. Hettinga, eds., *Sitting at the the Feet of the Past*. Westport, CT: Greenwood, 1992: 5–14.

Haley, Gail E. "From the Ananse Stories to the Jack Tales: My Work with Folktales." *Children's Literature Association Quarterly* 11 (Fall, 1986): 118–121.

Kellogg, Steven. "The Heritage of the American Tall Tale." In Gary D. Schmidt and Donald R. Hettinga, eds., *Sitting at the Feet of the Past*. Westport, CT: Greenwood, 1992: 191–194.

Lester, Julius. "The Storyteller's Voice: Reflections on the Rewriting of Uncle Remus." *New Advocate* 1 (Summer 1988): 137–147.

Lewis, C. S. "On Three Ways of Writing for Children." In Sheila Egoff, ed., *Only Connect: Readings on Children's Literature*. New York: Oxford University Press, 1969: 206–220.

Lüthi, Max. *Once upon a Time: On the Nature of Fairy Tales*. Bloomington, IN: Indiana University Press, l970.

May, Jill. "Illustration as Interpretation: Trina Hyman's Folk Tales." *Children's Literature Association Quarterly* 10 (Fall, 1985): 127–131.

McGlathery, James M., ed. *The Brothers Grimm and Folktale*. Urbana, IL: University of Illinois Press, 1988.

McGrath, Robin. "Words Melt Away Like Hills in Fog: Putting Inuit Legends into Print." *Children's Literature Association Quarterly* 13 (Spring, 1988): 9–12.

Milner, Joseph O. and Loraine Moses Stewart, "Flossie Ebonics: Sociolinguistic Messages in *Flossie and the Fox*." *New Advocate* 10 (Summer, 1997): 211–214.

Moustakis, Christian. "A Plea for Heads: Illustrating Violence in Fairy Tales." *Children's Literature Association Quarterly* 7 (Summer, 1982): 26–30.

Propp, Vladimir. *Morphology of the Folktale*. Bloomington, IN: Indiana University, 1958.

———. *Theory and History of Folklore*. Anatoly Liberman, ed. Minneapolis: University of Minnesota Press, 1984.

Sanfield, Steve. "Across Cultures: Stories That Say *L'Chaim*." In Gary D. Schmidt and Donald R. Hettinga, eds., *Sitting at the Feet of the Past*. Westport, CT: Greenwood, 1992: 69–76.

Tatar, Maria. "Tests, Tasks, and Trials in the Grimms' Fairy Tales." *Children's Literature* 13 (1985): 31–48.

Temple, Charles. "Seven Readings of a Folktale: Literary Theory in the Classroom." *New Advocate* 4 (Winter 1991): 25–35.

Thompson, Stith. *The Folktale*. New York: Dryden, 1951.

Trousdale, Ann. "The True Bride: Perceptions of Beauty and Feminine Virtue in Folktales." *New Advocate* 2 (Fall, 1989): 239–248.

Warner, Marina. *From the Beast to the Blonde: On Fairy Tales and Their Tellers*. New York: Farrar, Straus and Giroux, 1994.

Zarucchi, Jeanne Morgan. "Audiences and Messages in Perrault's Tales." *Children's Literature Association Quarterly* 12 (Winter, 1987): 162–164.

Zipes, Jack. *The Brothers Grimm*. New York: Routledge, 1988.

———. "The Changing Function of the Fairy Tale." *Lion and the Unicorn* 12 (1988): 7–31.

———. *Fairy Tale as Myth*. Lexington, KY: University Press of Kentucky, 1994.

———. *Fairy Tales and the Art of Subversion*. New York: Routledge, 1991.

———, ed. *The Trials and Tribulations of Little Red Riding Hood*. New York: Routledge, 1993.

6

Myths and Epics: Tales of Universal Truths

In *The Lost Children* (1993), Paul Goble retells the Native American Blackfoot story of the origin of the Pleiades. These stars are the lost children from the tribe, lost because their mothers and fathers did not care for them. "Nobody was kind to the brothers. Nobody wanted them. Other children chased them, and threw stones, and laughed at their ragged clothes and tangled hair." Finally, in despair, they escaped to the Above World, where they became the Pleiades.

This story, among others that Goble tells, appears on the painted tipis of the Blackfoot. Each tipi tells the ancient tales of the tribe in a patterned fashion. The lost children are found on the south flap at the top of the tipi. The cross on the back flap represents the morning star, who is the son of the sun and the moon. On the North flap is a line of seven disks representing the seven brothers of the Big Dipper. In the middle of the tipi are pictures of the animals who gave the Blackfoot the vision of the tipi's design. The bottom part of the tipi is painted as the earth with jagged mountains, smooth plains, and round puffballs known to appear in the land overnight. Each part of the natural world is explained in the tipi drawings.

Those explanations are myths. They are stories a culture establishes to answer the questions that the world around them engenders. They are stories that come out of the particular circumstances of a people, molded to that people's needs and hopes, shaped by their world. Often, they are the stories a culture uses to define itself.

David Leeming, in *The World of Myth* (1990), writes, "As we explore the world of myth, we should remember that we are journeying not through a maze of falsehood but through a marvelous world of metaphor that breathes life into the essential human story: the story of the search for identity in the context of the universal struggle between order and chaos" (p. 8). It is this understanding of myth as metaphor that establishes the boundaries of mythology in children's literature.

Definitions and Boundaries

Myth

A myth is a folk story of communal origin, whose intent is to explain the cosmos and the world, to instruct people in how to live together, to illustrate the ways of the gods to humanity, to explain communal and individual origins and ends.

Myths and epics are not simply grand stories of cultures' beginnings and their heroes' exploits. The word *mythos* means "tale" or "speech," though that word in contemporary society has come to mean "an old wives' tale," a quaint story patently untrue, such as the myth of the Loch Ness Monster. But myth in its older, fuller sense means a story that answers questions about the nature of life, about the nature of community, about the nature of the world. Insofar as a myth is an attempt to answer questions, insofar as myth tries to tell us something of who human beings are, it is by definition true.

Mythic Questions.   The questions that myths from all cultures ask are the questions that every society has asked.

Who am I? Where was I before I was born?

What is beyond the realm of the senses? Is there a spiritual world?

What happens to me after I die?

How did my people, my community, begin?

What is the meaning of the religious exercises of my community?

How is it that my people are different from another? Are those differences significant?

How did this place come to be? What is its future?

How did the world begin? How will the world end?

What is the origin and what is the meaning of the natural phenomena I see around me? Clouds, rain, the seasons, the mountains, the sun, the moving stars, a comet, a volcano?

Who governs the world?

If there is one who governs the world, is that one interested in my people? Is that one interested in me?

These questions are central to every culture, and every culture has established mythic stories to answer them.

The human need to tell stories is confirmed by anthropologists such as Ernst Cassirer and Claude Levi-Strauss. They argue that myth becomes a self-contained symbol system that exists because humanity has an inborn desire to establish meaning by ordering natural phenomena and interpreting elements in the world. Myth answers humanity's desire to make sense of the natural world. When humans see salmon swimming upstream, that action becomes a metaphor for a life of struggle against a difficult world. When humans see a sparrow fly through a lighted barn, they create a metaphor for the brevity of life. Myths, in this sense, use the imagination to make sense of the world and its meanings.

Myth and the Phenomena of Nature. Many myths are stories that explain the phenomena of nature in terms of the experience that a culture sees around itself. The sun comes up every morning and sets every evening, and so cultures construct stories to account for its movement. The seasons change, the moon waxes and wanes, the tide rises, and a culture uses story to explain what otherwise cannot be explained. Often, such myths attempt to explain the mysteries of the earth by stories of divine intervention or leading.

Why the seasons change is the subject of the Greek myth of *Persephone,* retold and illustrated by Warwick Hutton (1994). She and her mother Demeter, the goddess of nature, live happily and enjoy summer weather all year long, until Hades sees Persephone and snatches her into the underworld to live with him. Without Persephone, Demeter is lost and allows the world to become barren; finally she demands that Zeus help her find Persephone or she will allow the world to be destroyed. He consents, but, when they find out that Persephone has eaten Hades's pomegranate seeds, a compromise has to be struck between Demeter and Hades: Each will have Persephone for half the year. When she is with her mother, the earth will be warm and productive; when she is with Hades, the earth will be brown and barren. Thus, the changing location of the goddess accounts for the natural phenomenon of the changing seasons.

How Night Came from the Sea (1994) by Mary Joan Gerson is a Caribbean myth explaining night's origin. A goddess's daughter marries a human and comes to live on Earth where she is almost happy. What she misses most about home is the cool night time. As she says to her mortal husband, "Night is like the quiet after crying or the end of the story. It is a dark, cool blanket that covers everything." Her mother decides to send night and puts it in a bag to be opened only by her daughter, because she is the one who can keep the night calm. However, the men who go to pick up the bag cannot restrain their curiosity, so they open it and out jumps night. To this day, night leaps out quickly in the Caribbean.

Fire Came to the Earth People (1988) by Susan Roth is a Dahomean story that explains how humanity received fire. The people live in a cold world because Manu, the moon god, is too selfish and will not share his fire. The people who have tried to steal it from him are not successful until Chameleon and Tortoise help. Tortoise steals the fire and then hides it under his shell when Manu tries to rain it out.

Such stories explain the workings of nature, but they also work to form an integrated whole, a cosmos that reflects the culture. The natural world is explained in a manner that reflects the understandings of the culture. And, often, the natural world is explained in such a way as to suggest that its workings are somehow in concert with that culture. Drought may come because of evil acts; floods may come as a sign of judgment. The natural world, then, is not apart from human activity, but closely respondent to it. Or, to put it another way, myth is shaped by the geography, nature, and activities of the people from whom it comes.

Myth and the Community, Myth and the Individual.   Myth may instruct its culture concerning life within the community. It may explain certain rituals and traditions; it may show how to live in community; it may suggest the origins and meanings of communal life. It may show what is the good and what is the evil on a cosmic scale, but it also may show what might be proper on a domestic scale. Children learn how to interact with parents, with siblings, and with extended family. Myth demonstrates how men and women should act in particular communal situations. It shows how individuals fit into a society's system of living together. Seeing the totality of what myth encompasses makes it difficult to dismiss its stories as merely quaint. This is not simply entertainment, not a frivolous addition to society; it is at the very center of the structure of society, dealing with a culture's deepest concerns.

In *Beyond the Ridge* (1989), Paul Goble portrays a Native American view of death—a universal theme. He illustrates one of the Plains Indians' metaphors for death, that of climbing up a long difficult slope towards a high, pine-covered ridge, by showing the journey of a dying grandmother. She prepares for her journey with sage in her hands to please the spirits; covered with a trade blanket, she is announced to the new spiritual world by crows, who are messengers of the spirit. Then the grandmother begins her trek to the land that is better than this one. The recognition that death is inevitable and natural, coupled with the understanding of the brevity of human life, demonstrates that it is appropriate to approach death calmly.

Family relationships are the subject of *The Magic Tree: A Tale from the Congo* (1973). Gerald McDermott unfolds the story of an unloved twin son who leaves home to make his own way. He finds a huge tree whose leaves turn into people when they are plucked. When a princess is magically freed and comes to live with him, she makes him promise not to tell his family about their life together. However, unable to resist the temptation to show off his good fortune, the young man returns home and quickly brags about his new life. When he tries to return to his princess, she and the rest of his life are gone. The lesson for the tribal society is that unrestrained pride will devastate not only the individual, but the fuller family.

In a Cambodian tale, *The Tale of the Spiteful Spirit* (1991) by Carole Tate Kampuchean, the importance of passing on the stories of the people is underscored by the tale of a young boy who hears the ancient stories of his culture but keeps them to himself. He hides them in a bag where the spirits of the stories plot their revenge: They will ruin his wedding day. However, an old man saves the young one from the spirits and he, in turn, realizes he must tell the stories of his people, thus respecting a tradition that calls for deference to one's elders and to the culture's myths.

While mythic tales may suggest truths about communal activities, they also speak to the growth and journey of the individual. In these stories, questions dealing with the nature and concerns of the single individual dominate, though the answers to the questions may become archetypal for the community.

In *Arrow to the Sun* (1974) a Pueblo tale retold by Gerald McDermott, the Sun-God sends a spark to Earth; it falls into the house of a maiden and becomes a boy who, when he grows up, is laughed at because he has no father. He leaves home to search for him, stopping at several places to see if someone can help. Finally he comes to the arrow-maker. Seeing that this boy is special, the wise man sends him to his father, the sun, by turning him into an arrow. Once there, the boy has to prove himself by enduring three trials. Having successfully completed these, he stands once again before his father. "Now you must return to earth, my son, and bring my spirit to the world of men." Obediently, the boy becomes an arrow again and returns to Earth with his father's spirit. The story functions on the communal level by dealing with the relationship between God and humanity, but it also recounts the necessary growth and maturation of the individual.

Myth as Cultural and Religious Artifact.   Most mythologists agree that world mythologies are marked by distinct similarities. While differences may be explicit, likenesses below the surfaces are implicit and can be seen in certain typologies as well as archetypal human actions. Sources of life are found in water, earth, air, fire, or the human body. Dark forests are fearful places where anything is liable to happen. Single trees, however, represent the opposite.

These more than coincidental patterns have been explained by C. C. Jung in his theory of the collective unconscious. He believes in the power of mythology in terms of the root meaning of the word *educate, e-ducere,* referring to life-binding images that come not from the surface and current features of any culture but from the deep structure of all. Thus, the hero/heroine cycle, the basic images of male and female, and the individual's complex makeup can be found with similar meanings in all cultures. He called these "a priori inborn forms of intuition" that were not incidental in human life but were fundamental to it.

Jung also posited that we are religious beings, and that myth forms the base of all organized religion and, as such, holds the key for humanity's relationship to the divine. While the surfaces of the myths are attached to particular cultures in particular times, the deeper structures embody the mystery of our eternal search to know and speak about the transcendent. In these terms, myth tells truth in ways that science cannot. While science is limited by the concrete from which it hopes to extract abstract principles, myth works in the reverse manner by putting concrete clothes on abstract beliefs. With this understanding as a base, myths take on new meaning. They are no longer stories fabricated by primitive people, but genuine attempts to speak about and connect with the divine through revelation about the nature of the world.

Myth continues to attract through the potent power of its ability to speak to our deepest selves. The child who holds up Medusa's head to freeze a classmate, or who draws the winged Pegasus, or who pretends to wield the hammer of Thor is participating in their strong narrative in a way similar to that of a child of long ago. And, as North Americans create their own stories to explain the nature of the world, the community, the individual, and their society's relationship to the divine, they participate in mythmaking in a manner not completely dissimilar to that of ancient ancestors.

Pointers for Teachers

Interactive Possibilities
- Discuss the following questions after reading a retelling of a myth: How would you respond to the hero or heroine? Were the actions of the protagonist predictable? Would you have done something similar, given equal abilities?
- Are there parts of the mythic story that you find distasteful? Why?
- Bring a bag of objects into class containing such things as straws, walnuts, cotton balls, balloons, and gum wrappers. Have each student reach into the bag and pull out an object. The hero or heroine of a mythological tale has just been transformed into this object. What problems does the student foresee for the character?

Writing Possibility
- Sketch the main actions of a protagonist on the board. Break the students into groups and have them change one of the central actions in the plot. They then should write the new ending to the story that results from that change.

Hands-On Possibility
- Break students into groups of four or five. Assign to each group an event from a particular mythological story, assigning the same story to pairs of groups. One group should dramatize the story as if it were occurring within the parent culture; the other group should dramatize it as if it were occurring in a contemporary North American culture. Afterwards, discuss the differences in the productions and what might have caused them.

Epic

Though epics include a cast of characters similar to those of myths, they focus much more decidedly on human characters. Epics are national stories in which characters may battle with the gods or larger-than-life adversaries, defying them, matching wits with them, and, in the end, being grandly defeated by them. It is always the human character who remains in the forefront. This character endures greatly, perseveres greatly, suffers greatly, and dies nobly. The epic hero is drawn in a larger-than-life outline, and fills that outline with a larger-than-life persona engaged in a larger-than-life quest.

Epics are peculiarly national; they focus not on humanity as a whole, but, instead, on their own particular society. As such, they are indicators of the values held by that society. What is the role of the hero? What is the noble act, the gracious act, the honorable act? What is the ignoble, ungracious, and cowardly act? What are the heroic codes of this world, and how do they reflect the larger collectively held values of the society?

Joseph Campbell, in *The Hero with a Thousand Faces* (1949), synthesizes the basic similarities of the epic hero's character and actions from many different cultures. The hero begins in the comfort of his own society, is called from either inside or outside of himself to search for a particular boon for his society, and decides whether to accept or reject that call. If he accepts, he begins a series of trials. In the midst of his adventures he meets a woman who will teach him inner truths, and then a father who teaches him outer truths—that is, how to succeed in capturing the boon his people need. Once the hero succeeds, he takes the boon back to his own society. There he is sometimes welcomed for this truth, sometimes killed for it, and often simply ignored for it. If he does not succeed, his failure is still a noble one.

The Anglo-Saxon story of the hero *Beowulf* (1982) is retold by Kevin Crossley-Holland, who uses the storyteller, Gangleri, to tell of the monster Grendel and his mother, who are terrorizing the Danes. There follows a tale of an untried warrior, Beowulf, leaving the comforts of his own society in order to test his mettle. And tested it is. Impervious to slights, focused on the task at hand, Beowulf kills Grendel and his mother, proving his worth to return to his homeland and become king. The young man fulfills most of the hero cycle readily.

When Beowulf goes to fight Grendel and then his mother, he does battle alone. He has come to relieve Hrothgar of his woe, but his coming is not motivated by charity, but by a desire to prove himself, to assert his own manhood. Repeatedly he claims that he yearns for unending glory, which he gains by the end of the poem. In the end, he goes to fight a dragon, again alone, because this is what the Anglo-Saxon hero must do if he is to attain glory. The fact that he knows that he is going to his death makes the glory all the greater.

In fact, great odds are precisely what make the epic hero larger than life. Beowulf battles his dragon. Odysseus battles the huge and powerful Cyclops. Roland, with his small band, battles the entire Saracen army. El Cid lifts a siege against an enormous and powerful foe. St. George battles an impervious dragon. Robin Hood

Pointers for Teachers: Evaluating Collections of Myths and Epics

Text
- How does the retelling help the child reader to learn about and enjoy the culture being portrayed?
- How does the literature show that humanity has common characteristics, both good and ill? What unique cultural characteristics are depicted?
- How does the retelling maintain the original oral quality of the tale? What does the language reflect about the culture?
- How does the retelling challenge the child reader, encouraging growth and the development of a new and wider vision of the world?

Illustrations
- How do the visual elements of line, color, shape, and texture complement and extend the tale?
- How do the illustrations come out of and reflect the cultural origins of the tale?
- How do the illustrations contribute to the child's understanding of what may be a very complex and multilayered story?

hides out in Sherwood Forest and fights against all the might of Prince John. All of these battles—whether they are engaged in physically or through the epic hero's innate wit—are larger-than-life encounters.

Like myths, epics are stories told by adults to adults. They are frequently violent and bloody, often erotic and bawdy. They are hardly, it would seem, the stuff of children's literature. Yet they have, indeed, entered into the boundaries of children's literature. It remains to be seen how those boundaries have changed epics in order that they might adapt to a new audience.

Issues in the Retelling of Myths and Epics

How do writers structure a collection of myths for a child audience?

In examining how representative collections of myths have been put together, readers can see that the collectors show their own beliefs about myth as much as they inform about the myths themselves. Many early collections rearranged and truncated myths and made judgments about the people from whom they came, contorting the myths so that their meanings suited the contemporary and cultural mindset. There is an unexamined and assumed presumption of superiority in those collections. In 1855, for example, Charles Kingsley collected Greek myths in *The Heroes*. He wanted his audience to make the connection between Greek culture and Christian British culture. These myths, he argued, form the base of the intellectual subjects of geometry, astronomy, geography, and logic; they give readers "beauty, wisdom, truth, and…make…children love noble deeds, and trust in God to help them through." Kingsley further argued that "the stories are not all true…you are not simple enough to fancy that; but the meaning of them is true," and that this meaning is "'Do right, and God will help you!'" There is an easy Victorian reductionism here, though also, at least, some sense of the potency of the myth's meanings.

Amy Cruse, in *The Young Folk's Book of Myths* (1927), invited her audience to remember when the world seemed new and wonderful to them, when they looked at natural phenomena and wondered where all of it came from. She compared this attitude to the peoples who made up explanations for the workings of the natural world, calling them "childlike adults." "In those days the first lesson of science had not been learnt" and so mythologies filled that gap with fantastical stories. Claiming that all mythologies grew in this fashion, Cruse looked for the commonalities among the stories as well as the rational explanations for their formations. In introducing the Greek pantheon, she reminded the reader that the geographical location in a sunny and beautiful country made it so that the people loved beauty and proportion in nature, in buildings, in the human body. Thus, their gods were beautiful because they made them in their own image.

In thinking about the Norse pantheon, Cruse noted that the hard, cold, frozen world the Vikings lived in formed the basis for their view of life as fleeting, and that, in order to exist, humans and gods had to be physically and mentally tough. Thus, strength was the most important measure of the gods. The Native Americans, on the other hand, lived the free and easy life of the "savage," reflecting another primitive view of religion. Their "hunt or starve" culture pitted humans against animals, and many times humans lost because they were not strong enough or cunning enough in the ways of the animal world. These people respected animals so much that they came to regard the animals as literal ancestors; thus the totem pole came into existence.

In each case the myths were told from the point of view of an outsider who saw them as the products of an ignorant, inferior people. They are the stuff of legend, the stuff of pagan insecurity and darkness.

In the 1960s, myths began to be presented without accompanying interpretation and almost no commentary on the originating peoples and their civilization. Their power, editors claimed, came from their power as stories. Here the stories were collected for their ability to reach the audience through their drama, their structure, their intriguing incident and character. Thus, in *Hibernian Nights* (1963), Seumas MacManus innocently explained his purpose in collecting myth by suggesting that the stories should simply be kept alive by good storytellers, an ancient vocation that he has seen fall into modern disdain. In Joseph Jacobs's *The Book of Wonder Voyages* (1967), the editor suggests that these myths, centered around a journey theme, are "to be read in the middle of winter or anytime when your spirit wants to move beyond horizons."

In the 1980s there was a greater reliance on the cultural context that surrounded the myths. For instance, *The World Mythology* series (1982) set its stories of the Norse mythology in a complex nexus of visual and verbal symbols. The introductory illustrations showed the major symbols of the mythology, and, although there is no explanation for them at this point, readers are drawn into the ancient world of the Vikings. A map showing where the myths originated followed, and, at the end of the collection of stories, there was a short essay entitled, "Who were the gods?" The editor offered several choices. Perhaps these early stories contain the exploits of specially gifted human beings whom people later turned into gods. Perhaps these gods came into being in order to explain the ways of nature to humanity. Or perhaps the landscape itself shaped the gods and their activities.

At the turn of the millennium, the emphasis is not only on the multiplicity of beliefs about myths but also on their irretrievable cultural context. In *The Illustrated Book of Myths* (1995), Neil Philip writes that "every myth is a shaft of human truth…People believe it with all their heart and soul"; his definition of truth allows that myth may be religion or fiction. His thematic arrangement by subject matter stresses the similarities and differences between the audience's beliefs and the mythological system. The new addition is the impossibility of an outsider who is able to comprehend completely what those beliefs mean to an insider in both time and place. For instance, the Australian aboriginals who enter Dreamtime connect physically and spiritually with their ancient ancestors through chanting and singing; however, such an entrance is only an intellectual exercise for the nonaboriginal. In an effort to cross the gap, Philips includes a great deal of cultural information in the form of photographs of the culture as well as its history and geography.

Cynthia O'Neill's *Goddesses, Heroes, and Shamans* (1994) also presents a culture's entire context. This collection of over five hundred characters from various world mythologies demonstrates recurring themes and patterns among the myths; it also includes sectional maps, time lines, and essays to introduce peoples and their myths, a dictionary for unfamiliar words, and sidebars to include interesting tidbits of information. O'Neill's inclusive work reminds readers that myth may be a religious, social, historical, or symbolic representation of a culture's alignment with its natural surroundings. Despite her encyclopedic approach, she does not include Christian, Jewish, or Muslim myth, although she acknowledges myth's religious dimension. While her avowed desire is to objectively present the cultures of the world, her work shows that she knows objectivity is impossible.

However they are structured, a collection of myths must have some organizing principle to give unity. Mary Hoffman, in *Earth, Fire, Water, Air* (1995) uses the four elements as an arranging device for stories from around the world. Hoffman shows how different cultures have worshipped these elements or tried to control them. She is not merely using the elements as an organizing tool; the organization is also a way for her to present her thesis: People have polluted the earth. Thus, the earth has a "song," but it is one that she thinks we can hardly hear in this century. Pleasant DeSpain in *Eleven Turtle Tales* (1994), on the other hand, has limited herself to an innocuous thematic collection of turtle tales from around the world to show the ancient nature of the turtle symbol. She makes a metaphorical transference: The turtle that carried the world on its back in many cultures, now carries humankind's stories.

Jacket cover from *Eleven Turtle Tales* by Pleasant DeSpain, illustration by Joe Shlichta (August House, 1994). Used by permission.

What relevance do myth and epic have for a child reader today?

Are there any compelling reasons for reading ancient stories? What could the young reader of today possibly have in common with the tales of good and evil, of worlds crashing to an end, of heroes who give their lives for the good of the community?

The most obvious answer is that these stories are grand entertainment! As early as 1905, Lilian Stoughton Hyde reasoned, in her preface to *Favourite Greek Myths* (1905), that the Greek stories appeal to a young child's imagination. Two generations later, Gwyn Thomas and Kevin Crossley-Holland brought together some of the better-known Welsh stories in their *Tales from the Mabinogion* (1984), also in an explicit effort to entertain. They invoke the power of the storyteller who gathers his audience around him and then captivates the listeners. So the book emphasizes with dialogue and plot structure the fast-moving elements of the oral stories.

Myths also offer a child patterns for behavior in community and personal living. Lilia Melani, in "A Child's Psyche: Recollections of Fairy Tales, Myths, and Romances," remembers that she saw in the stories of the gods her own limitations and limitlessness, both the good things in her personality and the bad things. Bruno Bettleheim, in *The Uses of Enchantment* (1975), argues that the stories give a moral education to children that answers the question, "Whom do I wish to be like?" not "Do I want to be good?"

Kris Waldherr's *The Book of Goddesses* (1995), for example, deliberately explores the feminine concept of the divine in order to stand as a model for readers. In her introduction to the text, Linda Schierse Leonard writes that, when an audience has an opportunity to examine different ways of being in the world, it is stretched not only by the information but also by the implicit value attached to the subject. The book itself has twenty-six illustrations of goddesses from around the world and an informative text about them. Child readers are encouraged to make up their own stories by using the facts and the details in the watercolors.

On a personal, ethical scale, *The Knight with the Lion* (1996) by John Howe relates the story of a knight who defeats the Black Knight and wins the love of the Lady. Later, he carelessly breaks a promise to her and she punishes him by throwing him out of the kingdom. If he wishes to be reinstated, he must perform a noble deed for anyone who needs one. This the knight undertakes and eventually regains the lady and her kingdom. The reteller himself speculates that children will read the tale and learn about keeping promises.

If the myths are to be relevant to a contemporary North American child audience, then that audience must somehow perceive a connection between the activities, motivations, and values of these ancient tales and their own contemporary situation. In other words, they must be able to perceive the universality of these stories. *Favorite Greek Myths* (1989) by Mary Pope Osborne addresses the likenesses between gods and humankind explicitly. She asks readers to imagine how much they are like the heroes and gods they will read about. Perhaps the audience can never perform such actions as the gods perform, but it can imagine similarities in feelings.

Osborne's *Favorite Norse Myths* (1996) rests on the same premise: that children read these myths because they recognize the emotions and reactions of the protagonists as being their own emotions and reactions; they share in the core humanity of the story. In an unusual effort to demonstrate the layeredness of this link, Troy Howell, the illustrator, combines primitive one-dimensional drawings with lush paintings. Thus, the stylized drawings taken from cave walls and stelae serve as rough guides for Howell's interpretation of each myth. Children can connect the sticklike primitive figures, which are difficult to relate to, and Howell's representational paintings, which are easier to relate to.

What is the mythic role of the trickster figure?

It would seem from this description that myths and epics are inexorably high-toned and serious in their moral purpose. But laughter, too, is a part of the human experience, and mythic stories recognize this facet of experience as well. Certainly this is evident in the stories of the tricksters.

Once again the faces may change as a child reader moves from Hermes in the Greek world, to Coyote in the Native American culture, to Krishna in India and Loki in the Norse cosmos, but the meaning of the trickster stays the same. They are popular figures who disturb the seriousness and the locked-in concepts of the culture. Their outrageous, often amoral behavior offers the people a healing laugh and a new way of looking at the world.

The trickster speaks to the physical self, the one who must take care of bodily functions, who loves to undercut the staid citizen, the comic who can spontaneously shake up the entire community. Paul Goble has retold several tales about Iktomi the trickster, although it is Iktomi who is usually tricked in the end. Readers see him doing silly things like jumping into the water to get berries in *Iktomi and the Berries* (1989) only to find they are reflections. He gets his head stuck in a buffalo skull in *Iktomi and the Buffalo Skull* (1991). When readers know that the skull is a sacred object in Native American culture, they understand why native readers would gasp at the audacity of Iktomi's actions. Goble also presents Iktomi as a brave full of his own opinion of himself; he is sure everyone is impressed with his riding abilities and with his elaborate costumes. His frequent falls carry with them a pleasing and proper irony.

Gerald McDermott's *Zomo, the Rabbit* (1992) is another trickster who regularly outwits much larger foes. When he sets out to gain wisdom, he is successful in the end because he uses his speed. McDermott also retells the tale of *Raven: A Trickster Tale from the Pacific Northwest* (1993). Here, the story of the god that helps humanity obtain fire, famous to the West in the form of Prometheus, comes in the form of the bird who changes himself into a baby among the gods. As a baby he pretends to play with various objects but is really looking for the lighted box. Once he finds it, he takes out the ball and throws it into the sky. Thus, the sun will now warm mankind. Gayle Ross' *How Rabbit Tricked Otter and Other Cherokee Trickster Stories* (1994) continues Raven's exploits of completing creation. Here the world is frightened by a giant, Flint. Rabbit stands up in council meeting and speaks (mainly because he likes the sound of his own voice) promising to kill Flint. By using trickery, Rabbit does carry through on his promise, and the giant's body turns into arrowheads for the people. Unfortunately, these split Rabbit's nose.

The trickster plays to the human desire for power, for being noticed. But he also plays to the desire to create disorder, for disturbing the careful, composed pattern. Such audacious exploits—comic when successful, even more comic when unsuccessful—are all recognizably part of the human experience.

What happens to the oral nature of myth when it is written down?

Myths by their very definition are oral. The ancient stories were told to a community around campfires, during religious rituals, throughout the daily lives of the people. In fact, in Egypt, the story of Isis and Osiris was so well known that for thousands of years it was not written down; it was assumed that everyone was well acquainted with the cultural story.

As with all oral folktales, the ability of myth to grow and take on the colorations of the teller end when the myth is written down. It becomes constricted to the page, unable to control the situation in which it is read. It may be picked up by a child who needs background information on the culture before the stories are understandable, or a child who has chosen something too difficult for his or her current ability level, or a child who off-handedly will read parts of the myth while traveling in the car or sitting in a doctor's office. When a myth is written down, removed from its culture, and brought to a child audience, something dramatic has happened. That new audience generally lacks the context for the myth's meanings, the sophistication for its deepest subtleties, and the analytical skills to understand its structure. In addition, it comes to an audience unaware of the cultural assumptions and allusions that lie behind the story. Can a North American child coming to the character Loki for the first time understand the complex role of the trickster who is sometimes malevolent, sometimes benevolent, and who is finally condemned by the gods to lie beneath dripping poison for all eternity? What will a North American child make of all this?

Alice Mills offers, in "Two Versions of *Beowulf*" (1986), a commentary on the impossibility of transmitting the stories of an oral culture evenhandedly and fully. By comparing Rosemary Sutcliff's retelling of *Beowulf* (1961) with Kevin Crossley-Holland's version, she argues that readers can see that cultural understanding plays a vital role in understanding heroic behavior. Sutcliff tells a sanitized tale of man against monster. The original story emphasizes doom and dread of the unknown, punctuated by only a brief time of happiness. It balances itself between a Christian view of the world where God has designed all and rules all, and a more pessimistic and fatalistic Nordic view. Death comes as fate wills and man is judged on his actions in this world alone. Sutcliff makes the entire story brighter and more optimistic, avoiding the fatalism of the ending. She changes the identity of the mother of Grendel to a "sea-hag" rather than mother, perhaps to avoid the notion of the monstrous mother, but also to simplify the complex situation of the feud, in which Grendel's relation has every right to exact vengeance for the death of a son.

But if Sutcliff simplifies and avoids difficulties, Kevin Crossley-Holland coarsens the poem. Mills argues that he emphasizes the primitive nature of the story, using illustrations to suggest the rugged nature of Anglo-Saxon days. Crossley-Holland devalues the glorious language of the text and places the story firmly in the world of half-civilized tribes. They are shown to be coarse, crude, and deformed human beings who battle for mere survival.

In the case of the two *Beowulf* retellings, there is a culture that has been lost, particularly for a child audience. The original oral context is gone. There is no opportunity for the interaction between the teller and audience that can occur in the original oral culture, where the teller has control not only of the tale but also of the situation in which it is told. Like a teacher, the teller can adapt the tales to the audience. There is a spontaneity, within limits, that is given up once the tale has been written down.

Paul Goble battles both of these impulses in his work. In *Adopted by the Eagles* (1994), for example, Goble tells the tale of two young men who were *kolas*; he recognizes that this relationship is central to his story, because both young men must decide between their status as *kola* and their mutual love for the same young woman. However, he also realizes that most North American children will not be familiar with the term; it will be outside of their cultural arena. So he begins the story with an explanation, set in distinct italic type, to establish the relationship and its meaning:

> *During the old Buffalo days two young men sometimes formed a special friendship. They became kolas, friends. Kolas swore to do everything together, to look after each other's family, to help each other hunt, to share everything to the last morsel of food; and, if it had to be, even to die in the defense of his friend. They tried to kept the Four Virtues in their thoughts: Bravery, Patience, Kindness, and Wisdom. Being kolas was a difficult, and sacred relationship.*

This opening, almost an introit, serves to establish the meaning of the term for a new audience, but also serves to introduce the principal themes of the story.

In *Iktomi and the Ducks* (1990), Goble deals with the issue of the oral retelling. In such a retelling, a story is told to a communal audience, and, traditionally, that audience is very active. The storyteller will ask questions and wait for responses. The audience will interject comments, will call out, and will actually be a part of the retelling. To replicate this experience, Goble uses three typefaces. The large roman type carries the main plot line; a gray italic type represents the questions and interjections where listeners are to be participating; the small roman type suggests Iktomi's thoughts, another narrative thread added to the first. The result is a telling that captures the oral feel of the tale, as the gray type asks, "What do you think he wants that branch for?" and "He is fooling the ducks, isn't he?"

The question of the relationship of the oral tale to its printed version is at the very heart of what each reteller must decide as principles are established for the new retelling. How much of the cultural history may be assumed? Should any be assumed? Should the collection include material that provides historical background: a glossary, a listing of the pantheon of the gods, a history of the culture?

However these questions are answered, those writers trying to preserve the orality of the stories usually find that their first principle must be the creation of a vivid narrative. In writing *Back in the Beforetime* (1987), Jane Louise Curry knew that her audience was not going to be aware of the pantheon of the gods of the California Native American tribes, but she was committed first to the telling of story, and begins with this emphasis:

> Back in the Beforetime, when the World was new as new and flat as flat, Old Man Above, who had made it, sat above the sky and puzzled what to do with it. The World floated far below, wrapped up in the deep dark, for it was so new that the stars were still unlit.
>
> Old Man Above wondered if his World would do to live in. For how was he to tell? His eyes were sharp—sharp enough to spy the Wind—but he could not see down through the dark. (1)

The emphasis here is on plot narrative, in drawing the audience into the tale.

The work of Jean Guard Monroe and Ray Williamson represents a very different approach. Where Curry tries to take on the role of the oral storyteller, in *They Dance in the Sky* (1987), Monroe and Williamson take a much more distant approach, telling the stories as examples, almost artifacts, of Native American culture. Each story is introduced by an explanatory passage, as this one about the Pleiades: "Throughout North America, Native Americans have told stories about this tiny constellation and used it to organize their calendars. Some tribes watched the unique bunch of stars before it disappeared in the sunsets of early spring for clues about when to begin their yearly planting" (2). This stance is completely different from that of Goble and Curry; it suggests that the role of the oral teller cannot be completely recaptured, and that the stories must, instead, be viewed from a distance.

In *Wings* (1991), Jane Yolen suggests the orality of these stories—or at least the presence of a responsive audience—by creating alternate speakers and audiences. The powerful rhythmic text, which establishes repeating motifs and images, carries the principal plot narrative. But, beneath each page of text, is a short response set in italic type, suggesting the response of a choruslike character from Greek drama. Thus, we are told, for example, that the people of Athens loved Daedalus and knew that the gods would love him forever. "The gods listened," the choric response reads, "and did not like to be told what to do." In fact, the gods themselves are a clear audience for the story. They react with pleasure at the sight of the birth of Icarus, with thoughtfulness at the battle with the Minotaur that makes Daedalus flee, and with horror at the death of Icarus as he falls from the sky. Here, Yolen has created, in addition to the reader, responders that suggest the oral quality of the story.

Regarding this issue, illustrations, too, play a role; they can contribute to the recovery of an oral tradition by reproducing for a modern audience the artistic motifs of the parent culture. No illustrator is more effective at using illustration to suggest the nature of a culture than Gerald McDermott. He incorporates pottery designs, sandpainting patterns, bright colors and bold shapes, and any motifs that apply to the artwork of a given culture in order to establish that culture as the originator of the story. In *Arrow to the Sun*, he uses the square motifs of Pueblo art, along with its desertlike colors. In *The Magic Tree* (1973), McDermott, using bold African designs and primary colors, retells the story of the man whose bragging cost him the life he loved. The story fairly undulates across the page, stretching the audience's ideas of representational art. In *The Stone Cutter: A Japanese Folk Tale* (1975), McDermott cuts his colorful designs from paper he has painted and then mounts them in collage style to evoke the art of Japan. In *The Voyage of Osiris: A Myth of Ancient Egypt* (1977), McDermott uses the shapes and symbols of Egyptian culture. His innovative technique of painting and then cutting the story pieces into frames to be photographed blends a primitive style with modern skills. *The Knight of the Lion* (1979) delves into Arthurian mythology to retell the adventures of Yvain and his lion. This time McDermott chooses black-and-white illustrations reminiscent of woodcuts to embody the power of the story. In *Sun Flight* (1980) and *Daughter of the Earth: A Roman Myth* (1984), McDermott turns to abstract shapes and symbols to tell his stories visually, representing not only the seasons symbolically, but the very characters as well, all in an effort to show how the symbols might have been used by the parent culture.

Whichever principle is embraced—becoming the oral teller or abandoning that role, using the artistic motifs of a culture or turning to contemporary representations—the reteller must recognize that, as with all folk tales, the stories do begin as oral tales, and their refinements and subtleties, developed through generations, are peculiar to a given culture. It is virtually impossible to recover that original retelling for a contemporary audience through a print medium.

How do retellers adapt what were adult myths and epics for adult audiences to a child audience in contemporary North America?

In the Norse myth of Thor and Geirrod, Thor and Odin come to the Vimur—a wide river composed of water and menstrual blood. In Kevin Crossley-Holland's *The Norse Myths* (1980), the episode poses some difficulties in a retelling for a child audience: "Thor paused to regain his breath and looked upstream into a rocky ravine. And there he saw the cause of their hardship: Geirrod's daughter, Gjalp, was standing astride the torrent and blood was streaming from her, increasing the depth of the river." Thor hurls a rock at Gjalp. "He aimed well. Gjalp was maimed." The focus on menstrual blood here would be outside the boundaries of children's literature, so, when Crossley-Holland wrote a collection of Norse myths specifically directed at a child's audience, *Axe-Age, Wolf-Age* (1985), he changed this image to the giant's melting a torrent of water to sweep Thor and Odin away.

In making the change, Crossley-Holland has followed the lead of many retellers of myths. Myths and epics were adult stories, told to an adult audience. They are erotic and sexual, filled with the bawdy (Loki tying a thong behind his testicles) and vulgar (Odin boasting of plunging his "shaft" into heroes and virgins). In Greek myth there are the not infrequent abductions and rapes by Zeus, the violence of the sexuality presenting yet another difficulty.

Some have not shrunk from these elements. Charles Mikolaycak's *Orpheus* (1992), for example, retells the tale of Orpheus's search for his beloved Eurydice, finally finding her in hell, only to lose her again when his curiosity overcomes him. Mikolaycak creates a very sensual story in which all the characters are nude; the illustrations are vivid and erotic, as he plays up the scale of the sexuality. The closing illustration—following the penultimate illustration of Orpheus's bleeding naked body—shows the head having been torn off by the frenzied Maenads. Here the violence and eroticism of the story have been given full play.

Most writers of children's literature would see such an approach as having exceeded—perhaps having far exceeded—the boundaries of children's literature. If the retelling is to be appropriate to a child audience, then the sexuality and violence of the tales must be handled in such a manner that the child audience will focus, not on these elements, but on the larger narratives and meanings of the story.

In general, however, most retellers of myths for children avoid this problem simply through selection; there are few retellings of the rape of Europa for a child audience, and, where they do appear, they are in longer collections for older children. The dominant concern is to find a way to retell the tale so as to overcome the cultural barriers that lie before the North American child reader and the original tellers of the tale. This usually means that the work will provide context not obtrusively, but as an inherent part of the narrative.

Ingri and Edgar Parin D'Aulaire, in their *Book of Greek Myths* (1962) and *Norse Gods and Giants* (1967), remove the violence and sexuality of the stories, both in their texts and in their gentle illustrations. The rape of Europa becomes Zeus's benevolent act: He has "come to earth to make her his bride and the Queen of Crete," and, in fact, she lived in Crete, "in glory and delight to the end of her days." The story of Geirrod's daughter is changed to the giantess making the river rise by straddling it; Thor throws a rock and "screaming, the giantess raced off." The illustration shows a giantess whose smile is too silly to look malignant. In fact, the D'Aulaires are careful throughout their book to eliminate problematic passages and to use illustrations that delight through their bright color, simple forms, foreshortened perspective, and imaginative details.

Perhaps most important in the conversion of an adult tale to a tale retold to children is the preservation of the larger meanings of the story. In such conversion, the child's retelling will often have its meanings more explicitly portrayed. In Mordicai Gerstein's *The Shadow of a Flying Bird* (1994), Gerstein retells a Kurdistani tale about the death of Moses. It is a story that explores a love of life and the qualities of God. In the end, when Moses's soul has finally been persuaded to leave him, Gerstein shows God mourning the passing of Moses, even though his soul comes to heaven. "In death as in life, Moses is yours. His soul will be with you forever and always." This is true, and something to rejoice in. But the terrible pain of his death is also true, and not to be neglected. This is a paradox that is central to the story, and Gerstein makes it explicit both in text and illustration.

Whether handling a tale's sexuality and violence, or making a tale's original culture and meanings clearer, the reteller of a myth or epic for a child audience is faced with the task of conveying a tale not only to a different culture, but to an entirely different audience in terms of age. While practically speaking this realization has meant that some tales are simply not retold, it has also meant that tales have been adapted to the needs of the audience. In fulfilling this adaptation, contemporary retellers are continuing the technique of an oral reteller adapting to his or her specific audience at a specific time in a specific place.

Authors and Illustrators of Myths and Epics

> Stories were told after dark when the mind's eye sees most clearly. Winter evenings were best, when the children were lying under their buffalo robes and the fire was glowing at the center of the tipi. After the sounds in the camp had grown quiet and the deer had come to graze, the storyteller would smooth the earth in front of him; rubbing his hands together, he would pass them over his head and body. He was remembering that the Creator had made the people out of the earth, and would be witness to the truth of the story he was going to tell.

This opening to Paul Goble's *Her Seven Brothers* (1988) establishes several of the issues that any reteller of myth and epic must confront. There is the sense here that myths are experiential, tied to a particular culture and its experience. The act of telling the myth or epic also involves some sense of separation, here suggested by ritual, to give the notion that this is an act separate from mere day-to-day speech. And there is the sense here that the telling of myth is an act demanding responsibility and accountability. Insofar as these are true stories, attempting explanations for true events, the telling of them matters.

All of these are elements that the reteller must consider.

Retellers of Native American Myths

John Bierhorst (b. 1936)

John Bierhorst began his professional career as a concert pianist, but, during a field trip to Peru, he became interested in native cultures and decided to pursue anthropology, specializing in the Aztec language. He does not call himself an anthropologist but a translator who wishes to make the native cultures of the world better known. Noted for his accurate translations and his attention to detail, as well as exhaustive crediting of sources, he first published *Four Masterworks of American Indian Literature* (1974), which presents four myths that Bierhorst declares have heretofore been "hidden." He recreates for readers the hero myth of Quetzalcoatl from the Aztecs, a Ritual of Condolence from the Iroquois, the prophetic Cuceb from the Maya, and the Night Chant from the Navajo. In the introduction to the book, Bierhorst stresses that he is presenting each of these particulars in order to showcase a universal. Thus, the myth speaks not only to the culture, but to all humanity.

With *Black Rainbow: Legends of the Incas and Myths of Ancient Peru* (1976), Bierhorst moved to the more particular. He included more background of the native peoples, explaining the difficult terrain and the history of the Inca tribe itself. By focusing on the Incan ability to conquer other native tribes by arms or bribery, then to force the conquered people to learn the Incan language, to accept the new governmental system, and, sometimes, even to relocate, Bierhorst related geography, religion, history, and literature to present native cultures. This technique would be part of his work from this book on.

The Hungry Woman: Myths and Legends of the Aztecs (1984) and *Mythology of North America* (1985) established Bierhorst's interest in the sacred aspects of myths. These oral myths told of the beginnings of the Aztecs, of the creation of four worlds before this fifth, and of the people's belief that Quetzacoatl would reappear to them. In *Mythology of North America,* Bierhorst suggests the human quality of mythology, arguing that myths come from the past and reflect the desires, dreams, fears, realities of a particular group of people. Here though, Bierhorst goes further to carefully situate these myths historically by tracing the process by which they were written down.

Because his aim in this book is to not only tell myths, but talk about myths, he discusses the attempts in the late 1880s to preserve the Native American legends before they were gone. He presents their oldest sources, maps that follow their dissemination, pictures of cult objects, and a glossary and index. In addition, Bierhorst speculates about the nature of storytelling by suggesting that it is an art, bringing together the teller and truth and the audience. He argues that, although storytelling is an ephemeral art that takes place in a particular time and location, it is no less valuable than later printed versions. In fact, in many ways, Bierhorst gives the impression that he prefers the oral presentation to the printed one.

This attention to the unique qualities of storytelling marks Bierhorst's transition into the 1990s. In *The White Deer and Other Stories Told by the Lenape* (1995), he argues that folktales are both kept from oblivion and given new forms as they are retold. In this volume Bierhorst includes full-page pictures of storytellers as well as recounting the rules for storytelling. All stories should be told after dark during the cold months, so bugs, snakes, and lizards do not join the group. The audience sits around a campfire or in the middle of a ring of fires and looks expectantly to the storyteller. As the teller opens his or her bag of pebbles, a tale is told for each pebble. When the bag is empty, the session is over. The storyteller uses set phrases, set beginnings and endings, and so links himself to earlier storytellers as well as to this audience, who also know these phrases. Sometimes they may even shout in chorus as the story progresses.

Here, in addition to his careful maps, glossaries, indexes, and background information, Bierhorst immerses the reader in the culture by trying to recreate the role of the storyteller.

Paul Goble (b. 1933)

Paul Goble is another author/illustrator who came to Native American mythology from an unusual direction. He is an Englishman whose interest in native cultures began when he collected artifacts as a small boy. That grew into a lifelong desire to know more about Native Americans. Early in his career he visited the West during summer months, but in 1977 he moved his entire family to the American West and has lived there since that time.

His first book came about because he noted a deficiency in Western literature: As he looked around for reading material for his family, he found that most of it concentrated on the white man's point of view; he decided to correct that. His first book, *Red Hawk's Account of Custer's Last Battle* (1969), argues that Native Americans can be proud of this battle because of the bravery and intelligence of their warriors. The story is told from fifteen-year-old Red Hawk's point of view. The illustrations, although not as numerous as in Goble's later books, show the signature design for which Goble has become famous. He takes his stylized designs from patterns he has seen on tipis and other objects in Native American culture and from early ledger-book art, with its illustration on the left-hand side and its interpretation on the right. The text is fairly formal, almost poetic, as Goble tries to evoke the oral tradition.

In *Brave Eagle's Account of the Fetterman Fight* (1972), Paul Goble continues to challenge the accepted historical perspective by telling the story from the Native American side. Once again, the Indians won the battle, and once again Goble wants children to hear about the glorious deeds of their ancestors, both so that they can be proud, but also so that they can emulate their heroes' character traits. In *Death of the Iron Horse* (1987), Goble tells the story of the only train wrecked by Indians. Although they have been blamed for many train wrecks, this is the only substantiated instance. Goble's account of this event begins mythically, with the medicine man's prediction that white men will come to the Indian's territory. It moves through the terror the warriors feel at seeing the long snake with smoke that blows against the wind, to their chopping up the rails, and, finally, the derailing of the train. But he ends with the warriors facing away because they see more white men coming.

This sympathetic but honest presentation of a culture that has almost been lost hallmarks each of Paul Goble's books. His books are marked by a kind of urgency; in the face of so much loss, some may be saved. But, even beyond this, it is Goble's belief in the usefulness of myth today that defines his purpose. Truths conveyed through myths do not change with the years, he argues. And these essential truths are human truths, translatable from one culture to the next. *Buffalo Woman* (1984) establishes this by reminding readers that the story will not simply entertain; its retelling yields the power to change, so that listeners might be worthier persons.

This immediate connection between the mythic story and the listener can be seen in *Her Seven Brothers* (1988), where first the storyteller smoothes the earth in front of him, rubs his hands together, and pats them over his body so as to remember that, in the same manner, the creator made man out of the dust and would be the witness of the truth of the story. That storyteller's audience of children snuggled under a buffalo robe turns into contemporary readers. In *The Lost Children* (1993), the storyteller pulls a weed from the ground and points out to his audience that, just as the weed has several branches, so does the story he is about to tell; but, just as those branches are connected to the main stem, so is his story.

Perhaps nowhere is this linkage of myth and immediate concern more vivid than in *Beyond the Ridge* (1989), in which Goble uses the metaphor of a journey over rocky ground to tell the story of the beloved grandmother who leaves this world at her death. Her dogs are the only ones who see her get up from the body to leave as she hears her mother's voice and follows. She is surprised to find that she is wearing her favorite dress and moccasins, and, though the climb up the ridge is hard, she is encouraged by the voice and, at the top, by a glimpse of a beautiful country "stretching blue and green into the distance." It is a paradise with flowers and rivers and herds of buffalo, and she heads to a circle of tipis where those who had died before her wait. "She felt strong again. The way down from the top was so easy and beautiful. She even wanted to run. There was no other path to take." The concern is universal; the metaphor is particular. But, in capturing the larger meaning of that metaphor, Goble has moved from the particular to the universal, showing customs unique to a certain people, but concerns that mark all.

Goble also retells more humorous stories about the trickster Iktomi: *Iktomi and the Berries* (1989), *Iktomi and the Ducks* (1990), *Iktomi and the Buffalo Skull* (1991). He includes these trickster tales for several reasons: They are old and have been found on tipis, they show children what not to do in this society, they relieve tension that can build up when everything is too serious, and they indeed entertain. Here, too, Goble has brought Iktomi up to current times and metafictively shows that Iktomi is aware of the impropriety of "this white guy" telling stories about him, ones that he doesn't like.

Deborah Nourse Lattimore

In bringing unfamiliar stories from relatively unfamiliar cultures into the arena of children's literature, Deborah Nourse Lattimore faces the difficulty of finding a way to introduce an entire culture to a child audience without intrusive heavy-handedness. She chooses not to include an explanatory introduction, but, instead, to concentrate on the style of the artwork to introduce the culture. Thus, the opening of *The Prince and the Golden Ax* (1988) uses an introduction that does not so much explain as entice:

> Once, in ages now long past, an ancient people called the Minoans ruled the Aegean Sea. The beauty of their time filled the isles of Crete and Thera long before the arrival of the Greeks and all the gods of Olympus. Yet one day they vanished. Among the ruins were found a statue of a goddess and a double-bladed ax. Who is she, and what mystery lies behind her shining weapon? No one knows. But those who dream of such things tell this tale… (3)

The story is of Akros and his boasting, a boasting that leads to the anger of the gods and the destruction of the island in volcanic furor. The illustrations capture the Minoan culture, with elongated forms, one-dimensionality, and profiled characters.

In *The Flame of Peace* (1987) and *Why There Is No Arguing in Heaven* (1989), Lattimore turned to very different cultures. *The Flame of Peace* is an Aztec story in which a young boy called Two Flint decides to journey to Lord Morning Star in order to bring peace to his land and avoid the ravages of an invading army. Two Flint encounters the enemy, Lord Volcano, Lord Earthquake, and Lord Smoking Mirror, and is able to outwit each and bring back the sacred flame of peace. The motif of the journey allows Lattimore to illustrate all of these characters and, to introduce the culture, she turns to the bright, square, stylized forms of Aztec art. In fact, many of the characters, with their square forms and elongated features, reflect the sculpted stone artwork of the culture. The extravagant decorations and headdresses, the postures, the designed architecuture, all introduce young readers to the world of the Aztecs. To complement these spreads, Lattimore includes endpapers that identify the meanings of many of the pictoral motifs that appear in the picturebook.

In *Why There Is No Arguing in Heaven,* Lattimore turns to the Mayan culture; here, too, she uses the artwork of that culture, with its more elongated, sinuous, and less stylized forms. Much of the artwork looks as if it were made of stones, both in shape and color, and the placement of those forms against the lush background of the rain forest is striking. The story is a creation tale in which alternate possibilties for the creation of humanity are presented. Each of the gods creates man to worship Hunab Ku, but most are unsuccessful. The Lizard god uses mud, but it is washed away. The Moon goddess uses the wooden boughs of trees, but they can only screech. Finally, the Maize god plants his seeds, and from those seeds come the race of bronze men and women, and Hunab Ku is pleased. In her depiction of the scene, Lattimore is careful to color the new human with the glowing colors of fire.

Though the texts of her stories are quite similar and do not replicate the oral quality of a teller, the intimate wedding of the artwork with the culture creates a story for a child reader that distances the reader from the familiar and introduces a world that is of a piece with the tale. The potent visual illustrations create a landscape that would have been familiar to the original listeners of the myths, but that now is recreated for an audience unfamiliar with it.

Retellers of Greek Myths

Leonard Everett Fisher (b. 1924)

Leonard Everett Fisher's retellings of Greek myths are marked by dramatic, bold, huge illustrations in which the forms are seemingly crude, the shapes large and dominant, and the texture grainy, as though the illustrations might be found on rock faces. Background detail is minimal; the principal action alone draws the eye, and that action is always presented in a very human guise. Fisher's retelling of *Theseus and the Minotaur* (1988) rests mainly on the emotional connections among characters and a heightened presentation of the action. Thus, the minotaur is huge and wild-eyed; set against a darkened background, he fills an entire page. On the opposite page is Theseus, cowering most unherolike behind rocks and trying to gather his courage to attack. The same dramatic, primitive presentation holds true in *Jason and the Golden Fleece* (1990), in which readers see Jason in a very human stance; he holds up the golden fleece with great effort. While Jason is triumphant, as a hero ought to be, the strain of winning shows. Fisher's representation of *Cyclops* (1991) underscores his attitudes. He shows the Cyclops as a huge hairy man who lumbers into his cave at the end of the day, pops one of Odysseus's men in his mouth, and later pitifully gropes after his sheep with Odysseus's sharpened red-hot poker stuck in his eye.

Fisher does not back away from the violence of the stories, and the large shapes and prominent figures create a dramatic stage for that violence. At the same time, those very qualities give his retellings their power, their ability to show the nobility of the human endeavor.

Warwick Hutton (1939–1994)

Warwick Hutton moves in a direction very different from that of Leonard Everett Fisher in his depiction of the Greek myths. He uses brightly, thinly lined sketches to capture action. He chooses to concentrate his illustrations on calmer moments in the mythic tales. For instance, his *Theseus and the Minotaur* (1989) notes that everyone wept to see Theseus depart, including his father, but the illustration shows a distant frame of a ship leaving the harbor. The minotaur, though larger than Theseus, is downplayed; Hutton sketches him as a huge bull with only a token of the human side seen in the arms and legs. In his retelling of *Odysseus and the Cyclops* (1995), Hutton shows the Cyclops the moment before he eats one of Odysseus's men, and shows Odysseus at work sharpening and heating the stake he will use; he shows neither the actual eating nor the spearing. In *The Trojan Horse* (1992), *Persephone* (1994), and *Perseus* (1993), Hutton uses light watercolors and bright action that diminish the dark questions of Greek mythology. Fisher and Hutton retain details of the stories they use, but differ greatly about how and what to represent to children.

Retellers of the Epic Tradition

Rosemary Sutcliff (1920–1992)

Rosemary Sutcliff, well known for writing historical fiction centered in Britain, is equally well known for retelling Britain's epic tales. Her stories of King Arthur and his court, taken from the account of Sir Thomas Malory, have been read with pleasure since they came out. In 1971, *Tristan and Iseult* was published. Sutcliff decided to tell the story of the famous lovers, and she also decided to depart from hundreds of years of tradition and not include their drinking the love potion meant for Iseult and the king. Sutcliff declared that the addition had been made during the Middle Ages in order to give the two lovers an excuse that Sutcliff felt was unlikely. So her interpretation caused the two to flout vows and good intentions and commit themselves to each other out of their own wills.

Putting her own stamp on the stories was something Sutcliff continued to do as she wrote. Not only did she insist that storytellers traditionally had that right, to shift and change the elements somewhat, but she also insisted that the language used should be formal so that readers would know they had entered a world unlike their common everyday one. Her trilogy on the Arthurian cycle, *The Light beyond the Forest: The Quest for the Holy Grail* (1980), *The Sword and the Circle* (1981), and *The Road to Camlann: The Death of King Arthur* (1982), demonstrate her high style, as in this excerpt from *The Light beyond the Forest:*

> Now Sir Lancelot was as odd and ill-matching in his hidden inmost self as he was in his face for all to see.... He had a great and terrible hope in him, more fitted to a monk than to a knight, that one day, if he proved himself worthy, God would let him perform a miracle. But for that to happen, he would have to be the best knight in the world. So kneeling there in the moon-whitened chapel all night along, he prayed that he should become not just the strongest and bravest and most skilled knight, but the best. He prayed that he might never do anything to stain his honor or anybody else's; and he prayed for his miracle (87).

The language is not so formal as to discourage readers, but it is enough removed from the everyday vernacular that readers find themselves in places they have not been before. The meaning also underscores the irony of Lancelot's life: That the very thing he desired not to do, he could not resist doing. Indeed, it is the love affair between the queen and him that eventually brings down all of Camelot. Sutcliff brings those long ago times to modern readers with skill and passion.

The same commitment can be seen in an earlier work, *Beowulf* (1961). Speaking of the monster's terrifying mother, Sutcliff says,

> She was of the same kind as Grendel, monstrous evil, a Death-Shadow-in-the-Dark; but she had possessed the power to love, and she had loved her son, and was therefore more terrible than he had ever been. Now, mad with grief as a bitch-wolf whose cubs are taken from her, panting for revenge, she followed the day-old blood trail in the threshold of Heorot and hurled back the door (46).

Once again the formal, balanced language is rhythmic and subtle. Sutcliff shows that a mother's love for her child leads to her hatred of the man who killed him. A mother's love thus, ironically, makes the motive for killing stronger.

Geraldine McCaughrean (b. 1951)

One of the foremost retellers of epic tales, Geraldine McCaughrean has retold epics for the older child. In books like *Saint George and the Dragon* (1989) and *The Odyssey* (1993), McCaughrean has focused on the larger-than-life qualities of the epic heroes who will not shrink from fighting gods. Though Saint George is metamorphosed into a superhuman character at the end of the book, throughout the short tale he is very much the human, but the human who will not admit limitations. The battle scene suggests his dominance, as his bright shield turns aside the dragon's flames, and the imperturbability of the hero allows him to strike quickly at the dragon's heart. But still—and this is crucial in the epic—there is a real chance of loss, as at one point the dragon almost topples on him.

In *The Odyssey,* McCaughrean retells the familiar epic and mythic journey of Odysseus, and, though she does not play up the scale of the violence and sexuality of the tales, neither does she withhold these elements. Ulysses is clearly unfaithful to Penelope, and the temptations he endures are more often sexual in character than not. The illustrations coordinate with this approach, suggesting the violence of the stories, as well as the nature of the temptations. The language often lacks the formal diction and structures of Sutcliff's prose; in fact, it can, at times, be colloquial. But, even so, the retelling captures the spirit and varying tones and moods of the original.

With *El Cid* (1988), McCaughrean turned to an epic tale less familiar to children. Here the national hero of Castile fights against the Moors and captures the stronghold of Valencia. As with *The Odyssey,* McCaughrean writes for older readers, and so she does not hesitate to include the violence of the tales, particularly the horrific, climactic image of El Cid mounted, dead, on a horse, riding out to strike fear into the hearts of the invading Moors.

In all of these works, McCaughrean depends heavily on action scenes, and particularly on dialogue. There is little introspection and minimal description, in keeping with the epic tone of these tales.

Thinking and Writing about and from within Myth and Epic

Thinking and Writing about the Genres of Myth and Epic

1. Choose a type of character that appeals to your imagination: hero, heroine, trickster, monster. Then examine its representation in six cultures. What similarities do you see? What differences do you see? What is the meaning of these similarities and differences? Which culture's representation of the character type do you prefer? Why?

2. Write a book review of Diane Wynne Jones's *Eight Days of Luke* (1975), focusing on the appropriateness of taking characters out of their original mythological contexts.

3. Examine the images of the harpies and the blinding of the cyclops from Rosemary Sutcliff's *The Wanderings of Odysseus* (1995). Are these appropriate images for the retelling of a tale for a child audience?

Thinking and Writing from within the Genres of Myth and Epic _____

1. Mythology perhaps began as stories around a campfire. Choose a story that has already captured your interest and prepare it for a retelling. Think about the audience and what it needs to hear; learn, rather than memorize the story, and tell it.

2. Choose a favorite story from one of the mythologies presented in this chapter. Find as many retellings of it as possible and compare them for content and illustration. Then rewrite the story yourself for a young audience. Keep a journal of the decisions you made about such subjects as audience level, parts of the plot to leave in or take out, how much background to include, what scenes and characters you chose to illustrate, and the difficulties you encountered.

Selected Bibliographies

Works Cited _____

Crossley-Holland, Kevin. *Axe-Age, Wolf-Age.* London: André Deutsch, 1985.

———. *Beowulf.* Illustrated by Charles Keeping. New York: Oxford University Press, 1982.

———. *The Norse Myths.* New York: Random House, 1980.

Cruse, Amy. *The Young Folk's Book of Myths.* Boston: Little, Brown, 1927.

Curry, Jane Louise. *Back in the Beforetime.* New York: Margaret McElderry, 1987.

D'Aulaire, Ingri and Edgar Parin. *Book of Greek Myths.* Garden City, NY: Doubleday, 1962.

———. *Norse Gods and Giants.* Garden City, NY: Doubleday, 1967.

DeSpain, Pleasant. *Eleven Turtle Tales.* Illustrated by Joe Shlichta. Little Rock: August House, 1994.

Gerson, Mary Joan. *How Night Came from the Sea.* Illustrated by Carla Golembe. Boston: Little, Brown, 1994.

Gerstein, Mordicai. *The Shadow of a Flying Bird.* New York: Hyperion, 1994.

Hodges, Margaret. *The Kitchen Knight.* Illustrated by Trina Schart Hyman. New York: Holiday House, 1990.

———. *Saint George and the Dragon.* Illustrated by Trina Schart Hyman. Boston: Little, Brown, 1984.

Hoffman, Mary. *Earth, Fire, Water, Air.* Illustrated by Jane Ray. New York: Penguin, 1995.

Howe, John, *The Knight with the Lion.* Boston: Little, Brown, 1996.

Hyde, Lilian Stoughton. *Favorite Greek Myths.* London: George G. Harrap, 1905.

Jacobs, Joseph. *The Book of Wonder Voyages.* Illustrated by John Batten. New York: Arno, 1967.

Jones, Dianne Wynne. *Eight Days of Luke.* New York: Alfred A. Knopf, 1975.

Kampuchean, Carole Tate. *The Tale of the Spiteful Spirits.* New York: Bedrick/Blackie, 1991.

Kingsley, Charles. *The Heroes.* Illustrated by Ron King. Chicago: Children's Press, 1968.

Low, Alice. *The Macmillan Book of Greek Gods and Heroes.* Illustrated by Arvis Stewart. New York: Macmillan, 1985.

MacManus, Seumas. *Hibernian Nights.* Illustrated by Paul Kennedy. New York: Macmillan, 1963.

McDermott, Gerald. *Arrow to the Sun.* New York: Viking, 1974.

———. *Daughter of the Earth: A Roman Myth.* New York: Delacorte, 1984.

———. *The Knight of the Lion.* New York: Four Winds, 1979.

———. *The Magic Tree: A Tale from the Congo.* New York: Holt, Rinehart & Winston, 1973.

———. *Raven: A Trickster Tale from the Pacific Northwest.* San Diego: Harcourt Brace Jovanovich, 1993.

———. *The Stone Cutter: A Japanese folk tale.* New York: Viking, 1975.

———. *Sun Flight.* New York: Four Winds, 1980.

———. *The Voyage of Osiris: A Myth of Ancient Egypt.* New York: E. P. Dutton, 1977.

———. *Zomo, the Rabbit.* San Diego: Harcourt Brace Jovanovich, 1992.

Mikolaycak, Charles. *Orpheus.* New York: Harcourt Brace Jovanovich, 1992.

Monroe, Jean Guard and Ray Williamson. *They Dance in the Sky.* Boston: Houghton Mifflin, 1987.

Moorse, Christopher. *Ishtar and Tammuz.* Illustrated by Christina Balit. New York: Kingfisher, 1996.

Nunukul, Oodgeroo. *Dreamtime: Aboriginal Stories.* Illustrated by Bronwyn Bancroft. New York: Lothrop, Lee, and Shephard, 1972.

O'Neill, Cynthia, Peter Casterton and Catherine Headlam, eds. *Goddesses, Heroes and Shamans: The Young People's Guide to World Mythology.* New York: Kingfisher, 1995.

Osborne, Mary Pope. *Favorite Greek Myths.* Illustrated by Troy Howell. New York: Scholastic, 1989.

———. *Favorite Norse Myths.* Illustrated by Troy Howell. New York: Scholastic, 1996.

Philip, Neil. *The Illustrated Book of Myths.* Illustrated by Nilesh Mistry. London: Darling Kindersley, 1995.

Ross, Gayle. *How Rabbit Tricked Otter and Other Cherokee Trickster Stories.* New York: HarperCollins, 1994.

Roth, Susan. *Fire Came to the Earth People.* New York: St. Martin's, 1988.

Sabuda, Robert. *Arthur and the Sword.* New York: Atheneum, 1995.

San Souci, Robert D. *Young Lancelot.* Illustrated by Jamichael Henterly. New York: Doubleday, 1996.

Talbott, Hudson. *King Arthur and the Round Table.* New York: Morrow, 1995.

Thomas, Gwyn and Kevin Crossley-Holland. *Tales from the Mabinogion.* Illustrated by Margaret Jones. Woodstock, NY: Overlook, 1984.

The Usborne Book of Greek and Norse Legends. Illustrated by Rodney Matthews. Tulsa, OK: EDC, 1987.

Waldherr, Kris. *The Book of Goddesses.* Hillsboro, OR: Beyond Words, 1995.

Wood, Douglas. *Old Turtle.* Illustrated by Cheng-Khee Lee. New York: Pfeifer-Hamilton, 1992.

The World Mythology Series. New York: Peter Bedrick, 1982.

Yolen, Jane. *Wings.* Illustrated by Dennis Nolen. New York: Harcourt Brace Jovanovich, 1991.

Works of Selected Retellers

John Bierhorst

Black Rainbow: Legends of the Incas and Myths of Ancient Peru. New York: Farrar, Straus, and Giroux, 1976.

Four Masterworks of American Indian Literature. New York: Farrar, Straus, and Giroux, 1974.

The Hungry Woman: Myths and Legends of the Aztecs. New York: William Morrow, 1984.

Mythology of North America. New York: William Morrow, 1985.

The White Deer and Other Stories Told by the Lenape. New York: William Morrow, 1995.

The Woman Who Fell From the Sky. Illustrated by Robert Andrew Parker. New York: William Morrow, 1993.

Leonard Everett Fisher

Cyclops. New York: Holiday House, 1991.

Jason and the Golden Fleece. New York: Holiday House, 1990.

The Olympians: Great Gods and Goddesses of Ancient Greece. New York: Holiday House, 1984.

Pyramid of the Sun, Pyramid of the Moon. New York: Macmillan, 1988.

Theseus and the Minotaur. New York: Holiday House, 1988.

Paul Goble

Adopted by the Eagles: A Plains Indian Story of Friendship and Treachery. New York: Bradbury Press, 1994.

Beyond the Ridge. New York: Bradbury, 1989.

Brave Eagle's Account of the Fetterman Fight: 21 December, 1866. New York: Pantheon Books, 1972. Lincoln, Nebraska: University of Nebraska Press, 1992.

Buffalo Woman. New York: Bradbury, 1984.

Death of the Iron Horse. Scarsdale, New York: Bradbury, 1987.

Her Seven Brothers. New York: Bradbury, 1988.

Iktomi and the Berries. New York: Orchard, 1989.

Iktomi and the Buffalo Skull. New York: Orchard, 1991.

Iktomi and the Ducks. New York: Orchard, 1990.

The Lost Children. New York: Bradbury, 1993.

Love Flute. New York: Bradbury, 1992.

Red Hawk's Account of Custer's Last Battle. New York: Pantheon Books, 1969. Rpt. Lincoln, NE: University of Nebraska Press, 1992.

The Return of the Buffalo. Washington, DC: National Geographic Society, 1996.

Star Boy. Scarsdale, New York: Bradbury, 1983.

Warwick Hutton

Odysseus and the Cyclops. New York: Margaret K. McElderry, 1995.

Persephone. New York: Margaret K. McElderry, 1994.

Perseus. New York: Margaret K. McElderry, 1993.

Theseus and the Minotaur. New York: Margaret K. McElderry, 1989.

The Trojan Horse. New York: Margaret K. McElderry, 1992.

Deborah Nourse Lattimore

The Flame of Peace. New York: Harper and Row, 1987.

The Prince and the Golden Ax. New York: Harper and Row, 1988.

Why There Is No Arguing in Heaven. New York: Harper and Row, 1989.

Geraldine McCaughrean

El Cid. New York: Oxford University Press, 1988. Illustrated by Victor G. Ambrus.

The Golden Hoard. Illustrated by Bea Willey. New York: Margaret K. McElderry, 1995.

The Odyssey. New York: Oxford University Press, 1993. Illustrated by Victor G. Ambrus.

Saint George and the Dragon. Garden City, NY: Doubleday, 1989. Illustrated by Nicki Palin.

The Silver Treasure. Illustrated by Bea Willey. New York: Margaret K. McElderry, 1996.

Rosemary Sutcliff

Beowulf. New York: Dutton, 1961.

The Black Ships of Troy: The Story of the Iliad. Illustrated by Alan Lee. New York: Delacorte, 1995.

Dragon Slayer: The Story of Beowulf. Illustrated by Charles Keeping. New York: Macmillan, 1980.

The Light beyond the Forest: The Quest for the Holy Grail. Illustrated by Shirley Felts. New York: Dutton, 1980.

The Road to Camlann: The Death of King Arthur. Illustrated by Shirley Felts. New York: Dutton, 1982.

The Shining Company. New York: Farrar Straus, 1990.

The Sword and the Circle. Illustrated by Shirley Felts. New York: Dutton, 1981.

Tristan and Iseult. New York: Dutton, 1971.

The Wanderings of Odysseus. Illustrated by Alan Lee. New York: Delacorte, 1995.

Works on the Retelling of Myth and Epic in Children's Literature _____

Austin, Norman. *Meaning and Being in Myth.* University Park: Pennsylvania State University Press, 1990.

Aylwin, Tony. "Using Myths and Legends in School." *Children's Literature* 12 (1981): 82–89.

Baeten, Elizabeth M. *The Magic Mirror: Myth's Abiding Power.* Albany, NY: State University of New York Press, 1996.

Bettleheim, Bruno. *The Uses of Enchantment: The Meaning and Importance of Fairy Tales.* New York: Knopf, 1976.

Biallas, Leonard. *Myths: Gods, Heroes, and Saviors.* Mystic, CT: Twenty-Third Publications, 1986.

Campbell, Joseph. *The Hero with a Thousand Faces.* Princeton, NJ: Princeton University Press, 1949.

———. *The Flight of the Wild Gander.* New York: Viking, 1951.

Eliade, Mircea. *Myth and Reality.* New York: Harper & Row, 1963.

Ewers, Hans-Heino. "Old Heroes in New Dress." *Lion and the Unicorn* 9 (1985): 170–174.

Goble, Paul. "On Beaded Dresses and the Blazing Sun." In Gary D. Schmidt and Donald R. Hettings, eds., *Sitting at the Feet of the Past* (Westport, CT: Greenwood, 1992): 5–14.

Leeming, David. *The World of Myth.* New York: Oxford University Press, 1990.

Lowry, Shirley Park. *Familiar Mysteries: The Truth in Myth.* New York: Oxford University Press, 1982.

Mahy, Margaret. "A Dissolving Ghost." In Sheila Egoff, Gordon Stubbs, Ralph Ashley, and Wendy Sutton, eds., *Only Connections: Readings on Children's Literature.* New York: Oxford University Press, 1996: 135–53.

McDermott, Gerald. "Caldecott Award Acceptance." *Horn Book* (August 1975): 349–354.

Melani, Lilia. "A Child's Psyche: Recollections of Fairy Tales, Myths, and Romances." *Lion and the Unicorn* 3 (1979): 14–27.

Mills, Alice. "Two Versions of *Beowulf.*" *Children's Literature in Education* 17 (1986): 75–87.

Otten, Charlotte, and Gary Schmidt, eds. *The Voice of the Narrator in Children's Literature.* New York: Greenwood, 1989.

Russell, David L. "Pinocchio and the Child: Hero's Quest." *Children's Literature in Education* 20 (1989): 203–213.

Sidwell, R. T. "Rhea Was a Broad: Pre-Hellenic Greek Myths for Post-Hellenic Children." *Children's Literature in Education* 12 (1981): 171–176.

Thomas, Joyce. "Woods and Castles, Towers, and Huts: Aspects of Setting in the Fairy Tale." *Only Connect: Readings on Children's Literature.* In Sheila Egoff, . . . eds., New York: Oxford University Press, 1996: 122–129.

Vickery, Gill. "The Authurian Antecedents of Gene Kemp's *The Turbulent Term of Tyke Tiler.*" *Children's Literature in Education* 24 (1993): 185–193.

Wilson, Raymond. "*Slake's Limbo:* A Myth-Critical Approach." *Children's Literature in Education* 18 (1984): 219–226.

Wrightson, Patricia. "Deeper Than You Think." In Sheila Egoff, . . . eds., *Only Connections: Readings of Children's Literature.* New York: Oxford University Press, 1996: 154–161.

7

The Retelling of the Biblical Tale

A number of years ago, the British author Peter Dickinson was approached by a publisher eager to have him write a collection of Bible stories. Dickinson instantly rejected the idea. Such stories, he felt, had been told over and over again in innumerable Bible storybooks. He felt that they were almost cultural clichés, and that there was little chance of finding a way into such stories, of making them fresh and new, of invigorating them with a dramatic narrative so that they would become vibrant.

What Dickinson faced was the problem of too much familiarity. In retelling the myths of other cultures, North American authors may generally assume that few children will know the stories; such authors do not first have to overcome the sense that these are tales that need no telling. Not many children know the Taino creation story or the epic of Gilgamesh. But many biblical stories have entered into the culture in such a way that they are almost clichés, devoid of any real power because their endings are so well known, their characters so well understood. How could Dickinson find a new way to retell the story of Noah and the Flood, or Moses and the Red Sea, or Abraham and Isaac?

But the idea nagged at Dickinson. These are, after all, the great foundational stories of the culture. They are stories that are told generation after generation, stories that have become clichéd because they have become so widespread. As myths, the stories do indeed engage with life's most elemental questions, striving to find answers to such questions or, at least, the correct means of framing those questions. And, for many in the culture, the stories of the Old and New Testaments carry a special meaning, in that they are part of a faith heritage, as other myths might work in another culture. For many, these stories speak of the relationship of humanity to God, the source of all meaning. The stories are, thus, both mythic and historical.

Dickinson wrestled with the problem of the familiar, and, not long after the initial request, he called his publisher to accept the project. He remembered that the stories of the Bible, like all myths, were first told orally. So, in writing *City of Gold* (1980), he retold the stories by putting them into the mouths of those who would have told the stories orally. The story of Eden, for example, is told by an exiled Hebrew slave in the days of the Babylonian Captivity; the story of Egypt's plagues is told by a father to his family while in hiding from Antiochus Epiphanes. In each case, Dickinson de-familiarized the stories of the Bible by casting them into the mouths of unexpected narrators, narrators for whom the stories were immediately applicable and moving. A pilgrim describing Jerusalem captures this sense of immediacy:

> But sometimes, drawing a stillness round myself in the clamour and jostling of the courtyard, it is almost as though my soul were standing, eyes closed, by a great fire, whose heat throbbed out towards me. I do not need even to be there to feel it, because always I carry in my heart the vision of Jerusalem, lying in gold and stillness along its ridge, which my father gave me on my first pilgrimage. (140)

Creating such narrators erases familiarity for the contemporary reader.

It is the task of all retellers of biblical tales to erase familiarity, to create a meaningful distance so that the stories may be told with power and meaning. But, even as he or she de-familiarizes, the reteller of a biblical tale must still tell the authentic tale, so that the story's ethos—its basic meaning and context—are preserved. At times these two impulses—distancing and preserving—vie with each other; the successful biblical retelling crafts the aesthetics and meaning of the story in the crucible of that tension.

Boundaries and Definitions of the Retold Biblical Tale

Though the claims for historicity are more marked in biblical tales than in some other mythologies, Bible stories do share with other mythic tales the search for answers to the large questions of existence. They ask about the nature of the world, both in terms of its creation and governance. They ask about the nature of God. They ask about the world beyond the senses, and about the nature of death, and about existence after death. They ask about the immediacy of the relationship between God and humanity, and about the impact of that relationship on moral behavior. They ask questions about the nature of a community, about the nature of an individual, and about their mutual responsibilities and roles. And, like most mythic stories, the answers they give are at times immediate and overt, at times hidden and subtle.

It would seem that the boundaries of the biblical tale would be obvious: The retelling is bound by the text with which it deals. Thus, a retelling of the story of Miriam and the baby Moses is bound by the scriptural version of that story, and the reteller looks for ways of giving vitality to details already established in an ancient text.

In *Esther's Story* (1996), however, Diane Wolkstein expands on the traditional story of Esther by using her both as protagonist and narrator. She develops the character of Esther by adding a tale about her childhood to explain her commitment to her people, and by imagining scenes that are only suggested in the biblical text. When the king sends for Esther to decide if she is to be the new queen, the biblical text is quite sparse in terms of the events of their first meeting: "Now the king was attracted to Esther more than to any of the other women, and she won his favor and approval more than any of the other virgins" (Esther 2.17). But Wolkstein adds significantly to that sketch:

> The king was standing by the window. He looked a little lonely. His arms were folded. I folded mine in the same way. He scratched his head. I scratched mine, and a tiny pink rose fell to the floor. As I bent to pick it up, the king said, "How beautiful you are!"
>
> I put the rose in his curly hair and said, "How beautiful *you* are!"
> He laughed. I liked his laugh. It was deep and growly and unexpected.
> "Laugh again," I said, and I tickled him.
> A big happy laugh came bursting out of him, like water from a fountain.
> When he stopped laughing, he picked up the crown from the table and, without asking my name, said, "You, my shining one, shall be queen."

This scene is Wolkstein's addition, her imagining of what won the heart of Xerxes. Another author might have yet a different understanding, perhaps arguing that a young girl meeting the king for the first time would probably not be so playful as the Esther of this scene. In either case, the author has expanded the biblical text to flesh out characters and situations.

In Philip Turner's collection, *The Bible Story* (1968), yet another boundary is stretched. This text covers many biblical tales, often quite quickly and with strict adherence to the details. But, not infrequently, Turner expands on a text, not simply to flesh out a story, but in order to comment on the story's meaning. In a scene from the temptations of Jesus, for example, he wants to suggest the nature of Satan's third temptation: the world itself.

> Jesus was on a high mountain; like Sinai, or Mont Blanc, or Everest. It was a high place of the mind from which he could see all the earth from the beginning to the end of time: Adam in the garden, Solomon in Jerusalem, the hanging gardens of Babylon, the white pillars of imperial Rome, skyscrapers in New York, motor-cars in London, and pinnacles like onions in Moscow.... Out of this pageant of all the kings of all the world came the temptation: "All this shall be yours—if you will kneel and worship me." (94)

Here the expansion of the biblical passage—"The devil led him up to a high place and showed him in an instant all the kingdoms of the world" (Luke 4.5)—suggests that the temptation is not simply one that deals with the present, but one that transcends time itself. To do this, he adds the images of both ancient and modern cities, and these become part of the real temptation.

In both of these cases, the edges of the traditional tale have been blurred. In *Esther's Story,* the author has gone well beyond the confines of the textual narrative to move towards historical fiction, endowing protagonists and antagonists with fuller characters and creating narrative plotlines that spring from but do not adhere to biblical material. In *The Bible Story* Turner has added material for the purposes of interpreting, so that the retelling is not so much a dramatization of a plotline as it is a fleshing out of an interpretive model.

The Boundaries of a Retelling

On the one hand, biblical tales may be defined as stories that adhere strictly to their corresponding biblical texts. Under this definition, retellings would include material that was defined by the text alone. Characterization, questions of motivation, contextual definition, the role of minor characters—all of these would be strictly subordinate to the biblical text. Some retellings are, in fact, hardly retellings at all, but instead take their texts directly from versions of the Bible. Jane Ray's *Noah's Ark* (1990), Julie Vivas's *The Nativity* (1988), and Elizabeth Winthrop's *He Is Risen: The Easter Story* (1985) take as their text the King James Version of the Bible, choosing that version for its muscular cadences, though each of them, particularly Winthrop, modifies the text somewhat for ease of reading. *Tomie DePaola's Book of Bible Stories* (1990) uses the New International Version of the Bible, and here he makes no changes at all, given that version's more contemporary and familiar language. In these books there is very little distinction between the scriptural version of the text and that presented for the child reader.

In his preface to *The Book of Adam to Moses* (1987), Lore Segal expressed the difficulty of working with a text such as that of King James, of adapting such a text to a child audience.

> [H]ow do we translate the word the King James text renders as "behold," Luther as *siehe*? Some moderns translate "look." "Look" will do—though we are more likely to say "listen" when one human wants another to pay attention. But "look" does not *feel* right when it occurs in a dialogue between God and man, in either direction. Why not leave it out, then, since it adds nothing to content? Because we would lose a looseness in the rhythm, the sense of presence, of connectedness between the divine and the human having a conversation.
>
> And so one broods over each recurrence of each problem and keeps trying it this way and that, unable, ever, entirely, to abandon hope of, sooner or later, getting it exactly right. (x)

Even the reteller who stays very close to the biblical text, then, finds difficulties in the relationship of language and meaning, in the task of preserving poetic rhythm and reverence through the language, in the work of matching diction to tone and meaning.

On the other hand, the reteller of a biblical tale may move away from a pre-scribed text in order to de-familiarize or to interpret. Here the goal of the reteller is both to make the text more dramatic and to show its meaning more clearly to a contemporary child audience. Or the goal might be to show the larger contexts of the story, or to suggest possibilities about the action that the reader may not have gleaned from the spare biblical text. Here, the reteller is not so invested with the purpose of simply repeating the details already given in the text as he or she is invested with the purpose of suggesting meanings that the reader may not have anticipated, or may have overlooked because of the familiarity of the story.

Thus, though Julie Vivas's *The Nativity* strictly adheres to the King James Version's text, her illustrations depart in dramatic fashion from what might be ex-pected. In other words, they de-familiarize and, in so doing, suggest new nuances and meanings about the Nativity story that are not suggested in other versions that adhere more closely to the biblical narrative in both text and illustration. Here, the stress of the illustrations is on the humanity of the event, when the Christ child comes to poor, lowly people who are homely and wretched. Mary's pregnancy is played to humorous scale, and the annunciation of the angel Gabriel is handled over a bowl of soup, with a rooster clucking nearby. Mary is herself startled and amused by her growing disproportion, and, when the child is finally birthed, she sits, sweaty and exhausted, as the child is cradled in the arms of Joseph. The shep-herds who come to visit, balding and with unkempt hair, peer into the manger with the same bemused expression that any adult approaching a newborn will bring, and, when Joseph finally heaves Mary onto the donkey to begin the escape to Egypt, a bedraggled Gabriel, worn out with all the news and wearing unlaced boots, holds the Christ child until she has settled herself. Judged as irreverent in some quarters, the book reinvests the story of the Nativity with its central mes-sage: that the Christ child was born a human birth.

James Daugherty's *In the Beginning* works similarly; he, too, uses the King James Version for the text of the creation story, and then interprets that story through the use of muscular allegorical figures. His opening image pictures a gender-neutral God, eyes downcast, a finger set at the lips. God pauses before beginning the work of creation to consider what is about to be done. Here, Daugh-erty extends the text so that it begins before the opening of Genesis, putting into human form the notion of God's considering. For both Vivas and Daugherty, the illustrations suggest new ways of seeing old forms.

And it is at the interface of old forms and new ways of seeing that the author and illustrator work to de-familiarize, to maintain the integrity of the story but to tell its slant by changing its stance or its point of view, by rearranging familiar details in new patterns, by shifting the emphases, by fleshing out larger meanings through new details, by doing whatever they can to bring out the original story's vividness and meaning.

Boundaries are pushed not so much when authors and illustrators de-fa-miliarize in these ways as when they shift meanings and purposes of the tales, when they remove stories from their cultural and spiritual contexts, when they subordinate the stories to other kinds of agendas quite apart from the stories as stories. A biblical retelling—like the retelling of any myth—will be one of integrity if the author and illustrator are conscious of the literal meaning of the story, are committed to maintaining the cultural context of the tales, are aware that, inevitably, a retelling interprets and that the interpretation should be consonant with larger biblical themes, and understand that in their roles as storytellers they must speak to their audience vividly and dramatically in ways that enhance the tales. When retellings leave these criteria and move towards historical fiction or fable, they have extended past the boundary of a retelling and moved to stories that employ biblical motifs, a wholly legitimate approach, but not a biblical retelling.

De-Familiarizing the Biblical Tale

In order to de-familiarize the tales, writers and illustrators have turned to a wide variety of methods. A number of retellers have shifted the nature of the narrator, so that the tale may be told from an unusual narrative perspective, often limiting the knowledge of the teller and, thus, creating a situation in which the reader knows more than the teller. In Barbara Cohen's *I Am Joseph* (1980), for example, Joseph himself tells his story but often seems unaware of the implications of what he says: "When I was seventeen, my father gave me a glorious coat, a coat of many colors. We were twelve brothers, and we were all handsome, but I was the handsomest and I knew it." In Gary Schmidt's *The Blessing of the Lord* (1997), the narrative stance is shifted to minor characters who know only a portion of the tale, so that the reader, with fuller knowledge, provides the missing context. The story of Abraham and Isaac is told by the two servants who accompany the principals of the story to the sacrificial mountain, but who are not witnesses of the event. One of the most moving and creative of these shifts in narrative perspective comes in Patricia and Frederick McKissack's *Let My People Go* (1998), in which Charlotte Jeffries and her father Price tell a dozen stories, each introduced and inspired by a short section on the horrors of slavery times. The connection between the biblical tale and the life of Price as a slave gives each of the retellings a profoundly moving context.

Other narrators are even more distant from the actual texts. In Nancy White Carlstrom's *I Am Christmas* (1995), the Nativity story is told by the voice of the personified Christmas, and the Christ child is virtually equated with Christmas itself: "I am the gift God gives to his children sent down from above to the world. I am Christmas." And James Weldon Johnson's *The Creation* uses the voice of an African American storyteller to tell of the first seven days of the world. As illustrated by James E. Ransome (1994), the poem is a lyrical and evocative poetic sermon in which the storyteller uses colloquial, rhythmic, and repetitive language to make the story come to life for a group of children who sit gathered around him. Ransome alternates illustrations of the storyteller and the children with illustrations of the images that he has conjured up in the minds of the children. In this case—and in the case of each of these texts—the shifting of the narrator has created a new perspective, making the story itself something seen through new eyes.

Other writers and illustrators have chosen to shift traditional understandings and nomenclature, de-familiarizing by having the reader see the familiar in a completely new guise. Both Cynthia Rylant in *The Dreamer* (1993) and Eric Carle in *Draw Me a Star* (1992) engage in this shifting by imaging God as an artist. In *The Dreamer,* God is "a young artist who lived all alone, quietly, and who spent his days as most young artists do: daydreaming." In the end he creates other artists "who might listen and understand." Barry Moser's illustrations show only the hands of God, quietly cutting out stars like a young child, but then holding the spanned globe of the world in his single hand. Eric Carle also pictures God in *Draw Me a Star,* but he begins with God as a child who gradually ages through the book until he becomes the more traditional image of God as a bearded older man. Here, the motion of creation is unlike the Genesis account: Instead, each creation asks for the next creation so that it might find some kind of completion. When the star is drawn, it asks for a sun, which asks for a tree, which asks for a couple, which asks for a house, which asks for a dog, until, in the end, the moon asks for another star, which travels with the artist, now old, across the night sky. In picturing God as artist, Rylant, Moser, and Carle have shifted the usual depictions to emphasize a specific quality of God, creativity.

Other retellers depend heavily on their illustrations to extend their texts, to de-familiarize the well-known. Sarah Waldman's *Light* (1993) retells the creation story of Genesis, using simple language whose rhythms and even diction suggest their King James Version origin. But, against the familiar language, Neil Waldman illustrates the book with bright watercolors whose textured skies move, picture by picture, from dark formlessness to bright concreteness. He populates the world anachronistically with antelope and dinosaurs, and concludes the book with Adam and Eve riding zebras through a rainbow landscape, completing the transition to a bright world full of light, the overall theme of the book.

Katherine Paterson's *The Angel and the Donkey* (1996) retells the story of the prophet Balaam, who is asked by the king of Moab to curse the approaching Hebrew army. Alexander Koshkin's illustrations capture the tension between the human and the supernatural in the tale. On the one hand, his illustrations are stylized, evoking the colorful and stilted poses of early Middle Eastern

Illustration by Alexander Koshkin for Katherine Paterson's *The Angel and the Donkey.* Copyright © 1996. Reprinted by permission of Clarion Books.

Pointers for Teachers: Evaluating Retellings of Biblical Tales

- How does the author make these familiar stories fresh? Through a new narrator or narrative perspective? Through additional details? Through vivid illustrations? Through a mix of the biblical and another culture? How does this "freshening" enhance the story's meaning?
- What large questions about humanity and life in this world does the story address?
- If the retelling does not strictly adhere to the biblical version, do the differences expand or contract the meaning of the original story?
- How does the author avoid didacticism?
- How does the illustrator depict God? Would this imaging offend readers?

art. He uses this stylized form to depict the large and fearsome angel who confronts the donkey and the prophet. But, at the same time, this is a very human and even humorous story, and Koshkin uses detail within that stylization to capture those moments: Balaam's irritation at being called from his home by the king, the embarassment and surprise the mighty Balaam feels when he is thrown from the back of his donkey, the reverence that both Balaam and the donkey pay to the angel. This movement back and forth from the supernatural to the human world continues right to the final illustration, in which Balaam leaves behind forever the wealth of Moab and turns, humbly, to the world he inhabits with his donkey. Here the illustrations have worked with the text to de-familiarize the retelling.

Issues in the Retelling of Biblical Tales

Like other tales with oral origins, biblical stories pose a number of difficulties. There is, for example, the question of variant stories, as in the two creation accounts, or the two very different stories about Goliath's death. The retelling of Bible stories raises the issue of authorial motivation; if the motive behind the telling is an act of proselytizing, rather than telling the story as a story, perhaps the book may not be appropriate for all libraries. But there is also the difficulty of retelling stories that, in their origin, were told to an adult, not a child, audience. It is the case that many Biblical tales are beset with sexual and violent content. (It is this difficulty that leads to regular censoring of the Bible from school libraries.)

But, with biblical stories in particular, there is the issue of rescuing the stories from heavily didactic contexts that threaten to wring the life and drama from them. Biblical retellings for children began with these intentions: to teach, and not necessarily to delight. The intent was to move a child to a religious position and to inform the child of a religious heritage. Without impugning such motives, it is nonetheless difficult to write a dramatic text in which such motivation is preeminent.

In 1833, *First Lessons, or, The Great Principles of Religion* set out to teach young Sabbath students the rudiments of Christianity through asking a series of directed questions. At times, such questions would pause for retellings of a biblical tale, as in the following:

> [Jesus] became a little babe, and was born in a stable. His mother was a poor young woman. Then he grew up to be a little boy, like some of you, only he had no wickedness in him. Though he was so good, yet he suffered a great deal. When he became a man, he was often hungry and thirsty; he was often tired and weak; often he had no place to lie down in at night. He was always doing good to people, curing the sick, and lame, and blind, and deaf; but the Jews abused him...and scarcely ever let him alone, until they caught him and killed him. They hung him on a cross, and drove great nails through his hands and feet. Oh, how much he suffered.... After he had been dead part of three days, he came to life again; and after forty days more he went up to heaven. (64–65)

The text here is sparse and flat; details are cursory, and the focus one-dimensional. More disturbing is the manipulative nature of the text; the writer uses the emphasis on suffering not to tell a story, but to establish the kind of response he hopes for in the young child. This is a retelling in which didacticism has triumphed over the nature of story itself. At issue is whether biblical tales can be extricated from such a context, and whether the means of extrication are themselves legitimate or damaging to the text.

How far afield may a biblical retelling move from its scriptural context?

Strictly speaking, a retelling of a Bible story is intimately bound to the scriptural context. As with the retelling of any mythic tale, the reteller is responsible for establishing that context in the body of the retelling, so that the retelling does not conflict with the essential meaning and plot narrative of the story as recorded in the source.

This does not mean, however, that retelling must rigidly adhere to such plot narratives; it can be expanded and developed in imaginative ways and still not conflict with the original story's meaning. In *The Deep Blue Sea* (1990), Bijou Le Tord retells the story of creation, but her quiet and evocative retelling is not at all meant to follow the chronological account of Genesis; instead, it evokes images of the beauty and meaningfulness of creation, suggesting that each created element finds its place and meaning in the world. Similarly, Nancy White Carlstrom's *I Am Christmas*, though its illustrations follow the chronological narrative of the Nativity, uses a text that is not so concerned with the flow of the narrative but, instead, seeks to connect that birth to prophetic pronouncements about the meaning of the birth. In each of these cases, the plot narrative is subordinate to the author's interest in the meaning of the story.

Other authors move farther afield to explore traditions of storytelling that may begin with the Bible, but then add other cultural traditions. In Sandy Eisenberg Sasso's *But God Remembered* (1995) and *A Prayer for the Earth: The Story of*

Naamah, Noah's Wife (1996), the author uses tales of the Jewish midrash, which develop sparse hints in biblical stories. Thus, in *But God Remembered,* Sasso tells, for example, the story of Lilith, the first woman whom Adam betrayed, and Bityah, the daughter of Pharaoh who plucked Moses from the Nile. In *A Prayer for the Earth,* Sasson focuses on Noah's wife, who, while Noah goes about saving the animals of the world, is called by God to save all the plants of the world. The story has a strong environmental message, but also suggests the power of the world's plants, which bring calm and healing to Noah and Naamah.

In his *When the Beginning Began* (1999), Julius Lester combines the midrashic elements with a storytelling voice derived from the African American storytelling tradition. The result is a playful, expansive vision that he offsets with his own literal translations of the Old Testament.

> Making the world was not easy. If God hadn't been careful, there might be fish that bark, alligators walking into grocery stores and buying kosher hot dogs, and people sitting on nests and laying eggs. However, we do have mosquitoes, hay fever, cold sheets, brussels sprouts, and hiccups. Maybe God was not as careful as he could have been.
>
> God would not have gotten into the creation business if he had had something to do. But there was just him and the angels—sitting in the dark. The darkness was unlike anything that ever was or will be. It had no top, bottom, or middle and was thick, like a question that could never be answered. Not only was it impossible to see through, you couldn't move against it. But since there was nowhere to go, that did not cause a problem. (1)

Lester is inserting questions that the midrash would ask: What did God do before creation began? But to those questions he adds imaginative details with a slight irreverence that together contribute to the humor, power, and vividness of the piece.

Other tellings of Biblical stories use Jewish lore to contribute to our understanding of it. In Fran Manushkin's *Miriam's Cup* (1998), the story of the Passover is retold from the point of view of Miriam; her role is significantly expanded. In Mordicai Gerstein's *Jonah and the Two Great Fish* (1997), the author turns to Jewish folklore to tell of the first fish that swallowed Jonah and provided him with a home that was too comfortable; in his *Noah and the Great Flood* (1999), Gerstein fills the very familiar tale with details derived from midrashic sources: Noah is born with sunlight streaming from his eyes; as a man he invents the hoe, plowshare, and shovel; he preaches for 120 years to the rebellious giants who do not fear a flood because they are so tall; he designs his ark according to plans given to him by the angel Raphael in a sapphire book. The same midrashic sources are used by Eric Kimmel in *Be Not Far from Me* (1998), a striking collection that Kimmel sees as the epic story of God's love for man. In these stories, Abraham destroys the idols in the shop of his father to proclaim their impotence, God makes the midwives of the Hebrew slaves invisible so that Pharaoh cannot stop them from birthing babies, and Elijah bargains back and forth with God for the key to rain, birth, and raising the dead. Kimmel's is a seamless mixing together of the Biblical tales and midrashic legends. Barbara Diamond Goldin uses more modern Jewish folkloric sources for her *Journeys with Elijah* (1999), a collection of eight tales in which the prophet comes into the lives of people from many different cultures.

Some retellers use sources from further afield. Shulamith Levey Oppenheim's *Iblis* (1994) and *And the Earth Trembled* (1996), for example, retell the stories of the creation of the world and the creation of woman and man from an Islamic perspective, with material drawn from the Koran. John Bierhorst's *Spirit Child: A Story of the Nativity* (1984) retells the story of the Nativity from an Aztec perspective, using a sixteenth-century missionary text that combined the traditional biblical tales with Aztec traditions and motifs.

Retellings such as these translate the traditional tales through the eyes of a distinct culture. In this sense, the tales are retold twice, and, thus, distanced more from their original source than a retelling that simply goes back to the original texts. They remain, however, retellings of Bible stories because of their insistence on the basic meanings and import of the stories, though they will change the narrative lines to accord with a second culture's understandings and traditional additions.

Given that many biblical tales are sexual or violent in content, how might such tales be retold to a child audience?

Sex and violence are indeed at the heart of some biblical stories. The stories of Samson, for example, cannot be told without reference to his violent nature or the sexual temptation that led him away from his prophetic tasks. Stories of the temptation of Joseph by Potiphar's wife, of Sodom and Gommorah, of Jacob and Esau, of the crucifixion of Jesus, of the stoning of Stephen, all are stories told originally for an adult audience, with very adult themes and content.

Artists have chosen to handle this tension in quite different ways. Charles Mikolaycak represents one end of a spectrum; his illustrations are graphic and shocking. His illustration for the temptation by Potiphar's wife in *I Am Joseph* (1980) shows a transparently clad woman and a naked Joseph, his loincloth having been just torn away. For Elizabeth Winthrop's *He Is Risen* (1985), Mikolaycak decided to depict the suffering of Jesus with terrible clarity. In the scene in which he is nailed to the cross, his virtually naked body is stretched out on a red cloth, and huge wooden stakes are being driven through his upper wrists; blood pours out. In *David and Goliath* (1993), Leonard Everett Fisher has the victorious David hold the head of Goliath high above him. The cleanly severed neck shows the cut esophagus; the hole in his whitened head shows the entrance of the fatal stone. David holds the bloodied sword beside it in triumph. Here, certainly, are retellings in which the sexuality and violence of the stories is not denied at all.

In contrast, Scott Cameron's corresponding illustration for Beatrice Schenk de Regniers's *David and Goliath* (1993) shows David standing over the fallen Goliath, holding the sword that will sever the head. Throughout the text, even beginning with the cover, Cameron emphasizes the distinction in size between David and Goliath, using a high perspective to show the dominance of the giant. But, in this illustration, Cameron switches that and uses a low perspective so that David, standing over the fallen giant, now seems huge by comparison. Here, the change in perspective carries the meaning of the moment: David has triumphed over the one who was judged to be the stronger. Cameron avoids the gore.

On this end of the spectrum, retellers—and, particularly, illustrators—do not focus on the sexuality and violence of the stories. Violence and sexuality are not negated, or even denied, but they play a much more implicit role and lie behind the meanings, rather than act as meanings themselves. This is particularly evident in depictions of the crucifixion. In Jan Pienkowski's *Easter* (1989), a silhouette of Jesus on the cross fronts a sky strangely and disturbingly striped with red and gray. The outline of Jesus' body is shown, but with none of Mikolaycak's gore, and the focus is, instead, on the moment when the disciple John takes the aged Mary as his own mother. In the following illsutration, the violence of the scene is suggested by a rent tree destroyed by the ensuing earthquake, as well as the browned background. Brian Wildsmith and Tomie DePaola similarly depend on the background to convey meaning, rather than on the details of Jesus' torment. Wildsmith, in Turner's *The Bible Story,* paints a black background, spreading it over dark greens and blues to suggest the unnatural atmosphere; the scene is crowded with figures, but Jesus is placed in the background, his face impressionistically depicted. For the three spreads depicting the Passion in his *Book of Bible Stories,* DePaola uses a solid red; the scene on the cross is placed far away, and the reader looks from behind the event. The most moving scene is the full-page depiction of Mary holding the body of Jesus, which has just been taken from the cross. The emphasis is not on the physical suffering of Jesus—the wounds to his hands and feet are shown only as red dots—but on the terrible emotional suffering of his mother.

On each end of the spectrum the reteller is concerned with meaning. For those on one end, the violence and sexuality of a story may, in fact, be much of its meaning, and, thus, to depict the story in a way that denies that violence and sexuality would be to do an injustice to the tale. Those on the other end of the spectrum would argue that, though violence and sexuality do lie behind the stories, their meaning is not tied to those qualities, but goes beyond them. Thus, Joseph's temptation is part of the larger story of God's providential care, and David and Goliath's confrontation the story of a young man's faith and God's corresponding faithfulness.

Certainly any retelling of a story originally told for an adult audience—and this must be true for folktales and epics alike—must consider the new audience of the stories. This does not mean that a tale must be sanitized, but it does mean that the reteller must consider whether a child reader has the maturity and emotional discipline to understand the place of the violence or sexuality in a tale, and whether the depiction of those qualities will detract from the child's ability to discern the larger meanings of the tale. A story that focuses singularly on the violence of David and Goliath will certainly have missed the larger meanings of the tale, and, in this sense, the reteller will not have communicated the mythic story fully.

Should God be depicted in a picture book retelling?

The retelling of a Bible story is, for many groups of faith, a most serious business; certainly one of the most serious elements of that business is the depiction of God. Many readers would suggest that God not be depicted at all; others would argue that there is a long tradition in Western art of depicting God, and that images such as those of Michaelangelo are part of the cultural consciousness.

Most Bible retellings do not include an image of God; in creation stories such as those in Bijou Le Tord's *The Deep Blue Sea,* Philip Turner's *The Bible Story,* and Lore Segal's *The Book of Adam to Moses,* the moment of creation is depicted through an illustration of chaos; in Brian Wildsmith's illustration for Turner's *The Bible Story,* the page is simply black. Here the illustrators have avoided the problem altogether by not depicting God at all. But in books such as Jane Ray's *Noah's Ark,* the artist has chosen to illustrate God abstractly; here God is depicted with a face surrounded by the flares of sunlight; he holds in his hand a scepter topped with a crescent moon. In Tomie DePaola's *Book of Bible Stories,* God is depicted as a single hand that reaches down from the clouds to begin the work of creation. In Brian Wildsmith's *Exodus* (1999), God is depicted as an abstract six-pointed star, first seen in the burning bush that Moses witnesses; this motif is then carried throughout the book. In these cases the illustrators have decided not to illustrate God in human guise, but to find ways to suggest his suprahuman nature.

If the artist does decide to depict God, then it is important to realize that the stories are mythic, and, like all myths of all cultures, deserve a reverential and dignified treatment. That is, an illustrator, while not subverting his or her vision of the text, should recognize the needs and sensitivities of the audience of the texts. In choosing to depict God abstractly or symbolically—through the use of a hand, for example—the artist responds to the ineffable quality of God that most faith communities would affirm.

In Cynthia Rylant's *The Dreamer,* Moser has used the technique of DePaola: He indicates God's presence through a focus on the hands of God, though where DePaola's hand is stylized, Moser's is realistic. Moser also depicts God abstractly, as a bright light emanating from a single pointed star. In addition, Moser depicts God realistically as a robed figure walking beneath a pine; the silhouette stands out against a foggy green background. In each of these Moser has depicted God with the reverence and dignity due to a mythic tale. In contrast, the depictions of God in Martha Whitmore Hickman's *And God Created Squash* (1993) and Helme Heine's *One Day in Paradise* (1986) show God as a comic, somewhat doddering figure who is humorously bumbling and half-surprised that things turn out so well as they have. These two versions have a very different purpose than that of *The Dreamer,* and, with it, a very different depiction of God, one that does not carry with it the mythic seriousness of biblical retellings, but instead the lighter stance of the humorous folktale.

Pointers for Teachers

Interactive Possibilities

- Choose a biblical tale and read it aloud to the class. Break the students into groups of four or five and ask them to cast the tale's characters into a film using popular stars. Have each group be prepared to tell why they made such a choice. Then ask each group to pitch their concept to the large group of producers (the rest of the class). After each group has made its pitch, have the class vote on the favorite listing.
- Read aloud a biblical tale that creates significant distance between itself and the original text. Discuss their reactions to the plot and character, given the distinctions.

Writing Possibilities

- Allow students to choose a biblical tale and write a biography for one of its characters. Encourage them to use sources outside of the tale itself.
- Choose a biblical tale and ask students to write a last will and testament for the main character. Model the assignment first by using a transparency to show the parts of a will: how to distribute the money and goods, what to do with the deceased's body, and last bits of advice.
- Bring to class several classified sections from the local newspaper. Allow students to pair up and ask them to analyze the ads for types of jobs, information in the ad about the company, requirements for the job. Have the pairs of students write job descriptions for the main characters in a biblical tale.

Hands-On Possibilities

- Tell the class that they will be throwing a party for the characters from a biblical tale. Make and send invitations, construct the banners, choose food and appropriate games.
- Bring several old magazines to class. Break the students into groups of four or five and allow each group to choose a biblical story. Ask each group to select a character and create a scrapbook for him or her as if the character were in the same grade as the class. Be sure to have the groups spend some time brainstorming about parts of the character's life: home, vacation spot, school, neighborhood.

Authors and Illustrators of Biblical Retellings

Peter Spier (b. 1927)

The illustrator Peter Spier is best known for the Caldecott-winning *Noah's Ark* (1977). It is, for the most part, a book without text, the meanings of the story suggested by the dense detail of the images. The opening endpage juxtaposes images of violence—a city burning; a victorious army; destroyed fields and houses; the dead bodies of horses, cattle, and people; all depicted in browns—with the green images of Noah's cultivated vineyards, with Noah himself gathering the grapes in peace and plenty. This kind of juxtaposition occurs throughout the text, as Spier extends the biblical text of Noah's story by adding a wealth of detail to suggest the smaller, very human moments of Noah's adventure.

One of the larger opening illustrations depicts the entry of pairs of animals into the ark, but Noah's sons stand beside them, holding off the other animals who have gathered; the opening pages of the flood will show that they have drowned. In this sense, Spier brings to bear the hard questions of the tale, the loss of creatures who died innocently merely because they could not fit on the ark, the frustration and worry of Noah over the events, the doubting that must have occurred.

Spier is eager to affirm life in this retelling, not destruction, so in his speculations on the events on the ark during the voyage, he emphasizes life and birth. There is a new colt, new hatchlings, a baby giraffe, puppies, kittens, ducklings, chicks, owlets—all suggesting that life will be renewed once the flood ends. When the animals are released, they rush out in droves, preceded by dozens and dozens of rabbits, as well as flocks of birds. And Noah, in the final endpage, is planting a vineyard, and his sons plow and watch over a small flock of sheep, while Vs of birds fly overhead. The details suggest Spier's affirmation of life, his view that the meaning of the story is primarily one of providential protection.

But the book is memorable also for the humorous details that Spier adds to augment the events on the ark; few biblical retellings can be said to be humorous. Noah has to drag the donkey onto the ark, and closes the door just as the two snails finish their journey up the ramp; they are also the last to leave the ark. An elephant steps on a rat's tail, a cow chews on the olive branch brought back by the dove, and a dog sniffs at the door when it first opens. But to this humor is also added poignancy, as Spier interrupts the flow of interior pictures with double spreads of the ark as it floats, very alone and very small, on a huge ocean, suggesting the vulnerability of the boat. In this way, Spier expands the biblical narrative while maintaining the focus on the theme of providential care that he has established.

In *The Book of Jonah* (1985), Spier similarly uses his illustrations to expand the story of Jonah and his three-day sojourn in the fish's belly. In this more complicated story, however, he uses more text, retelling the story through a simplified version of the biblical tale. He tells the entire story, moving beyond the familiar portion of the sea storm to the withering of the vine that teaches Jonah tolerance and mercy.

The expansion of the illustration works in two ways. First, it expands on the theme of loyalty and disloyalty that is so much a part of the Jonah story. When Jonah hears the call to Nineveh, he is standing in front of his home, where his wife, two children, and dog are waiting for him. In a succession of poignant illustrations, Spier depicts Jonah's abandonment of them and their consequent despair. The dog faithfully travels with him to Joppa, but then he, too, is abandoned once Jonah boards ship. Once the storm has raged and Jonah is thrown into the sea, Spier dwells on the sailors, who, through exaggerated expressions of prayer and homage, express a new loyalty to God.

But the illustrations also develop the physical settings of the story. Spier takes pains to reproduce accurately a ship of the period, its cargo, and its sailors.

The city scenes are similarly developed, particularly the city of Nineveh, which is depicted in strong contrasts: the bright Assyrian art set against the brown and gray sackcloth and ashes into which the citizens of Nineveh plunge after hearing the prophetic pronouncement against them. Spier also develops the ribbed interior of the great fish, filling its guts with seawater filled with eels, fish, jellyfish, and seaweed. Spier contrasts the surrounding sea's abundance of life with the tomb-like belly of Jonah's prison. It is hardly a surprise that the prophet quickly turns to prayer.

In each of Spier's books he has fleshed out the spare telling of a familiar biblical story to express its detailed context, and, most importantly, to suggest the humanity that lies behind the mythic story. Here's how Jonah and Noah would react as real people in these mythic situations, he seems to suggest, and so the tale gains an added poignancy, humor, and drama than it might otherwise have.

Tomie DePaola (b. 1934)

Tomie DePaola is best known for his many works in folklore; within that field, however, he has been one of the very few artists to retell Christian stories, both Biblical and legendary stories. In books like *The Lady of Guadalupe* (1980), *Francis, the Poor Man of Assisi* (1982), *Patrick, Patron Saint of Ireland* (1992), and *Christopher, the Holy Giant* (1994), DePaola explores the lives of the Christian saints, showing the miraculous attestations of their holy lives, but focusing particularly on their humanity. In other texts, such as the *Book of Bible Stories* (1990) and the companion volumes, *The Parables of Jesus* (1987) and *The Miracles of Jesus* (1987), DePaola retells biblical tales by staying very close to the language of the Bible.

Like Peter Spier, DePaola depends on his illustrations for his effects. Each of the books opens with a double-page spread that brings the reader into the world of these stories: the *Book of Bible Stories* begins with a rabbinic storyteller, who speaks to three children, a lamb, and a dove; the world to which he speaks is one of innocence and youth, and suggests the stance of the book. *The Miracles of Jesus* opens with a picture of a nimbus-ed Jesus poised by a stylized tree, looking out at the reader and holding his hand in a gesture of invitation; the opening of *The Parables of Jesus* shows a lamb under a stylized bush, with a shepherd standing off in the distance, suggesting the parable of the lost sheep. In each of these cases DePaola implies his artistic role: He will interpret visually what the reader will find in the text, but he will not add to or amend that text.

In this sense DePaola differs enormously from Spier. Where Spier will add details to a sparse text, will develop and expand on suggestions through a fleshing out of the humanity of the characters involved, DePaola will not. His pictorial interpretations are quite literal. Those depicting Abraham's sacrifice of Isaac in the *Book of Bible Stories,* for example, show Isaac bound on a stone altar, a pot with the fire and the sticks nearby; an angelic arm waves down from heaven to stop the knife, and Abraham holds his arms out in response. All of the elements are from the biblical text, and the flattened background focuses the reader's eye on those elements.

This is true throughout the texts; all of the illustrations are quite literal. In *The Parables of Jesus,* the illustration for the parable of "The Laborers in the Vineyard" shows five panels in which more and more laborers go out to prune in the vineyard; the passage of time is suggested by the falling sun. The story of "The Prodigal Son" is illustrated with two panels, one showing the despairing son taking care of a pig, the second showing the father negotiating the relationship between the two brothers after the return of the prodigal. The parable of "The Sower" shows, again very literally, the three possible alternatives to the seed: withered, destroyed by thistles, or grown full and fertile. The illustrations thus serve as a visual narrative of the parable, not only reinforcing meaning, but establishing characterization through stylized posing.

Many of DePaola's illustrations for these biblical retellings use medieval and Renaissance models and patterns. In the illustration for Abraham and Isaac, DePaola uses the narrative technique common to medieval painting of having several layers of action occurring simultaneously: Isaac's despair, Abraham's acceptance, the preparation of the knife, and the ending of the test all occur simultaneously. The stylized plants and trees, the prayerful postures, the staging and bounding of the illustrations, all of these techniques accentuate not only the age of the stories, but also place them within the larger context of Christian art.

Though each of the books is drawn closely from biblical texts, the illustrations for *The Parables of Jesus* and *The Miracles of Jesus* suggest that these two books are drawn for a younger audience. In the illustration of Jesus walking on the water and the near drowning of Peter in the *Book of Bible Stories,* DePaola paints a wild and dark blue sea. Jesus' clothes and hair are churned by the wind, and the sea covers his feet. In the illustration for the same story in *The Miracles of Jesus,* DePaola has calmed the sea and given it a gentler green color. He has benimbed Jesus, who stands completely unruffled by the wind and not within the water at all. His body has been shortened in such a way as to suggest that a child is acting the role, as is true for most of the characters in these books. In all, it is a less threatening, more secure world that DePaola paints in these two books.

In *Mary, the Mother of Jesus* (1995), DePaola combines "scripture, legend, and tradition" to craft a book to praise Mary, the mother of Jesus. The book is a collection of vignettes about Mary's life. Some, like her presentation at the Temple and details about her betrothal to Joseph, are apocryphal; most, however, are scriptural. Each is illustrated with a panel at the bottom of the text and a full-page picture opposite. They are marked by the solemn stateliness of the figures, who all seem to be posing, frozen for the moment of the text. The most effective of these is that of Mary following the crucifixion, holding the crown of thorns and comforted by the disciple John, standing before a reddened sky and three empty crosses. Mary stands quite still and quite straight, though her head is bowed; the picture is saved from sentimentality by the dignity and seriousness of the figures.

Dignity and seriousness might be adjectives used for any of the Biblical retellings by DePaola. His task is to literally depict, but also to suggest a kind of reverential tone for these stories. In the apparent simplicity of his designs, in the spare use of detail, in the literalism of his pictures, DePaola stands quite apart from both Peter Spier and Charles Mikolaycak.

Warwick Hutton (1939–1994)

Like Tomie DePaola and Charles Mikolaycak, the British painter Warwick Hutton is known for his renditions of myths, particularly those of Greece and Wales. But, like those picture book illustrators, Hutton wrestled with adapting biblical stories to a child audience, producing in just a few years *Adam and Eve* (1987), *Noah and the Great Flood* (1977), *Moses in the Bulrushes* (1986), and *Jonah and the Great Fish* (1984). Each of these is marked by the same format: a text simplified from the King James Version, set against a full-page illustration. Hutton will, at times, vary this format with a double-page spread; these spreads are most effective in *Noah and the Great Flood,* where they are unaccompanied by text. The goal of each book is the same, though: To tell the mythic tale as a story, and not at all as a vehicle for didactic meaning.

While the text has been greatly simplified, it retains some of its very formal structures to heighten the diction of the story, and, thus, to heighten the quality of the tone. "So Jonah rose up"; "The Lord God sent them forth from the garden of Eden to till the ground from whence they were taken"; "Then the fountains of the great deep were released"; "Behold the people of Israel are more numerous and mightier than we are"—each of these phrases suggests the high tones of the King James Version. But attached to those very formal sentences are other sentences that are equally plain and simple in their structure: "There was a Hebrew family called Levi, and when a son was born to them, the mother, seeing that he was a healthy child, decided to hide him carefully for three months, hoping to save his life." Though the sentence is complex, its clauses are broken down over four pages and six illustrations.

With the exception of *Adam and Eve,* in which Hutton changes the order of the creation story to fit his narrative, the text stays quite close to the biblical story. But, like Peter Spier, Hutton expands the limits of the text through his illustrations, crafting scenes that have a highly narrative quality. In *Moses in the Bulrushes,* for example, he pictures the empty house of Moses's mother. She sits bereft and hopeless beside an empty cradle, because the child is now floating in the river. Completely covered by shadow, she stares at the family of chicks being guarded by their mother, a poignant comparison. But the sadness of the scene is relieved for the reader by the sight of Miriam, who is seen through the open doorway, sprinting back to tell her mother that Pharaoh's daughter has asked her to nurse her own child. In *Noah and the Great Flood,* Hutton plays with the irony of seaweed and crabs on mountain peaks, but suggests the totality of the flood's devastation by also including a human skull and femur outside the grounded ark. In *Jonah and the Great Fish,* Hutton suggests the disparity between the fleeing prophet, who rushes about in terrible fear, and the pleasures of the routines felt by those going about their daily taks without such a burden. At the port of Joppa, two boys swim happily; four small boats sail past, perhaps on pleasure, perhaps on business; and the sailors make preparations for sailing to Tarshish—all perfectly calm and unaware of the terror of Jonah. In each case, Hutton has worked out some of the implications of the story.

In *Adam and Eve,* Hutton faced two difficulties: depicting God and the nudity of the first couple. His solution to the first mirrors one of the solutions Barry Moser chose for *The Dreamer:* He pictures God as a fully robed figure. But, in order to avoid humanizing God, Hutton crafts the figure in a bright, bright white, so that he seems to exude light that shines all about him. He is also pictured at a distance, his back to the reader; when he does face the reader the light is so bright as to obscure his face. He remains defined yet amorphous, like the human he has created, but unlike. This creates a terrible sadness in the scene of the expulsion from the Garden, for Adam and Eve walk away from the light given off by God himself, their shadows thrown ahead of them into darkness.

Because Hutton is principally interested in focusing on Adam and Eve—unlike other creation stories, they appear by the third spread—he is faced with the difficulty of depicting them nude. The traditional solution of polite obscurity afforded by leaves would become stilted and repetitive if used on each page, and the resolution of the problem would become more diverting than the story itself. Hutton cuts through the problem by representing Adam and Eve unabashedly and innocently nude. However, as with the figure of God, Hutton generally distances the two, so that the pictures never seem to dwell on the sexuality of the characters as much as they focus on the continuance of the narrative.

Aware that the picture book format limits the extent of his tales, Hutton opts to focus on a small segment of his tales, rather than to condense a larger tale. The story of Moses, consequently, is confined to the episode in the bulrushes, though a final page summarizes Moses's life in the exodus. The tale of Jonah similarly focuses only on the episode with the great fish, rather than continuing, as does Peter Spier, to Jonah's sullen response to the acceptance of his prophetic message. But this is all in keeping with the simplicity of the stories, and places Hutton's work closer to that of DePaola than to that of Mikolaycak.

Leon Garfield (1921–1996)

The British writer Leon Garfield is best known for his historical fiction set in the eighteenth and nineteenth centuries. His language and plot situations often capture the diction and machinations of Charles Dickens, and, indeed, he finished the work that Dickens failed to complete before his death so well that the writing of the two authors is seamlessly interwoven in *The Mystery of Edwin Drood* (1980). While many of his books are for older, even young adult audiences, he collaborated with the artist Michael Bragg to produce three retellings of biblical tales remarkable for the ways in which they stretch the boundaries of such retellings.

Each of the three books adds a single child protagonist to the biblical tale. On the one hand, the tale comes closer to the child reader's world as a child engages in the action of the plot narrative, though that action does not change the biblical narrative. On the other hand—and more important to what Garfield is about—the meaning of that tale comes only in the context that that child represents. Thus, the meaning that comes out of the tale is not necessarily the meaning one familiar with the tale might expect.

In *King Nimrod's Tower* (1982), for example, a young boy in Babylon encounters a dog.

> "I'll take you home with me," said the boy, "if you learn how to behave."
>   The dog bit his shoe; and whooped like anything.
>   "But I'll leave you here in the fields if you don't learn to behave."
>   The dog bit his trousers; and whooped again.
>   And all the brickmakers, carpenters, stone-workers, architects and surveyors who were working in the fields, laughed till they were told to stop laughing and get on with their work.

The passage introduces the boy and his aggressive desire to control the dog, but also introduces the building in Babylon; in fact, they are building the Tower of Babel. The two stories continue: The boy continues to pursue the dog, who refuses to allow himself to be caught by such aggression. The tower continues to grow higher and higher, and Nimrod prouder and prouder. Both stories work simultaneously around the same site. They are also combined by the attention they receive from heaven; the angels worry about the coming of the tower, but God, drawn as a Blakean figure, is only concerned with watching the boy and his dog.

When God causes the linguistic difficulty that ends the building of the tower, Bragg depicts the boy still trying to control the dog. Nimrod's pride is swept away, and God's authority established: This is certainly the traditional understanding of the tale's meaning. But then, in the conclusion of the text, Garfield smashes the two stories together to yield a surprising twist on that meaning. The boy gives up his aggression and tells the dog that he is not trying to control: "I only want to be your friend," he says. Once that new stance is established, the dog and boy become close and go home together.

> "How did it happen?" marvelled the angels. "At last!"
>   "Because My Kingdom of Heaven is better reached," said God, "by a bridge than by a tower."

The ending shifts the meaning to a larger one about the nature of relationships, both on the human and on the divine level. That shift comes about only as the two stories are fused. The retelling thus becomes larger in scope with the addition of the child character and his story.

In *The King in the Garden* (1984), Garfield tells the story of Nebuchadnezzar; here the young Abigail finds the king in her garden, eating the grass. "The king in the garden was strange and wild. His toe-nails were as long as spoons, his fingers were as sharp as forks. His hair was frantic, and his black burly beard was speckled all over with dandelion clocks. As he munched and chewed, and nibbled and grazed, the sunshine winked on the chinks of gold, which was all you could see of his overgrown crown." The meaning of the narrative is here established by the contrasts between the king that Abigail expects—a king so great that no one is allowed to see him—and the king that Abigail finds. Through Abigail's innocent and un-awed ministrations to him—in contrast to the distant oblations paid by his courtiers—Abigail brings the king to the memory of himself and takes him back to his palace, where no one has missed him for seven years. The meaning again comes in the last page, when the story of Abigail and the biblical narrative fuse. When Abigail asks him why he has not been missed, the king whispers to her, "A king may leave his kingdom, even for seven long years, and nobody need notice that he isn't there; but if God leaves a man, even for a single minute, all the world sees that he's become less than a beast."

In *The Writing on the Wall* (1983), Garfield retells the story of Belshazzar and the mysterious hand that writes a prophecy of doom on the wall. The biblical tale is set against the story of Sam.

> Just as Sam is short for Samuel, so Samuel was short for a boy. Very short. When he fetched the dishes in, all you could see was roast goose and legs. When he took the dishes out, all you could see were dirty plates and legs. The most you ever saw of his other end was a tuft of hair sticking up over the top of sprouts or dumplings, like a sprig of black parsley. He was a nothing, a nobody; he was a kitchen-boy in Babylon, and he was rushed off his feet.

The wealth, power, and dominance of Belshazzar are contrasted with the tiny, unimportant status of Samuel, both in the text and illustrations. When Samuel befriends the starving cat Mordecai, he finds it difficult to feed him until everyone's eye is attracted to the prophetic hand; in the silence that follows, Samuel pours some cream for the cat, and then is overwhelmed with guilt for his theft. When the prophet Daniel arrives and clears the room with his interpretation of the writing, he finds Samuel under the table and reinterprets the writing for him: "Samuel and Mordecai have been weighed in the balances and found NEEDING." He sends Samuel home and tells him that "God punishes greed, not need."

In each of these stories Garfield parallels the biblical tale with the tale of the child. The meaning of the two is changed by their fusion, and the meaning of the biblical tale not only made accessible to a child audience, but broadened to a larger scope. Michael Bragg's illustrations augment this fusion by placing the children almost as a recurring melody against a larger cacophony of sound. The melody comes to the forefront only at the end, when it takes that cacophony and resolves it.

Charles Mikolaycak (1937–1993)

In books like Miriam Chaikin's *Exodus* (1987), Elizabeth Winthrop's *He Is Risen* (1985), and Barbara Cohen's *I Am Joseph* (1980), Charles Mikolaycak illustrates a biblical tale with vivid, sensual, and dramatic illustrations. Where the illustrations of Peter Spier are bright and light, those of Mikolaycak are dark and brooding, often disturbing in their interplay of violence and sexuality. Known for illustration of many myths—the Norse myths in Cynthia King's *In the Morning of Time* (1970), Hawaiian myths in Jay Williams's *The Surprising Things Maui Did* (1979), and Greek myths in Margaret Hodges's *The Gorgon's Head* (1972), and his own *Orpheus* (1992)—Mikolaycak brings a larger-than-life, bold vision, creating human and more than human characters to fit the mythic tones of the biblical tales.

In muted browns and reds, Mikolaycak's illustrations for *He Is Risen* retell the story of Jesus' passion and resurrection by playing up the dark tones of the tale. Each of the illustrations has a grainy, gritty quality, suggesting the mystery of the passion, as well as the darkness of the setting—both physical and metaphoric. Even the resurrection scene is darkened, so that the angel wings that overpower the tomb are brown and stained, and the light representative of the risen Jesus seems to shed no illumination over the gathered disciples.

Mikolaycak does not shrink from depicting scenes that show the violence and sexuality of the biblical scenes; in *He Is Risen*, the crucifixion scene is one of great suffering and humiliation, as the nearly nude figures struggle and bleed on the crosses, close to the foreground of the illustration. In *Exodus*, Mikolaycak dwells particularly on the almost titillating nudity of the Egyptians, whose gaudy paint is seen as a stark contrast to the desert browns and rough clothing of Moses and the escaping Hebrews. In *I Am Joseph*, Mikolaycak depicts the bleeding and nearly nude figure of the young Joseph, just thrown into a pit by his brothers. Later, a nude Joseph stands awkwardly in front of Potiphar's wife, who has just torn his loincloth from him. In his illustrations for Bernard Evslin's *Signs and Wonders: Tales from the Old Testament* (1981), Mikolaycak deals with this same moment, but he has muted the sexuality to some extent. Potiphar's wife still wears the flimsy gauze that barely concealed her in *I Am Joseph*, but now a fanged cobra belt encircles her waist, as if in warning, and only Joseph's face is shown in the reflection of a mirror.

This disturbing quality of Mikolaycak's work underscores the sometimes disturbing stories and their sometimes disturbing meanings. If the work may not be appropriate for the very young child, or even as an initial investigation into biblical retellings, it is nonetheless challenging for those who already know the tales and might be eager for new understandings.

In *Signs and Wonders*, Mikolaycak also had to deal with the question of how he might depict God. He settled on the same solution as Tomie DePaola—representing God by his hand—though here the solution was also suggested by Evslin's text: "God reached down and took a handful of dust and breathed His own life into it. There in the palm of His hand lay a man asleep. God set him down in a garden and let the darkness come. That was the end of the sixth day" (11). The emphasis on the hand leads naturally to Mikolaycak's illustration, which depicts a huge and smoking hand descending from a darkened sky. Curled into a fetal position, Adam lies securely in the palm. The author's text is matched, while the illustrator has used the position of his characters to suggest birth.

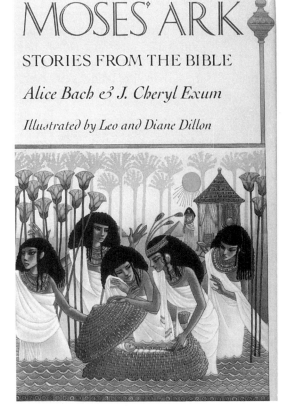

From *Moses' Ark* (Jacket Cover) by Alice Bach and J. Cheryl Exum. Illustrated by Leo and Diane Dillon. Copyright © 1989. Used by permission of Delacorte Press, a division of Random House, Inc.

Alice Bach (b. 1942) and J. Cheryl Exum

In *Moses' Ark: Stories from the Bible* (1989) and *Miriam's Well: Stories about Women in the Bible* (1991), Alice Bach and J. Cheryl Exum bring one of the most scholarly approaches to bear on biblical texts. Often their use of research into the texts involves what they call "filling in the gaps," or adding material to tales where the biblical text is sparse. Thus, they employ the resources of archeology, writing about city defenses, water systems, and Babylonian ziggurats. At other times they use descriptions of physical objects that are taken from other sections of the Bible; for example, details about Solomon's feast welcoming the Queen of Sheba are taken from the feast of Ahasuerus in the Book of Esther. At other times details are added from scholarly material about the surrounding cultures, so, when the biblical texts suggests that Solomon gave great wealth to the Queen of Sheba, Bach and Exum describe the nature of those gifts: jewels, gold, and spices.

But the most important element of these retellings is their use of language; Bach and Exum decided to return to the original Hebrew text of the Old Testament, rather than to English translations, in order to capture some of the puns, the wordplay, the interconnections between stories that the original language makes but which are necessarily lost in a translation.

> Working from the original Hebrew text, we have highlighted features of the stories available only to readers of the original. A prime example is found in the story of Moses' birth. We are all familiar with Noah's ark, but the reader of the Hebrew text knows that Moses, too, has an ark. The Hebrew word *tevah* used for Noah's ark appears in only one other place in the Bible, referring to the "basket" Moses' mother makes before setting him afloat on the Nile. The allusion, lost in most translations, is extremely important: both "arks" are vehicles of salvation. (*Moses' Ark,* 2)

This concern for language has a strong impact on the meaning of the stories. In the tale of the creation of Adam and Eve, for example, Bach and Exum are careful to match gender-neutral English words with gender-neutral Hebrew words.

God stood back and watched the human being in its new home. The human picked some ripe fruit and ate it. It touched the pale petals of flowers and the rough bark of a tree. Then it sat in the shade of a broad-leafed tree, looking at its own fingers.

"It is not good that the human is alone," God thought. "I shall make a companion to share this luscious garden, a companion that is just right for it." (10–11)

Here the story matches the Hebrew's insistence that Adam is neither male nor female, that Adam was designated male only after Eve was created. In this way, the language has shaped and even provided the larger meanings of the retelling.

In *Moses' Ark,* Bach and Exum decided to include some lesser known stories from the Old Testament in which female characters figure prominently; to this end they include some of the stories of David's "less admirable adventures," as well as the encounter between Saul and the Witch of Endor. In *Miriam's Well* they expand this concern so that each of the thirteen stories contains a female protagonist. "In telling the stories of biblical women," they write, "we have tried to give the women a voice where the Bible often relegates them to silence, to tell the stories from their point of view" (xiv). For some, the telling is easier: Ruth, Esther, and Judith each have biblical books in which they are the most prominent figures. For others, the retellers use material from other biblical books to flesh out stories; sometimes they turn to rabbinic stories. In one story, "A Mosaic for Miriam," the authors put together a series of references to biblical women who are only mentioned, but never developed. Here, they seek to answer questions, such as the response of Job's wife to his trials or the nature of the compulsion that drove Lot's wife to turn one more time to Sodom:

"Move again," our mother moaned. "I am tired of moving from place to place, being an outsider and having to make friends all over again." She clutched one of her delicately embroidered cushions. "Must we give up all our possessions—our household goods and even our livestock. Where would we go?" (164)

This motivation is not given in the biblical text, but any child who has changed homes will understand the impulse.

In their concern for research into the lifestyle and setting of the biblical characters, in their linguistic care, in their inclusion of female characters, Bach and Exum have retold the tales for an older audience than that of the picture books of DePaola and Spier. They have also tried to capture the mysterious nature of scriptural stories, which seem to have an inexhaustible depth that allows and even demands such deep probing and exploration as Bach and Exum provide.

Brian Wildsmith (b. 1930)

The work of Brian Wildsmith is done in one of the most recognizable styles in all of children's literature. His colors are bright and strong, clashing, conflicting, and challenging each other against brilliant and very articulated backgrounds. The busy-ness of the page is composed strongly of these clashes, as well as the detailed lines and shapes that fill his large spreads. For Bible stories such as *Joseph*

(1997) and *Exodus* (1999), this means that the large double spreads are dominated either by large shapes that are intricately decorated—the walls of an Egyptian city, the pillars of an Egyptian bedroom or courtyard—or by large open spaces tinted by spreading watercolors. His biblical retellings are, in the end, visually engaging in their depictions of the cultures out of which the stories come.

In *Joseph* and *Exodus,* Wildsmith stays close to the biblical texts in order to convey his stories. Unlike many Bible retellers, he chooses to give the large dimensions of the story, rather than focusing on a smaller, more compact dramatic unit. In *Exodus* he includes the large structures of the entire Old Testament book, ending with the death of Moses and the beginning of the movement of the Hebrew nation into the Promised Land. *Joseph* too is very complete in its telling, including the complex series of tricks that Joseph plays on his hapless brothers.

But these two retellings are particularly arresting in their visual representation. As in many of Wildsmith's works, the characters seem almost dwarfed by their settings, almost incidental to the lush, detailed, many-colored illustrations whose scale is enormous. In particular, Wildsmith plays up the scale of Egyptian structures, placing them in stark contrast to the tents of the Hebrews. In the same way he contrasts the fertility of Egypt, with its luxurious growth of plants, to the sparse and barren desert of the Hebrews. That Joseph can come to have a home in this place, and that the Hebrews can overcome the scale of Egypt, suggests implicitly the power of the Hebrew God.

In books like *Professor Noah's Spaceship* and *A Christmas Story* (1989), Wildsmith comes at the biblical tale from an unusual angle. *Professor Noah's Spaceship* is really an ecological tale set in the future; its power lies in its echoes of the biblical tale. *A Christmas Story* is a tale of Rebecca, who brings the colt of the donkey that Mary rides to Bethlehem after the Holy Family. For Rebecca, the story is off to the side; she is interested in bringing the colt and its mother back together. But, along the way, she questions people to find the Holy Family, and in her questions she comes across all of the characters of the Christmas story: the innkeeper, the shepherds, and even the kings, who give her a ride back to Nazareth on a camel. Though Rebecca does not see the story unfolding, the reader does, in startling ways: The illustrations are dominated by a flat gold that is striking amidst the complexity of watercolor that dominates the rest of the spreads. Rebecca does not seem to spy the gold, but the reader's eye is certainly drawn to it, as the familiar story takes place side by side with Rebecca's quest.

Wildsmith also illustrated Philip Turner's *The Bible Story* (1968), and here his technique is somewhat different. There is much more text than in one of Wildsmith's picture books, and so his illustrations are smaller, more self-contained. There are only a few spreads, many containing text. All are marked by the dramatic moment of the story, however. The moment before creation is completely black, then a burst of light challenges the darkness, a light filled with every color drawn with sharp angles. The ark of Noah floats over the towers of a drowned city. David's rock, drawn as a white circle, strikes the forehead of Goliath. Bright lightning strikes the altar of Elijah and ignores the altar of Baal. At the Transfiguration Jesus is surrounded with the same colors that had marked creation, only here their edges are softened.

In all of his illustrations Wildsmith depends on his colors for his dramatic effects. And those effects, in turn, highlight the appropriateness of his choice of scenes to illustrate. His sense of the dramatic moment matches his choice of a brilliant palette.

Thinking and Writing about and from within the Biblical Retelling

Consider the following familiar passage from the seventeenth chapter of the Book of Samuel. The text is taken from the King James Version of the Bible.

> Now the Philistines gathered together their armies to battle, and they were gathered together at Shochoh, which belongeth to Judah, and pitched between Shochoh and Azekah, in Ephes-dammim. And Saul and the men of Israel were gathered together, and pitched by the valley of Elah, and set the battle in array against the Philistines. And the Philistines stood on a mountain on the one side, and Israel stood on a mountain on the other side: and there was a valley between them. And there went out a champion out of the camp of the Philistines, named Goliath, of Gath, whose height was six cubits and a span. And he had an helmet of brass upon his head, and he was armed with a coat of mail; and the weight of the coat was five thousand shekels of brass. And he had greaves of brass upon his legs, and a target of brass between his shoulders. And the staff of his spear was like a weaver's beam; and his spear's head weighed six hundred shekels of iron: and one bearing a shield went before him.
>
> And he stood and cried unto the armies of Israel, and said unto them, "Why are ye come out to set your battle in array? am not I a Philistine, and ye servants of Saul? choose you a man for you, and let him come down to me. If he be able to fight with me, and to kill me, then will we be your servants: but if I prevail against him, and kill him, then shall ye be our servants, and serve us." And the Philistine said, "I defy the armies of Israel this day; give me a man, that we may fight together." When Saul and all Israel heard those words of the Philistine, they were dismayed, and greatly afraid…. And the Philistine drew near morning and evening, and presented himself forty days….
>
> And David spake unto the men that stood by him, saying…"Who is this uncircumcised Philistine, that he should defy the armies of the living God?"… And David said to Saul, "Let no man's heart fail because of him; thy servant will go and fight with this Philistine." And Saul said to David, "Thou art not able to go against this Philistine to fight with him: for thou art but a youth, and he a man of war from his youth." And David said unto Saul, "Thy servant kept his father's sheep, and there came a lion, and a bear, and took a lamb out of the flock: and I went after him, and smote him, and delivered it out of his mouth: and when he arose against me, I caught him by his beard, and smote him, and slew him. Thy servant slew both the lion and the bear:

and this uncircumcised Philsitine shall be as one of them...." And Saul said unto David, "Go, and the Lord be with thee."

And when the Philistine looked about, and saw David, he disdained him: for he was but a youth, and ruddy, and of a fair countenance. And the Philistine said unto David, "Am I a dog, that thou comest to me with staves?" And the Philistine cursed David by his gods. And the Philistine said unto David, "Come to me, and I will give thy flesh unto the fowls of the air, and to the beasts of the field." Then said David to the Philistine, "Thou comest to me with a sword, and with a spear, and with a shield: but I come to thee in the name of the Lord of hosts, the God of the armies of Israel, whom thou hast defied. This day will the Lord deliver thee into my hand; and I will smite thee, and take thine head from thee.... For the battle is the Lord's, and he will give you into our hands...." And David put his hand in his bag, and took thence a stone, and smote the Philistine in his forehead, that the stone stuck into his forehead; and he fell upon his face to the earth...Therefore David ran, and stood upon the Philistine, and took his sword, and drew it out of the sheath thereof, and slew him, and cut off his head therewith. And when the Philistines saw their champion was dead, they fled.

1. Consider the above story as it is told through a third-person narrative. What details would be eliminated, which details emphasized, if the story was to be told emphasizing the perspective of David? How would this story change if the emphasis was on the point of view of Saul, who watches this young champion who will eventually displace him as king?

2. Would it be legitimate to retell the story from the viewpoint of Goliath, with the giant himself the narrator of the tale? What meanings and details would change in this story if this were the case?

3. There are times when minor characters can be witnesses to events in which they play little part, and yet they too may have an important perspective to give on a story. Consider the role of the shield bearer who goes before Goliath in this passage. He is mentioned only briefly and not developed in any way. How might he be developed? What possible stances might he take toward these events?

   In considering this figure, think about questions such as the following:

   - Why is the shield bearer not there to protect the fallen Goliath?
   - What attitudes might he have toward Goliath? Is he proud of his duties?
   - Does he flee with the rest of the Philistines?

As you answer these, you are doing what the authors of the midrash stories do: speculating and developing story from sparse texts.

4. Consider what details you might include or delete depending on your choice of one of the following emphases, any one of which will shape your retelling:

   - David as the young champion come to assert his prominence and Saul's decline
   - the contrast between the forces of light and darkness
   - the contrast between the forces of apparent weakness and apparent strength
   - the providential care of God to those of faith

How will a retelling with one of these foci differ from a retelling with another focus? How will one emphasis dictate a different set of details than another? How might the narrative voice change?

5. The language of the King James Version is now almost four centuries old. What advantages does the reteller gain by keeping all or some of this language? What specific disadvantages does a reteller face? Revise the following passage for a retelling aimed at a very young audience:

> And the Philistine said unto David, "Am I a dog, that thou comest to me with staves?" And the Philistine cursed David by his gods. And the Philistine said to David, "Come to me, and I will give thy flesh unto the fowls of the air, and to the beasts of the field."

Be ready to justify the decisions you have made in your changes. What have you gained, and what have you lost?

6. Consider the following revisions of the above passage. The first is from Leonard Everett Fisher's *David and Goliath:*

> When Goliath saw David he burst out laughing. "Israelites! You insult me," he bellowed. "You have sent a boy to fight a man. His flesh and bones will feed birds and beasts."

The second is from Beatrice Schenk de Regniers's *David and Goliath:*

> Goliath looked all around, and when he finally saw little David standing there with his shepherd's staff, the giant said, "Am I a dog, that you come after me with a stick?" Then Goliath laughed scornfully, and said in a voice like thunder: "Come, come a little closer, and I will feed your flesh to the birds of the air and to the beasts of the field."

The third is from Philip Turner's *The Bible Story:*

> When Goliath saw David he threw back his head so that the bronze helm glittered like the sun itself, and he laughed. How he laughed. Great rumbling belly laughter like tumbling rocks sounding across the plain. "Am I a dog," he roared, "that you come with a stick? Come to me"—he beckoned with a finger like a bull's horn—"Come to me, little one, and I will feed your flesh to the crows."

What choices have these three authors made, and how have those choices defined their emphases and meanings?

Selected Bibliographies

Works Cited

Bierhorst, John. *Spirit Child: A Story of the Nativity.* New York: Morrow, 1984. Illustrated by Barbara Cooney.

Carle, Eric. *Draw Me a Star.* New York: Philomel, 1992.

Carlstrom, Nancy White. *I Am Christmas.* Grand Rapids, MI: Eerdmans, 1995. Illustrated by Lori McElrath-Eslick.

Daugherty, James. *In the Beginning.* New York: Oxford University Press, n.d.

de Regniers, Beatric Schenk. *David and Goliath.* New York: Orchard, 1993. Illustrated by Scott Cameron.

Dickens, Charles. *The Mystery of Edwin Drood.* New York: Pantheon Books, 1980. Completed by Leon Garfield.

Dickinson, Peter. *City of Gold*. New York: Pantheon, 1980. Illustrated by Michael Foreman.

First Lessons, or, The Great Principles of Religion. Philadelphia: American Sunday-School Union, 1833.

Fisher, Leonard Everett. *David and Goliath*. New York: Holiday House, 1993.

Gerstein, Mordicai. *Jonah and the Two Great Fish*. New York: Simon and Schuster, 1997.

———. *Noah and the Great Flood*. New York: Simon and Schuster, 1999.

Goldin, Barbara Diamond. *Journeys with Elijah*. New York: Harcourt, Brace, 1999. Illustrated by Jerry Pinkney.

Heine, Helme. *One Day in Paradise*. New York: Atheneum, 1986.

Hickman, Martha Whitmore. *And God Created Squash*. Morton Grove, IL: Albert Whitman, 1993. Illustrated by Giuliano Ferri.

Johnson, James Weldon. *The Creation*. New York: Holiday House, 1994. Illustrated by James E. Ransome.

Kimmel, Eric A. *Be Not Far from Me: The Oldest Love Story*. New York: Simon and Schuster, 1998. Illustrated by David Diaz.

Lester, Julius. *When the Beginning Began*. New York: Harcourt, Brace, 1999.

Le Tord, Bijou. *The Deep Blue Sea*. New York: Orchard, 1990.

Manushkin, Fran. *Miriam's Cup*. New York: Scholastic, 1998. Illustrated by Bob Dacey.

McKissack, Patricia and Fredrick. *Let My People Go*. New York: Atheneum, 1998. Illustrated by James E. Ransome.

Oppenheim, Shulamith Levey. *And the Earth Trembled*. New York: Harcourt, Brace, 1996. Illustrated by Neil Waldman.

———. *Iblis*. New York: Harcourt, Brace, 1994. Illustrated by Ed Young.

Paterson, Katherine. *The Angel and the Donkey*. New York: Clarion, 1996. Illustrated by Alexander Koshkin.

Pienkowski, Jan. *Easter*. New York: Alfred A. Knopf, 1989.

Ray, Jane. *Noah's Ark*. New York: Dutton, 1990.

Rylant, Cynthia. *The Dreamer*. New York: Scholastic, 1993. Illustrated by Barry Moser.

Sasso, Sandy Eisenberg. *But God Remembered*. Woodstock, VT: Jewish Lights, 1995. Illustrated by Bethanne Andersen.

———. *A Prayer for the Earth: The Story of Naamah, Noah's Wife*. Woodstock, VT: Jewish Lights, 1996. Illustrated by Bethanne Andersen.

Schmidt, Gary. *The Blessing of the Lord*. Grand Rapids, MI: Eerdmans, 1997. Illustrated by Dennis Nolan.

Segal, Lore. *The Book of Adam to Moses*. New York: Schocken, 1987. Illustrated by Leonard Baskin.

Turner, Philip. *The Bible Story*. New York: Oxford University Press, 1968. Illustrated by Brian Wildsmith.

Vivas, Julie. *The Nativity*. New York: Harcourt, Brace, 1988.

Waldman, Sarah. *Light*. New York: Harcourt, Brace, 1993. Illustrated by Neil Waldman.

Wolkstein, Diane. *Esther's Story*. New York: Morrow, 1996. Illustrated by Juan Wijngaard.

Works of Selected Retellers

Peter Spier
The Book of Jonah. New York: Doubleday, 1985.
Noah's Ark. New York: Doubleday, 1977.

Tomie DePaola
Book of Bible Stories. New York: G. P. Putnam's Sons and Zondervan, 1990.
Christopher, the Holy Giant. New York: Holiday House, 1994.
Francis, the Poor Man of Assissi. New York: Holiday House, 1982.

The Lady of Guadalupe. New York: Holiday House, 1980.
Mary, the Mother of Jesus. New York: Holiday House, 1995.
The Miracles of Jesus. New York: Holiday House, 1987.
The Parables of Jesus. New York: Holiday House, 1987.
Patrick, Patron Saint of Ireland. New York: Holiday House, 1992.

Warwick Hutton

Adam and Eve. New York: Margaret K. McElderry, 1987.

Jonah and the Great Fish. New York: Margaret K. McElderry, 1984.

Moses in the Bulrushes. New York: Margaret K. McElderry, 1986.

Noah and the Great Flood. New York: Margaret K. McElderry, 1977.

Leon Garfield

The King in the Garden. New York: Lothrop, Lee & Shephard, 1984. Illustrated by Michael Bragg.

King Nimrod's Tower. New York: Lothrop, Lee & Shepard, 1982. Illustrated by Michael Bragg.

The Writing on the Wall. New York: Lothrop, Lee & Shephard, 1983. Illustrated by Michael Bragg.

Charles Mikolaycak

Chaikin, Miriam. *Exodus.* New York: Holiday House, 1987. Illustrated by Charles Mikolaycak.

Cohen, Barbara. *The Binding of Isaac.* New York: Lothrop, 1978. Illustrated by Charles Mikolaycak.

———. *I Am Joseph.* New York: Lothrop, Lee, & Shepard, 1980. Illustrated by Charles Mikolaycak.

Evslin, Bernard. *Signs and Wonders: Tales from the Old Testament.* New York: Four Winds, 1981. Illustrated by Charles Mikolaycak.

Hodges, Margaret. *The Gorgon's Head.* Boston: Little, Brown, 1972. Illustrated by Charles Mikolaycak.

King, Cynthia. *In the Morning of Time.* New York: Four Winds, 1970. Illustrated by Charles Mikolaycak.

Mikolaycak, Charles. *Orpheus.* New York: Harcourt, Brace, 1992.

Williams, Jay. *The Surprising Things Maui Did.* New York: Four Winds, 1979. Illustrated by Charles Mikolaycak.

Winthrop, Elizabeth. *A Child is Born: The Christmas Story.* New York: Holiday House, 1983.

———. *He Is Risen: The Easter Story.* New York: Holiday House, 1985. Illustrated by Charles Mikolaycak.

Alice Bach and J. Cheryl Exum

Miriam's Well: Stories about Women in the Bible. New York: Delacorte, 1991. Illustrated by Leo and Diane Dillon.

Moses' Ark: Stories from the Bible. New York: Delacorte, 1989. Illustrated by Leo and Diane Dillon.

Brian Wildsmith

A Christmas Story. Oxford: Oxford University Press, 1989.

The Creation: A Pop-Up Book. Highland Park, NJ: Millbrook, 1996.

Exodus. Grand Rapids, Michigan: Eerdmans, 1999.

Joseph. Grand Rapids, MI: Eerdmans, 1997.

Noah's Ark: The Pop-Up Book. New York: HarperCollins, 1994.

Professor Noah's Spaceship. New York: Oxford University Press, 1980.

Turner, Philip. *The Bible Story.* New York: Oxford University Press, 1968. Illustrated by Brian Wildsmith.

Works on the Retelling of Biblical Tales in Children's Literature

Bottigheimer, Ruth B. "An Alternative Eve in Johann Hubner's Children's Bible." *Children's Literature Association Quarterly* 16 (Summer, 1991): 73–78.

———. "Religion for the Young in Bible Story Collections." *Fabula* 32 (1991): 19–32.

Dickinson, Peter. "The Oral Voices of *City of Gold.*" In Charlotte F. Otten and Gary D. Schmidt, eds., *The Voice of the Narrator in Children's Literature.* Westport, CT: Greenwood, 1989: 78–80.

Natov, Roni. *Leon Garfield.* New York: Macmillan, 1994.

Piehl, Kathy. "'By Faith Noah': Obedient Servant as Religious Hero." *Lion and the Unicorn* 13 (June, 1989): 41–52.

Potter, Joyce Elizabeth. "Beautiful for Situation: Bible Literature and Art in Modern Books for Children." *Children's Literature Association Quarterly* 11 (Winter, 1986–1987): 186–192.

———. "Manger and Star: The Christmas Story in Modern Picture Books." *Children's Literature Association Quarterly* 13 (Winter, 1988): 185–191.

Sawyer, Ruth. "On Reading the Bible Aloud." In Norma R. Fryatt, ed., *A Horn Book Sampler.* Boston: The Horn Book, 1959: 168–177.

Spier, Peter. "Caldecott Award Acceptance for *Noah's Ark.*" *Horn Book* 54 (August, 1978): 372–378.

8

Fantasy: Conceiving Truth through the Imagination

Hugh Lofting begins *The Story of Doctor Dolittle* (1920) with a description that distances the story in time and establishes the setting.

> Once upon a time, many years ago—when our grandfathers were little children—there was a doctor; and his name was Dolittle—John Dolittle, M. D. "M. D." means that he was a proper doctor and knew a whole lot.
>
> He lived in a little town called, Puddleby-on-the-Marsh. All the folks, young and old, knew him well by sight. And whenever he walked down the street in his high hat everyone would say, "There goes the Doctor!—He's a clever man." And the dogs and the children would all run up and follow behind him; and even the crows that lived in the church-tower would caw and nod their heads. (1–2)

Such a beginning might be the start of any realistic novel. But Lofting is about to tell a fantasy: This is the story of a man who can talk with the animals. So he gives clues even in the opening that all is not as it might be in a realistic world. He places the story in that nebulous long ago time that begins so many folktales—though still, such a setting is plausible. He creates a man so beloved that all the children and dogs follow him—still this is plausible. But he is also a man to whom the crows caw and nod their heads, and here we have moved into a slightly different realm. But the movement is subtle, hardly to be detected at all. In fact, the next few pages seem to return to realism, as the Doctor becomes disenchanted with tending the imagined ailments of people and finds his interest taken up more and more with the ills of animals, so much so that his practice begins to fail and his sister abandons him. The fantasy begins anew only when his parrot Polynesia addresses him, and his reaction again shows Lofting's subtle hand.

> "Be an animal-doctor[," Polynesia said. "]Give the silly people up—if they haven't brains enough to see you're the best doctor in the world. Take care of animals instead—*they'll* soon find it out. Be an animal-doctor."

> "Oh, there are plenty of animal-doctors," said John Dolittle, putting the flower pots outside on the window-sill to get the rain. (9)

His reaction here does not give any clue that something fantastic has just happened. He speaks to her as though speaking to the neighbor next door. The result is that the reader tends to react similarly, to enter into the gentle fantasy even before he or she knows that the entering has occurred.

Readers who turn to E. B. White's *Charlotte's Web* (1952) find something similar. For the first two-and-a-half chapters, this too might be a realistic novel. Fern, having saved the runt of a litter from her father's ax, treats the pig as though he were an infant. Forced to give him to her uncle to be raised in his barn, Fern visits the pig, whom she has named Wilbur, each day, watching the pig's antics and frolics among the other animals. The entrance into the fantasy is again very subtle, so subtle as to be almost missed.

> Mr. Zuckerman did not allow [Fern] to take Wilbur out, and he did not allow her to get into the pigpen. But he told Fern that she could sit on the stool and watch Wilbur as long as she wanted to. It made her happy just to be near the pig, and it made Wilbur happy to know that she was sitting there, right outside his pen. But he never had any fun—no walks, no rides, no swims. (15–16)

White moves from the inner consciousness of Fern, who is happy just being near the pig, to the inner consciousness of Wilbur, who is happy that Fern is sitting beside his pen. This soft leap then leads to the next sentence, in which Wilbur wishes he might have walks, rides, and swims.

The leap into the animal's consciousness is a leap into fantasy, and it prepares the reader for the very next paragraph in which the pig is standing "lonely and bored" (16). In granting the pig these qualities, in allowing the reader to understand the state of Wilbur's mind, White prepares the reader for the following paragraph, in which Wilbur speaks for himself.

> "There's never anything to do around here," he thought. He walked slowly to his food trough and sniffed to see if anything had been overlooked at lunch. He found a small strip of potato skin and ate it. His back itched, so he leaned against the fence and rubbed against the boards. When he tired of this, he walked indoors, climbed to the top of the manure pile, and sat down. He didn't feel like going to sleep, he didn't feel like digging, he was tired of standing still, tired of lying down. "I'm less than two months old and I'm tired of living," he said. He walked out to the yard again. (16)

The opening of the paragraph is clearly fantasy; the pig is now able to articulate his thoughts in language. The large middle section is closer to realism, following the habits of a pig, though here those actions are endowed with emotion and conscious understanding. At the conclusion of the paragraph, the speech only summarizes what the actions have established, and so the speech itself is readily accepted even though it comes from an animal. Having merged the real with the fantastic, the fantastic becomes less jolting when it is introduced.

Lofting and White prepare the reader for the entrance into fantasy by providing a realistic opening and establishing not only a means, but a cause for the entrance to the fantastic. In essence, both of these writers move readers from their familiar worlds to fantastic worlds. It is in the moment of that movement that much of the success of the book lies. If that movement is not convincing, then the fantasy will have failed to achieve what Wordsworth called the "suspension of disbelief" that allows the reader to enter into the narrative in such a way that the fantasy can speak to the reader's very real experience.

In this sense, fantasy is quite firmly grounded in reality. Certainly, it moves in a world other than that of the real world, or at least in a world where the normal, expected, understood rules of experience no longer apply. But, at the same time, it refers back to the world of the reader's experience, as it must because any creation must be explained in reference to the known. (It would be impossible, for example, to describe a color in a fantasy world that does not appear in this world without reference to something in this world.) But, more fully, fantasy takes its cues, its foundations, its distinctions, and even its meaning from reality; it is itself, primarily, because it is not the real. Readers understand fantasy in terms of its reverse relationship to reality.

Boundaries and Definitions of Fantasy

The meanings that fantasy generates come out of the author's ability to refer to the "real world" recognized by the reader and, at the same time, to create an "other world" that the reader can accept in its context. The movement back and forth between the "real" and "other" worlds lies within much of the plot narrative, of course, but also affects the overall meanings of the fantasy and how they are conveyed. In Natalie Babbitt's *Tuck Everlasting* (1975), for example, Babbitt is able to create a realistic child protagonist, Winnie Foster, who responds with impulses that might be recognizable in any child; that is, she is a narrative creation that connects the reader to the real world. Yet she is placed in a fantasy situation: She discovers a spring that grants eternal life, as well as a family that has drunk from that spring. The central meaning of the novel lies with the tension between the real world and the fantasy world. Should Winnie Foster live out her life as a mortal child of the race, or should she become an immortal and join the Tucks? The tension between the fantasy and reality of the novel reflects the tension in Winnie's own choice.

If the reader fails to accept the fantasy element of the novel—if the reader cannot suspend disbelief—then the fantasy will fail. The successful fantasy is the one that bridges that leap of disbelief and that uses the "real" and the "other" to create its meanings.

In *Charlotte's Web*, the principal action of the story concerns Wilbur and his new friend Charlotte. Recognizing that it is a pig's lot to be slaughtered, Wilbur and Charlotte the spider work together to show that Wilbur is no ordinary pig, and, using her web, Charlotte convinces the local townspeople that Wilbur is "radiant" and "some pig." Wilbur will, in turn, prove that worth when he rescues the dying Charlotte's egg sac. All of this is in the realm of fantasy—and yet, not quite completely in that realm. The world of animal speech is fantasy, but the world of the barnyard, the world of the small farm, the world of the county fair, all of these are familiar and real.

> After the heat of the day, the evening came as a welcome relief to all. The Ferris wheel was lighted now. It went round and round in the sky and seemed twice as high as by day. There were lights on the midway, and you could hear the crackle of the gambling machines and the music of the merry-go-round and the voice of the man in the beano booth calling numbers. (138)

Such a passage could appear in a work of realistic fiction as well; the fantasy of *Charlotte's Web*, then, is firmly grounded in the elements of the real world, and these elements include the fact that pigs are, indeed, slaughtered for food. The fantasy allows this realistic element to be subverted, but the fantasy could not exist if that realistic peril were not there.

At the same time, *Charlotte's Web* is the story of Fern, who, in the beginning of the novel, is young, imaginative, willing to put in long hours watching the animals. By the end of the novel, she has withdrawn from this world and, at the climactic fair scene, is on the Ferris wheel with Henry Fussy; later, when Fern thinks about the fair, she will think about getting caught at the top of the Ferris wheel with Henry Fussy, not about Wilbur, and not about Charlotte. In this narrative strand, White has crafted the story of a young girl maturing, coming into new interests and awarenesses, moving away from the world of the imagination that had so dominated her childhood.

The fantasies of *The Story of Doctor Dolittle* and *Charlotte's Web* involve a movement into a narrative moment that depicts a scene impossible in the world as the reader knows it. Doctors do not talk to animals and spiders do not weave words into their webs. No matter how connected these events are to the "real" world—a world in which animals do communicate and where kindness between animals is evidenced—these events do not occur as real events in a real setting. It is not sufficient for events to be merely improbable; in the genre of fantasy, events must occur that cannot occur in the known physical world.

Fantasy, then, is that genre in which the narrative action includes elements of plot, character, or setting that are not bound by the limitations of reality as it is generally perceived. It is a genre that depends on the reader's willingness to suspend disbelief, a genre that uses the interplay between reason and the imagination to create its meanings.

The Subgenres of Fantasy: Low Fantasy

One set of boundaries in this genre is suggested by the terms *low* or *light* fantasy and *high* fantasy; there are, in fact, several forms of "other" worlds to which the writer of fantasy turns. Low fantasy is represented by such works as Robert Law-

Pointers for Teachers: Evaluating Fantasy

- How does the author help readers suspend disbelief? By beginning in this world? By creating a strong narrative voice? By creating consistent and complete characters and settings? Why is the author's choice for a given novel successful or not?
- How does the author successfully work the interplay between the real and the unreal elements of the story?
- How has the author created a whole and consistent setting?
- How can the structure of the fantasy be seen as a vehicle for truth?
- What truths about humanity and the world are being conveyed through the fantasy?

son's *Rabbit Hill* (1944), which opens with the animals excited over what might be happy news.

> All the Hill was boiling with excitement. On every side there rose a continual chattering and squeaking, whispering and whistling, as the animals discussed the great news. Through it all could be heard again and again the words, "New Folks coming."
>
> Little Georgie came tumbling down the Rabbit burrow, panting out the tidings. "New Folks coming," he shouted. "New Folks coming, Mother—Father, New Folks coming into the Big House." (11–12)

At issue here is whether the New Folks will be planting Folks, or whether they will come with dogs. In fact, they are planting Folks, and the animals plan their division of the spoils as the huge garden nears harvest time. What they do not anticipate, however, is what kind of planting Folks have come; in fact, the garden has been planted for them, and, one evening, under the watchful eyes of St. Francis and the New Folks, the animals enjoy the bounty heaped so generously on them.

This is low or light fantasy in which the fantasy takes place in the real world, and in which it is generally lighthearted, perhaps even comical, in its workings out. It is generally centered on concerns that mark younger children, principally on the situations of the family, or defining the nature of one's home, or even of one's own incipient identity. The hope that dominates these fantasies is the hope for a secure, centered world, where there is warmth and caring and good food and acceptance.

It was the creation of low fantasies—and the term is not at all meant to be pejorative—that marked the great Victorian and Edwardian age of children's literature in England. Writers such as Beatrix Potter worked to establish very specific subgenres, creating tales of personified animals such as her *The Tale of Peter Rabbit* (1902). Here, animals such as those in Robert Lawson's *Rabbit Hill* act anthropomorphically at the same time that they retain their animal characteristics. Peter Rabbit is, on the one hand, the naughty, disobedient boy who gets into trouble for his mischief, and, at the same time, very much a rabbit who will get into Mr. MacGregor's garden. It is this subgenre of talking animals that E. B. White turned to with *Charlotte's Web,* and which is represented in more contemporary works by such books as Cynthia Rylant's *Gooseberry Park* (1995), in which a labrador helps the squirrel Stumpy to find her babies, Avi's *Poppy* (1995), in which the mouse Poppy tries to convince her family to overcome their fear of an owl so that they might move closer to the cornfield that would feed their community, Kevin Henkes's *Lily's Purple Plastic Purse* (1996), which uses mice to suggest the realistic, if sometimes unpleasant, relationships of very young schoolchildren, and Dick King-Smith's *Babe: The Gallant Pig* (1983), which follows the adventures of Babe the sheep pig, who uses his natural politeness and ability to communicate with sheep to turn in an impressive performance at the sheepdog trials. Usually in this genre the "real" world remains very familiar; the only fantasy is the entrance into animal consciousness.

A. A. Milne's *Winnie-the-Pooh* (1926) and *The House at Pooh Corner* (1928) are in the subgenre of personified toys and objects, a tradition continued in such works as Virginia Lee Burton's *Mike Mulligan and His Steamshovel* (1939) and *The Little House* (1942), Margery Williams's *The Velveteen Rabbit* (1922), and, in a more contemporary vein, Pam Conrad's *The Tub People* (1989) and *The Tub Grandfather* (1993), and Lynn Reid Banks's *The Indian in the Cupboard* (1981). The tension and suspense of these works often lie with the gap between living and nonliving characters, between the "real" and the "toy."

P. L. Travers' *Mary Poppins* (1934) works within a subgenre of fantasy that has a looser boundary, but is characterized by humor, magical elements, and exaggerated characters, all firmly held within the real world. Mary Poppins may be able to bring her young charges, Jane and Michael Banks, up to the stars, but she is equally able to bring them up to the nursery and tuck them in at night. Here belong works such as Mary Norton's *The Borrowers* (1953), in which a tiny race adapts human objects to their own needs, Natalie Babbitt's *Tuck Everlasting* (1975), Roald Dahl's *Charlie and the Chocolate Factory* (1964), and Sylvia Waugh's *The Mennyms* (1993).

Fantasies such as John Bellairs's *The House with a Clock in Its Walls* (1973) and Madeleine L'Engle's *A Wrinkle in Time* (1962) also fit into this subgenre, though here the comical elements are subordinate to the more serious elements of the novels. Each of them, as low fantasy, introduces a specific set of elements into a very real world. Bellairs uses witchcraft to focus on the difficulties that Lewis Barnevelt has in adjusting to a new home; L'Engle uses theoretical physics to introduce the elements of time and space travel. In each case, the novelist uses a circumscribed set of fantasy elements while maintaining the authenticity and familiarity of the dominant setting.

In a novel such as John Christopher's *The White Mountains* (1967), the earliest-written volume in a quartet of books about the alien Tripods, Christopher chooses a very different set of elements to create his fantasy. He still uses a familiar setting—a small village in England—but he has distanced it in time and type: It is a medieval village, but paradoxically set in the future. In fact, Tripods have come to Earth and destroyed technology, reducing humanity to a nontechnological world and destroying its will. The protagonist of the novel, suitably named Will, refuses to succumb and searches for an escape. The futuristic setting and the alien technology bring this series of books into science fiction, which calls for a very different set of fantasy elements than animal fantasy. And though the world of this book—as is true of many science fiction books—is quite different from the "real" world, still, the central problems of the novel—the question of human will and freedom, and the nature of that freedom's responsibilities—are familiar elements of the "real" world.

Finally, low fantasy will also include works that use time slippage as their means of entering the fantasy world. Perhaps the most well-known of these is Philippa Pearce's *Tom's Midnight Garden* (1984), in which a young boy discovers a garden that brings him back to meet his own grandmother as a child. Similarly, Cynthia Voigt's *Building Blocks* (1984) brings the young protagonist back in time to meet his father as a child. In Belinda Hurmence's *A Girl Called Boy* (1982) and Jane Yolen's *The Devil's Arithmetic* (1988), a child comes face-to-face with a frightening historical period: slave times and the Holocaust. In such time fantasies the child protagonist learns about himself or herself through the movement backwards, and is changed forever by the time of the return.

All of these works are bounded by the definition of low fantasy in that they are all ultimately inward looking; all contain characters whose central focus is on establishing home and identity.

The Subgenres of Fantasy: High Fantasy

If the central focus of low fantasy is inward looking, the focus of high fantasy is turned outward. Much of high fantasy turns to mythic archetypes to create the secondary world of the fantasy, and the protagonist involved with this world is usually on some form of heroic or romantic quest, often recreated by the author's turning to older epics and legends for the necessary structure and elements. High fantasy involves difficult and arduous journeys, supernatural characters who are both benign and malignant, a gathered set of companions who will contribute to the fulfilling of the quest, a quest object that is often magical, a cause that is just and right, and tasks that test the worth of the protagonist.

In novels such as Lloyd's Alexander's *The Book of Three* (1964)—the first novel of the Prydain Chronicles—and Susan Cooper's *Over Sea, under Stone* (1965)—the first novel of the Dark is Rising Quintet—the authors turn to Welsh mythology to introduce fantasy elements into their worlds. In the case of Alexander, *The Book of Three* creates an entirely "other" world, though still recognizable not only because of its geographical features, but because of the nature of Taran, the protagonist, who yearns for the heroic. Cooper uses the "real" world of contemporary England, but that world is invaded by mythological forces that threaten characters who do not even know their connections to those myths. Such novels, with their sometimes heightened language and use of mythic archetypes, use an altogether distinct set of fantasy elements.

Some fantasists set out to create an entirely other world as the ground for their high fantasy, a world that is not a balance of the "real" and the "unreal," but, instead, an entirely new beginning. In *Heart's Blood* (1984), for example, Jane Yolen creates Austar IV, the fourth planet in a solar system in the Erato Galaxy. She encourages the suspension of disbelief by beginning the novel with an excerpt from *The Encyclopedia Galaxia,* and then moves to the plot narrative of Jakkin and his dragon, Heart's Blood. Like other novels of this sort, this is a world completely removed from the "real" world of the reader, though, still, it responds to and comes out of that real world. Jakkin, for example, recalls the protagonists of *Old Yeller,* of *The Yearling,* of *A Day No Pigs Would Die,* all realistic novels that deal with a boy and his animal. There is the element of expectation, of hope, of adventure, all of which are familiar emotions and elements in a realistic novel. Here, however, the familiar is distanced into an entirely new world.

It is important to note that, in high fantasy, the protagonist is not necessarily superhuman; Bilbo Baggins of J. R. R. Tolkien's *The Hobbit* (1937) is very much the stay-at-home hobbit, and the four children of C. S. Lewis's *The Lion, the Witch, and the Wardrobe* (1950) are most ordinary, until they meet Aslan in the land of Narnia. Similarly, Taran is simply a young man who has yet to prove his worth, and Susan Cooper's Will is, in many respects, an ordinary, and somewhat bewildered, eleven-year-old boy. Their success in this genre depends on their willingness to rise above that ordinariness in order to meet the demands that the quest requires of them. They return, at the end of such quests, changed, having grown towards maturity and independence, not towards the security of home.

Fantasy as the Creation of Distance

In the end, fantasies are all similar in their technique of de-familiarizing the familiar, not in order to hide, but to make the familiar all the more clear in its meaning. Through the distancing of fantasy, the reader should learn of his or her own world, of his or her own humanity.

Going to a wide-screen theater, a viewer may decide to sit quite close, perhaps in the front row. If so, he or she is faced with the difficulty of keeping the entire screen in focus, of looking to the left while missing what is going on to the right. The sound will be huge and difficult to shut out. If the viewer moves back in the theater, he or she will be distanced from the actual screen, but able to see it all better, having a fuller perspective and being better able to discern the distinctions in sound.

Fantasy moves the reader towards the back of the theater. It grants the reader the distance to see what is true about the "real" world in a new, perhaps unexpected, guise, as the author employs a given set of fantasy elements. By moving out of our world, yet staying connected to the life and meanings of our world, the fantasist creates an arena where he or she can speak more clearly about something that may be clichéd or trite in a work of realism, or too close to our own experience for it to have the kind of impact for which a writer hopes.

Pointers for Teachers

Interactive Possibility
- Discuss with the class the ways in which the protagonist grows. Find some decision that the protagonist makes that distinguishes his earlier from later character.

Writing Possibilities
- Take the class outside and ask them to write down in great detail elements of the setting, including smells, tastes, sounds, and feelings. After your return to your classroom, have the students write up their observations as if they were beginning a work of realism. But, somewhere in that opening, they will introduce some element that will lead readers to the fantasy.
- After reading a fantasy, have the students speculate in their journals about the choice of title. Have them offer some suggestions for a different name.
- Have students establish a fantasy setting that has no connection to elements in this world. Discuss why or why not this may be very difficult.

Hands-On Possibility
- After reading a fantasy, break the students into groups of four or five. Give them paper lunch bags, yarn, markers, scissors, construction paper, and glue. Have each group create a set of puppets for the fantasy and then practice their telling of the story. Have the students present their shows to younger students in the school.

Issues in Fantasy

Perhaps the most difficult issue in the genre of fantasy is the question of how a work of fantasy can convey reality and truth through the means of what is patently unreal. It is this particular issue that has led some—particularly religious groups—to question the authenticity and appropriateness of the genre. It is also this very question that has led to heavy censorship of such books as Madeleine L'Engle's *A Wrinkle in Time* (1962). In that novel, three children are conducted by guardian angels to a distant planet, where they see their own world, though covered with a terrible darkness.

> "I hate it!" Charles Wallace cried passionately. "I hate the Dark Thing!"
>
> Mrs. Whatsit nodded. "Yes, Charles dear. We all do. That's another reason we wanted to prepare you on Uriel. We thought it would be too frightening for you to see it first of all about your own, beloved world."
>
> "But what is it?" Calvin demanded. "We know that it's evil, but what is it?"
>
> "Yyouu hhave ssaidd itt!" Mrs. Which's voice rang out. "Itt iss Eevill. Itt iss thee Ppowers of Ddarrkknesss!"
>
> "But what's going to happen?" Meg's voice trembled. "Oh please, Mrs. Which, tell us what's going to happen."

"Wwe wwill cconnttinnue tto ffightt!"

Something in Mrs. Which's voice made all three of the children stand straighter, throwing back their shoulders with determination, looking at the glimmer that was Mrs. Which with pride and confidence. (88)

In this passage, L'Engle wants to say something about her perceptions of the nature of this world—that it is covered with evil, but that that evil is being fought against by those who are aware of it and by those who refuse to surrender to it.

Though this seems like a truth that many readers could affirm, in fact *A Wrinkle in Time* is one of the most censored novels in North America, censored principally by religious groups that disapprove of, among other things, the use of fantasy to convey such truths. But L'Engle, like other writers of fantasy, is arguing metaphorically, using her fantasy creations to think seriously about the world and our lives in it. The argument is carried through the metaphor; if the reader rejects this approach, then the genre of fantasy ceases to have any real meaning.

In what ways does the writer of fantasy enable the reader to willingly suspend disbelief?

One of the advantages for the writer in beginning the narrative in the real world and then moving the narrative into the fantasy world lies in just this issue: By beginning in a realistic setting, the author has, from the inception of the story, begun to help the reader move past disbelief. The reader begins in a world that he or she knows on some level, where all the expected rules and situations apply. The shift comes when those rules and situations that are already established are warped, or changed, or negated on some level, but the fact of their earlier establishment makes the change less jarring, more of a piece.

In Audrey Wood's *Heckedy Peg* (1987), for example, both the author and illustrator—Don Wood—use traditional folktale motifs to tell the story of a mother and her seven children, each named after one of the days of the week. The story opens with an untexted illustration showing the mother holding a child as she stirs a pot; the other children lie in various stages of wakefulness about her. The yellows and browns of the image suggest warmth and security, the maternal world of wholeness and safety. The opening spreads show the children at their chores—airing mattresses, taking baths, gathering eggs, milking the cow—as the mother sweeps. When she leaves for the market, she promises to bring back something for each of them, and they are told to stay away from the fire and not to allow anyone in. Once she leaves, the children fall into mischief and the room becomes darker. In the background, the witch Heckedy Peg comes with her cart. All of this has been realistic, and prepares for the entrance of the witch, who only shows her true nature once the children have violated their mother's prohibition about both strangers and fire. Only after that moment does the fantasy enter the story, having been prepared for by the realistic opening so that the entrance into the witch's spell seems both convincing and, on some level, only the natural outcome of what has gone on before.

In Nancy Willard's *Pish, Posh, Hieronymus Bosch* (1991) and *The Sorcerer's Apprentice* (1993), both illustrated by Leo and Diane Dillon, a female protagonist begins in a fantasy setting where there is little distinction between the inanimate and the animate, or between the cute and the monstrous. In the first, the creatures all stem from the imagination of Hieronymus Bosch; in the second, they stem from the imaginations of the Dillons, though they have also included familiar creatures such as the fox and cat from *Pinnochio*. The fantasy elements begin almost immediately and are visually overwhelming. But the text centers on the protagonist, and the protagonist is close to the reader in her situation. In *Pish, Posh,* she has grown frustrated at her inability to control her world, and decides to leave in a huff, only returning when she realizes that she need not control her world as much as she needs to accept and love it for what it is. In the familiar story of *The Sorcerer's Apprentice,* Sylvia must learn that frustration is not a good teacher, and that she must come to understanding through patient practice. In these books, the reader moves past disbelief by finding, not a situation as in *Heckedy Peg,* but a character whose emotional and personal situation is realistic and familiar.

One of the most important elements in suspending disbelief is the creation of a wholly consistent world: Once having established the rules by which this world is governed, the writer of fantasy needs to maintain those rules rigorously. This is true for fantasies in which an entire world is created, and it is true for fantasies in which unreal elements occur within the realistic world. In *Blitzcat* (1989), for example, Robert Westall tells the tale of Lord Gort, a cat, who searches all of Britain for her master Geoffrey, not understanding that he has been called away to fight as a pilot in World War II. Westall mixes fantasy and realism as he describes the effects of the Blitz on Great Britain. But when he turns to the inner consciousness of Lord Gort, he is very careful to limit himself to the perceptions that a cat might have, and only to those perceptions: "Lord Gort wriggled over on her back, careful not to fall off his knee. Idly, she swung a paw in the direction of his tie. In her small mind, all the places, all the people were fading. Even the memory of Mrs. Sample were very dim.... She was home with her person; she was warm, dry, full. That was all that mattered." (230)

The perceptions of the characters—the ways in which they react to the fantasy—also play a large role in helping readers suspend disbelief. Patricia Wrightson's *The Nargun and the Stars* (1974) begins with the half-inarticulate perceptions of the Nargun, a mythic Australian creature, all set in italic type in a prologue. With the beginning of Chapter One and the return to the expected Roman type, the angle of perception shifts to Simon. The reader follows Simon's perceptions, and will eventually shift to the perceptions of other mythic creatures, notably the trickster Potkoorok. But these shifts are not jarring because the reader reacts to them with Simon; he becomes the reader's mediator between the mythic and the real worlds, working, as a stranger to himself, to create normalcy in a world that is coming apart, both on the personal and mythic levels. In keeping readers close to the perceptions of her most realistic character, Wrightson is able to lessen the disbelief that fantasy may create.

The perceptions of the narrator with regard to the elements of fantasy can also contribute to the suspension of disbelief. Certainly the great British fantasy writers of the first half of the twentieth century knew this, writers such as Beatrix Potter, J. R. R. Tolkien, C. S. Lewis, in his *Narnia Chronicles,* and A. A. Milne. Their narrative voices were strong, dominant, and controlling; they suspended disbelief through a strong presence that offered plausibility and demanded acceptance, as in the opening from *Winnie-the-Pooh* (1926).

> Here is Edward Bear, coming downstairs now, bump, bump, bump, on the back of his head, behind Christopher Robin. It is, as far as he knows, the only way of coming downstairs, but sometimes he feels that there really is another way, if only he could stop bumping for a moment and think about it. And then he feels that perhaps there isn't. Anyhow, here he is at the bottom, and ready to be introduced to you. Winnie-the-Pooh.
>
> When I first heard his name, I said, just as you are going to say, "But I thought he was a boy?"
>
> "So did I," said Christopher Robin.
>
> "Then you can't call him Winnie?"
>
> "I don't."
>
> "But you said—"
>
> "He's Winnie-ther-Pooh. Don't you know what 'ther' means?"
>
> "Ah, yes, now I do," I said quickly; and I hope you do too, because it is all the explanation you are going to get. (3–4)

The narrative presence here is so strong that the narrator is virtually another character; the narrator also is the very clear intermediary between the reader and the other characters, and, in that capacity, he enables a suspension of disbelief.

However the writer of fantasy chooses to help the reader move beyond disbelief, the writer must help the reader to bridge that gap if the fantasy is to work. Whether this is through the presence of a strong narrator, or through the creation of a wholly consistent world, the reader must move beyond questions of credibility if the metaphoric meanings of the fantasy are to be potent.

In what ways does the writer of fantasy speak of the real in terms of the unreal? How is the fantasist able to use the imagination to convey truth?

Fantasy as a genre has not been well served by the common perception that it represents an escape from reality. The labeling of it as escapism, and the suggestion that it represents a movement away from the real world in which we find ourselves, leads to the conclusion that it has little of substance to say about our real world. But, in fact, the genre uses that distancing, that de-familiarizing to find a perceptive and powerful way of speaking to the issues of the real world.

What is crucial to realize is that fantasy speaks metaphorically, presenting, like the poet, one thing in terms of another in order to clarify the first. Just as the diverging road in Robert Frost's famous poem is more than simply a road, so does the fantasy world suggest that the event or element or situation is more than what it simply seems to be. At the same time, it is indeed what it seems to be. The diverging path really is a diverging path, even as it comes to represent the element of choice in our lives.

In this sense, a work of fantasy can speak about the real world very potently, while at the same time retaining the integrity and wholeness of its fantasy world. Eloise McGraw's *The Moorchild* (1996) is a poignant capturing of this equation. Young Moqul is the daughter of a human father and fairy mother, and, though she is brought up in the Hill, where the Little Folk dwell, she is never fully part of that community. She cannot, for example, disappear entirely when humans arrive. So the Fairies, against her will, substitute her as a changeling, and she becomes Saaski. As she grows, she tries desperately to fit into the village life, but the villagers see her as different, as unnatural. They blame her for various illnesses in the village, and refuse to accept her as one of them. In the end, even her parents recognize that she must leave, because she is not theirs, and, in one final act of love, she rescues their human child held under the Hill and returns it to them.

The conclusion of the novel is heavy with loss and renewal. Saaski must leave, but she leaves with Tam, a human child who, also, has never been accepted. Abandoned by two worlds, Saaski finds that she and Tam will make their own, and the novel closes with the sound of their two shepherd's pipes playing in unison. McGraw has created a complete and whole world as she describes the interactions of humans and fairies, and on one level the novel works as a mystery, as Saaski tries to find out who she is in the context of the two worlds. But the novel also is a telling statement on distinctions and acceptance. Despite her many gifts and her essential kindness, Saaski cannot exist in either world because neither sees her as a part of itself. Neither world will accept the differences that mark her, and the easy and unquestioned cruelty of their abandonment says much about our society's—or any society's—willingness to accept the other.

Jacket cover from *The Giver*, by Lois Lowry. Copyright © 1993. Reprinted by permission of Houghton Mifflin Company.

In her novel *The Giver* (1993), Lois Lowry creates a world of no pain, no starvation, no war, no disease, and no worries. It is a world where each child has a parent watching conscientiously over his or her development. It is a world where each child knows that he or she is observed through the childhood years and that that observation will lead to a considered, informed selection of a future career; there is no worry here about choosing a vocation or finding a job: that choice is provided for by those who know the child best. It is a world of safety, of security.

It is also a world with no love, no passion. There are no choices to be made, no independent thought, no sexuality, no color, no real sorrow—but no real joy, no spontaneity, no acceptance of otherness. And beneath that world is the well-kept secret of how others are dealt with. Into this arena comes Jonas, who will be the next Giver, the one who holds all of the memories of the community. These are memories of pleasure and joy and color, but they are also memories of pain and war and loss. The community has entrusted all of the intensity of these memories to its Giver, allowing them perfect bland freedom. But Jonas will not accept the rules of this world when he discovers that those rules also include killing a baby who will not conform, and, as he races away from the community, he sends back to them the memories that will change their ordered ease forever.

The ending is ambiguous. Does Jonas, whose name suggests his prophetic role, escape with the child Gabriel to find a new life? Or does he die in the snow, frozen with the baby? And in either case, what happens to the community once its memories return to it? All these are left unanswered, so that the novel begs not to be closed, but to be considered. In fact, the novel explores major issues that confront North American society, issues such as euthanasia, the care of the elderly, human choice and freedom versus the need to enforce community laws and standards, even, some argue, the issue of abortion rights. The ambiguity of the ending, together with the powerful narrative drive of the story, provide contexts for such thought and discussion that might otherwise not be available, or available only in a worn, clichéd setting.

Fantasies find different ways of exploring the real world; one way, certainly, is the creation of an ostensibly other world. Another way comes through the use of a form similar to a parable, a story with a strong moral meaning that maintains its narrative strength and dominance. Wanda Gág's *Millions of Cats* (1928) tells the story of the very old man who goes in search of a cat so that he and his wife will not be lonely. He encounters "hundreds of cats, thousands of cats, millions and billions and trillions of cats," but decides he can only keep the one that is prettiest. Hearing this, the cats turn on one another, each claiming to be the prettiest, until they have eaten each other up, all except for the smallest, who is not eaten because he believes himself to be "a very homely little cat." The couple bring it inside, and love it, and feed it, and find that, in the end, it is the prettiest cat after all. The ending carries the meaning that love should not come with beauty, but beauty with love.

Sarah Stewart's *The Money Tree* (1991) tells of Miss McGillicuddy, who finds a tree growing in her yard with leaves of money. Miss McGillicuddy cannot understand her neighbors' frantic efforts to harvest the leaves; instead, she continues with the routines that have enriched her life and the lives of the children around her: gardening, building fires, making quilts, putting up strawberry preserves, making cherry cobbler, reading, planting, caring for the land and for her animals. With illustrations by David Small that are both comic and poignant, the book challenges the contemporary North American desire for wealth by the posing of a very different kind of life.

The Money Tree, Millions of Cats, The Moorchild, and *The Giver* speak very directly to the question of how life is hard. They do it through establishing a fantasy world, then allowing the issues that touch readers to play themselves out in that world, all the while adapting those issues to those worlds so that the novel is whole and of a piece, and not simply a veneer for a didactic lesson. In this sense, the authors have used an imaginative venue for the examination of familiar reality.

Why is the genre of fantasy so subject to censorship, particularly by religious groups and organizations?

It is the case that no genre is so frequently attacked from religious sources as fantasy. In large part this derives from the very means through which fantasy works. If a religious group sees the development of something patently unreal as a lie—or a story as in some measure an untruth—then, by its very nature, they would argue, fantasy is working within an unethical arena. It is crafting its own reality, and, even if it is acknowledged that that new reality is being used to talk about the real world, still, there is the difficulty of the writer usurping the privileges of creation and crafting something that is in essence untrue. Spiders do not weave webs with language embedded; toads do not drive motorcars; doctors cannot speak to animals; and rabbits and mice certainly do not make pilgrimages. To say that they do is to create falsehood. Thus, the book becomes subject to censorship, because the vehicle of meaning for the genre is rejected as unacceptable.

There are, of course, less philosophical reasons for the attacks on fantasy. One is that fantasy, in using ancient archetypes, dabbles in mythologies that are essentially pagan, and, therefore, subject to some suspicion. In this same way, fantasy uses images that are seen as unacceptable to many religious groups. C. S. Lewis's *The Lion, the Witch, and the Wardrobe* (1950), despite its explicitly Christian meaning, is sometimes censored because of the presence of the White Witch, on the understanding that children should not dabble in witchcraft. John Bellairs's *The House with a Clock in Its Walls* (1973) similarly is censored for the presence of witches, although at least two of those are meant to be good in nature, and the others are more the stuff of horror flicks than true witchcraft. Even Madeleine L'Engle's *A Wrinkle in Time* (1962) faces frequent opposition on the grounds that Mrs. Who, Mrs. Whatsit, and Mrs. Which are witches, given their dress, when in fact the three are meant to be angelic beings. And J. K. Rowling's *Harry Potter* series is frequently attacked for its focus on Hogwarts, a school for witches.

If a group limits truth to the confines of mere fact—if it plays the role of Dickens's Mr. Gradgrind and cannot accept the role of the imagination in presenting truth—then it is unlikely that fantasy will be an acceptable genre; that group will instead turn to biography and nonfiction. If the group objects to mythic elements because they are inconsistent with their own religious stand, then the case is harder. For the fantasist reaching for old metaphors and images to show our current real world in a new, potent guise, such a stance is stultifying. It negates some of the culture's most powerful images and refuses to allow the reader's imagination to use those ancient images to create new meanings about the current world. In short, that stance prohibits story from acting as story.

However, while it is easy to react negatively to such a stance, such objections should not be dismissed as mere contrariness, either. On its deepest level, this is a clash of philosophies, as well as a clash about the role of literature in a child's life.

Authors and Illustrators of Fantasy

Maurice Sendak (b. 1928)

In Maurice Sendak's trilogy of fantasies, the reader begins in the real world, but the fantasy world is located in the interior life of the child protagonist. Max, in *Where the Wild Things Are* (1963), is making mischief of one kind or another because he is quite alone; no one pays attention to him. When his mischief causes a spat with his mother, the person he loves most in all the world, he is suddenly faced with the huge contradictory emotions of love and hate. Mickey, the protagonist of *In the Night Kitchen* (1970), is faced with the frustration of being put to bed and, thus, kept away from the adult secrets; it is a frustration that will lead him into the night kitchen to see what it is that grown-ups do at night. And Ida, of *Outside Over There* (1981), must deal with the anger that comes on her as her father leaves, her mother turns her attention inward, and she is left with the care of the screaming baby.

In each case, Sendak begins with a child in an inner conflict, one familiar to many children. Most of these conflicts involve contradictions in which the child is confronted with emotions that do not seem to match, that, it seems, cannot coexist. In the face of these conflicts, Sendak suggests, children invent a world around themselves to give order and meaning to disorder and meaninglessness. In short, they create fantasy.

In *Where the Wild Things Are*, Max's room is transformed into a forest, then an ocean, then the land of the Wild Things, as gradually the illustrations get larger and larger, eventually taking over one page, then reaching across the spread, and finally coming to the borders of the double-page spread. In this new land, Max encounters the monsters, who at first threaten him; but his response is one of control: He tames all of the Wild Things, and then romps with them through their world, though even then they stare at him as though he is not completely in control.

In *In the Night Kitchen*, Mickey abandons his bed and falls, somewhat helplessly, into the night kitchen, where three bakers are baking the morning cake. The sensuality of the experience is heightened as a naked Mickey falls into bread dough, swims through milk, and crows on top of a milk jug. He moves from helpless falling to complete control as he undertakes the quest for milk when the despairing bakers realize they do not have enough.

Ida, in *Outside Over There*, sees her deep desires fulfilled, desires that she cannot even articulate. Even as the illustrations outside her window suggest that she believes her father has abandoned them forever, the baby for which she is responsible is stolen, and she is freed. But, even beneath these desires, there is one deeper. Ida wants to find her brother, and so she moves into the fantasy world of Outside Over There to track him down. She finds him amidst the kidnapping goblins, and, after dispelling them with her magic horn, she finds one baby left: It is her brother, and his presence in a broken eggshell suggests a new relationship between them. Holding him tightly, she returns to the arbor and her mother.

Each of the three books ends with a resolution that suggests that Max, and Mickey, and Ida have dealt with their conflicting emotions and are now ready to return home. Max realizes that he cannot stay in this world of disorder, and that he wants to be "where someone loved him best of all." So he rejects the land of the Wild Things, though they do not let him go easily, and he returns to his very own room, where his mother has left his hot supper as a sign of her love. His costume falls off as he walks back wearily into his own room. Mickey, having crowed his crows and learned what was in the night kitchen, is able to slide off the milk bottle and fall back into bed, where he snuggles into a satisfied sleep. And Ida is able to return to her mother's clasp, while the baby plays with the dog beside them; the whole book has perhaps taken only a moment of time.

Of the three, however, Ida's situation is most problematic. Her father has still not returned, and, in fact, has sent a note suggesting that Ida must be brave, and that she must take care of her mother and the baby. Her mother's enclosing arm suggests that there is at least that connection reestablished, though her mother's eyes are on Papa's letter, not on Ida. But the last page shows that Ida is teaching the baby to walk, and the boulders looming nearby are frighteningly reminiscent of the goblins who lurk just below her consciousness.

The realistic world that Sendak portrays is an interior world; the fantasy is inaugurated when the character moves into it to deal with emotions that are contradictory, or unfamiliar, or too terrible to handle in a realistic setting. Fantasy is the place where such contradictions can coexist and be resolved, leaving the character free to return to the real world. Perhaps nowhere else in picture books is the concept of fantasy used with such perception and depth of insight, where the inner world is played out on a fantasy stage and brought to fitting conclusions that allow the lights to come back on and the audience to return home.

Jacket cover from *Jumanji,* by Chris Van Allsburg. Copyright © 1981. Reprinted by permission of Houghton Mifflin Company.

Chris Van Allsburg (b. 1949)

With *The Garden of Abdul Gasazi* (1979) and *Jumanji* (1981), Chris Van Allsburg thundered onto the stage of children's literature. These two black-and-white books merged a mysterious, sometimes threatening, always curious tone with a deep, insightful vision of childhood. Both begin in a world that might be just around the corner, but quickly turn that world into a place where the rules of the "real" world are undercut. It is in this undercutting that the power of Van Allsburg's fantasy lies, the refusal of the story and the illustrations to succumb to what is normal, or to suggest that what appears to be fantasy in these books is, in fact, fantasy. In that refusal lies Van Allsburg's probing into the nature of childhood.

In *The Garden of Abdul Gasazi*, Alan Mitz is commissioned by Miss Hester to tend her dog, Fritz, for an afternoon. When the dog escapes into Abdul Gasazi's garden, Alan must trespass to find him. He implores Gasazi for help, but the magician assures Alan that the dog has been turned into a duck. Later, while bringing him home, the duck steals Alan's hat and flies away. Distraught, Alan returns to Miss Hester's house, only to find the dog waiting for him, Miss Hester beside him. She chides him for believing that a magician might change a dog to a duck, and, when Alan leaves, chides the dog for holding Alan's hat.

The key to this fantasy lies in its ending; the reader is not permitted the easy explanation that the dog simply made his own way back out of Gasazi's garden, because he has come with the hat taken by the duck. The familiar, expected world—a boy caring for a neighbor's dog—has indeed come up against a mysterious world, as is suggested by the illustrations. The statues by the doorway into Gasazi's garden, for example, mirror Alan's strides into the forbidden place, but they also hold up warning hands. This is still within the realm of the real. The transformation of the dog into a duck might be explained as the imagination of a naive boy, an imagination encouraged by the unusual surroundings of the garden. But the final page, showing that the dog does indeed have the hat, undercuts such an interpretation. It may be that the mysteries pooh-poohed by Miss Hester are, in fact, true after all, and it is this possibility that the fantasy might have a kind of reality—Van Allsburg's playful blurring of the distinctions between the real and unreal—that forges his means of entry into fantasy.

In both *The Garden of Abdul Gasazi* and *Jumanji,* fantasy is quite clearly the realm of children; adults are often screened from it; at least they do not openly participate in it. If Miss Hester can reject the notion that Abdul Gasazi can transform a dog into a duck, then in *Jumanji* the adults could never believe that their house had been transformed into a jungle adventure. In fact, in the one illustration in which the adults appear, they are shown only from their necks down, as if almost entirely out of the world of childhood. Judy and Peter, on the other hand, exchange knowing looks: They have participated in something that they can never share with that adult world.

Jumanji also introduced a fantasy technique that Van Allsburg would call on again and again in later books. There is nothing fantastic about a lion, a hunter, a rhinoceros, a snake, or a group of monkeys. Nor is there anything fantastic about the overstuffed chairs, beds, mantlepieces, pianos, and kitchen of Peter and Judy's house. However, once those disparate elements are joined together, they merge into fantasy. A lion roaring atop a piano, a rhino rushing down a hallway, a snake coiling around the mantlepiece, fog broiling up from the floor, these are elements that are fantastic. Whereas Gasazi's garden might be explained as the reflection of a young boy's imagination, here the suggestion is quite strong that fantasy has broken into reality by the bringing together of two elements that should not be together, though only the children are able to perceive this joining.

Van Allsburg uses this technique often in his work. In *The Polar Express* (1985), Van Allsburg places a train down the center of a 1930s-style street. The young boy who stays awake listening for the sounds of Santa's reindeer instead hears "the sounds of hissing steam and squeaking metal." In several of the books, Van Allsburg alters this technique by bringing characters into worlds that are not their own—worlds that are familiar to the reader, but strange to the character. In *Bad Day at Riverbend* (1995), Van Allsburg brings the flat, empty characters of a coloring book into a realm in which they live and react to the coloring of a young child that is applied to them. In *The Stranger* (1986), a character who combines the qualities of Jack Frost and the legendary New England "man clothed in leather" is struck by a car and forgets his identity. The mythic character suddenly enters the "real" world of a New England farm, where he encounters such strangeness as music and hot soup, a reversal of the expected notion of a realistic character entering a fantasy world. In *The Wreck of the Zephyr* (1983), a young boy finds his sailboat being sailed nonchalantly above the waves, so that it is taken out of its normal element. And, in *Two Bad Ants* (1988), the insect protagonists encounter the dilemma of moving into a world that is not their own and finding themselves threatened by cups of coffee, electric toasters, and garbage disposals, all viewed as huge from the perspective of the ants.

The blurring between fantasy and reality begun in *The Garden of Abdul Gasazi* continues in most of Van Allsburg's books, so that, as he moves from the "real" world to the fantasy world, there is no distinct line, no door in a wardrobe or flash of light. Does the young boy of *The Polar Express* simply dream all the adventure? Do the protagonists of *Just a Dream* (1990) and *Ben's Dream* (1982) similarly fall asleep and dream the entire sequence of the picture book? Van Allsburg leaves the possibility open; it is a possibility that invites the reader to deny the fantasy element of those books. At the same time, he undercuts that possibility, as he had in *The Garden of Abdul Gasazi*. Ben's dream of the architectural wonders of the world is also shared with Margaret; in fact, Ben has seen her there. And, in *The Polar Express*, the fact remains at the end of the book that the child is, indeed, holding the bell that he received—perhaps in a dream—from Santa.

In all of the books, Van Allsburg continues his exploration of the world of childhood. It is a world in which the unexpected can happen, in which the powerless find themselves pitted against enormity, in which innocence and joy and simple pleasure can prevail. These are the qualities that appear even when Van Allsburg uses adult characters. In *The Widow's Broom* (1992), for example, the widow's innocent and childlike dependence on the broom for company and support is pitted against the fearful superstition of the adult world, which cannot perceive the goodness of the broom. In *The Sweetest Fig* (1993), the long-suffering dog Marcel endures the clear savagery of his master Monsieur Bibot, until fantasy allows him to exchange their roles.

Perhaps the unique feature of Van Allsburg's fantasy is his ability to bring the reader into that blurred world between reality and fantasy, where the reader must make a decision about the reality of the story or—and perhaps this is preferable—live in the ambiguity of that blurred line. Van Allsburg never identifies the protagonist of *The Stranger;* the reader must decipher the clues and interpret his fantastic ability to blow frigid air. The mutual dreams of Ben and Margaret, the trick of the widow in preserving her broom, the exchange of positions between Marcel and Bibot—all of these are left to the reader to decipher, just as Van Allsburg leaves the mysterious stories in *The Mysteries of Harris Burdick* (1984) to the reader to create. There is, in short, a participatory quality to his blurring of the real and the unreal that calls for an active readership, one that does not end at the turning of the last page. Fantasy, in Van Allsburg's world, lies not only in the juxtaposition of two elements that should be apart, but also in the recognition of the mysterious interaction that we all have with the world, with each other, and with ourselves.

William Steig (b. 1907)

If Chris Van Allsburg blends the real and the unreal world to create his fantasy, Steig, instead, begins directly in the unreal world; his is not the process of Hugh Lofting or E. B. White. In picture books like *Roland the Minstrel Pig* (1968), *The Amazing Bone* (1976), *Sylvester and the Magic Pebble* (1987), and *Doctor DeSoto* (1982), Steig uses animal characters who play human roles—often adult roles—in human dress, with human voice. What is often startling is the mixture of the human and the animal, so that Roland is a marvelous singer, but he is also a pig and liable to be eaten by a fox. Similarly, Doctor DeSoto is a dentist who "did very good work," but he is also a mouse, and therefore in very real danger when one of his patients is a fox. Here the fantasy has come not through a blending, but through a movement of the human role out of that sphere and into the arena of animals, who are given speech and emotion to accompany those human roles.

In the work of Chris Van Allsburg, fantasy suggests a world of mystery and surprise; in Steig's work, fantasy heralds a world of very real danger. But juxtaposed with that danger is the security offered by the family—though at times that security is impotent—and a setting that is visually bright, colorful, and attractive. When Pearl comes home from school in *The Amazing Bone*, she dawdles through the forest whose light greens are set off by flowering trees: "[S]pring was so bright and beautiful, the warm air touched her so tenderly, she could almost feel herself changing into a flower. Her light dress felt like petals." The fantasy element of this sunny world—in addition to the fact that Pearl is a pig—is a talking bone who can imitate any sound; the afternoon becomes even more pleasant with such a companion.

But Steig never leaves his worlds merely pleasant. When a gentlemanly fox kidnaps Pearl, the bone is powerless to help. The danger of the scene is quite real; Pearl has been kidnapped by an adult fox who plans to kill her. This is not often the stuff of children's books when the story is taken out of the context of a folktale.

And the fox is malicious: "It would be amusing to gnaw on a bone that talks…and screams with pain." Only at the very moment of crisis does the bone remember the magic that will dispel the fox and save Pearl. She returns to her home and receives the frantic greeting that any parent would give afer having searched fruitlessly for a child: "The moment the door swung open she was in her mother's arms, and right after that in her father's."

Sylvester and the Magic Pebble works with a similar motif of separation. When Sylvester the donkey finds a magic pebble that grants all of his wishes, he is overjoyed and eager to show his parents. But, encountering a lion on the way home, he panics and turns himself into a rock, the pebble falling on the ground. With no way to change himself back and no way to communicate, it seems that Sylvester is doomed to remain a rock, and, in fact, as the seasons pass, he falls into a more and more profound sleep. Steig focuses not only on his despair, but also on the despair of his parents, who finally, almost a year later, go on a picnic to see if they might be happy again. There, by chance, they find the very rock that is Sylvester, set out their picnic lunch, and then find the red pebble that Sylvester had wished on. They place it on the rock that is Sylvester, and he is able to wish himself back into his donkey form. The terrible despair and loneliness of separation is at the center of this fantasy, despite the gentle colors and the humorous animals that inhabit the narrative.

The ending of *Sylvester and the Magic Pebble* suggests much about the world of Steig's fantasy; underneath the apparent bucolic nature and the comic animals, there is a deeply serious moral underpinning. When Sylvester shows his parents the quality of the pebble they have found, they do nothing but put the pebble in a safe. "After all, what more could they wish for? They all had all that they wanted." The real danger has been averted, and the terrible fear of the book resolved; but the moral seriousness remains.

It is up to the characters of William Steig's books to make their way through this dangerous world, much as a character in a folktale might. In *Doctor DeSoto*, the Doctor and his wife succeed because of their pluck and wit. A fox, having had his toothache cured, comes back for the final treatment; he has every intention of eating the little mouse working in his jaws. But he is foiled by the glue that the dentist spreads over his teeth, clamping his jaws shut. "All he could do was say, 'Frank oo berry mush' through his clenched teeth, and get up and leave. He tried to do so with dignity." The DeSotos, Steig writes, "had outfoxed the fox. They kissed each other and took the rest of the day off." Where Sylvester had succeeded through his recognition of his parents' love, the DeSotos succeed through their cleverness.

Though brighter visually and seemingly less mysterious than Van Allsburg, Steig, in actuality, explores a darker world, using his fantasy to subvert the very real dangers with which he deals, to tone down the dark potentialities of his tales. While this toning down does not affect their moral seriousness, it does—as in some folktales—set up an arena in which the reader expects the characters to come out all right in the end. But, even here, Steig will not play the expected role. When Pearl brings the Amazing Bone to her house, she is at first pleased with this constant companion. But the ending of the book suggests that not all is always well: "Anyone who happened to be alone in the house always had the bone to converse with. And they all had music whenever they wanted it, and sometimes even when they didn't."

Susan Cooper (b. 1935)

Unlike Chris Van Allsburg and William Steig, Susan Cooper, a novelist, uses the archetypes of myth and legend to inform her fantasy work. In her Dark is Rising quintet, Cooper uses Welsh and British mythology to invest stories that seem, at first, to be realistic stories, but then become larger and more universal as Cooper introduces the mythic elements. In her fantasy, Cooper does not leave the real world so much as she—like Chris Van Allsburg—brings two worlds into juxtaposition; she uses the interface of the two to create the plot narrative and even the meanings of the novels.

In *Over Sea, under Stone* (1965), Cooper introduces Barney, Jane, and Simon Drew, three normal if perceptive children who discover an ancient map while on vacation in Cornwall. Though this situation seems utterly realistic—even clichéd—it takes on enormous complication and import when the map leads the children into the Arthurian legends and, behind them, into the eternal struggle between the Light and the Dark, the Good and the Evil. Their guide into these legends, and an active participant, is their Uncle Merriman, who soon takes on mythic overtones: "How old he was, nobody knew. 'Old as the hills,' Father said, and they felt, deep down, that this was probably right. There was something about Great-Uncle Merry that was like the hills, or the sea, or the sky; something ancient, but without age or end" (9). This impression of eternality is confirmed when it becomes clear that this is Merlin.

In *The Dark Is Rising* (1973), Cooper introduces Will Stanton, who, on his eleventh birthday, discovers that he is the last of the Old Ones, immortal characters whose lot it is to protect the world from the dominion of the Dark. On many levels Will is a normal boy, with a very normal family. When he goes to feed the rabbits, unaware that he has come into his powers, he is surprised at their fear of him. His brother, however, has an explanation: "They've never smelt you clean before. Probably all will die of shock" (5). But on the other side, Will becomes aware of his new role through a series of visions, and also comes to realize some of the complications of his new life: The distinction between the Light and the Dark is not so easy as it might appear, a fact he learns again in *The Grey King* (1975), when he comes near to death so that the Light might use his illness in its cause.

It is this combination of myth and realism that gives these novels much of their power. The threatening power of ravens, the Hunter Hern, the female strength of the Greenwitch, the High Magic of the Grey King, the Sleepers under the Hill—all of these elements weave in and out of images of Will's family, of the Drew children, of the peace and serenity of the Welsh countryside. But the conclusion of the novels is a rejection of this juxtaposition, a recognition that life does not occur in the mythic realm forever. In the end, there is a return to the necessity of realism. Uncle Merry bids them all farewell, leaving the safekeeping of the earth in human hands, and even taking their memory of him away. In fact, the Drew children forget all of the mythic realm except their resolve to keep the Good.

Even the language of the novel suggests the mythic realm within the human realm. As Merry prepares to part from them in *Silver on the Tree* (1977), the concluding novel, he tells the children,

> For Drake is no longer in his hammock, children, nor is Arthur somewhere sleeping, and you may not lie idly expecting the second coming of anybody now, because the world is yours and it is up to you. Now especially since man has the strength to destroy the world, it is the responsibility of man to keep it alive, in all its beauty and marvelous joy. (267)

The high and formal stance of this passage, the long, balanced sentences, the careful, though not stylized, diction—all these suggest the tones of epic fantasy. But, when Will Stanton speaks at the end of the novel, he speaks both as an Old One and as a young boy: "I think it's time we were starting out…. We've got a long way to go." On one level he speaks of the hike back down the hills they have climbed, but on another level he speaks metaphorically of the task that lies ahead of them. The last line becomes emblematic of the movement back out of fantasy and into the real world, though the presence of the fantasy is never wholly dispelled.

In her two Boggart books, *The Boggart* (1993) and *The Boggart and the Monster* (1997), Cooper again turns to Welsh myth, here using the character of the Boggart, a playful, mischievous creature who can disappear. In the first novel, the Boggart is transported out of his ancient setting to contemporary Toronto. There, the juxtaposition of this ancient, mythical creature and the contemporary chaos of a busy modern city leads to humorous confusion, out of which develops the narrative goal: to return the Boggart to his castle. In *The Boggart and the Monster,* the Boggart goes to the aid of his friend Nessie, the Loch Ness monster, as Cooper brings two fantastic creatures together.

The Boggart novels lack the high seriousness of the Dark is Rising sequence, but each works along similar lines: the use of ancient archetypes in a realistic setting. The suspense of each of the stories lies with Cooper's ability to bring distanced stories into the immediate present, so that the world of myth no longer seems very far away. This combination of ancient and modern, of mythic and realistic, suggests Cooper's approach to fantasy.

Lloyd Alexander (b. 1924)

Like Susan Cooper, Lloyd Alexander employs the archetypes of myth and legend to create his fantasy; in fact, the five books of his Prydain series began as an adaptation of Welsh myth. The books, however, quickly became, instead, an examination of personal heroism. And the method of this examination was to create a landscape infused with Welsh lore and to place within it a character who wishes that, indeed, he were a part of the heroic, epic world that he sees so close to him.

In fact, however, Taran is always apart from that world. In the first book of the series, *The Book of Three* (1964), Taran is an assistant pigkeeper who yearns to be a great warrior and who, in fact, does journey on a quest. Quests continue in *The Black Cauldron* (1965), in which he journeys to the Land of Death, and *The Castle of Llyr* (1966), in which he rescues the Princess Eilonwy.

But it is in *Taran Wanderer* (1967) that Taran finally comes to the devastating understanding that he is not of royal blood, that he will not be a part of the magical epic world that he so desires. However, in *The High King* (1968), the final book of the series, he does indeed become King of Prydain when he learns that it is not royal blood or magical power that enables a man to become noble, but his deeds and accomplishments. The fantasy of the chronicles has carried this one character who, in the end, is not a part of the fantasy, and who steps out from it to show a larger meaning than might have been anticipated.

Unlike Susan Cooper, Alexander's novels can read sometimes like high tragedy, sometimes like vaudeville. There is a kind of slapstick about this world that undercuts the terrible seriousness of the epic world, particularly in the interactions of Taran's companions. Princess Eilonwy is a scrappy, witty, sharp-tongued girl who eventually falls in love with Taran, though she can hardly admit that a princess should fall in love with an assistant pigkeeper. The harpist Fflewddur Fflam strives his utmost not to boast, but he cannot overcome this weakness, though he is reminded of it when, each time he boasts, a string on his harp breaks. And Gurgi, the half-animal, half-human companion, is the child–adult, always hungry, always sensitive, always speaking in rhymes.

In the Westmark Trilogy, *Westmark* (1981), *The Kestrel* (1982), and *The Beggar Queen* (1984), Alexander uses a similar underlying proposition: One of the characters is trying to discover an identity. This time the character is female, and Mickle does indeed turn out to be Queen Augusta. Though Alexander again fills his stories with humor, he is also willing to show the grim side of human reality, with a vividness that can, at times, be startling, as in *The Kestrel* when Theo comes on the body of the poet Stock: "Theo jumped down from his mare. What looked like a side of beef had been propped against a tree trunk. The eyes were open, staring at him. The mouth seemed full of red mud. It took him several moments to realize it was Stock" (132). In Alexander's world this kind of vivid horror exists side by side with raucous humor.

More recently, Alexander has written fantasies such as *The Remarkable Journey of Prince Jen* (1991) and *The Iron Ring* (1997), in which he uses real settings, such as ancient China and India, as the landscape for epic adventures. The length of these novels is much greater than the novels of the Prydain and Westmark series, and their interweaving patterns are complex. In each, though, there is the quest for something larger than the individual. In *The Remarkable Journey of Prince Jen*, for example, Jen wants to leave his palace to find the legendary court of T'ien-kuo, where the great Yuan-ming rules in peace and prosperity. But, when he leaves the palace, he is betrayed, his kingdom wrenched from him. Abandoned, he meets several unlikely companions who gather around him and suffer with him all the indignities and injustices that his land can offer. In the end, they are able to retake the kingdom and Jen has become a different person; having suffered the worst abuses of his kingdom, he can put them to rights. Thus, when Jen finally does try to make his second journey, he discovers that he has no need of leaving to find a kingdom that is paradisal; there is his own already. The deep moral sense of what constitutes a noble, rich, and flourishing community is not imparted didactically, but is woven into the fabric of the fantasy itself.

This last is perhaps Alexander's greatest quality: a sense that there are ethical and moral choices to be made, and that real human beings make them. By placing the making of those choices in the arena of fantasy, Alexander has distanced them and let readers see them all the more clearly for the distancing.

Madeleine L'Engle (b. 1918)

In her use of elements such as time and space travel, alien worlds, and technological advances, it might seem that Madeleine L'Engle is squarely in the genre of science fiction. In fact, however, it is difficult to set generic boundaries on her Time Quartet. There are elements of science fiction, certainly; when Meg, Calvin, and Charles Wallace are whisked away to Uriel in *A Wrinkle in Time* (1962), or when the children are transported in time in *A Swiftly Tilting Planet* (1978) and *Many Waters* (1986), this is the stuff of science fiction. But that generic boundary starts to become blurry when L'Engle turns to the philosophers among the physical scientists, such as Einstein and Fritjof Capra. Here are elements that are not only scientific: the theoretical fusion of time and space; the elimination of the straight line as the shortest distance between two points; elements that are neither real nor unreal, but have a tendency to exist. Here L'Engle has merged into philosophical, even, in her hands, mystical territory that distinguishes her from other writers of science fiction.

Like John Christopher, L'Engle will use the constructs of science fiction to deal with powerful thematic issues. But, unlike Christopher, she will include antagonists who are not the typical fare of science fiction. Instead, her novels are populated with creatures who share—or do not share—in the heavenly dance, and who carry a great deal of theological weight. In *A Wrinkle in Time* she will include three weird sisters who dress and act the part of witches, but who are angelic comforters. In *A Wind in the Door* she includes a cherubim, Proginoskes, who teaches her characters the theological concept of naming. In *Many Waters* Meg's brothers encounter the fallen angels, the Nephilim, and, in *A Swiftly Tilting Planet,* the children come across creatures singing the words of the Doxology.

In that final book, L'Engle sets out one of the central tenets of her work: "They moved through the time-spinning reaches of a far galaxy, and he realized that the galaxy itself was part of a mighty orchestra, and each star and planet within the galaxy added its own instrument to the music of the spheres. As long as the ancient harmonies were sung, the universe would not entirely lose its joy" (72). The metaphor of music and harmony suggests the larger theme that Engle pursues: that joy and harmony lie at the center of the universe, and that, while there are forces that fight for its continuity, there are also forces that fight for its destruction—in L'Engle's works, the mysterious and shadowy Ecthroi. In the theological, scientific, fantasy worlds that L'Engle creates, the central incarnation of good and evil is represented by the forces that fight for the light against the darkness, or the angelic forces versus the ecthroi, the destroyers. It is absolutely crucial to see that the children are battlers also, and, though they might not have the same supranatural powers of some fighters, they are nonetheless equally important in the battle.

In the first two novels of the series, *A Wrinkle in Time* and *A Wind in the Door*, L'Engle sets her fantasy in a very familiar world: Meg is unhappy with her teachers, unhappy with the school principal, and, for the most part, without friends. This changes with the advent of Calvin, but that set of difficulties portends the larger difficulties that Meg faces: the rescue of her father and the safety of Charles Wallace, whose mitochondria are dying. In the last two novels, the adventures and quests become larger: Charles Wallace must travel through time, though not space, to resolve a family line that has led to a South American tyrant with nuclear capabilities, and the twins, who have travelled back to the time of Noah, must find a way to escape before the coming flood.

But what is markedly L'Engle is that she does not make distinctions between the apparently mundane quests and the much more global ones; throughout her work she insists that there is little distinction in size that is meaningful, and this is true of the quests as well. Meg's difficulties in school are just as much disharmony as Mad Dog Branzillo's threats. This strong religious and philosophic stance, this suggestion that these novels are dealing with moral and ethical choices that are of enormous consequence to both the individual and corporate worlds, is at the very heart of L'Engle's fantasy, and accounts in large part for its theological dimensions.

John Christopher (b. 1922)

The work of John Christopher (the pseudonym used by the author C. S. Youd) is generally regarded as the coming of age of science fiction in Great Britain. In books like *The Guardians* (1970), in which everyone in Britain is manipulated and ruled from a secret source, and *The Lotus Caves* (1969), in which two boys escape from a moon research station and discover an intelligent plant that offers perpetual rest and youth, Christopher explores the nature and costs of human will and independence. Of his many works, the Tripods Trilogy is perhaps his most popular in North America. In this series, which became a quartet with the addition of *When the Tripods Came* (1988), a prequel, Christopher uses the motifs of science fiction to explore these fundamental questions of human freedom. It would be easy for such questions to become mere clichés; Christopher avoids that debasement, however, by using the distancing that fantasy can provide. In short, he moves his readers back in the theater.

The White Mountains (1967) begins, it would seem, as historical fiction rather than fantasy. The action is set in a small village that is isolated, accessible, it seems, only by horse. But references to "Capping" and to Tripods show that this novel is, in fact, set in the future, during a time when alien Tripods have conquered the earth and used metallic caps to curb human beings' will. The protagonist of the novel—named, significantly, Will—finds himself loathe to undergo such a capping, and eventually discovers that there are others like him who have escaped and who are organizing resistance to the Tripods. Will, together with two other boys, resolves to flee. The novel chronicles their hazardous escape from their village to the White Mountains.

If fantasy distances, then it must distance for a purpose. Here, the purpose is to clarify a difficult question. The Tripods have brought with them an end to hunger, an end to poverty, an end to human war and strife. But the cost of that is the complete loss of human will. Christopher asks, Are war and poverty and hardship worth the price of human will and freedom? In *When the Tripods Came*, it seems that the human race is all too willing to yield the responsibilities of freedom. But in the conclusion to *The White Mountains*, Will believes that freedom is worth the costs it engenders, and, from his hard refuge in the White Mountains, he decides that, though the life of the people down in the valley is easy and secure, he is blessed with freedom and hope—two distinctly human qualities.

The trilogy—and its questions—continue in *The City of Gold and Lead* (1967) and *The Pool of Fire* (1968). Here, Will is able to infiltrate one of the domed cities of the Tripods and finds a race that uses humans to serve it, and a race that intends to change the atmosphere of the earth to make it habitable for them, but for them alone. Again, Christopher does not make the plot situation clichéd; there is a curious gentleness about some of the aliens that Will finds poignant. But, in the end, he escapes the city with some concept of how to destroy them, and that campaign is carried out in the final novel. But, even in the conclusion, Christopher poses hard questions. The battle has been won, despite the hint of a possible later invasion, but now the free groups of humanity are already divided on how to govern themselves. Freedom's costs come quickly and explicitly.

To create his fantasy world, the arena in which he will ask his questions, Christopher brings together two levels of technology. There is, first, the high level of the Tripod technology, a technology that the humans are barely able to comprehend. Opposed to that is the human technology, that has been brought back to a medieval level. Will and his friends do get occasional glimpses of human technology—his father has a Watch that could never be duplicated, and they see tunnels made for engines that carried people underground—but this is a human technology that is virtually out of reach. Beanpole, one of the characters who escapes with Will, does have some sense that it might be re-created; he imagines a steam engine, for example. But, in the end, the boys have to rely on primitive means to defeat mighty technology; in fact, their final assault comes as a hot-air balloon attack. Christopher has here created a fantasy future world based squarely on an older, nontechnological world, so it is at once familiar and unfamiliar, comforting in its simplicity yet frightening in its losses.

Nancy Farmer (b. 1941)

Nancy Farmer has shown herself to be one of the most inventive of recent fantasists, for, while she has maintained a consistency in her settings—her books are set in Zimbabwe—she has crafted very different kinds of fantasies, though all of them are marked by a mixture of intensity and humor, and sometimes almost raucous comedy. In *The Warm Place* (1995), she tells the story of Ruva, a baby giraffe who has been kidnapped by poachers. Her escape and journey back towards her home are certainly poignant, but what is perhaps not expected is that the episodes on the journey can be so comic as well. Similarly, *The Ear, the Eye, and the Arm* (1994) is a sprawling epic of a novel with very intense and even frightening moments, but at the center of the book is a trio of mutated detectives who are comic, bumbling, always just one step or so behind. Yet, in the end, they are the ones who help to save the day through their bumbling.

Farmer's fantasy comes through a melding of the spiritual world of Zimbabwe's mythology with the real world of Zimbabwe. In fact, in her novels, there seems to be no boundary between the two, so that they pass easily backwards and forwards. In Farmer's *A Girl Named Disaster* (1996), Nhamo flees an impending marriage with a man who will certainly be cruel to her, and in her flight she is aided by the spirit of her mother, as well as the spirits of African mythology. When she is stranded on an island in Lake Cobora Bassa, she must share her refuge with a leopard, who kills a threatening baboon and, later, an antelope that Nhamo is able to share in order to survive. Only later does she realize that the leopard is the spirit of her father.

The presence of that spirit world is never questioned; it is both threatening and helpful, something to be feared, something to be appeased, something for which to be grateful. For Nhamo it is what keeps her alive, and what drives her on in her search for a better life. For the three children of *The Ear, the Eye, and the Arm*, it is something that gives courage in the midst of real danger and threatens Tendai with a tortuous death. In both cases, the spirit world is very close to the real world, breaking through often and easily.

To recreate the world of Zimbabwe, the other world that must be created in fantasy, Farmer moves backwards and forwards in time. In *A Girl Named Disaster*, it seems that she has set the story in a much earlier time, but references to electric lights, land mines, and health clinics show that this is not so; in fact, the story is set at the beginning of the 1980s. Still, there is a jarring union of past and present when Nhamo, with such an acute awareness of the spirit world, meets with contemporary researchers who have lost that vision. The jarring is plainer in *The Ear, the Eye, and the Arm*, which is set two centuries ahead, when Zimbabwe has been devastated by nuclear disaster and where plastic is now an incredibly expensive commodity. Here the three children find a nightmare of a world in the future, but, when they enter pastoral Resthaven, they find a world that is purposefully set back in the past. Yet, here too, they find nightmares, where children are killed out of superstition. Neither place seems an adequate home, but both places are intensely aware of the spiritual realm and its workings out in real life.

To read Nancy Farmer is to be educated in Shona mythology; her books come complete with explanatory histories and glossaries. Like Madeleine L'Engle, she is concerned with showing the lack of real distinction between spiritual and physical things, and she has found a potent other world in which she can clarify this point.

Donna Jo Napoli (b. 1948)

In books such as *The Prince of the Pond* (1992) and *Jimmy, The Pickpocket of the Palace* (1995), Donna Jo Napoli creates fantasies based on folktales. While maintaining the principal outlines of the folktale, she expands the plot narrative to craft a text that recreates the folktale in an entirely new guise, giving her the opportunity to establish fuller characters, more developed settings, and—this last most important—more fully worked out implications of the plot. In *The Prince of the Pond* and *Jimmy, The Pickpocket of the Palace*, Napoli retells the story of the frog prince, developing, in the first novel, the prince's dual nature: He is, in many ways, both prince and frog, and can never entirely leave one side alone.

In *Jimmy, The Pickpocket of the Palace*, the protagonist—a frog named Jimmy—is, in fact, the prince's son. He comes to the palace to find the hag's magic ring, kept by the prince, and to find news of his father, who disappeared when the prince appeared. The tone of the adventures he encounters is comic and suspenseful, not far from the tone of many of Lloyd Alexander's works. Jimmy, who has been turned into a boy by a delayed spell, tries to adapt froglike to his new surroundings, hiding in the horse trough, eating caterpillars, and trying to cope with clothes, new limbs, and only a stump of a tongue. But beneath that humor lies the poignancy of a broken family; the prince comes to the pond to call out to them, but he is no longer of their world and there is no real connection. In the end, Jimmy, having succeeded in thwarting the hag, returns to his frog state, having discovered that the prince is indeed his father but that he will never be part of their world.

It is this development of matters only implied in the folktales that marks the strength of Napoli's fantasies. She takes what is most familiar and then develops the fuller plot line to make explicit what had perhaps been only hinted in the barer narratives of the folktales. In *Zel* (1996) and *The Magic Circle* (1993), Napoli explores deeper and more disturbing implications, so disturbing that she abandons the lightheartedness of the Frog Prince novels and, instead, engineers much darker worlds. *Zel* is a retelling of the folktale of Rapunzel, but here she explores the nature of love itself. Zel and her mother live alone, and her mother insists that, because they have each other, they have enough. When Zel grows up and encounters a man by chance, she sees that perhaps she and her mother are not enough for each other. Terrified of the future loss she will endure, the mother locks Zel in a tower, and so develops the exploration of harm and evil done in the name of love, of love as distinct from possessiveness, of love as something that leads to ill and to redemption.

In *The Magic Circle*, Napoli retells the story of Hansel and Gretel through the first-person narrative of the witch. But here, the Ugly One is in fact a witch who has been tempted into evil by a drive for goodness. In order to heal, she is convinced by her neighbor that she should learn to control demons. So the

Ugly One draws the Magic Circle about herself to protect her while she controls; unfortunately, she is tricked and then possessed, with the result that this healer suddenly is a witch. To defy the demons and escape her new nature, she flees to the woods so that she may avoid doing what her new nature forces her to do: Eat children. There she escapes, for a time, until two children come and the demons rediscover and repossess her. This is a novel about temptation, and a novel about someone who refuses to yield to the furious demands of her new nature. In this refusal to yield, she is able to reject that nature and connect herself once again to something quite different. In the end, after she shows Gretel that she must push her into the oven, she finds that, in her refusal to yield, she has found a new nature. Her powerful and vivid writing create a very different image of the witch than the traditional folktale yields. In the fantasy, Napoli has created a character at war with herself, a character who is determined to overcome what has been foisted on her. Napoli's other world, then, is the world of the folktale writ large, and crafted so as to free the implicit concerns of those tales.

Thinking and Writing about and from within the Genre of Fantasy

Thinking and Writing about the Genre of Fantasy

1. Consider this passage from the opening of L. Frank Baum's *The Wizard of Oz* (1899), one of the best-known of U.S. fantasies.

    > The cyclone had set the house down, very gently—for a cyclone— in the midst of a country of marvelous beauty. There were lovely patches of green sward all about, with stately trees bearing rich and luscious fruits. Banks of gorgeous flowers were on every hand, and birds with rare and brilliant plumage sang and fluttered in the trees and bushes. A little way off was a small brook, rushing and sparkling along between green banks, and murmuring in a voice very grateful to a little girl who had lived so long on the dry, gray prairies.
    >
    > While she stood looking eagerly at the strange and beautiful sights, she noticed coming toward her a group of the queerest people she had ever seen. They were not as big as the grown folk she had always been used to; but neither were they very small. In fact, they seemed about as tall as Dorothy, who was a well-grown child for her age, although they were, so far as looks go, many years older.

    If a fantasy is to succeed, the writer must help the reader to suspend disbelief. Is Baum successful in this opening in his attempt to bring the reader convincingly into Oz?

2. Choose one of Virginia Lee Burton's picture books from the middle of the century: *Mike Mulligan and His Steamshovel, Katy and the Big Snow, The Little House*. If fantasy is to speak metaphorically about the real world, then how does Burton use her personifications of inanimate objects as a way to tell us about the world?

3. Lloyd Alexander's *The Fortune Tellers* (1992), set in the West African country of Cameroon, tells the story of a young carpenter who, unhappy with his lot, visits the local fortune-teller. "Rich you will surely be," he tells the carpenter, if "you earn large sums of money." He will become famous "once you become well known," and he shall marry his true love "if you find her and she agrees." Soon afterwards, the carpenter is himself mistaken for the fortune-teller, and he decides to play the role by giving the same sort of answers he had heard. He soon becomes famous for his skill, and wealthy, and does indeed marry his true love. "Despite his wealth and fame, the carpenter never forgot his benefactor. Although in time he gave up wondering what had happened to the fortune-teller, the carpenter thought of him frequently with warmth and gratitude for having seen the future so clearly."

The story is all told tongue-in-cheek, and there is never any sense that the fortune-telling business is in any sense real. Yet the book has been attacked and censored because it deals with matters of fortune-telling. How might you answer someone who attacked the book on these grounds?

Thinking and Writing from within the Genre of Fantasy

1. The creation of a secondary world in fantasy demands the creation of a whole world, a world that is consistent and that accords with the rules by which it is established. You, as an author of fantasy, have decided to create an underwater world, perhaps on this planet, perhaps on another. Consider such questions as the following:

- How will those inhabitants of this underwater world have adapted themselves to the needs of their underwater life? How will they differ physically from humans? How will their eyes adjust to the dimmer light? How will they dress, if they are dressed at all?
- How will the inhabitants communicate? How might their language differ from human language? What idioms might develop in such a world? How will their metaphors differ from those of a land dweller?
- Who are their enemies, and who their friends?
- How do they adapt to warmer and cooler climates? Is their watery life under the polar caps, or just in the more temperate zones?
- Can these inhabitants communicate with other species? If so, how? Can they communicate with humans? Why would they?
- Do they hunt, or gather, or farm?

Think of other questions that you might have to ask about these people so that you might create a whole and consistent world even before you put pen to paper.

2. After reading one of the texts by William Steig, such as *The Amazing Bone*, rewrite the story using human characters instead of the animal characters. Think about what has been lost with such a revision.

3. Create a character that might be in a low fantasy—perhaps an animal, or a personified toy—and then craft a setting from a high fantasy in which that character might find himself or herself. Is the result tragic, horrific, comic, romantic? Why?

Selected Bibliographies

Works Cited

Picture Book Fantasies

Alexander, Lloyd. *The Fortune-Tellers*. New York: Dutton, 1992. Illustrated by Trina Schart Hyman.

Burton, Virginia Lee. *Katy and the Big Snow*. Boston: Houghton Mifflin, 1943.

———. *The Little House*. Boston: Houghton Mifflin, 1942.

———. *Mike Mulligan and His Steamshovel*. Boston: Houghton Mifflin, 1939.

Conrad, Pam. *The Tub Grandfather*. New York: HarperCollins, 1993. Illustrated by Richard Egleiski.

———. *The Tub People*. New York: HarperCollins, 1989. Illustrated by Richard Egleiski.

Gág, Wanda. *Millions of Cats*. New York: Coward-McCann, 1928.

San Souci, Robert D. *Nicholas Pipe*. New York: Dial, 1997. Illustrated by David Shannon.

Sendak, Maurice. *Where the Wild Things Are*. New York: Harper and Row, 1963.

Stewart, Sarah. *The Money Tree*. New York: Farrar, Straus and Giroux, 1991. Illustrated by David Small.

Willard, Nancy. *Pish, Posh, Hieronymus Bosch*. New York: Harcourt Brace, 1991. Illustrated by Leo, Diane, and Lee Dillon.

———. *The Sorcerer's Apprentice*. New York: Scholastic, 1993. Illustrations by Leo and Diane Dillon.

Wood, Audrey. *Heckedy Peg*. New York: Harcourt Brace, 1987. Illustrations by Don Wood.

Non-Picture Book Fantasies

Avi. *Poppy*. New York: Orchard, 1995.

Babbitt, Natalie. *Tuck Everlasting*. New York: Farrar, Strauss, 1975.

Banks, Lynne Reid. *The Indian in the Cupboard*. Garden City, NY: Doubleday, 1985.

Baum, L. Frank. *The Wizard of Oz*. Indianapolis: Bobbs-Merrill, 1899.

Bellairs, John. *The House with a Clock in Its Walls*. New York: Dial, 1973.

Christopher, John. *The White Mountains*. New York: Simon and Schuster, 1967.

Cooper, Susan. *Over Sea, under Stone*. New York: Harcourt, Brace, 1965.

Dahl, Roald. *Charlie and the Chocolate Factory*. New York: Knopf, 1964.

Henkes, Kevin. *Lily's Purple Plastic Purse*. New York: Greenwillow, 1996.

Hurmence, Belinda. *A Girl Called Boy*. New York: Clarion, 1982.

King-Smith, Dick. *Babe: The Gallant Pig*. New York: Random House, 1983.

Lawson, Robert. *Rabbit Hill*. New York: Viking, 1944.

L'Engle, Madeleine. *A Wrinkle in Time*. New York: Farrar, Straus and Giroux, 1962.

Lewis, C. S. *The Lion, the Witch, and the Wardrobe*. New York: Macmillan, 1950.

Lofting, Hugh. *The Story of Doctor Dolittle*. New York: Frederick A. Stokes, 1920.

Lowry, Lois. *The Giver*. Boston: Houghton Mifflin, 1993.

McGraw, Eloise. *The Moorchild*. New York: McElderry, 1996.

Milne, A. A. *The House at Pooh Corner*. London: E. P. Dutton, 1928.

———. *Winnie-the-Pooh*. London: E. P. Dutton, 1926.

Norton, Mary. *The Borrowers*. New York: Harcourt, 1953.

Pearce, Philippa. *Tom's Midnight Garden*. Philadelphia: Lippincott, 1959.

Potter, Beatrix. *The Tale of Peter Rabbit*. London: Warne, 1902.

Rowling, J. K. *Harry Potter and the Chamber of Secrets*. New York: Scholastic, 1999.

———. *Harry Potter and the Goblet of Fire*. New York: Scholastic, 2000.

———. *Harry Potter and the Prisoner of Azkaban*. New York: Scholastic, 1999.

———. *Harry Potter and the Sorcerer's Stone*. New York: Scholastic, 1997.

Rylant, Cynthia. *Gooseberry Park*. New York: Harcourt Brace, 1995.

Tolkien, J. R. R. *The Hobbit*. London: Allen and Unwin, 1937.

Travers, P. L. *Mary Poppins*. New York: Harcourt, 1934.

Waugh, Sylvia. *The Mennyms*. New York: William Morrow, 1993.

Westall, Robert. *Blitzcat*. New York: Scholastic, 1989.

White, E. B. *Charlotte's Web*. New York: Harper and Brothers, 1952.

Williams, Margery. *The Velveteen Rabbit*. New York: George H. Doran, 1922.

Wrightson, Patricia. *The Nargun and the Stars*. New York: Macmillan, 1974.

Voigt, Cynthia. *Building Blocks*. New York: Scholastic, 1984.

Yolen, Jane. *The Devil's Arithmetic*. New York: Viking, 1988.

———. *Heart's Blood*. New York: Delacorte, 1984.

Works of Selected Writers and Illustrators of Fantasy

Maurice Sendak

The Animal Family. New York: Pantheon, 1965. Randall Jarrell, author.

The Bat-Poet. New York: Macmillan, 1964. Randall Jarrell, author.

The Bee-Man of Orn. New York: Holt, Rinehart, and Winston, 1964. Frank Stockton, author.

Dear Mili. New York: Farrar, Straus and Giroux, 1988.

Fly By Night. New York: Farrar, Straus and Giroux, 1976. Randall Jarrell, author.

In the Night Kitchen. New York: Harper and Row, 1970.

Outside over There. New York: Harper and Row, 1981.

Where the Wild Things Are. New York: Harper and Row, 1963.

Chris Van Allsburg

Bad Day at Riverbend. Boston: Houghton Mifflin, 1995.

Ben's Dream. Boston: Houghton Mifflin, 1982.

A City in Winter. New York: Viking, 1996. Written by Mark Helprin.

The Garden of Abdul Gasazi. Boston: Houghton Mifflin, 1979.

Jumanji. Boston: Houghton Mifflin, 1981.

Just a Dream. Boston: Houghton Mifflin, 1990.

The Mysteries of Harris Burdick. Boston: Houghton Mifflin, 1984.

The Polar Express. Boston: Houghton Mifflin, 1985.

The Stranger. Boston: Houghton Mifflin, 1986.

Swan Lake. Boston: Houghton Mifflin, 1989. Written by Mark Helprin.

The Sweetest Fig. Boston: Houghton Mifflin, 1993.

Two Bad Ants. Boston: Houghton Mifflin, 1988.

The Widow's Broom. Boston: Houghton Mifflin, 1992.

The Wreck of the Zephyr. Boston: Houghton Mifflin, 1983.

The Wretched Stone. Boston: Houghton Mifflin, 1991.

William Steig

Abel's Island. New York: Farrar, Straus and Giroux, 1976.

The Amazing Bone. New York: Farrar, Straus and Giroux, 1976.

Brave Irene. New York: Farrar, Straus and Giroux, 1986.

Doctor DeSoto. New York: Farrar, Straus and Giroux, 1982.

Doctor DeSoto Goes to Africa. New York: HarperCollins, 1992.

Dominic. New York: Farrar, Straus and Giroux, 1984.

The Real Thief. New York: Farrar, Straus and Giroux, 1976.

Roland the Minstrel Pig. New York: HarperCollins, 1986.

Shrek! New York: Farrar, Straus, 1990.

Sylvester and the Magic Pebble. New York: Simon and Schuster, 1987.

Susan Cooper

The Boggart. New York: Simon and Schuster, 1993.

The Boggart and the Monster. New York: Simon and Schuster, 1997.

The Dark is Rising. New York: Simon and Schuster, 1973.

Greenwitch. New York: Simon and Schuster, 1976.

The Grey King. New York: Simon and Schuster, 1975.

Over Sea, under Stone. New York: Simon and Schuster, 1965.

Silver on the Tree. New York: Simon and Schuster, 1977.

Lloyd Alexander

The Beggar Queen. New York: Dutton, 1984.
The Black Cauldron. New York: Holt, 1965.
The Book of Three. New York: Holt, 1964.
The Castle of Llyr. New York: Holt, 1966.
The High King. New York: Holt, 1968.
The Iron Ring. New York: Dutton, 1997.
The Kestrel. New York: Dutton, 1982.
The Marvelous Misadventures of Sebastian. New York: Dutton, 1970.
The Remarkable Journey of Prince Jen. New York: Dutton, 1991.
Taran Wanderer. New York: Holt, 1967.
Westmark. New York: Dutton, 1981.

Madeleine L'Engle

Many Waters. New York: Farrar, Straus and Giroux, 1986.
A Swiftly Tilting Planet. New York: Farrar, Straus and Giroux, 1978.
A Wind in the Door. New York: Farrar, Straus and Giroux, 1973.
A Wrinkle in Time. New York: Farrar, Straus and Giroux, 1962.

John Christopher

Beyond the Burning Lands. New York: Macmillan, 1971.

The City of Gold and Lead. New York: Macmillan, 1967.
Dragon Dance. New York: Dutton, 1986.
Empty World. New York: Dutton, 1978.
Fireball. New York: Dutton, 1981.
The Guardians. New York: Macmillan, 1970.
The Lotus Caves. New York: Macmillan, 1969.
New Found Land. New York: Dutton, 1983.
The Pool of Fire. New York: Macmillan, 1968.
The Prince in Waiting. New York: Macmillan, 1970.
The Sword of the Spirits. New York: Macmillan, 1972.
When the Tripods Came. New York: Viking, 1988.
The White Mountains. New York: Macmillan, 1967.
Wild Jack. New York: Macmillan, 1974.

Nancy Farmer

The Ear, the Eye, and the Arm. New York: Orchard, 1994.
A Girl Named Disaster. New York: Orchard, 1996.
The Warm Place. New York: Orchard, 1995.

Donna Jo Napoli

Jimmy, The Pickpocket of the Palace. New York: Dutton, 1995.
The Magic Circle. New York: Dutton, 1993.
The Prince of the Pond. New York: Dutton, 1992.
Zel. New York: Dutton, 1996.

Works about the Genre of Fantasy

Alexander, Lloyd. "Fantasy and the Human Condition." *New Advocate* 1 (Spring, 1988): 75–83.

———. "A Manner of Speaking." In Charlotte F. Otten and Gary D. Schmidt, eds., *The Voice of the Narrator in Children's Literature* (Westport, CT: Greeenwood, 1989): 123–131.

Blackburn, William. "Madeleine L'Engle's *A Wrinkle in Time:* Seeking the Original Face." In Perry Nodelman, ed., *Touchstones: Reflections on the Best in Children's Literature* 1

(West Lafayette, IN: Children's Literature Association, 1989): 123–131.

Bottner, Barbara. "William Steig: The Two Legacies." *Lion and the Unicorn* 2 (1978): 4–16.

Cech, John. *Angels and Wild Things: The Archetypal Poetics of Maurice Sendak.* University Park: Pennsylvania State University Press, 1995.

DeLuca, Geraldine. "Exploring the Levels of Childhood: The Allegorical Sensibility of Maurice Sendak." *Children's Literature* 12 (1984): 3–24.

Evans, Gwyneth. "Harps and Harpers in Contemporary Fantasy." *Lion and the Unicorn* 6 (December, 1992): 199–209.

Ford, Elizabeth A. "Resurrection Twins: Visual Implications in *Two Bad Ants*." *Children's Literature Association Quarterly* 15 (Spring, 1990): 8–10.

Gauch, Patricia Lee. "A Quest for the Heart of Fantasy." *New Advocate* 7 (Summer, 1994): 159–167.

Hettinga, Donald R. *Presenting Madeleine L'Engle.* New York: Twayne, 1993.

Hughes, Monica. "Science Fiction as Myth and Metaphor." *ALAN Review* 19 (Spring, 1992): 2–5.

Hunt, Caroline. "Form as Fantasy—Fantasy as Form." *Children's Literature Association Quarterly* 12 (Spring, 1987): 7–10.

Kuznets, Lois. "'High Fantasy' in America: A Study of Lloyd Alexander, Ursula LeGuin, and Susan Cooper." *Lion and the Unicorn* 9 (1985): 19–35.

Lanes, Selma. *The Art of Maurice Sendak.* New York: Abrams, 1980.

May, Jill. *Lloyd Alexander.* Boston: Twayne, 1991.

Neumeyer, Peter. "How Picture Books Mean: The Case of Chris Van Allsburg." *Children's Literature Association Quarterly* 15 (1990): 2–8.

Nodelman, Perry. "Text as Teacher: The Beginning of *Charlotte's Web*." *Children's Literature* 13 (1985): 109–127.

Perrot, Jean. "Maurice Sendak's Ritual Cooking of the Child in Three Tableaux: The Moon, Mother, and Music." *Children's Literature* 18 (1990): 68–86.

Quinn, Dennis B. "The Narnia Books of C. S. Lewis: Fantastic or Wonderful?" *Children's Literature* 12 (1984): 105–121.

Riga, Frank P. "Mortals Call Their History Fable: Narnia and the Use of Fairy Tale." *Children's Literature Association Quarterly* 14 (Spring, 1989): 26–30.

Rollin, Lucy. "The Reproduction of Mothering in *Charlotte's Web*." *Children's Literature* 18 (1990): 42–52.

Rushdy, Ashraf H. A. "'The Miracle of the Web': Continuity, Desire, and Narrativity in *Charlotte's Web*." *Lion and the Unicorn* 15 (December, 1991): 35–60.

Schmidt, Gary D. *Hugh Lofting.* New York: Twayne, 1992.

———. *Robert Lawson.* New York: Twayne, 1997.

Stanton, Joseph. "The Dreaming Picture Books of Chris Van Allsburg." *Children's Literature* 24 (1996): 161–179.

Steig, Michael. "Reading *Outside Over There*." *Children's Literature* 13 (1985): 139–153.

Stott, Jon C. "Lloyd Alexander's Chronicles of Prydain: The Nature of Beginnings." In Perry Nodelman, ed., *Touchstones: Reflections on the Best in Children's Literature* 1 (West Lafayette, IN: Children's Literature Association, 1989): 21–29.

——— and Teresa Krier, "Virginia Lee Burton's *The Little House:* Technological Changes and Fundamental Verities." In Perry Nodelman, ed., *Touchstones: Reflections on the Best in Children's Literature* 3 (West Lafayette, IN: Children's Literature Association, 1989): 28–37.

Tunnell, Michael O. "An Interview with Lloyd Alexander." *New Advocate* 2 (Spring, 1989): 83–95.

Waller, Jennifer. "Maurice Sendak and the Blakean Vision of Childhood." *Children's Literature* 6 (1977): 130–140.

Wilner, Arlene. "'Unlocked by Love': William Steig's Tales of Transformation and Magic." *Children's Literature* 18 (1990): 31–41.

9

Realism: Truth, Whether It Happened or Not

In Taro Yashima's *Crow Boy* (1965), young Chibi is scorned by his classmates for his quiet ways, strange clothing and food, and odd interests. Unable to connect with the children or with the studies, Chibi is left alone, except when he is taunted. Then, at the end of his six years of schooling, Chibi encounters a loving and sensitive teacher who is able to draw out his artistic skills. In the school talent contest, Chibi imitates the voices of crows, and the children are amazed at his skills—and equally amazed that every day for six years he has left home at dawn and arrived home at dusk so that he could come to school. After his graduation, they rename him Crow Boy, a term of honor.

In Chris Soentpiet's *Around Town* (1994), a young girl and her mother spend a day in New York City, where they celebrate the life around Central Park, "where houses are built close together and backyards are tiny and streets are always busy, and where sometimes it feels like there's everything under the sun." The final clause of this opening page suggests the nature of this book: It does seem as if the city offers more than can hardly be imagined, and it is a place under the sun, with its suggestion of warmth and fullness. The mother and daughter pass children playing in the spray from an open hydrant, a toyshop on the street, street musicians, the birds and chess players of the park, and an open-air Italian restaurant. They take a ride through the park and watch the clowns and jugglers, carry balloons, have their portraits drawn, their faces painted, their backs massaged. Some people "don't like a city," the narrator concludes, but "some people live in the city and think it's the best place of all."

Both of these books are quiet; neither has the dramatic plot narrative that drives a reader on through the pages. Instead, both explore their subjects deeply and richly. For Taro Yashima, this means the exploration of character, as she portrays six lonely years in the life of a young boy who develops skills to pass the time and avoid the loneliness that surrounds him. In the end, the six years are not wiped away—there is still pain in those memories—but they do grow to a blossoming as a new teacher helps Chibi—Crow Boy—come into his young manhood, proud of his abilities. Chris Soentpiet, on the other hand, explores place, and his view is expansive. He does not insist that everyone must love the city, but clearly his work demonstrates a love on his part. The city is a place of raucous wonder, of quiet and intimate pleasure, of excitement. It is a place where there is everything under the sun.

Both Taro Yashima and Chris Soentpiet are working within the genre of realism. It is a genre that sets its boundaries at the edges of our own experience, at the edges of the known world. To move beyond that would be to move to fantasy. To move to an earlier time, outside our own, would be to move into historical fiction, a subgenre of realism. But realism itself must deal with the real world in the contemporary period. At the same time, its boundaries may not be so easily and sharply defined. Realism is not simply the objective presentation, not simply the straightforward presentation of the facts of everyday life, as Jerry Spinelli suggests in his opening to *Maniac Magee* (1990): "[T]he history of a kid is one part fact, two parts legend, and three parts snowball. And if you want to know what it was like back when Maniac Magee roamed these parts, well, just run your hand under your movie seat and be very, very careful not to let the facts get mixed up with the truth." (2)

Boundaries and Definitions of Realism

A number of works within the genre of realism have been inspired by a real-life situation. Cynthia Voigt's *Homecoming* (1981) was suggested when the author saw a car full of kids in the parking lot of a mall and wondered what they would do if their parents did not return. When Robert Cormier's son decided not to sell chocolates at his school, the author turned the event into powerful fiction. When Pat Brisson watched friends die of cancer, she wondered how their mother prepared her children for death and so began *Sky Memories* (1999). Writers use these ideas to begin a work of fiction, interpreting that moment in the contemporary world, energizing its artistic potentialities. The writer's materials may be the experiences of the real world, but the writer's goal is to uncover from those materials the story—and the truth—resting beneath them. The writer of realism must make sense out of the flood of everyday events; he or she must step back from this rush and see the truth that lies beneath it.

If a metaphor for fantasy is a theater in which the viewer is moved back away from the screen—away from real life—so that the viewer might bring the totality of the screen into clearer and sharper focus, then it might seem that the appropriate metaphor for realism might be some sort of moving closer, or perhaps some metaphor that involves immersion in the real stuff of life. But a work of art is not itself real life; it is a reflection of real life, an re-creation through the artistic eye of real-life experience. In this sense, the appropriate metaphor might better be a mirror, in that this genre reflects real life, or, in a more classical sense, works as an imitation of the real world.

But realism is not merely an imitation, not merely a mirror. The experience has been translated by the artist, who shapes it, who re-creates it, who gives it sharper meanings than might at first be apparent, who endows it with new meanings, who allows the art to show the reader his or her own experience—or experience that is part of his or her world and nature—but to see it more clearly, more sharply, more significantly than he or she had seen it before. It may be that many child readers have visited the city, even New York's Central Park, but in *Around Town* Soentpiet has established and shared his vision of the city and its unending possibilities "under the sun." His reflection has been one of joy and celebration, and he holds it up to the reader so that the reader can see this real world as portrayed in his vision. He has controlled and shaped the vision that appears in the mirror.

Insofar as it holds the mirror before the reader, a work of realism calls on the reader to see the world that lies all around—and to see the experiences that surround and mold the reader—in new, sometimes startling ways.

The Necessity of the Possible

In looking for ways to show the real world, Taro Yashima might have taken *Crow Boy* in a very different direction. Chibi, having been scorned by his classmates, might have developed an even stronger affinity for the crows to whom he listened on his long daily walks. Tired of this world, he might have stretched his arms, arched his shoulders, and flown into the sky, a crow himself among other crows, where he would finally have found acceptance. But if Yashima had changed the plot in this way, then the book would have escaped the boundaries of realism. The plot line would no longer have met with the expectations and limitations of this world, of human experience.

For a book to be a work of realism, every element of the plot must be possible in the real world as it is known by contemporaries. If Yashima's book had taken a turn in which Chibi becomes a crow, then the artist would have been using the motifs of folklore to create a fantasy. But, in fact, everything that happens in the work can happen in the real world, and, as such, it is a work of realism. Every element of the book reflects possible direct experience.

There are two significant parts of this definition. First, every element in the plot, characterization, setting—in fact, throughout the text—must be possible. The boundaries of realism are quite stern. Every element must be within the realm of possibility. This does not mean, however, that every element must be probable. It may very well be the case that some elements in the work are highly improbable. In Helen Cresswell's *Ordinary Jack* (1977), for example, Jack is the only sibling in his family who seems to have no extraordinary talents. With the help of his uncle, he decides to find a way to become extraordinary and resolves to become a prophet. Through a series of circumstances, he succeeds beyond his imaginings and becomes nationally known, until the whole enterprise is finally shown to be a hoax. Here Cresswell has moved into the world of the highly improbable for comic effect, but she has remained in the realm of the possible. It may be a very unlikely possibility, yet it is still a possibility.

In staying within the boundaries of the possible, realism deals with the world as it truly is, not as the idealistic might like to paint it. This means that realism will not always deal with the noble and the good, but sometimes with the ignoble and the evil. Though characters are certainly seen acting nobly and honorably, there are also characters who fail, who must face the darker sides of life. Parents abandon children, parents abuse children, children are faced with realities beyond their years, friends die or leave—all of these elements come into the genre because it must face this world squarely.

The Necessity of the Contemporary Perspective

The sense that everything must be possible in the real world is balanced by the second half of the definition, that everything must be possible in the real world as it is known by contemporaries. This means that the events and elements of the book must reflect the experience of humanity in the world as it is currently known. The difficulty in this second half is the fact that the nature of the world is constantly shifting, that what is known about the universe grows daily, at astonishing rates. What is known of experience by one generation of writers will certainly be eclipsed by the next. Yet, for there to be any boundaries at all around the genre of realism, it must be the case that the genre reflects the known.

When Jules Verne wrote *Twenty Thousand Leagues under the Sea* in 1870, he certainly anticipated the many advances in underwater exploration that would occur in the next century. But authors place their works within genres quite consciously, and, from Verne's point of view, the work was a fantasy. It may be the case that humans will one day travel to Mars, or that humans will one day be able to transplant human brains. But these elements are beyond current human experience. So Ray Bradbury's *The Martian Chronicles* (1958) and Peter Dickinson's *Eva* (1988) are works of fantasy rather than realism. The time may come when contemporary authors are able to use those experiences as part of the real world, and those authors will be writing in the genre of realism. But writing and definitions are not retroactive, and Bradbury and Dickinson's work will always be works of fantasy.

Given these two sides of the definition—that everything must be possible in the real world, that the real world that is being perceived is the real world of the contemporary writer—the author who works in this genre approaches the sharpening, the focusing of experience under certain kinds of limitations. He or she must write a story that obeys the realities of the given world. He or she must create characters who work within the realities of the given world. He or she must establish settings that are consonant with the given world. It would seem that, under such circumstances, the writer of realism would be hard-pressed to be original, to press boundaries, to surprise.

In fact, however, it is the very conventions of the genre that allow the writer of realism to be original, to press boundaries, to surprise. Writers of realism do work within the concrete world, a world that is generally recognizable. But in shifting the scale of meaning in the recognizable, the writer of realism has made the child reader see the ordinary as something quite extraordinary. Beverly

Cleary's *Dear Mr. Henshaw* (1983) seems, on the one hand, to be about an ordinary child, Leigh Botts, who has a dog and a mother and a broken home. Many readers would recognize all of these elements. But Cleary is able to shape the ordinary, so that the journal that Leigh keeps becomes a record of a soul's growth, and each of the seemingly ordinary events of his life lead almost inexorably to the final scene, in which his father returns for a time and in which Leigh gives his dog to his estranged father. The conclusion of the novel shows Leigh's growing self-awareness, something established by the accumulating "ordinary" events he has already lived through: "Maybe it was broccoli that brought Dad to Salinas, but he had come the rest of the way because he really wanted to see us. He had really missed us. I felt sad and a whole lot better at the same time" (134). The willingness to recognize and accept this ambiguity as part of normal experience comes only when he has worked through many other, smaller elements.

In establishing characters, the writer of realism turns to the real world, the physical world. Here, perhaps more than anywhere else, the writer needs to be aware of the presence of that real world. In that real world, characters are not all good, or all bad. They are not sweetly sentimental, or one-dimensional, or entirely vicious. They are not only bullies, not only the lonely child, not only the vacuous blond, not only the clueless teacher or the principal whose mindless discipline is his or her only reason for being. Characters are full and rich and multidimensional. They are not stereotypes; they do not neatly fit into conventions. They do not always understand all parts of their experience; they do not lead unambiguous lives.

For the writer of realism, this means that the characters of the work must be full and real, with multiple sides, with lives that are not too neat for this world. For a writer like Mary Stolz in *A Dog on Barkham Street* (1960) and its companion volume *The Bully of Barkham Street* (1963), this means that even a bully has a reason for being what he is—perhaps he is ashamed and lonely, furious at a world that treats him as it does. For Katherine Paterson this means that her characters will be imperfect, as in *The Great Gilly Hopkins* (1978), in which Gilly is a most unlovable foster child. For Suzanne Staples, this means that, in books such as *Shabanu* (1989) and *Dangerous Skies* (1996), characters will live within their culture at the same time that they fight against it. For Bruce Brooks in *What Hearts* (1992) and Myron Levoy in *Pictures of Adam* (1986), it will mean the refusal of characters to allow pain to decide how their lives will be lived. In all of these ways the writer has found ways to make the character real, a living being who is recognizable, at least in part, for his or her complexity rather than flat simplicity.

In Tomie dePaola's *The Art Lesson* (1989), young Tommy looks forward eagerly to school and his first real art lesson. He has watched his older cousins paint, and has already begun to recognize his own talent and passion for painting. To create this world, to make it show vividly, dePaola evokes a typical classroom, complete with its awful dusty paint and its somewhat stereotyped teacher. The physical setting of the story interacts strongly with the events and the characters, so that when Tommy is dismayed that he will have only a single sheet of paper and that he will be asked to copy, the reaction is a realistic one: His authoritarian teacher determines that he is troublesome. The art teacher, however, recognizes his need, and this recognition leads to the resolution of the story, in which Tommy is permitted, and even encouraged, to exercise his extraordinary skills.

Here, in a short picture book, is a work of realism that mirrors the real world, that includes complex and multidimensional characters, that uses a setting that is recognizable and made sharper and more vivid through the artist's eye. In the end, the child reader sees his or her own world better for having seen this world through dePaola's eye.

In creating a realistic setting, the writer of realism is not only creating a place, though such creation is crucial. Katherine Paterson's evocation of Ras Island in the Chesapeake Bay for *Jacob Have I Loved* (1980), Gary Paulsen's creation of a small Kansas town for *The Monument* (1991), and Phyllis Reynolds Naylor's creation of Friendly, West Virginia, for *Shiloh* (1991) are all critical to the success of those novels. Each evocation must be accurate and filled with life-giving details without seeming to be a travelogue. At the same time, those settings need to play back and forth with the characters to create a realistic world, so that fully rounded characters can exist in a fully rounded world. In both *Jacob Have I Loved* and *The Monument,* the setting takes on metaphoric qualities as each of the protagonists feels entrapped in a shrinking or shrunken landscape. In *Shiloh,* the name of the town takes on ironic proportions as Marty has to deal with an abusive neighbor. The settings are not merely places for the action to occur; they are landscapes that contribute to and respond to the action and the characters.

The Subgenres of Realism

Contemporary or modern realism uses plot narratives and situations that are set in the present world. Within this arena there are a number of smaller subgenres, each with its own boundaries and distinctions. The survival story, for example, is a work of realism with a central plot motif that focuses on the survival of the individual or the group. The protagonist is often placed in a vulnerable position and must overcome enormous odds in order to stay alive. Gary Paulsen's *Hatchet* (1987) is perhaps the best-known of these stories, a tale in which young Brian's plane crashes into the wilderness and he must survive with only a hatchet at hand. Often, in such genres, there are surprising enemies to overcome, but in *Hatchet* Paulsen is able to make the wilderness itself both abundant provider and enemy; the wilderness is as much a character as Brian.

The mystery story is another genre within realism, often set in a series. Though this genre for a child audience can often be predictable, the best mysteries are able to establish an intriguing setting, a very engaging cast of characters—any of whom could be the villain of the piece—and a twisting plot line that is marked by surprise. Ellen Raskin's *The Westing Game* (1978) is a mystery with a large inheritance at its center; the comic, bumbling cast of characters fumble after the money in a plot that turns and turns again. Zilpha Keatley Snyder's *The Egypt Game* (1967) has a more sinister plot in which an innocent game about Egypt begins to connect to a murderer.

Pointers for Teachers: Evaluating Works of Realism

- How does the author use setting, plot structure, and characterization to establish a realistic setting?
- How does the author use symbol, ambiguity, or theme as a way to take ordinary experience and give it a larger meaning?
- How does the author capture a community's values? The larger society's values?
- How does the author help readers identify or empathize with the main character?
- How does the author acknowledge and respond to the developmental level of the audience? Is such a response important?
- If the subject matter of the work is controversial, how does the author handle the matter?
- How do the illustrations enhance the realistic quality of the text?

Like both the survival novel and the mystery, the adventure novel centers on surprise and vulnerability. Here the protagonist finds himself or herself in a world other than his or her usual, normal existence, battling towards some objective in an environment that poses both difficulties and dangers. For it to work, this subgenre depends on the strange, the unfamiliar, the unexpected, even the exotic. Gary Paulsen's *Dogsong* (1985) works in this manner, as Russel Suskitt leaves the familiar and modern ways of his village and goes with a dogsled team on a mystical adventure to find his "song." Richard Armstrong's ocean stories work similarly, as in *The Secret Sea* (1966), in which young Thor Krogan goes out on his first whaling expedition to the Antarctic and is caught in the enclosing ice, or *The Big Sea* (1964), in which Jonty Lammerton engages in a three-day struggle to save the ship he is on.

Comedies work quite differently than the adventure story in that they often turn the normal, expected world upside down, rather than posing an entirely new, exotic world. Here the humor is generated by taking the expected and exaggerating it or subverting it. In Helen Cresswell's Bagthorpe series—*Ordinary Jack* (1977), *Absolute Zero* (1978), *Bagthorpes Unlimited* (1978), *Bagthorpes v. the World* (1979)—the comedy is generated through hyperbole: Normal impulses are exaggerated to a ridiculous point. A family visit becomes a war with saboteurs, a desire to become self-sufficient leads to the front lawn being plowed up and the summerhouse cleared for chickens. In *Misery Guts* (1991) and *Worry Warts* (1991), Morris Gleitzman takes the pain of a broken family and explores it through comedy, as young Keith Shipley desperately tries to hold his parents together. Convinced that they need to leave gray England for the tropics of Australia, he works to bring color and warmth to their lives; it is these attempts and their comic failures that brings humor to the novels, though the end of *Worry Warts* shows that even this humor has not been enough to keep his parents united.

All of these genres must, in the end, remain in the real world; they may create improbabilities, but they may not create impossibilities. It is this stern boundary that establishes the ways in which this genre may work, and also sets certain limits on the ways in which it may deal with the real world. It is these limits that often give rise to certain kinds of controversies, just as it is the nature of the genre—reflecting the real world—that even more often gives rise to heated conflict.

Issues in the Genre of Realism

Sugary endings, shallow characters responding in stereotypical ways, oversimplification, avoidance of that which may cause offense—these are all potential difficulties in a genre that is perhaps, along with fantasy, one of the genres that attracts more criticism than its rightful share. In avoiding such difficulties, the artist chooses to picture the world as it is. But, in picturing it as such, he or she may very well create a novel that raises the hackles of readers, teachers, librarians, reviewers, and many others associated with children and books.

Realism is fraught with challenges. Some people might argue that their child ought not be exposed to vulgar language or subject matter. Teachers might refuse to recognize that, in a sense, a selection process involves some censorship. Realism as a genre demands that readers think hard and articulately about what they are doing and what they want to accomplish. The many answers to these questions are, at times, decidedly in conflict.

Why does the genre of realism attract so much criticism?

When Katherine Paterson wrote *The Great Gilly Hopkins,* she wrote it as the story of a young foster girl who, against all hope, retains the belief that one day her mother will come for her. In the meantime, she defends herself against the terrible pain of her abandonment through her violence, her swearing, her stealing, and her control of all the adults in her life. But one day she is placed with Trotter, who is physically huge but also huge in her capacity for love. It is this overwhelming, gracious love that brings Gilly into a family, and, though in the end she must leave it, she brings with her the memory and the lessons of love that will enable her not to leave her pain and sense of betrayal behind—these she will always have with her—but to live with those hurts in the knowledge that love is stronger still.

It is a story of extraordinary power, a story of love and its fulfillment, of trust earned and given, of hope. In fact, this is a retelling of the story of the prodigal son, in which a young boy abandons his father and family so that he may squander his inheritance; when he returns, penniless and chastened, having lived with pigs, he finds to his astonishment his father with his arms held wide to welcome him with love.

Yet, despite the power and meaning of the story, despite its biblical echoes and allusions, *The Great Gilly Hopkins* is one of the more frequently attacked and censored books in North America. Gilly is hardly a role model. She lies and swears. She sends racist messages. She is filled with hate. She manipulates those younger than her through fear; she manipulates those older than her through her cleverness. For some readers, these traits—particularly her swearing—make this an inappropriate book for the child reader.

Paterson, however, would claim the opposite. If a writer is going to tell the story of a character who goes to the pigpen, having lost love, then, to make the story real, the writer needs to tell about the pigpen. In this sense Gilly is a very realistic, honest portrayal of a young child filled with anger at abandonment, driven to defend herself against similar betrayals by shoving all other proffered love aside, and doing that by making herself as unlovable as possible. After all, Paterson was not trying to present a model child, but a real one. To find euphemisms for Gilly's swearing, or to have her say *sugar* instead of something more colorful, negates her reality. In the same way, if she went to school and fell in love with a teacher and instantly became good and sweet and kind, she would have lost her reality. To show Gilly's movement to hope and love, Paterson had to show her first rejecting it. This means that, Paterson acknowledges, in depicting an imperfect person, the writer will always run the risk of offending and disappointing those who look to characters for role models.

The genre of realism runs into difficulties precisely because of its boundaries and conventions. On the one side, the reader who is expecting characters to be models, or who believes that a literary work confers a certain kind of authority for behavior or language, will argue that unseemly language and incidents are inappropriate to a work of children's literature. Certainly, there is a sense for most adult writers and readers that there are some scenes that would be inappropriate to include in a work of children's literature. In other words, the nature of the audience does call for some boundaries, it would seem.

On the other hand, realism also demands realistic portrayals, and writers must be able to depict realistically scenes and characters if they want them to be developed fully and honestly. In this sense the writer is trying to show the real world to the child, to suggest its limitations and realities. Here the writer is not being titillating, or voyeuristic, but honestly presenting experiences that any child reader might, indeed, confront. It may not be that every child reader will confront an angry foster child virtually destroyed by the hurt of abandonment. But every child will know pain, will know loneliness, will know hurt, and every child will know some means, in himself or herself, or in others, of defending against that hurt.

Realism may be the most pointed genre in its ability to suggest to readers that they are not alone, that they are not the only ones to whom awful things have come. It can offer a kind of identification, and, to those readers who have not experienced the kinds of hurts dealt with in this genre, it offers the choice of an empathetic expansion of experience. It offers the reader the chance to identify with the humanity of another person.

In showing the reader the bent world, the mirror of realism can sometimes show ugliness. If that mirror is angled merely to revel in that ugliness, or merely to nuzzle in the unseemly, the grotesque, the bawdy, the obscene, then realism has lost its purpose. It no longer seeks to reflect reality as much as it seeks to show only a single warped perspective of it. If the mirror is meant to show a full character, a full story, then that mirror willy-nilly must show the bent world for what it is, a mixture of joy and sorrow, gladness and despair, beauty and ugliness, responsibility and manipulation. What realism can show most vividly, in fact, is the suggestion that great joy, great gladness, great beauty, great responsibility may come out of a reaction to their opposites.

Is there a place for a depiction of sexuality in a work of realism for the child reader?

There is no greater flashpoint in a work of children's literature than that of sexuality. When Maurice Sendak depicted the young boy David as a nude in his illustrations for Randall Jarrell's *Fly by Night* (1976), he called down a firestorm of criticism for his realism, as he had earlier for his illustrations for *In the Night Kitchen* (1970). Any author who includes a scene in a work of children's literature that involves a discussion of sexuality must be ready for similar criticism. Here, too, is one of the reasons that realism so often invokes so much criticism.

As with any potentially controversial issue, the writer needs to consider purpose and audience. If the purpose of including controversial material is mere voyeurism, then the work is deeply flawed. If, though, the purpose is an honest, realistic exploration of a subject, with the writer keenly aware of its sensitivity, then the inclusion is legitimate. In creating a character that may be a young adolescent, for example, it would be absolutely legitimate for a writer to show his or her growing awareness of his or her own sexuality. This does not mean that the entire work points to nothing but this growing awareness, though, to the exclusion of all else.

This leads to the author's second consideration: audience. Given the audience of children's literature, the writer and illustrator need to consider what the child reader can understand, what the child reader can interpret. A work for a young child is a work for a reader who has not necessarily explored his or her own sexuality, for whom that world is remote and untouched. There will simply be much about sexuality that a child reader has not experienced, and so it becomes, in that sense, something outside the boundaries of children's literature.

This does not mean that the boundaries of children's literature exclude representations of the body, however. A child is intensely aware of his or her own body, and the author and illustrator of children's literature who are sensitive to the life of the child may use this awareness in a work of children's literature. Sendak's use of nudity in *In the Night Kitchen* is of a piece with his exploration of a child's love of sensory experience; it is a picture book filled with physical sensation, and the nudity of Mickey contributes to that meaning. Similarly, Robie Jarris's *Happy Birth Day!* (1996) uses lifesize illustrations of a newborn infant to depict the wonder and glory of birth. The baby is, of course, naked, the umbilical cord still attached. But the nudity is not voyeurism; it is, instead, an open marveling at the extraordinary event—the perfect birth of a child.

Perhaps the test of appropriateness might be this: If the illustration or scene calls attention to itself and detracts from the overall meaning and progression of the work, then it may be that the illustration or scene is not intrinsic to the work or is aimed at the wrong audience. If the illustration or scene, on the other hand, is part of the fabric of the entire work, contributing to its overall meanings and developments, then it is included more appropriately. In any case the writer needs to discern the needs of his or her audience and the appropriateness and purpose of the inclusion of sexuality in a work of children's literature.

Are there certain issues that are inappropriate for a child audience in this genre?

In asking this question, one is acknowledging that the act of reading has consequences. Where education is seen as protection, or childhood is seen as idealized, this is a dangerous question indeed. Of all the genres, realism has been the genre to move more quickly to deal with issues that had been seen as taboo in earlier years. Where issues of sexuality, violence, drug use, emotional illness, the elderly, physical handicaps, divorce, child abuse had all seemed to have no part in the world of children's literature for the first half of the twentieth century, the last half has seen a greater willingness to explore these topics. And, though certainly there are some works that exploit these topics, many others are serious considerations of those elements that do touch children's lives but which are frequently ignored or hidden in embarrassment.

When Ursula Nordstrom, the children's book editor at Harper and Row, first read the manuscript of Louise Fitzhugh's *Harriet the Spy* (1964), she found in the text a scene that openly treated a young girl's first period. In the margin of the manuscript she wrote, "Thank you Louise Fitzhugh." She did not mean by that comment that Fitzhugh had written a passage that would titillate readers and so sell many books. Instead, she meant that, for the first time in children's literature, a topic that young girls were intimately concerned about was being treated with some openness, not as though it were a dirty secret. Her "thank you" was on behalf of the child readers.

In this sense, realism can work as a genre that does allow the writer to explore all issues that might touch on a child's experience, a genre that allows a writer to press against taboos and silence, so that the writer is free to explore and deal with elements that many children will recognize in their own lives. When Beverly Cleary, in *Dear Mr. Henshaw,* and Bruce Brooks, in *What Hearts,* write of divorce and the brokenness of families, they write of experience that many, many children will recognize. When Katherine Paterson writes of infidelity and betrayal in *Come Sing, Jimmy Jo* (1985), when Jerry Spinelli, in *The Library Card* (1997), and Paula Fox, in *Monkey Island* (1991), write of homelessness, when Doris Buchanan Smith, in *Tough Chauncey* (1974), writes of the anger of a foster child, when Miriam Bat-Ami in *Dear Elijah* (1995), Stephanie Tolan in *Save Halloween* (1993), and Cynthia Rylant in *A Fine White Dust* (1986) write of growing religious awareness, and when Doris Buchanan Smith, in *A Taste of Blackberries* (1973), Gary Paulsen, in *Tracker* (1984), Lois Lowry, in *A Summer to Die* (1977), and Cynthia Rylant, in *Missing May* (1992) write about death, they are all writing about experiences that touch the lives of many, many children.

Realism as a genre allows writers to explore areas that may not have been seen as appropriate to children's literature at the midpoint of the century. Today, this genre is seen as perhaps the most open to new subjects. The significant consideration here is that the treatment of those subjects be linked to the child audience and its ability to understand and perceive the meaning of those treatments.

How should a school instructor or librarian respond to issues of censorship in the genre of realism?

There is, perhaps, no issue more difficult that faces those who would bring books to children than the issue of censorship. It is, too often, a fear that leads to self-censorship, where a teacher or a librarian will not purchase or recommend or even read a book to his or her students for fear that the book will be attacked. Better not to buy the book in the first place than to raise the spectre of a censorship battle, the argument goes. Those who do take the opportunity of bringing some of the best books to children are also taking the chance of real criticism, or charges that they are insensitive to children, that they are usurping parental rights, that they are encouraging and affirming the breakdown of the moral life. No teacher or librarian who has faced such attacks has faced them cavalierly.

Before a censorship case looms, administrators, teachers, librarians should have prepared for it. The aesthetic qualities of realistic fiction should be a part of their repertoire. They should be able to articulate the developmental nature of character, that often a character who begins in one situation or mindset is moving, through the course of the novel, to another. They will need to know how questions of appropriateness and age group are decided, and how books and children are brought together in their school specifically. In addition, they need to know their community, its history, its value systems, its range. That community should be able to expect a well-articulated vision for education from its school system, as well as a sense that community participation is welcome, and more than welcome.

With this as background, the best place to begin in censorship disputes is on common ground, though at first it may not seem like there is much of it. Certainly, both sides in a censorship battle acknowledge two positions, however. First, both sides are invested in the healthy development and growth of the child. Second, both sides recognize that reading can be a powerful and influential act in a child's life. Beginning there suggests real commonality.

But, having begun there, both sides have legitimate questions that suggest their diverging points of view. Those who would censor a book might ask the following sorts of questions:

> Isn't it the case that there are standards that need to be applied to the choice of books? And, if it is the case that books are influential, shouldn't those standards deal with more than matters of aesthetics?

> Isn't it the case that teachers and librarians should respond to a community's standards? Shouldn't a library reflect the interest and standards and affirmations of its community?

> Aren't there some books that everybody would find noxious and inappropriate for all audiences, let alone a child audience?

Those who would argue against censorship would ask questions that are not so dissimilar.

> Isn't it the case that a library's collections should be open to all points of view? Shouldn't a library's holdings not only come out of a community's standards, but also reflect on those standards, push them somewhat?
>
> Isn't it the case that as soon as a single small group begins to make decisions about a library's holdings, then it, in effect, has made decisions for a much larger group? If one parent removes a book, then that book is no longer available for any child.
>
> Isn't it the case that books should encourage discussion, new thought, new understandings, not just affirm what is already held to be true?
>
> If any book might be removed for any complaint, then no book is safe except for the most bland. In a society where books such as *Huckleberry Finn, To Kill a Mockingbird, Bridge to Terabithia, Little Women,* and the Bible are regularly attacked and banned, what book of any dimension and quality would be safe from the censor's hands?

Both sides, of course, can be taken to extremes. No reasonable person in favor of community censorship of books would argue that any book vetoed by any person must therefore without question be eliminated from the library's holdings so that no child may be exposed to it. Similarly, even those ardently against censorship in any form would be hard-pressed to argue that any book at all should be included in a school library, including material that most reasonable readers would deem pornographic, obscene, or racist hate literature. Extremism of this sort on this issue is hardly useful. It leads to the kind of intransigent position that one school board in Tennessee faced when a parent attacked *The Lion, the Witch, and the Wardrobe* as pornographic, arguing that the blood and hair left on Peter's sword after he has killed a wolf suggest the weapon's phallic meaning.

How, then, should a teacher or librarian respond to questions of censorship? Beginning with the common ground, rejecting extremist positions, the teacher needs to understand and to take seriously a parent's objection to a work. It is easy to dismiss objections as ignorant, or as coming from someone not an expert in the field. But, if the parent has read and understood the book, and if the parent has thoughtful and meaningful objections, then the teacher needs to take those into account.

The teacher, on the other hand, is obligated to have thought through such issues long before the book comes into the hands of the students. The teacher should know what the objectionable material might be, though, as in the Tennessee case cited above, one can never anticipate all of these. But no teacher should be surprised to hear that a parent might object to the word *nigger* in *Huckleberry Finn,* or the nudity in *Fly by Night,* or the swearing in *The Great Gilly Hopkins,* or the sexuality of *Beyond the Chocolate War,* or the language that borrows from spiritual movements in the work of Madeleine L'Engle. The teacher and librarian should anticipate all of these and be ready to respond.

This response is critical. Even as the instructor is obligated to take seriously the objections of a parent, so the instructor has a right to expect that the parent take seriously the issues that the teacher advances. The teacher and librarian should both be able to articulate the reasons for including the work in the collection or in a classroom. They should be able to articulate its merits as a work of literature. They should be able to articulate the way in which the book works as a literary work, and why the objectionable scene is included, is, in fact, an intimate part of the book's meaning.

There are certainly larger issues to deal with as well. Should the objections of a single parent remove the availability of the book for an entire class, or from all children in the school? The answer here must clearly be "no." At the same time, the instructor needs to be willing, with the backing of other teachers and administrators, to be vulnerable, to allow parents to know when a book that might find fierce objections will be read. This might mean a letter home, it might mean a parental meeting, it might mean some kind of open forum for discussion. But, if a censorship issue is not to turn into a battle, both sides must be honest, even-handed, and open with their divisions while understanding the other's position.

If a school system is to be truly responsive to its constituency on the matter of reading and literature, it must be willing to hear that constituency. It must also be willing to educate that constituency. If, on the other hand, that constituency wants its children to develop and mature fully, then it must give teachers and librarians the room to use the very best in children's literature, to build a collection that reflects multiple viewpoints, that honestly mirrors real life and, through the eye of the artist, shapes that real life so that the child reader comes away from it having grown. This means avoiding the safe, easy, bland, completely unobjectionable book in favor of the book that dares to be literature, that dares to take a stand, that speaks to the soul.

Is it possible for a work of realism to switch genres? Can a work set in the contemporary period become a work of historical fiction when that period is past?

In general, works do not switch genres with time. Historical fiction is a genre in which an author has consciously moved back in time, creating a setting and cast of characters within that earlier time. The author of modern realism has no such intention; instead, he or she is working within the contemporary period to craft a work that speaks to the contemporary child about his or her own time.

Many works of realism do not depend particularly on the specifics of a time. Katherine Paterson's *Bridge to Terabithia* (1977), for example, though written more than two decades ago, may be read as though set in the contemporary period; there is nothing that ties it inexorably to the time in which it was written. Even as the years pass and the society in which the novel is set changes, the book will remain a work of realism, because that was the distinct intention of the author.

Pointers for Teachers

Interactive Possibilities
- Before reading a work of realism, explore the meaning of the word *culture*. As the teacher, model what role several elements of a person's culture play in daily life: family, schoolwork, hobbies, play, spiritual beliefs. Have children explore some of the same questions in small groups.
- Choose a realistic text and, after reading it aloud, have students in pairs note how the author used the senses in his or her description. Ask them to find several examples for each sense, then read the work aloud again.

Writing Possibilities
- Assign one character from the work of realism to a group of four or five students. Each group will write a biography for its character, including physical description, hobbies, least favorite thing, what the character did last night, dreams for the future. One group member will read the biography to the entire class, who will guess the character's identity.
- Ask each student to write a letter to the protagonist as if he or she were a significant person in the student's life. Allow the students to choose their own character.
- Break the students into groups of four or five and ask them to write another ending to the story. After the groups have finished reading their new endings to the class, ask the class to vote on its favorite new ending, explaining why they made that choice. You might point out to students that Gary Paulsen did the same thing when he wrote *Brian's Winter* as a rewrite for *Hatchet*.

Hands-On Possibilities
- Ask each student to choose a favorite object from the protagonist's life. Have students pretend to carry that object around with them throughout the day, without telling other classmates what it might be. At the end of the day, have students guess.
- Have the students in groups decide on the kind of award they would like to give to several characters from a work of realism: "Most Likely to Succeed," "Most Popular," "Funniest Character," "Most Likely to be Remembered." Break students into groups and ask them to construct the award from materials provided.

But this issue is cloudier than it first appears. Some novels are indeed attached to a particular time, as suggested by several set in South Africa. Dianne Case's *Love, David* (1986) depicts the loving relationship between Anna and her half-brother David in the midst of terrible poverty and oppression. Maretha Maartens's *Paper Bird* (1989) deals with Adam's crisis as he must decide whether he will join in a strike or go to the city to sell newspapers and gather the money his family needs. Michael Williams's *Into the Valley* (1990) has young Walter Hudson leaving Johannesburg to make connections with a rebel leader in Zululand. Sheila Gordon's *Waiting for the Rain* (1988) paints the picture of a friendship between Tengo and Frikke, one African American, the other Caucasian; that friendship is threatened as they grow older and must face the restrictions of their culture. Each of these four novels was written as a work of contemporary realism. Each of them depicts life as it would be seen by a contemporary in South Africa, the first two working from the perspective of a black South African, the third from the perspective of a white South African, the final novel working from both perspectives.

But each of these novels was written before the huge changes in South African society in which apartheid was finally eliminated. Though these are works of realism, the system of apartheid that generates much of the tension in the novels no longer exists. This, then, seems to date the novels, or, in some way, places them between genres. They are no longer works of contemporary realism in the sense that they no longer accurately depict the society in which the plot narrative works itself out. At the same time, they are not works of historical fiction because the author made no attempt to set the plotline back in another historical period.

Because of the authors' intentions, these hybrids must, in the end, be classified as realism. But for the child reader the work may also function in a manner similar to that of historical fiction, in that the novel can depict the situations and conflicts of another time.

Writers of Realism for Children

Eve Bunting (b. 1928)

In Eve Bunting's *The Wall* (1990), a young narrator and his father visit the Vietnam War Memorial. The boy's voice is simple and powerful: "Dad runs his fingers along the rows of print and I do, too. The letters march side by side, like rows of soldiers. They're nice and even. It's better printing than I can do. The wall is warm." He watches as his father finally finds his own father's name, then takes a rubbing. The boy holds his head still for a time, but then looks up and down to see that some people are mere tourists, while others are here to remember. He leaves, wishing that his grandfather was here with him.

The stark simplicity of the picture book, with its short sentences, belies its powerful emotional appeal. And this is the great strength of Eve Bunting as

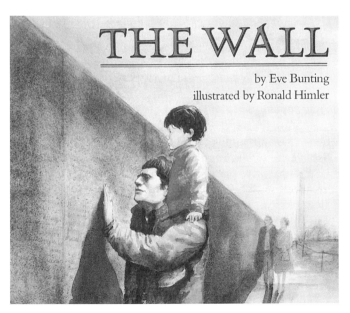

Illustration by Ronald Himler for Eve Bunting's *The Wall.* Copyright © 1990. Reprinted by permission of Clarion Books.

she comes to the genre of realism. She takes characters in situations of enormous emotional upheaval, situations that are quite real in the contemporary world, such as the loss of a family member who is remembered on the Vietnam Memorial. She is able to avoid sentimentality and mawkishness by having the perspective be a child's, and, thus, somewhat naive. Usually the child does not see the entire horror or sadness of the larger situation—here, the loss of a generation of young men.

A number of Bunting's books work in a similar vein. *A Day's Work* (1994) tells of the plight of a Mexican laborer in the United States who misunderstands the instructions of his American boss; though his grandson is able to rectify the mistake, there is the lingering sense of the unfairness of the situation, where the older man is put in a situation of such difficulty. In *Smoky Night* (1994), Bunting tells of Daniel and his mother, who are caught in the middle of the Los Angeles riots. As their neighborhood is burned and looted, they flee to a shelter, where they see Mrs. Kim, whose shop has been destroyed. Both families have lost their cats, and, when a fireman brings them in together, they eat from the same bowl. Daniel, astonished, remarks that now that they know each other, they like each other, and the adults are shamed by the obvious comparison.

Sometimes the poignancy of the stories is not linked to a particular contemporary situation. In *The Day before Christmas* (1992), Allie and her grandfather board a train to go to the city and Allie's first *Nutcracker* ballet. Her pleasure is hardly to be contained, but it is muted slightly by the knowledge that her grandfather used to bring Allie's mother to the same ballet, and now she was dead. But Allie learns that this is not a sad time for her grandfather, since he is now building new happy memories. In *Ghost's Hour, Spook's Hour* (1987), a young boy wakes up and finds that the electricity is out and his parents are missing. Slowly, frightened, he searches through the house until he finds them in the living room, asleep by a candle. The quick shift from lonely fear to full security is mirrored by the boy's running patter with Biff, the dog, who, he assures, should not be afraid at all.

Bunting's strength is her depiction of the interior life of a child who is struggling and who will survive either a fear, or a loss, or a sadness. In *Fly Away Home* (1991), a boy and his father are trapped into living in an airport, having no job and no home. They establish a kind of community with others in the same situation who watch over the boy as the father goes daily to look for work. The boy is usually not angry, but there are times when he finds it terribly unfair that he and his father should have to live in an airport. But, one day when he sees a trapped bird escape, he comes to believe that they will leave also. "And when the bird left, when it flew free, I know it was singing." The boy here is proud of a loving father, and frustrated and sometimes angry, and, at the same time, hopeful, a realistic mixture.

The mirror that Bunting holds up shows a great deal of pain, a great deal of sorrow. But it also shows the resilience that lies in a child's voice. Her first-person narratives carry with them simplicity and strength, and the suggestion that the child will survive, particularly if surrounded by a loving community.

Beverly Cleary (b. 1916)

Where Eve Bunting chronicles the sometimes painful sides of childhood, Beverly Cleary, in her work in realism, usually chronicles the more uproarious, comical side of childhood. Her books often depict the lives of ordinary children by entering into their perspective, so that the events of their lives are heightened as they would be to a child. The result is that names like Henry Huggins, Ramona Quimby, and Ribsy are, for many children, part of their vocabulary.

Cleary's first book dealt with Henry Huggins, a third-grade boy who lives on Klickitat Street in Portland. The events that she pours into his life have all the semblance of ordinariness: a paper route, breeding fish, a fishing trip, a backyard clubhouse. Henry also finds a stray dog whom he names Ribsy. All of these elements seem natural and almost clichéd, but, by heightening them according to the importance they assume to Henry, Cleary instead gives the ordinary a kind of freshness that recalls the way children come to those events.

Not all of Cleary's characters are ordinary, however. In *Beezus and Ramona* (1955) Cleary introduced the character of Ramona, the little sister of Henry's best friend Beatrice. She comes to full development in *Ramona the Pest* (1968), in which Cleary tells of her life from kindergarten through third grade, and in *Ramona the Brave* (1975), in which Cleary chronicles her life in first grade. In these books she emerges as someone who needs love and affection, certainly, but also someone who is very imaginative and creative, with the result that she is often misunderstood. She is also someone who seems to highlight the comic side of everyday events—keeping up with an older sister, lording it over a younger brother, riding a school bus, interacting with the other kids at school. In *Ramona and Her Father* (1981) and *Ramona Forever* (1984), Cleary deepens the nature of the events that Ramona encounters, as her father loses his job and she faces death and birth for the first time.

For both Henry Huggins and Ramona Quimby, Cleary holds up a mirror that reflects the neighbor next door, the child in the next seat, the kid on the playground. There is a sense of familiarity about these characters, a sense that they are known.

In *Dear Mr. Henshaw* (1983), Cleary writes of Leigh Botts, taking him from early grades through several years. Leigh's family has broken; his parents are divorced and his father is a trucker, gone most of the time. In coping with this brokenness, Leigh uses his own imagination and creative abilities, as in this journal entry that Leigh writes after an unsatisfactory phone call with his father.

> Today is Saturday, so this morning I walked to the butterfly trees again. The grove was quiet and beautiful, and because the sun was shining, I stood there a long time, looking at the orange butterflies floating through the gray and green leaves and listening to the sound of the ocean on the rocks. There aren't as many butterflies now. Maybe they are starting to go north for the summer. I thought I might write about them in prose instead of poetry, but on the way home I got to thinking about Dad and one time when he took me along when he was hauling grapes to a winery and what a great day it had been (107–108).

The memory is a way of coping with the loss, but the sensitivity to the surrounding world and the connecting of that sensitivity to story marks Leigh as a potential writer; in fact, the piece he does come to write wins him a meeting with an author who praises his work.

Perhaps, in the end, Beverly Cleary's characters are not ordinary. They only seem so because they are so recognizable; they deal with situations that many, many children face. But, in addition, they are perceptive, sensitive, imaginative characters who react with compassion and interest and enthusiasm and understanding to the world around them.

Jean Craighead George (b. 1919)

For most of her writing career, Jean Craighead George has held her mirror of realism to reflect the interactions of humanity and the natural world. They are interactions that are realistically portrayed. Nature is not the sentimental park, not the romantic forest where wood nymphs play and bluebirds perch on a character's shoulder. Neither is it the implacable enemy of a Jack London story in which there is a mindless malevolence that seeks to destroy. Instead, nature is quite simply itself. It acts according to its own kind, according to its own rhythms.

In *My Side of the Mountain* (1959) and its sequel, *On the Far Side of the Mountain* (1990), a young boy lives in the Catskills on his own, accompanied predominantly by a falcon whom he befriends, or who befriends him. In some ways this is a survival story that might be compared to Gary Paulsen's *Hatchet*. But, in another way, it is quite different from *Hatchet*. Nature here is not something to be overcome in its harsh wildness, but, instead, something whose rhythms one must learn, whose patterns one must discover and fit into. George continues this theme in books like *Water Sky* (1987), which tries to establish a balance between the hunting needs of the Eskimos and the concern of environmentalists for the whale population, and *The Talking Earth* (1983), in which a young Seminole girl spends time in the woods alone so that she may be able to listen to the voice of the earth.

George's most powerful evocation of this theme comes in *Julie of the Wolves* (1972), set on the Alaskan tundra. When Julie faces a changing village life, a father who has lost his connection to the old ways, and the prospect of marriage to someone she does not love, she runs away to the tundra and there enters into a relationship with a wolf pack. The opening of the novel suggests the coming union between the human character and the wolf pack as well as the physical setting:

> Miyax pushed back the hood of her sealskin parka and looked at the Arctic sun. It was a yellow disc in a lime-green sky, the colors of six o'clock in the evening and the time when the wolves awoke. Quietly she put down her cooking pot and crept to the top of a dome-shaped frost heave, one of the many earth buckles that rise and fall in the crackling cold of the Arctic winter. Lying on her stomach, she looked across a vast lawn of grass and moss and focused her attention on the wolves she had come upon two sleeps ago. They were wagging their tails as they awoke and saw each other. (5)

Julie must learn to read their signs, must learn to communicate as a wolf, and must learn the complicated relationships that exist among members of the pack. In the end she returns to her village, knowing that her place is not out on the tundra, but brings with her the sense that humans can coexist with the natural world, and that the old ways worked hard towards doing just that. The story is continued in *Julie* (1994), in which Julie struggles to deal with the changes in her Arctic world and helps the wolves find new food during a caribou famine, and in *Julie's Wolf Pack* (1997), told mostly from the point of view of the wolves, in which the new leader, Kapu, must protect his pack from famine and disease and keep it organized under his leadership.

In each of these books there is the powerful sense that nature must be shown in its reality. The wolves must be wild; they are not pets. Predators and prey must work to their own rhythms. In short, everything in the natural world—even humans—must be true to their own nature if the cyclical rhythms will be kept.

Katherine Paterson (b. 1932)

Although Katherine Paterson began her writing career as a novelist in historical fiction with such works as *Of Nightingales That Weep* (1974) and *The Sign of the Chrysanthemum* (1973), and though some of her most recent work, such as *Lyddie* (1991) and *Jip: His Story* (1996) mark a return to that genre, Paterson is perhaps best known for her work in contemporary realism. Novels such as *Bridge to Terabithia* (1977), *The Great Gilly Hopkins* (1978), *Jacob Have I Loved* (1980), *Come Sing, Jimmy Jo* (1985), *Park's Quest* (1988), and *Flip-Flop Girl* (1994) have established her as one of the foremost writers of realism for the young reader.

The consistent theme throughout her work—both in realism and in historical fiction—is of hope. Again and again her characters find themselves in situations that seem hopeless, where the burden of the world and of themselves is so great that it seems as if it must be impossible to bear. But through grace, their own natures, the help of others, they begin to find a way to, if not shed the burden, lighten it enough to carry. Hers is a world where bad things do happen, where there is real unhappiness, and where conventionally happy endings do not abound. Brokenness may be healed, but the cracks remain, and characters must learn to live in the presence of those reminding cracks.

In *Park's Quest,* Park, who perceives himself as the knight Parsival, makes a journey to his grandfather's estate; he has never been there before, and has had no contact with that side of the family since his father was killed in Vietnam. There he begins to find the truth of what happened years before, a pain that has affected him in ways he never knew. When his father returned from Vietnam, he had fathered a daughter; Park's mother, devastated at the betrayal, rejected him. He returned to Vietnam and was killed. His brother, Park's uncle, then sought out the mother of his niece, married her, and brought her back to the estate.

The guilt and anger of Park's mother, the terrible guilt of Park's grandfather, who blames himself for his son's military career, the web of silence that has been flung over all relationships—all these elements would seem to lead to nothing but destruction. Whom can Park trust? How should he relate to Thanh, his half-sister, knowing that his father went back to Vietnam because of her and was killed? How guilty is his mother in his father's death? In the end, Park and Thanh are able to affirm life, are able to articulate guilt and sorrow, and are able to help their grandfather to do the same. The conclusion of the novel sets them in a holy moment, as each drinks from a coconut that may indeed be the holy grail, having spoken their sorrow and established their love.

In *Come Sing, Jimmy Jo,* James is a young, very talented singer who prefers to stay at home with his beloved grandmother while his family goes off to sing. When their agent brings him into the circle of the singing, however, it is clear that he is the most talented of them all. In fact, if they hope to make it big, they must include him. And so they do, heading to Nashville where they find tremendous success. However, James's mother is driven by terrible jealousy, and, in fact, will steal a song written by James's father and record it with his uncle, with whom there is a love interest. As the family starts to spin out of control, James learns of his mother's angry jealousy, and he learns that his father is not his biological father. It is his decision whether he will destroy the fragile bonds that hold the family together. He decides not to sever the bonds, but to hold onto them, fragile as they might be.

Neither of these novels ends in a conventionally happy manner, but this is a huge element of Paterson's vision of the genre. We live, she points out, in a broken world, among broken people, and in the midst of that, we maintain hope, we search for hope, we hold onto hope as a way of ordering and giving meaning and beauty and charity to our lives.

The vigor of Paterson's contemporary realism lies particularly with her characters. This is true in her historical fiction as well: the inconclusive but finally resolute characters of her Japanese novels, Louise of *Jacob Have I Loved* who is seared with jealousy, the determined and closed Lyddie who will not yield, the gentle and sweet Jip whose every instinct impels towards kindness. But in her works of contemporary realism Paterson is also able to create vigorous characters whose perspectives undergo tremendous change and growth. Jess of *Bridge to Terabithia* begins as a somewhat shy and inward-looking boy whose greatest goals are to be invisible in a classroom and to be the fastest kid in fifth grade. Through his interactions with Leslie, he comes to recognize and, more importantly, affirm his own artistic and imaginative side; in the imaginary world of Terabithia, his soul opens. In *The Great Gilly Hopkins,* Gilly begins as an angry foster child. When she confronts real love for the first time, she fights against it, determined to believe that her neglectful mother will come for her. But, in the end, she can accept that love even as she recognizes the limitations of her own mother.

Neither of these books ends in a conventionally happy way either. Yet, Paterson plants the seeds, establishes the possible routes of happiness and healing. Park's grandfather has acknowledged his sorrow and guilt, but there is still not full healing, and there is still the anger and guilt that beset Park's mother. Jimmy Jo's parents are still close to a break, but the betrayals in the adult world, while not his to expose, are also not his to heal. Jess has grown and been able to pass on his love at the end of the novel, despite Leslie's death, but Gilly has not yet come to that lesson. It is not clear how she will react to a mother who disappoints her so cataclysmically. There is hope, but not easy, complete, neatly tied-up endings. This, Paterson would argue, is the way of the world.

The end result of a journey for a Katherine Paterson character is not so much happiness as it is insight. The character is able to perceive the realities of his or her situation, and, instead of being weighted down or even destroyed by those realities, is able to come to some kind of understanding of how one should address those realities, or continue to live in the face of them. At the end of *Bridge to Terabithia*, for example, Jess has lost his best friend through accidental death. All that she had awakened in him through her influence is threatened, and it would not be astonishing to see Jess turn inward, bitter and cynical, willing to become a harsh caricature of his father. But he does not do this; the insights he has gained will not allow this. Instead, he builds a bridge into Terabithia for his younger sister, and in so doing he passes on the vision that Leslie had given to him.

Doris Buchanan Smith (b. 1934)

Like Katherine Paterson, Doris Buchanan Smith writes of characters who are struggling, who try desperately to deal with the events that suddenly surround them. And, like Paterson, Smith will often bring her characters close to resolution, suggesting the ways in which they too will find hope, or at least direction, given the circumstances of their lives.

In what is perhaps her best known work, *A Taste of Blackberries* (1973), the narrator must deal with the death of his closest friend, Jamie. Jamie is unpredictable, surprising, excited, exciting, always dancing happily around trouble, always dancing away at the last minute. But the mirror of realism that Smith holds up shows that sometimes terrible things do happen, even to young children who seem immune from such dangers. When Jamie is stung and falls down, the narrator does not believe that Jamie is doing anything but joking. But soon the word comes that Jamie has, in fact, died from the sting, and the guilt of his first reactions, merging with the despair and sadness over the loss, show the narrator to be a young boy who is sensitive and aware.

At first he finds it hard to understand how his friends can go on playing in such a world, but he comes to recognize that he must continue to live on. He picks the blackberries that he and Jamie had planned to pick together and brings them to Jamie's mother; then he too goes to play. And, in so doing, he lives. "In my relief I felt that Jamie, too, was glad the main sadness was over," he concludes (85). The hurt is still there, but there is also some sense of resolution.

Tough Chauncey (1974) tells of Chauncey Childs, who is sent away by his mother; he has never known his father. He comes to live in Georgia with his grandparents, but soon finds that they are abusive, and that his reputation has quickly, for them, become reality. Chauncey has indeed become toughened, though physically small; yet he knows that there is a different Chauncey inside him, and he hopes it will grow out. Finally, when the abuse becomes more than he can bear, he runs away, resolved, at first, that he will be alone. Only when he recognizes and believes that the inside of him can grow to the outside does he finally seek help.

The novel concludes with Chauncey going to find foster care. He turns to the cabman who has brought him and smiles for one of the first times in the book as he is about to enter the social services building: "You haven't seen the complete me yet!" he calls back (222). Clearly, this is a new beginning for Chauncey, but, just as clearly, the pain of his life has not gone away, though his resolution will carry him forward.

In *Return to Bitter Creek* (1986), a young girl comes back to her mother's Appalachian home to face the scorn of her family: Her mother ran off and has now returned unmarried but with a lover. The bitterness of the title is suggested in the family relationships, which are quite strained. When the lover dies tragically, the young girl must deal with this loss as well, and finds surprising strength and support in a community that had, at one point, only offered rejection.

For Smith, the world is a world of pain and surprising love, of grief and joy, of tragedy and the resolution to pass beyond that tragedy. Her characters are marked by great strength, great resilience; like Paterson's characters, they lead toward hope.

Judy Blume (b. 1938)

Judy Blume was one of the early writers to insist that children be presented as they really are: imperfect human beings who worry and wonder about everything from wearing a bra to understanding who God is. In works like *Are You There God? It's Me, Margaret* (1970), in which Blume explores the changes in a young girl's life, and in *Blubber* (1974), in which Blume explores the humiliations of an overweight girl, Blume creates characters who give voice to readers' own inner fears and anxieties.

With a slightly irreverent view of the world, her characters splash their way through life, bringing up problems with no easy solutions and venting their frustrations. They face situations that their readers will instantly recognize, as when Peter deals with his life with a baby brother, Fudge, the one who gets all the attention, in *Tales of a Fourth Grade Nothing* (1972):

> Mrs. Yarby left the room again. This time she came back with a flat package. It was wrapped up too—red ribbon and all. She handed it to me. Fudge stopped playing with his train long enough to come over and see what I got. I took off the paper very carefully in case my mother wanted to save it. And also to show Mrs. Yarby that I'm a lot more careful about things than my brother. I'm not sure she noticed. My present turned out to be a big picture dictionary. The kind I liked when I was about four years old. My old one in is Fudge's bookcase now (11).

Readers quickly perceive the kind of guest Mrs. Yarby represents, as well as the strong judgment that only a nine-year-old can make. The vividness of these characters and situations is enhanced by the strong and sometimes unyielding first-person narrators, who give an immediacy to situations.

Blume is one of the more controversial authors in the genre, principally because of her willingness to be very explicit about teenage sexuality. In *Forever* (1975), she pictures Michael and Katherine at the moment of their first sexual encounter. In *Deenie* (1973) and *Just as Long as We're Together* (1987), she discusses masturbation and menstruation. In *Starring Sally J. Freedman as Herself* (1977), Sally has one final summer when the adult world remains mysterious to her. She does not understand why her mother and father want to stay in a hotel, or how "an addition" can mean a baby and not another room in the house. Readers leave her deciding to make up one more story with her Margaret O'Brien paper dolls, and recognize that Sally will grow up when she is ready.

At issue here is the question of audience. Blume contends that she is dealing with those issues that her readers are confronting, and that her treatment is an honest depiction of child and adolescent interest in sexual matter. Others argue that the explicit nature of the scenes suggests a kind of juvenile voyeurism that is objectionable. In either case, the rich complexity of Blume's characters and their dealing with real and recognizable issues continues to make her work popular.

Gary Paulsen (b. 1939)

The energy in a Gary Paulsen novel pulses off the pages. Readers encounter young protagonists who find adventure in both the ordinary and the unusual, all drawn from the life that Paulsen and his wife lead. *Dogteam* (1993) captures Paulsen's sense of adventure and the poetic language he uses to describe those adventures, usually engendered as a union of the natural world and human emotion. It is an Alaskan night, and, as the narrator harnesses the dogs for their run, the dogs romp and pull; the metaphor that Paulsen uses is a dance.

> Through the trees, in and out, the sled whipping after them through the trees with no sound but the song of the runners, the high-soft-shusshh-whine of the runners and the soft jingle of their collars.

The text suggests the sensory pleasure of the run, and it is a pleasure that Paulsen seeks to impart to his readers.

Gary Paulsen is perhaps best known for works with young male protagonists who must survive, must endure, must pit themselves against the environment in order not only to live, but to live fully as young men. They are stories of survival and more than survival, as the characters come to completely new understandings of who they are.

Of these, perhaps the best known of Paulsen's books is *Hatchet* (1987), in which Brian is forced to live on his own in the Canadian wilderness with nothing but a hatchet he has saved from an airplane crash. At first it seems he cannot survive, beset as he is by the lack of food, by clouds of mosquitoes, by even a small tornado that destroys his shelter. But Brian is determined to survive, and little by little he comes to know the ways of the woods. He learns to use smoke to keep the mosquitoes away; he learns the proper technique of spearing "foolbirds"; he learns how to account for the refraction of the water as he fishes with a spear. He quickly learns that food is everything, but, by the end of the novel, he has also learned more about his own life, about what can be stripped away, about what is most important. These are lessons that serve him well in the sequels to *Hatchet: The River* (1991), in which Brian, accompanied by a survival expert, must navigate the river with a wounded companion, and *Brian's Winter* (1996), in which Paulsen changes the ending of *Hatchet* to allow Brian to live at his shelter through the winter.

The Haymeadow (1992) similarly uses the motif of survival, but this time the young protagonist comes purposefully to care for his father's sheep. He has had little relation with his father since the death of his mother, and goes out alone with some fear. And the fear is justified; he must endure coyotes, bears, and flash floods, all of which seem to spring on him so that he has hardly a moment between disasters. But, when his father returns to see him, there is a new kind of relationship that allows them, for the first time, to talk about the mother and wife missing from their family.

Paulsen's *Dogsong* (1985), perhaps his most mystical and eloquent book, takes young Russel on a rite of passage; he leaves his Inuit village where the men now hunt with snowmobiles and goes on a journey in search of his own song. He uses a dogsled team, and brings only ancient weapons along, weapons he will need to fight a polar bear. In following the old stories, the old songs, the old ways, Russel comes to know himself, so that when he begins to dream of his ancestors, he recognizes his own place among their line.

> The man was him: Russel, with more hair, longer hair, and a small beard and a mustache, but he was Russel and Russel knew fear, deep fear, because with the knowledge that he was the man in the dream he knew that he would have to fight the mammoth. He would have to fight it and kill it.
>
> And the mammoth charged.
>
> The head and tusks thrashed in angry arcs and the huge feet trampled the earth, tearing up clods of dirty snow, as the mighty animal bore down on the man and the dogs and sled.
>
> There was no time for escape, no time for dodging. The man had to face the beast.
>
> The dogs ran to the side, but turned back in as the mammoth rushed by them, heading for the man. But their action caused the animal to swing its head slightly to the side and that revealed the center of its chest. (96–97)

The quick pace of this writing is typically Paulsen. There are an abundance of short paragraphs, marked by short sentences with some repetitions. And then suddenly there will be a long, breathless sentence as the narrative rushes towards a climax. The staccato effect of this complements the quick pace of the action.

Not all of Paulsen's books are marked by this kind of pacing, however, nor are they all marked by questions of physical survival. In *Tracker* (1984), Paulsen told of John Borne (a significant name) who must deal with the imminence of his grandfather's death. He goes out to hunt alone for the first time, and does so to track and touch—but not kill—a doe. The affirmation of life that follows shows Paulsen in a meditative mode. *The Monument* (1991) is set in a small town in Kansas, where Rocky, handicapped, feels that she has no real place. But when Mick, an artist, comes to town to design a memorial for the war veterans there, he shows her her own artistic sensibilities and how art can move and change a person. And, in *The Tent* (1995), Paulsen tells of a father and son who ride the revival circuit and preach Jesus so that they can make money. Only after they become well known and wealthy do they begin to think about the reality of what they have been preaching and, astonishingly, turn to begin the circuit all over again, this time to preach honestly of God's love.

In *Harris and Me* (1993), Paulsen turns to uproarious comedy, though it is comedy laced with pain. The eleven-year-old boy is sent from relative to relative to keep him from his alcoholic parents. With that history he comes to Harris's farm to spend a summer. He longs to be a part of this family, with its hard work and good humor and, particularly, Harris, who will try and dare anything, with comically disastrous consequences. When he leaves at the end of the summer, he leaves with a terrible longing for what might have been.

The mirror that Paulsen holds up in using the genre of realism is a mirror that focuses on growth. At times that growth will come about because of physical hardships overcome; at times that growth will come about as inner hardships are overcome. But in all cases Paulsen is depicting characters whose souls are strengthened by the events of the plot, and who come out larger human beings in the end.

Lois Lowry (b. 1937)

Though Lois Lowry has been most celebrated for her historical fiction (*Number the Stars* [1989]) and fantasy (*The Giver* [1993] and its companion novel, *Gathering Blue* [2000]), she is also known for her work in realism; in fact, most of her work is in this genre. Her earliest novel in realism was *A Summer to Die* (1977), in which thirteen-year-old Meg struggles with the onset of her sister's illness and, by the end of the summer, death. Though she is befriended by an elderly neighbor and a young couple who both show her something of the cycles of life, Meg is caught up in her despair and even guilt at her sister's disease. Only in the end is she able to come to acceptance and resolution, painful as it is: "Somewhere, for Molly, I thought suddenly, it would be summer still, summer always."

Later novels like *Rabble Starkey* (1987) and *Autumn Street* (1980) are similarly powerful in their situations. In *Rabble Starkey,* a mother and daughter struggle to find a place for themselves in a world that seems to have no place for them. In *Autumn Street,* a young girl experiences the murder of her close friend Charles, and, at the same time, has her father come home from war wounded. In fact, the wounds are more than physical for both of them, but in the end they are able to make the "impossible promise" that they will heal. Yet—and here Lowry shows the honesty of her writing—they recognize that they will never be completely healed. Instead, they will hold to hope rather than truth.

With *Anastasia Krupnik* (1979), Lowry introduced a new character whose adventures are much more comic, though just as poignant, as those of characters in her other novels. Anastasia lives in Cambridge, Massachusetts, the daughter of a remarkably gifted and creative couple, the brother of younger Sam. Hers is a world of discovery, though sometimes that discovery is painful. In *Anastasia Krupnik*, she deals with the news of a new child, but also comes to a growing awareness of her own imaginative abilities. When she writes a poem that is derided by her teacher, for example, her father, a poet himself, recognizes it for its excellent combination of meaning and sound. In the end, she comes to love almost all those things that she had listed as hating in her journal, suggesting her new delight in the world around her.

Lowry continues Anastasia's growth in later novels. *Anastasia at Your Service* (1982) chronicles her first job, while *Anastasia's Chosen Career* (1987) describes her search for a vocation. *All About Sam* (1988) describes life from Sam's point of view, beginning with his impressions as a newborn and leading to the delightful sensation of squishing things into his hair and hiding something awful behind the curtains.

In all of these novels Lowry is not afraid to deal realistically and honestly with the pain in life. But she is also willing to show the abundance of life, its delights, its fulfillments.

Thinking and Writing about and from within the Genre of Realism

Thinking and Writing about the Genre of Realism _____

1. Read Katherine Paterson's *The Great Gilly Hopkins* (1978) or Robert Cormier's *The Chocolate War* (1974). Draft a letter from you as a teacher or librarian that explains to parents the reasons why you believe this work must be included in the school library. You will need to deal with those issues raised by the novels that you believe some readers might find objectionable.

2. Write the review for Eve Bunting's *Ducky* (1998) that explores the genre to which this work belongs. A picture book, it tells the story of a crate full of toys that was washed overboard in the Pacific Ocean.

3. One metaphor for the way in which realism works is the metaphor of the mirror; realism is a mirror that sharpens the image of real life. In a short essay, establish a different metaphor for the workings of realism, and apply that metaphor to the work of Doris Buchanan Smith or Jean George.

4. Read Katherine Paterson's *Bridge to Terabithia* (1977). Write a critical essay that explores the ways in which Paterson uses the notion of bridges—physical and metaphorical—in this novel.

5. Read one of the works by Judy Blume discussed in this chapter. Write an editorial in your school newspaper considering whether or not that work should be in-

cluded in your school library. Consider as well whether it has a place in classroom libraries, or even on the assigned curriculum.

Thinking and Writing from within the Genre of Realism

1. In *Smoky Night* (1994), Eve Bunting wrote a picture book about the Los Angeles riots. She did this by focusing on a particular group of people; she did not try to write an information book, but to make the event meaningful by zooming in on the particular. Choose a contemporary event and write the text for a picture book that uses Bunting's method.

2. Outline a story about a boy and his backyard treehouse. The situation is a clichéd one, so you will need to find some means of avoiding the expected plot, the expected scenarios.

3. In *Water Sky* (1987), Jean George presented an issue by placing characters on two sides of it. She did not bias the issue by placing good characters on one side, unlikable characters on the other. Nor did she allow the story to be dominated by a didactic purpose. Choose an issue that interests you and write a précis for a story you might draft that sets characters in conflict over the issue.

4. Using a normal week from your life, write a realistic story about it. Include all the elements of good fiction: character, plot direction, setting, point of view. At the end, include a short description of how you chose incidents and details.

Selected Bibliographies

Works Cited

Armstrong, Richard. *The Big Sea*. New York: David McKay, 1964.

———. *The Secret Sea*. New York: David McKay, 1966.

Bat-Ami, Miriam. *Dear Elijah*. New York: Farrar, Straus, 1995.

Bradbury, Ray. *The Martian Chronicles*. New York: Doubleday, 1958.

Brisson, Pat. *Sky Memories*. NY: Delacorte Press, 1999. Illustrated by Wendell Minor.

Brooks, Bruce. *What Hearts*. New York: HarperCollins, 1992.

Case, Dianne. *Love, David*. New York: Lodestar, 1986.

Cleary, Beverly. *Dear Mr. Henshaw*. New York: William Morrow, 1983.

Cormier, Robert. *Beyond the Chocolate War*. New York: Knopf, 1985.

———. *The Chocolate War*. New York: Pantheon, 1974.

Cresswell, Helen. *Absolute Zero*. New York: Macmillan, 1978.

———. *Bagthorpes Unlimited*. New York: Macmillan, 1978.

———. *Bagthorpes v. the World*. New York: Macmillan, 1979.

———. *Ordinary Jack*. New York: Macmillan, 1977.

dePaola, Tomie. *The Art Lesson*. New York: Putnam, 1989.

Dickinson, Peter. *Eva*. New York: Delacort, 1988.

Fitzhugh, Louise. *Harriet the Spy*. New York: Harper and Row, 1964.

Fox, Paula. *Monkey Island*. New York: Orchard, 1991.

Gleitzman, Morris. *Misery Guts*. New York: Harcourt, Brace, 1991.

———. *Worry Warts*. New York: Harcourt, Brace, 1991.

Gordon, Sheila. *Waiting for the Rain.* Toronto: Bantam, 1989.

Harris, Robie H. *Happy Birth Day!* Cambridge, MA: Candlewick, 1996. Illustrated by Michael Emberley.

Hathorn, Libby. *Way Home.* New York: Crown, 1994. Illustrated by Gregory Rogers.

Jarrell, Randall. *Fly by Night.* New York: Farrar, Straus, 1976. Illustrated by Maurice Sendak.

Jarris, Robie. *Happy Birthday!* Cambridge, MA: Candlewick Press, 1996.

Lee, Harper. *To Kill a Mockingbird.* Philadelphia: Lippincott, 1960.

Levoy, Myron. *Pictures of Adam.* New York: Harper and Row, 1986.

Lewis, C. S. *The Lion, the Witch, and the Wardrobe.* London: Geoffrey Bles, 1950.

Lowry, Lois. *A Summer to Die.* Boston: Houghton Mifflin, 1977.

Maartens, Maretha. *Paper Bird.* New York: Clarion, 1989.

Naylor, Phyllis Reynolds. *Shiloh.* New York: Atheneum, 1991.

Paterson, Katherine. *Bridge to Terabithia.* New York: Crowell, 1977.

———. *Come Sing, Jimmy Jo.* New York: Lodestar, 1985.

———. *The Great Gilly Hopkins.* New York: Crowell, 1978.

———. *Jacob Have I Loved.* New York: HarperCollins, 1980.

Paulsen, Gary. *Dogsong.* New York: Bradbury, 1985.

———. *Hatchet.* New York: Bradbury, 1987.

———. *The Monument.* New York: Delacorte, 1991.

———. *Tracker.* New York: Bradbury, 1984.

Raskin, Ellen. *The Westing Game.* New York: Dutton, 1978.

Rylant, Cynthia. *A Fine White Dust.* New York: Bradbury, 1986.

———. *Missing May.* New York: Orchard Books, 1992.

Sendak, Maurice. *In the Night Kitchen.* New York: Harper and Row, 1970.

Soentpiet, Chris. *Around Town.* New York: Lothrop, Lee and Shepard, 1994.

Smith, Doris Buchanan. *A Taste of Blackberries.* New York: Harper and Row, 1973.

———. *Tough Chauncey.* New York: Viking, 1974.

Snyder, Zilpha Keatley. *The Egypt Game.* New York: Atheneum, 1967.

Spinelli, Jerry. *The Library Card.* New York: Scholastic, 1997.

———. *Maniac Magee.* Boston: Little, Brown, 1990.

Staples, Suzanne. *Dangerous Skies.* New York: Farrar, Straus, 1996.

———. *Shabanu, Daughter of the Wind.* New York: Knopf, 1989.

Stolz, Mary. *The Bully of Barkham Street.* New York: Harper and Row, 1963.

———. *A Dog on Barkham Street.* New York: Harper and Row, 1960.

Tolan, Stephanie. *Save Halloween!* New York: Morrow, 1993.

Verne, Jules. *Twenty Thousand Leagues Under the Sea.* New York: Tor Books, 1995.

Voigt, Cynthia. *Homecoming.* New York: Atheneum, 1981.

Williams, Michael. *Into the Valley.* New York: Philomel, 1990.

Yashima, Taro. *Crow Boy.* New York: Viking, 1965.

Works by Selected Writers of Realism

Eve Bunting

The Day before Christmas. New York: Clarion, 1992. Illustrated by Beth Peck.

A Day's Work. Boston: Houghton Mifflin, 1994. Illustrated by Ronald Himler.

Ducky. New York: Clarion, 1998. Illustrated by David Wisniewski.

Fly Away Home. New York: Clarion, 1991. Illustrated by Ronald Himler.

Ghost's Hour, Spook's Hour. New York: Clarion, 1987. Illustrated by Donald Carrick.

Smoky Night. New York: Harcourt, Brace, 1994. Illustrated by David Diaz.

The Wall. New York: Clarion, 1990. Illustrated by Ronald Himler.

Beverly Cleary

Beezus and Ramona. New York: William Morrow, 1955.

Dear Mr. Henshaw. New York: William Morrow, 1983.

Henry Huggins. New York: William Morrow, 1950.

Ramona and Her Father. New York: William Morrow, 1977.

Ramona Forever. New York: William Morrow, 1984.

Ramona Quimby, Age 8. Boston: Houghton Mifflin, 1991.

Ramona the Brave. New York: William Morrow, 1975.

Ramona the Pest. New York: William Morrow, 1968.

Ribsy. New York: William Morrow, 1964.

Strider. New York: William Morrow, 1991.

Jean Craighead George

Julie. New York: HarperCollins, 1994.

Julie of the Wolves. New York: Harper and Row, 1972.

Julie's Wolf Pack. New York: HarperCollins, 1997.

My Side of the Mountain. New York: Dutton, 1959.

On the Far Side of the Mountain. New York: Dutton, 1990.

The Talking Earth. New York: Harper and Row, 1983.

Water Sky. New York: Harper and Row, 1987.

Katherine Paterson

Bridge to Terabithia. New York: Crowell, 1977.

Come Sing, Jimmy Jo. New York: Dutton, 1985.

Flip-Flop Girl. New York: Lodestar, 1994.

The Great Gilly Hopkins. New York: Crowell, 1978.

Jacob Have I Loved. New York: Crowell, 1980.

Jip: His Story. New York: Lodestar, 1996.

Lyddie. New York: Dutton, 1991.

Of Nightingales That Weep. New York: Crowell, 1974.

Park's Quest. New York: Dutton, 1988.

The Sign of the Crysanthemum. New York: Crowell, 1973.

Doris Buchanan Smith

Return to Bitter Creek. New York: Viking, 1986.

A Taste of Blackberries. New York: Harper and Row, 1973.

Tough Chauncey. New York: Viking, 1974.

Judy Blume

Are You There, God? It's Me, Margaret. New York: Dell, 1970.

Blubber. New York: Dell, 1974.

Deenie. New York: Laurel Leaf, 1973.

Forever. Bradbury, 1975.

Just as Long as We're Together. New York: Orchard, 1987.

Starring Sally J. Friedman as Herself. New York: Bradbury, 1977.

Tales of a Fourth Grade Nothing. New York: E. P. Dutton, 1972.

Gary Paulsen

Brian's Winter. New York: Delacorte, 1996.

Dogsong. New York: Bradbury, 1985.

Dogteam. New York: Delacorte, 1993.

Harris and Me. New York: Harcourt, Brace, 1993.

Hatchet. New York: Bradbury, 1987.

The Haymeadow. New York: Delacorte, 1992.

The Monument. New York: Delacorte, 1991.

The River. New York: Delacorte, 1991.

The Tent. New York: Harcourt, Brace, 1995.

Tracker. New York: Bradbury, 1984.

Lois Lowry

All about Sam. Boston: Houghton Mifflin, 1988.

Anastasia at Your Service. Boston: Houghton Mifflin, 1982.

Anastasia Krupnik. Boston: Houghton Mifflin, 1979.

Anastasia's Chosen Career. Boston: Houghton Mifflin, 1987.

Autumn Street. Boston: Houghton Mifflin, 1980.

Gathering Blue. Boston: Houghton Mifflin, 2000.

The Giver. Boston: Houghton Mifflin, 1993.

Number the Stars. Boston: Houghton Mifflin, 1989.

Rabble Starkey. Boston: Houghton Mifflin, 1987.

A Summer to Die. Boston: Houghton Mifflin, 1977.

Works on Realism in Children's Literature

Age, Hugh. "Preserving Intellectual Freedom: The Principal's Role." *ALAN Review* 20 (1993): 7–9.

Apseloff, Marilyn Fain. "Abandonment: The New Realism of the Eighties." In Sheila Egoff, ed., *Only Connect: Readings on Children's Literature.* New York: Oxford University Press, 1996: 359–364.

Becker, George J. *Realism in Modern Literature.* New York: Frederick Ungar, 1980.

Bosmajian, Hamida. "Tricks of the Text and Acts of Reading by Censors and Adolescents." *Children's Literature in Education* 18 (1987): 89–96.

Chaston, Joel. "The Other Deaths in *Bridge to Terabithia.*" *Children's Literature in Education* 23 (1992): 238–241.

Davis, James E. "What Principals and Other Administrators Have Done and Can Do in Defending Intellectual Freedom." *ALAN Review* 20 (1993): 11–13.

DeLuca, Geraldine. "'Composing a Life': The Diary of Leigh Botts." *Lion and the Unicorn* 14 (1990): 58–65.

Fisher, Margery. *The Bright Face of Danger.* Boston: Horn Book, 1986.

Giblin, James Cross. "Esthetic or Functional, Saccharine or Shocking? An Editor Looks at Values in Children's Books." *Children's Literature in Education* 8 (1977): 120–126.

Gooderham, David. "Still Catching Them Young? The Moral Dimension in Young Children's Books." *Children's Literature in Education* 24 (1993): 115–122.

Klein, Norma. "Growing Up Human: The Case for Sexuality in Children's Books." *Children's Literature in Education* 8 (1977): 80–84.

Lukens, Rebecca. "From Salinger to Cormier: Disillusionment Is Despair in Thirty Years." *ALAN Review* 9 (1981): 38–42.

Lynch, Chris. "If You Show Me Yours, I'll Show You Mine." *ALAN Review* 24 (1996): 7–9.

Marcus, Leonard, ed. *Dear Genius: The Letters of Ursula Nordstrom.* New York: HarperCollins, 1998.

May, Jill P. *Children's Literature and Critical Theory.* New York: Oxford University Press, 1995.

Meyer, Michael. "Problems and Prescriptions: Child Abuse in the Novels of Paul Zindel." *Children's Literature Association Quarterly* 17 (1992): 11–14.

Paterson, Katherine. *A Sense of Wonder.* New York: Penguin, 1995.

Paul, Lissa. "The Feminist Writer as Heroine in *Harriet the Spy.*" *Lion and the Unicorn* 13 (1989): 67–73.

Pflieger, Pat. *Beverly Cleary.* Boston: Twayne, 1991.

Phinney, Margaret Yatsevitch. "Eve Bunting: A 'Wonderful Happenstance.'" *New Advocate* 10 (Summer 1997): 195–202.

Pipken, Gloria Treadwell. "Challenging the Conventional Wisdom on Censorship." *ALAN Review* 20 (1993): 35–37.

Plotz, Judith. "The Disappearance of Childhood: Parent–Child Role Reversals in *After the First Death* and *A Solitary Blue.*" *Children's Literature in Education* 19 (1988): 67–79.

Sawyer, Walter and Jean. "A Discussion with Suzanne Fisher Staples: The Author as Writer and Cultural Observer." *New Advocate* 6 (Summer 1993): 159–170.

Schmidt, Gary D. *Katherine Paterson.* New York: Twayne, 1994.

Shannon, Patrick. "Overt and Covert Censorship of Children's Books." *New Advocate* 2 (Spring 1989): 97–104.

———. "Unconscious Censorship of Social and Political Ideas in Children's Books." *Children's Literature Association Quarterly* 11 (1987): 103–105.

Simmons, John. "Censorship in the Schools: No End in Sight." *ALAN Review* 18 (1993): 6–8.

Smedman, M. Sarah. "Springs of Hope: Recovery of Primordial Time in 'Mythic' Novels for Young Readers." *Children's Literature* 16 (1988): 91–107.

Snow, C. P. *The Realists.* New York: Charles Scribner's Sons, 1978.

Stoehr, Shelley. "Controversial Issues in the Lives of Contemporary Young Adults." *ALAN Review* 24 (1997): 3–5.

Stott, Jon C. "Jean George's Arctic Pastoral: A Reading of *Julie of the Wolves.*" *Children's Literature* 3 (1974): 131–139.

Tod, Robert. "The Treatment of Childhood Stress in Children's Literature." *Children's Literature in Education* 5 (1971): 24–45.

Veglahn, Nancy. "The Bland Face of Evil in the Novels of Robert Cormier." *Lion and the Unicorn* 12 (1988): 12–18.

Waddy, Lucy E. "Cinderella and Pigman: Why Kids Read Blume and Zindel Novels." *ALAN Review* 10 (1983): 6–9.

Wolf, Virginia L. "*Harriet the Spy:* Milestone, Masterpiece?" *Children's Literature* 4 (1975): 120–126.

10

Historical Fiction: Recasting the Past

Historical fiction melds fact and fiction, joining the fact of the event, the writer's vision of the meaning of the event, and the fictional tale with which the writer surrounds the event. The success of a work of historical fiction depends on the success of these three elements. Their fusion is what brings the spirit of the age to the forefront of the story, so that the action and characters do not seem to be merely those of contemporary characters set back into an earlier setting, but the actions and attitudes of characters who are truly from an earlier period.

To accomplish this fusion, the writer needs to help the child reader feel an overwhelming sense of the past's presence, so that it exists in a totality, and so that it exists convincingly. The writer of historical fiction must have a good sense of the historical material, certainly. He or she must be able to capture the essence of that period and setting with deftness and accuracy. In addition, historical fiction implies fiction; there must be the narrative. He or she is not just recounting historical events, but using those events and settings as the context for a narrative. The writer of historical fiction blends history and imagination, and blends them seamlessly.

The historical writer's story must merge with established historical fact and present the writer's vision of the meaning of those facts, all in the context of an engaging narrative that strays neither into fantasy nor nonfiction. A story of the American Revolution would become fantasy if a stray bullet were to pick off George Washington; the book would stray into nonfiction if it included long passages unimportant to the action about conditions at Valley Forge. A work of historical fiction must remain true to the facts while telling a fictional narrative that uses those facts as linchpins.

But here historical fiction moves to an important truth. Though the story may be about characters well separated from the reader in terms of time and setting and culture, still, the story is about human characters who have the same essential nature as the reader, a nature that does not change over time. Historical fiction shows distinctions, certainly. Different cultures will lead to different under-

260

standings, beliefs, actions, motivations. But historical fiction also shows the commonalities of humanity. Leon Garfield uses a different metaphor to suggest the effects that historical fictional has on the reader: "History becomes a mirror in which we see ourselves, for a fleeting instant, as others see us." (1988)

Boundaries and Definitions of Historical Fiction

Historical fiction is bound on the one side by historical fact and on the other by fiction. Within these boundaries a writer crafts a narrative that is both fictional and suggestive of the meaning of the historical facts included in the tale. Thus, historical fiction is a story rooted in a particular time and place by observation and illustration that deliberately evoke and clarify the spirit of a past culture.

Historical fiction is story, with all the fictive structuring that that word entails. It functions within the broad arena of realism, in that everything that occurs within the story must be possible, if not necessarily plausible. However, historical fiction has sterner strictures than the broader genre of realism, in that everything in the story must conform to historical reality. The writer of historical fiction must look at the mass of detail related by chronology to his or her story and decide how those details will contribute to the tale. Which details should be kept, and which deleted? Which details are to be emphasized, and which included subtly? How are the details to be integrated into the fictional story?

The Integration of Fact and Fiction

Integration comes about through the observant, accurate eye of the writer. In order to create an accurately evoked scene, the writer of historical fiction must have the observant eye that comes through research. For example, a writer trying to describe a New England inn at the turn of the eighteenth century would have to know how that inn was constructed, how the doors opened, where the plates were stored, what kind of food would be served, and how it would be cooked. What kind of rugs are on the floors, prints on the walls, herbs hanging from the beams? What are people wearing, what are they talking about, how do they pay for their lodging? The writer needs to integrate these and hundreds of other details into the story, not so that readers feel as if they are touring the inn, but as if they are watching a scene unfold by having stepped back into the past.

Consider how James Lincoln Collier and Christopher Collier integrate details into the narrative in this opening scene of *My Brother Sam Is Dead* (1974), set during the opening of the American Revolution.

> It was April, and outside in the dark the rain whipped against the windows of our tavern, making a sound like muffled drums. We were concentrating on our dinner, and everybody jumped when the door slammed open and banged against the wall, making the plates rattle in their racks. My brother Sam was standing there, wearing a uniform....

"We've beaten the British in Massachusetts," he shouted.
"*Who* has beaten the British?" Father said.
Sam shut the door. "We have," he said, with his back to us as he slipped the latch in place (2).

The Colliers have, in this short section, established the time—that of the battles of Lexington and Concord—as well as several facts about the tavern: that the door is closed with a latch, and that the plates are stored in racks on the wall. The simile used by the narrator suggests something else about the kinds of sounds he has heard before. None of these details are obtrusive; all easily flow into the action of the narrative, and, in fact, contribute to that action.

Writers make this fusion between history and story invisible by arranging the historical events within the story's design. The literary elements that contribute to this arrangement can seem artificial when placed against the flow of history, which does not arrange itself neatly into exposition, complication, rising action, climax, and resolution. History is not narrative in itself. The writer of historical fiction arranges historical events in the pattern of the story to create the narrative. While not free to invent historical events or to change them significantly, the writer nevertheless is free to choose and arrange within his or her story.

This sounds straightforward, and most readers are comfortable enough with their understanding of the necessities of story writing that this fusion may go almost unnoticed. However, the apparently effortless fusion of fact and story, of history and fiction, represents the high artistry of this genre. In *The Lotus Seed* (1993), Sherry Garland chooses certain facts from recent Vietnamese history and arranges them in the context of the narrator's grandmother's individual story. The loss of the dragon throne, the destructive war, a desperate escape by boat, the confusion of a new life in the United States—all of these are historical events for many Vietnamese immigrants. But the power of *The Lotus Seed* as historical fiction lies in its arrangement of those facts within the pattern of the fictional grandmother's concern for the preservation of her culture, a concern metaphorically treated in the lotus seed that will eventually blossom. That metaphor and the fictional story of the grandmother swirl about the linchpins of the historical facts that Garland has chosen.

The fusion of history and story may be crafted through the evocation of emotional response on the part of a protagonist. The protagonist reacts for the reader, in this sense, and brings together what might have been dry fact and a plot line that demands response. In *The Eagle of the Ninth* (1954), the story of a Roman boy's search for the fate of his missing father, Rosemary Sutcliff fuses history and story by linking historically accurate descriptions with the emotional responses of the protagonist, as in this description of a Roman barracks:

Through the doorless opening Marcus could see almost the whole of the sleeping-cell, the narrow cot piled with gay native rugs, the polished oaken chest, the lamp-bracket high on the bare wall, and nothing more. The outer room held the battered writing table on which Marcus was sitting, a cross-legged camp-stool, the cushioned bench to represent comfort, another chest for the record rolls, and a bronze pedestal lamp of peculiarly hideous design.

> In the little silence that had fallen between them, Marcus looked round him at the austere room in the yellow flood of lamplight, and to him it seemed beautiful (8–9).

Sutcliff carefully envisions the setting by stringing together details, an act she calls "fleshing out," "molding," "sifting," and "imaginative bridging." This "bridging," all the more effective for its invisibility, allows her to set the emotion of the story: Marcus's seeing this stark room as beautiful.

The fusion of history and story may also be created by evoking a fictional character's response, not to a setting, but to a historical character, as in Jill Paton Walsh's *The Emperor's Winding Sheet* (1974).

> There was a silence. The agonized silence made by many men holding their breath. A hundred eyes were bent upon the Despot Constantine; they watched, they commanded. The boy shivered. He could feel the tension in the sunlit afternoon air, something fateful happening, some terrible bond being forged. Then the Despot reached out his hand, and lightly touched his crown. Voices rang out (10).

This story of a young boy's introduction to the emperor Constantine and his attachment to him begins at this point. The writer has used a character's emotional reaction to tie the narrative of her story together with the historical events within it, a tying that will ultimately suggest the meaning of those historical events.

Historical fiction is firmly rooted in a particular time and place. In order for readers to believe that they have been transported to another time and place, writers create settings that are realistic and appropriate to the period. Maps, careful description, intimate detail, and period illustrations all make the settings come to life. In Jill Paton Walsh's *Fireweed* (1969), the period of the London blitz is evoked through vivid description.

> Later we sat in St. James's Park, on the grass beside the water. There was barbed wire all over the Horse Guards' parade, and the soldiers on guard there were in khaki; but we had been to Trafalgar Square and Whitehall. There were wardens' posts and shelters covered in sandbags set up around the edge of the park, but the middle was the same as it used to be. We were eating lunch: sandwiches and mugs of hot tea bought from a W. V. S. canteen in a lorry parked in the Mall. There was some sort of fire-fighting exercise going on, and people marked A. F. S. were swarming over from Green Park, and the canteen was for them really, but they didn't mind serving us. They were hearty women in green overcoats, very cheerful (33).

The description does not particularly advance the plot narrative, but it does create a realistic context within which the narrative moves. The descriptive details suggest much about the mindset of the characters and the people around them as well. On the one hand, there are all the preparations for a bombing, including the fire-fighting exercise and the presence of official groups. Sandbags and soldiers are on the Mall. But, at the same time, there is an insistence on normalcy; the characters observing the Mall are not panicking, but are eating sandwiches and drinking tea; the women who serve them are cheerful.

Thus, the writer of historical fiction is faced not only with the question of which details should be kept and which discarded, but with the question of how the details that are kept may be artfully and unobtrusively integrated into the story in such a way that they accurately reflect the period and culture.

Historical fiction, like the genre of fantasy, creates an other world, a deliberately evoked world quite different from our own, but with strong connections to our own. The writer of historical fiction creates an other world, but it is a world firmly rooted in the real world. The power of historical fiction lies in the ability of the writer to create that other world and, in creating it, to allow the reader to see his or her own world more fully, from more perspectives, from deeper inside.

Working in Two Time Periods

In evoking a past time, the writer of historical fiction is doing more than simply setting a story in the past. The writer of historical fiction works within two time frames for particular reasons. On the one hand, the writer works in the present and uses the privileged view of the present to comment on the past. Novels like *Friedrich* (1970) and *I Was There* (1972) by Hans Peter Richter comment on the terrible growth of Nazism from the perspective of a young German boy; such a story would have been impossible to write in the late 1930s, but, from the perspective of the present, Richter can comment on the subtle horror of that growth.

On the other hand, the writer uses the past to clarify the present, or to comment on his or her own time. When Esther Forbes wrote *Johnny Tremain* in 1943, she wrote to encourage Americans to "stand up," a phrase used over and over again in the novel, for their freedoms against the Nazi war machine. In *The Fighting Ground* (1984), Avi has his protagonist discover the horror and brutality of war by battling the Hessians during the American Revolution; the conclusion of the protagonist is that all war is dreadful, no matter what its time period. In *Catherine, Called Birdy* (1994), *The Midwife's Apprentice* (1995), *The Ballad of Lucy Whipple* (1996), and *Matilda Bone* (2000), Karen Cushman creates four strong female protagonists not only to suggest the presence of such women during the Middle Ages and the California Gold Rush, but to suggest to the child reader that one's life does not always have to be molded by society's expectations, no matter what the time period.

In all of these stories the writer uses the past to speak to readers of the present about their own lives and situations. The writer of historical fiction is uniquely qualified to show how the past of all cultures impacts and gives meaning to the present of all cultures, and that, even as we interpret the past through the eyes of the present, the past has much to teach us about ourselves.

Certainly, one way in which historical fiction uses the past to inform the present is the forum it provides for voices drowned out by the clamoring, neglect, or malice of a majority culture. In 1960 Scott O'Dell's *Island of the Blue Dolphins* brought a Native American voice to the forefront, a voice deeply affected by the nonnative culture that was sweeping the continent but that was not a part of that culture. O'Dell followed that book with novels like *Sing Down the Moon* (1970), about the destruction of the Navajo culture, and *Streams to the River, River to the Sea* (1986), the story of the Lewis and Clark expedition from the point of view of Sacagawea.

In 1975, Mildred Taylor's *Song of the Trees* established a strong African American voice. In this novel set during the Depression, Cassie Logan tells the story of her strong family and its struggle to overcome the brutal hostility and prejudice of most of its neighbors. It is their determination to maintain their self-respect and to tell their stories that gives Cassie the strength to deal with the humiliations that she faces as she grows up. This growth is charted in novels like *Roll of Thunder, Hear My Cry* (1976), *Let the Circle Be Unbroken* (1981), and *The Road to Memphis* (1990). In each of these works of historical fiction, the genre allows the reader to enter into the time period and to experience the action from the inside; when this experiencing allows the reader to understand another culture's perspective, it is especially valuable.

Many writers have worked to pave the road that O'Dell and Taylor have travelled, and this has allowed many new voices to emerge, many new perspectives to be seen. James Lincoln Collier and Christopher Collier's *War Comes to Willy Freeman* (1983), *Jump Ship to Freedom* (1981), and *Who is Carrie?* (1984) introduced the perspective of the Arabus family, an African American family whose perspective on the American Revolutionary War is quite different from that generally accepted. Minfong Ho's *The Clay Marble* (1991) allows a forum for twelve-year-old Dara, a Cambodian refugee. Katherine Paterson's *Of Nightingales That Weep* (1974) shows the life of a samurai's daughter in medieval Japan. Eloise Jarvis McGraw's *The Golden Goblet* (1961) shows an even remoter life in ancient Egypt. Patricia Hermes's *On Winter's Wind* (1995) depicts the experience of a poverty-stricken ship's captain's daughter in early New England. Laurence Yep's *The Star Fisher* (1991) follows the life of Joan Lee as she tries to straddle the two worlds of West Virginia and China, her parents' homeland. And Katherine Lasky's *Beyond the Divide* (1983) and *The Night Journey* (1981) both follow changes in the life of a young girl, the first as Meribah Simon abandons her Amish community to head west with her shunned father, and the second as Sashie escapes from tsarist Russia.

The Role of Illustration in Historical Fiction

Illustration further deepens the reader's experience, for it allows visual access to the period. Sometimes this access can come through the addition of details not specified in the text. In *Hattie and the Wild Waves* (1990), for example, Barbara Cooney's detailed illustrations evoke the life of wealth and privilege led by Hattie, which stands in contrast to her determination to forge a life of her own. The elaborate wallpaper, the fine upholstered furniture, the cut glass, the marble-topped tables, the stained-glass windows, the flowers under glass—all suggest something about Hattie's life that is not at all mentioned in the text, but says much about the time period and the nature of Hattie's battle for self-identification.

Illustrations can convey much of the thematic meaning even as they convey details of the period. In Eve Bunting's *Dandelions* (1995), the story of a family's move to Nebraska is heightened by Greg Shedd's illustrations. His sepia-tinted impressionistic pictures add to the feeling of nostalgia, but details such as the wilted dandelions the daughters plant for their homesick mother hint at the hope that, though this year will not be an easy time for the mother, perhaps next year's blooming will accompany a new love for this flat land. Diane Goode's illustrations for Cynthia Rylant's *When I Was Young in the Mountains* (1982) complement the text by stressing the deep contentment of the narrator in her life in the mountains. The expressions on the faces of the congregation as they witness a baptism show their love for the child and their sense of the meaning of this ceremony. Tony Johnston's *The Wagon* (1996) focuses on a young slave boy's terrible frustration about his slavery, symbolized for him by the wagon that his father has crafted but may not own. James Ransome's oil illustrations focus on the first-person narrator, who is often pictured behind the action or behind his family. The starkness of their surroundings and the pain of their struggle is vividly depicted through expression and body language, as well as through the landscape. In the concluding picture, the slave family takes the wagon to head towards Mr. Lincoln's funeral; the young boy is saddened and even quizzical; the sun is either rising or setting: They are heading to freedom, but also to the funeral of the one responsible for it, and so the illustration remains ambiguous.

Creating a Sense of the Totality of the Past

Writers must find ways other than visual to create the overwhelming sense of the past, the totality of the historical moment. They have solved this problem in numerous ways. *Constance: A Story of Early Plymouth* (1968) by Patricia Clapp uses the journal structure to create a sense of realism. The journal chronicles the settlement of the community in New England at the same time that it focuses on the growing but reluctant acceptance of her new life by Constance.

> *November 1621 continued*
> The first I knew aught out of the way was when I saw Squanto running past our house and up the Street. Squanto rarely runs now, feeling it beneath his dignity in his new position as adviser and constant help to Plymouth, but when he chooses—as at the races on our feast days—he covers ground with his long easy lope at an unbelievable speed. I was sitting just inside the open doorway, the day being bright and mild for November, sewing on a little coat for Oceanus, who—now that he can walk—can no longer wear swaddling clothes. (And what we should have done for clothing without the garments left by those who died during the Sickness, I do not know!) (81).

Readers are shifted to the seventeenth-century Pilgrim experience by the concerns of a fifteen-year-old girl who is limited in terms of her historical perspective but who allows the reader a sense of the real-life experience—even to the point of finding some good in the sickness that killed so many of the Pilgrims. While journals do have their shortcomings—sentences filled with information that a contemporary writer might never have bothered to include, the description of items that would never have occurred at the time, the use of modernized language and spelling—still, the journal form allows the writer of historical fiction an avenue into the past. Patricia Clapp suggests that the journal is an intimate way to let readers in on history, that they are pulled in almost unawares.

Another way into a sense of the past is through the creation of period language. Rigid adherence to earlier speech patterns and diction can cause problems if the language interferes with readers' understanding, but, if the writer can balance the creation of authentic language with the reader's understanding, then he or she will have found a way to create a strong sense of the past. In Mary Stolz's *Bartholomew Fair* (1990), for example, Stolz wants to suggest something of the flavor of Elizabethan speech, but she does not want to distance her dialogue from her child readers to the point that they would not understand it. She achieves this balance with a moderate use of Elizabethan vocabulary and sentence structuring in this scene in which Queen Elizabeth is not pleased by the carriage prepared for her.

> "Mr. Secretary, I liketh this not!" she said, coming up against him, staring upward into his eyes, her own flinty with anger.
> "I like it little myself, Madam. It was not I—" he began, and broke off. The first councillor to the Majesty of England did not put the onus, however deserved, on others. "If Your Majesty will, perhaps, walk in the orchard, I will assay to reason with her Master of the Horse—"
> "Assay? What means this *assay*! Tell the Earl of Essex that he oversteps himself. Clear all this out—" She waved a hand at the great gilded coach, the grooms, the mounted equerries, the Guardsmen.
> "Get a small, open carriage—" (66).

The one unfamiliar word—*assay*—is defined within its context; the dialogue is distanced by the unfamiliar word orders, but the meanings are not hindered by that unfamiliarity. The diction suggests as well something of the relationship between the two speakers, as well as something of their characters. In so doing, Stolz has used her dialogue to do more than advance the story; it tells of something of the historical period from which it derives.

In the opening of *Jack Holborn* (1964), Leon Garfield creates a narrator whose diction instantly signals the period of the action.

> My story must begin when I boarded the *Charming Molly* at Bristol. Before that there's little to tell. My name is Jack, surnamed "Holborn" after the parish where I was found: for I had neither father nor mother who'd cared enough to leave me a name of their own.
> When I was old enough to stand without the aid of my hands, employment was found for them with a stony-fisted cobbler who did nothing but prate about my good fortune in being with him—and curse his own lack of it in having me. When I was old enough to run, I left him. But now, looking back on it, he must have been a virtuous man, who did his charitable duty according to his lights. It was ill-luck that those lights never shone on me.
> So I came to Bristol, which I judged to be the best place for leaving this hard-hearted, scornful land, where money alone in your purse serves you for honor, justice, and pity; and a good heart in your breast serves you for nothing but to break (3).

The language of the first-person narrator suggests the earlier time: the references to *parishes* and *cobblers,* the use of words like *prate, hardhearted,* and *purse.* But even the sentence structures suggest the earlier period, such as the use of the infinitive at the conclusion of the passage.

Writers of historical fiction can also create a sense of realism in their work by allowing fictional characters, perhaps even characters who serve as narrators, to give their responses to significant historical events. In this way the event is not merely what Laurence Yep calls "dead" history, but comes alive because of the character's responsiveness, a responsiveness that may echo that of the reader. Theodore Taylor's *The Bomb* (1995) is a striking account of the nuclear testing on the island of Bikini in 1946, written by an author who was aboard the *Sumner* when the experiment was conducted. The novel is told from the point of view of a young native boy, who experiences all the frustration, outrage, and puzzlement that the reader might experience in trying to understand why a culture was destroyed and an island infected forever merely for the sake of an explosion. Carolyn Reeder's *Grandpa's Mountain* (1991) examines one girl's response to the creation of the Shenandoah National Park and the loss of her grandparents' farm and a way of life in the Blue Ridge Mountains. Whereas it would seem that the creation of such a park would be universally applauded, the perspective of this novel suggests that not everyone thought the park a boon. Christopher Paul Curtis's *The Watsons Go to Birmingham—1963* (1995) dramatizes the early days of the Civil Rights Movement by focusing on the tension and its effects on one Michigan family travelling in the South. In each case the genre of historical fiction allows the writer to create a character to respond to a major historical event, and in responding, to create an effect on the reader.

In making these sorts of decisions about how to make a historical period come alive for the reader, the writer of historical fiction is working to present a brisk narrative with well-developed characters who speak with authentic voices about concerns that would be germane and appropriate to the period. Such a task makes the writing of historical fiction one of the more difficult writing tasks to undertake.

Pointers for Teachers: Evaluating Historical Fiction

- What is the author's vision of the time period being presented? Does it match what is known about the time period itself?
- How do the characters' actions fit with the time period of the work?
- How does the author use language to make the characters vivid? Does the author attempt to replicate the language of the period? Does that replication come through diction, rhythm, phrasing, or word placement?
- How does the author establish the setting of the events? Does the author use familiar historical people, or stay away from such uses?
- How do the illustrations contribute to the establishment of the historical period?

Issues in the Genre of Historical Fiction

If historical fiction clarifies the past through its fusion of fact and fiction, so, too, does it clarify the present. While it shows the "otherness" of another time, another culture, it also shows that history is made up of those who share much of what we are. They may hold very different cultural assumptions, but they also show human needs and desires that seem unchanging. While some of the issues in historical fiction reflect a concern with the interface of fact and fiction, others reflect a concern with understanding and dealing with cultural assumptions different from our own, all within the context of understanding the role of those assumptions within our common humanity.

If historical fiction is bound by the strictures of historical fact, how does it borrow from other genres without stretching those strictures?

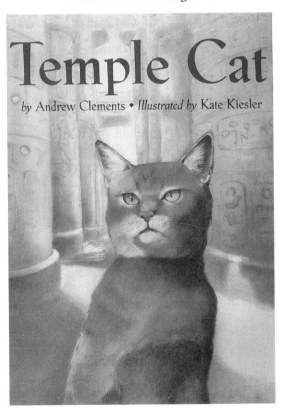

Illustration by Kate Kiesler for Andrew Clements' *Temple Cat*. Copyright © 1996. Reprinted by permission of Clarion Books.

Like other genres, historical fiction will borrow from outside the strict confines of its own sphere, and, in so doing, it will stretch the strictures that define it. In this sense historical fiction may be said to work within a spectrum, one end of which stretches towards fantasy, the other towards nonfiction. In Andrew Clements's *Temple Cat* (1996), a cat worshiped as a god in the ancient Egyptian city of Neba tires of the constant attention. Fleeing the temple and its luxuries, he reaches the coast and is there adopted by a poor fisherman's family: "[B]efore the cat even knew what his dearest wish was, it came true. He played with the children, and they loved him." The response of the children is a universal one; we expect the children to play with the cat. The cat's own search, not for worship, but for personal love, similarly reflects a universal need. The setting and context of the story places the picture book within historical fiction, for it tells much of the practices of temple worship of the time. The difficulty comes as the narrator enters into the consciousness of the cat. As soon as this happens, the book leans towards fantasy. Nevertheless, the book is primarily historical fiction in its intentions.

Insofar as a book consciously recreates a historical setting and places its characters and plot narratives in the context of that setting, it is primarily a work of historical fiction. If it violates that recreation by shifting away from historical reality, its ties to the genre are significantly looser.

John Bellairs's *The Trolley to Yesterday* (1989) uses fantasy to pique his readers' interest in history, using such elements as a talking statue and a time machine that allows his characters to travel back to fifteenth-century Constantinople and first-century Egypt. His presentation is whimsical, designed to suggest an unexpected entry into history. Jane Yolen's *Devil's Arithmetic* (1990) similarly uses fantasy, this time to suggest the meaning and significance of the past. The protagonist, bored with yet another Jewish Seder dinner, protests that she does not want to hear the same old stories. Only when she is transported back in time to the Holocaust does she begin to understand how the traditional stories of suffering and rescue keep her family and her people alive.

Writers of historical fiction have also turned to folklore to craft a compelling tale. Jane Yolen's *Briar Rose* (1992) uses the story of Sleeping Beauty as a metaphor for the Holocaust, arguing that the fairy tale has the ability to tell terrible truths in meaningful ways. She uses the fairy tale as chapter counterpoints placed at the beginning of several chapters, making it possible for the reader to see where the fairy tale fits with the historical story. The narrative of the Holocaust is told through the grandmother's tale, which is not a first-person account but a version pieced together by a curious granddaughter. Placed in conjunction, the two tales convey a single universal truth: the darkness of the human heart.

Such hybrids remain within the arena of historical fiction because their primary purpose is deliberately to create historically accurate representations of another time, another place. Though they may borrow heavily from other genres, they are still committed to accurate portrayals of the historical period. The borrowed elements add to the depictions by offering another way in to the truth of the material.

A novel of historical fiction needs to create characters whose attitudes and assumptions mirror those of their culture. But how should a writer deal with attitudes antithetical to contemporary beliefs and understandings?

It is easy enough to say that historical fiction should reflect the values of the age and culture being written about. Part of what a writer is trying to accomplish is to recreate a particular society's view of life and the world. What is admired and honored in a community? How are the elderly treated? What is the place of women in the society? Who has the power in the culture and what checks are on it? How is life valued? What is the nature of the culture's spiritual life? Writers research these attitudes and faithfully reproduce them in the context of a novel.

But what if the characters' attitudes are abhorrent to a contemporary North American society? Imagine if the character is a young child growing up in Nazi

Germany. Should that character uncritically reflect the anti-Semitic mindset of his time? Should the characterization of an antebellum slaveholder be presented without question, because the slaveholder himself would not question his beliefs? Should a young girl growing up in the South of the 1920s uncritically reflect that period's attitudes about African Americans?

Most books that include characters who hold such views also include a protagonist who reacts strongly against those commonly held views. In Paula Fox's *The Slave Dancer* (1973), young Jesse is kidnapped in order to play his flute on a slave ship; the slaves will exercise to his music. All around him are men who have no qualms about the slave trade, who see the slaves as mere chattel. But Jesse learns from his experience and is repelled by slavery. Once he comes to know one of the young slaves, he discovers a bond of friendship. Similarly, in Hans Peter Richter's *I Was There* (1972), the protagonist is caught up in the world of Nazi propaganda, and, though he will become a soldier in the war and a member of the Hitler Youth, he will react strongly against the horrors of Nazism.

However, a book like William Armstrong's *Sounder* (1969) presents a more difficult question. In this novel, the African American characters are placed in very subservient roles. We do not see them respond against those roles, caught as they are in the webs of prejudice and hatred that mark the time. The attitudes projected by the main characters are consistent with the period, and, in that sense, the book is indeed an accurate portrayal. But this portrayal raises an ethical question: Should books for children present African American characters in subservient roles? While the presentation may be historically accurate, the audience of the novel may not realize the error of the stereotyped views.

Another facet of this same problem appears in James Lincoln Collier and Christopher Collier's *Jump Ship to Freedom* (1981), in which the authors use certain language in order to capture the attitudes of Birdsey, who questions young Daniel, a slave, about money that his father earned fighting for the American cause during the revolution.

> "It was his army pay. He was six years fighting for that money."
> "Niggers can't own money," Birdsey said.
> "Sure they can," I said.
> He thought about that for a minute. "Well, free niggers, sure, they can own money. But not slave niggers. How could a nigger own money if he can't even own himself?" (37)

The two authors explain in the afterward that the word *nigger* was used extensively during that time period; historical accuracy demands its use. They also note that they use the word to show a growth in the protagonist: At the beginning of the novel he uses the word to describe himself, but by the end he has a different vision of who he is and rejects the use of *nigger.* Thematically and historically, then, the word is appropriate. But, as with *Sounder,* one needs to consider audience. Will the use of that word suggest its inappropriateness to a child audience, or can the writer assume that that audience will have the discernment to catch the subtle thematic role of the term?

The writing of historical fiction raises the same issue as the writing of folklore: Can someone from outside the culture accurately and fairly re-create another culture for the reader?

As with folklore, the question of authorship and culture is a dilemma. Can outsiders write realistically about cultures of which they are not a part? The heart of the matter is that writers are unable to remove themselves completely from their own culture. Subjectivity isn't simply a personal word; it is a collective one. Even as the writer of historical fiction re-creates another world, he or she recognizes that assumptions held by his or her own culture will inevitably affect his or her vision of the period that is being re-created.

From *NightJohn* (jacket cover) by Gary Paulsen, illustrated by Jerry Pinkney. Copyright © 1993 by Lynn Braswell. Used by permission of Delacorte Press, a division of Random House, Inc.

Here is where writers such as Minfong Ho, Hans Peter Richter, and Mildred Taylor have been valuable in historical fiction; each of these is able to write from within the culture that he or she is re-creating. In *Rice without Rain* (1990), Minfong Ho uses her position in the culture to articulate the small details of traditional rituals. In *Roll of Thunder, Hear My Cry* (1976), Mildred Taylor recreates the oral quality of the tales that she herself heard as a child. In working from within, as it were, such writers are able to articulate assumptions with which they themselves have always been familiar. These assumptions about a culture are naturally made explicit by these inside writers. They encourage and enable readers to see and feel the texture of life in another culture.

Nevertheless, if historical fiction is able to speak to a contemporary North American society, it is able to do so not by fragmenting the human experience, but by speaking about its universality. Perhaps this is why a number of writers have had such success writing about cultures other than their own, having thoroughly researched those cultures. Novels like Ouida Sebestyen's *Words by Heart* (1979), James Lincoln Collier and Christopher Collier's Arabus family series, Gary Paulsen's *NightJohn* (1993), Graham Salisbury's *Blue Skin of the Sea* (1994), and *Under the Blood Red Sun* (1994)—all were written by authors outside the culture of the novel, but all have successfully captured that culture.

If historical fiction allows many cultures, many forgotten voices to speak, what does that suggest about the quality of truth in history?

All historical writing, including historical fiction, is written by a writer with a point of view. That means that that writing comes from a single lens, a single perspective. But historical events do not always affect only a single perspective; in fact, they rarely affect only one culture, one people. Historical fiction can show the multitude of peoples that are affected by any one event. In Avi's *The Fighting Ground* (1984), for example, we see the perspective of the revolutionaries during the American Revolution, the perspective with which most are familiar. But the novel also suggests the perspective of the Tories, who are ripped from their loyalties and their homes, and the perspective of the Hessians, who have no stake in the battles in which they are fighting. In being granted these multiple perspectives, the protagonist comes to new awarenesses about war itself. Avi has not suggested that the perspective of the Revolutionaries is untrue; he does show, however, that it is only one perspective among several.

Where one perspective dominates, others may be pushed into the background, or simply ignored. In this process, historical fiction in fact highlights what is true of all history—the writer inevitably writes from a limited perspective. In her *Witches' Children* (1982), Patricia Clapp gives readers only one reason for the Salem witch trials: Puritan girls who were psychologically repressed became bored. They wanted excitement and found that they could create their own by shrieking, fainting, and recounting "visions." When their elders take these histrionics seriously, the girls, in a frenzy of excitement, accuse more and more people of witchery. The role of religious belief in the Salem phenomenon is not explored in the novel, nor are any alternate possibilities examined. The whole truth of these trials includes additional aspects, but the point of view of the novelist curtails such exploration. The perspective is limited, as would be the perspective of any participant.

But, at times, that limited perspective can open up new understandings. Jane Yolen's *Encounter* (1992) gives a voice to the Taino culture, which was wiped out by the Spanish migration to the New World. The picture book tells the story of the New World's "discovery" from the point of view of one of its young natives. The meeting between two totally different cultures is presented visually through the imagination of the native culture. Thus, illustrator David Shannon's representation of Columbus's three ships makes them seem at first to be three huge birds, the vision in the narrator's dream; later, they appear as three large canoes. The Spaniards look like parrots, so that when the native chief presents them several parrots as a gift, he is joking with Columbus and his crew. The narrator notes that these strangers hide their feet as well as their bodies; even their chins are hidden with bushes of hair. The strangers' skin is "moon to my sun," and they have "darts that sprang from sticks with a sound like thunder that could kill a parrot many paces away." All of these details are seen through the perspective of the Taino culture, making the conclusion all the more poignant: At the end of the story, the narrator, now an old man, thinks longingly of the old days and the old ways; he sits staring at the ocean, dressed in white man's clothes, knowing that his culture has ended. The illustration shows him sitting on the stump of a tree in a forest that exists no more, an acrid land around him, a city in the distance, and himself literally fading away.

The story presents an alternative view to the common one of Columbus's glorious discovery. It does not negate the common view, but suggests the vision of another people deeply affected by what Columbus did.

Paul Fleischman's *Bull Run* (1993) groups several voices together in a single novel to suggest the multiple perspectives on the beginning of the Civil War. Readers hear from stable boys, generals, slaves, families who send their men to war, and children in the war, giving a sense of the number of disparate personalities who took part in the battle. This story is not just presented from the viewpoint of the victors. The resultant picture, a crowded one with many participants seemingly speaking at once, asks that its readers listen carefully, filtering the information through their own minds, and coming to individual conclusions about the meaning of so many competing voices.

In works such as these, the writer asserts that history has no single truth, that truth often depends on the perspective of the teller, that every historical tale has multiple sides, multiple understandings. In short, history is not merely fact, but interpretation of fact.

Are there historical facts and events too harsh for children to read about? Should history be given in all of its bare realism, or softened for the child audience?

The issue for historical fiction for a child audience is whether a subject presented in graphic fashion is appropriate for the audience. As with writers of all genres, writers of historical fiction must consider their audience. What kinds of subjects are appropriate for children? How should those subjects be handled? Should children bear the devastating details of history, or should they be sheltered from them for a time?

Paula Fox's *The Slave Dancer* (1973) tells of the Middle Passage: the terrible thirst, the stacking of bodies, the stench, the abuse, the throwing of the slaves to sharks. What saves the book from mere horror is that the action and response is always mediated through Jesse, who reacts with horror equal to the horror around him. That mediation creates some distance. In this way the book is a more effective presentation to a child audience.

One way for the writer of historical fiction to mitigate the harshness of the past is to provide a mediating voice and consciousness that has suffered through the events and now comes to tell their meaning. In this sense the events, horrible as they might be, do not lead to despair, but hope. At least one person has survived to make sense of it all. Katherine Lasky, in *The Night Journey* (1981), creates a teenager bored with her family and life in general. She becomes interested in Nana Sashie's stories of escape from Russia in the 1900s. As she listens to the story of Sashie's escape underneath crates of chickens while the family gold is hidden inside freshly baked cookies, the stories become vivid for Rache, and eventually she can imaginatively identify with Nana Sashie's memories. Rache learns that yesterday can seem closer than today, and that forty years can seem only a month. But the high emotion of the escape is mediated. Rache's connection with the past is real but without the harsh physical realities of those earlier hurts and emotional pains.

Sheldon Oberman, in his *The Always Prayer Shawl* (1994), illustrated by Ted Lewin, will not be as explicit as Feelings in his presentation; he mediates the action through the context of the family. This story of a Russian Jewish family's survival of the oppressive tsarist regime concentrates on the hope, love, and tradition of the family. The threat of the tsar is suggested through the presence of soldiers in many of the early illustrations; they are not mentioned in the text, but loom over the early action, present but not overwhelming. The grandfather who cannot leave Russia gives his grandfather's prayer shawl to his grandson as a gift of continuity. Adam, the grandson, replies, "I am always Adam and this is my always prayer shawl. That won't change."

However, many things do change. Adam grows up, marries, raises a family—but he keeps the prayer shawl. He adds new material when it is worn, puts on a new fringe and new collar. But when he changes and ages, he gives the shawl to his own grandson, also named Adam, who promises that he will give it to his grandson. The symbolic use of the name Adam, the first man, suggests that this story stands as a powerful testament to the survival of the Jews and their traditions, and that, for each new generation, those traditions are both newly experienced and a symbol of continuity with the past.

Michelle Magorian's *Good Night, Mr. Tom* (1981) is explicit in examining and presenting very disturbing details. During World War II, children from London are taken to the country so they can escape the Blitz. Young Willie is billeted with Mr. Tom. The two grow close, and, when Willie returns home, they both are devastated and promise to write. When no word comes, Mr. Tom, who has suspected that Willie's mother was abusing him, sets out for London to find him. He finally does, breaking down a wall with a warden to discover that Willie has been abused yet again.

> The small alcove stank of stale urine and vomit. A thin emaciated boy with matted hair and skin like parchment was tied to a length of copper piping. He held a small bundle in his arms. His scrawny limbs were covered with sores and bruises and he sat in his own excrement. He shrank at the light from the torch and made husky gagging noises. The warden reached out and touched him and he let out a frightened whimper. An empty baby's bottle stood by his legs (213).

The atrocity of this abuse is jolting; certainly some child reader would be deeply disturbed by this. And perhaps here is the center of the question. Whether a child reader can handle the difficulties of historical details depends on the age and maturity of the child, the relationship of the adult offering the book, the community in which both live, and the purpose for which the book is offered. In *Good Night, Mr. Tom*, Magorian is not simply playing the voyeur; she contrasts the abuse of Willie by his mother with the tender love of Mr. Tom, and, in the contrast, suggests something of the nature of a family.

If history is to be presented honestly, it cannot be prettified. If history is to be accurate, it may not be warped and manipulated so that the writer is presenting facts, but presenting them in such a way as to hide their import. Nevertheless, at the same time the writer needs to be aware that the audience is a child audience. This means that his or her handling of the details must take into consideration the levels of maturity children might have, their ability to understand and make sense of the story, and their ability to cope with the meanings of what has been presented. The story must be told in such a way and couched in such a context that this understanding and coping is possible.

In teaching about the past, how does historical fiction teach about the present?

The ancient writers of history believed that history should teach the young men of society how to live the moral, upright life. Facts were explicitly put to the service of teaching values to the next generation. Today, in an age when openly didactic literature is often seen as suspect, historical fiction does not presume to have as its primary goal the teaching of values. Nevertheless, much historical fiction does teach, in the sense that it communicates the nature, contexts, and values of another time, another culture. It allows that other culture to stand in opposition to our own, or perhaps as a complement. In doing so, the presentation of that other culture becomes in some measure a commentary on our own, at the same time that it suggests the universality of human needs and values. In short, historical fiction shows us ourselves by showing us the other.

In the Obadiah series, Brinton Turkle creates a young Quaker hero who looks at the world with a presumed religious sensibility. In *Obadiah the Bold* (1965), Obadiah declares his wish to be a pirate. When he discovers that they are robbers who walk the plank if captured, he loses his dream. That dream is sensitively replaced by his father with the story of his grandfather's bravery in rounding Cape Horn.

> "Which way is the Horn, Father?"
> "Away off yonder," Father said, pointing.
> "Farther than France?"
> "Much farther."
> "Someday I'll see it," said Obadiah.
> Father put his hand on Obadiah's shoulder. "I expect thee will," he said.

The affirmation between this father and son works on the particular level of the story; Obadiah is bold, and his father does recognize that he will travel and see the Horn. But the affirmation also works on the larger scale to show the continuity of human concerns, hopes, and wishes.

The illustrations in *Obadiah the Bold* are at their most powerful when depicting the storm in which Obadiah's grandfather showed his unusual courage. The small scale of the ship in comparison to the huge sky and ocean gives the reader a sense of what the captain and his crew underwent. The size of the illustration, the only one that completely fills the page, shows that this dream is not only acceptable to Obadiah, but every bit as dramatic and adventuresome as the piracy he had previously imagined. Obadiah also knows that he will pursue this dream with his father's support. Basic human desires for meaningful work and for good relationships remain the same no matter what the time period.

Paul Fleischman deals with this matter of universality in *Dateline: Troy* (1996), whose collages by Gwen Frankfeldt and Glenn Morrow push the connections between ancient and contemporary times explicitly. Fleischman retells the Greek myth of the Trojan War on the left side of each spread; the illustrators set modern newspaper headlines on the right side. The modern stories, left in their newspaper format and set against a bland background, join to carry the theme suggested by the Trojan War into a contemporary setting. For example, on one side is the story

Pointers for Teachers

Interactive Possibilities
- After reading a portion of the novel, allow students to choose a partner. Assign a character from the story to each pairing and ask them to find three examples of emotion that their character displayed during the story. Have them be prepared to identify those emotions and talk about why the character displayed them. Were they appropriate?
- After concluding a novel, discuss with the class the ways in which men, women, children, and the elderly were presented. Are these appropriate presentations in contemporary society?

Writing Possibilities
- Have the class work together on a project in which they create a newspaper for the time period from which the book comes. Bring several local newspapers to class and have students study them for their structure and parts. Choose the elements you want the newspaper to contain and assign different parts to small groups to create for the class paper. Be sure to give them the time to research the period and perhaps even to see newspapers from that period.
- Bring several eulogies from newspapers or books. Read these aloud and analyze the kinds of elements to be found in them. Then ask students to write a eulogy for any of the characters who have died in the narrative.

Hands-On Possibilities
- Choose a holiday that would come during the sequence of the novel. Research the ways in which people celebrated the holiday in that society and prepare a similar celebration for your classroom on the appropriate day. Assign groups of students to such concerns as food, decorations, entertainment, and gifts.
- Ask students to role-play a character from the novel. After choosing the character, students should develop the ways in which the character dresses, speaks, gestures, eats. In particular, the student should develop a model for how the character treats other people. Each of the students should be prepared to introduce themselves to the rest of the class as that character.

of Paris, the most beautiful of human beings, whose beauty earned him trouble when three goddesses demanded that he choose between the three of them. His judgment puts him in the same kinds of impossible situations readers see in the newspaper clippings: "Studies on beauty raise a number of ugly findings." The novel suggests that human nature is the same throughout the ages.

Writers of Historical Fiction

The writer of historical fiction is both a writer of fiction and a historian; those two roles are intimately and inextricably bound together. The writer creates the characters, the plotlines, and the appropriate settings. But the historian contributes the realism of the period, the mindsets that determine the plot, the historical events around which the plot twists and curves. The successful balancing of these two sides is essential to the success of a work of historical fiction.

Jacket cover for *The Witch of Blackbird Pond,* by Elizabeth George Speare. Copyright © 1958. Reprinted by permission of Houghton Mifflin Company.

Elizabeth George Speare (1908–1994)

Though Elizabeth George Speare wrote only four novels for a child audience, in each she was able to create vivid, startling characters who are strongly influenced by the various cultures from which they spring, but who are also, because of their strong natures, able to stand apart from that culture. Three of the books were set in pre-Revolutionary America: *The Witch of Blackbird Pond* (1958), *Calico Captive* (1957), and *The Sign of the Beaver* (1983). In each Speare depicted the period and the setting with precise and accurate detail, the kind of detail that comes of the observant eye of the historian. And, within the context of those details, Speare created characters who show historical moments from the inside out, allowing readers a glimpse of how figures in those settings might have reacted to the events that swirl about them.

In *The Witch of Blackbird Pond,* Speare tells the story of Kit, a young English girl from Barbados who must make her way in the cold New England north. She is slow to understand and accept the strange ways of these northerners. They sit in a cold church for hours, refuse to wear anything brightly colored, speak in riddles, and shun anything unusual. She is particularly frustrated with their slow acceptance of her ways, and puzzled by the unfounded hatred for the Quaker, Hannah.

Speare might have let the story be dominated by the witchcraft scare and trials that marked this period, and, in fact, these do play a role in the story. But, in focusing on Kit, Speare gives the reader an entry into the culture she is portraying. Just as Kit is, so is the reader an outsider to this world, and the reader's reactions to the Puritan severity might echo those of Kit. As she comes to understand and deal with that severity, so, too, does the reader, so that the historical event is perceived by both character and reader in a similar manner.

In *The Sign of the Beaver*, thirteen-year-old Matt has come to the Maine territories with his father; he will remain in the wilderness with their house while his father fetches the rest of the family. But when his rifle is stolen and the winter stretches on, Matt realizes that he will die unless he befriends the Native American folks around him. Once again, Speare avoids having the larger issues overwhelm the book by focusing on the developing friendship between Matt and Attean, a friendship that begins with reluctance but ends with closeness. It is this relationship, and not the larger issues, that dominate the novel. In this sense the reader sees the historical moment as Matt might have.

Speare's opening suggests her method.

> Matt stood at the edge of the clearing for some time after his father had gone out of sight among the trees. There was just a chance that his father might turn back, that perhaps he had forgotten something or had some last word of advice. This was one time Matt reckoned he wouldn't mind the advice, no matter how many times he had heard it before. But finally he had to admit that this was not going to happen. His father was really gone. He was alone, with miles of wilderness stretching on every side (1).

The focus here is on Matt and his mindset; the context is a vivid one, but it does not overwhelm the first impression the reader has of Matt, who is resourceful and trustworthy, independent and ready, but also, right now, lonely and a little afraid.

In *The Bronze Bow* (1961), Speare moves her setting to first-century Palestine. Daniel, an embittered orphan and zealot, comes in contact with a powerful historical figure: Jesus of Nazareth. Once again the temptation here would be to focus on the historical figure, but Speare instead focuses on Daniel, on his hatred of the Romans who killed his father, on his preoccupation with his sister's illness, on his own disenchantment with the outlaw leader. His search is a search for purpose and meaning, and, though Jesus figures prominently, Daniel is the protagonist who stays at center stage.

If mere historical fact takes over a character, readers are given a textbook-like accounting of disembodied events rolling but leaving little effect. The question to ask is what it was like to have been alive during a particular period; the answer to that question must be authentic in terms of the period and authentic in terms of the character. This allows the reader to experience the age and culture through the eyes and mindset of a participant in that culture. It is this particular quality that is so strong in Speare's work.

Leon Garfield (1921–1996)

Like Elizabeth George Speare, Leon Garfield creates a strong background set in a particular historical period. For Garfield, however, the setting is not pre-Revolutionary America, but eighteenth-century Britain, particularly centered around London, though he has also set novels in the Renaissance as well as the Victorian period. His are stories of intrigue and mystery, in which young protagonists are caught up in secret plots and must work out, not only their own escape, but somehow their own identity. In the process they encounter an exuberant adventure.

The opening of his *Smith* (1967) shows that Garfield is conscious not only of the details of the period, but most particularly of the language:

> He was called Smith and was twelve years old. Which, in itself, was a marvel; for it seemed as if the smallpox, the consumption, brain-fever, gaol-fever and even the hangman's rope had given him a wide berth for fear of catching something. Or else they weren't quick enough (7).

The language here, with its unconventional grammatical structures and its eighteenth-century references, evokes the period as much as the individual details. It also sets up the context within which the character must move.

The adventures of the novels recall the adventures of a Robert Louis Stevenson romance. In *Smith,* the young boy, a pickpocket, is given a home by a blind magistrate, only to be plunged into a murder mystery when that magistrate is killed and the blame placed on Smith himself. In *Black Jack* (1968), the villain of the title cheats the hangman's noose by inserting a silver tube in his throat, then enlists the young apprentice Tolly to be his accomplice. In *Devil-in-the-Fog* (1966), young George, part of a band of strolling players, is catapulted into danger when it is suggested that he is the long-lost son of a nobleman. And in *Jack Holborn* (1964), the young Jack finds himself in the company of a twin who has mistakenly exchanged places with his brother, a fierce pirate. The tales, sometimes macabre, sometimes uproariously funny, are always marked by high adventure.

As suggested by their plotlines, the novels are often explorations of identity, in which the young protagonist's task is to negotiate himself through the complex world as he tries to define who he is. In *Jack Holborn* this issue is at the very heart of the novel, as the protagonist sees two possibilities for a single identity—one good, the other evil—laid before him with startling clarity. It is left to him to resolve the tension.

The most complex and beautiful of the novels is actually a collection of twelve short linked stories entitled *The Apprentices* (1978). The stories are linked by their mutual exploration of sin and evil in the most dank and awful parts of the city of London; the evil is both corporate and individual, the fault of the city at large and the characters. But opening the sequence and appearing between the stories and in the conclusion is the lamplighter and his apprentice Possul; their presence takes on metaphorical meaning as they begin to throw light into the dark corners of the city. *The Apprentices* is a challenging read for a child, and, in its use of eighteenth-century linguistic structures, causes the plotline to be difficult, at times. But the overriding metaphor and the connecting characters bring what seems to be disparate into a joyful whole by the novel's conclusion.

Though Elizabeth George Speare, too, writes of young protagonists about to discover more and more of themselves, this theme of self-discovery is central to the work of Garfield. It is a theme that might also appear in a work of realism, as well as a work of fantasy. But in Garfield's work the theme is set off against a dramatic background with a cast of characters that might have stepped from a Dickens or a Fielding novel. That creates a sense of remoteness, of strangeness, that allows the self-discovery to go on in a highlighted manner, as the reader sees it occurring, not against the mundane background of the contemporary world, but against the high drama of eighteenth-century London.

James Lincoln Collier (b. 1928) and Christopher Collier (b. 1930)

The Collier brothers, the first a writer for children, the second a professor of history, first wrote together with *My Brother Sam Is Dead* (1974). Like other writers of historical fiction, the Colliers worked to produce a seamless text in which story and historical details are blended together. But they have a very different purpose than either Elizabeth George Speare or Leon Garfield. They wish to show the discrepancies of history, the fact that history is not black and white, that history may be told by many different voices. In *My Brother Sam Is Dead,* for example, they want to show the varying responses to the American Revolution. To that end, their description of the war is a description of unending privation. Resources are low because all of the soldiers—American and British—must eat. The narrator, Tim, has a father who is ambivalent about the war; he begins as a Tory, but is so offended by what he sees that he becomes ambivalent. The mother hates the war from the very beginning, knowing that it will bring only death and disruption. When Sam is put to death in a meaningless sacrifice for the theft of cattle—executed even though the general who condemns him knows he did not commit the crime but must suffer as an example—all violent action is condemned. "War is never fair," explains the general. "Who chooses which men get killed and which ones don't?" But the question is not enough left alone; the implied answer is that one should not have to choose at all.

The historical fiction of the Colliers is based loosely on real events, and this is true also of the Arabus family trilogy, which tells the story of an African American family whose participation in the war had seemed to promise release from slavery. In *War Comes to Willy Freeman* (1983), Willy must struggle to secure her family's freedom when her father, a slave, is killed fighting for the American side, but whose master refuses to keep his promise to free the family. (The plotline is based on a real Connecticut court case.) As in the work of Leon Garfield, the protagonist here struggles to establish self-identity, a struggle made infinitely more difficult by the culture around her.

The sequels to *War Comes to Willy Freeman* continue to follow extended branches of the family, and continue to explore the growth of self-identity within a culture that seeks to erase it. In *Jump Ship to Freedom* (1981), the authors base the plot on the enactment of the Fugitive Slave law, as Daniel struggles to escape from a ship bound for the West Indies, a ship that will lead him to slavery. In *Who Is Carrie?* (1984), a young servant girl who is befriended by Daniel tries to help him find how he might buy his mother's freedom; at the same time she struggles to understand some mysterious clues about her own past, her own family.

In each of these stories the writers use a point of view that has not often been heard: the point of view of the slaves who were not freed by the American Revolution. The words *revolution, freedom, libery, independence* take on new and unpleasant meanings here, as the reader encounters a new perspective and sees that history has not always been fully explored. Here are writers of historical fiction who strive very consciously to teach the reader something of the slippery nature of history itself.

Scott O'Dell (1898–1989)

Those who do not know the historical past, Scott O'Dell has written, live lives that are limited in their promise and vision. It is a sentiment that explains some of O'Dell's passion for the work that he has done in historical fiction, though it must be put together with his equal passion for story. In writing his many novels set in the Americas, O'Dell was chronicling his country's development for young readers, creating vivid and engaging stories of seemingly small, inconsequential folks who, in fact, founded this land. Though most of the stories are about characters who names are unknown, these characters, in their skills, endurance, and perseverance, take on epic qualities that make them larger than life; in fact, they become emblematic of the vastness of the land itself.

In order to make this work, O'Dell needs to ground his story in historical fact, and then create a vivid character and plot narrative that will draw the reader into his tale, so that the learning of history and the pleasure of the plotline become a single event. This, O'Dell claims, is an advantage when writing historical fiction for children; it allows the storyteller to avoid the sometimes dull predictability and tones of many history texts and, instead, allows the writer to be creative and dramatic. He writes that "history has a very valid connection with what we are now. Many of my books are set in the past, but the problems of isolation, moral decisions, greed, need for love and affection are problems of today as well" (1984).

Jacket cover for *The Island of the Blue Dolphins,* by Scott O'Dell. Copyright © 1960. Reprinted by permission of Houghton Mifflin Company.

The question for O'Dell is how to create that kind of identification. Certainly one way in which he chooses to do that is to create an admirable character who dares greatly and who overcomes greatly. In *Island of the Blue Dolphins* (1960) and *The King's Fifth* (1966), O'Dell uses two historical figures, neither well known, to tell tales of extraordinary endurance and survival. The first is set on an island off the California coast; here Karana, left behind when her tribe leaves, survives alone for eighteen years, fighting rounds of natural enemies and establishing the routines of survival. In *The King's Fifth*, Estaban struggles with the trials of conquering what he hopes are cities of gold, as well as with his own inner turmoil about what he is doing. In each, a vivid protagonist calls towards identification.

O'Dell works towards that identification through a first-person point of view. A work like *Sing Down the Moon* (1970), about the destruction of the Navaho nation both by Spanish slavers and the U.S. army, O'Dell uses the voice of Bright Morning to focus the reader on the forced hardships, as well as to suggest the strength and resilience and perseverance of a single individual. It also allows O'Dell to suggest some of the greatest yearnings of this people: "I stood alone in the orchard, where the peaches grow. It was a miracle. Yesterday there was nothing to see save bare trees and wide stretches of yellow sand. In one night everything had changed. The trees had begun to bud and the sand lay deep under blue, rushing water" (8). This kind of voice allows the reader of historical fiction access to the past, suggesting the fullness and humanity of characters. O'Dell similarly uses this technique in *Sarah Bishop* (1980), a novel set during the Revolutionary War. Again O'Dell uses a historical figure and the first-person point of view to trace the abandonment of civilization that Sarah Bishop is forced to undertake. The poignancy of her losses comes through this voice, as well as her intense hopefulness.

To create identification, O'Dell normally avoids using a prominent figure as his protagonist, though in *Streams to the River, River to the Sea* (1986) O'Dell used Sacagawea to tell her own story, depending on the first-person narrative to overcome the barrier of using a well-known historical person. More often he uses unknown figures, or figures who are connected to significant people. In *The Serpent Never Sleeps* (1987), for example, O'Dell centers the character of Serena, who flees first to Bermuda, then to North America, and comes to know Pocahontas. It is this friendship that leads Pocahontas more and more into the English world, until finally she converts to Christianity, wears English clothing, and marries an Englishman. Nevertheless, Serena keeps center stage, and the child reader sees Pocahontas through her eyes. In creating this sense of identification, O'Dell has used story to convey history; but he is first a storyteller, and it is the vivid tales of history that most attract him, and that he fully develops.

Mildred Taylor (b. 1943)

In *Song of the Trees* (1975), Mildred Taylor introduced Cassie Logan, the narrator of this novel and future novels about her family. An African American family living in the South, they face terrible persecution, terrible injustice, terrible prejudice, but they face it all together. The story and its sequels are paeons of praise to the strong family that is centered in its traditions and stories, and that is committed to each member. The strength of that family unity is what allows Cassie and her brothers to refuse to accept the culture's vision of them as inferior.

In *Roll of Thunder, Hear My Cry* (1976), Cassie discovers that her own vision of herself does come into conflict with that of the culture, and that the culture is powerful and threatening—as well as threatened. Messages are sent to Cassie in a multitude of ways: She must get off the sidewalk when a young white girl passes, she must refer to a white girl as Miss, she must accept the most damaged books in the school system. But larger threats come as well, threats that threaten their very lives.

These same kinds of threats continue in the sequels, *Let the Circle Be Unbroken* (1981) and *The Road to Memphis* (1990). In each the characters struggle with the injustice that is constantly being thrown in their way, and they are able to overcome that injustice through the union of their family. In *The Road to Memphis*, however, Cassie is now older, and, for the first time, she must confront injustice without the strong help of her father. It is his legacy that allows her to help a young boy escape from vigilante terror. In later books, Taylor turned back to the younger days of Cassie.

In *The Friendship* (1987), she created a relationship between two men, one African American and old, the other white and young; it is a relationship that breaks apart when one demands the sign of respect the other refuses to give. In *The Gold Cadillac* (1987), Taylor wrote of the fierceness of stereotypes and prejudice, a theme also played out in *Mississippi Bridge* (1990), in which an African American woman is forced to yield her seat on a bus that later plummets over a bridge. In *The Well* (1995), Taylor went to the youth of Cassie's father to tell a story of rivalry and prejudice, in which African American boys are placed in the humiliating position of allowing an injustice to occur in order to prevent further injustice.

In all of these works, Taylor writes of such injustices. Though she creates several white characters who refuse to participate in such injustice, she is more concerned with how that injustice affects the family, and how the family responds. In the case of the Logan family, the inevitable response is one of love, strength, and unity, elements that enable them all to withstand the difficulties they face.

Taylor's stories come out of her own past. "From my father the storyteller," she writes in the preface to *Roll of Thunder, Hear My Cry,* "I learned to respect the past, to respect my own heritage and myself" (vii). Certainly the events of the stories of her own past are here, and the terrible and frustrating prejudice that the family must deal with gives the plotlines a strong driving rhythm. But, more important, in some ways, is the presence of the strong narrative voice, a voice that echoes that of her father and speaks of the past to the present and to the future. It is the voice from the front porch, from the Sunday dinner table, from the oak tree, from any situation where a family gathers to express its unity and connectedness.

Uri Orlev (b. 1931)

Because the Israeli writer Uri Orlev sets his stories during the Holocaust, he must deal with the issue of history's violence and horror. He does this by creating very real characters—his tales are usually based quite closely on true events—and then by focusing not so much on the horror as on the suspense of the event, thus drawing the reader in. In *The Man from the Other Side* (1991), for example, Orlev tells the story of the Warsaw Ghetto uprising, using the secret of the narrator's birth to at first keep the narrator as "other," and then to draw him intimately into the event.

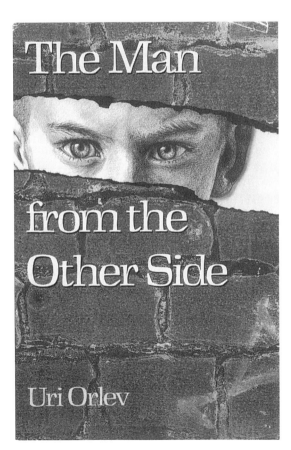

Jacket cover for *The Man from the Other Side,* by Uri Orlev, translated by Hillel Halkin. Copyright © 1993. Reprinted by permission of Houghton Mifflin Company.

Orlev begins in the sewers, where Marek's stepfather, who smuggles food to the Jewish ghetto, now wants to enlist Marek's help: "My mother was dead set against it, because she thought it was too dangerous. With my ear pressed to a hollow in the wall through which I could hear them better, I felt a twinge of fear. I had always pictured the sewers as a ghastly underground world beneath the streets and houses of the city, the closest thing to hell I could imagine" (5). The suspense is already established, as is the boy's sense of fear. By putting the narrative in Marek's voice, Orlev will try to express the scenes of the sewer vividly: water up to the waist, the residue, the rat-infested gloom, the friend's voice that suddenly turns into the call of an enemy. All of this is only a prelude to the scenes in the ghetto, where sad faces of starving children—as opposed to those who still have the money to buy

Marek's food—present a powerful picture. The chaos, the dirt, the inhumanity, the orthodox believer mixing with the Gentile—all are given a color in Orlev's palette.

The writer of historical fiction must not only paint a setting, however, but give a sense of the ethos of the place. Here, Jews are seen as less than human, a rationalization that allows others to make money from their misfortune. Marek shares in this to a point, but, when his stepfather reveals that Marek's own father was Jewish, Marek sees the world in a wholly different light; he begins to help those trapped in the ghetto, even hiding a refugee for a time. It is this refugee—Josef—whom Orlev uses to suggest not only the plight of those in the ghetto, but the need for Marek—and the reader—to respond. The first-person narrator engages the perceptions and perspective of the reader, so that both reader and character are forced to make certain kinds of decisions.

Thus, when Josef returns to fight in the uprising—Marek smuggles him back into the ghetto—Marek too choses to become part of that hopeless fight. He learns that men and women must fight for what they believe, for who they are, despite costs.

Orlev also uses the Warsaw Ghetto in *The Island on Bird Street* (1984). The protagonist is an eleven-year-old boy whose mother has already disappeared sometime ago and who now faces his father's disappearance. When Alex tentatively asks for help from former neighbors, they will not even share the crust of bread that they have stolen from his own house. Alex retreats to the site where his father had hoped to meet him, the house on Bird Street, and there, alone but for his mouse, he lives through the long winter, cold, hungry, sustained by the belief that his father will return. He fends off looters, finds food and water for himself, and hides from the Germans.

The novel moves closer and closer to despair, as Alex refuses to leave and finally runs out of kerosene. When, by accident, his quilt catches on fire, it is clear that Alex has reached the end of his resources. And then, unbelievably, his father does return. The implausibility of the ending may offend, but in fact the story is based on a true one, in which the father and son did reunite and then join the resistance.

At issue here is the nature of the historical world into which Orlev brings his readers. It is a world of horrible pain and suffering, of senseless and awful cruelty and violence. But, in the middle of this situation, Orlev places characters who react with strength and nobility; one way to read his novels is to see them as triumphal hymns of the human spirit in a world gone mad.

Karen Cushman (b. 1941)

In faithfully re-creating the worlds of medieval England and California during the Gold Rush, Karen Cushman has put strong female protagonists in the swirl of events. Though those protagonists act out of and accept much of the mindset of their surrounding culture, they are also strong enough to stand against parts of it. It is in the interplay of acceptance and tension that Cushman forges her plotlines, as characters who are thoroughly medieval, for example, struggle against aspects of the medieval culture. In doing this, they display a sensibility that would not be foreign to a contemporary reader.

In Cushman's first novel, *Catherine, Called Birdy* (1994), Catherine writes a journal to describe her life in the late thirteenth century during a period when her father, whom she despises, is trying to marry her off. There is much that she rebels against in her world. She would like to be a scholar, a Crusader, a doctor, a monk, a *jongleur*, but none of these options are open to her as a woman. Part of a noble house, she must marry, but she refuses to blithely accept that fate, or the choices of her father, and in hilarious scenes subverts her father's suitors again and again. In all of this she stands against her world. But, at the same time, she is thoroughly a part of it. It is clear throughout the novel that her closest soulmate, the one person she might love, is Perkin, the goat boy. But, because he is a goat boy, it never occurs to Catherine that she might love him, that she might marry him. The assumption of her class status is too large to allow for such an idea.

The novel is an evocation of the late thirteenth century, but Catherine herself dominates the text with her energy, her wit, her astonishing and funny narrative voice: "Last night I tucked a pin into an onion and put it under my pillow so I would dream of my future husband. I dreamed only of onions and in the morning had to wash my hair. It near froze before it dried" (57). Catherine's journal reflects her desire for a better life and her refusal to allow the rules of society to govern that life. Her struggle against marriage is one she must lose, she knows, but in her struggle she becomes a humorously noble figure, strong in her defiance and vivid in her wide-ranging fascination with her world.

In *The Midwife's Apprentice* (1995) Cushman opens with a very different kind of narrative voice.

Jacket illustration for *The Midwife's Apprentice,* by Karen Cushman, illustration by Trina Schart Hyman. Copyright © 1995. Reprinted by permission of Clarion Books.

When animal droppings and garbage and spoiled straw are piled up in a great heap, the rotting and moiling give forth heat. Usually no one gets close enough to notice because of the stench. But the girl noticed and, on that frosty night, burrowed deep into the warm, rotting muck, heedless of the smell. In any event, the dung heap probably smelled little worse than everything else in her life—the food scraps scavenged from kitchen yards, the stables and sties she slept in when she could, and her own unwashed, unnourished, unloved, and unlovely body (1).

Here Cushman has evoked a very different kind of girl, and one who is not speaking in the first-person. The scene is vivid and dramatic, and, though the young girl is the center here, the setting is still used to evoke the period, most particularly through the language.

This time the young protagonist—Beetle—is not as strong as Catherine, and certainly not in the kind of position Catherine occupies. But, like Catherine, she stands against the way the culture has chosen to view her. She struggles to become a midwife herself, and, despite a terrible failure, she is able to overcome her sense of worthlessness and resolve to try again, even when it seems the midwife to whom she is apprenticed will not have her: "Jane Sharp! It is I, Alyce, your apprentice. I have come back. And if you do not let me in, I will try again and again.... I will not go away" (116). Here, too, the focus is on the growth of the individual, though that growth comes about quite clearly from within the medieval culture.

The result of this focus is Cushman's strong message that, despite the strangeness and otherness of another culture, another period, people do not change. The needs of Catherine and Beetle/Alyce to be accepted for who they are and not to be defined entirely by the larger culture are needs that are shared by the contemporary child as well.

In *The Ballad of Lucy Whipple* (1996), Cushman again sets a strong female protagonist in a riotous time, but this period is California during the years of the Gold Rush. When Lucy's mother takes her family to California to find a life, Lucy—who is also a narrator who speaks in the first person—refuses to accept her fate, though she is dragged along. Much of the novel is taken up with her horror of the chaotic, mostly male world around her. She is resolved that she will return to Massachusetts. But, by the end of the novel, she has come to find a place in the small mining town that is itself struggling to establish an identity. When the opportunity finally does come for her to leave, she stays and founds a library, having made her own choice and having established her own personhood.

Cushman's novels are funny, moving, deadly serious, raucously vaudevillian examinations of a character in the middle of change, both in her own life and that of her culture. Each of the protagonists' goal is to find her own individual way, and not to be defined otherwise. It is a concern shared by children of any period, and, though the working out of that concern is here set in distant cultures, that distance helps to clarify the struggle.

Thinking and Writing about and from within Historical Fiction

Thinking and Writing about the Genre of Historical Fiction

1. Choose a work of historical fiction and examine the sources the writer used for his or her research. How does the writer use those sources? How does the writer find a means to make sources that may seem as dry as dust work in a novel to create a lasting impression?

2. Choose a work of historical fiction about an event or period that some might find inappropriate for a young child. In a letter to the school board, explain why that

book should or should not be included on the shelves of the school library or of the public library.

3. Read *Johnny Tremain* by Esther Forbes. Written in 1943, the book is marked by patriotism, willing sacrifice, and an eagerness for revolution. Johnny gives up personal relationships for a cause, and watches his close friend die, so that "a man can stand up." Coming as the story does during World War II, readers understand the optimism and the call to arms, as well as the call to sublimate the personal in favor of the corporate. Is this a book still valuable to today's contemporary audience? If you were to teach it, would it be with certain caveats, or with full approval? Write a report on the book that you will present to other teachers in your grade as you plan a semester's work.

Thinking and Writing from within the Genre of Historical Fiction _____

1. For her *A Gathering of Days* (1979), a novel set in the 1830s and written as a journal, Joan Blos researched the actual sites of the events by reading old county and courthouse records, letters, newspapers, and history books. She conducted interviews and visited local museums, as well as investigating libraries and historical societies. Using primary sources—autobiographies, letters, diaries, songs, poetry, newspapers, town records, public hearing transcripts, speeches, trials, almanacs—come to an understanding of a setting and period in North America. And for this, understand not just the important people and events of the age, but the people and events of common life. Having done this, write a work of historical fiction that will function as the text for a picture book.

2. Research your hometown's history, using as many local sources as possible. Be sure to include interviews, if appropriate, and a visit to the town's historical society and museum. Having chosen a date, tell a story of a young child who is just coming into the town. Perhaps, if the town is on the coast, the child will be an immigrant. Perhaps, if the town is in the middle of the continent, the child will be coming with a pioneering family.

3. Choose an issue that has some currency today: a nation's willingness to go to war, moral decline, the role of religion in corporate life, the place of sport in a culture. Examine that same issue in another historical and cultural setting, and outline the chapters of a novel in this genre that uses that issue as a central theme.

Selected Bibliographies

Works Cited _____

Armstrong, William. *Sounder.* New York: Harper and Row, 1969.

Avi. *The Fighting Ground.* New York: Lippincott, 1984.

Bellairs, John. *The Trolley to Yesterday.* New York: Dial, 1989.

Blos, Joan. *A Gathering of Days: A New England Girl's Journal,* 1830–32. New York: Scribners, 1979.

Bunting, Eve. *Dandelions.* New York: Harcourt, Brace, 1995. Illustrated by Greg Shedd.

Clapp, Patricia. *Constance: A Story of Early Plymouth*. New York: Lothrop, Lee and Shepard, 1968.

———. *Witches' Children*. New York: Lothrop, Lee and Shepard, 1982.

Clements, Andrew. *Temple Cat*. New York: Clarion, 1996.

Cooney, Barbara. *Hattie and the Wild Waves*. New York: Viking, 1990.

Curtis, Christopher Paul. *The Watsons Go to Birmingham—1963*. New York: Delacorte, 1995.

Fleischman, Paul. *Bull Run*. New York: HarperCollins, 1993.

———. *Dateline: Troy*. Cambridge: Candlewick, 1996. Illustrated by Gwen Frankfeldt and Glenn Morrow.

Forbes, Esther. *Johnny Tremain*. Boston: Houghton Mifflin, 1943.

Fox, Paula. *The Slave Dancer*. New York: Bradbury, 1973.

Garland, Sherry. *The Lotus Seed*. New York: Harcourt, Brace, 1993. Illustrated by Tatsuro Kiuchi.

Hermes, Patricia. *On Winter's Wind*. Boston: Little, Brown, 1995.

Ho, Minfong. *The Clay Marble*. New York: Farrar, Straus, 1991.

———. *Rice without Rain*. New York: Lothrop, Lee and Shepard, 1990.

Johnston, Tony. *The Wagon*. New York: Tambourine, 1996. Illustrated by James Ransome.

Lasky, Katherine. *Beyond the Divide*. New York: Macmillan, 1983.

———. *The Night Journey*. New York: Warne, 1981.

Magorian, Michelle. *Good Night, Mr. Tom*. New York: Harper and Row, 1981.

McGraw, Eloise. *The Golden Goblet*. New York: Coward-McGann, 1961.

Oberman, Sheldon. *The Always Prayer Shawl*. Honesdale, PA: Boyds Mills, 1994. Illustrated by Ted Lewin.

Paterson, Katherine. *Of Nightingales That Weep*. New York: Crowell, 1974.

Paulsen, Gary. *NightJohn*. New York: Delacorte, 1993.

Reeder, Carolyn. *Grandpa's Mountain*. New York: Macmillan, 1991.

Richter, Hans Peter. *Friedrich*. New York: Holt, 1970.

———. *I Was There*. New York: Holt, 1972.

Rylant, Cynthia. *When I Was Young in the Mountains*. New York: Dutton, 1982. Illustrated by Diane Goode.

Salisbury, Graham. *Blue Skin of the Sea*. New York: Delacorte, 1994.

———. *Under the Blood Red Sun*. New York: Delacorte, 1994.

Sebestyen, Ouida. *Words by Heart*. Boston: Little, Brown, 1979.

Stolz, Mary. *Bartholomew Fair*. New York: Greenwillow, 1990.

Sutcliff, Rosemary. *The Eagle of the Ninth*. New York: H. Z. Walck, 1954.

Taylor, Theodore. *The Bomb*. New York: Harcourt, Brace, 1995.

Turkle, Brinton. *Obadiah the Bold*. New York: Viking, 1965.

Walsh, Jill Paton. *The Emperor's Winding Sheet*. New York: Farrar, Straus, 1974.

———. *Fireweed*. New York: Farrar, Straus, 1969.

Yep, Laurence. *The Star Fisher*. New York: Morrow, 1991.

Yolen, Jane. *Briar Rose*. Doherty Associates, 1992.

———. *Devil's Arithmetic*. New York: Viking, 1990.

———. *Encounter*. New York: Harcourt, Brace, 1992. Illustrated by David Shannon.

Works by Writers of Historical Fiction

Elizabeth George Speare

The Bronze Bow. Boston: Houghton Mifflin, 1961.

Calico Captive. Boston: Houghton Mifflin, 1957.

The Sign of the Beaver. Boston: Houghton Mifflin, 1983.

The Witch of Blackbird Pond. Boston: Houghton Mifflin, 1958.

Leon Garfield

The Apprentices. New York: Viking, 1978.
Black Jack. New York: Penguin, 1968.
Devil-in-the-Fog. New York: Pantheon, 1966.
Jack Holborn. New York: Pantheon, 1964.
Smith. New York: Penguin, 1967.
The Sound of Coaches. New York: Viking, 1974.

James Lincoln Collier and Christopher Collier

The Bloody Country. New York: Four Winds, 1976.
Jump Ship to Freedom. New York: Delacorte, 1981.
My Brother Sam Is Dead. New York: Four Winds, 1974.
War Comes to Willy Freeman. New York: Delacorte, 1983.
Who Is Carrie? New York: Delacorte, 1984.
The Winter Hero. New York: Four Winds, 1978.

Scott O'Dell

Island of the Blue Dolphins. Boston: Houghton Mifflin, 1960.
The King's Fifth. Boston: Houghton Mifflin, 1966.
Sarah Bishop. Boston: Houghton Mifflin, 1980.
The Serpent Never Sleeps Boston: Houghton Mifflin, 1987.
Sing Down the Moon. Boston: Houghton Mifflin, 1970.

Streams to the River, River to the Sea. Boston: Houghton Mifflin, 1986.

Mildred Taylor

The Friendship. New York: Dial, 1987.
The Gold Cadillac. New York: Dial, 1987.
Let the Circle Be Unbroken. New York: Dial, 1981.
Mississippi Bridge. New York: Dial, 1990.
The Road to Memphis. New York: Dial, 1990.
Roll of Thunder, Hear My Cry. New York: Dial, 1976.
Song of the Trees. New York: Dial, 1975.
The Well. New York: Dial, 1995.

Uri Orlev

The Island on Bird Street. Boston: Houghton Mifflin, 1984. Trans. Hillel Halkin.
Lydia, Queen of Palestine. Boston: Houghton Mifflin, 1993. Trans. Hillel Halkin.
The Man from the Other Side. Boston: Houghton Mifflin, 1991. Trans. Hillel Halkin.

Karen Cushman

The Ballad of Lucy Whipple. New York: Clarion, 1996.
Catherine, Called Birdy. New York: Clarion, 1994.
Matilda Bone. New York: Clarion, 2000.
The Midwife's Apprentice. New York: Clarion, 1995.

Works about the Genre of Historical Fiction

Adamson, Lynda. *Recreating the Past: A Guide to American and World Historical Fiction for Children and Young Adults.* Westport, CT: Greenwood, 1994.

Aiken, Joan. "Interpreting the Past: Reflections of an Historical Novelist." *In Only Connect,* Sheila Egoff, Gordon Stubbs, Ralph Ashley, and Wendy Sutton, eds., (New York: Oxford University Press, 1996): 62–73.

Blos, Joan. "Assessing Historical Fiction." *School Library Journal* (November, 1985): 38–39.

Bosmajian, Hamida. "Mildred Taylor's Story of Cassie Logan: A Search for Law and Jus-

tice in a Racist Society." *Children's Literature* 24 (1996): 141–160.

———. "Vastness and Contraction of Space in Little House on the Prairie." *Children's Literature* 11 (1983): 49–63.

Brown, Joshua. "Telling the Story of All Americans: Milton Meltzer, Minorities, and the Restoration of the Past. *Lion and the Unicorn* 11 (1987): 9–20.

Cai, Mingshui. "Variables and Values in Historical Fiction for Children." *New Advocate* 5 (1992): 279–291.

Clapp, Patricia. "Letting History Speak for Itself." In Charlotte F. Otten and Gary D. Schmidt, eds., *The Voice of the Narrator in Children's Literature* (New York: Greenwood, 1989): 269–275.

Corbin, Denee. "Bringing Social Studies to Life through Children's Fiction." *Social Studies Review* 311 (1991): 22–25.

Garfield, Leon. "Historical Fiction for our Global Times." *Horn Book* 64 (November/December, 1988): 736–742.

Goldman, James. "Selling American History." *Lion and the Unicorn* 6 (1982): 48–53.

Lasky, Katherine. "The Fiction of History: Or, What Did Miss Kitty Really Do?" *New Advocate* 3 (1990): 157–166.

Maher, Susan. "Laura Ingalls and Caddie Woodlawn: Daughters of a Border Space." *Lion and the Unicorn* 18 (1994): 130–142.

Miller, Miriam Youngerman. "'Thy Speech Is Strange and Uncouth': Language in the Children's Historical Novel of the Middle Ages." *Children's Literature* 23 (1995): 71–90.

Moore, Rosa Ann. "Laura Ingalls Wilder's Orange Notebooks and the Art of the Little House Books." *Children's Literature* 4 (1975): 105–119.

Natov, Roni. "Re-Imagining the Past: An Interview with Leon Garfield." *Lion and the Unicorn* 15 (1991): 89–115.

Rahn, Suzanne. "An Evolving Past: The Story of Historical Fiction and Nonfiction for Children." *Lion and the Unicorn* 15 (1991): 1–26.

Roop, Peter. "Profile: Scott O'Dell." *Language Arts* 61 (November, 1984): 50.

Rudman, Masha Kabakow and Susan P. Rosenberg. "Confronting History: Holocaust Books for Children." *New Advocate* 4 (1991): 163–177.

Russell, David. "Reading the Shards and Fragments: Holocaust Literature for Young Readers." *Lion and the Unicorn* 21 (1997): 267–280.

Self, David. "A Lost Asset? The Historical Novel in the Classroom." *Children's Literature in Education* 22 (1991): 45–49.

Tarr, C. Anita. "'A Man Can Stand Up': *Johnny Tremain* and the Rebel Pose." *Lion and the Unicorn* 18 (1994): 178–189.

Zornado, Joseph. "A Poetics of History: Karen Cushman's Medieval World." *Lion and the Unicorn* 21 (1997): 251–266.

11

Biography: The Telling of a Life's Story

The art of biography is the art of telling a life. It is the art of interweaving the stories of a single individual together with the stories of the world around him or her—the world both close in and far away—so that they become one story with several dimensions. It is the art of taking from among thousands and thousands a small, significant handful of details that can be shaped into a coherent story, for no one's life is totally coherent from one moment to the next, day in and day out. It is an art that must carefully balance the mixture of fact and story, so that the facts are true and verifiable and the story shows what those facts mean and signify.

Biography seems, on the one hand, to be the simplest of the genres: The writer only needs to go out and collect data, which is then narrated in the form of a story. But it is in the narration that the genre begins to complicate itself. Consider this passage from James Daugherty's *Abraham Lincoln* (1943):

> As he worked alone in the tall timber, Abe made his acquaintance with the forest singers and talkers. He listened to the woodpecker's drum and the redbird's rich note, the wood dove's melancholy cry, the cherry quail's "bob white," the harsh clamor of the crows, the blue jay's scolding whine, and the meadow lark's free ecstasy. He could read in the soft earth or snow shorthand autobiographies written by the deer, the wolf, and the ambling bear. He could say to the veined hands of the leaf multitude, I know you and all your family. He knew the good snakes from the bad, and dealt swiftly with the rattler and the deadly copperhead. (20)

The passage strikes the senses in several ways. Daugherty has captured the many sounds of the birds of the woods. He has not simply written that "Abe heard a host of songbirds as he worked in the tall timber." He has listed the specific birds with their specific calls. And Daugherty evokes images, both explicitly, as with the veins on the leaves, and implicitly, as with the suggested striking out against the rattlers and copperheads.

But how does this work as biography? On the one hand, the passage suggests the things that Lincoln would have seen and heard around him as he grew up. On the other hand, this is a biographer's interpretation of those sights and sounds, as well as an interpretation of Lincoln's reaction to them. Could Lincoln have said to the leaves, "I know you and all your family"? Possibly. But did he say such a thing? If so, it has never been recorded. Would he have agreed with Daugherty that the quail is "cheery" and that the meadow lark is a bird of "free ecstasy"? Again, possibly, but, if so, that reaction has not been recorded.

In short, Daugherty is like any biographer in that he is interpreting. No biographer is purely objective, without interpretation. In choosing certain facts, in presenting those facts in a certain order, in deleting facts judged to be less important, in suggesting the meaning for those facts, the biographer is interpreting. The biographer is always aware that he or she is creating a vision, an impression of a figure. The reader is obligated to be aware that what he or she is receiving is only that.

Boundaries and Definitions

In that biography is a work of nonfiction, it attempts, as accurately as possible, to portray the life of a figure. The biographer is obligated to historical accuracy, to precision of detail, to the recording of verifiable data. The biographer is working with facts that are matters of historical record, and, therefore, may not be fictionally construed.

In this sense, biography is not historical fiction. The biographer is not free to create entirely imaginative scenes and claim that they are true, at least true in the sense that the figures depicted actually said and did the things that are recorded in these scenes. Based on this criterion, the reader might question a scene in Ruth Belov Gross's *True Stories about Abraham Lincoln* (1990) in which Dennis Hanks comes to his sister's house to see the new-born child. When Abe starts to cry, Dennis hands him back to his mother, certain that the baby won't amount to very much. The scene reads like a family story, told down through the years. But, despite the title of the book, which suggests that the stories are all true, the text is not reassuring. Are their words recorded verbatim? Was Dennis's prophetic line real, or was it imagined ironically in later years?

Yet, like any family story, there is a kernel of truth here—the sense that Lincoln came from origins so humble that no one could seriously imagine that he would one day aspire to the presidency itself. In order to point out that kernel of truth, this biographer has been willing to use the imagination to fill in gaps, to create scenes and relationships as they might have been in order to make the larger point.

The art of biography is an art that gathers verifiable facts. Yet it is not an empirical art. The biographer is always at the task of using art not just to record facts, but to express truth.

At the beginning of *Homesick: My Own Story* (1982), Jean Fritz writes a foreword to express her idea of what she has written. It is, on the one hand, an autobiography, detailing the author's childhood in China. Yet, she found that as she became caught up in literal accuracy, in getting all the facts exactly in a row, she lost the life of the story. Abandoning the actual sequence of events, she wrote the tale of her childhood as a story. The events are all true events, in the sense that they actually happened, but they may not have happened in precisely the order or way that they are recorded in the work. "The people are real people; the places are dear to me. But most important, the form I have used has given me the freedom to recreate the emotions that I remember so vividly. Strictly speaking, I have to call this book fiction, but it does not feel like fiction to me. It is my story, told as truly as I can tell it" (7). The line between fiction and biography in this case is very blurred.

The same tension between literal facts and an artistic rendering of those facts to suggest their meaning holds true for illustrations in biographies, because illustrations interpret as well. When Russell Freedman chronicles Lincoln's life in *Lincoln: A Photobiography* (1987), he relies completely on contemporary photographs of Lincoln to illustrate his text, realizing that photographs themselves, as well as his juxtaposition of them, are interpretive. When, for example, Freedman groups several photographs of Lincoln taken during the war years to show Lincoln's aging face, he is interpreting the effects of the war on the president. When Ingri and Edgar D'Aulaire conclude their *Abraham Lincoln* (1939) with an illustration of Lincoln sitting back in his rocking chair to rest after the task of preserving the Union, they are interpreting his state of mind at the end of the war. They are not arguing that this is literally what he did; they are presenting a vision of what his life was about at that time.

Biography is not, then, encyclopedic. It presents factual details, but in such a way that the meaning of those details is apparent. So we come to this definition: The art of biography in children's literature is a narrative and illustrative art. It details the events and the world of a figure's life and interprets those events in such a way as to show their larger meaning and significance for the child reader.

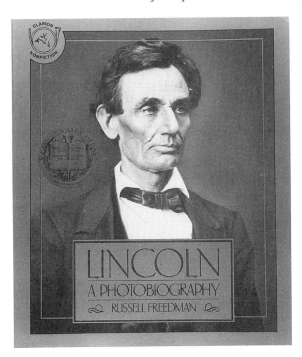

Jacket cover from *Lincoln: A Photobiography*, by Russell Freedman. Copyright © 1987. Reprinted by permission of Clarion Publishers.

Biography as Narrative

Biography is, first, a *narrative* art. The biography is, like any other narrative, a series of events that are brought together into a tale. However, no life falls naturally into a pattern; there are too many jerking, halting movements—or periods when there is no movement at all—to allow any writer to simply record what happened on a day-to-day basis and claim that he or she has written biography. It is the writer's task to select, delete, and arrange events so that, together, they move forward in telling a story.

This means that, like any story, biography needs some underlying structure that provides the context for all the events. Because this structure is rarely apparent—and perhaps not even existent—in a figure's real life, it is something that must be provided by the writer. In *Carry On, Mr. Bowditch* (1955), Jean Lee Latham tells the story of the famous New England mathematician and navigator by using the recurring theme of "carrying on" despite the obstacles placed in one's way. This structure is suggested by several phrases—such as "sailing by an ash breeze," meaning using one's own strength through oars rather than relying on the wind—but it is always underlying the events, so that the events Latham has chosen to include are not random, but brought together by the notion of persistence. Jean Fritz uses a similar technique in books like *Traitor: The Case of Benedict Arnold* (1981), *The Great Little Madison* (1989), and *Stonewall* (1979). In each she finds one persistent character trait that she uses to structure her narrative; all of the episodes she tells come back, sometimes explicitly, sometimes implicitly, to that character trait. This allows her to take seemingly random events and create a narrative from them.

The Role of Illustration in Biography

Biography in children's literature is also *illustrative*. One of the distinctions between biography for children and biography for adults is the strong dependence of the former on illustration; this need is more pronounced as the biography is aimed at a younger and younger audience. The illustrations must do more than decorate; they should be attuned to the vision of the figure of the biography that the biographer is trying to develop. They should add narrative information that is consonant with the author's interpretation of the figure. They should contribute to the establishment of a historical context. In their presentation, they should suggest styles with which the figure would have been familiar. In content and form, they must contribute to the telling of a life's story.

To fulfill this need, biographers have turned to a range of techniques. Russell Freedman, in books like *Lincoln: A Photobiography* and *Indian Chiefs* (1987), and Howard Greenfeld, in *The Hidden Children* (1993), depend almost exclusively on contemporary photographs. *The Hidden Children* chronicles the lives of several children who were hidden by Catholic families during the Holocaust, and Greenfeld chooses to illustrate their accounts with snapshots of them. Freedman depends on archival research for his texts, using photographs of events and figures that were taken at the time of his figures' lives.

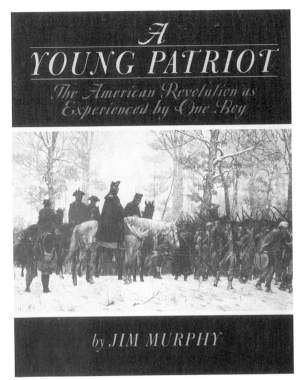

Jacket cover from *A Young Patriot,* by Jim Murphy. Copyright © 1996. Reprinted by permission of Clarion Books.

Jim Murphy also illustrates with photographs, but not all of his photographs were taken during the events they document. Instead, he photographs archival material to illustrate his narrative. In *A Young Patriot: The American Revolution as Experienced by One Boy* (1996), Murphy photographs old etchings and prints to tell the story of the Revolution in Massachusetts. Dennis Fradin's *Samuel Adams: The Father of American Independence* (1998), in addition to using pictures and documents contemporary to Adams, includes a series of contemporary images of Adams, all derived from a Copley painting, noting that each of the images—and many contemporary accounts—concentrates on Adams's striking eyes.

There are times, of course, when photographs are not available. Books like David Adler's *George Washington: Father of Our Country* (1988) and Alice Fleming's *George Washington Wasn't Always Old* (1991) are aimed at very young audiences, and it may have been that the illustrators would have decided that photographs were not appropriate for the age level they wished to reach. But in any case, none are available. They have used charcoal and pen-and-ink drawings to capture moments in Washington's life. *George Washington: Father of Our Country* focuses on the Revolutionary events in Washington's life, so the illustrations all seem posed, as though the characters are pausing for a moment in the midst of this important historical event so that they might be recorded. The effect is to give a kind of grandeur and weight to the illustrations. *George Washington Wasn't Always Old* is written in a much more playful mood, so the illustrations capture informal moments in Washington's childhood: his love of swimming, his horsemanship, and the pleasure of the race.

Ordering the Events

Biography is the recounting of *events in a figure's life*. There are two decisions a biographer makes as he or she decides on events. First, there is the question of selection. In choosing to portray a figure's life, the biographer must choose those events that are most significant in depicting the figure. This means that certain events may be chosen, others not chosen because they are judged to be less significant, or outside the vision of the figure that the biographer is trying to portray. In either case, the biographer is obligated to give fair, impartial judgments, not using the deletions or choices to bias the reader for or against a figure.

For example, in writing a biography of William Bradford, the biographer might want to stress the antagonism that developed among the native peoples against these colonists. Such a biographer might include episodes in which the Pilgrims stole native seed corn when they first landed at Cape Cod, or when the Pilgrims fought with a group of Nausets on the arm of the Cape, or when they attacked a group of Wampanoag Indians late one night, wounding three.

But if the biographer chose only those details, then he or she would have done an injustice to Bradford, and to the reader. The biographer should also include the fact that, six months later, the Pilgrims repaid the tribe from whom they took the corn, to mutual satisfaction, that the fight with the Nausets began over a misunderstanding and was settled peacefully, that the attack on the Wampanoags was an attempt to rescue Squanto, whom the Pilgrims thought had been murdered. If these details are ignored, then the image that the reader would take away from Bradford would be incorrect.

A number of children's biographies focus, not on an entire life, but on a single period in a figure's life, often to suggest the critical importance of a certain event or series of events in a figure's life. Leonard Everett Fisher uses this focused strategy in his *Prince Henry the Navigator* (1990), beginning the biography with Henry's twenty-first year, the time when he began serious navigational studies. Barbara Cooney examines Eleanor Roosevelt's childhood and adolescence in *Eleanor* (1996), showing how the terrible sadness and loss of her youth affected her understanding for those less privileged than her. And Kathryn Lasky's *A Brilliant Streak* (1998)—the title refers to Haley's Comet—recounts the childhood of Mark Twain, which Lasky portrays as lasting up until he became a writer and which provided him with the material for his later books centered on the Mississippi River.

This kind of strategic focus succeeds by using a small selection of events to suggest something about the whole of the figure's life. In her *More Than Anything Else* (1995), for example, Marie Bradby focuses on a few days in Booker T. Washington's childhood. She describes his yearning to read, as well as his first book (given by his mother, who could not read herself) and his first sense of the meaning of letters. The illustrations by Chris Soentpiet are dark, lit only in a small area by the bright light of a lantern, suggesting how this one skill—reading—will illuminate the darkness. In this focus, Bradby has said much about Washington's character.

But, in recounting a figure's life, the selection of details is not the only decision the biographer makes; the biographer must also decide on the ordering of those details. The most frequent order is, of course, chronological, but that is not the only ordering. Beverly Gherman, for example, begins her biography on the author of *Charlotte's Web*—*E. B. White: Some Writer!* (1992)—with a chapter about White's later life and successful career in journalism and children's books. In each case the biographer needs to find a way to order the details that is most suited to the vision of the figure that he or she is trying to present. All of the details in their combination must support the thematic principle that guides the biographer's sense of the figure.

The Context of the Figure's Life

In telling a figure's life, the biographer recognizes that no life—even the life of a hermit—exists in isolation; the biographer therefore places the figure's life in the *context of his or her world.* Whether a figure changes the world, challenges it, brings progress to it, works against its injustices—in all cases the figure affects and is affected by the world around him or her. The biographer needs to be able to articulate the nature of this context to give a full picture of the figure. It would be impossible, for example, to deal fully with William Bradford without discussing the Separatist movement that gave him so much energy and purpose.

Elizabeth Partridge's *Restless Spirit: The Life and Work of Dorothea Lange* (1998), for example, tells the story of Lange's difficult life, beginning with her strained family situation, her inability to effectively juggle her own family situation, and the drive that gave her art its edge and power. At the same time, Partridge cannot simply leave that life as if it were isolated, with no historical context. Thus, she is careful to set Lange's life and work within the context of the Great Depression in the opening two paragraphs.

> Dorothea Lange tightened her grip on the steering wheel and peered through the rain beating against the windshield. It was the end of a cold, miserable winter. She had been traveling alone for a month photographing migrant farmworkers in California. Now her camera bags were packed and she was heading home. On the seat beside her was a box full of exposed film, ready to be mailed back to Washington, D.C. Her time was up, and she was worked out, tired to the bone.
>
> It was early March 1936. The Great Depression and terrible dust storms in the Midwest had torn tens of thousands of farmers from their land. They had packed up a few belongings and come to California, driving battered old cars or pickup trucks, riding the rails, or tramping along the road, thumbing rides. Some came alone, but many brought families. They were looking for work, any kind of work, to keep from starving. What they knew was farming, so they headed for the rich agricultural fields of the West. (1)

The first paragraph focuses on Lange, using narrative to bring the reader directly into her story. The second paragraph provides context, the world within which Lange worked. Both are essential for a full, well-developed biographical account.

In *The Great Little Madison* (1989), Jean Fritz uses a very different technique. Instead of prefacing the book with the historical context, she interweaves the context with her telling of the life of James Madison. The first chapter, for example, opens with a focus on her main character: "James Madison was a small, pale, sickly boy with a weak voice" (7). The second chapter opens with a focus on the world in which he lived: "Americans had actually been at war a little more than a year when the Declaration of Independence was signed." (17)

In children's biography, providing the necessary context is often difficult, but most biographers acknowledge the necessity of this context. The difficulty comes in determining how much should be included, and in what detail. In writing *Homesick: My Own Story,* Jean Fritz had to struggle with the level of detail she would use in describing the political situation in China, given that she already had so much to discuss in telling her own family's story. In *Prince Henry the Navigator,* Leonard Everett Fisher had to struggle with the level of detail he would include about the spirit of travel and investigation that dominated Europe during the Renaissance. Should he include, for example, stories of similar voyagers who must have inspired Prince Henry? In *The Last Princess: The Story of Princess Ka'iulani of Hawai'i* (1991), Fay Stanley struggled with the inclusion of the detailed political maneuvering that threatened the independence of the Hawaiian islands, trying not to allow those details to overshadow her focus on the young girl who was at the center of her story, being sure that the details illuminated the life, and were not in the narrative for their own sake alone. And in *Friend: The Story of George Fox and the Quakers* (1972), Jane Yolen had to struggle with the amount of detail she would include about the very complex religious visions of the Quaker leader. How much time should she take to describe his notions of the inner light? In each case the biographer, aware of his or her audience, gauges the balance between the dramatic story of the individual figure and the contextual world of that figure.

The Interpretive Nature of Biography

In creating this balance, the biographer is aware that biography is *interpretive, not empirical work.* This means that the biographer is a writer who brings his or her own interpretive analysis to the events and details of a figure's life. When, at the beginning of *Make Way for Sam Houston* (1986), Jean Fritz writes that "All his life Sam Houston liked to do things in a big way or not at all" (9), she is interpreting the events of his life. Hope Irvin Marston, in writing *Isaac Johnson: From Slave to Stonecutter* (1995), wanted to tell a story about someone who overcomes the crippling effects of slavery, so she, too, interprets events: "Many slaves crumbled under the terrors of cruel slaveholders and bloodthirsty slave catchers. Isaac's determination to be a free man enabled him to escape the hardships that slaves endured. He rose above the indignities, the hopelessness, and the frustrations which his people suffered" (73). His determination is expressed as a character trait that motivates and explains his actions, according to Marston's interpretation.

The art of interpretation means that any two biographies of the same figure may be radically different. In James Daugherty's *Daniel Boone* (1939), Boone is a larger-than-life hero, almost a figure out of a tall tale. Daugherty's purpose is to suggest that Boone's life was the life of all North America in its pioneering drive westward:

> Boone's story was the story of a whole people. It had all their griefs and tragedies and restless longings and rich half-fulfilled dreams, all their ranging freedom and mortal bondages. It rang with the roaring laughter and boisterous fun; it was dark

with the unfathomable silent anguishes by new-made graves; it was full of lost hopes and dreams of grandeur. Through it rushed the winds and the voices of the valley, the vast Ohio valley. (52)

The large, superhuman vision here is Daugherty's interpretation of Boone's life. The grave diction, the clausal structure, the decorum of the piece all lend themselves to that vision. It is also complemented by the bold lithographs that illustrate the text, one of which envisions Boone almost as a god plowing out the new country.

In her *Daniel Boone* (1989), however, Laurie Lawlor is much more interested in interpreting Boone's life not on a national, but on an individual scale. Her interpretation suggests that Boone was not a tall tale character, but a brave, though flawed, pioneer. She notes, for example, the frequency with which he abandoned his family, sometimes for years on end. She details his sometimes murderous ways, a foolhardy episode that led to the death of Boone's son, and his courtmartial. Her goal in this interpretation is not simply to debunk, but to reestablish the humanity of the figure.

At times, the author of a biography has no choice but to interpret certain events, even to guess at certain elements of a subject's life. In such a case, the biographer should base these interpretations on solid factual knowledge about the culture and the characters with whom he or she is working. When, in *Behind the Mask: The Life of Queen Elizabeth I* (1998), Jane Resh Thomas writes of Elizabeth I's reaction to the execution of her mother by her father, she is careful to set the events within a certain stance:

> Elizabeth may not have known her mother well enough to miss her greatly when she died, for servants had tended the princess from the day she was born. Queens and other highborn women were considered above changing their children's diapers, guiding them, disciplining them. Anne had provided the child with fine clothing, but she had never cared for her physical needs. The women who breast-fed Elizabeth and kept her clean, who rocked her and put her to bed, were still with her. Whatever turmoil occurred around Elizabeth, even the death of her mother, the circle of people who loved her and tended her every day remained stable. She probably adjusted quickly.
>
> Nevertheless, the princess undoubtedly heard gossip about Anne and eventually drew her own conclusions about the execution. Her governess probably warned her that it would be prudent to distance herself from the woman who had been convicted of treason against the king; if Elizabeth ever mentioned her mother at all, for the rest of her life, she did so privately. (25)

There is much here that Thomas can never document: How did Elizabeth react? Had she known her mother well? Did she adjust? Had she heard gossip? Did the governess warn her? Did Elizabeth mention her mother at all? Thomas writes her interpretation, her version of the answers to these questions after she had established the strong cultural context of the period; she makes educated guesses about what must have happened. At the same time, she hedges her interpretation by using words like *may, if,* and *probably.*

This element of interpretation means that no one biography will exactly match another, and for children this is not an easy concept. After all, isn't the story of someone's life the same, no matter who tells it? But the teller is crucial. Any teller will have a unique interpretive vision. Any given biography is only one account shaped by the vision of one writer.

Two recent picture book biographies of Joan of Arc suggest this distinction. In *Joan of Arc* (1998), Josephine Poole wants to depict Joan as a saint, as someone who truly did hear voices that came from God. Everything in the work, including the details Poole chose to include or not include, inclines to this particular vision. Thus, in the scene depicting Joan's death, Poole focuses on the execution as a martyrdom.

> The Voices said, "Take all in good part, do not complain over thy martyrdom. By it thou shalt come at last to the Kingdom of Paradise."
>
> The English carried out the sentence. But it was an Englishman who, at the last, made her a little cross of wood, which she kissed and hid inside her clothes. So she died by fire, and the ashes of her body were thrown into the river.
>
> But that was not the end. A saint is like a star. A star and a saint shine forever.

The political side of the event is downplayed; instead, Poole elevates her focus on the religious implications of the event.

In contrast, Diane Stanley's *Joan of Arc* (1998) focuses on the political context of the event, and is marked by a much fuller use of historical details taken from the transcripts of Joan's trial to flesh out what is left quite bare in Poole's account.

> Joan was to go to her death in proper women's clothes, but on her head she was forced to wear a tall paper cap with the words *heretic, relapsed, apostate, idolatress* written on it. Under close guard, she was brought to the Old Market Square, where a restless crowd awaited the spectacle. There, frightened and heartsick, she endured yet another sermon. Then she knelt and began to pray aloud, begging God's mercy and forgiving those who had wronged her. Her terrible grief and devout words moved the crowd so deeply that "even several Englishmen...most bitterly wept at it." Others with harder hearts grew impatient. "Do you mean to have us dine here?" one shouted.
>
> Finally, for the second time, Cauchon pronounced Joan cast out of the Catholic Church and turned over to the state for justice. Then, without waiting for the sheriff of Rouen to sentence her, the guards hastily took her to the scaffold and bound her to the stake.
>
> Joan asked for a cross, so someone in the crowd tied two sticks together for her. A sympathetic priest hurried into the church and brought out the crucifix, which he held up to comfort her in her last, dreadful moments. When it was all over, the English had her ashes gathered and thrown into the Seine.

The scene is much more vivid in its detail than Poole's corresponding scene, not because Poole was a poor researcher, but because Stanley had an entirely different vision of what the biography was to be about. Stanley does not include the reassuring presence of the Voices—this is not within her focus—and ends with Joan on the scaffold facing "her last, dreadful moments."

Each biography is the vision of one artist. In that sense, each biography must be interpretive in its essence. If this means that no biography can be considered as utterly objective, it also means that biographers are enjoined to show their own interests, predilections, and imaginative, creative inclinations in the production of an artistic whole.

When a reader recognizes the interpretive quality of biography, then he or she has made an important leap. There is now a recognition that authors make choices, even in biographies, and that those choices must be analyzed. As a child reads biographies—particularly biographies about the same figure—he or she develops the kind of critical comprehension skills that allow for comparison and mature judgement.

The Balance of Fact, Meaning, and Significance

In addition to being interpretative, the writer needs to show *the meaning of the events* in a person's life. On a given day in the early 1900s, for example, Dorothea Lange walked by the studio of Arnold Genthe, on Fifth Avenue in New York. Impressed by his work, she went upstairs and asked him for a job. He immediately agreed. Now, if the biographer simply left these facts to stand, they would not mean much to the child reader beyond the simple narrative information. But in *Dorothea Lange: Life through the Camera* (1985), Milton Meltzer shows what those facts mean, noting that it was extraordinary for a woman to secure a job such as this, and the fact that Lange did secure one suggests something about her intensity. But the meaning of these facts goes even further, for they point the way to Lange's vocation: "He was a real artist, she thought. He made pictures that went below the surface. He showed the true character of the sitter. Here was someone who did what he wanted to do, and loved it" (12).

Closely allied to the question of meaning is significance: The biographer must show the child reader why *the life about which he or she is reading is significant* in some manner. Certainly, on the one hand, a biography is read for its narrative; biography functions like any story in presenting dramatic material in an engaging way. But, in addition, biography should show the reader why the life was important, and why it is worth considering today. At the beginning of her biography of George Fox, Jane Yolen writes that "though he was a product of the 1600s, he has much to say to us today.... His message of the Inner Light and the brotherhood of men is as timely now as when he first cried it in the wildernesses of England" (x). The biography, then, is not simply about a long-dead fellow with quaint religious ideas; it is about a man with a message that thunders down to the present day.

In recent years, a number of autobiographies have focused on the significance of events as they contribute to the life of the writer. In books like Beverly Cleary's *A Girl from Yamhill* (1988) and *My Own Two Feet* (1995), Marion Dane

Pointers for Teachers: Evaluating Biographies

- What makes the subject of the biography worth reading about?
- How does the author construct a complete picture of the subject? Is the subject a complete human being, with both strengths and weaknesses presented?
- How does the author present the culture and times within which the subject lived? Is the full culture represented in terms of its social, religious, economic, political, and artistic elements?
- What sources has the author used to investigate the subject? How would you evaluate those sources? Are those sources adequate? reliable? factual?
- How does the author address the question of dialogue? Does the author use only direct quotes, or are dialogues included that are likely but essentially constructed?
- How does the author use illustrations to support the text? What kinds of illustrations are included? Are they appropriate to the text and period? Are they contemporary to the period or modern representations? Which would be more appropriate to this period?

Bauer's *A Writer's Story: From Life to Fiction* (1995), Betsy Byars's *The Moon and I* (1992), Phyllis Reynolds Naylor's *How I Came to Be a Writer* (1987), Jean Little's *Little by Little: A Writer's Childhood* (1988) and *Stars Come Out Within* (1991), Gary Paulsen's *Wood-Song* (1990), Sid Fleischman's *The Abracadabra Kid* (1996), and Roald Dahl's *Boy: Tales of Childhood* (1984) and posthumously published *My Year* (1993), writers of children's literature have examined the ways in which their lives have been shaped by their desire to write as well as their need to write. Each of these writers works not so much to show the meaning of their own lives, but to show the child reader the meaning of the small, tiny details in one's life and how they lead to the choice of a vocation. The significance that these works try to make explicit is the importance of following the vocation.

The success of any biography for children lies in how well all of these elements come together.

Issues in the Genre of Biography

As a work of nonfiction, a children's biography serves the dual role of both telling a compelling story and conveying information in an artistic and effective manner. Many of the issues that emerge with the writing of biography lie on the interface of story and information. The biographer delights as well as informs, and the questions arise when the desire to delight overwhelms the desire to inform, or when the desire to inform neglects the desire to delight.

Are children's biographies limited in terms of their subjects? For example, are there inappropriate subjects for a children's biography? Are there limits to the kinds of details that can be used in a biography for children?

In general, there are no limits or boundaries on the subjects of a biography for children. In fact, recent years have seen an extraordinary widening of subjects to which biographers have turned. Recent series have focused on Western outlaws and gunfighters (Carl Green and William Sanford's *Bat Masterson* [1992] and *Wyatt Earp* [1992]) and women whose spiritual lives have governed and led to their accomplishments (Jennifer Fisher Bryant's *Lucretia Mott: A Guiding Light* [1996] and Beatrice Gormley's *Maria Mitchell: The Soul of an Astronomer* [1995]). Biographers have turned to world leaders in biographies like Leonard Everett Fisher's *Gandhi* (1995), Fay Stanley's *The Last Princess: The Story of Princess Ka'iulani of Hawai'i* (1991), and Diane Stanley and Peter Vennema's *Cleopatra* (1994); they have examined artists and writers in books like Keith Ferrell's *John Steinbeck: The Voice of the Land* (1986), Diane Stanley and Peter Vennema's *Charles Dickens: The Man Who Had Great Expectations* (1993), and Christina Björk and Lena Anderson's *Linnea in Monet's Garden* (1987). Recent biographers have examined great scientists (Leonard Everett Fisher's *Marie Curie* [1994]), aviators (Jim Haskins' *Black Eagles: African Americans in Aviation* [1995]), musicians (Patricia and Fredrick McKissack's *Louis Armstrong: Jazz Musician* [1991]), athletes (Patricia and Fredrick McKissack's *Jesse Owens* [1992] and *Satchel Paige* [1992]), and immigrants (Michael Cooper's *Bound for the Promised Land* [1995]). No area is automatically outside the boundary of children's biography.

Still, given that this is a literature defined by its audience, there are important questions to ask about the nature of the chosen subjects. For example, in that biography is obligated to suggest the significance of a life so that a child reader can perceive its meanings, one wonders if figures such as Dolly Parton or Martina Navratilova, both of which appeared in Puffin's "Women of Our Time" series, are significant enough to warrant a biography. Perhaps in some circles they are, but the question can be asked as to whether children are in those circles.

Additionally, it seems clear that historical objectivity and distance are important qualities of a biography. Without such distance, the biographer works very closely to the subject and finds it harder to sift through the clues that suggest the figure's significance. In writing a biography of a very recent figure, the biographer also runs the danger of giving what may quickly become an inaccurate picture. For example, soon after Corazon Aquino came to be the leader of the Philippines, expelling the Marcos family, two biographies were written about her life: James Haskins' *Corazon Aquino: Leader of the Philippines* (1988) and Laurie Nadel's *Corazon Aquino: Journey to Power* (1987). Using very contemporary sources, principally news journals, the two books glowed with praise for Aquino. They would have been different books had they been written several years later, following an administration that was fraught with ineptitude and corruption. Read today by a child reader, they would present an inaccurate view of Aquino's presidential role.

An issue related to the choice of subject is the choice of details that might be judged to be unseemly. Is a biographer writing for children obligated to relate those details about a figure's life that suggest the figure's weaknesses, moral lapses, or errors? In the days when biographies were seen principally as the telling of stories of lives that were to function as role models, including such details would have been a problem, given that they would detract from the figure's stature. Stewart Edward White's *Daniel Boone: Wilderness Scout* (1922), for example, was a book formally approved by the Boy Scouts; it depicts Boone as a man who has all the skills for which a scout should strive: resourcefulness, independence, preparedness, woodcraft. But the book never mentions the kinds of flaws that Lawlor examines in her biography; such details would have been inconsistent with the purpose of the book: to present Boone as a model for behavior.

However, hiding or omitting such details may skew the presentation of a life, so that the figure may seem to be heroic, almost Olympian, with absolutely no flaws that suggest the reality of his or her humanity. Jean Fritz led the way, showing that her figures were real humans, not only by discussing their character traits—traits such as John Hancock's inordinate desire to be noticed, in *Will You Sign Here, John Hancock?* (1976)—but also by including details that other children's biographers might not have included. If such material is included merely to debunk, or to mock, or to titillate the reader, then the inclusion of such material seems inappropriate. But, if the material is cast in such a way that it is comprehensible to a child reader, and if the material is important for an understanding of a character's motivations and actions, then it may be appropriate. In writing of the marriage of Franklin and Eleanor Roosevelt in *Eleanor Roosevelt: A Life of Discovery* (1993), Russell Freedman shows Eleanor discovering the love letters that revealed the affair between Lucy Mercer and Franklin Roosevelt. But the story is not there simply to demean; it is there to explain some of the reasons for the ways in which Eleanor and Franklin arranged their married lives from that time on. The detail is there to explain what could not otherwise be explained; as such, it is appropriate.

What role may fictive contexts play in a biography?

The question of whether one may fictionalize within a biography is one that lies directly at the center of the balance between the desires to delight and to inform. At the beginning of *The Story of Columbus* (1952), Nina Brown Baker quotes Columbus's sister Bianca, who has come in search of Christopher and his brother. She yells at them for covering themselves with dye instead of using long sticks to color the cloth. Even his red hair is dyed red, she complains. In this, Baker does convey narrative information—Christopher's family is one of dyers, his hair is red, he has a brother and sister—and she tries to do this in the form of a story. But this is certainly not a verifiable record of a real incident.

James Cross Giblin's *Thomas Jefferson* (1994) suggests an approach that allows the details to create the dramatic story. In this picture-book biography, Giblin adheres strictly to facts about Jefferson's life, never giving dialogue when the quote is not documentable; still, he is able to use details to suggest much about Jefferson's character, and he is able to present those details in an engaging style.

> At the President's House, Thomas did away with formal gatherings and entertained at small private dinners. The table was round so that no guest would sit in a more important place than another.
>   A mockingbird kept Thomas company in his study. He loved to listen to its cheerful songs while he worked. If he had no visitors, he let the bird out of its cage so that it could fly freely around the room. Often it would land on his shoulder and chirp in his ear. (31)

Giblin could have written that Jefferson, in his republicanism, was eager to show that he thought no man better than another. He could also have made up a fictional dinner at which several were invited and surprised that they were not accorded places of honor. Instead, the one detail of the round table establishes the very same point.

But fictive contexts are not to be dismissed too easily. David Kherdian's *The Road from Home* (1979) is, in many senses, fictional, in that Kherdian establishes the fictional context of a diary written by his mother. Yet it remains an accurate and moving biographical account of a child who witnessed the atrocities committed by the Turks against the Armenians. Kherdian felt that the first-person narrative would bring the reader closer to the action and make the action all the more horrific and compelling. In the following scene, the narrator has been walking for three days in the desert on a forced march, after having been exiled from her home.

> We had been heading south into hot, muggy weather. We soon ran out of water, and our food supply was very low. Papa was able to buy water at the villages, but only when the guards were willing to stop for food or water for themselves. We were stopping to rest more and more often, and I didn't know how the ones who were walking could go on. I tried not to think of all the people who were no longer with us. (73–74)

The narrator's matter-of-fact voice, almost the voice of a reporter who has seen too much horror to react, is startling. The voice is not a whine, not a voice of despair, but the voice of one who has no more emotion to spend.

One biography that assaults the boundary between historical fiction and biography even more aggressively is Alan Schroeder's *Minty: A Story of Young Harriet Tubman* (1996). Schroeder takes several of the very few facts known about Tubman's early life—that she was "difficult," that she worked in the fields because she was not docile enough to work in the Big House, that she tended muskrat traps—and weaves these into a narrative. When Schroeder writes about her freeing a captive muskrat, he has no evidence that this actually occurred, but he wants to suggest something about her character. Some scenes are, thus, invented, yet the foundational facts are accurate. Most would argue, however, that, in inventing scenes, Schroeder has gone beyond the boundaries of biography; he himself calls the book "a fictional account of Harriet Tubman's childhood."

Deborah Hopkinson presses this point even further in *Maria's Comet* (1999), a picture book biography about Maria Mitchell, the first female astronomer in the United States. The first-person narrative tells of Maria's father, who ascends to the roof each night and sweeps the sky with his telescope. When her brother runs away to sea—the family lives on Nantucket—Maria decides that she will stay home, but that she, too, will take a journey to a distant land. That night, she ascends with her father and begins the studies that will take her on that journey. Up to this point, the illustrations have been quite literal, but, as the book ends, the final illustration takes on a metaphorical quality as Maria holds onto a star as it travels across the sky: "I can go wherever it takes me." In its essence, the work captures the spirit of Maria Mitchell, who came from a family that supported her interest in science and astronomy and encouraged her to take the kind of journey that the narrator here takes. But the perspective and the monologue are constructed by Hopkinson, so that she writes in the afterward that, while she "tried to capture Maria Mitchell's wonderful questioning spirit and dedication to women's education," the work is still fiction, though "inspired by a real person."

At times, biographers use a narrator based on a real character to focus the selection of events, as in F. N. Monjo's *Poor Richard in France* (1973) and Barbara Nichol's *Beethoven Lives Upstairs* (1993). Both are narrated by a child narrator who is, for the time of the book, intimate with the major figure, but the narration is not a series of documented quotes. Instead, the biographer uses the narrator's perspective to direct the reader's perspective. *Poor Richard in France* is told by Benny, a young grandson of Benjamin Franklin, and recounts his life with Franklin while he was being lionized by the people of France, aristocrat and peasant alike: "All the ladies in Paris want to kiss Grandfather. But Grandfather says it isn't so easy to kiss French ladies. Here's why you can't kiss them on the lips. It's impolite. And you can't kiss them on the cheeks, either, because they wear big, bright circles of rouge there. That means you have to kiss them on the neck! So that's what Grandfather does." (27) Benny recounts those things that might impress a young child, such as the exotic ladies and odd customs of another country, particularly when they so closely affect his grandfather. This means that the reader has a single, somewhat narrow perspective on a small part of Franklin's life, but it is, nonetheless, an intimate perspective that gives real insight into Franklin.

Beethoven Lives Upstairs is a series of letters from young Christoph, whose father has just died, to his uncle, recounting the embarrassing things that the new lodger is doing. The new lodger is, in fact, Beethoven, who is just finishing his Ninth Symphony. In one of his last letters to his uncle, Christoph writes of the first performance, to which Beethoven has invited him.

> And when the music ended, the audience was on its feet. Everyone was standing and cheering and clapping and waving scarves and crying and trying to make Mr. Beethoven hear them.

But he couldn't hear us and he didn't know that we were cheering until one of the sopranos took his sleeve and turned him to face the crowd. Four times the audience finished their clapping and then began to clap and cheer again. Up on the stage Mr. Beethoven bowed and bowed.

As the carriage took us home, I could hear the music in my head. But my thoughts kept turning back to Mr. Beethoven himself.

He has so many troubles, how can he have a heart so full of joy?...

This short picture book covers only a very short time in Beethoven's life, but it gives a picture of the terrible torment of a man who is able "to feel so much inside" yet who is physically deaf. Christoph is the reader's interpreter, giving a moving impression of Beethoven that coincides with growth on his own part as well.

The boundary between a novel, particularly a work of historical fiction, and a biography is blurred in another way by Emily Arnold McCully's *The Bobbin Girl* (1996), about life in the Lowell mills, and *The Ballot Box Battle* (1996). McCully based her protagonist in *The Bobbin Girl,* Rebecca, on the real Harriet Hanson Robinson, who worked in the mills of Lowell in the nineteenth century. Rebecca is a fictional character, but everything she does has been suggested by Robinson's account of her own life. In *The Ballot Box Battle* McCully creates a fictional character, Cordelia, to interact with Elizabeth Stanton, who tells the story of her life to Cordelia and encourages her to defy the social boundaries that oppress women. In McCully's books, the dialogue is invented, but all of the scenes, the characters' actions and motivations, are accurate.

Monjo, Nichols, Hopkinson, and McCully press the boundaries of biography. Their techniques suggest those of historical fiction, but their reliance on biographical techniques suggests that the distinction between the two genres is not always easy to define. That distinction is even further complicated when an author's prologue or afterward draws explicit connections between the work at hand and the life of a biographical figure who has "inspired" the current handling.

Is it legitimate for the biographer to manipulate narrative perspectives by using stances that are not meant to be objective?

For many young readers, biographies can speak with encyclopedic voices; they assume the stance of authority, as though they are doing no less than revealing truth. But recent biographies for children have varied this narrative stance to suggest a very different perspective: The narrator is not the objective encyclopedia, but the engaged voice that speaks with many different tones to the reader.

There is, for example, the humorous voice of Alice Fleming's *George Washington Wasn't Always Old* (1991), which addresses the child reader directly: "You probably won't believe this—hardly anyone does—but George Washington wasn't always old. Once upon a time, he was young enough to turn somersaults and tease his little sister and throw tantrums when he couldn't have his own way" (1). The direct address and the overturning of stereotypical visions of Washington is accomplished through the narrative perspective.

A similar tone is used by Kathryn Lasky in her biography of the Greek thinker and geographer, Eratosthenes: *The Librarian Who Measured the Earth* (1994). Her subject is a weighty one and not one that seems readily adaptable to a child audience. But, by using a light and humorous tone, Lasky is able to avoid heavy description and lengthy explanation and, instead, maintain a lively narrative pace, as in this description of the museum at Alexandria:

> At the museum there were laboratories and libraries, dining halls and private studios. There were special promenades that wound through quiet gardens for thoughtful strolls. Great minds were supposed to come to this place to read, study, and be inspired. And if the stomachs of these great minds started to growl with hunger, there were meals—porridge, fruit, nuts, and cheese. (21)

The careful pairing in the first two sentences, as well as the undercutting humor of the last, all convey information, but do it with a briskness that does not slow down the narrative. The full-page illustrations by Kevin Hawkes contribute to the undercutting humor: In one, while Eratosthenes strolls through the gardens past tall Ionic columns, his servant, burdened with the luggage that the mathematician has just brought, eyes the fruit, nuts, and cheese hungrily.

Of course, not all narrative voices in biographies for children are humorous, but they must find some manner of engaging the child reader. The narrators of Rhoda Blumberg's *Commodore Perry in the Land of the Shogun* (1985) and *The Incredible Journey of Lewis and Clark* (1987) are much more traditional; there is no humor, and the voices are closer to that of the authoritative teacher. Yet, they are not that. Blumberg carefully constructs her descriptions and narrative paragraphs so that she is not merely listing details, but showing their meaning and significance in the context of the worlds of Commodore Perry and Lewis and Clark. In the following passage from *The Incredible Journey of Lewis and Clark*, Blumberg discusses Lewis' meeting with the Mandan and Hidatsas tribes.

> The captain was under the impression that Black Cat was the villages' most powerful chief. Unfortunately, despite all the briefings about big chiefs and lesser chiefs, Lewis persisted in believing that one head chief was the decision maker. He and Clark never understood that one Indian tribe often had many chiefs of equal importance, and that chiefs' powers were usually limited. The Mandans, for example, were governed by a council of elders. However, the council didn't have absolute authority. It acted as an advisory board to all the people. Tribespeople usually accepted the council's opinion, but were not obligated to obey. (68)

This passage is meant both to convey information about how the Mandan and Hidatsas tribes were governed and to describe the explorers' inability to understand that system. Blumberg could have stepped outside the narrative and given a short history of the system; instead, she weaves it into the narrative, beginning with the explorers who are the focus of her book and then moving outward to a discussion of the tribes, preceded by the reaction of the explorers. In this way she balances the giving of information and the narrative line through the narrative voice that she has constructed.

The construction of the narrative voice, then, greatly affects how the biographer will present the figure to the child reader. Whether that voice is that of a third-person narrator, or whether that voice is manipulated in less traditional ways, the biographer needs to find the best way to present the vision of the figure that he or she wishes to project.

Many biographies have appeared in the context of a series. How does this affect the writing and crafting of an individual biography?

Perhaps the most popular way of marketing biographies is through a series; certainly this was true even through the 1980s, and the practice continues today unabated. This practice was particularly useful to publishers when schools and libraries bought biographies through subscription to a series, and, in the 1950s and 1960s, most biographies were written as part of a series. Today, those series biographies of two and three decades ago are looked at askance, and series themselves have changed in response to the criticisms of the earlier biographies.

The difficulty facing the biographer whose work is part of a series is that the creative process is reversed. Normally, a writer will conceive of a subject and a way of treating that subject that leads to a meaningful book. This means that the biographer chooses the voice, format, level of treatment, and diction that is most suitable to his or her subject and methods. But, when a biographer becomes part of a series, he or she is guided, instead, by the vision of the series editor, which may or may not be consistent with what the biographer had hoped to do with a subject. This means, for example, that if one of the authors of the Bobbs-Merrill *Childhood of Famous Americans* series of the 1950s and 1960s wanted to add a great deal more material on the later life of the subject, he or she would have gone beyond the boundaries of the series and this material would most probably have been edited out. If a biographer is to craft a biography in a series and make it truly his or hers, then the writer will have to find a way within the boundaries of the editor's format to craft something that is unique and individual, appropriate to the subject that the biographer is treating.

Not all biographical series were as stringent in their boundaries as the Bobbs-Merrill series. Beginning in 1950, Random House published the Landmark Books, whose boundaries were determined, not according to format, but vision. The books were meant to celebrate U.S. democracy, and subjects were chosen who were seen to have contributed to that democratic vision. Eager for acceptance, Random House sought out well-known authors already proven to be popular, and orchestrated very readable, if at times imaginative, biographies. They included Sterling North's *Abe Lincoln: Log Cabin to White House* (1956) and *George Washington: Frontier Colonel* (1957), Margaret Cousins's *Ben Franklin of Old Philadelphia* (1952), James Daugherty's *The Landing of the Pilgrims* (1950) and *Trappers and Traders of the Far West* (1952), Armstrong Sperry's *The Voyages of Christopher Columbus* (1950) and *John Paul Jones, Fighting Sailor* (1953), Dorothy Canfield Fisher's *Paul Revere and the*

Minute Men (1950), and Jim Kjelgaard's *The Explorations of Pere Marquette* (1951). They included as well biographies by popular adult novelists of the 1950s: Thomas Costain, who would become famous for his novel of Jesus' life, *The Silver Chalice* (1952), wrote *The Mississippi Bubble* (1955); C. S. Forester, who was becoming known for his *Horatio Hornblower* books, wrote *The Barbary Pirates* (1953); and Robert Penn Warren wrote *Remember the Alamo!* (1958).

Grosset and Dunlap, not to be outdone, launched its Signature Books, a collection of biographies of those who shaped history. It was a curious mix of the Bobbs-Merrill and Random House books: "Expert authors of children's books, leading artists, simple sentences, scientific word-choice, easy-to-read type plus realistic, human story structure distinguish these true-life stories which emphasize the beginning years of famous men and women in history," read the advertisement. It quickly published biographies of figures like Buffalo Bill, Davy Crockett, Ulysses Grant, Robert E. Lee, and Florence Nightingale, but the authors were not nearly as distinguished as the advertisement claimed, and few today would remember Enid LaMonte Meadowcroft, Alida Sims Malkus, or Nina Brown Baker.

Today, nothing on the scale of the series by Bobbs-Merrill or Random House during the 1950s is being published, but the notion of a series is still guiding the publication of a number of biographies. In 1993 Oliver Press established its Profile series with Robert Pile's *Top Entrepreneurs and Their Businesses* (1993); as a series, it used the model of a collective biography, bringing in a number of similar figures to discuss as a group. In a similar vein, Chelsea Publishers has printed North American Indians of Achievement and Hispanics of Achievement series. Enslow Publishers created its Outlaws and Lawmen of the Wild West in 1992, and later issued the Great African Americans and Sports Greats series. The mid-1980s saw the publication of books in Puffin's Women of Our Time series, and the mid-1990s saw the beginning of William B. Eerdmans Publishers's Women of Spirit and Men of Spirit biographies. Though these latter two series worked to establish consistent formats and audiences, neither had the kind of stern strictures that governed the earlier series.

If it is the case that series biographies hinder the freedom and creativity of the biographer, it nevertheless is true that they have continued, despite the increase by trade publishers of biographies that are not part of a series. Certainly this kind of packaging eases a publisher's marketing, but perhaps there are other elements from a reader's perspective that are pleasing in a biography series. After all, why is it that so many adults who decry the Bobbs-Merrill series as biographies remember with pleasure the hours they spent devouring those same books?

Certainly there is the pleasure of the familiar, an aspect of any series. Though readers do not return to the same characters in a biography series, still they return to the familiar format, the familiar handling. There is the comfortable pleasure in knowing what to expect; suspense is not the only pleasure in reading. In addition, the limits that series place on the handling of a figure's life can themselves be pleasurable; readers know precisely what they will encounter and within what limits they are working. A consistent vision brings readers back to further novels in a series if that vision has been successful in the first read.

Pointers for Teachers

Interactive Possibilities
- Before reading the biography, brainstorm what the class already knows about the subject. Keep a record of ideas on an overhead; then, after reading the text, compare the earlier ideas with the author's presentation.
- Choose five illustrations from several points in the biography. Make slides of these. Then, before reading the text, have the class look at these projected images and talk about how they might view the subject.

Writing Possibilities
- Have students choose an important event from the subject's life and write two weeks of journal entries about that event as though the writer were the subject.
- Have each student act as reporter for his/her school newspaper; write lead articles on the subjects of the biographies as teasers for school visits later that week.

Hands-On Possibilities
- Write on slips of paper the names of all significant characters from the biography. Have the students, working in pairs, choose a name and create a mask that represents that significant character. Have the appropriate materials ready at hand, and, afterwards, have the rest of the students guess the identity of the character. Display the masks for a week or two.
- Place the students in "advertising" groups of five. Based on their knowledge of the biography, they should prepare a campaign to "sell" it to another group of students, or to another classroom. After they have chosen a target group and thought about its interests and needs, the groups should each make a poster, a brochure, a video, and a script for a book talk. Finally, each of the groups should try their sell on their target audience.

> ### As a biography becomes dated, it may also become less palatable to a later age that sees, in its judgments and assumptions, attitudes that are problematic.

The issue of a datedness of a biography's attitudes and assumptions is as problematic in children's literature as it is in adult literature. Here again the intersection of the need to delight as well as inform affects the issue. If the biography were purely to delight, then the issue of datedness would not be so enormous, as long as the biography were seen as a product of its particular time. But biographies necessarily play a dual role, and, insofar as they inform, then, when they do work on assumptions that are problematic, they pose a difficulty to anyone interested in bringing together children and books.

Consider, for example, Robert Lawson's Caldecott-winning *They Were Strong and Good* (1940), a picture book biography of the two sides of Lawson's own family. In describing his father's childhood, Lawson writes that "[w]hen my father was very young he had two dogs and a colored boy. The dogs were named Sextus Hostilius and Numa Pompilius. The colored boy was just my father's age. He was a slave, but they didn't call him that. They just called him Dick. He and my father and the two hound dogs used to hunt all day long." The accompanying illustration shows that Dick's role in the hunting was to carry the dead animals over his shoulder; his broad smile suggests that he is delighted with this role.

Most would find this passage problematic, not only in the easy acceptance of ownership, but particularly in the assumption that slavery doesn't seem all that awful as long as you don't use the word. On the one hand, this is a text written in 1940, about a time before the Civil War, in which questions such as the ethics of slavery might not have been raised by a young boy. In that sense this text is a document of its time, and one cannot expect assumptions at the turn of the millennium to be reflected in a text written so long ago. Yet, if biographies are to inform, the question arises as to whether a child reader can make the leap of understanding that suggests that this attitude is part of the time from which the writing arose, but is no longer part of society's understanding of the meaning of these events.

Authors and Illustrators of Biographies

Unlike most other genres, biography does not boast a long and prestigious string of writers; it is a genre that attracted major writers only within the last two decades, though with some notable exceptions.

Ingri (1904–1980) and Edgar Parin D'Aulaire (1898–1986)

The D'Aulaires were among the first writers of children's literature who crafted biographies for the very young, effectively combining text and illustration to portray their subjects. Though Ingri was Norwegian, born in Köngsberg, near Øslo, and Edgar Parin was the son of an Italian artist, it would be the United States that they would adopt, settling first in New York, then in Connecticut. There they produced a series of biographies about figures associated with their adopted country: *George Washington* (1936), *Abraham Lincoln* (1939), which won the Caldecott Medal, *Pocahontas* (1946), *Benjamin Franklin* (1950), *Buffalo Bill* (1952), and *Columbus* (1955). The books are all in a picture book format, each spread self-contained. On one side of a spread, the D'Aulaires placed a full-page illustration, alternating between sepia or monotones and full color. On the opposing page is the text, accompanied by smaller illustrations above or below, as well as fanciful pictures marching up and down and around the text that comment on the action. The D'Aulaires' perspective was flattened, and their drawings suggested a strong, vital simplicity.

As the D'Aulaires experimented with their biographies, the books became more and more complex, so that the diction of the text of *Benjamin Franklin* is markedly more difficult than that of *George Washington,* and the biographies become fuller as well. In *George Washington,* the D'Aulaires focus almost wholly on Washington's Revolutionary War experiences and neglect the years of his presidency. In *Abraham Lincoln,* the D'Aulaires choose not to include the assassination of the president. But in *Benjamin Franklin* the D'Aulaires include much more detail, and a much fuller account of Franklin's life. In *Columbus,* they include accounts even of the bitter final voyages: "Columbus was a great man. But he was not a modest man. He wanted too much and so he did not get enough…. People soon forgot that no one had dared to cross the Atlantic before Columbus had proved that it could be done. That irked the aging Columbus." This kind of detail suggests that the D'Aulaires allowed their vision of how to deal with the meaning and significance of a life's details to evolve.

The early books would never have included a criticism of a figure; in fact, books like *George Washington* and *Abraham Lincoln* verge on hagiography. In *George Washington,* for example, the D'Aulaires write that "he was tall and strong, and rode his horse better than any other boy of his age, and he beat them all in races and games." Later, as a surveyor, Washington is frequently forced to camp in the wilderness. "Often wind and rain tore the tent from over his head, but he did not mind, for he was strong as a bear." This, needless to say, is hard to believe.

The vision that the D'Aulaires carry for biography for the young child includes a belief in presenting essentially optimistic, secure stories of the figures with which they deal; this strongly affects their choice of details. In *Abraham Lincoln,* for example, the D'Aulaires take care to omit details that might be frightening to a young reader. When the Lincoln family moves to Little Pigeon Creek, they set up a three-walled shelter for the winter. It is a dangerous time for the family, out in the open in the wilderness, but the accompanying illustration shows a cozy shelter, warmly lit under a beautiful canopy of trees. The land in front is cleared and nicely grassed, and the family is contentedly busy about their chores. There is no real sense of hardship here. Later, when the D'Aulaires turn to the Civil War, there is no sense of the bloody horrors of that war; no battles are specifically described. When Lincoln calls again and again for soldiers, they come eagerly to "Father Abraham"; there is no mention of the New York draft riots, or of the North's anger at Lincoln's prosecution of the war. None of these details would have fit into the optimistic vision of the D'Aulaires.

Each of the books spends a good deal of time on the childhood of these figures, not only because the D'Aulaires believed these stories appealed to child readers, but because they found in these stories the seeds of what their figures would later become. Benjamin Franklin, even as a young boy, is marked by his wit: When he sits down for daily prayers, he suggests to his father that he "think of all the time you could save if you would thank the Lord, once and for all, for the whole larder." When Abraham Lincoln sits eating a gingerbread man, he "wondered why the things he liked best were always the hardest to get," a philosophical position that would later trouble him during the Civil War. When, as a young man he arrives in New Orleans and sees the slave auctions for the first time, he is outraged. The accompanying illustration shows slaves lined up for sale beside horses, cattle, and hogs, and the poignant reaching of a young child for her mother suggests the horror of the trade. This, the D'Aulaires later show, suggests much of Lincoln's motivation in his presidency.

Several of the D'Aulaires' books remain in print, though some are sixty years old now. If their optimistic vision does not always yield an entirely accurate portrayal of the complexities of a figure's life, still, it is a vision that appealed, the D'Aularies felt, to children who are not yet ready for the subtleties and complexities that make even the simplest action full of possible motivations. They wanted to celebrate U.S. heroes, to see in them the models for action and behavior that spawned a new country.

Leonard Everett Fisher (b. 1924)

Like the D'Aulaires, Leonard Everett Fisher has successfully combined text and illustration in the creation of his picture book biographies. His subjects have ranged more widely than that of the D'Aulaires, as Fisher has written biographies of subjects from around the world. He began with historical subjects from the Renaissance: *Prince Henry the Navigator* (1990), *Galileo* (1992), and *Gutenberg* (1993). From there he worked on more contemporary subjects: *Marie Curie* (1994) and *Gandhi* (1995). In each he maintained a similar format: one large black-and-white illustration that covers a double-page spread, with the text inserted into the illustration.

In a form that necessarily limits the amount of detail, Fisher has tried to capture a life in a text much simpler and much more concise than that of the D'Aulaires. This means that Fisher does not include many of the small details that the D'Aulaires included, but he has a very different purpose. While the D'Aulaires maintain a steady focus on the life of the figure, Fisher is much more interested in the significance of the life within its world context. After discussing the motivations and navigational improvements of Prince Henry the Navigator, for example, Fisher concludes his biography with a final assessment of that figure's signficance.

> Prince Henry's school of navigation was the first maritime institute in the world for deepwater research. There information was gathered and studied, and expeditions were sent out to chart the unknown. While Henry himself never sailed on his ships, he is called Henry the Navigator because he made it possible for sailors to find their way at sea with greater accuracy. Prince Henry expanded the oceanic frontier, leading to the discovery of the Americas.

The life of Prince Henry itself is not particularly dramatic; the D'Aulaires might have been hard put to deal with it in their style. But, as Fisher places that life in the context of its significance to later explorations, the life takes on drama and meaning.

Fisher maintains this same focus in his other biographies. In *Marie Curie*, he deals with her scientific discoveries as well as her overcoming of gender barriers, but he concludes again with her large significance in terms of later history: "The Curies, Marie and Pierre," he writes, "revolutionized modern science and opened wide the door to the study of the atom." In *Gandhi,* Fisher writes of Gandhi's legacy in the Civil Rights movement in the United States and concludes with a quote that suggests something of Gandhi's character as well as his lasting impact on social movements: "Love of the hater is the most difficult of all. But by the grace of God even this most difficult thing becomes easy to accomplish if we want to do it."

To augment this focus on context and significance, Fisher begins each of his biographies with a chronology that merges the life of the figure with corresponding events in his or her time; on the facing page he adds a simplified map to show the geographical context of the figure.

Fisher's black-and-white toned illustrations are not especially detailed. Whereas the D'Aulaires included many colors and many small illustrations and details to capture the eye, Fisher uses large shapes and solid spaces to focus the eye on the central figure. The result is that the perspective seems always to mirror that of the figure, as in *Prince Henry the Navigator,* in which Henry stares out to sea, trying to discern the mysteries that escape him, or in *Gandhi* where Gandhi, the largest figure in the spread, walks directly towards the reader at the head of a protest march. The effect is to keep the figure central even in the midst of the swirling events of his or her historical context.

David A. Adler (b. 1947)

Like the D'Aulaires and Leonard Everett Fisher, David Adler has crafted picture-book biographies. And, also like the D'Aulaires, he has turned principally to U.S. figures. He entitles his works "First Biographies," and, in that sense, they are meant to give an accurate story of the lives with which he deals in books such as *Thomas Alva Edison: Great Inventor* (1990), *Jackie Robinson: He Was the First* (1989), *Thomas Jefferson: Father of Our Democracy* (1987), *George Washington: Father of Our Country* (1988), *Martin Luther King, Jr.: Free at Last* (1986), and *Christopher Columbus: Great Explorer* (1991).

Like Leonard Everett Fisher, David Adler includes a chronology of the figure's life, again set against the historical period in which he or she lived, but his format is somewhat different. He adds an index and divides the text into four- to six-page chapters. Unlike Fisher and the D'Aulaires, he is committed to writing of the figure's entire life, and so neither *George Washington* nor *Thomas Jefferson*—nor any of the biographies—focuses only on a single period.

The two-page spreads are dominated either by one or two large illustrations, done in pen and ink. They are, in general, crucial in depicting the details of the story not covered by the texts. In *Christopher Columbus,* for example, they are important in their depiction of the three ships Columbus uses. In *George Washington* and *Thomas Jefferson* they are important in depicting the progression of houses, leading to Mount Vernon and Monticello.

Adler balances the sort of detailed narrative used by the D'Aulaires with the contextual material that is prominant in Fisher's work. In using both, his biographies are generally fuller than those of other biographers for young children. He writes in *Christopher Columbus,* for example, that "[t]he Atlantic Ocean, the large body of water to the west of Portugal, was called the Sea of Darkness. The legends surrounding it were frightening. Sailors told tales of boiling water and of giant sea monsters. People in Europe didn't know of the land and people living on the other side of the Atlantic" (6). Soon after that, Adler moves from the general to the specific in dealing with the young Christopher: "Christopher and Bartholomew helped their father. They combed raw wool to clean it and untangle the fibers" (9). In *George Washington,* Adler, in two successive paragraphs, includes the names of Washington's dogs—"Topsey, Musick, Drunkard, Sweetlips, and Rockwood"—and then notes that "the peace in the colonies following and French and Indian War was coming to an end" (31). This movement back and forth from the general to the particular helps to set the life in its context.

Adler is very explicit about the meanings of his details. Instead of citing an episode and then abandoning it for the next, he suggests the larger significance of that episode in the figure's life, an important trait for a child reader. When George Washington witnesses an Indian wardance during his surveying trip to the wilderness of Virginia, Adler remarks that "[h]e was learning firsthand about the American frontier" (16). When, at the age of twenty-one, he is made a major in the Virginian Army, Adler notes that he was now "a soldier and a leader of men" (19).

Adler uses the same technique to point out even larger significances to the reader; he will, at times, stop his narrative flow and suggest the larger meaning that a detail will hold for the future. After Adler points out Jefferson's abhorrence of slavery as a child, he leaps forward in time to the period when Jefferson inherits his father's slaves: "He was known to be a good master, but he was also criticized for not letting his slaves go free" (13). After Columbus meets the natives in the New World for the first, time, Adler stops the narrative to note that "[t]he arrival of Columbus was a tragic happening for the Indians.... In the years ahead, millions of Indians would be brutally killed by the conquering people from across the ocean" (31). In *Our Golda* (1984), a biography of Golda Meir, Adler writes that Golda gave her first speech when she was only eleven years old, and, despite her mother's pleas, she did not write it out. "Over the years," Adler concludes, "Golda made thousands of speeches. She almost always spoke the same way, from her heart, without notes." It is a technique that Adler uses effectively to emphasize the larger meanings of what might otherwise be seen as small details.

In writing for a young audience, Adler uses a stripped-down style, with simple, repetitive sentence structures, that allows him to keep the diction and reading simple, but also to establish dramatic pauses. In writing of the assassination in *A Picture Book of Martin Luther King, Jr.* (1989), Adler's technique makes his sentences vibrate with a staccatolike rhythm.

> Dr. King stood outside his hotel room. Another man, James Earl Ray, was hiding nearby. He pointed a rifle at Dr. King. He fired the gun. An hour later Dr. King was dead.

In *Our Golda,* Adler uses a simple, repetitive sentence structure to quickly cover a great deal of information, as well as to make a point about the nature of Golda Meir's life.

> Golda Meir was one of the great leaders of our time. She was the Prime Minister, the leader of Israel. She was also a shopkeeper, schoolteacher, librarian, almond picker, and fund raiser. She was a chicken farmer, hunger striker, and freedom fighter. She was a mother and grandmother. She was Golda. (3)

The final very simple sentence summarizes what is obviously a most complicated life. In using this writing style, Adler has found a form that appeals to young readers who are coming to their first biographies, and a form that effectively conveys the information he wishes to impart.

Diane Stanley (b. 1943)

Like David Adler, Diane Stanley is concerned with telling the story of a figure's life in the context of that figure's world. Believing passionately that every culture can contribute to everyone's learning, she seeks to enrich children by allowing them to look through the eyes of another culture or another time. This dramatically affects her choice of figures; she avoids the common figures that one might expect in a picture book biography published in North America, and chooses lives that are not at all common in biographies for children. Two of her biographies focus on authors: *Bard of Avon: The Story of William Shakespeare* (1992) and *Charles Dickens: The Man Who Had Great Expectations* (1993). Other biographies focus on world leaders, again including uncommon choices: *Shaka, King of the Zulus* (1988), *Good Queen Bess: The Story of Elizabeth I of England* (1990), *Cleopatra* (1994), and *Joan of Arc* (1998).

Stanley's reference to "story" in the titles in significant. In the preface to *Cleopatra,* she writes that "[a]t the time our story opens, Julius Caesar had effective control of Rome and all its provinces." There is a strong sense here that the biography is really a story, a narrative telling of a life. This strongly affects the ways in which this biographer organizes her material. *Cleopatra,* for example, begins with the claim that the queen was eager to bring Egypt back to its old prominence in the world, and almost succeeded. The rest of the biography is a charting of her schemes for Egypt, and the eventual loss of her power and place. In *Charles Dickens,* Stanley opens with Charles's father suggesting that his son might one day own a fine house like Gad's Hill Place if he worked hard enough; the rest of the biography shows the drive that eventually leads Dickens to own that very home. In fact, he would die there. In *Shaka, King of the Zulus,* Stanley focuses on Shaka's innovative sense of an army's organization, an organization that leads to Shaka's powerful position. In her narrative, Stanley tries to strip away mythic images of her figures—that Cleopatra was especially beautiful, that Leonardo was only a great artist. Instead, she examines them in the context of their complex cultural positions, trying to give a picture of a whole person, rather than a mythic re-creation. This means that Stanley must simultaneously narrate the story of a life and narrate the story of a culture.

In none of the other picture book biographies are the illustrations as crucial to the work of the biography as they are in these books. Drawn by Diane Stanley, they add details to the narrative, particularly in terms of setting. This frees the biographer in that she does not need to devote long spaces to description, and can use visual details to show what might otherwise be difficult to envision. In *Cleopatra*, Stanley painstakingly illustrates the austere Roman Senate and the luxurious apartments of Cleopatra, establishing striking visual distinctions between the two ways of life. In *Charles Dickens*, Stanley suggests the tension between Charles and his new wife Catherine by showing the disorder of the dining room: Charles works at carving a burnt roast in a room where pictures hang askew, books and newspapers lie about on the floor, and laundry is piled up under the furniture. In *Good Queen Bess* Stanley is able to show effectively the effusive Elizabethan costuming of the queen and her courtiers without lengthy descriptions, a technique she uses again in *Bard of Avon*. In that latter book, Stanley suggests visually the central focus of the plays through depicting a set of characters from many of them, showing at the same time the nature of the costuming and staging of the plays. In *Joan of Arc*, she suggests the art of the period by creating the effects of an illuminated text, complete with golden frames for both illustration and text.

The strong narrative voice of these books makes them dramatic; though the books are equipped with prefaces, afterwards, maps, and bibliographies—the only picture book biographies to have such—they read as tales. This is Stanley's great success. In capturing the story of a life, she captures its high drama and potential for art. That she can, at the same time, suggest the significances of that life within its culture—and outside of its culture—is a testimony to how story can convey significance without necessarily being explicit.

Jean Fritz (b. 1924)

The titles of Jean Fritz's biographies for the young child suggest the perspectives that she takes: *Why Don't You Get a Horse, Sam Adams?* (1982), *What's the Big Idea, Ben Franklin?* (1982), *Will You Sign Here, John Hancock?* (1976), *Where Was Patrick Henry on the 29th of May?* (1982). There is a kind of brash irreverence in these titles, a demanding levity that a reader does not usually associate with biography. In her work for younger readers, Jean Fritz uses this tone to capture attention and to rescue her figures from the stiff stances that historical perspective may sometimes confer. Fritz is not at all interested in the kind of hagiographic approach that the D'Aulaires used; instead, she wants to present her characters as they were: imperfect figures striving to do something great.

Fritz also rejects the use of biographical fiction, the kind of approach used by so many of the series biographies that preceded her work. Instead, she argues that anything that appeared in her work—anything—should be absolutely verifiable through her research. This means that none of her characters should speak words that had not actually been recorded in their own writings or through the writings of contemporaries. The result is that Fritz works very hard to find the perfect, apt quotation, as in *You Want Women to Vote, Lizzie Stanton?* (1995).

> Her weight had become a problem, so she spent most of her hours, she said, "in the horizontal position…few in the perpendicular."… She made no effort to reduce, so she must have known that she was still gaining weight and would find it increasingly difficult to get around. She was still able to work, however, and after eighteen months she returned home and took up where she had left off. She continued to write speeches for Susan [B. Anthony], and even joined her in yet another campaign for suffrage in New York State. "What a set of jackasses we have at Albany this winter," she reported. "I have written several of them and they simply bray in return." And as usual the vote on suffrage was a resounding no. (72)

Rather than invention, Fritz argues, the biographer looks for emotional involvement through a judicious selection of detail, theme, and quotation. This principle puts certain limitations on her writing, limitations that actually gave her the form that would make her biographies so successful.

In rejecting any fictitious additions to her biography, Fritz turned instead to the establishment of a specific vision that would consistently be examined throughout the biography. All the details, all the episodes she includes, work together to create and support this central vision. In *Will You Sign Here, John Hancock?* Fritz suggests that Hancock was a man eager to be praised.

> Actually, what John Hancock wanted most was for people to like him. Not just some people. Everybody. It wasn't hard to like him. He was nice-looking, friendly, kind, generous, and he gave fantastic parties. But he wanted people to like him so much that they would elect him to office. He wanted to march at the head of parades, to sit in the seat of honor, and to stand on the center of platforms. (8)

The rest of the page suggests how Hancock went about getting noticed so that he would be liked: his vivid clothing, his extravagant lifestyle, his elegant house on Boston Commons. The details throughout the text work towards presenting this single vision of Hancock's character, so that, even in death, the detail Fritz includes was the fact that he missed one final parade that he had hoped to attend.

The other biographies in this series work similarly. In *Where Do You Think You're Going, Christopher Columbus?* (1981), Fritz paints Columbus as a man of arrogant stubbornness, a man who, she concludes, was angry to discover a New World, because he had never intended to set out to do it. In *Make Way for Sam Houston* (1986), Fritz opens the biography by noting that "[a]ll his life Sam Houston liked to do things in a big way or not at all"; the remainder of the biography shows how Houston went about doing things in a big way. This approach allows Fritz to present a coherent vision and creates a structure within which she can accumulate pointed details.

In writing a number of biographies for older children, Fritz has followed these same patterns. Books like *Stonewall* (1979), *The Great Little Madison* (1989), *Traitor: The Case of Benedict Arnold* (1981), and *Harriet Beecher Stowe & the Beecher Preachers* (1994) continue her focus on U.S. figures, and continue to organize their details around a central vision of the figure under study. In dealing with Benedict Arnold, Fritz chronicles the way his life was organized around his almost manic desire to show how brave he was, to win the support of others through demonstrations of his own daring: "Oh, there was nowhere he couldn't go now! Nothing he couldn't do! Bravery: it was the answer to everything" (10). In writing about Stonewall Jackson, Fritz concentrated on his extraordinary will and determination to proceed as he thought he should: "He decided very early that he had to find rules for his life and then follow them strictly. He wasn't going to let life just happen to him" (17). In *The Great Little Madison,* Fritz centers on the paradox of a small, unimposing figure with a small, unimposing voice filling the Constitutional Convention with passion and dominating the vision that would lead to the union of the colonies. As with her biographies for younger readers, these biographies are captivating in their use of details to suggest relationships between the figures and their world, and to suggest the truth and validity of Fritz's central vision.

Russell Freedman (b. 1929)

In 1988, Russell Freedman's *Lincoln: A Photobiography* (1987) received the Newbery Award, the first biography to receive this award in over thirty years. Like Jean Fritz, Freedman writes for an audience of older children, and, like her works, his are the product of extensive archival research and, at times, interviews with contemporaries who knew the figures with whom he deals. Freedman, too, has chosen to focus on U.S. figures, writing books like *Franklin Delano Roosevelt* (1990), *Eleanor Roosevelt: A Life of Discovery* (1993), *Indian Chiefs* (1987), *Kids at Work: Lewis Hine and the Crusade against Child Labor* (1994), and *The Wright Brothers: How They Invented the Airplane* (1991).

Like those of Diane Stanley, Freedman's biographies are notable for their extensive illustration, but, unlike any of the picture book biographies, and unlike Jean Fritz's work, all the illustrations of Freedman's biographies are contemporary photographs, amassed through the research he had done. The photographs are aptly chosen and appear on virtually every spread; in many cases they work as picture-book illustrations do to contribute to the narrative movement of the book. *Kids at Work* uses the photographs of Lewis Hine himself to illustrate the ways in which Hine captured the conditions of North America's working children and used those photographs to push for laws against child labor. *Lincoln: A Photobiography* uses photographs of contemporary illustrations to depict Lincoln's childhood, but then uses many photographs of Lincoln himself to show the devastating effects of the Civil War on him. Both *Franklin Delano Roosevelt* and *Eleanor Roosevelt: A Life of Discovery* combine public photographs from newspapers and magazines with the very private photographs of the Roosevelt family to give a portrait of the tensions between public and private life.

At the same time, he works to take what are generally very complicated lives deeply immersed in a tumultuous culture or period and, through the simplicity of his style, makes those lives understandable to his child audience. In his *Martha Graham: A Dancer's Life* (1998), Freedman tries to evoke the meanings of a complicated series of dances that Graham has choreographed.

Appalachian Spring had its premiere at a Library of Congress concert on December 30, 1944. Graham, who had turned fifty that year, danced the role of the young bride. Hawkins portrayed her proud young farmer-husband. Merce Cunningham, who would soon leave the company to form his own modern dance troupe, was cast as a mesmerizing revivalist preacher. And May O'Donnell played a seasoned pioneer woman modeled on Graham's great-grandmother, who was "very beautiful and was always very still." Each of these characters dances a solo that expresses his or her personality traits and feelings. And as the work ends, the newlyweds are left alone in their farmhouse, quiet and strong, with the suggestion of a baby yet to come. (99–100)

In this one passage, Freedman has given something of the history of the dance, has followed the continuing career of several of the dancers he has focused on earlier, and gives a sense of how Graham constructed the dance. All of this is conveyed in a spare prose style that will not lose the child reader, even a child reader not accustomed to reading about dance.

Freedman consciously balances the role of the storyteller with the role of the teacher. He wants to give information, but at the same time he is aware that information as mere information can be dull. History, he argues, is story, and the storyteller entertains. He also argues that no historian is objective; with the advantage of hindsight, the historian judges and evaluates. But this judgment has to be a fairminded one, setting the realities of a given time against social and ethical ideals that have not yet been reached even today.

Freedman's are the most extensive, most detailed of the biographies written for children. This research is suggested not only by the inclusion of details, but in the frequent and fruitful use of quotations from the figures' own writings and recorded speech. Accompanied by extensive bibliographic material, as well as comments on the sites associated with his figures and their availability to the public, the biographies are careful and complete accounts of very complex lives. Freedman does not focus on a central vision, as does Jean Fritz, but instead focuses on the development and growth of the person, particularly in the Roosevelt and Lincoln biographies. Though he suggests the contexts within which his figures worked, Freedman is careful to center on the responses of his figures, so that his text never leaves them for long, and the eye of the reader, captured by the photographs, never wanders from the figure.

Thinking and Writing about and from within the Genre of Biography

1. You are crafting a children's biography of William Bradford, the Pilgrim governor of Plymouth Colony for over thirty years. In the course of your research, you come across the following facts about Bradford's life. Which of these would you include, and which omit, in a picture book biography of Bradford?

   - Bradford's loss of his parents at an early age
   - Bradford's strict Separatist beliefs that led him to abandon the Church of England
   - Bradford's giving of his inheritance to the Pilgrims so that they might build a church in Leyden

- Bradford's ridicule of Robert Cushman, who made all the arrangements that allowed the Pilgrims to migrate, but who himself was too fearful of the sea to come with them
- Bradford's decision to leave his son behind in Leyden when he and his wife migrated to the New World; his son was five years old
- The death of the "lustie sailor" who had mocked the Pilgrims aboard the Mayflower and Bradford's belief that this came about due to God's providence
- The suicide of Bradford's wife, Dorothy
- The Pilgrims' theft of the Indian seed corn on Cape Cod
- Squanto's befriending of the Pilgrims and his conversion to their faith
- The refusal to allow any celebrations of Christmas
- Bradford's attack on a rival colony led by Thomas Morton, an attack motivated by fear of Morton's trading of guns to the Indians, but also because of his Church of England sympathies and his economic threat
- Bradford's delight in the defeat of his enemies, and his sense of "wonder" at hearing them shrieking and frying in fires the Pilgrims had set
- Bradford's loving role as father/governor to Plymouth, and his almost single-handed maintaining of the vision of the colony

Which of these details might be better conveyed by the illustrations rather than through the text? Are there any of these details that would not be appropriate for a biography for an older child?

2. Can a biography written for children be a basically unsympathetic portrayal of a figure? Is it appropriate, for example, for a children's biography to be written about Mao Tse Tung if the writer's basic aim is to attack Mao's effect on Chinese culture?

3. If a biographer chooses to work from the perspective of one of the characters in the figure's life, has the biographer fictionalized? To what extent? What issues must a biographer deal with if he or she chooses to write from such a perspective? Consider the effectiveness of this technique in Jane Yolen's *Encounter* (1992). How does the cover illustration of that book suggest the importance of narrative perspectives?

Selected Bibliographies

Works Cited

Picture Book Biographies
Bradby, Marie. *More Than Anything Else.* New York: Orchard, 1995. Illustrated by Chris Soentpiet.
Cooney, Barbara. *Eleanor.* New York: Viking, 1996.
Giblin, James Cross. *Thomas Jefferson: A Picture Book Biography.* New York: Scholastic, 1994.
Hopkinson, Deborah. *Maria's Comet.* New York: Atheneum, 1999. Illustrated by Deborah Lanine.

Lasky, Kathryn. *A Brilliant Streak: The Making of Mark Twain.* New York: Harcourt, Brace, 1998. Illustrated by Barry Moser.
———. *The Librarian Who Measured the Earth.* New York: Little, Brown, 1994.
Lawson, Robert. *They Were Strong and Good.* New York: Viking, 1940.
McCully, Emily Arnold. *The Bobbin Girl.* New York: Dial, 1996.
———. *The Ballot Box Battle.* New York: Knopf, 1996.

McKissack, Patricia and Fredrick McKissack. *Jesse Owens: Olympic Star*. Hillsdale, NJ: Enslow, 1992.

———. *Langston Hughes: Great American Poet*. Hillsdale, NJ: Enslow, 1992.

———. *Louis Armstrong: Jazz Musician*. Springfield, NJ: Endslow Pub, 1991.

———. *Satchel Paige: The Best Arm in Baseball*. Hillsdale, NJ: Enslow, 1992.

Monjo, F. N. *Me and Willie and Pa*. New York: Simon and Schuster, 1973.

———. *The One Bad Thing about Father*. New York: Harper, 1970.

———. *Poor Richard in France*. New York: Holt, 1973.

Nichol, Barbara. *Beethoven Lives Upstairs*. New York: Orchard, 1993.

Poole, Josephine. *Joan of Arc*. New York: Alfred Knopf, 1998. Illustrated by Angela Barrett.

Schroeder, Alan. *Minty: A Story of Young Harriet Tubman*. New York: Dial, 1996. Illustrated by Jerry Pinkney.

Stanley, Fay. *The Last Princess: The Story of Princess Ka'iulani of Hawai'i*. New York: Four Winds, 1991.

Yolen, Jane. *Encounter*. New York: Harcourt, Brace, 1992. Illustrated by David Shannon.

Non-Picture-Book Biographies

Baker, Nina Brown. *The Story of Christopher Columbus*. New York: Grosset and Dunlap, 1952.

Bauer, Marion Dane. *A Writer's Story: From Life to Fiction*. New York: Clarion, 1995.

Björk, Christina, and Lena Anderson. *Linnea in Monet's Garden*. New York: R & S, 1987.

Blumberg, Rhoda. *Commodore Perry in the Land of the Shogun*. New York: Lothrop, 1985.

———. *The Incredible Journey of Lewis and Clark*. New York: Lothrop, 1987.

Bryant, Jennifer Fisher. *Lucretia Mott: A Guiding Light*. Grand Rapids, MI: William B. Eerdmans, 1996.

Byars, Betsy. *The Moon and I*. New York: Julian Messner, 1992.

Cleary, Beverly. *A Girl from Yamhill*. New York: Morrow, 1988.

———. *My Own Two Feet*. New York: Morrow, 1995.

Cooper, Michael L. *Bound for the Promised Land*. New York: Lodestar, 1995.

Costain, Thomas. *The Mississippi Bubble*. New York: Random House, 1955.

———. *The Silver Chalice*. Cutchague, NY: Buccaneer Books, 1998.

Cousins, Margaret. *Ben Franklin of Old Philadelphia*. New York: Random House, 1952.

Dahl, Roald. *Boy: Tales of Childhood*. New York: Farrar, Straus, 1984.

———. *My Year*. New York: Viking, 1993.

Daugherty, James. *Abraham Lincoln*. New York: Viking, 1943.

———. *Daniel Boone*. New York: Viking, 1939.

———. *The Landing of the Pilgrims*. New York: Random House, 1950.

———. *Trappers and Traders of the Far West*. New York: Random House, 1952.

Ferrell, Keith. *John Steinbeck: The Voice of the Land*. New York: M. Evans, 1986.

Fisher, Dorothy Canfield. *Paul Revere and the Minute Men*. New York: Random House, 1950.

Fleming, Alice. *George Washington Wasn't Always Old*. New York: Simon and Schuster, 1991.

Fleischman, Sid. *The Abracadabra Kid*. New York: Greenwillow, 1996.

Forester, C. S. *The Barbary Pirates*. New York: Random House, 1953.

Fradin, Dennis. *Samuel Adams: The Father of American Independence*. New York: Clarion, 1998.

Gherman, Beverly. *E. B. White: Some Writer!* New York: Atheneum, 1992.

Gormley, Beatrice. *Maria Mitchell: The Soul of an Astronomer*. Grand Rapids, MI: William B. Eerdmans, 1995.

Green, Carl R. and William R. Sanford. *Bat Masterson*. Hillsdale, NJ: Enslow, 1992.

———. *Wyatt Earp*. Hillsdale, NJ: Enslow, 1992.

Greenfeld, Howard. *The Hidden Children*. New York: Ticknor and Fields, 1993.

Gross, Ruth Belov. *True Stories about Abraham Lincoln*. New York: Lothrop, 1990.

Haskins, Jim. *Black Eagles: African Americans in Aviation*. New York: Scholastic, 1995.

———. *Corazon Aquino: Leader of the Philippines*. Hillsdale, NJ: Enslow, 1988.

Kherdian, David. *The Road from Home: The Story of an Armenian Girl.* New York: Morrow, 1979.

Kjelgaard, Jim. *The Explorations of Pere Marquette.* New York: Random House, 1951.

Latham, Jean Lee. *Carry On, Mr. Bowditch.* Boston: Houghton Mifflin, 1955.

Lawlor, Laurie. *Daniel Boone.* Niles, IL: Albert Whitman, 1989.

Little, Jean. *Little by Little: A Writer's Childhood.* New York: Viking, 1988.

———. *Stars Come Out Within.* New York: Viking, 1991.

Marston, Hope Irvin. *Isaac Johnson: From Slave to Stonecutter.* New York: Dutton, 1995.

Meltzer, Milton. *Dorothea Lange: Life through the Camera.* New York: Viking, 1985.

———. *Underground Man.* New York: Harcourt, Brace, 1990.

Murphy, Jim. *A Young Patriot: The American Revolution as Experienced by One Boy.* New York: Clarion, 1996.

Nadel, Laurie. *Corazon Aquino: Journey to Power.* New York: Julian Messner, 1987.

Naylor, Phyllis Reynolds. *How I Came to Be a Writer.* New York: Macmillan, 1987.

North, Sterling. *Abe Lincoln: Log Cabin to White House.* New York: Random House, 1956.

———. *George Washington: Frontier Colonel.* New York: Random House, 1957.

Partridge, Elizabeth. *Restless Spirit: The Life and Work of Dorothea Lange.* New York: Viking, 1998.

Paulsen, Gary. *Wood-Song.* New York: Bradbury, 1990.

Peet, Bill. *Bill Peet: An Autobiography.* Boston: Houghton Mifflin, 1989.

Pile, Robert. *Top Entrepreneurs and their Businesses.* Minneapolis, MN: Oliver Press, 1993.

Sperry, Armstrong. *John Paul Jones: Fighting Sailor.* New York: Random House, 1953.

———. *The Voyages of Christopher Columbus.* New York: Random House, 1950.

Thomas, Jane Resh. *Behind the Mask: The Life of Queen Elizabeth I.* New York: Clarion, 1998.

Warren, Robert Penn. *Remember the Alamo!* New York: Random House, 1958.

White, Stewart Edward. *Daniel Boone: Wilderness Scout.* Garden City, NY: Doubleday, 1922.

Yolen, Jane. *Friend: The Story of George Fox and the Quakers.* New York: Seabury, 1972.

Works of Selected Biographers

David Adler

Benjamin Franklin: Printer, Inventor, Statesman. New York: Holiday House, 1992.

Christopher Columbus: Great Explorer. New York: Holiday House, 1991.

George Washington: Father of Our Country. New York: Holiday House, 1988.

Jackie Robinson: He Was the First. New York: Holiday House, 1989.

Martin Luther King, Jr.: Free at Last. New York: Holiday House, 1986.

Our Golda: The Story of Golda Meir. New York: Viking, 1984.

A Picture Book of Anne Frank. New York: Holiday House, 1993.

A Picture Book of Eleanor Roosevelt. New York: Holiday House, 1991.

A Picture Book of Florence Nightingale. New York: Holiday House, 1992.

A Picture Book of Frederick Douglas. New York: Holiday House, 1993.

A Picture Book of Harriet Tubman. New York: Holiday House, 1992.

A Picture Book of Martin Luther King, Jr. New York: Holiday House, 1989.

A Picture Book of Paul Revere. New York: Holiday House, 1995.

Thomas Alva Edison: Great Inventor. New York: Holiday House, 1990.

Thomas Jefferson: Father of Our Democracy. New York: Holiday House, 1987.

Ingri and Edgar Parin D'Aulaire

Abraham Lincoln. Garden City, NY: Doubleday, 1939.

Benjamin Franklin. Garden City, NY: Doubleday, 1950.

Buffalo Bill. Garden City, NY: Doubleday, 1952.

Columbus. Garden City, NY: Doubleday, 1955.

George Washington. Garden City, NY: Doubleday, 1936.

Leif the Lucky. Garden City, NY: Doubleday, 1941.

Pocahontas. Garden City, NY: Doubleday, 1946.

Leonard Everett Fisher

Galileo. New York: Macmillan, 1992.

Gandhi. New York: Atheneum, 1995.

Gutenberg. New York: Macmillan, 1993.

Marie Curie. New York: Macmillan, 1994.

Moses. New York: Holiday House, 1995.

Prince Henry the Navigator. New York: Macmillan, 1990.

Russell Freedman

Cowboys of the Wild West. New York: Clarion, 1985.

Eleanor Roosevelt: A Life of Discovery. New York: Clarion, 1993.

Franklin Delano Roosevelt. New York: Clarion, 1990.

Immigrant Kids. New York: Dutton, 1980.

Indian Chiefs. New York: Holiday House, 1987.

Kids at Work: Lewis Hine and the Crusade against Child Labor. New York: Clarion, 1994.

Lincoln: A Photobiography. New York: Clarion, 1987.

Martha Graham: A Dancer's Life. New York: Clarion, 1998.

The Wright Brothers: How They Invented the Airplane. New York: Holiday House, 1991.

Jean Fritz

And Then What Happened, Paul Revere? New York: Coward-McGann, 1973.

Brendan the Navigator: A History Mystery about the Discovery of America. New York: Coward-McGann, 1979.

Bully for You, Teddy Roosevelt. New York: Putnam, 1991.

Can't You Make Them Behave, King George? New York: Coward-McGann, 1982.

China Homecoming. New York: Putnam, 1985.

The Double Life of Pocahontas. New York: Puffin, 1987.

The Great Little Madison. New York: Putnam, 1989.

Harriet Beecher Stowe and the Beecher Preachers. New York: Putnam, 1994.

Homesick: My Own Story. New York: Putnam, 1982.

Make Way for Sam Houston. New York: Putnam, 1986.

Stonewall. New York: Putnam, 1979.

Traitor: The Case of Benedict Arnold. New York: Putnam, 1981.

What's the Big Idea, Ben Franklin? New York: Coward-McGann, 1982.

Where Do You Think You're Going, Christopher Columbus? New York: Putnam, 1981.

Where Was Patrick Henry on the 29th of May? New York: Coward-McGann, 1982.

Who's That Stepping on Plymouth Rock? New York: Coward-McGann, 1975.

Why Don't You Get a Horse, Sam Adams? New York: Coward-McGann, 1982.

Will You Sign Here, John Hancock? New York: Coward-McGann, 1976.

You Want Women to Vote, Lizzie Stanton? New York: Putnam, 1995.

Diane Stanley

Bard of Avon: The Story of William Shakespeare. New York: Morrow, 1992. With Peter Vennema.

Charles Dickens: The Man Who Had Great Expectations. New York: Morrow, 1993. With Peter Vennema.

Cleopatra. New York: Morrow, 1994. With Peter Vennema.

Eléna. New York: Hyperion, 1996.

Good Queen Bess: The Story of Elizabeth I of England. New York: Four Winds, 1990. With Peter Vennema.

Joan of Arc. New York: Morrow, 1998.

Leonardo da Vinci. New York: Morrow, 1996.

Michelangelo. New York: HarperCollins, 2000.

Peter the Great. New York: Four Winds, 1986.

Shaka: King of the Zulus. New York: Morrow, 1988. With Peter Vennema.

The True Adventure of Daniel Hall. New York: Dial, 1995.

Works on Biography in Children's Literature

Alberghene, Janice. "Artful Memory: Jean Fritz, Autobiography, and the Child Reader." In Charlotte F. Otten and Gary D. Schmidt, eds., *The Voice of the Narrator in Children's Literature* (New York: Greenwood, 1989): 362–368.

Bigelow, Bill. "Good Intentions Are Not Enough: Children's Literature in the Aftermath of the Quincentenary." *New Advocate* 7 (Fall, 1994): 265–279.

Bober, Natalie S. "Writing Lives." *Lion and the Unicorn* 15 (1991): 78–88.

Carr, Jo. "What Do We Do about Bad Biographies?" *School Library Journal* 27 (May, 1981): 19–22. Reprinted in Jo Carr, ed., *Beyond Fact* (Chicago: American Library Association, 1982): 119–128.

Epstein, William H. "Inducing Biography." *Children's Literature Association Quarterly* 12 (Winter, 1987): 177–179.

Forman, Jack. "Biography for Children: More Facts, Less Fiction." *Library Journal* 97 (September 15, 1972): 2968–2969.

Fritz, Jean. "The Voice of One Biographer." In Charlotte F. Otten and Gary D. Schmidt, eds., *The Voice of the Narrator in Children's Literature* (New York: Greenwood, 1989): 337–340.

Girard, Linda. "Series Thinking and the Art of Biography for Children." *Children's Literature Association Quarterly* 14 (Winter, 1989): 187–192.

———. "The Truth with Some Stretchers." *Horn Book* 64 (July/August, 1988): 464–469.

Huse, Nancy. "Of Nancy Hanks Born: Meridel LeSueur's Abraham Lincoln." *Children's Literature Association Quarterly* 18 (Spring, 1993): 13–17.

Ingber, Bonnie Verbrug. "The Writing of *Encounter:* The Editor's Perspective." *New Advocate* 5 (Fall, 1992): 241–245.

Jurich, Marilyn. "What's Left Out of Biography for Children." *Children's Literature* 1 (1972): 143–151.

Klatt, Beverly. "Abraham Lincoln: Deified Martyr, Flesh and Blood Hero, and a Man with Warts." *Children's Literature in Education* 23 (September, 1992): 119–129.

Marcus, Leonard. "Life Drawing: Some Notes on Children's Picture Book Biographies." *Lion and the Unicorn* 4 (1980): 15–31.

Meltzer, Milton. "The Designing Narrator." In Charlotte F. Otten and Gary D. Schmidt, eds., *The Voice of the Narrator in Children's Literature* (New York: Greenwood, 1989): 333–336.

———. "Notes on Biography." *Children's Literature Association Quarterly* 10 (Winter, 1986): 172–175.

Monjo, F. N. "Great Men, Melodies, Experiments, Plots, Predictability, and Surprises." *Horn Book* 51 (October, 1975): 433–441.

Moore, Ann W. "A Question of Accuracy: Errors in Children's Biographies." *School Library Journal* 31 (February, 1985): 34–35.

Quackenbush, Robert. "Laughter in Biography: Narrating for Today's Children." In Charlotte F. Otten and Gary D. Schmidt, eds., *The Voice of the Narrator in Children's Literature* (New York: Greenwood, 1989): 341–346.

Segel, Elizabeth. "In Biography for Young Readers, Nothing is Impossible." *Lion and the Unicorn* 4 (1980): 4–14.

West, Jane, et al. "Expectations and Evocations: Encountering Columbus through Literature." *New Advocate* 5 (Fall, 1992): 247–263.

Wilms, Denise. "An Evaluation of Biography." *ALA Booklist* (September 15, 1978): 218–220. Reprinted in Pamela Barron and Jennifer Burley, eds., *Jump Over the Moon* (New York: Holt, Rinehart, 1984): 220–225.

Yolen, Jane. "Past Time: The Writing of the Picture Book *Encounter*." *New Advocate* 5 (Fall, 1992): 235–239.

Zanderer, Leo. "Evaluating Contemporary Children's Biography: Imaginative Reconstruction and Its Discontents." *Lion and the Unicorn* 5 (1981): 33–51.

12

Nonfiction: A Pack of Facts in Pursuit of Truth

Nonfiction is a genre that has, in the past, raised up spectres of encyclopedic books that attempted to present large areas of knowledge in a compressed space, with dull, dense prose and poorly reproduced photographs. It was treated as a poor relation to fiction, with its wide variety of genres and rich permutations. Nonfiction has been called utilitarian, useful, practical, fact-based—all terms essentially designed to consign it to the back shelves of the library.

Even a short history of the genre will show that bias against it has caused problems. It is true that, in 1922, the very first Newbery was awarded to a nonfiction book, *The Story of Mankind* by Hendrik Willem Van Loon. But, since 1922, only six of the Newbery Awards have gone to a work of nonfiction. It seems that the genre's reliance on a factual foundation interferes with its being taken seriously as imaginative work. After all, if students need to know about the world of insects, they only need facts given in a clear fashion, not story.

Milton Meltzer was one of the first to ask why informational books were not being considered as works of art. In his "Where Do All the Prizes Go?" he makes a strong case for the bias against informational books and an equally strong case that informational books are, indeed, art forms. Critics, he argued, tend to ignore or too easily dismiss informational books. Either the books never make any list of consideration or they are reviewed in unhelpful ways, mainly by summarizing their contents. This lack of thoughtful attention causes them to be ignored, not just by prize committees, but by the entire critical world.

When Meltzer decided to write his *Never to Forget: The Jews of the Holocaust* (1976), he needed an appropriate form that would reflect the point he wanted to make about the Holocaust. As he researched, as he read diaries, letters, memoirs, eyewitness accounts, testimonies at hearings, songs, poems, a form finally suggested itself to him. He did not merely piece together a collection of children's experiences during the war, but carefully crafted a work whose purpose was to mark the Holocaust on readers' minds indelibly. Meltzer shows that the foundation of informational literature may be fact, but the structures of the genre are just as imaginative as those of a novel.

Boundaries and Definitions of the Informational Book

Facts by themselves are dead, boring strings of unrelated data that have no meaning until they are selected, grouped, and infused with a writer's imagination. It is that creative process that gives meaning to the facts, and makes informational books into literary works.

Certainly, the author of a work of nonfiction must begin in the real world. That author must draw materials from subjects that are found about him or her. If these works are to be accurate and full, the writers must do the extensive research necessary for them to become expert on the subject at hand. All of this is axiomatic. But the distinction that marks the finest writer of an information book is that writer's ability to gather the research and then create a vivid world, a creation marked by a narrative, characters, settings, thematic interests—all of the elements of fine fiction. Out of the mélange of research comes a strong personal vision that organizes the material, not only for clarity, but so that the reader might catch a sense of what meanings the writer perceives in the material.

Russell Freedman demonstrates the way that meaning can be derived from mere fact in *Kids at Work: Lewis Hine and the Crusade against Child Labor* (1994). Using Hine's startling black-and-white photographs from the early twentieth century, Freedman recreates the horrific world of child labor. Readers are not assaulted with heavy moralistic language; rather, they are presented with the reality of the photograph. One such photo is given an innocuous caption, "Breaker boys at a Pennsylvania coal mine," (3) but, when readers begin to scan the faces of the "boys," they can draw their own conclusions about the effects of working in a mine on children. Stoicism and dulled indifference stare back at the camera.

In his *Indian Chiefs* (1987), Freedman set out to suggest a revisionary view of Native Americans and the history of the West. He recounts the stories of six chiefs from the West. By using art from the period he is discussing, Freedman takes readers back to when George Caitlin's photographic images and Remington's drawings fixed haunting interpretations of their subjects. Their view of the wild West is a romantic one. But, in his text, Freedman shows the other side of the West, whose reality rested on physical strength and endurance. In dismissing the romantic vision, Freedman affirms his own vision of the West as a world of hardships and change.

S. Beth Atkin, in *Voices From the Fields: Children of Migrant Farmworkers Tell Their Stories* (1993), uses photographs to establish her settings and poetry to structure her plot. She brings the field of farm workers to life by using photos that begin with the knowledge readers already have of migrant workers—many bodies, young and old, male and female, bending over a crop and picking—and ends with a look into the eyes of one of the workers. This glimpse shocks readers into acknowledging the common humanity between themselves and the field workers.

The text, then, moves that glimpse into the intimate world of poetry, as Atkin turns her interviews with migrant workers into poetic accounts of life in the fields.

The Foundation of Fact and the Expository Style

The factual basis of the material is the first important marker for informational books. Authors do not create fiction in their minds; they find something in the real world that engages them, that sends them to more research. Eventually, they discern what they want to say about the subject, and, finally, how they want to say it.

The expository style of informational books has, for some time now, been regarded with suspicion. Perhaps it is the style that lends itself to dry, boring accounts. However, recent writers of informational books have found ways to enliven that style, to use it judiciously in order to convey the information of a book in an engaging manner. An expository presentation must have some kind of organizing center, some strategy for presenting the facts.

Jerry Stanley organizes his *Children of the Dust* (1992) by revivifying the Okies' journey west and their heartbreaking experiences in the Dust Bowl. Stanley details the life and school of Weed Patch camp, and, by using a combination of photos, maps, journals, and expository prose, he brings to life a piece of our nation's history. *The Bone Detectives* (1996) introduces readers to forensic anthropologists, doctors who can determine the physical characteristics of a person just from the skeleton. The author, Donna Jackson, follows Dr. Charney as he reconstructs what happened to humans who have died either from natural or unnatural causes. Patricia Lauber's *Dinosaurs Walked Here and Other Stories Fossils Tell* (1987) reverses typical chronology in order to make its point. Showing her readers present-day remains, such as preserved footprints, Lauber demonstrates how these remains can unlock the secrets of the prehistoric world. She uses art and photographs extensively as she moves step by step back into the past to consider the kinds of creatures who would make such footprints or have such bones.

Designing the Structure

Authors search for the story within the subject, selecting, arranging, rearranging the material until the list of facts comes to life. For this reason, authors constantly look for the telling detail, the luminous anecdote, the perfect illustration that will give exactly the impression the author is searching for in order to clarify or establish the meaning. No reader will be absorbed by mere fact. The informational book must delight and show meaning—not necessarily an easy union.

Kathryn Lasky in *Sugaring Time* (1986) strives to recreate solely the parts of the sugaring process that will make a point indelibly; to do this, she chooses the vivid and telling detail: "Breaking out is the hardest part of sugaring. After three months of easy barn living with no loads to pull and not even a fly to swish away, the horses are winter lazy and stubborn." In the accompanying photograph, the two horses shed their winter laziness; one drags a bit behind the other, while the lead horse's head is turned to its mate as if urging him on. Here Lasky has depended on the union of text and photograph to show meaning. In his *To Be a Slave* (1968), Julius Lester uses anecdote from firsthand accounts to create a vivid story. For example, Granny Judith tells the story of the slaves' use of red cloth. Because Africans had no such cloth, they were intrigued by it. As the slave-catchers dropped piece after piece, laying a fateful trail to the ship, the soon-to-be slaves were tricked out of their freedom. Such stories, arranged in a sequence that mirrors the experiences of the slaves, generates more meaning than a set of statistics.

All writers of informational books depend on vivid prose, not only to draw the reader into the world of the material, but to express artfully their vision of the material's meaning; gone are the days of encyclopedic texts. In *Talking Walls* (1992), Margy Burns turns to simile in the introductory paragraph.

> According to an old tale, the only structure on earth that can be seen from the moon is the magnificent Great Wall of China. For about fifteen hundred miles this ancient fortress twists and turns like a massive stone serpent across the mountains, plains, and deserts of China. Chinese children and their families and people from many other countries love to visit the wall where they walk along a path, as wide as five horses, that winds along the top of the wall.

Her sentences are carefully crafted with introductory phrases and parallelism. Burns also uses metaphor in some verb choices (*twists, turns*) and simile (*like a massive stone serpent*) in order to expand the readers' understanding of the look of the Great Wall.

David Macaulay's *Ship* (1993) combines the accounts of the building of a seventeenth-century coastal ship with the modern account of its archeological recovery. The account of the recovery, accompanied by detailed illustrations of all parts of the archeological expedition, reads as part adventure, part detective story.

> By the end of the month, everyone has readjusted to a floor that doesn't move, dry clothes, and friendly food. The artifacts are soaking in tanks of solution to reduce deterioration caused by salt water. Like anything removed from one environment and thrust into another each object recovered from the Brazos reef, whether wood, metal, ceramic, glass, or stone requires great care and plenty of time if it is going to adapt and survive. (34–35)

An interesting feature of this book is the inclusion of the archeologist's hands in many of the illustrations. As readers look at maps where the divers are considering going, they see hands holding that map. This metacognitive device helps keep the book in the realm of informational literature and not fiction. The scientists are in control of each step of the search, and it is their knowledge and expertise that allows the caravel to be recreated. Here is fact and story, structure and meaning.

The strength of this genre today lies in the many imaginative approaches that writers have used and continue to use to present fact, not only clearly and accurately, but engagingly. If, at one time, this was a genre mired in poor writing, uninteresting illustration, and mediocre insight, today it is one of the genres that has blossomed into full flower, principally because of writers' willingness to merge their roles as instructors and artists. That merger allows for the conveying of information even as the conveyance is itself a source of imaginative delight.

A number of books on the Civil War, for example, work to personalize the war so that it does not seem merely to be a distant, bloodless event marked by lists of battles. Delia Ray in *Behind the Blue and the Gray* (1991) tells a balanced story of the Civil War from the viewpoints of the North and South. Using photos, drawings, and personal accounts, she establishes the rationale behind each position by using a human touch. Milton Meltzer's *Voices from the Civil War* (1989) quotes extensively from diaries, using drawings and photos strategically. By framing each diary entry with an authorial commentary, Meltzer deftly selects and arranges his material, allowing the participants to speak for themselves as much as possible. *The Boys War* (1990), by Jim Murphy, takes readers even deeper into the realization that war requires human sacrifice. Juxtaposing heartwrenching photos of young soldiers on both sides with battle scenes demonstrates to the readers that the warriors "standing gloriously to the colors" were boys.

The use of such sources supports the interpretive elements of the book. Thus, Donna Brook's *The Journey of English* (1998) uses maps to show the breadth of the language's spread. Frederick L. And Patricia McKissack's *Rebels against Slavery* (1996) uses songs, photographs, contemporary illustrations, personal testimony, and contemporary newspaper accounts to recreate the story of slave revolts in North America. Jim Murphy's engaging *Gone A-Whaling* (1998) brings to life the early days of the whaling industry by casting the story in the voices of the boys who went to sea, allowing them to speak from their own letters and journal entries and illustrating those texts with contemporary photographs, engravings, and prints. Each of these writers uses original material to support an interpretive view of the event or matter.

Borrowing from Other Genres

If the factual base is the common ground for informational literature, then how will child readers know what is factual if imagination is counted as a necessary ingredient? How will they trust the specifics if they know the framework cannot be real? After all, if the readers have never been to the town's water works before (and chances are good that they haven't) how will that look any less like fantasy than the magic school bus that Joanna Cole invented to take Ms. Frizzle and her class on such an excursion?

To arrange and select this material in order to make a world live for its readers, informational literature takes lessons from fiction; it re-creates believable characters, discovers plotlines, establishes points of view, describes settings carefully, and orders the material around a theme. Authors may look closely at an event and see its complexity, its inextricable entanglement in the culture and setting from which it comes. Thus, authors focus on an event or a person and work at reproducing complexity, not reductive simplicity.

Discovering a valid plotline in informational literature is a bit different from constructing a plotline in fiction: nonfiction authors are bound by their researched material for their matter. Yet, in informational literature these plotlines can still take many forms: straight chronology, reverse chronology, concurrent plots, inverted plots. In *Pyramid of the Sun, Pyramid of the Moon* (1988), Leonard Everett Fisher uses a straight chronological approach to describe the building of the ancient city of Teotihuacán. His illustrations show the workforce constructing the pyramids, the priests sacrificing there, and the masses of people as they look at the finished product. David Macaulay's *Ship* (1993) works its way from the end to the beginning as it follows underwater archaeologists piecing together a caravel from the seventeenth century. Jason Gaes, in *My Book for Kids with Cansur* (1987), uses a flashback technique to tell his story of battling cancer, using his own language and even invented spelling. Julie Downing, in *Mozart Tonight* (1991), begins with Mozart and his wife riding in a carriage to his opera premier in a Prague concert hall in 1787; then she uses the flashback technique to incorporate the rest of the story of Mozart's life. *The Wing on the Flea* (1961), by Ed Emberly, skips across time periods by juxtaposing triangle shapes such as a rocket's tail and a dragon's tail. He places unlikely objects side by side—such as fish tails and ice cream cones—and keeps them all together with rhyme. Each of these authors chooses a plot strategy suitable to the subject and the audience.

At the heart of the endeavor is the well-drawn character and the believable world. Readers expect to identify with characters who experience, discover, learn about the past and the world around them. They also expect to be immersed in a world that completely fills their senses. They should see that world with paintings, drawings, and photographs as well as finely crafted descriptions. They should hear that world through songs, dialects, and everyday sounds. They should smell that world through descriptions and taste it the same way. Even touch can be conveyed through illustrations and language.

Leonard Everett Fisher's *The Wailing Wall* (1989) for example, uses the twentieth-century symbol of the remaining temple wall in Jerusalem to retell Jewish history. Through text and black-and-white paintings, Fisher leads his readers through the complicated and ancient world of the Fertile Crescent. Maps and diagrams clearly set forward the outlines of Jewish history while paintings of people worshiping at the wall add an emotional element to the story. Fisher means to give as much context as possible to the wall so that readers will understand its importance to the Jewish people.

Walter Wick's *A Drop of Water* (1997) combines science of the late nineteenth century with today's science to produce a lush, beautiful, simple and engaging book. Using early science experiments for children, Wick recreated the procedures and photographed the results. The illustrations depict the entire world of a drop of water, showing it in its beautiful, elegant transformation. The graphic displays show ice, snowflakes, a drop entering a larger body of water, condensation, prismatic effects, and all manner of bubbles to suggest the wonder of, not only water, but the earth and the field of science itself.

Establishing the point of view from which the story will be told is crucial in informational literature. First person draws readers close to the subject matter. For instance, Julius Lester's *To Be a Slave* (1968) uses first-person slave narratives extensively. This serves to give the readers eyewitness accounts of slavery. Choosing this form also underscores the slaves' rights to tell their own stories, something that was not automatically granted to them at the close of the Civil War. In fact, historians did not want to take down personal histories of slaves during that time period, so Lester's choice gives a voice to people not previously heard.

Third person allows an omniscient narrator to select, arrange, and interpret the events. When Patricia and Frederick McKissack decided to write *Rebels against Slavery* (1996), they chose a third-person narrator that allowed them to present with authority their findings about five different slave revolts, including those of Nat Turner, Cinque, and John Brown. The McKissacks use song lyrics, pictures, photographs, testimonies, and newspaper accounts to tell their stories of a people who refused to remain in slavery. It is the reasonable voice of the third-person narrator that brings order to the mass of material.

No strategy open to the writer of fiction is necessarily closed to the writer of the informational book. The boundary is one of fact, but that boundary does not prohibit an engaging, imaginative presentation of that fact. The trick in this is the balance between the material and the presentation.

The Necessity of Personal Vision

Because it would be literally impossible to relate everything known about a particular topic, a personal vision is necessary as an organizing tool alone. But, even if this were not true, the author would still need to find a way to create his or her own personal vision if the book is to be more than a mere literal recitation. This means that writers of information books need to think about what a fact means. In contemporary information books, there is a need for an informed human mind creating a personal vision. This means, in addition, that the author shares his or her vision of the subject, even in his or her tone, whether that vision is whimsical, humorous, or serious.

One result of the explicitly personal vision is a willingness in authors of information books to abandon breadth of coverage for depth. Snippets of fact, strings of dates, bloodless short paragraphs on a range of topics have been replaced with in-depth ruminations about the nature of the event or person under examination. *Commodore Perry in the Land of the Shogun* (1985), by Rhoda Blumberg, is an example of a book that examines in depth both a person and an event. Readers see through the eyes of Japanese drawings the alarm that went through Japan when Commodore Perry tried to open its harbors. Readers also hear the panic through the text.

> People in the fishing village of Shimoda were the first to spot four huge hulks, two streaming smoke, on the ocean's surface approaching the shore. "Giant dragons puffing smoke," cried some. "Alien ships of fire," cried others. Surely something horrible was happening on this day, Friday, July 8, 1853. (13)

The tone and stance here are closer to the novel than to the encyclopedia.

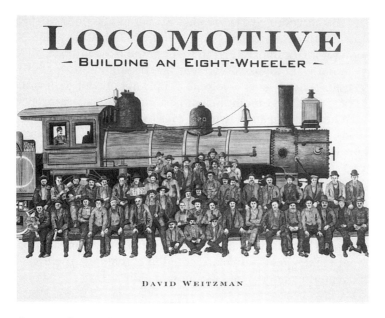

Illustration by David Weitzman for his *Locomotive: Building an Eight-Wheeler.*
Copyright © 1999. Reprinted by permission of Houghton Mifflin Company.

Some informational books work towards allowing children to establish their own personal visions on a given subject. *I Never Saw Another Butterfly* (1973) is a collection of drawings and poems from the State Jewish Museum in Prague. Firi Weil chose from over 1,000 such drawings and poems to vividly illustrate what life was like for these children. Completely devoid of authorial commentary, seemingly placed in haphazard fashion, this combination of text and illustration tells the harrowing tale of innocence destroyed, but beauty cherished. Readers must make their own sense of the material, must complete the picture for themselves. In this sense the reader takes on the same role as the writer to find meaning and significance in fact.

When the author develops a strong personal vision of the factual material and conveys that vision, the information book is likely to have a strongly personal stance that encourages the reader to participate in the passion of the writer. The purpose of the book is thus much more than the conveying of information; it is the sharing of an entire sense of purpose, of meaning, and even of excitement. David Weitzman's *Locomotive: Building an Eight-Wheeler* (1999), for example, may not seem at first to be the kind of topic suitable for a young reader; it is, after all, about a nineteenth-century technology. But Weitzman, himself a skilled craftsman, is also paying homage to the precise and meticulous skills of the men who built these machines, and this sense of homage dominates the book. The illustrations are black-and-white line drawings with extremely fine lines that allow for

Pointers for Teachers: Evaluating Information Books

- What is the author's personal vision for the body of facts on which the book is based? Would that vision be accessible to a child audience?
- What emotions does the author want the reader to take away, given this reading? How does the author balance those emotions with a sense of objectivity?
- How has the author made the work appropriate to the intended audience?
- How has the author used illustrations throughout the text to supplement, extend, or enhance the meanings of the text? Are the illustrations photographs, charts, drawings, contemporary works that have been reproduced?
- What does the author do in the book to suggest his or her expertise? How might the reader learn about the kinds of research the author has done?

---

the kind of precise and specific images that show the craftsmanship of the building. This same precision marks his text:

> The planer is used for making flat surfaces, such as the main and side rods, and for cutting slots. The rod is clamped down to the table. The machinist adjusts the tool for the first cut and then turns on the planer. The table glides back and forth under the tool, planing off long strips of metal. After each cut, the tool moves over and makes another cut right next to the previous one, producing a smooth surface. There are large planers that can machine engine frames more than twenty feet long.

The sentences are uncomplicated and spare, with few adjectives and simple verb structures. All of this is purposeful, because the text is meant to clarify the illustration beneath it: a very precise drawing of a most complicated machine. The simplicity combined with the precision of the illustrations marks Weitzman's approach to what he sees as a wonderful, extraordinary, and artistic creation: the locomotive.

Issues in the Genre of Information Books

Is it legitimate to use fictional material in an informational book?

At first blush it would seem that the answer to this question must be no. An informational book is by definition a work of nonfiction, and, though it may use some of the techniques of a work of fiction, the material in it—its contents—should not be fictional.

Yet, informational books have, in fact, used fictional elements to contribute to the ways in which they present their material. In effect, this is a working out of the dual roles of informational books: to instruct and, at the same time, delight.

The fictional elements are usually used to create an effective means of bringing the reader or viewer into the work, to engage that reader so that he or she may find the informational material enticing. That is, the addition of fictional material is a means of organizing, supporting, introducing, or presenting the information.

In the study of the natural world, perhaps no one does this better than Toshi Yoshida, a Japanese artist who has used colored pencils to capture the wildlife of Africa. In *Rhinoceros Mother* (1991), Yoshida begins with a wounded rhinoceros, attended by her young baby. Yoshida asks his reader how she may have been wounded, and, in a series of black-and-white sketches, shows certain possibilities: a cheetah, a gnu, an antelope. Finally, he goes back into the past and tells the story of how a baby elephant wandered over to the baby rhinoceros, and this led to a clash of the two mothers, a clash in which the rhinoceros was wounded by the elephant's tusk. In *Young Lions* (1989), Yoshida tells of the first hunt of a trio of young lions. Their surprising lack of success suggests their need for practice but also the fact that the predators are not always successful in the hunt.

In both texts Yoshida uses fictional constructs—two stories of a group of African animals—in order to convey information about those animals. He might have avoided this fiction and simply used statistics about hunting success, or simply used photographs to accompany descriptions of life on the African plains, focusing on the potential enemies of a rhinoceros. Instead, he conveys this same information vividly through the use of a fictional tale that is based strongly on his research.

In this sense, Yoshida has employed fiction to create nonfiction. It is not an infrequent technique. In *Walter Dragun's Town* (1989), Sheila Sancha tells the story of the medieval English town of Stanford, focusing on the crafts and trade of the town. All of the events, the figures, the names, even the illustrations of the main characters, are all based on material from the town's history. But to enliven the material, Sancha tells the history as a story, emphasizing especially the unfairness and corruption of Walter Dragun. This corruption is a matter of historical record, but, as Sancha pictures real characters who suffer because of that corruption, Dragun becomes even more of a villain.

Sometimes it is only the narrator who carries the fictional elements of the story. In *Africa: Brothers and Sisters* (1993), Virginia Kroll tells of a number of African tribes and their distinguishing characteristics to make the point that there are many distinctions among the African peoples. She uses the context of a conversation between a fictional father and son to support the emotional power of the information. In *Barn* (1996), Debby Atwell uses a most unusual narrator: the barn itself speaks to take the reader through its century-long history.

In using such a technique, the writer needs to be careful to delineate fact from fiction. The purpose of using the fictional material must be clear and potent, principally serving as a means for engaging the reader so that he or she will find the information of the book more vivid.

What role does illustration play in the genre of the information book?

In the earlier days of informational literature, authors included few illustrations, but currently illustrations are an inseparable part of the art form. Authors are careful to create detailed settings with text and with photographs, facsimiles, drawing, and graphics. The richness of the context will enable the readers to be transported to the world of the book, so particular attention is given here.

Because of the visual nature of our society, authors can take as much time selecting illustrations and writing captions as writing the text itself. There are many roles that illustration plays, each important, not only in establishing setting in the minds of the readers, but also in creating meaning. Illustrations can give a lot of information quickly, much more quickly than pure text. For instance, the meeting between the Pilgrims and the Wampanoogs in Marcia Sewall's *Thunder from the Clear Sky* (1995) is given an ironical twist in the illustration of the Indians rowing out to the Pilgrims' ship. Although the ship is small, readers who know their history realize that its size here masks its true import. So, too, the eager Indians leaning forward in their canoes and paddling hard toward the ship will find destruction to their way of life, camouflaged in bright beads and colorful cloth.

Illustrations also create the emotional tone the author wishes. Seymour Simon's *Storms* (1989) uses a dramatic black sky illumined by lightning and swirling clouds to suggest the force and size of the electrical storm. His *Whales* (1989) has the same effect. He has the bodies of these mammals fill up the horizon of the sea as they leap across two pages of illustration at a time. The effect is quite different from Carol Carrick's *Whaling Days* (1993), whose history of whaling from ancient times to today is punctuated with striking woodcuts by David Frampton. Their strong lines convey the mystery and size of whales as well.

Illustrations will certainly amplify and extend the text, but they can also suggest the background of the culture or experience behind the text. Susan Campbell Bartoletti's *Growing Up in Coal Country* (1996) and *Kids on Strike!* (1999) work well in this way. Both cover illustrations show a group of children, one having just come out of the mine, the other holding placards begging for the opportunity to go to school. Both show children in crisis; the mining children are covered with grit and dust, while the striking children hope simply to have some free hours in their childhood in which to do more than work at the most awful, boring jobs. Yet, surprisingly, the children stand with fortitude, with camraderie, with strength. Their lives are harsh and difficult, but they have not been destroyed. This is a balance that Bartoletti maintains throughout her choice of illustrations: the harshness of the conditions that maim and kill and wither, and the refusal of the children to succumb.

Hiroshima No Pika (1980) by Toshi Maruki, for example, takes the complex subject of the U.S. bombing of Hiroshima during World War II and presents a single unified vision of it—the vision of the victims. His expressionist paintings first show people living normally, going to work, riding bikes, jumping on streetcars; then he shows human beings in various stages of flight, in various settings, always with the posture and expression of terror. He discolors both the landscape and the bodies of the characters, so that the first appears orange, the second a horrible sickly green. The overall effect is one of disgust and makes a strong case against war of any sort. Although not everyone will share the perspective here, most readers will affirm the interpretation that Maruki has given to these facts as both valid and powerful.

In informational books, photography often plays a key role. Here, as with any picture book, the elements of design help the artist highlight or play up the scale of any single element, thus affecting the entire meaning of the work. In *Let There Be Light: A Book about Windows* (1988), James Cross Giblin tilts the camera up to look at Rome's Pantheon from the point of view of an onlooker; it is an angle that emphasizes size and grandeur. In Margy Burns's *Talking Walls* (1992), large-scale images of the Great Wall of China encourage a sense of participation by including close-ups of young boys on the Wall, one of whom, with arms outstretched, takes up fully a third of the illustration. Raymond Bial uses the exquisite clarity of his photographs in *The Strength of These Arms* (1997) to bring to life the time of slavery, as he photographs slaves' homes, tools, cooking utensils, and clothing, shows the glory of the lush simplicity of Shaker architecture in *Shaker Home* (1994), evokes the rigorous charm of early American education in *One-Room School* (1999), and involves the reader in the sights that would have greeted a fearful and desperate runaway slave in *The Underground Railroad* (1995). In each of these works the illustrator marries the text to the illustration to present a consistent and unified vision of the event.

Perhaps no two works demonstrate the interpretive quality of photography better than Kathleen Kenna's *A People Apart* (1995) and Leslie Ann Hauslein's *The Amish: The Enduring Spirit* (1991). Hauslein's full-color book begins with a cover that shows the silhouette of a carriage against a spectacular sunset. In fact, all of the illustrations are spectacular, the kind one might find on a postcard; the text is, for the most part, limited to explanatory captions. The photographs are clear and lush, connecting the people to the land. They are very much the tourist shots, however, very much the view point of the outsider. The photographs of Kathleen Kenna's *A People Apart*, in contrast, are all black and white, and they accompany chapters organized around the life of the Amish. The portraits here are intimate and personal, very much the insider's point of view. The focus is not so much on the land as on the complexities of living as an Amish person, with all of its seeming simplicity and seeming contradiction.

Are there, as in biography, effective and artistic series that are a part of this genre?

Any work within a series must in some way deal with the reputation that a series book still has. In the genre of informational books, series are indeed alive and well, however, and they are responding to the same kind of impulses that other books in the genre are responding to. This means that any given book in a series does not necessarily have to walk lockstep with any other given book in the series. Given that an informational book must, in some manner, represent a personal vision of the author, it would be almost impossible for such a limited approach to work.

The result of this is a number of series that approach their intriguing topics interestingly and engagingly.

Trains: The History of Railroads (1991) by David Jeffers is part of a well-done series on wheels. The text informs about the history of the subject and its current status around the world. But it is the author's inclusion of photographs and drawings, all with interesting captions, that pulls readers into the subject matter.

The Colonial Craftsman series, written by Leonard Everett Fisher, focused on different professions found in early U.S. society such as doctors, schoolmasters, tanners, and papermakers. Fisher gives a broad view of how society worked then. He also chose to use woodcuts as illustrations and their primitive feel lends the distance Fisher wanted between a modern audience and this earlier time.

How It Feels to Fight for Your Life (1989) is one in a series of "How It Feels" books. This particular book tells the stories of fourteen young people fighting for their lives with diseases ranging from cancer to spina bifida. Not only does Jill Krementz present the medical issues but she also presents little discussed ones like sibling rivalry, which can develop when one child receives all the attention of parents or a young person's fight for independence that is rendered impossible by a disease that forces the child to be dependent for care. Paying special attention to the emotional side of illness brings it into the realm of readers' experiences.

If popularity is any indication of acceptance, then *The Magic School Bus* series stands as good evidence. Joanna Cole's work has avoided any of the stodginess left in science study, as unforgettable and unflappable Ms. Frizzle takes her children on hair-raising adventures through the town's waterworks, the inside of the earth, the human body, the universe. No subject is too broad or too well known for Cole to tackle. It is the unique presentation that keeps readers interested: the cartoon style art, the dialogue bubbles, the labels, even the text itself. There are so many stimulants that any child can be entertained, and it is that element of entertainment that teaches at the same time.

The trick in any of these series books is to be sure to allow for personal vision. Certainly there is a gain in using the same format, the same layout, the same kinds of voices, perhaps even the same kinds of approaches to topics in a given series. At the same time, the books, to be excellent informational works on an individual basis, need to bear the mark of the personal vision of the author.

How does informational literature work to encourage a moral viewpoint in a child reader?

The answer to this question lies in the nature of the author, the type of audience targeted, and the degree of knowledge an audience has about the subject matter. Behind it lies the assumption that informational books are not just presenting information, but are encouraging responses.

Laurence Pringle in *Death Is Natural* (1977) seeks to illustrate his belief that death is part of a natural cycle, not an event that ushers the person to eternity. Using multiple examples from nature, Pringle argues that, although human beings are the only ones who remember their dead and have a consciousness that can project their own annihilation, humans are still part of the natural world at the time of death. He asks the reader to consider the meaning of such a position.

Eleanor Coerr's *Sadako* (1993), illustrated by Ed Young, asks the question, What lengths should a country go in order to win a war? Coerr tells the story of Sadako, a young Japanese girl who died of leukemia caused by the atom bomb dropped during World War II. The story of Sadako's fight for life is presented

Pointers for Teachers

Interactive Possibilities
- After reading an information book aloud, discuss with the class the nature of the narrator. What kind of person is speaking? How do you know? Whose voices are you not hearing? Are those silent voices problematic?
- Discuss the balance between fact and interpretation in a given text you have read.
- Choose an illustration from an information book. Ask the class to point out what they see in the picture, and then to speculate on why the author included that particular illustration.
- Find pairs of recent and older information books on the same topic. Have students compare the two in small groups of three or four. Then have them think about how it is that researchers make progress in a given field.

Writing Possibility
- Break the class into writing pairs to construct an annotated calendar based on research they have done related to a theme that the students have chosen. The themes may deal with anything that can be organized chronologically, such as life cycles, historical periods, any process that is located in specific seasons.

Hands-On Possibilities
- As a class, construct a time capsule. Bring in newspaper stories and have the students read them to see what sorts of things are generally included. Then break the students into groups of four or five to have each group choose an object for the capsule. You will open it as a class at the end of the year.
- Working in pairs, have students research games or recipes from a period studied in an information book that you have read. Have them share these with the class.

---

through the outlines of an old Japanese legend: If the person who is ill can fold 1,000 paper cranes, the gods will grant her the wish to be well. Sadako falls short of her goal and so dies. The question of morality in wartime has been focused by the heartwrenching death of a young girl. Ed Young adds more emotional weight to the story with his 300 pastel illustrations, which are expressionistic renderings of Sadako's life.

Certainly one manifestation of the moral voice in nonfiction for children must be a cry for justice and peace. This is suggested in two books about Native Americans. *To Live in Two Worlds* (1984) by Brent Ashabranner is a contemporary look at the Navajo nation. Here readers are given facts, figures, and personal accounts about the life of poetry and despair that the Navajos lead. Their collective cry that they are real people is extended repeatedly in the photography, the range of age, mood, and style in the people shown. Russell Freedman's *An Indian Winter* (1992) recreates the journey to North Dakota taken by Prince Alexander Philipp Maximilian and Karl Bodmer in 1815. Freedman uses Bodmer's illustrations and Maximilian's text to bring back to life the Mandans in all their uniqueness. When readers find out that this tribe was wiped out by smallpox, they are asked to consider the prices natives paid so that white men could expand their land holdings.

A different kind of call for justice is also found in Mary Ann Fraser's *Sanctuary* (1994). She tells the story of the first wildlife sanctuary, Three Arch Rock, created by Teddy Roosevelt in 1903. At that time, two naturalists were appalled at the sea lion's destruction and the destruction of other wild animals' habitats, so they decided to photograph the wildlife that depended on Three Arch Rock for survival. Fraser uses original photographs and pieces of the naturalists' journals in order to make her point.

Yet another call for justice and charity comes in *Voices from the Streets* (1996) by S. Beth Atkin, in which readers are given a shocking look at former gang members. Atkin shows how and why young people join gangs and the fragmented families most of the members come from through text, photographs, poems, journal entries, and scrapbook keepsakes. The insider's view tells a chilling tale of how easy it is to get into a gang and how difficult it is to get out.

Should children read books of integrity and beauty? Yes.

Should children ignore the distasteful when it is aimed at their reading level? No.

Should books have a moral voice that calls for a response? Yes, as long as such books call for a considered response, and do not manipulate this response from the child reader.

Authors and Illustrators of Informational Literature

Writers of informational books make the complex easy to understand, interpreting concepts for the child reader. They also write about what interests them, finding their subjects in newspaper stories, in photographs, and in the casual comment made by a friend. These writers then thoroughly research their material to be as accurate as possible in their reporting. Once the project is researched, the writers look for the fresh angle, the new approach to show the significance of the project. In other words, they move away from viewing a subject as simply a conglomeration of facts and toward understanding the ideas that give the subject life.

Holling Clancy Holling (1900–1973)

In his *Paddle-to-the-Sea* (1941), Holling Clancy Holling tells the story of a young boy who carves a canoe and paddler that he puts in at the headwaters of Lake Superior. The book recounts the canoe's four-year journey to the sea, traveling through each of the Great Lakes and along the St. Lawrence Seaway until it finally reaches the Grand Banks and the Atlantic Ocean. Along the way it encounters a logjam, frozen waters, the system of locks at the Soo, a forest fire, Niagra

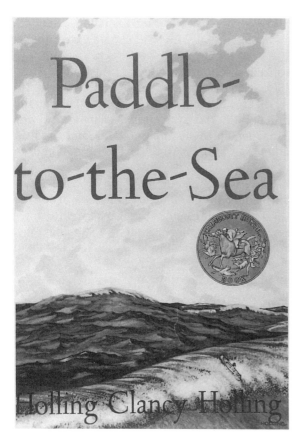

Illustration by Holling Clancy Holling for his *Paddle-to-the-Sea*. Copyright © 1941. Reprinted by permission of Houghton Mifflin Company.

Falls, and pulping mills. It survives all of these, aided by friendly fishermen, until it finally does reach the ocean.

Holling's interest here is to recreate the environment of the Great Lakes. He wants his readers to finish the book with a sense, not only of the geography of the lakes, but with an understanding of their complex ecosystems and the ways of life that they support. To do so he uses the techniques of fiction. He writes what might be considered a quest, as the small canoe, set dramatically in the illustrations against the huge scale of the Great Lakes, takes on a kind of representative life: Just as the reader hopes for the success of the hero, so does the reader hope for the success of this tiny craft.

In all of his books, Holling creates an environment through the focus on a single character. In focusing on that character's exploits, the reader is also learning much about the world of that figure. In *Minn of the Mississippi* (1951), Holling follows the Mississippi River by concentrating on a small turtle who is found by a young Indian boy. Focusing on the role of instinct, Holling tells of the life of the turtle, who leaves the headwaters of the river and travels south. At the same time that he tells of the turtle's life, he also tells of the surrounding environment, at times blending the two together.

> Minn liked the smell of the new streams as they joined the River. Some raced from far forests tawny with wood-mold, holding a bitter-sweet tang of timber and roots. Some crawled from flat prairies, scented with lush green plants. Marshy creeks smelled and tasted of muck, rocky streams brought odors of granite, shale or limestone. There were strong tastes of copper and iron in this fresh, north-wilderness river. (28)

Though the focus here is on the tastes and smells that the turtle experiences, Holling has also passed on information about the nature of the Mississippi—that it is made of a series of smaller streams—and about the nature of the water that flows into the river.

In *Pagoo* (1957), Holling turns to the life of a hermit crab and his surrounding tidal pools. Here Holling focuses on the dangerous life of the crab who faces enemies all around, particularly when he is in the process of trying to find and fit into a new shell. Here Holling is even closer to the consciousness of the principal character.

> Though now he was a young boy-Hermit, Pagoo did not feel very important. Somehow he felt unprotected, not quite secure, and the unprotected feeling, he was certain, crept over him from the rear. Surely something was missing back there—his tail was not complete—he needed a—
>   "Scoot!" hissed Instinct. "Go find some sort of cover for that bare and tender behind!" (18)

The personification of Instinct is here done to make a vivid point: that Pagoo reacts instinctively to certain needs and dangers. This characterization continues throughout the text as Pagoo faces a number of dangers in his quest, not only to survive, but to find a mate and reproduce.

Holling is aware of the tension involved in using fictional patterns in his work. "We chose this small Hermit Crab as our main character," he writes, "because these clownish creatures are found along the beaches of many seas. We have tried to tell Pagoo's story against a factual background" (5). It is that mixture of "story" with "factual background" that mark's Holling's work. His is an approach that represented a distinct shift, and, though numbers of informational book writers argue against the inclusion of such material, suggesting that the truth is marvelous enough to hold the attention of a reader, still Holling's approach merges instruction and delight.

Patricia Lauber (b. 1924)

Patricia Lauber's work in the sciences is distinctly different from that of Holling Clancy Holling. Lauber includes nothing that smacks of story, though at times she will turn from her work to address the reader directly. In her *Seeds Pop, Stick, Glide* (1981), she organizes her material around a simple question: How do seeds travel? The text moves easily from a straightforward omniscient narrator to an intimate *you*: "You have been for a fall walk. Home again, you find you are covered" with sticking seeds (2). Lauber also relies on easily imagined similes and metaphors to help her readers see what she sees. Thus, lines like "bracts are as stiff and sharp as fishhooks" (6) and "Each has the shape of an umbrella" (8) enliven the text. The flow from text to picture is managed with design, subject matter, and the angle of the camera. The photographs range from children playing around seeds to close-ups of the seed carriers themselves. Readers begin far away, but move in for these close-ups. At these moments, the little-known world of seeds comes into focus.

Lauber's attention to detail found a subject in the eruption of Mt. St. Helens in *Volcano: The Eruption and Healing of Mt. St. Helens* (1986). This time her story centers around the life that inevitably pushes its way up through the destruction. In fact, it was the last picture of the book, the tiny Alpine pink flowers, that startled her into researching the volcano. Using photographs and drawings, she sets the stage for the blast. The text and photographs thoroughly examine every part of the region where the blast occurred, using photographs of the mountain before and after the eruption to imprint on the readers' minds the breadth of the eruption. The eruption itself is shown in a series of photographs as well as through images of the destruction around it. Lauber uses the well-known picture of the trees that had been leveled by the blast and explains how they were destroyed: It was not through wind, because not even a 200-mile-an-hour windstorm could have dropped those huge trees. Instead, it was through a "stone wind," ranging in size from "grains of sand to blocks as big as cars." Once again, her clear language uses understandable similes. In the end, Lauber shows life. True, no humans could have survived, but some plants and animals did. She even helps her readers to be thankful for the lowly termite by celebrating its tenacity for life.

In much of her work, Lauber portrays the scientist as something of a detective. Science is the art of unlocking mysteries. Lauber's *Snakes Are Hunters* (1988) carefully details the life and habits of several kinds of snakes. She answers implicit questions: How do snakes move without legs to help them? How can they eat animals bigger than they are? With a clear text and helpful illustrations, Lauber encourages her readers to understand the answers to such questions. In *Living with Dinosaurs* (1991), Lauber invites readers to imagine themselves moving back through 75 million years to when the dinosaurs lived. At the end of the book Lauber closes with an explanation of "how we know what we know." She reminds readers of how fossils are formed and can speak to a scientist about origins. "By using our brains, we can learn about worlds that existed long before people did. By using our imaginations, we can go back 75 million years" (47). This concentration allows the child reader to perceive something of the workings of the detective scientist.

Applying that same combination of imagination and detection, Lauber examines the facts of Amelia Earhart's last flight in *Lost Star* (1988). She tells Earhart's story from her early tomboy exploits to her later desire to defy societal expectations and become a pilot. Lauber carefully grounds her story in fact remembered by Earhart herself. "What mattered was setting herself a challenge and meeting it. What mattered was showing that women could do what men could do and enouraging other women to do what they were capable of. That was why she was flying over the Pacific, looking for a speck of land. Fame was never her goal" (3).

With a judicious use of family photographs, Lauber builds the tale of the plucky young woman who looked at life's challenges. Lauber examines the mystery of Earhart's last flight as a scientist, putting forth several hypotheses and testing them for accuracy. Had she been lost at sea? Was she taken prisoner by the Japanese? Had she been on a secret mission? Had she died of a disease in prison? Lauber finds that, in the end, there is no conclusive answer.

In *Seeing Earth from Space* (1990), Lauber takes another decidedly unusual point of view. Using the vantage point of space, Lauber instructs the child reader about storms, clouds, man-made pollution; she explores through remote sensing. In doing this, she also demonstrates the ways that geologists and weatherpersons try to understand both natural patterns and the ways in which humanity is affecting the earth. Seeing the whole, the child reader learns just how fragile the planet is. At the end, Lauber uses for the first time the inclusive *we* when she asks readers to treasure and protect the earth.

In all of her books, Lauber shows an awareness of her audience's needs, ranging from her engaging narrative voice to her bold and sometimes unusual photography. For her, the use of fictional elements is not necessary: Her narrative voice will itself engage the reader.

Joanna Cole (b. 1944) and Bruce Degen (b. 1945)

In creating their Magic School Bus series, Joanna Cole and Bruce Degen moved well beyond Holling Clancy Holling in their use of fantasy elements to convey information. The central conceit in each of the books is the role of Ms. Frizzle, who, with her Magic School Bus, brings children all around the solar system to examine phenomena. The series has been put on CD–ROM, picked up by Public Broadcasting Station, and is generally known for its lighthearted approach to science, providing students with so much fun that they do not realize that they are learning. Cole and Degen use color, busy page designs, and facts mixed with outrageous episodes. But, at the conclusion of each book, they undercut their technique by separating fantasy from fact.

In *Lost in the Solar System* (1990), Cole and Degen begin with Ms. Frizzle's unforgettable person. None of her students can wait to see what she has on today; her apparel hints at where the school bus will go. The large text relates the facts the students are learning; the small text is the exchange going on between the teacher and children or among themselves. The familiar school talk about assignments, the teacher, each other, puts readers in a world that they know well, but the unusual field trips catapault readers into the unknown with the students. Cole and Degen keep this tension until the last page, when characters and readers are brought back into the world of reality.

Inside the Earth (1987) uses the same format, and suggests reactions students might have to the new and the strange. The students go on the field trip to collect rocks firsthand. When one of the students says, "I'm not used to Ms. Frizzle yet" (16), readers can empathize humorously—Ms. Frizzle has just handed out jackhammers. As they are floating on a lava flow, one student complains, "My mother said I'm not allowed to go inside the earth" (28), suggesting an apprehension about the new. In *Inside the Human Body* (1989), the children have to put up the bus window when they are in the stomach to avoid the food being digested. When the bus comes to the nose, a student shouts, "We're in the nose? I'm so grossed out!" Once again Cole and Degen use the same closing format to bring the fantasy science lesson gently back to the real world.

It is Cole and Degen's awareness of how children's feelings affect their learning that endear them to readers' hearts. From close observation they know how children in and out of school behave and they weave that behavior into the stories. They also know how much children love the unusual, and so include more than the unusual in each text.

David Macaulay (b. 1946)

David Macaulay, a trained architect, has made his name by explaining how things work, by making the abstract concrete, by bringing technology to the untutored. In one of his early books, *Underground* (1976), he shows his readers the workings of a city beneath the ground, demonstrating the complex systems that are necessary in order for a city to deliver services to its inhabitants. Macaulay begins with a street scene, marking the sites where he will go underground in subsequent drawings. The manhole cover that no one even glances at will be one of his subject areas. Another is the foundation of a huge building. He shows that some foundations are built on bedrock while others "float" on piles. Then Macaulay unpacks the utilities—water, sewer, drainage pipes, steam gas, and telephone lines. As readers see the complexity of lines and conjunction points, they are impressed with what makes up the unseen part of a city. Macaulay even manages a bit of humor with a dog sniffing the fire hydrant, a crocodile in the sewer lines, and rats scurrying along the pipes. All of these are sight gags; no mention of them is made in the text.

Illustration by David Macaulay for his *Pyramid*. Copyright © 1975. Reprinted by permission of Houghton Mifflin Company.

Macaulay's most typical approach is seen in *Pyramid* (1975), where he turns his attention to these Egyptian wonders. He begins with a short introduction to the Egyptian way of life, necessary as an underpinning for why these people would spend so much time, energy, and money on the great pyramids. Their preoccupation with eternity gives weight to the argument that a new pharaoh would begin his tomb the day he became ruler. The extreme care of the engineers in designing the pyramids, the hard work of the gangs of laborers, and the process itself are the subjects of this book. Macaulay trvaeled to Egypt himself so that he could get a firsthand sense of the culture and climate where the great edifaces of the pyramids tell the story of the people as well as the pharaoh.

In *Pyramid*—and in a number of works to follow—Macaulay focused on the construction of a large structure

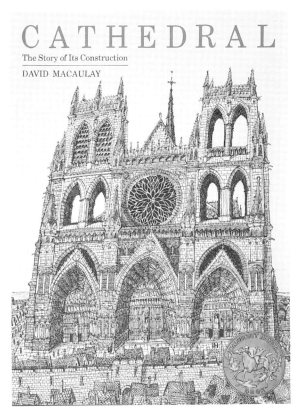

CATHEDRAL
The Story of Its Construction

DAVID MACAULAY

Illustration by David Macaulay for his *Cathedral.* Copyright ©
1973. Reprinted by permission of Houghton Mifflin Comapny.

through the creation of a fictional
context—here, the death of a particular
pharaoh. Though the context is fictional, the construction is representative
of many of the pyramids in terms of
its building, just as in *Cathedral* (1973)
and *Castle* (1977) the buildings stand as
representative of their types. Macaulay
begins with the choice of a site, then
shows the beginnings of the construction, including material on the foundation, the tools, and the workmen and
administrators of the project. He returns
periodically to the same site, using precisely the same perspective, so that the
child reader can see the growth of the
building from its foundation to the completed structure.

In this approach Macaulay follows
the lead of a writer like Holling Clancy
Holling, using a fictional context to give
shape to the information. This is most
certainly true in his *Rome Antics* (1997),
in which Macaulay tours the reader
through the ancient and contemporary
streets of Rome by putting the reader in
the position and perspective of a carrier
pigeon who is bringing an acceptance of
marriage from a woman outside the city
to an artist working within his studio in the old city. Along the way the bird
flies in and about and around Rome's buildings, giving the reader an unusual
perspective.

Macaulay's strength is the clarity of his text and illustration. In *Cathedral,* Macaulay is faced with the difficult task of explaining the complexities of the vaulted
ceiling; he succeeds because of the straightforward simplicity of his text.

> The carpenters then installed pieces of wood, called lagging, that spanned the space
> between two centerings. On top of the lagging the masons laid one course or layer
> of webbing stones. The lagging supported the course of webbing until the mortar
> was dry. The webbing was constructed of the lightest possible stone to lessen the
> weight on the ribs. (55)

The technical terminology is defined in context, and the word is then used in
the immediately following sentence to support its meaning. The two pen-and-
ink illustrations of the interior work show the centering, the wood lagging,

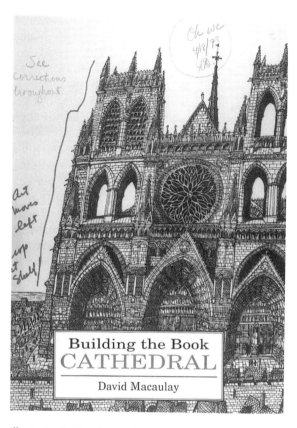

Illustration by David Macaulay for his *Building the Book Cathedral*. Copyright © 1999. Reprinted by permission of Houghton Mifflin Company.

and then, in the second illustration, the course of stones that have been laid over the wooden support. His recent *Building the Book Cathedral* (1999) explores the development of the book, as Macaulay takes the reader on a tour through his process, including rough drafts, research photos, and many revisions to develop the focus and the power of the book. This unique unveiling of the creative process in information books enables the reader to learn, not only the craft of building a cathedral, but the craft of building a book.

Macaulay's *City: The Story of Roman Planning and Construction* (1974) takes an extra step in presenting its subject matter: Macaulay argues that city planning is something modern architects and planners could learn from the Romans. In this book Macaulay invents Verbena, then recreates the steps the Romans would have taken in its planning and construction. First, they determined a city's size; when the population grew too large for the city, they simply built a new city elsewhere. Macaulay's full-page illustrations render the walls, gates, watchtowers, homes, businesses, temples, sewers, water pipes, public baths, forum, central market, public entertainment center, and a theater with a canvas roof. The Roman genius for practical solutions to living is given full range in this book.

In *Ship* (1993), Macaulay uses a unique approach both in subject matter and in his manner of portrayal. The ships he refers to are seventeenth-century ships that were used to deliver goods at lightning speeds. Macaulay, in what he calls a work of fiction, attempts to recreate one of these ships from the scraps of information at hand. Using a fictional framework—a log—he presents the building of one of the ships. Readers are also taken undersea to find remnants. Macaulay uses drawings, documents, maps, and diagrams to suggest the nature of underwater archeology.

Macaulay's *The Way Things Work* (1988) and his revised *The New Way Things Work* (1998) are encyclopedias of movement. The first version took three years to complete and is filled with subjects such as harnessing the elements, working with waves, electricity, automation, and the invention of machines. To add color and humor, Macaulay included a woolly mammoth belonging to the inventor/scientist who appears often throughout the book. In this way, Macaulay delights his readers and brings them into his material, which, again, is dominated by clarity of presentation.

Milton Meltzer (b. 1915)

Working in the social sciences, Milton Meltzer is well known for his study of oppressed peoples. In his three-volume work about the history of the African American *The Black Americans: A History in their Own Words* (1984), for example, Meltzer covers the time from the first slave landing in North America—1619—to the midpoint of the Civil Rights Movement—1966. His technique has, over the years, been one of the most vivid and riveting techniques used in the recreation of a culture's history: He uses the words of that culture, taking material from "letters, diaries, journals, autobiographies, speeches, resolutions, newspapers, pamphlets" to allow the documents to tell the story of the culture. As Meltzer notes, history is written by the pen of the victor, and he means to set the record straight on slavery times, telling the tale of men and women who yearned to be free.

Thirty years earlier, Meltzer published, with Langston Hughes, *A Pictorial History of the Negro in America* (1968). Both Meltzer and Hughes saw that history had not taken into account the African contribution to North America, so they worked together to right this wrong by collecting drawings, photographs, and reproductions to tell the stories of the slave ships, slavery, and abolition. Another book with Langston Hughes—*Black Magic* (1967)—told the story of the African American in the performing arts.

In *Bread and Roses* (1967), Meltzer told the story of the U.S. worker from the Civil War until World War I. He recounts the ways in which the United States left its farm heritage behind and catapulted into the life of the industrialized city. Meltzer agains draws on original sources depicting the life of the miner, the millworker, and the sweatshop worker. Not only does he recount the working life of these people, but also their personal lives, bound up in tenement and shack living. Meltzer sees the anger at such living as erupting into the union struggles, and deftly portrays the gulf that divided the employer from the employee.

In two books—*Never to Forget: The Jews of the Holocaust* (1976) and *Rescue: The Story of How Gentiles Saved Jews in World War II* (1988)—Meltzer turned his attention to the plight of Jews during the Nazi terror. Both testify about the atrocities of the Holocaust. Using his trademark diaries and testimonials, Meltzer recreates the lives of individuals who suffered during that time. In *Rescue,* he focused on rescuers, examining their individual and varied reasons for engaging in such desperate work.

In two books, Meltzer focused on the topic of immigration. *The Hispanic Americans* (1982) situates that people geographically and then follows their lives to New York City. Using photographs, Meltzer emphasizes North America's need for cheap labor, but then turns to all citizens to decry the stereotypes that have oppressed the Hispanic American: "If we are out of touch with what has happened to a people so central to American life, then we cannot know where we are now, and where we may be heading" (140). In *The Jewish Americans* (1982), Meltzer argues that history must be filled with people and their stories if we are to make any sense of events. Meltzer again uses personal texts to tell the story of what it means to be a Jewish American.

In all of his work, Meltzer insists on the personal. History is people, and his task is to recapture voices long silent, or bring forward voices that have never been heard.

Jim Murphy (b. 1947)

Whereas Milton Meltzer works by bringing together a community of voices and perspectives, suggesting a plurality of visions, Jim Murphy works in the opposite direction. He takes a period or event that may boast many, many voices and focuses on just a few that he makes representative. In this approach the experience of a single individual marks the experience of the whole; complexity has become simplicity.

In *A Young Patriot* (1996), Murphy tells about the experience of the Revolutionary War by focusing on the experience of Joseph Plumb Martin, who was fifteen when the war began. Using a book Martin wrote in his old age, Murphy takes the reader through the changes in the war, beginning with Concord and Lexington—which Martin refused to attend—to the battles along the coast, Valley Forge, and the surrender at Yorktown. Martin was present at each of these events. His life becomes the skeleton on which Murphy builds the story of the war. The effect is twofold. First, it gives structure to the large mass of material. Second, it emphasizes the human aspect of the struggle, so that the war is not impersonal but the endeavor of a group of real individuals who fought for many different reasons.

Murphy uses a similar technique in each of his works. In *The Boys' War* (1990), Murphy tells the untold story of boys who fought in the Civil War. Again he uses a limited number of specific stories as representative of the whole, hanging generalizations about the boys' duties on the skeleton of those specific stories.

> Drumming wasn't the only thing these boys did, either. While in camp, they would carry water, rub down horses, gather wood, or cook for the soldiers. There is even evidence that one was a barber for the troops when he wasn't drumming. After a battle, most drummers helped carry wounded soldiers off the field or assisted in burial details. And many drummer boys even got their wish to fight the enemy. (41)

Here Murphy is generalizing, but the power of his text lies in the telling specifics he is able to bring to bear.

> [Johnny] Clem ran away from home in 1861 when he was eleven years old. He enlisted, and the Twenty-second Michigan Regiment took him in as their drummer, paying him thirteen dollars a month for his services. Several months later, at the Battle of Shiloh, Clem earned the nickname of "Johnny Shiloh" when a piece of cannon shell bounced off a tree stump and destroyed his drum. When another drum was shattered in battle, Clem found a musket and fought bravely for the rest of the war, becoming a sergeant in the fall of 1863. (41)

Clem became a sergeant at the age of thirteen or fourteen. It is this kind of specific detail that makes Murphy's text so vivid.

In *The Great Fire* (1995), Murphy tells the story of the Chicago fire by focusing on four lives. He chooses four out of thousands, and chooses a group that is quite varied in its perspectives: Joseph Chamberlin, a twenty-year-old reporter; Horace White, the editor of the *Chicago Tribune;* Alexander Frear, a visitor to the city; and Claire Innes, a twelve-year-old child. Again, Murphy hangs his larger story of the fire on the skeleton of these four voices, voices that are quite vivid: "The storm of falling fire seemed to increase every second.... Looking back... toward the Opera House, I saw the smoke and flames pouring out of State Street, from the very point we had just left, and the intervening space was filled with the whirling embers that beat against the houses and covered the roofs and window-sills." (67)

In *Gone A-Whaling* (1998), Murphy expands his voices and allows many boys to speak in describing the history of North American whaling. Murphy's range in this book is a wide one; he follows the industry from its beginnings up until the present. But, once again, it is the telling quote that brings life to his story.

> Turning upon his side, he began to move in a circular direction, slowly at first, then faster and faster, until he was rushing round at tremendous speed, his great head raised quite out of the water at times, clashing his enormous jaws. Torrents of blood poured from his spout-hole, accompanied by hoarse bellowings...caused by the laboring breath trying to pass through the clogged air passages.... In a few minutes he subsided slowly into death, his mighty body reclined on one side, the fin uppermost waving limply as he rolled to the swell, while small waves broke gently over the carcass in a low, monotonous surf, intensifying the profound silence that had succeeded the tumult of our conflict with the late monarch of the deep. (80–81)

The vividness of this description speaks for itself, and Murphy's ability to write vivid descriptions creates a whole that is quite moving, It leads naturally to the concluding chapter, which is a passionate plea for the protection of whales.

In fact, Murphy, like Meltzer, allows people to speak for themselves, and, though his technique is different from Meltzer's, the end result is the same: History becomes vivid and real.

Thinking and Writing about and from within the Genre of Nonfiction

Thinking and Writing about the Genre of Nonfiction

1. Read Russell Freedman's *Indian Chiefs* (1987) and *Kids at Work* (1994). For an entry in a critical encyclopedia of writers of children's literature, write a three-page article that describes Russell's techniques as a writer of informational books.

2. Gather together a grouping of books about the same subject, either scientific or historical, and examine the ways in which they present their material. Then draw

up a list of recommendations for the librarians and teachers in your school district that lists criteria for evaluating the effectiveness of an informational book.

3. Examine an informational book published before 1960 with an informational book on the same subject published after 1990. In a critical essay, focus on the perceived differences between these two texts and speculate on what might have caused such differences.

Thinking and Writing from within the Genre of Nonfiction

1. After studying the work of Holling Clancy Holling, draft a dummy for a picture book for a younger audience that follows the monarch butterfly.

2. After reading two or three books from Jean George's *One Day in the...* series, choose a site that you would like to investigate and write a similar text. For the purposes of this project, there should be no human characters in the work.

3. An editor has proposed that you write a book about horses. The topic is vast and wide, and the editor has not set any guidelines other than that of audience, which she sees as one of early readers. Write back with a description of the angle that you will take to make this topic into a focused and centered informational book.

4. For the same editor, you decide to write a book about sea lions that uses a fictional context. Draft a proposal for that context.

Selected Bibliographies

Works Cited

Atwell, Debby. *Barn*. Boston, MA: Houghton Mifflin Company, 1996.

Ashabranner, Brent. *To Live in Two Worlds*. New York: Dodd, Mead, 1984.

Atkin, S. Beth. *Voices from the Fields: Children of Migrant Farmworkers Tell Their Stories*. Boston: Joy Street, 1993.

———. *Voices from the Streets*. Boston: Little, Brown, 1996.

Bartoletti, Susan Campbell. *Growing Up in Coal Country*. Boston: Houghton Mifflin, 1996.

———. *Kids on Strike!* Boston: Houghton Mifflin, 1999.

Bial, Raymond. *One-Room School*. Boston: Houghton Mifflin, 1999.

———. *Shaker Home*. Boston: Houghton Mifflin, 1994.

———. *The Strength of These Arms*. Boston: Houghton Mifflin, 1997.

———. *The Underground Railroad*. Boston: Houghton Mifflin, 1995.

Blumberg, Rhoda. *Commodore Perry in the Land of the Shogun*. New York: Lothrop, Lee, and Shepard, 1985.

Brook, Donna. *The Journey of English*. New York: Clarion, 1998.

Burns, Margy. *Talking Walls*. Gardiner, ME: Tilbury House, 1992.

Carrick, Carol. *Whaling Days*. Boston: Houghton Mifflin, 1993. Illustrated by David Frampton.

Coerr, Eleanor. *Sadako*. New York: G. P. Putnam's Sons, 1993. Illustrated by Ed Young.

Downing, Julie. *Mozart Tonight*. New York: Bradbury, 1991.

Emberly, Ed. *The Wing on a Flea*. Boston: Little, Brown, 1961.

Fisher, Leonard Everett. *Pyramid of the Sun, Pyramid of the Moon*. New York: Macmillan, 1988.

———. *The Wailing Wall*. New York: Macmillan, 1989.

Fraser, Mary Ann. *Sanctuary.* New York: Henry Holt, 1994.

Freedman, Russell. *Indian Chiefs.* New York: Holiday House, 1987.

———. *An Indian Winter.* New York: Holiday House, 1992.

———. *Kids at Work: Lewis Hine and the Crusade against Child Labor.* New York: Clarion Books, 1994.

Gaes, Jason. *My Book for Kids with Cansur.* Aberdeen, SD: Melius and Peterson, 1987.

George, Jean Craighead. *One Day in the Desert.* New York: Crowell, 1983.

Giblin, James Cross. *Let There Be Light: A Story about Windows.* New York: Crowell, 1988.

Hauslein, Leslie Ann. *The Amish: The Enduring Spirit.* New York: Crescent, 1991. Illustrated by Jerry Irwin.

Jackson, Donna. *The Bone Detectives.* New York: Little, Brown, 1996.

Jeffers, David. *Trains: The History of Railroads.* New York: Franklin Watts, 1991.

Kenna, Kathleen. *A People Apart.* Boston: Houghton Mifflin, 1995. Illustrated by Andrew Stawicki.

Krementz, Jill. *How It Feels to Fight for Your Life.* New York: Knopf, 1989.

Kroll, Virginia. *Africa: Brothers and Sisters.* New York: Four Winds, 1993. Illustrated by Vanessa French.

Lasky, Kathryn. *Sugaring Time.* New York. Macmillan, 1986.

Lester, Julius. *To Be a Slave.* New York: Dial, 1968.

Maruki, Toshi. *Hiroshima No Pika.* New York: Lothrop, Lee and Shepard, 1980.

McKissack, Patricia and Frederick. *Rebels against Slavery.* New York: Scholastic, 1996.

Pringle, Laurence. *Death Is Natural.* New York: Morrow, 1977.

Ray, Delia. *Behind the Blue and the Gray.* New York: Lodestar Books, 1991.

Sancha, Sheila. *Walter Dragun's Town.* New York: Crowell, 1989.

Simon, Seymour. *Saturn.* New York: Morrow, 1988.

———. *Storms.* New York: Morrow, 1989.

———. *Whales.* New York: Crowell, 1989.

Stanley, Jerry. *Children of the Dust.* New York: Crown, 1992.

Sewall, Marcia. *Thunder from the Clear Sky.* New York: Atheneum, 1995.

Van Loon, Hendrik Willem. *The Story of Mankind.* New York: Boni and Liveright, 1921.

Weil, Firi. *I Never Saw Another Butterfly.* New York: Schocken, 1973.

Weitzman, David. *Locomotive: Building an Eight-Wheeler.* Boston: Houghton Mifflin, 1999.

White, Laurence B. and Ron Broekel. *Optical Illusions.* New York: Franklin Watts, 1986.

Wick, Walter. *A Drop of Water.* New York: Scholastic, 1997.

Yoshida, Toshi. *Rhinoceros Mother.* New York: Philomel, 1991.

———. *Young Lions.* New York: Philomel, 1989.

Works by Selected Writers of Nonfiction

Holling Clancy Holling
Minn of the Mississippi. Boston: Houghton Mifflin, 1951.

Paddle-to-the-Sea. Boston: Houghton Mifflin, 1941.

Pagoo. Boston: Houghton Mifflin, 1957.

Patricia Lauber
Dinosaurs Walked Here and Other Stories Fossils Tell. New York: Bradbury, 1987.

Living with Dinosaurs. New York: Bradbury, 1991.

Lost Star. New York: Scholastic, 1988.

Seeds Pop, Stick, Glide. New York: Crown, 1981. Illustrated by Jerome Wexler.

Seeing Earth from Space. New York: Orchard, 1990.

Snakes Are Hunters. New York: Crowell, 1988. Illustrated by Holly Keller.

Volcano: The Eruption and Healing of Mount St. Helens. New York: Bradbury, 1986.

Joanna Cole and Bruce Degen
The Magic School Bus inside the Earth. New York: Scholastic, 1987. Illustrated by Bruce Degen.

The Magic School Bus Inside the Human Body. New York: Scholastic, 1989. Illustrated by Bruce Degen.

The Magic School Bus Lost in the Solar System. New York: Scholastic, 1990. Illustrated by Bruce Degen.

David Macaulay

Building the Book Cathedral. Boston: Houghton Mifflin, 1999.

Castle. Boston: Houghton Mifflin, 1977.

Cathedral. Boston: Houghton Mifflin, 1973.

City: The Story of Roman Planning and Construction. Boston: Houghton Mifflin, 1974.

The New Way Things Work. Boston: Houghton Mifflin, 1998.

Pyramid. Boston: Houghton Mifflin, 1975.

Rome Antics. Boston: Houghton Mifflin, 1997.

Ship. Boston: Houghton Mifflin, 1993.

Underground. Boston: Houghton Mifflin, 1976.

The Way Things Work. Boston: Houghton Mifflin, 1988.

Milton Meltzer

The Black Americans: A History in Their Own Words. New York: Harper and Row, 1984.

Black Magic. With Langston Hughes. Englewood Cliffs, NJ: Prentice-Hall, 1967.

Bread and Roses. New York: Knopf, 1967.

The Hispanic Americans. New York: Crowell, 1982.

The Jewish Americans. New York: Crowell, 1982.

Never to Forget: The Jews of the Holocaust. New York: Harper and Row, 1976.

A Pictorial History of the Negro in America. With Langston Hughes. New York: Crown, 1956.

Rescue: The Story of How Gentiles Saved Jews in World War II. New York: Harper, 1988.

Voices from the Civil War. New York: Crowell, 1989.

Jim Murphy

The Boys' War. Boston: Houghton Mifflin, 1990.

Gone A-Whaling. New York: Clarion, 1998.

The Great Fire. New York: Scholastic, 1995.

A Young Patriot. New York: Clarion, 1996.

Works about Informational Books _____

Bacon, Betty. "The Art of Non-Fiction." *Children's Literature in Education* 12 (1981): 3–14.

Barratt, Edward. "Writing the Literature of Fact." *Lion and the Unicorn* 6 (1983): 91–96.

Carter, B. and Abrahamson, R. F. *Nonfiction for Young Adults: From Delight to Wisdom.* Phoenix: Oryx, 1990.

DeLuca, Geraldiner and Roni Natov. "Who's Afraid of Science Books? An Interview with Seymour Simon." *Lion and the Unicorn* 6 (1983): 10–27.

Ellis, W. Geiger. "To Tell the Truth or at Least a Little Non-Fiction." *ALAN Review* 14 (1987): 39–41.

Fisher, Margery. *Matters of Fact.* New York: Crowell, 1972.

Freeman, Evelyn B. and Diane Goetz Person. *Using Nonfiction Trade Books in the Elementary Classroom: From Ants to Zeppelins.* Urbana, IL: National Council of Teachers of English, 1992.

Fritz, Jean. "The Very Truth." In Betsy Hearne and Marilyn Kaye, eds., *Celebrating Children's Books.* New York: Lothrop, Lee and Shepard, 1981: 81–86.

Giblin, James Cross. "Trends in Chidlren's Books Today." In Sheila Egoff, ed., *Only Connect.* New York: Oxford University Press, 1996: 337–342.

Goldman, James. "Selling American History." *Lion and the Unicorn* 6 (1983): 48–53.

Haskins, Jim. "Racism and Sexism in Children's Nonfiction." *Children's Literature* 5 (1976): 141–147.

Lasky, Kathryn. "Shuttling through Realities: The Warp and the Weft of Fantasy and Nonfiction Writing." *New Advocate* 6 (Fall, 1993): 235–242.

Lauber, Patricia. "What Makes an Appealing and Readable Science Book?" *Lion and the Unicorn* 6 (1983): 5–9.

Leal, Dorothy. "Storybooks, Information Books, and Informational Storybooks: An Explication of the Ambiguous Grey Genre." *New Advocate* 5 (Winter, 1993): 61–70.

Lounsberry, Barbara. *The Art of Fact.* New York: Greenwood, 1990.

Macaulay, David. "How to Create a Successful Children's Nonfiction Picture Book." In Betsy Hearne and Marilyn Kaye, eds., *Celebrating Children's Books.* New York: Lothrop, Lee and Shepard, 1981: 97–107.

Marcus, Leonard. "Nature into Art: An Interview with Anne Aphelia Dowden." *Lion and the Unicorn* 6 (1983): 28–40.

Meltzer, Milton. "Where Do All the Prizes Go?" *Horn Book* 52 (1976): 16–23.

Pringle, Laurence. "Science Done Here." In Betsy Hearne and Marilyn Kaye, eds., *Celebrat-*

ing Children's Books. New York: Lothrop, Lee and Shepard, 1981: 108–115.

Raymo, Chet. "Dr. Seuss and Dr. Einstein: Children's Books and the Scientific Imagination." *Horn Book* 68 (1992): 560–567.

Spink, J. Kevin. "The Aesthetics of Informational Reading." *New Advocate* 9 (Spring, 1996): 135–149.

Tremper, Ellen. "Grabbing Them by the Imagination." *Lion and the Unicorn* 6 (1983): 41–47.

Zarnowski, Myrc. "Learning History with Informational Storybooks: A Social Studies Educator's Perspective." *New Advocate* 8 (Summer, 1995): 183–196.

Caldecott Medal and Honor Awards

1938 Helen Dean Fish, ill. Dorothy P. Lathrop, *Animals of the Bible* (Stokes)
Honor Books: Boris Artzybasheff, *Seven Simeons: A Russian Tale* (Viking)
Helen Dean Fish, ill. Robert Lawson, *Four and Twenty Blackbirds: Nursery Rhymes of Yesterday Recalled for Children of Today* (Stokes)

1939 Thomas Handforth, *Mei Li* (Doubleday)
Honor Books: Laura Adams Armer, *The Forest Pool* (Longmans)
Munro Leaf, ill. Robert Lawson, *Wee Gillis* (Viking)
Wanda Gág, *Snow White and the Seven Dwarfs* (Coward)
Clare Newberry, *Barkis* (Harper)
James Daugherty, *Andy and the Lion: A Tale of Kindness Remembered or the Power of Gratitude* (Viking)

1940 Ingri and Edgar Parin d'Aulaire, *Abraham Lincoln* (Doubleday)
Honor Books: Berta and Elmer Hader, *Cock-a-Doodle Doo: The Story of a Little Red Rooster* (Macmillan)
Ludwig Bemelmans, *Madeline* (Simon & Schuster)
Lauren Ford, *The Ageless Story* (Dodd)

1941 Robert Lawson, *They Were Strong and Good* (Viking)
Honor Book: Clare Newberry, *April's Kittens* (Harper)

1942 Robert McCloskey, *Make Way for Ducklings* (Viking)
Honor Books: Maud and Miska Petersham, *An American ABC* (Macmillan)
Ann Nolan Clark, ill. Velino Herrera, *In My Mother's House* (Viking)
Holling C. Holling, *Paddle-to-the-Sea* (Houghton Mifflin)
Wanda Gág, *Nothing at All* (Coward)

1943 Virginia Lee Burton, *The Little House* (Houghton Mifflin)
Honor Books: Mary and Conrad Buff, *Dash and Dart* (Viking)
Clare Newberry, *Marshmallow* (Harper)

1944 James Thurber, ill. Louis Slobodkin, *Many Moons* (Harcourt Brace Jovanovich)
Honor Books: Jessie Orton Jones, ill. Elizabeth Orton Jones, *Small Rain: Verses from the Bible* (Viking)
Lee Kingman, ill. Arnold E. Bare, *Pierre Pigeon* (Houghton Mifflin)
Berta and Elmer Hader, *The Mighty Hunter* (Macmillan)
Margaret Wise Brown, ill. Jean Charlot, *A Child's Good Night Book* (W. R. Scott)
Chih-Yi-Chan, ill. Plato Chan, *Good Luck Horse* (Whittlesey)

1945 Rachel Field, ill. Elizabeth Orton Jones, *Prayer for a Child* (Macmillan)
Honor Books: ill. Tasha Tudor, *Mother Goose: Seventy-Seven Verses with Pictures* (Walck)
Marie Hall Ets, *In the Forest* (Viking)
Marguerite de Angeli, *Yonie Wondernose* (Doubleday)
Ruth Sawyer, ill. Kate Seredy, *The Christmas Anna Angel* (Viking)

1946   Maud and Miska Petersham, *The Rooster Crows…* (Macmillan)
    Honor Books: Golden MacDonald, ill. Leonard Weisgard, *Little Lost Lamb* (Doubleday)
        Opal Wheeler, ill. Marjorie Torrey, *Sing Mother Goose* (Dutton)
        Becky Reyher, ill. Ruth Gannett, *My Mother Is the Most Beautiful Woman in the World* (Lothrop)
        Kurt Wiese, *You Can Write Chinese* (Viking)

1947   Golden MacDonald, ill. Leonard Weisgard, *The Little Island* (Doubleday)
    Honor Books: Alvin Tresselt, ill. Leonard Weisgard, *Rain Drop Splash* (Lothrop)
        Marjorie Flack, ill. Jay Hyde Barnum, *Boats on the River* (Viking)
        Al Graham, ill. Tony Palazzo, *Timothy Turtle* (Viking)
        Leo Politi, *Pedro, the Angel of Olvera Street* (Scribner's)
        Opan Wheeler, ill. Marjorie Torrey, *Sing in Praise: A Collection of the Best Loved Hymns* (Dutton)

1948   Alvin Tresselt, ill. Roger Duvoisin, *White Snow, Bright Snow* (Lothrop)
    Honor Books: Marcia Brown, *Stone Soup: An Old Tale* (Scribner's)
        Dr. Seuss, *McElligot's Pool* (Random)
        George Schreiber, *Bambino the Clown* (Viking)
        Lavinia Davis, ill. Hildegard Woodward, *Roger and the Fox* (Doubleday)
        ed. Anne Malcolmson, ill. Virginia Lee Burton, *Song of Robin Hood* (Houghton)

1949   Berta and Elmer Hader, *The Big Snow* (Macmillan)
    Honor Books: Robert McCloskey, *Blueberries for Sal* (Viking)
        Phyllis McGinley, ill. Helen Stone, *All Around the Town* (Lippincott)
        Leo Politi, *Juanita* (Scribner's)
        Kurt Wiese, *Fish in the Air* (Viking)

1950   Leo Politi, *Song of the Swallows* (Scribner's)
    Honor Books: Stewart Holbrook, ill. Lynd Ward, *America's Ethan Allen* (Houghton Mifflin)
        Lavinia Davis, ill. Hildegrad Woodward, *The Wild Birthday Cake* (Doubleday)
        Ruth Krauss, ill. Marc Simont, *The Happy Day* (Harper)
        Dr. Seuss, *Bartholomew and the Oobleck* (Random)
        Marcia Brown, *Henry Fisherman* (Scribner's)

1951   Katherine Milhous, *The Egg Tree* (Scribner's)
    Honor Books: Marcia Brown, *Dick Whittington and His Cat* (Scribner's)
        William Lipkind, ill. Nicholas Mordvinoff, *The Two Reds* (Harcourt Brace Jovanovich)
        Dr. Seuss, *If I Ran the Zoo* (Random)
        Phyllis McGinley, ill. Helen Stone, *The Most Wonderful Doll in the World* (Lippincott)
        Clare Newberry, *T-Bone, the Baby Sitter* (Harper)

1952   William Lipkind, ill. Nicholas Mordvinoff, *Finders Keepers* (Harcourt Brace Jovanovich)
    Honor Books: Marie Hall Ets, *Mr. T. W. Anthony Wood: The Story of a Cat and a Dog and a Mouse* (Viking)
        Marcia Brown, *Skipper John's Cook* (Scribner's)
        Gene Zion, ill. Margaret Bloy Graham, *All Falling Down* (Harper)
        William Pène du Bois, *Bear Party* (Viking)
        Elizabeth Olds, *Feather Mountain* (Houghton Mifflin)

1953   Lynd Ward, *The Biggest Bear* (Houghton Mifflin)
    Honor Books: Charles Perrault, ill. and tr. Marcia Brown, *Puss in Boots* (Scribner's)
        Robert McCloskey, *One Morning in Maine* (Viking)
        Fritz Eichenberg, *Ape in a Cape: An Alphabet of Odd Animals* (Harcourt Brace Jovanovich)
        Charlotte Zolotow, ill. Margaret Bloy Graham, *The Storm Book* (Harper)
        Juliet Kepes, *Five Little Monkeys* (Houghton)

1954   Ludwig Bemelmans, *Madeline's Rescue* (Viking)
          Honor Books: Ruth Sawyer, ill. Robert McCloskey, *Journey Cake, Ho!* (Viking)
                 Miriam Schlein, ill. Jean Charlot, *When Will the World Be Mine?* (W. R. Scott)
                 Hans Christian Anderson, ill. Marcia Brown, *The Steadfast Tin Soldier* (Scribner's)
                 Ruth Krauss, ill. Maurice Sendak, *A Very Special House* (Harper)
                 A. Birnbaum, *Green Eyes* (Capitol)
1955   Charles Perrault, ill. and tr. Marcia Brown, *Cinderella, or the Little Glass Slipper* (Scribner's)
          Honor Books: ill. Marguerite de Angeli, *Book of Nursery and Mother Goose Rhymes*
                 (Doubleday)
                 Margaret Wise Brown, ill. Tibor Gergely, *Wheel on the Chimney* (Lippincott)
                 Alice Dalgliesh, ill. Helen Sewell, *The Thanksgiving Story* (Scribner's)
1956   ed. John Langstaff, ill. Feodor Rojankovsky, *Frog Went A-Courtin'* (Harcourt Brace
          Jovanovich)
          Honor Books: Marie Hall Ets, *Play with Me* (Viking)
                 Taro Yashima, *Crow Boy* (Viking)
1957   Janice May Udry, ill. Marc Simont, *A Tree Is Nice* (Harper)
          Honor Books: Marie Hall Ets, *Mr. Penny's Race Horse* (Viking)
                 Tasha Tudor, *1 Is One* (Walck)
                 Eve Titus, ill. Paul Galdone, *Anatole* (McGraw)
                 Benjamin Elkin, ill. James Daugherty, *Gillespie and the Guards* (Viking)
                 William Pène du Bois, *Lion* (Viking)
1958   Robert McCloskey, *Time of Wonder* (Viking)
          Honor Books: Don Freeman, *Fly High, Fly Low* (Viking)
                 Eve Titus, ill. by Paul Galdone, *Anatole and the Cat* (McGraw-Hill)
1959   adapted from Chaucer and ill. Barbara Cooney, *Chanticleer and the Fox* (Crowell)
          Honor Books: Antonio Frasconi, *The House That Jack Built: A Picture Book in Two Languages*
                 (Harcourt Brace Jovanovich)
                 Sesyle Joslin, ill. Maurice Sendak, *What Do You Say, Dear?* (W. R. Scott)
                 Taro Yashima, *Umbrella* (Viking)
1960   Marie Hall Ets and Aurora Labastida, ill. Marie Hall Ets, *Nine Days to Christmas* (Viking)
          Honor Books: Alice E. Goudey, ill. Adrienne Adams, *Houses from the Sea* (Scribner's)
                 Janice May Udry, ill. Maurice Sendak, *The Moon Jumpers* (Harper)
1961   Ruth Robbins, ill. Nicolas Sidjakov, *Baboushka and the Three Kings* (Parnassus)
          Honor Book: Leo Lionni, *Inch by Inch* (Obolensky)
1962   Marcia Brown, *Once a Mouse…* (Scribner's)
          Honor Books: Peter Spier, *The Fox Went Out on a Chilly Night: An Old Song* (Doubleday)
                 Else Holmelund Minarik, ill. Maurice Sendak, *Little Bear's Visit* (Harper)
                 Alice E. Goudey, ill. Adrienne Adams, *The Day We Saw the Sun Come Up* (Scribner's)
1963   Ezra Jack Keats, *The Snowy Day* (Viking)
          Honor Books: Natalia M. Belting, ill. Bernarda Bryson, *The Sun Is a Golden Earring* (Holt)
                 Charlotte Zolotow, ill. Maurice Sendak, *Mr. Rabbit and the Lovely Present* (Harper)
1964   Maurice Sendak, *Where the Wild Things Are* (Harper)
          Honor Books: Leo Lionni, *Swimmy* (Pantheon)
                 Sorche Nic Leodhas, ill. Evaline Ness, *All in the Morning Early* (Holt)
                 ill. Philip Reed, *Mother Goose and Nursery Rhymes* (Antheneum)
1965   Beatrice Schenk de Regniers, ill. Beni Montresor, *May I Bring a Friend?* (Antheneum)
          Honor Books: Julian Scheer, ill. Marvin Bileck, *Rain Makes Applesauce* (Holiday)
                 Margaret Hodges, ill. Blair Lent, *The Wave* (Houghton Mifflin)
                 Rebecca Caudill, ill. Evaline Ness, *A Pocketful of Cricket* (Holt)

1966 Sorche Nic Leodhas, ill. Nonny Hogrogian, *Always Room for One More* (Holt)
  Honor Books: Alvin Tresselt, ill. Roger Duvoisin, *Hide and Seek Fog* (Lothrop)
    Marie Hall Ets, *Just Me* (Viking)
    Evaline Ness, *Tom Tit Tot* (Scribner's)
1967 Evaline Ness, *Sam, Bangs & Moonshine* (Holt)
  Honor Book: Barbara Emberley, ill. Ed Emberley, *One Wide River to Cross* (Prentice)
1968 Barbara Emberley, ill. Ed Emberley, *Drummer Hoff* (Prentice-Hall)
  Honor Books: Leo Lionni, *Frederick* (Pantheon)
    Taro Yashima, *Seashore Story* (Viking)
    Jane Yolen, ill. Ed Young, *The Emperor and the Kite* (World)
1969 Arthur Ransome, ill. Uri Shulevitz, *The Fool of the World and the Flying Ship* (Farrar)
  Honor Book: Elphinstone Dayrell, ill. Blair Lent, *Why the Sun and the Moon Live in the Sky: An African Folktale* (Houghton Mifflin)
1970 William Steig, *Sylvester and the Magic Pebble* (Windmill)
  Honor Books: Ezra Jack Keats, *Goggles!* (Macmillan)
    Leo Lionni, *Alexander and the Wind-Up Mouse* (Pantheon)
    Edna Mitchell Preston, ill. Robert Andrew Parker, *Pop Corn and Ma Goodness* (Viking)
    Brinton Turkle, *Thy Friend, Obadiah* (Viking)
    Harve Zemach, ill. Margot Zemach, *The Judge: An Untrue Tale* (Farrar)
1971 Gail E. Haley, *A Story-A Story: An African Tale* (Atheneum)
  Honor Books: William Sleator, ill. Blair Lent, *The Angry Moon* (Atlantic-Little)
    Arnold Lobel, *Frog and Toad Are Friends* (Harper)
    Maurice Sendak, *In the Night Kitchen* (Harper)
1972 Nonny Hogrogian, *One Fine Day* (Macmillan)
  Honor Books: Janina Domanska, *If All the Seas Were One Sea* (Macmillan)
    Muriel Feelings, ill. Tom Feelings, *Moja Means One: Swahili Counting Book* (Dial)
    Cheli Duran Ryan, ill. Arnold Lobel, *Hildilid's Night* (Macmillan)
1973 retold by Arlene Mosel, ill. Blair Lent, *The Funny Little Woman* (Dutton)
  Honor Books: adapted and ill. Gerald McDermott, *Anansi the Spider: A Tale from the Ashanti* (Holt)
    Hosea Tobias and Lisa Baskin, ill. Leonard Baskin, *Hosie's Alphabet* (Viking)
    trans. Randall Jarrell, ill. Nancy Ekholm Burkert, *Snow White and the Seven Dwarfs* (Farrar)
    Byrd Baylor, ill. Tom Bahti, *When Clay Sings* (Scribner's)
1974 Harve Zemach, ill. Margot Zemach, *Duffy and the Devil* (Farrar)
  Honor Books: Susan Jeffers, *Three Jovial Huntsmen* (Bradbury)
    David Macaulay, *Cathedral: The Story of Its Construction* (Houghton Mifflin)
1975 adapted and ill. Gerald McDermott, *Arrow to the Sun* (Viking)
  Honor Book: Muriel Feelings, ill. Tom Feelings, *Jambo Means Hello: A Swahili Alphabet Book* (Dial)
1976 retold Verna Aardema, ill. Leo and Diane Dillon, *Why Mosquitoes Buzz in People's Ears* (Dial)
  Honor Books: Byrd Baylor, ill. Peter Parnall, *The Desert Is Theirs* (Scribner's)
    retold and ill. Tomie de Paola, *Strega Nona* (Prentice-Hall)
1977 Margaret Musgrove, ill. Leo and Diane Dillon, *Ashanti to Zulu: African Traditions* (Dial)
  Honor Books: William Steig, *The Amazing Bone* (Farrar)
    retold and ill. Nonny Hogrogian, *The Contest* (Greenwillow)
    M. B. Goffstein, *Fish for Supper* (Dial)
    Beverly Brodsky McDermott, *The Golem: A Jewish Legend* (Lippincott)
    Byrd Baylor, ill. Peter Parnall, *Hawk, I'm Your Brother* (Scribner's)

1978   Peter Spier, *Noah's Ark* (Doubleday)
        Honor Books: David Macaulay, *Castle* (Houghton Mifflin)
           retold and ill. Margot Zemach, *It Could Always Be Worse* (Farrar)
1979   Paul Goble, *The Girl Who Loved Wild Horses* (Bradbury)
        Honor Books: Donald Crews, *Freight Train* (Greenwillow)
           Byrd Baylor, ill. Peter Parnall, *The Way to Start a Day* (Scribner's)
1980   Donald Hall, ill. Barbara Cooney, *Ox-Cart Man* (Viking)
        Honor Books: Rachel Isadora, *Ben's Trumpet* (Greenwillow)
           Uri Shulevitz, *The Treasure* (Farrar)
           Chris Van Allsburg, *The Garden of Abdul Gasazi* (Houghton Mifflin)
1981   Arnold Lobel, *Fables* (Harper)
        Honor Books: Ilse Plume, *The Bremen-Town Musicians* (Doubleday)
           Molly Bang, *The Grey Lady and the Strawberry Snatcher* (Four Winds)
           Joseph Low, *Mice Twice* (Atheneum)
           Donald Crews, *Truck* (Greenwillow)
1982   Chris Van Allsburg, *Jumanji* (Houghton Mifflin)
        Honor Books: Nancy Willard, ill. Alice and Martin Provensen, *A Visit to William Blake's Inn: Poems for Innocent and Experienced Travelers* (Harcourt Brace Jovanovich)
           Olaf Baker, ill. Stephen Gammell, *Where the Buffaloes Begin* (Warner)
           Arnold Lobel, ill. Anita Lobel, *On Market Street* (Greenwillow)
           Maurice Sendak, *Outside Over There* (Harper)
1983   Blaise Cendrars, ill. Marcia Brown, *Shadow* (Scribner's)
        Honor Books: Cynthia Rylant, ill. Diane Goode, *When I Was Young in the Mountains* (Dutton)
           Vera B. Williams, *A Chair for My Mother* (Morrow)
1984   Alice and Martin Provensen, *The Glorious Flight: Across the Channel with Louis Bleriot* (Viking)
        Honor Books: Molly Bang, *Ten, Nine, Eight* (Greenwillow)
           retold and ill. Trina Schart Hyman, *Little Red Riding Hood* (Holiday House)
1985   retold Margaret Hodges, ill. Trina Schart Hyman, *St. George and the Dragon* (Little, Brown)
        Honor Books: retold Rika Lesser, ill. Paul O. Zelinsky, *Hansel and Gretel* (Dodd)
           Nancy Tafuri, *Have You Seen My Duckling?* (Greenwillow)
           John Steptoe, *The Story of Jumping Mouse* (Lothrop)
1986   Chris Van Allsburg, *The Polar Express* (Houghton Mifflin)
        Honor Books: Audrey Wood, ill. Don Wood, *King Bidgood's in the Bathtub* (Harcourt)
           Cynthia Rylant, ill. Stephen Gammell, *The Relatives Came* (Bradbury)
1987   Arthur Yorinks, ill. Richard Egielski, *Hey, Al* (Farrar, Straus & Giroux)
        Honor Books: Suse MacDonald, *Alphabatics* (Bradbury)
           retold and ill. Paul O. Zelinsky, *Rumpelstiltskin* (Dutton)
           Ann Grifalconi, *The Village of Round and Square Houses* (Little, Brown)
1988   Jane Yolen, ill. John Schoenherr, *Owl Moon* (Philomel)
        Honor Book: John Steptoe, *Mufaro's Beautiful Daughters: An African Tale* (Lothrop, Lee & Shepard)
1989   Karen Ackerman, ill. Stephen Gammell, *Song and Dance Man* (Knopf)
        Honor Books: Dianne Snyder, ill. Allen Say, *The Boy of the Three-Year Nap* (Houghton Mifflin)
           David Wiesner, *Free Fall* (Lothrop, Lee & Shepard)
           retold and ill. James Marshall, *Goldilocks* (Dial)
           Patricia C. McKissack, ill. Jerry Pinkney, *Mirandy and Brother Wind* (Knopf)
1990   trans. and ill. Ed Young, *Lon Po Po: A Red-Riding Hood Story from China* (Philomel)
        Honor Books: Bill Peet, *Bill Peet: An Autobiography* (Houghton Mifflin)

Lois Ehlert, *Color Zoo* (Lippincott)

Eric Kimmel, ill. Trina Schart Hyman, *Hershel and the Hanukkah Goblins* (Holiday House)

Robert D. San Souci, ill. Jerry Pinkney, *The Talking Eggs* (Dial)

1991   David Macaulay, *Black and White* (Houghton Mifflin)

Honor Books: Vera Williams, *More, More, More Said the Baby* (Greenwillow)

Charles Perrault, ill. Fred Marcellino, *Puss in Boots* (Farrar, Straus & Giroux)

1992   David Wiesner, *Tuesday* (Clarion)

Honor Book: Faith Ringgold, *Tar Beach* (Crown)

1993   Emily Arnold McCully, *Mirette on the High Wire* (Putnam's)

Honor Books: Ed Young, *Seven Blind Mice* (Philomel)

Jon Scieszka, ill. Lane Smith, *The Stinky Cheese Man and Other Fairly Stupid Tales* (Viking)

Sherely Anne Williams, ill. Carole Byard, *Working Cotton* (Harcourt Brace Jovanovich)

1994   Allen Say, *Grandfather's Journey* (Houghton Mifflin)

Honor Books: Kevin Henkes, *Owen* (Greenwillow)

Elisa Bartone, ill. Ted Lewin, *Peppe, the Lamplighter* (Lothrop, Lee & Shepard)

Gerald McDermott, *Raven* (Harcourt Brace Jovanovich)

Denise Fleming, *In the Small, Small Pond* (Holt)

Chris Raschka, *Yo! Yes?* (Orchard)

1995   Eve Bunting, ill. David Diaz, *Smoky Night* (Harcourt Brace Jovanovich)

Honor Books: Julius Lester, ill. Jerry Pinkney, *John Henry* (Dial)

Anne Issacs, ill. Paul O. Zelinsky, *Swamp Angel* (Dutton)

Eric Rohmann, *Time Flies* (Crown)

1996   Peggy Rathman, *Officer Buckle and Gloria* (Putnam)

Honor Books: Stephen T. Johnson, *Alphabet City* (Viking)

Robert D. San Souci, ill. Brian Pinkney, *The Faithful Friend* (Simon & Schuster)

Janet Stevens, *Tops and Bottoms* (Harcourt Brace Jovanovich)

Lloyd Moss, ill. Marjorie Priceman, *Zin! Zin! Zin! A Violin* (Simon & Schuster)

1997   David Wisniewski, *Golem* (Clarion)

Honor Books: Minfong Ho, ill. Holly Meade, *Hush! A Thai Lullaby* (Orchard)

Dav Pilkey, *The Paperboy* (Orchard)

Peter Sís, *Starry Messenger* (Farrar, Straus & Giroux)

1998   Brothers Grimm, ill. Paul O. Zelinsky, *Rapunzel* (Dutton)

Honor Books: Sarah Stewart, ill. David Small, *The Gardener* (Farrar, Strauss & Giroux)

Walter Dean Myers, ill. Christopher Myers, *Harlem* (Scholastic)

Simms Taback, *There Was an Old Woman Who Swallowed a Fly* (Viking)

1999   Jacqueline Briggs Martin, ill. Mary Azarian, *Snowflake Bentley* (Houghton Mifflin)

Honor Books: Andrea Davis Pinkney, ill. Brian Pinkney, *Duke Ellington: The Piano Prince and His Orchestra* (Hyperion)

David Shannon, *No David!* (Scholastic)

Uri Shulevitz, *Snow* (Farrar Straus Giroux)

Peter Sís. *Tibet through the Red Box* (Farrar Straus Giroux)

2000   Sims Taback, *Joseph Had a Little Overcoat* (Viking)

Honor Books: David Wiesner, *Sector 7* (Clarion)

Hans Christian Anderson, adapted and ill. Jerry Pinkney, *The Ugly Duckling* (Morrow)

Molly Bang, *When Sophie Got Angry—Really, Really Angry* (Scholastic)

John Updike, ill. Trina Schart Hyman, *A Child's Garden* (Holiday House)

Newbery Medal and Honor Awards

1922   Hendrik Willem van Loon, *The Story of Mankind* (Boni and Liveright)
        Honor Books: Charles Hawes, *The Great Quest* (Little)
            Bernard Marshall, *Cedric the Forester* (Appleton)
            William Bowen, *The Old Tobacco Shop: A True Account of What Befell a Little Boy in Search of Adventure* (Macmillan)
            Padriac Colum, *The Golden Fleece and the Heroes Who Lived before Achilles* (Macmillan)
            Cornelia Meigs, *Windy Hill* (Macmillan)
1923   Hugh Lofting, *The Voyages of Doctor Dolittle* (Lippincott)
        Honor Books: no record
1924   Charles Hawes, *The Dark Frigate* (Atlantic/Little)
        Honor Books: no record
1925   Charles Finger, *Tales from Silver Lands* (Doubleday)
        Honor Books: Anne Carroll Moore, *Nicholas: A Manhattan Christmas Story* (Putnam)
            Anne Parrish, *Dream Coach* (Macmillan)
1926   Arthur Bowie Chrisman, *Shen of the Sea* (Dutton)
        Honor Book: Padraic Colum, *Voyagers: Being Legends and Romances of Atlantic Discovery* (Macmillan)
1927   Will James, *Smoky, the Cowhorse* (Scribner's)
        Honor Books: no record
1928   Dhan Gopal Mukerji, *Gayneck, the Story of a Pigeon* (Dutton)
        Honor Books: Ella Young, *The Wonder Smith and His Son: A Tale from the Golden Childhood of the World* (Longmans)
            Caroline Snedeker, *Downright Dencey* (Doubleday)
1929   Eric P. Kelly, *The Trumpeter of Krakow* (Macmillan)
        Honor Books: John Bennet, *Pigtail of Ah Lee Ben Loo* (Longmans)
            Wanda Gág, *Millions of Cats* (Coward)
            Grace Hallock, *The Boy Who Was* (Dutton)
            Cornelia Meigs, *Clearing Weather* (Little)
            Grace Moon, *Runaway Papoose* (Doubleday)
            Elinor Whitney, *Tod of the Fens* (Macmillan)
1930   Rachel Field, *Hitty, Her First Hundred Years* (Macmillan)
        Honor Books: Jeanette Eaton, *Daughter of the Seine: The Life of Madame Roland* (Harper)
            Elizabeth Miller, *Pran of Albania* (Doubleday)
            Marian Hurd McNeely, *Jumping-off Place* (Longmans)
            Ella Young, *Tangle-Coated Horse and Other Tales: Episodes from the Fionn Saga* (Longmans)
            Julia Davis Adams, *Vaino: A Boy of New England* (Dutton)
            Hildegarde Swift, *Little Blacknose* (Harcourt Brace Jovanovich)
1931   Elizabeth Coatsworth, *The Cat Who Went to Heaven* (Macmillan)
        Honor Books: Anne Parrish, *Floating Island* (Harper)

Alida Malkus, *The Dark Star of Itza: The Story of a Pagan Princess* (Harcourt Brace Jovanovich)

Ralph Hubbard, *Queer Person* (Doubleday)

Julia Davis Adams, *Mountains Are Free* (Dutton)

Agnes Hewes, *Spice and the Devil's Cave* (Knopf)

Elizabeth Janet Gray, *Meggy Macintosh* (Doubleday)

Herbert Best, *Garram the Hunter: A Boy of the Hill Tribes* (Doubleday)

Alice Lide and Margaret Johansen, *Ood-Le-Uk the Wanderer* (Little)

1932   Laura Adams Armer, *Waterless Mountain* (Longmans)
Honor Books: Dorothy P. Lathrop, *The Fairy Circus* (Macmillan)

Rachel Field, *Calico Bush* (Macmillan)

Eunice Tietjens, *Boy of the South Seas* (Coward)

Eloise Lownsbery, *Out of the Flame* (Longmans)

Marjorie Allee, *Jane's Island* (Houghton Mifflin)

Mary Gould Davis, *Truce of the Wolf and Other Tales of Old Italy* (Harcourt Brace Jovanovich)

1933   Elizabeth Foreman Lewis, *Young Fu of the Upper Yangtze* (Winston)
Honor Books: Cornelia Meigs, *Swift Rivers* (Little)

Hildegarde Swift, *The Railroad to Freedom: A Story of the Civil War* (Harcourt Brace Jovanovich)

Nora Burglon, *Children of the Soil: A Story of Scandinavia* (Doubleday)

1934   Cornelia Meigs, *Invincible Louisa: The Story of the Author of 'Little Women'* (Little)
Honor Books: Caroline Snedeker, *The Forgotten Daughter* (Doubleday)

Elsie Singmaster, *Swords of Steel* (Houghton Mifflin)

Wanda Gág, *ABC Bunny* (Coward)

Erik Berry, *Winged Girl of Knossos* (Appleton)

Sarah Schmidt, *New Land* (McBride)

Padraic Colum, *Big Tree of Bunlahy: Stories of My Own Countryside* (Macmillan)

Agnes Hewes, *Glory of the Seas* (Knopf)

Ann Kyle, *Apprentice of Florence* (Houghton Mifflin)

1935   Monica Shannon, *Dobry* (Viking)
Honor Books: Elizabeth Seeger, *Pageant of Chinese History* (Longmans)

Constance Rourke, *Davy Crockett* (Harcourt Brace Jovanovich)

Hilda Van Stockum, *Day on Skates: The Story of a Dutch Picnic* (Harper)

1936   Carol Ryrie Brink, *Caddie Woodlawn* (Macmillan)
Honor Books: Phil Stong, *Honk, the Moose* (Dodd)

Kate Seredy, *The Good Master* (Viking)

Elizabeth Janet Gray, *Young Walter Scott* (Viking)

Armstrong Sperry, *All Sail Set: A Romance of the Flying Cloud* (Winston)

1937   Ruth Sawyer, *Roller Skates* (Viking)
Honor Books: Lois Lenski, *Phoebe Fairchild: Her Book* (Stokes)

Idwal Jones, *Whistler's Van* (Viking)

Ludwig Bemelmans, *Golden Basket* (Viking)

Margery Bianco, *Winterbound* (Viking)

Constance Rourke, *Audubon* (Harcourt Brace Jovanovich)

Agnes Hewes, *The Codfish Musket* (Doubleday)

1938   Kate Seredy, *The White Stag* (Viking)
Honor Books: James Cloyd Bowman, *Pecos Bill* (Little)

Mabel Robinson, *Bright Island* (Random House)

Laura Ingalls Wilder, *On the Banks of Plum Creek* (Harper)

1939   Elizabeth Enright, *Thimble Summer* (Rinehart)
    Honor Books: Valenti Angelo, *Nino* (Viking)
        Richard and Florence Atwater, *Mr. Popper's Penguins* (Little)
        Phyllis Crawford, *"Hello the Boat!"* (Holt)
        Jeanette Eaton, *Leader by Destiny: George Washington, Man and Patriot* (Harcourt Brace Jovanovich)
        Elizabeth Janet Gray, *Penn* (Viking)

1940   James Daugherty, *Daniel Boone* (Viking)
    Honor Books: Kate Seredy, *The Singing Tree* (Viking)
        Mabel Robinson, *Runner of the Mountain Tops: The Life of Louis Agassiz* (Random)
        Laura Ingalls Wilder, *By the Shores of Silver Lake* (Harper)
        Stephen W. Meader, *Boy with a Pack* (Harcourt Brace Jovanovich)

1941   Armstrong Sperry, *Call It Courage* (Macmillan)
    Honor Books: Doris Gates, *Blue Willow* (Viking)
        Mary Jane Carr, *Young Mac of Fort Vancouver* (Crowell)
        Laura Ingalls Wilder, *The Long Winter* (Harper)
        Anna Gertrude Hall, *Nansen* (Viking)

1942   Walter D. Edmonds, *The Matchlock Gun* (Dodd)
    Honor Books: Laura Ingalls Wilder, *Little Town on the Prairie* (Harper)
        Genevieve Foster, *George Washington's World* (Scribner's)
        Lois Lenski, *Indian Captive: The Story of Mary Jemison* (Lippincott)
        Eva Roe Gaggin, *Down Ryton Water* (Viking)

1943   Elizabeth Janet Gray, *Adam of the Road* (Viking)
    Honor Books: Eleanor Estes, *The Middle Moffat* (Harcourt Brace Jovanovich)
        Mabel Leigh Hunt, *Have You Seen Tom Thumb?* (Lippincott)

1944   Esther Forbes, *Johnny Tremain* (Houghton)
    Honor Books: Laura Ingalls Wilder, *The Happy Golden Years* (Harper Mifflin)
        Julia Sauer, *Fog Magic* (Viking)
        Eleanor Estes, *Rufus M.* (Harcourt Brace Jovanovich)
        Elizabeth Yates, *Mountain Born* (Coward)

1945   Robert Lawson, *Rabbit Hill* (Viking)
    Honor Books: Eleanor Estes, *The Hundred Dresses* (Harcourt Brace Jovanovich)
        Alice Dalgliesh, *The Silver Pencil* (Scribner's)
        Genevieve Foster, *Abraham Lincoln's World* (Scribner's)
        Jeanette Eaton, *Lone Journey: The Life of Roger Williams* (Harcourt Brace Jovanovich)

1946   Lois Lenski, *Strawberry Girl* (Lippincott)
    Honor Books: Marguerite Henry, *Justin Morgan Had a Horse* (Rand)
        Florence Crannell Means, *The Moved-Outers* (Houghton Mifflin)
        Christine Weston, *Bhimsa, the Dancing Bear* (Scribner's)
        Katherine Shippen, *New Found World* (Viking)

1947   Carolyn Sherwin Bailey, *Miss Hickory* (Viking)
    Honor Books: Nancy Barnes, *Wonderful Year* (Messner)
        Mary and Conrad Buff, *Big Tree* (Viking)
        William Maxwell, *The Heavenly Tenants* (Harper)
        Cyrus Fisher, *The Avion My Uncle Flew* (Appleton)
        Eleanore Jewett, *The Hidden Treasure of Glaston* (Viking)

1948   William Pène du Bois, *The Twenty-One Balloons* (Viking)
    Honor Books: Claire Huchet Bishop, *Pancakes-Paris* (Viking)
        Carolyn Treffinger, *Le Lun, Lad of Courage* (Abingdon)

Catherine Besterman, *The Quaint and Curious Quest of Johnny Longfoot, The Shoe-King's Son* (Bobbs)

Harold Courlander, *The Cow-Tail Switch, and Other West African Stories* (Holt)

Marguerite Henry, *Misty of Chincoteague* (Rand)

1949 Marguerite Henry, *King of the Wind* (Rand)
Honor Books: Holling C. Holling, *Seabird* (Houghton Mifflin)

Louise Rankin, *Daughter of the Mountains* (Viking)

Ruth S. Gannett, *My Father's Dragon* (Random House)

Arna Bontemps, *Story of the Negro* (Knopf)

1950 Marguerite de Angeli, *The Door in the Wall* (Doubleday)
Honor Books: Rebecca Caudill, *Tree of Freedom* (Viking)

Catherine Coblentz, *The Blue Cat of Castle Town* (Longmans)

Rutherford Montgomery, *Kildee House* (Doubleday)

Genevieve Foster, *George Washington* (Scribner's)

Walter and Marion Havighurst, *Song of the Pines: A Story of Norwegian Lumbering in Wisconsin* (Winston)

1951 Elizabeth Yates, *Amos Fortune, Free Man* (Aladdin)
Honor Books: Mabel Leigh Hunt, *Better Known as Johnny Appleseed* (Lippincott)

Jeanette Eaton, *Ghandi, Fighter without a Sword* (Morrow)

Clara Ingram Judson, *Abraham Lincoln: Friend of the People* (Follett)

Anne Parish, *The Story of Appleby Capple* (Harper)

1952 Eleanor Estes, *Ginger Pye* (Harcourt Brace Jovanovich)
Honor Books: Elizabeth Baity, *Americans before Columbus* (Viking)

Holling C. Holling, *Minn of the Mississippi* (Houghton Mifflin)

Nicholas Kalashnikoff, *The Defender* (Scribner's)

Julia Sauer, *The Light at Tern Rock* (Viking)

Mary and Conrad Buff, *The Apple and the Arrow* (Houghton Mifflin)

1953 Ann Nolan Clark, *Secret of the Andes* (Viking)
Honor Books: E. B. White, *Charlotte's Web* (Harper)

Eloise McGraw, *Moccasin Trail* (Coward)

Ann Weil, *Red Sails to Capri* (Viking)

Alice Dalgliesh, *The Bears on Hemlock Mountain* (Scribner's)

Genevieve Foster, *Birthdays of Freedom, Vol. 1* (Scribner's)

1954 Joseph Krumgold, *...and now Miguel* (Crowell)
Honor Books: Claire Huchet Bishop, *All Alone* (Viking)

Meindert DeJong, *Shadrach* (Harper)

Meindert DeJong, *Hurry Home Candy* (Harper)

Clara Ingram Judson, *Theodore Roosevelt, Fighting Patriot* (Follett)

Mary and Conrad Buff, *Magic Maize* (Houghton Mifflin)

1955 Meindert DeJong, *The Wheel on the School* (Harper)
Honor Books: Alice Dalgliesh, *The Courage of Sarah Noble* (Scribner's)

James Ullman, *Banner in the Sky* (Lippincott)

1956 Jean Lee Latham, *Carry On, Mr. Bowditch* (Houghton Mifflin)
Honor Books: Marjorie Kinnan Rawlings, *The Secret River* (Scribner's)

Jennie Linquist, *The Golden Name Day* (Harper)

Katherine Shippen, *Men, Microscopes, and Living Things* (Viking)

1957 Virginia Sorensen, *Miracles on Maple Hill* (Harcourt Brace Jovanovich)
Honor Books: Fred Gipson, *Old Yeller* (Harper)

Meindert DeJong, *The House of Sixty Fathers* (Harper)

Clara Ingram Judson, *Mr. Justice Holmes* (Follett)
Dorothy Rhoads, *The Corn Grows Ripe* (Viking)
Marguerite de Angeli, *Black Fox of Lorne* (Doubleday)

1958 Harold Keith, *Rifles for Watie* (Crowell)
Honor Books: Mari Sandoz, *The Horsecatcher* (Westminster)
Elizabeth Enright, *Goneaway Lake* (Harcourt Brace Jovanovich)
Robert Lawson, *The Great Wheel* (Viking)
Leo Gurko, *Tom Paine, Freedom's Apostle* (Crowell)

1959 Elizabeth George Speare, *The Witch of Blackbird Pond* (Houghton Mifflin)
Honor Books: Natalie Savage Carlson, *The Family under the Bridge* (Harper)
Meindert DeJong, *Along Came a Dog* (Harper)
Francis Kalnay, *Chucaro: Wild Pony of the Pampa* (Harcourt Brace Jovanovich)
William O. Steele, *The Perilous Road* (Harcourt Brace Jovanovich)

1960 Joseph Krumgold, *Onion John* (Crowell)
Honor Books: Jean George, *My Side of the Mountain* (Dutton)
Gerald W. Johnson, *America Is Born* (Morrow)
Carol Kendall, *The Gammage Cup* (Harcourt Brace Jovanovich)

1961 Scott O'Dell, *Island of the Blue Dolphins* (Houghton Mifflin)
Honor Books: Gerald W. Johnson, *America Moves Forward* (Morrow)
Jack Schaefer, *Old Ramon* (Houghton Mifflin)
George Selden, *The Cricket in Times Square* (Farrar)

1962 Elizabeth George Speare, *The Bronze Bow* (Houghton Mifflin)
Honor Books: Edwin Tunis, *Frontier Living* (World)
Eloise McCraw, *The Golden Goblet* (Coward)
Mary Stolz, *Belling the Tiger* (Harper)

1963 Madeleine L'Engle, *A Wrinkle in Time* (Farrar)
Honor Books: Sorche Nic Leodhas, *Thistle and Thyme: Tales and Legends from Scotland* (Holt)
Olivia Coolidge, *Men of Athens* (Houghton Mifflin)

1964 Emily Cheney Neville, *It's Like This, Cat* (Harper)
Honor Books: Sterling North, *Rascal* (Dutton)
Ester Wier, *The Loner* (McKay)

1965 Maja Wojciechowska, *Shadow of a Bull* (Atheneum)
Honor Book: Irene Hunt, *Across Five Aprils* (Follett)

1966 Elizabeth Borten de Trevino, *I, Juan de Pareja* (Farrar)
Honor Books: Lloyd Alexander, *The Black Cauldron* (Holt)
Randall Jarrell, *The Animal Family* (Pantheon)
Mary Stolz, *The Noonday Friends* (Harper)

1967 Irene Hunt, *Up a Road Slowly* (Follet)
Honor Books: Scott O'Dell, *The King's Fifth* (Houghton Mifflin)
Isaac Bashevis Singer, *Zlateh the Goat and Other Stories* (Harper)
Mary H. Weik, *The Jazz Man* (Atheneum)

1968 E. L. Konigsburg, *From the Mixed-Up Files of Mrs. Basil E. Frankweiler* (Atheneum)
Honor Books: E. L. Konigsburg, *Jennifer, Hecate, Macbeth, William McKinley, and Me, Elizabeth* (Atheneum)
Scott O'Dell, *The Black Pearl* (Houghton Mifflin)
Isaac Bashevis Singer, *The Fearsome Inn* (Scribner's)
Zilpha Keatley Snyder, *The Egypt Game* (Atheneum)

1969 Lloyd Alexander, *The High King* (Holt)
Honor Books: Julius Lester, *To Be a Slave* (Dial)
Isaac Bashevis Singer, *When Shlemiel Went to Warsaw and Other Stories* (Farrar)

1970   William H. Armstrong, *Sounder* (Harper)
Honor Books: Sulamith IshKishor, *Our Eddie* (Pantheon)
Janet Gaylord Moore, *The Many Ways of Seeing: An Introduction to the Pleasures of Art* (World)
Mary Q. Steele, *Journey Outside* (Viking)

1971   Betsy Byars, *Summer of the Swans* (Viking)
Honor Books: Natalie Babbitt, *Kneeknock Rise* (Farrar)
Sylvia Louise Engdahl, *Enchantress from the Stars* (Atheneum)
Scott O'Dell, *Sing Down the Moon* (Houghton Mifflin)

1972   Robert C. O'Brien, *Mrs. Frisby and the Rats of NIMH* (Atheneum)
Honor Books: Allan W. Eckert, *Incident at Hawk's Hill* (Little)
Virginia Hamilton, *The Planet of Junior Brown* (Macmillan)
Ursula K. Le Guin, *The Tombs of Atuan* (Atheneum)
Miska Miles, *Annie and the Old One* (Atlanitc-Little)
Zilpha Keatley Sunder, *The Headless Cupid* (Atheneum)

1973   Jean Craighead George, *Julie of the Wolves* (Harper)
Honor Books: Arnold Lobel, *Frog and Toad Together* (Harper)
Johanna Reiss, *The Upstairs Room* (Crowell)
Zilpha Keatley Snyder, *The Witches of Worm* (Atheneum)

1974   Paula Fox, *The Slave Dancer* (Bradbury)
Honor Book: Susan Cooper, *The Dark Is Rising* (Atheneum)

1975   Virginia Hamilton, *M. C. Higgins, the Great* (Macmillan)
Honor Books: Ellen Raskin, *Figgs & Phantoms* (Dutton)
James Lincoln Collier & Christopher Collier, *My Brother Sam Is Dead* (Four Winds)
Elizabeth Marie Pope, *The Perilous Gard* (Houghton Mifflin)
Bette Greene, *Philip Hall Likes Me. I Reckon Maybe* (Dial)

1976   Susan Cooper, *The Grey King* (Atheneum)
Honor Books: Sharon Bell Mathis, *The Hundred Penny Box* (Viking)
Laurence Yep, *Dragonwings* (Harper)

1977   Mildred D. Taylor, *Roll of Thunder, Hear My Cry* (Dial)
Honor Books: William Steig, *Abel's Island* (Farrar)
Nancy Bond, *A String in the Harp* (Atheneum)

1978   Katherine Paterson, *Bridge to Terabithia* (Crowell)
Honor Books: Beverly Cleary, *Ramona and Her Father* (Morrow)
Jamake Highwater, *Anpao: An American Indian Odyssey* (Lippincott)

1979   Ellen Raskin, *The Westing Game* (Dutton)
Honor Book: Katherine Paterson, *The Great Gilly Hopkins* (Crowell)

1980   Joan Blos, *A Gathering of Days: A New England Girl's Journal 1830–1832* (Scribner's)
Honor Book: David Kherdian, *The Road from Home: The Story of an Armenian Girl* (Greenwillow)

1981   Katherine Paterson, *Jacob Have I Loved* (Crowell)
Honor Books: Jane Langton, *The Fledgling* (Harper)
Madeleine L'Engle, *A Ring of Endless Light* (Farrar)

1982   Nancy Willard, *A Visit to William Blake's Inn: Poems for Innocent and Experienced Travelers* (Harcourt Brace Jovanovich)
Honor Books: Beverly Cleary, *Ramona Quimby, Age 8* (Morrow)
Aranka Siegal, *Upon the Head of the Goat: A Childhood in Hungary, 1939–1944* (Farrar)

1983   Cynthia Voigt, *Dicey's Song* (Atheneum)
Honor Books: Robin McKinley, *Blue Sword* (Morrow)
William Steig, *Dr. DeSoto* (Farrar)
Paul Fleischman, *Graven Images* (Harper)

Jean Fritz, *Homesick: My Own Story* (Putnam's)
Virginia Hamilton, *Sweet Whisper, Brother Rush* (Philomel)

1984   Beverly Cleary, *Dear Mr. Henshaw* (Morrow)
Honor Books: Elizabeth George Speare, *The Sign of the Beaver* (Houghton Mifflin)
Cynthia Voigt, *A Solitary Blue* (Atheneum)
Bill Britain, *The Wish Giver* (Harper)

1985   Robin McKinley, *The Hero and the Crown* (Greenwillow)
Honor Books: Mavis Jukes, *Like Jake and Me* (Knopf)
Bruce Brooks, *The Moves Make the Man* (Harper)
Paula Fox, *One-Eyed Cat* (Bradbury)

1986   Patricia MacLachlan, *Sarah, Plain and Tall* (Harper)
Honor Books: Rhoda Blumberg, *Commodore Perry in the Land of the Shogun* (Lothrop)
Gary Paulsen, *Dogsong* (Bradbury)

1987   Sid Fleischman, *The Whipping Boy* (Greenwillow)
Honor Books: Cynthia Rylant, *A Fine White Dust* (Bradbury)
Marion Dane Bauer, *On My Honor* (Clarion)
Patricia Lauber, *Volcano: The Eruption and Healing of Mount St. Helens* (Bradbury)

1988   Russell Freedom, *Lincoln: A Photobiography* (Clarion)
Honor Books: Norma Fox Mazer, *After the Rain* (Morrow)
Gary Paulsen, *Hatchet* (Bradbury)

1989   Paul Fleischman, *Joyful Noise: Poems for Two Voices* (Harper)
Honor Books: Virginia Hamilton, *In the Beginning: Creation Stories from around the World* (Harcourt)
Walter Dean Myers, *Scorpions* (Harper & Row)

1990   Lois Lowry, *Number the Stars* (Houghton Mifflin)
Honor Books: Janet Taylor Lisle, *Afternoon of the Elves* (Orchard)
Susan Fisher Staples, *Shabanu, Daughter of the Wind* (Knopf)
Gary Paulsen, *The Winter Room* (Orchard)

1991   Jerry Spinelli, *Maniac Magee* (Little, Brown)
Honor Book: Avi, *The True Confessions of Charlotte Doyle* (Orchard)

1992   Phyllis Reynolds Naylor, *Shiloh* (Atheneum)
Honor Books: Avi, *Nothing but the Truth* (Orchard)
Russell Freedman, *The Wright Brothers: How They Invented the Airplane* (Holiday)

1993   Cynthia Rylant, *Missing May* (Orchard)
Honor Books: Patricia McKissack, *The Dark-Thirty: Southern Tales of the Supernatural* (Knopf)
Walter Dean Myers, *Somewhere in the Darkness* (Scholastic)
Bruce Brooks, *What Hearts* (HarperCollins)

1994   Lois Lowry, *The Giver* (Houghton Mifflin)
Honor Books: Jane Leslie Conly, *Crazy Lady* (HarperCollins)
Laurence Yep, *Dragon's Gate* (HarperCollins)
Russell Freedman, *Eleanor Roosevelt: A Life of Discovery* (Clarion)

1995   Sharon Creech, *Walk Two Moons* (HarperCollins)
Honor Books: Karen Cushman, *Catherine, Called Birdy* (Clarion)
Nancy Farmer, *The Ear, the Eye, and the Arm* (Jackson/Orchard)

1996   Karen Cushman, *The Midwife's Apprentice* (Clarion)
Honor Books: Jim Murphy, *The Great Fire* (Scholastic)
Christopher Paul Curtis, *The Watsons Go to Birmingham–1963* (Delacorte)
Carolyn Coman, *What Jamie Saw* (Front Street)
Carol Fenner, *Yolonda's Genius* (McElderry/Simon & Schuster)

1997   E. L. Konigsburg, *The View from Saturday* (Atheneum)
      Honor Books: Ruth White, *Belle Prater's Boy* (Farrar, Straus & Giroux)
            Nancy Farmer, *A Girl Named Disaster* (Jackson/Orchard)
            Eloise McGraw, *Moorchild* (McElderry/Simon & Schuster)
            Megan Whalen Turner, *The Thief* (Greenwillow/Morrow)
1998   Karen Hesse, *Out of the Dust* (Scholastic)
      Honor Books: Gail Carson Levine, *Ella Enchanted* (HarperCollins)
            Patricia Reilly Giff, *Lily's Crossing* (Delacorte)
            Jerry Spinelli, *Wringer* (HarperCollins)
1999   Louis Sachar, *Holes* (Farrar, Straus)
      Honor Book: Richard Peck, *A Long Way from Chicago* (Dial)
2000   Christopher Paul Curtis, *Bud, Not Buddy* (Delacorte)
      Honor Books: Audrey Couloumbis, *Getting Near to Baby* (Putnam)
            Tomie DePaola, *26 Fairmount Avenue* (Putnam)
            Jennifer L. Holm, *Our Only May Amelia* (HarperCollins)

Subject Index

Author, Illustrator, and Title Index